The pure flame of devotion

This excellent book serves as a double gift. First, it fulfills the biblical injunction to give honour where honour is due, and it is a fitting thing to honour a man like Dr. Michael A.G. Haykin, a Spirit-filled polymath who uses his considerable gifts to serve the church with tireless devotion. Second, it is a gift to the church, as several of Dr. Haykin's colleagues and friends demonstrate what he models: a Christian approach to the history of Christian spirituality. The result is a volume that should find its way on to our shelves, then on to our desks, and then into our hearts and minds.

JUSTIN TAYLOR, senior vice-president and publisher for books, Crossway; co-author of *The Final Days of Jesus*

From its account of Michael Haykin's remarkable conversion and career, to its stellar cast of essayists, Ian Clary and Steve Weaver's *The Pure Flame of Devotion* is a volume worthy of the scholar it honours. In the breadth and depth of its fascinating case studies, this book reflects the outstanding qualities of Professor Haykin's own writings on Christian spirituality. I recommend it highly.

THOMAS S. KIDD, professor of history, Baylor University, Waco, Texas

I have long admired Michael Haykin, both as a church historian and churchman, but in these last years it has been my privilege to come to know him personally. That has only made me respect him more. He is a magisterial historian of evangelicalism (would that his views were more widely known and appreciated), a stellar scholar of Baptist history, a master theological educator, an avid student of the Holy Spirit, a learned teacher of patristics (a rarity among modern evangelicals) and, as the Puritans would have said, an affectionate, practical divine. For these reasons and many more, I am delighted to commend *The Pure Flame of Devotion: The History of Christian Spirituality, Essays in Honour of Michael A.G. Haykin.* This volume is a treasure trove of rich, theological, biblical, devotional, gospel truth.

LIGON DUNCAN, chancellor and John E. Richards Professor of systematic and historical theology, Reformed Theological Seminary, Jackson, Mississippi

This collection of essays brings together an extraordinary group of distinguished scholars. The fact that they bring their expertise to bear on the topic of Christian spirituality throughout the history of the church renders the volume especially interesting and attractive to both scholars and students. This is a fine and fitting tribute to such an accomplished colleague.

GREGORY A. WILLS, dean of the School of Theology, The Southern Baptist Theological Seminary, Louisville, Kentucky

This collection of essays is a well deserved tribute to Dr. Michael A.G. Haykin, a noted scholar who has emerged in these days as a leading patristic and Baptist historian. Recognized in the academic world as having a commanding knowledge in all areas of church history, this professor-author is also a man with a keen interest in genuine spirituality and biblical piety in the Christian life. He has especially excelled in the classroom by implanting within his students an infectious love for church history. The church of the Lord Jesus Christ owes an enormous debt to the laborious and tireless efforts of this distinguished intellect.

STEVEN J. LAWSON, pastor of Christ Fellowship Baptist Church, Mobile, Alabama

Dr. Michael Haykin is not only a colleague and dear friend but he is a prolific writer and fascinating lecturer who makes church history come alive for his students and anyone else who listens. In a day in which the lessons of the past are either unknown or quickly forgotten, he reminds us that we are not the first Christians to grapple with the challenge of living for Christ in the world. If more historians wrote and taught with the clarity of Dr. Haykin, more Christians young and old would know more about their rich Christian heritage. This *Festschrift* is a celebration of Dr. Haykin's passion and interests when it comes to church history and a way of recognizing his contribution to this vital area of study. I highly recommend it to those who want to learn more about God's work among his people down through the ages.

KIRK WELLUM, principal, Toronto Baptist Seminary and Bible College, Ontario

This is more than a *Festschrift* and much more than a tribute to the fabulous work of Michael Haykin. The editors have managed to put together a team of qualified authors that present to us a fascinating overview of the history of true Christian spirituality. It is a long history and also a deep and broad spirituality, as each of the contributions teach. As Haykin himself has always done, this book demonstrates how solid scholarship can be made relevant and stimulating. This gift to Michael Haykin is a gift to all who enjoy church history and wish to learn from it.

HERMAN SELDERHUIS, director Refo500, professor of church history, Apeldoorn, Netherlands

Few scholars have been at ease with both Basil of Caesarea and Fuller of Kettering. Michael Haykin, however, is numbered in the select band of those who are as familiar with the early church fathers as with the classic Baptist theologians. It is appropriate that this volume in honour of Michael's achievement should range from patristics to Baptists of the modern era, taking in many other Christian groups and individuals inbetween. Throughout the book there is a concern to appreciate the authentic spirituality of the subjects—and that is highly appropriate for Michael, too.

DAVID BEBBINGTON, professor of history, University of Stirling, Scotland

Dr. Michael Haykin is a Christian scholar of the first rank. His important work in church history and theology has been a great gift to the church. And what makes Dr. Haykin's particular erudition so very important to the church today is his combination of rigorous scholarship and genuine Christian devotion. I am very thankful for Michael Haykin, both as a Christian scholar and as a faithful guide to the Christian life. He makes church history come alive and theology walk. And he does so with the keenest thinking and the warmest heart.

R. ALBERT MOHLER JR., president, The Southern Baptist Theological Seminary, Louisville, Kentucky

The pure flame of devotion
The history of Christian spirituality

*Essays in honour of
Michael A.G. Haykin*

EDITED AND INTRODUCED BY
G. Stephen Weaver Jr. and Ian Hugh Clary

CONTRIBUTORS
Douglas Adams, Peter Beck, Joel R. Beeke, Nathan A. Finn, Keith Goad,
Crawford Gribben, Francis X. Gumerlock, David S. Hogg, Erroll Hulse,
Clint Humfrey, Sharon James, Mark Jones, Sean Michael Lucas,
Tom J. Nettles, Dennis Ngien, Robert W. Oliver, Kenneth J. Stewart,
Carl R. Trueman, Austin R. Walker, Donald S. Whitney,
Malcolm B. Yarnell, Fred G. Zaspel

press

press

www.joshuapress.com

Published by
Joshua Press Inc., Kitchener, Ontario, Canada
Distributed by
Sola Scriptura Ministries International
www.sola-scriptura.ca

First published 2013

Cover and book design by Janice Van Eck

The publication of this book was made possible by the generous support of Michael A.G. Haykin's friends and colleagues.

Library and Archives Canada Cataloguing in Publication

The pure flame of devotion : the history of Christian spirituality : essays in honour of Michael A.G. Haykin / edited and introduced by Steve Weaver and Ian Hugh Clary ; contributors, Doug Adams, Peter Beck, Joel R. Beeke, Nathan A. Finn, Keith Goad, Crawford Gribben, Francis X. Gumerlock, David S. Hogg, Erroll Hulse, Clint Humfrey, Sharon James, Sean Michael Lucas, Tom Nettles, Dennis Ngien, Robert W. Oliver, Kenneth J. Stewart, Austin Walker, Don Whitney, Malcolm B. Yarnell, Fred G. Zaspel.

Includes bibliographical references.
Issued in print and electronic formats.
ISBN 978-1-894400-55-8 (bound).—ISBN 978-1-894400-54-1 (pbk.).—
ISBN 978-1-894400-56-5 (epub).—ISBN 978-1-894400-57-2 (mobi)

1. Spirituality--History. I. Weaver, Steve, 1974–, writer of introduction, editor of compilation II. Clary, Ian Hugh, 1978–, writer of introduction, editor of compilation

BV4490.P87 2013   248.09   C2013-905612-2
                                                 C2013-905613-0

To Michael A.G. Haykin, historian of the Spirit,
lover of Christ, faithful friend and colleague, tireless servant
—with deep thanksgiving to God for you

"Remember your leaders, those who spoke to you
the word of God. Consider the outcome of their
way of life, and imitate their faith."
HEBREWS 13:7

Contents

Contents

Foreword

I FIRST MET Michael Haykin years ago when I visited Toronto Baptist Seminary where he was then principal. I found a vibrant community of scholars, and a passionate corps of students committed to taking the gospel to the uttermost regions of Canada and around the world. But I also found a quiet, dignified principal, a man who exuded gospel warmth and gospel gravity. I had read Haykin's work, but watching him shepherd these students, talking to each one of them about where God was leading, convinced me that I was in the presence not only of a brilliant man but a holy man.

Liberal biblical critics tell us that the books of Genesis and Isaiah are not in fact the works of Moses or Isaiah, but instead are pieced together from various sources. They say the same about the Gospels, unwilling to attribute each Gospel to the named author. As a conservative evangelical, I reject all of that. When it comes to Michael Haykin though, sometimes I feel like a source critic. I often wonder if Haykin is one scholar or a conspiracy of brilliant minds masquerading as one man. After all, he is a pacesetter in the fields of spiritual formation, Baptist studies, patristic history and beyond. All of these are very different fields, demanding a high level of expertise. He is one of the most recognized scholars in the world in each of these fields, having written and lectured extensively in each area, even while serving as a seminary administrator, popular conference speaker and leader within the Canadian Baptist and Southern Baptist churches.

After Michael Haykin joined the faculty at Southern Seminary, he quickly distinguished himself as a scholar to be reckoned with and a shepherd to be loved. His scholarly firepower and personal piety were joined together in an incandescent combination, reminiscent of Haykin's hero, the Baptist leader Andrew Fuller. In a day when the academy, even some places within evangelicalism, tends to veer from dead rationalism to hyper-mystical enthusiasm, Haykin brought to Southern, and to the larger evangelical community, a combination of a Spirit-renewed mind and a Spirit-filled heart.

Once when a group of accreditors visited Southern Seminary, we had several bookshelves filled with the books of each faculty member. Haykin's works filled an entire shelf and a half on their own. When some of the accreditors looked at the number of classes that Haykin taught, they said to me that they wondered whether we were keeping him from pursuing his scholarship. When I pointed them to the amount of research and writing that Haykin had done, they looked at me with almost disbelief. I understood that completely, because I had felt the same way when I first saw the scholarly, whirling dervish of Michael Haykin.

The truth is, Haykin not only teaches, writes and instructs, he also *pastors*. He has pastored many students in Canada and at Southern Seminary, his doctoral students and those who have sat in his popular master's level courses. Beyond that, he has pastored with his pen. And since Michael Haykin's work is rooted in the ancient and permanent ways of forebears, such as Irenaeus and Edwards and Fuller and Carey, there is little doubt that he will be read for decades, and even centuries, to come. He is well deserving of this volume. As you read it, I hope that you will join me in praying for more Michael Haykins to be sent forth, calling us all back to the old paths.

RUSSELL D. MOORE
President
Ethics & Religious Liberty Commission
Southern Baptist Convention

Contributors

DOUGLAS ADAMS (M.Div., Toronto Baptist Seminary) is currently pursuing a Ph.D. in history at the University of Western Ontario. Doug studied at Toronto Baptist Seminary and graduated in 1977. He went on to serve as an associate pastor at Briscoe Street Baptist Church, London, Ontario, and later as pastor of East Williams Baptist Church, a position he occupied for twenty years. During that time, Doug also pursued further education at the University of Western Ontario and by the mid-1990s achieved his Master of Arts degree. Doug also served as professor of church history at Toronto Baptist Seminary for nearly twenty years. Doug is currently writing his dissertation on T.T. Shields.

PETER BECK (Ph.D., The Southern Baptist Theological Seminary) is associate professor of Christian studies and director of the honours program at Charleston Southern University. In addition to his book, *The Voice of Faith: Jonathan Edwards's Theology of Prayer* (Joshua Press, 2010), he has published numerous articles on Jonathan Edwards, the Puritans and Baptist studies. Additionally, Peter has ten years of pastoral experience and currently serves as pastor of Doorway Baptist Church in North Charleston, South Carolina.

JOEL R. BEEKE (Ph.D., Westminster Theological Seminary) is president and professor of systematic theology and homiletics at Puritan Reformed Theological Seminary, a pastor of the Heritage Netherlands Reformed Congregation in Grand Rapids, Michigan, editor of *The Banner of Sovereign Grace Truth*, editorial director of Reformation Heritage Books, president of Inheritance Publishers and vice-president of the Dutch Reformed Translation Society. He has written, co-authored or edited over seventy books (most recently, *A Puritan Theology: Doctrine for Life*; *Prepared by Grace, for Grace: The Puritans on God's Ordinary Way of Leading Sinners to Christ*; *Living Zealously*; *Friends and Lovers: Cultivating Companionship and Intimacy in Marriage*; *Getting Back Into the Race: The Cure for Backsliding*; *Parenting by God's Promises: How to Raise Children in the Covenant of Grace*; *Living for the Glory of God: An Introduction to Calvinism*; *Meet the Puritans*; and *Taking Hold of God*), and contributed 2,000 articles to Reformed books, journals, periodicals and encyclopedias. He is frequently called upon to lecture at seminaries and to speak at Reformed conferences around the world. He and his wife Mary have been blessed with three children: Calvin, Esther and Lydia.

IAN HUGH CLARY (Ph.D. cand., Universiteit van die Vrystaat, Blomfontein) served as research assistant to Dr. Michael A.G. Haykin from 2003 to 2006. Ian has a Th.M. from Toronto Baptist Seminary where he wrote a dissertation on the patristic influences on the Christology of the Irish Puritan James Ussher. His Ph.D. dissertation is on the evangelical historiography of Arnold Dallimore. Ian co-wrote two local church histories with Dr. Haykin and has contributed to two academic books. He has also published articles in the *Scottish Bulletin of Evangelical Theology*, *Southern Baptist Journal of Theology*, *Mid-America Journal of Theology* and others. Ian and his wife Vicky have three children and live in Toronto where they are members of New City Baptist Church.

NATHAN A. FINN (Ph.D., Southeastern Baptist Theological Seminary) is associate professor of historical theology and Baptist studies at Southeastern Baptist Theological Seminary. He is also a senior fellow of the Andrew Fuller Center for Baptist Studies at The Southern Baptist Theological Seminary. He has contributed a number of works to the field of Baptist studies, most recently editing an updated edition of Robert Hall Sr.'s *Help to Zion's Travellers* (BorderStone, 2011).

KEITH GOAD (Ph.D., The Southern Baptist Theological Seminary) is the pastor of Jefferson Park Baptist Church in Charlottesville, Virginia. He studied with Dr. Michael Haykin at Southern and his research and writing focuses on the theology and spirituality of the early church.

CRAWFORD GRIBBEN (Ph.D., University of Strathclyde) is professor of early modern British history at Queen's University, Belfast. He is the author of a number of studies of the literary cultures of Puritanism and evangelicalism, and is currently completing the forthcoming *John Owen and English Puritanism* (Oxford University Press, 2014).

FRANCIS X. GUMERLOCK (Ph.D., Saint Louis University) writes on the theology of grace and eschatology in early and medieval Christianity and teaches Latin and historical theology in Colorado. His books include *The Day and the Hour* (2000), *The Seven Seals of the Apocalypse* (2009), *Fulgentius of Ruspe on the Saving Will of God* (2009) and *Revelation and the First Century* (2012). www.francisgumerlock.com.

DAVID S. HOGG is the associate dean for academic affairs at Beeson Divinity School in Birmingham, Alabama. He teaches history and theology, but his special area of interest is in medieval theology. Among his publications is *Anselm of Canterbury: The Beauty of Theology*. Hogg also helps train pastors at the Biblický Teologický Seminár in the Czech Republic, as time allows. In addition to academic roles, Hogg has pastored in Raleigh, North Carolina.

ERROLL HULSE graduated in architecture from Pretoria University, South Africa. He studied theology under principal E.F. Kevan at the London Bible College and while in London benefited from the ministry of Dr. D. Martyn Lloyd-Jones. He was called to the ministry in 1962 and has served in four churches. He is presently associate pastor of Leeds Reformed Baptist Church. Since 1970, he been editor of *Reformation Today*, an international journal published bi-monthly. He has authored a dozen books including *Who Are the Puritans? ...and What Do They Teach?* (Evangelical Press, 2000), which has a foreword by Michael Haykin. His book *Give Him No Rest* (Evangelical Press, 1991) is in the tradition of Jonathan Edwards and calls for a concert of prayer for revival.

CLINT HUMFREY (M.Div.) has been the pastor of Calvary Grace Church in Calgary, Alberta, since its founding in 2006. Prior to that he was a professor of Greek at Toronto Baptist Seminary from 2003 to 2006. Clint is married to Christel and they have three cowboys.

SHARON JAMES (M.A., M.Div., Ph.D.) has degrees in history from Cambridge University, and theology from Toronto Baptist Seminary. She taught history for several years in the United Kingdom and in Malawi. Sharon has been involved in pastoral work among women for many years, has written a number of books and has spoken at conferences in several countries. She recently completed doctoral studies, looking at government family policy in England from 1960 to 2010 and the evangelical response.

SEAN MICHAEL LUCAS (Ph.D., Westminster Theological Seminary) is senior minister at the First Presbyterian Church, Hattiesburg, Mississippi, and adjunct professor of church history at Reformed Theological Seminary, Jackson, Mississippi. He is the author of several books, including *Robert Lewis Dabney: A Southern Presbyterian Life* (P & R, 2005) and *God's Grand Design: The Theological Vision of Jonathan Edwards* (Crossway, 2011).

TOM J. NETTLES (Ph.D.) and his wife Margaret have three adult children and five grandchildren and are active in volunteer capacities at LaGrange Baptist Church, LaGrange, Kentucky. Teaching since 1976, Tom presently is professor of historical theology at The Southern Baptist Theological Seminary. He has published a biography of James Petigru Boyce, co-authored *Baptists and the Bible* with the late L. Russ Bush, *By His Grace and for His Glory*, *The Baptists* (a three volume work on Baptist history) and, most recently, *Living by Revealed Truth: Biography and Pastoral Theology of Charles H. Spurgeon*.

DENNIS NGIEN (Ph.D.) serves as professor of systematic theology at Tyndale University College and Seminary, Toronto. He is the Founder of the Centre for Mentorship & Theological Reflection and the author of several monographs, including, *Luther as a Spiritual Adviser* and *Gifted Response*, both with Paternoster Press.

ROBERT W. OLIVER has a B.A. from University College London and was awarded a Ph.D. by the Council for National Academic Awards. He served as pastor of Bradford-on-Avon Baptist Church from 1971 to 2006 and lecturer in church history at the London Theological Seminary (LTS) from 1989 to 2013. He has also served as lecturer at the John Owen Centre, LTS, England, and as visiting professor of church history at Westminster Theological Seminary, Philadelphia, and Puritan Reformed Seminary, Grand Rapids. He is the author of *History of the English Calvinistic Baptists, 1771–1892* (The Banner of Truth Trust, 2006).

KENNETH J. STEWART (Ph.D., University of Edinburgh) is professor of theological studies at Covenant College, Lookout Mountain, Georgia, where he has taught theology and the history of Christianity since 1997. He is a graduate of the University of British Columbia and the University of Waterloo, and completed theological studies at Westminster Theological Seminary and the University of Edinburgh. His most recent book was *Ten Myths About Calvinism* (IVP, 2011) and he is near to completing the forthcoming *Evangelicalism Navigates the Past* (IVP).

AUSTIN R. WALKER is co-pastor of Maidenbower Baptist Church, Crawley, England, having served this congregation since 1972. He is a graduate of the University of Wales, Aberystwyth (1968) and Westminster Theological Seminary (1971). He has authored *The Excellent Benjamin Keach* and *God's Care for the Widow*. He and his wife Mai have four children and ten grandchildren.

G. STEPHEN WEAVER JR. (Ph.D., The Southern Baptist Theological Seminary) is pastor of Farmdale Baptist Church in Frankfort, Kentucky. Since 2008 he has served as research assistant to Dr. Michael A.G. Haykin for the Andrew Fuller Center for Baptist Studies at The Southern Baptist Theological Seminary. As a Ph.D. student in church history/historical theology, Steve's dissertation focused on the seventeenth-century English Baptist Hercules Collins. Along with Michael Haykin, Steve co-edited, *"Devoted to the Service of the Temple": Piety, Persecution, and Ministry in the Writings of Hercules Collins* (Reformation Heritage Books, 2007). Steve and his wife Gretta have been married for eighteen years and have been blessed with six children.

DONALD S. WHITNEY (Ph.D.) has been associate professor of biblical spirituality and senior associate dean at The Southern Baptist Theological Seminary in Louisville, Kentucky, since 2005. Before that, he held a similar position at Midwestern Baptist Theological Seminary in Kansas City, Missouri, for ten years. He is the founder and president of The Center for Biblical Spirituality. He is the author of *Spiritual Disciplines for the Christian Life* (NavPress, 1991), which has a companion discussion guide. He has also written *How Can I Be Sure I'm a Christian?* (NavPress, 1994), *Spiritual Disciplines within the Church* (Moody Press, 1996), *Ten Questions to Diagnose Your Spiritual Health* (NavPress, 2001), *Simplify Your Spiritual Life* (NavPress, 2003) and *Family Worship* (Center for Biblical Spirituality, 2006).

MALCOLM B. YARNELL III (D.Phil., University of Oxford), a husband, father and preacher of the gospel, serves as professor of systematic theology and director of the Center for Theological Research at Southwestern Baptist Theological Seminary in Fort Worth, Texas. He is the author of *The Formation of Christian Doctrine* (B & H Academic, 2007) and *Royal Priesthood in the English Reformation* (Oxford University Press, 2013), as well as editor of eighteen works, most recently, *Anabaptists and Contemporary Baptists* (B & H Academic, 2013). He is currently writing a book on the Trinity in Scripture.

FRED G. ZASPEL (Ph.D., Free University of Amsterdam) is one of the pastors at Reformed Baptist Church in Franconia, Pennsylvania, and is professor of systematic theology at Calvary Baptist Seminary. A recognized authority on Benjamin Breckinridge Warfield of Old Princeton, he is the author of *The Theology of B.B. Warfield: A Systematic Summary* and *Warfield on the Christian Life: Living in Light of the Gospel*. He is also co-author, with Tom Wells, of *New Covenant Theology*. He has published many articles and reviews on various biblical and theological themes, and he blogs regularly at www.credomag.com.

INTRODUCTION

Michael A.G. Haykin: a biographical sketch

By G. Stephen Weaver Jr. and Ian Hugh Clary

SOME HISTORIANS HAVE dabbled in what is called "counterfactual history," taking delight in asking the question, "What if?" Steve Tally wrote *Almost America: From the Colonists to Clinton: A "What If" History of the U.S.*, where he asks fun questions like, what if Robert E. Lee accepted Abraham Lincoln's proposal to command the U.S. Army instead of the rebel forces.[1] This kind of historiography has the benefit of not only entertaining readers, it also forces them to think through issues of history in an unconventional way. For Christians, it entices us to consider the providence of God in history. Michael Haykin has often expressed an interest in this way of doing history and so we might play the same historiographical game with him. "What if" might be asked about the life of a young Azad Hakim whose father Sahir Sabir Hakim, in 1955, nearly returned to his native Kurdistan. "What if" he did in fact move? This would have meant taking his family from England, the place of birth of his then two-year-old son, to pursue a life in wartorn northern Iraq. If this counterfactual history were the case, great books studying Basil of Caesarea, Andrew Fuller and John Sutcliff would never have been written and you would not be holding this book in your hand.

---

1 Steve Tally, *Almost America: From the Colonists to Clinton: A "What If" History of the U.S.* (New York: HarperCollins, 2000).

Azad Hakim would, in God's providence, grow up not in Kirkuk, Iraq, nor in the industrial city of Birmingham, where he was born on November 24, 1953. Rather, Azad grew up in nearby Coventry, a town once known for its beautiful and historic cathedral which was destroyed during the Second World War. After moving to Canada in 1965 he would, like his father Simon, anglicize his name. In Canada, he became Michael Anthony George Haykin. This new name makes sense not only because he identified himself as a Briton, but also because his mother, Theresa Veronica (née O'Gorman) was Irish, from the town of Bray near Dublin. He took the names of her relatives.

Michael Haykin lived the next six years of his life in another quaint town, Ancaster, Ontario, near Hamilton, an industrial town akin to his native Birmingham. Though his formerly Muslim father converted to the religion of his Irish Catholic wife, their son was only nominally Christian. As he matured, Michael became repulsed by what he saw as the hypocrisy of the Catholics he knew—those who lived lives of debauchery and drunkenness during the week, only to go to confession and receive communion on Sundays without an ounce of regret. As a child of the late sixties, Michael turned from organized religion to revolution, opting to follow the teachings of Marx, Lenin and Mao. His hero was the would-be guerrilla Ernesto "Che" Guevara. Though a quiet man, Michael fell in with a like-minded crowd of revolutionaries and together they plotted the violent overthrow of the American Dream that was alive and well in Canada. This meant the donning of paramilitary apparel and the making of Molotov cocktails.

In 1971, Michael carried his Marxist ideals with him to London, Ontario, where he entered the philosophy program at the University of Western Ontario. Instead of rooming with a group of revolutionaries, he boarded in the home of an elderly couple. Their musings were less about Castro's Cuba and more about the brevity of life and how quickly it all ends. Michael was now confronted not with the death of a capitalist society, but with the reality of his own death and its fast approach. Thoughts turned to fears and he embarked on a struggle that would last for much of his young adult life. In the face of such fears, the materialism of Marx offered him no comfort and slowly communism lost its hold.

Rather than turn to the Catholicism of his parents, Michael became interested in eastern religions and the New Age. The pantheism and

Michael A.G. Haykin
circa 1970/1971*

* *Thanks to George Puharich for this photograph.*

escapism of Zen Buddhism, Taoism and Transcendental Meditation would surely dissipate the fears of death. Are we not just "spirits in a material world" as one popular music group would put it? Do we not all become absorbed into the One after we leave our earthly shell of a body? But try as he might, the fear of death remained.

The year 1971 was momentous for Michael, not only because of his move into higher education, but this was also the year that he became a Canadian citizen. Two other events also occurred that God would use to make Michael a citizen of his kingdom. The first happened in the autumn of that year. He had to write a paper on the existence of God for a course in philosophy, but before putting pen to paper, Michael was suddenly convinced that there was a God. He went from being agnostic to the possibility of God one moment, to believing in God the next. This did not mean that he converted to Christianity, nor did it mean that there was any change in his lifestyle. The second event came through his friendship with a fellow student named Doug whom he had known before going to Western, and who, as it turned out, was a committed Christian. Because Doug was one his few friends in university, Michael spent time with him and, as a result, was introduced to other Christians on campus. Though he does not recall being on the receiving end of their evangelism, he did at this time begin to pray to God.

In 1972, Michael transferred from Western to the philosophy program at the University of Toronto. He did this primarily because he had friends in Toronto; he would move into a one-bedroom apartment with two of his closest friends in the city's downtown core. While in Toronto, he thought little about his belief in the existence of God and he continued to live an immoral lifestyle. Not surprisingly, all of this would become a recipe for disaster for the three friends; eventually they would go their separate ways. Michael moved out of the apartment to live by himself and, soon after, his life began to change. He cut his long hair and gave up smoking and drinking.

In the summer of 1973, Michael got a job at Mother's Pizza Parlour, a restaurant in the west end of Hamilton. This led to another momentous event. Also working at Mother's was a young Glaswegian girl named Alison Lowe. She was a cashier while Michael made pizzas. An attractive woman, she caught Michael's eye, and in God's providence it turned out that she was also a Christian. Alison attended Stanley Avenue Baptist Church in Hamilton and, as a part of his desire for change, Michael decided to attend church with her. In the following autumn he returned to university in Toronto, studying during the week and travelling back to Hamilton to make pizzas and go to church. He was now in the third year of his philosophy degree, living alone and immersed in the thought world of the German existentialist Martin Heidegger. Through his studies of Heidegger, his fear and anxiety over death re-emerged. (A hallmark of Heidegger's philosophy was the idea that authentic existence was only possible in the contemplation of one's death.)

On Sundays, however, he found himself sitting under the pulpit ministry of Bruce Woods, the pastor of Stanley Avenue. Unlike the Marxism and eastern religions of his past, the gospel that Woods preached did have answers to Michael's questions, and it did prove to alleviate his fears. The breaking point came in February 1974 after a series of nights where Michael would awaken in a cold sweat with a pounding heart. On the third of such nights he found himself on his knees in prayer, crying out to God for salvation. When he returned to Hamilton that weekend he knew that God was with him—he had been soundly converted to Christ. In April 1974, he took the step of obedience and was baptized by immersion as a believer at Stanley Avenue Baptist Church.

That same year, Michael graduated from Victoria College, University of Toronto—famous as the school of the literary critic and theorist Northrop Frye—with a bachelor's degree in philosophy. Knowing that philosophy required a lot of original thought, which was not his forte, and coupled with his new-found Christian faith, Michael switched into the history program at Wycliffe College, University of Toronto, a broadly evangelical school that trained ministers for the Anglican Church of Canada. During his time at Wycliffe, the school boasted a tremendous faculty that included Oliver O'Donovan and Richard Longenecker among others. Michael worked his way through the program, writing two theses: one on Augustine's philosophy of history, and another on the concept of the "eighth day" in patristic thought. It was also during his graduate studies that he and Alison were married, on Guy Fawkes Day, November 5, 1976. This was also an important year in Michael's life because his mother, a woman very dear to his heart, passed on to glory. Thankfully, in God's mercy and care, she had been converted to Christ not long before her passing.

After graduating with a master of religion, Michael continued in the doctor of theology program at Wycliffe, focusing on patristics. This course of study became a lifelong professional interest. He recalls that his first in-depth encounter with the writings of the early church came through an essay that he was assigned by Jakób Jocz (1906–1983), an important Hebrew Christian theologian and missiologist who had escaped Europe during the Nazi atrocities. Jocz had his student write on Novation's *On the Trinity*. "From that point on," Michael wrote, "I was hooked on the Fathers."[2]

Michael took his first course in patristics a year later, taught by John Egan, S.J., who was a world-renowned expert in patristic Trinitarianism, in particular that of Gregory of Nazianzus. Egan would supervise Michael's doctoral thesis that focused on a fourth-century controversy over the deity of the Holy Spirit, and was later published as *The Spirit of God: The Exegesis of 1 and 2 Corinthians in the Pneumatomachian Controversy of the Fourth Century*.[3] Of Egan's influence, Michael writes, "I will ever thank God that I had the enormous privilege of having this gifted man serve as my early mentor in the study of the church fathers. The course I took from him in 1976 was on the knowledge of God in the third- and fourth-century Greek and Latin fathers. John's focus on the primary sources and rigorous methods of study opened up the vast riches of Patristic literature."[4] The theology that Michael was learning from the great theologians of the early church helped him in battling his fears over death.

In the year that his mother passed away, he wrote a paper on the beatific vision in the works of Irenaeus of Lyons under the tutelage of Eugene R. Fairweather (1921–2002) of Trinity College, University of Toronto. Through this study, Michael's interest in the Holy Spirit was kindled—so much so that his doctoral dissertation was focused on this subject, and he also became heavily involved in the Toronto charismatic scene. Although he later came "to reject much of what passed for biblical Christianity in the Charismatic movement,"

---

2   Michael A.G. Haykin, *Rediscovering the Church Fathers: Who They Were and How They Shaped the Church* (Wheaton: Crossway, 2011), 150.

3   Michael A.G. Haykin, *The Spirit of God: The Exegesis of 1 and 2 Corinthians in the Pneumatomachian Controversy of the Fourth Century* (Leiden: Brill, 1994).

4   Haykin, *Rediscovering the Church Fathers*, 151.

Michael nevertheless retained an interest in the person and work of the Holy Spirit.[5] Happily, his studies in the Reformation/Puritan eras, along with his growing interest in the English Baptist communities of the seventeenth and eighteenth centuries, revealed a deep dependence upon the work of the Holy Spirit on the part of the key figures in these movements.

In 1989, Alison and Michael experienced the joy of becoming parents with the birth of their daughter Victoria. This joy was to be theirs again in 1991 when their son Nigel was born. (Both of them demonstrate their father's scholarly aptitude, including an interest in ancient history, as they are each excelling in classics degrees.)

After Michael graduated from the University of Toronto with a doctor of theology (Th.D.) in 1982, he was hired to teach church history at Central Baptist Seminary, then located in downtown Toronto. In 1993, Central merged with London Baptist Bible College to form Heritage Baptist College and Seminary, headquartered first in London and then in Cambridge, Ontario. He remained on faculty there until 2003.

Early in his teaching career, Michael came to realize that his expertise in the church fathers was not valued as an asset. At the time, evangelicals were just not interested in patristic studies. He believed that to be able to continue to teach in these institutions, he would need to develop other areas of expertise. This led to his aforementioned forays into Reformation, Puritan and Baptist studies. This experience, which must have been disappointing to a young professor, led to the development of a truly Renaissance man of church history. Among the nearly 100 publications of this well-rounded scholar are well-respected articles and monographs in not only his primary interest of patristics, but also in sixteenth-century Reformation, seventeenth-century Puritan, eighteenth-century Evangelicalism and seventeenth- and eighteenth-century Baptist studies. Though originally born both of necessity and his insatiable desire to learn, Michael's unique combination of areas of expertise would inadvertently lead to a demand for his services from multiple institutions.

By 2003, Michael had developed a reputation as a leading scholar through his many publications. He had also cofounded a publishing

---

5 Michael A.G. Haykin, *The Empire of the Holy Spirit* (Memphis: BorderStone Press, 2010), i.

company with Janice Van Eck in 1999, Joshua Press, where he served as editorial director until 2002. During these years, he continued to teach part time at Heritage. In 2003, Michael turned down an opportunity to serve as editorial director of The Banner of Truth Trust, a publisher of Reformed and Puritan literature in the United Kingdom. The same year he also turned down a full-time teaching position in the United States at The Southern Baptist Theological Seminary in Louisville, Kentucky. Instead, he chose to remain in Canada to take the position of principal at Toronto Baptist Seminary and Bible College (TBS). The school had gone through some struggles in the years preceding, but Michael's arrival brought a needed change, in terms of rebuilding the faculty, attracting a growing student body and regaining the support of churches.

As principal of Toronto Baptist Seminary, Michael also established the Jonathan Edwards Centre for Reformed Spirituality in 2003. It was later renamed the Jonathan Edwards Centre for Reformed Evangelicalism, before being labelled the Andrew Fuller Centre for Reformed Evangelicalism in 2006. From 2003 to 2010, Michael served as editor of the centre's academic journal, *Eusebeia*.

Throughout his academic career, Michael has taught in a variety of institutions as a visiting/adjunct/research professor, even while teaching full time elsewhere. Among the institutions where he has served in this capacity are the Irish Baptist College (Belfast, Northern Ireland), Knox Theological Seminary (Fort Lauderdale, Florida), Puritan Reformed Theological Seminary (Grand Rapids, Michigan), Tyndale Seminary (Toronto, Ontario) and the Séminaire Baptiste Évangélique du Québec (Montréal, Québec). From 2002 to 2007, Michael also served as a visiting professor of church history at The Southern Baptist Theological Seminary (Louisville, Kentucky).

In 2007, Southern, the flagship seminary of the Southern Baptist Convention, once again approached Michael to take a full-time teaching position. Michael had come to realize that his primary calling was as an academic, both writing and instructing students, and not as an administrator. He decided, therefore, to leave his administrative post at TBS and invest his considerable skills in the classroom and in a writing ministry. Where better to do this than at one of the largest evangelical seminaries in the world? At Southern, Michael served alongside a world-class faculty and had the opportunity to supervise doctoral students in his long-beloved area of early church history. No longer a liability, Michael's expertise in the patristic era was now a valued commodity. In fact, the article in the seminary newspaper announcing his hiring, while acknowledging his expertise in Baptist history and Christian spirituality, was headlined "SBTS appoints renowned early church scholar to faculty."[6] Things had certainly changed in the evangelical world in the twenty-five years since Haykin had graduated with a doctorate in patristics.

Michael was hired to teach and supervise doctoral students in early church history, as well as to pioneer Southern's new Ph.D. and D.Min. programs in biblical spirituality, the first such degrees offered by an evangelical institution. In this role, Michael's long settled interest in biblical spirituality—what Andrew Fuller, in a description of his friend Samuel Pearce, called "the pure flame of Scriptural devotion"[7]—and the early church would have their expression in a teaching opportunity seemingly perfectly fitted to his gifts and interests. The move to Southern was a difficult one personally, due to his deep-seated love for Canada and his burden for the kingdom to spread there. As a result, Haykin continued to be involved in Canadian Baptist church life and to teach part time at Toronto Baptist Seminary.

The move to Southern also allowed Michael to utilize the considerable resources of the seminary to promote his love for Baptist history, especially for the eighteenth-century English Baptist theologian of the modern missionary movement—Andrew Fuller. The Andrew Fuller Centre for Reformed Evangelicalism was rebranded the Andrew Fuller Center for Baptist Studies and began to promote Baptist studies through regular conferences and publications. Chief among the center's activities is the publication of a critical edition of the works of Andrew Fuller. *The Works of Andrew Fuller*, for which Haykin will serve as general editor, will total sixteen volumes and will be published by the academic publisher Walter de Gruyter. Haykin has assembled a team of respected scholars to edit the individual volumes, slated to be published over the next several years.

---

6   Jeff Robinson, "SBTS appoints renowned early church scholar to faculty," May 14, 2007 (http://news.sbts.edu/2007/05/14/sbts-appoints-renowned-early-church-scholar-to-faculty/; accessed August 5, 2013).

7   Andrew Fuller, *A Heart for Missions: The Classic Memoir of Samuel Pearce* (Birmingham: Solid Ground Christian Books, 2006), 171.

As a genuine polymath, Michael continues to make contributions in the fields of biblical spirituality, Baptist studies, Reformation/Puritan studies and patristics. The diversity of both the contributors and the topics covered in this volume, *The pure flame of devotion*, testify not only to Michael's extended network of friends, but also to the broad range of his interests. We pray this book will be a fitting tribute to our mentor and friend.

Aim of the book

When Michael Haykin wrote *Rediscovering the Church Fathers* in 2011, he not only encouraged evangelicals to look deep into their past, he also taught them *how* to read the early church. His book is not an introduction to patristics in the proper sense; it is not a treatment of every church father or controversy in the first centuries of the church, rather he *modelled* a way for Protestants to approach ancient texts.[8] Readers were shown how to handle representative figures from representative periods, with critical appreciation and an eye to contemporary usefulness. Likewise, this volume follows a similar course. More than a *Festschrift*, it is intended to serve as a model for students and educated laypeople for how to approach the history of Christian spirituality. As church history and spirituality are two of Dr. Haykin's great loves, and as he has been such a paragon of "remembrancing" to so many, we thought that this was the only appropriate way to pay homage to the years of labour he has put into bringing a "usable past"[9] to the church.

This book is divided into four key sections, each dealing with a major period in church history. While some chapters are dedicated to a particular person or persons, others deal with an entire period; and instead of treating the overall spiritual program of a person or period, only certain aspects of thought are dealt with. This demonstrates the way church history can be approached with an eye to issues of spirituality. This can take a variety of forms—for instance, Francis Gumerlock's intriguing chapter on how the apocalypse shaped the spirituality of God's people in the Middle Ages, or Crawford Gribben's literary com-

---

8   Ian Hugh Clary, "Review of Michael A.G. Haykin, *Rediscovering the Church Fathers*," *Credo Magazine* 2 (2012): 72.

9   Michael A.G. Haykin, *The Reformers and Puritans as Spiritual Mentors: "Hope is Kindled"* (Kitchener: Joshua Press, 2012), 7–9.

parison between the well-known John Owen and the relatively obscure Faithful Teate. In each chapter, reflecting Michael Haykin's own historical method, the emphasis is on how to cull ancient sources for spiritual benefit.

A note of appreciation

I (*Ian Clary*) first met Dr. Haykin (he has often asked me to call him Michael, but I can't bring myself to do it!) when he taught Church History II at the Windsor, Ontario, extension campus for Heritage College. I still look back at the paper I wrote on Oliver Cromwell and shudder to think that he was actually forced to read it. That was over ten years ago and since then—and in God's superabundant providence—he has played a number of important roles in my life: boss, mentor, dissertation supervisor, brother in Christ and friend. When I look back on the last ten or so years of my life, I am amazed at how profoundly I have been shaped by Michael Haykin—the depth of his influence on me is hard to fathom. His deep love for Christ's church, both historically and as she exists today, is exemplary. I have seen firsthand what a Christian scholar—or as Clint Humfrey says at the end of this volume, a historian of the Spirit—looks like, and learned the importance not only of how to read church history, but how to do so with a commitment to piety and godliness. Some of my most cherished memories are of simply reading Scripture and praying with him. This volume is only a small token of the unspeakable appreciation and love I have for Dr. Haykin—I hope it honours him in the way he deserves.

I (*Steve Weaver*) came to know Dr. Haykin through an email correspondence. I wrote to him requesting his advice for topics of historical research. He suggested, among a handful of other topics/individuals, a largely unknown seventeenth-century English Baptist named Hercules Collins. From the beginning of our relationship, I was struck by his graciousness and trust, which he gave to an untested and unrefined East Tennessee hillbilly. Words alone will never be able to repay the debt that I owe to Michael Haykin. Without him I would likely never have had the opportunity to pursue doctoral studies. God, in his providence, used this man to open the door for me to study at Southern. Dr. Haykin has been my teacher, boss, mentor and friend. In every relationship, he has been a model of Christian piety. Dr. Haykin is one of the rare individuals who, the better they are known, the more respected and appreciated they become. He truly embodies the spirit of this volume. His piety is the same piety as those Spirit-filled men and women who walk the pages of church history. I am honoured to dedicate this volume in honour of Dr. Michael A.G. Haykin.

Acknowledgments

Many people have been of tremendous help to us in the process of publishing this book and we would like to thank them. First, we want to offer a hearty thanks to all of the contributors, most of whom know Dr. Haykin personally, and who are all well-respected authors and scholars. Your willingness to be a part of this volume is humbling. We would like to show our appreciation to the people at Joshua Press— themselves longtime friends of Michael Haykin—who have made this a labour of love, in particular Heinz Dschankilic, the director, and Janice Van Eck, who designed this lovely book. Special thanks goes to Dustin W. Benge, Dustin Bruce, Joseph C. Harrod, Michael Plato and J. Ryan West for their proofreading assistance. We are also thankful to Jay Collier of Reformation Heritage Books and Justin Taylor of Crossway Books who offered helpful advice along the way. Susie Truax and Parkside Church (Cleveland) showed kind hospitality as we editors met to finalize drafts in the basement of the church, and we thank Mark and Jenn Nenadov for facilitating the accommodations. Finally, special thanks are due to our wives and children for allowing us the time needed to work on this project.

Church history as a pastoral discipline

By Sean Michael Lucas

WHEN ROBERT LEWIS Dabney (1820–1898) was thirty-three years old, he became professor of ecclesiastical history and polity at Union Theological Seminary in Virginia. As part of his inauguration, he gave a lecture on "The Uses and Results of Church History." In many ways, it was an amazing lecture. Although given in 1854, Dabney was already pointing out the problem of prejudice and personal history for "objective, scientific history;" noting that history provides an opportunity for cross-cultural thinking as a means for finding present-day blind spots; and wishing for a social history method that would complement more intellectual approaches. And yet, even with all of that, Dabney struggled to articulate one key point: What is the value of church history to pastoral ministry? Why bother with church history in training future ministers?[1]

Of course, Dabney was not and has not been the only church history professor who has struggled to justify his existence in a theological school. After all, most students come to seminary to study the Bible,

---

This paper was presented at the national meeting of the Evangelical Theological Society, San Francisco, November 17, 2011.

1   Robert Lewis Dabney, "The Uses and Results of Church History," in *Discussions*, 4 vols., ed. C.R. Vaughan (1891; reprint, Harrisonburg: Sprinkle, 1982), 2:1–25.

learn systematic theology or perfect their pastoral skills; relatively few come to take the required courses in church history (or history of Christianity, depending on the course title and description). Those few who do come specifically to take church history are often those who end up leaving seminary, not for congregational ministry but for further graduate work in history.[2]

As a result, professors of church history—and I was formerly numbered among them as a professor at Covenant Theological Seminary—have tried to explain to students who come to theological seminaries to become ministers why they need to bother with church history, why church history is not simply in the curriculum to provide professional historians with teaching positions and research opportunities or to make sure that there are a few hardy souls who can remember what happened ten years ago in a particular denomination or institution.

Central to my argument, both when I taught and now that I have returned to congregational ministry, is this: *I very much believe that church history is a pastoral discipline.* That is to say, there are few other theological disciplines as important and worthwhile for developing pastoral sensibilities and resources and for providing pastoral models (both good and bad) than studying church history. As a result, not only should church history be taught to aspiring pastors but also the theological curriculum would be poorer, and even incomplete, without it. In order to understand fully the impact of this claim, we must back up and think about church history as a historical, theological and cross-cultural discipline.

A historical discipline

It should be obvious that church history has value as a historical discipline. And there is value in training future ministers to think historically: such ways of thinking are actually important for ensuring that one survives and thrives in ministry. Pity the pastor who comes to a historic church and fails to understand and exegete the historical forces that have shaped that congregation for good and for ill.

---

2   This justification is required in the academy as well: see Henry Warner Bowden, *Church History in an Age of Uncertainty: Historiographical Patterns in the United States, 1906–1990* (Carbondale: Southern Illinois University Press, 1991).

But in saying that church history has value for ministers as a historical discipline, we have to step back and think about the purpose of history. Historian Grant Wacker reflected once on the challenges of teaching history at Duke Divinity School. One student, fresh out of the Marine Corps, told Wacker that he looked forward to hearing "the straight stuff" in his history class: "I don't pay ten grand a year to hear other students' opinions. I can get that in the lounge anytime. What I want is the true story, the way it really was, straight from you." A couple of days later, in the midst of a well-crafted lecture, a female student exploded, "I'm sick of all this Enlightenment crap! What I want to hear about are narratives, you know the stories of the oppressed." The differences between the ex-Marine and the postmodern female centred on the purpose of history, whether history was about "understanding the past" or "using the past."[3]

Of course, these distinctions represent a false dichotomy. What most people want, at the end of the day, is both to understand history and also to use history in ways that are appropriate and true. But this can only be done if we recognize that, because we tell history "from below," using human tools that can only account for human actions, all history is limited and fallible and hence contested history. From our fallible perspectives and our limited resources (even the best researchers cannot read or even find everything), we will necessarily tell a limited and fallible story. The stories we tell will be shaped by our cultural moments, identity and theological commitments and will be told for our own publics, purposes and problems. And these stories will be contestable and contested because there will be alternative perspectives and approaches that will highlight different angles of vision and use those stories for different purposes.

Because this is the case—because history represents an interpreted past that is contestable—we understand and use the past with a certain amount of caution, modesty and humility. This does not throw us into a postmodern, relativistic morass; we sift evidence and make propositional statements with "proper confidence" that what we say is true as far as we know. But we also speak recognizing that we are

---

3   Grant Wacker, "Understanding the Past, Using the Past," in *Religious Advocacy and American History*, ed. Bruce Kuklick and D.G. Hart (Grand Rapids: Wm. B. Eerdmans, 1997), 159–160.

constantly trying to piece together a knowledge that equivocates the "truth" (which God alone knows). In this we hope that we think God's historical knowledge after him.[4]

And when we think about it this way, the fact that church history teaches ministers and pastoral candidates caution, modesty and humility is actually a blessed thing. Such pastoral virtues can be extremely helpful in deciding not to replace a stained glass window of Jesus that was given by an elder's great-grandmother until the larger history, the local context, iconography and the Reformed tradition, are understood. Likewise, in the inevitable theological scraps with a local church or national denomination, caution, modesty and humility will cause us to look at situations with a longer historical view—both understanding and using history with appropriate caution, knowing that even our best understandings are contestable and contested.

A theological discipline

Of course, even in saying this, our understanding of history will necessarily be a relentless theological one. And so, we have to say that church history is a theological discipline and as such it is useful for pastoral ministry. By saying this, we do not mean that church history's value is found only when it does the history of doctrine, although undoubtedly church history does and must do this. Rather, we mean to say that church history forces us to own our theological commitments in ways that are pastorally healthy. We are forced to think through how our view of God, humanity, justice, sin, redemption and eschatology inevitably affect the stories we historians and pastors tell and the ways we tell them.[5]

For example, what view of ecclesiology lies behind the historical professions' focus on evangelicalism as a major interpretative lens for American religious history over the past thirty years? To be sure, there

---

4   Lesslie Newbigin, *Proper Confidence: Faith, Doubt, and Certainty in Christian Discipleship* (Grand Rapids: Wm. B. Eerdmans, 1995). The language of equivocation is a nod toward Thomas Aquinas, who teaches us that all our knowledge of God is necessarily approximate, analogous and limited, not univocal and comprehensive.

5   George Marsden notes that Christian perspectives will shape the selection of topics, the questions historians ask and the current theories accepted: see his "What Differences Might Christian Perspectives Make?" in *History and the Christian Historian*, ed. Ronald A. Wells (Grand Rapids: Wm. B. Eerdmans, 1998), 15–16.

is evidence that in some sections of the country, believers moved back and forth between Baptists, Presbyterians and Methodists with some ease. And yet, as historian Brooks Holifield has recognized, denominational labelling meant something to people in the eighteenth and nineteenth centuries: theological commitments were vital for the communions that most Americans joined. To put it baldly, historically speaking, people invested a great deal in being Baptist, Presbyterian or Methodist. To flatten those theological distinctions under the construct of "American evangelicalism" might actually say more about our own day than the past.[6]

For another example, how does one's theological perspective on humankind, and especially humans exercising power in church and state, shape our understanding of Constantine's Edict of Milan in 313? In that action, Constantine granted religious liberty to Christians throughout the Roman Empire, established Christianity as the official state religion and ended the persecution of Christians that had occurred under the reign of his predecessor. On the surface, all of this appears to be good: Christians moved from being oppressed to being secure and the gospel was now ascendant in the empire. But some groups—especially latter-day Baptists and Mennonites—have typically viewed this Constantinian settlement as a bad thing: it led to the merger of church and state, the influx of lapsed Christians and the moral and doctrinal downgrade of Christianity. One's theological commitments will inevitably affect how we think about these things.[7]

And our theological commitments will shape the way we think about the historical story and the nature of time. For those of us who grew up in the United States of America, we recognize the ways that our culture has taught us to tell time through our holidays—our holy days—reinforcing several things about being an American: it primarily tells us that being American means being successful in war, being on the winning team. Many of these days celebrate or remember those

---

6 E. Brooks Holifield, *Theology in America: Christian Thought from the Age of the Puritans to the Civil War* (New Haven: Yale University Press, 2003), 14.

7 For example, see Peter J. Leithart, *Defending Constantine: The Twilight of an Empire and the Dawn of Christendom* (Downers Grove: InterVarsity, 2010) and John Howard Yoder, *Christian Attitudes to War, Peace, and Revolution*, ed. Theodore J. Koontz and Andy Alexis-Baker (Grand Rapids: Brazos, 2009), 42–74.

who fought in the American Revolution, the Civil War or the First World War. This story also reminds us that Americans are for liberty and justice for all—both Martin Luther King Jr. Day and Independence Day highlight the centrality of these American virtues. However, our theological commitments should challenge our learned cultural story to see that there is a more biblical way of telling time with a different kind of war and a truer kind of liberty and justice.

All of this means that church history taught both as a historical and a theological discipline will train ministers to become much more self-critical and self-conscious about how our theological commitments shape the way we hear and tell stories. Along this line, I would suggest that a theologically reflective church history should make it impossible for ministers to embrace the type of "God and country" rhetoric so common in Protestant churches in the United States. In fact, such teaching should move us toward a more global understanding and appreciation of our world because Psalm 72 tells us that God's reign will extend from the River to the ends of the earth, not from America's "sea to shining sea."[8]

As a result, church history has a place in the theological curriculum for training ministers because it is a pastoral discipline that inculcates caution, moderation and humility and that encourages self-criticism and self-reflection in the light of hard won, biblically-based theological norms.

A cross-cultural discipline

Perhaps part of the way of meeting these concerns is to rethink what it means to think culturally. Borrowing from the anthropologist Clifford Geertz, we can suggest that religion operates within a culture or cultural system as the means by which people synthesize their ethos ("the tone, character, and quality of their life, its moral and aesthetic style and mood") and worldview ("the picture they have of the way things in sheer actuality are, their most comprehensive ideas of order"). Through their beliefs and practices, people are able to make sense of their worlds and their lives within those worlds.[9] By thinking in these terms, we can say

---

8   See Mark A. Noll, Nathan O. Hatch, and George M. Marsden, *The Search for Christian America* (Colorado Springs: Helmers and Howard, 1989).

9   Clifford Geertz, "Religion as a Cultural System," in *The Interpretation of Cultures* (New York: Basic Books, 1973), 89.

that religion conveys an identity (or even ideology) that provides meaning and purpose, charts directions and assimilates values.

As Christians, then, what we are trying to do in historical work is to tell stories about how Christians are. In other words, what we desire to trace is how Christian identity is formed and how this identity plays itself out in ways that are continuous and discontinuous with the biblical witness. Hence, some of the things in which church historians should be interested should include how Christianity has become incarnate or indigenous in discrete cultural systems; how these ways of being Christian have become traditioned and traditional (and hence, normative); and how these ways of being Christian continue (or do not continue) to shape Christian identity today.

When we begin to talk about Christian identity, we are especially interested in those beliefs, practices and stories which converge to form this identity. By beliefs, we particularly mean those core understandings that form and motivate what and how I practice. By practices, we speak of those ritual actions, those regular activities, that shape myself and my understanding of my world. These practices flow from my beliefs and reinforce those beliefs. And by stories, we think of those narratives which embed these beliefs and practices and make them all make sense.[10]

The problem comes, of course, in the reality that beliefs, practices and stories are not the only contributors to religious or personal identity. In fact, while religious commitments operate within a cultural system, they may not be the dominant force creating meaning, shaping ethos or informing worldview. Within that system, religious beliefs and practices mix with class, gender, race, region and geography, politics, education and other contributors. As historian D.G. Hart has pointed out, the failure of religious history generally has been its inability to present a compelling case for how religion actually makes a difference in historical figures' motivations or actions. But it is not simply the failure of religious history to make a case for how religion matters; rather, it is the complexity of the cultural systems themselves and the way religion can become captive to other concerns

---

10 See Sean Michael Lucas, *On Being Presbyterian: Our Beliefs, Practices, and Stories* (Phillipsburg: P & R Publishing, 2006).

that accounts for that failure. *Sometimes the story actually is how religious belief and practice fail to make a genuine difference.*[11]

I think part of the reason for this is that Christianity actually incarnates itself within the existing cultural system in ways that are surprising and unexpected, both for good and ill. As historian Andrew Walls suggested, taking seriously the "indigenizing principle" inevitably means that Christians, churches and Christianity itself will be "conditioned by a particular time and place, by our family and group and society, by 'culture' in fact." But God in his mercy still uses his people, even when their beliefs and practices are held captive by their cultural moment (remember, there is only one hero, Jesus; hence, God uses people even with their flaws).[12]

What is incumbent upon us is to be as self-critical as possible—to see where our cultural and personal blind spots might be and to seek to understand the ways in which we are captive to our own cultural moments. And so, church history is necessarily a cross-cultural work—a movement from our cultural moment/system to another—in order to have new eyes to see our own cultural blind spots, the ways our beliefs and practices are held captive by our commitments to our class, race, gender, region or whatever. Far from being inspirational, church history can actually serve a prophetic role—pointing out our failures to live the Christian life in ways consonant with the biblical witness.

Surely as church history serves to confront our cultural blind spots, it serves the pastoral role. Ministers are regularly called into situations where racial relations bear the strain of hundreds of years of inequality, where divorce and remarriage are easy fixes to deep generational patterns of sin, where local economies are built upon the exploitation of the creation. Learning how to engage these potential areas of blind-

---

11 D.G. Hart, "The Failure of American Religious History," *The Journal of The Historical Society* 1 (2000): 1–31. The cultural captivity theme was a major interpretative grid for historians of the American South during the Civil Rights era; the best of that literature was Samuel S. Hill's *Southern Churches in Crisis* (1966) (now titled *Southern Churches in Crisis Revisited* [Tuscaloosa: University of Alabama Press, 1996]) and John Lee Eighmy, *Churches in Cultural Captivity: A History of Social Attitudes of Southern Baptists* (1972; reprint, Knoxville: University of Tennessee Press, 1988).

12 Andrew F. Walls, "The Gospel as the Prisoner and Liberator of Culture," in *The Missionary Movement in Christian History: Studies in the Transformation of Faith* (Marynoll: Orbis, 1996), 7–8.

ness in our cultural moments happens best through historical work. And when this happens, the result should be a greater faithfulness in the present, a more sure identity for the challenges of today.

A discipline of wisdom

And so, church history has a great deal to offer ministers in their pastoral role: caution, moderation, humility, self-criticism and self-awareness, cultural awareness, pastoral compassion and prophetic voice. In doing all of this, I would suggest that church history offers ministers its greatest gift: wisdom.

And here we come back to the beginning with Robert Lewis Dabney and his inaugural address as Union Seminary's church historian. One of the central points that he makes is that "it is the knowledge of the past which gives to the young man the experience of age.... The man who undertakes to teach, to legislate, or to govern, either in church or state, without historical wisdom, is a reckless tyro." What does church history offer to ministers? Why should it be in the theological curriculum? It offers wisdom, the experience of age.[13]

In order to do this, church history professors have to learn to teach with an eye toward primarily inculcating not simply names, dates and places, but wisdom and insight. One of the unique design aspects of the main church history classes at Covenant Seminary when I taught there were the pastoral case studies that forced students to think through how historical situations relate to actual questions parishioners and seekers ask. As students wrestle with cases about friends captured by the New Age movement, worshipping in Oneness pentecostalism or at a free will Baptist church, or thinking that Allah and the Christian God are the same, they recognize that the historical moments that we studied actually help us see today more clearly; we find wisdom for the pastoral challenges we experience.

As we learn the stories of Israel and the church, as we learn the stories of the saints through the ages, we do so not for inspiration or for idolizing heroes. Rather, we learn these stories in order to gain wisdom and insight into what God has called us to be and to do in our present moment. As pastors, we need such wisdom and insight when dealing with the knotty issues of church life; and we gain it not only

---

13 Dabney, "Uses and Results of Church History," 12–13.

by listening to the wisdom of the celebrity pastor *du jour* or even of fellow pastors within our presbytery. Rather, we gain real insight by listening to the communion of the saints through the ages.

It is as we study the church's history—thinking historically, guided theologically, working cross-culturally—that we find new streams of wisdom to guide our pastoral practice. And so it is that church history is a profoundly pastoral discipline.

PATRISTICS · MEDIEVAL

The Spirit "worshipped and glorified" as the perfecting cause of our worship in Basil of Caesarea's De Spiritu Sancto

By Dennis Ngien

Introduction

THE MOST IMPORTANT work on the Holy Spirit in the fourth century came from the pen of Basil of Caesarea (*c.* A.D. 330–379).[1] The immediate occasion of Basil's *On the Holy Spirit* was a dispute with the Pneumatomachians (the "Spirit-fighters") over the doxology he introduced, glorifying the Father "*with* the Son, together *with* the Holy Spirit."[2] The apologetic intention of this treatise is clearly stated: "The one aim of the whole band of these enemies of sound doctrine is to shake the faith of Christ down to its foundations, by utterly leveling apostolic tradition to the ground.... But we will not surrender the truth; we will not betray the defense like cowards."[3] Basil's treatise was

---

1 Richard Hanson, "The Divinity of the Holy Spirit," *The Church Quarterly* 1 (1969): 300.

2 David Anderson, introduction to Basil the Great, *On the Holy Spirit*, trans. David Anderson (Crestwood: St. Vladimir's Seminary Press, 1980), 1.3. Hereafter cited as *On the Spirit*. See also Saint Basil, *De Spiritu Sancto*, trans. Blomfield Jackson, in *The Nicene and Post-Nicene Fathers*, Second Series, ed. Philip Schaff and Henry Wace, vol. 8 (Grand Rapids: Wm. B. Eerdmans, 1989). Hereafter cited as *De Spiritu Sancto*. See T.A. Noble, "Gregory Nazianzen's Use of Scripture in Defence of the Deity of the Spirit," *Tyndale Bulletin* 39 (1988): 106.

3 *On the Spirit* 10.25.

probably aimed at his former mentor, Eustathius, whose subordination doctrine of the Spirit was widespread.[4] This piece is Christocen-
tric in its focus, but trinitarian in its content. The Christological
formulation of Nicaea (A.D. 325) is the basis of Basil's pneumatology.
Just as the Son belongs rightly to the Godhead, so also the Spirit is
placed within the same Deity, not under or outside it. Because the
Spirit is indivisibly united in being and agency with the Father and the
Son, he is to be equally rendered that which only God should receive:
honour and worship.

Basil inculcated in the church's worship the form with which he
regarded as rooted not only in tradition but, most importantly, in
Scripture. He also saw this form not as contradictory, but complemen-
tary with the customary form of worship, "Glory to the Father through
the Son in the Spirit." The former admits of the immanental unity and
close communion of the members of the Trinity; the latter admits of
the way the triune God deals with us in the economy of salvation. That
the Spirit belongs intrinsically to the same Godhead as the Father and
Son must be believed for one's salvation, and concomitantly for the
possibility of true worship. The contemplation of the Spirit's titles,
operations and gifts is the dynamic of true worship. The saving import
of the Spirit's deity lies in this: the Spirit places us in Christ so that our
worship, as a participation in the Son's communion with the Father,
is found pleasing. The believer, "the place of the Spirit," is enabled to
offer doxology to God.[5] The church's worship is truly ours insofar as it
participates in the Spirit's unitive movement through the only begotten to the Father.

The aim of this chapter is to show how the confession of the Spirit's
deity in Basil's treatise is constitutive of a theology of worship, in
which the Spirit is not only the lawful object of worship, the one who
receives our praise, but also the perfecting cause, the one through
whom our worship in the Son finds admission into the heavenly choir
of angels.

---

4   Robert Letham, *The Holy Trinity. In Scripture, History, Theology, and Worship*
(Phillipsburg: P & R Publishing, 2001), 148.

5   *On the Spirit* 26.63.

Basil's reticence: Homoousios

It is historically accurate that one does not find in Basil's *On the Spirit* an explicit assertion of the deity of the Spirit as in Gregory of Nazianzus' (A.D. 329/30–389/90) *Fifth Theological Oration:* "What then? Is the Spirit God? Most certainly. Well, then, is he consubstantial? Yes, if he is God."[6] Both Richard Hanson and Gary Badcock argue that for fear of presumably creating a scandal, Basil was not as intransigent as Athanasius (c. A.D. 296–373) in predicating the term *homoousios* of the Spirit.[7] Alasdair Heron concurs with them, when he says, "Basil... drew back—at least in his official, public statements—from calling the Spirit 'God' because it could cause offence."[8] It was primarily his pastoral concern for church unity that caused his reticence. Cyril Karam stated: "Basil's reticence was for the sake of gaining the weak, making himself weak for them."[9] Basil perceived the danger of the theological controversies which might turn the church into a naval battlefield. The Arian controversy, for one, beset the church like a raging storm, creating schism, irreconcilable hatred and party spirits. Basil described the dangerous effects: "We attack one another, we are overthrown by one another. If the enemy does not strike us first we are wounded by our comrade; if he is wounded and falls, he is trampled by his fellow soldier. Although we are united in our hatred of common

---

6 Gregory of Nazianzen, *Orationes* 29.15; 40.43 as cited in Thomas F. Torrance, *The Christian Doctrine of God* (Edinburgh: T & T Clark, 1996), 127. See Tom A. Noble, "Gregory Nazianzen's Use of Scripture in Defence of the Deity of the Spirit," *Tyndale Bulletin* 39 (1988): 123; Frederick W. Norris, "Gregory the Theologian," *Pro Ecclesia* 2 (1993): 483.

7 R.P.C Hanson, *The Search for the Christian Doctrine of God* (Edinburgh: T & T Clark, 1988), 776; Gary D. Badcock, *Light of Truth and Fire of Love: A Theology of the Holy Spirit* (Grand Rapids: Wm. B. Eerdmans, 1997), 55. Jean Gribomont, "Intransigence and Irenicism in Saint Basil's 'De Spiritu Sancto,'" in *Word and Spirit: A Monastic Review. In Honor of Saint Basil the Great* (Still River: St. Bede's Publications, 1979), 118.

8 Alasdair Heron, *The Holy Spirit* (Philadelphia: Westminster, 1983), 81.

9 Cyril Karam, "Basil on the Holy Spirit—Some aspects of His Theology," in *Word and Spirit*, 143. However, Mark J. Larson, in his "A Re-examination of *De Spiritu Sancto*: Saint Basil's Bold Defence of the Spirit's Deity," *Scottish Bulletin of Evangelical Theology* 19 (2001): 65–84, argues for the contrary, that although Basil may have been somewhat reserved, a restrained style does not characterize his *On the Spirit*. Whether Larson's position is right or not is beyond the scope of this work.

foes, no sooner do they retreat, and we find enemies in each other."[10] Thus he stated: "Since no human voice is powerful enough to be heard in such an uproar, I reckon that silence is more profitable than words."[11]

Officially, the creedal term *homoousios* was reserved for the relationship between the Father and the Son. The Nicene faith constituted what Basil called the "kerygma," the publicly proclaimed teaching heard by all, which he distinguished from "dogma," the teaching "given to us secretly through apostolic tradition."[12] Here in his document, he observed the "kerygma," the church's established teaching. He applied the Christological defense of the Nicene faith to his doctrine of the Spirit, although without using the word *homoousios*. He refrained from attributing the same term to the Spirit, for that might create the adverse effect of alienating his supporters or contraries, through a misunderstanding of the terminology. So, at such a crucial moment, the unity of the orthodox position took priority over theological controversy or terminological clarification. In lieu of affirming categorically the deity of the Spirit, Basil preferred to repudiate the doctrine that held that the Spirit belongs to the creaturely order and bears no ontological status of God. In preserving the ecumenical spirit, his aim was to not drive away those who in principle rejected the creatureliness of the Spirit, but had not been convinced of the deity of the Spirit. Being interested in convincing rather than crushing his opponents, Basil sought to lead them through worship to an assertion of the divinity of the Spirit. For this reason he wrote *On the Spirit*, in which, in showing that his version of the doxology, "Glory be to the Father, with the Son and with the Spirit," is justifiable, he too demonstrates that the Spirit is God, although without forthrightly calling him "God."[13]

---

10 *On the Spirit* 30.77.

11 *On the Spirit* 30.78.

12 *On the Spirit* 17.65–66. For a discussion of Basil's use of tradition to develop his pneumatology, see Emmanuel Amand de Mendieta, "The Pair Kerygma and Dogma in the Theological Thought of St. Basil of Caesarea," *Journal of Theological Studies* 16 (1965): 129–142; Emmanuel Amand de Mendieta, *The "Unwritten" and "Secret" Apostolic Tradition in the Theological Thought of St. Basil of Caesarea* (Edinburgh: Oliver and Boyd, 1965); R.P.C. Hanson, "Basil's Doctrine of the Tradition in Relation to the Holy Spirit," *Vigiliae Christianae* 22 (1968): 241–255.

13 Justol L. González, *A History of Christian Thought*, 3 vol. (Nashville: Abingdon Press, 1970), 1:317. Basil explicitly used the term *homoousios* in one of his letters: "And if He is

Moreover Basil did not shrink from speaking the truth about the supreme nature of the Spirit. He declared: "We place our trust in the Spirit's help, and boldly proclaim the truth."[14] Basil marshalled his arguments against the Pneumatomachians, not desiring of their damnation but their salvation: "For my own part, I fervently pray that the good God will make His peace to reign in everyone's heart, so that these men who are swollen with pride and who bitterly rage against us may be calmed by the Spirit of gentleness and love."[15]

Christology as prolegomena to pneumatology

Historically, the assertion of the deity of the Son is not only the ground of a true knowledge of God, but also the presupposition of true worship. The indissoluble unity of revelation of God and piety means there is no speech about God without reverential worship. The Christological controversies of Nicaea adopted what Jaroslav Pelikan called "the standard disjunctive syllogism" as the method of argumentation: either he is God or a creature; if the former, he is the object of worship; if the latter, it is idolatry to worship him.[16] The line of absolute distinction between God and the creature in respect to the identity of the Son is determinative of orthodoxy or heresy. The Council of Nicaea affirmed that the Son belongs to the uncreated order, and is himself God as the Father is God, not a created intermediary between God and the world as is in Arius' thought. This mode of argumentation was meant to lead Arians to believe and "confess Him to be fully God, one with God, the object of worship," although they refused to concede his oneness with God.[17] Echoing the same method of syllistic argumentation, Basil questioned his opponents concerning whether the Spirit be placed on God's side of the line: "Will they rank Him with God, or

---

not a creature, He is consubstantial with God." See Saint Basil, Letter 8, trans., Roy J. Deferrari, in *Saint Basil: The Letters* (Cambridge, 1950), 1:81 as cited in Larson, "A Reexamination of *De Spiritu Sancto*: Saint Basil's Bold Defence of the Spirit's Deity," 67.

14 *On the Spirit* 30.79.

15 *On the Spirit* 29.75; 1.2.

16 Jaroslav Pelikan, "The 'Spiritual Sense' of Scripture: The Exegetical Basis for St. Basil's Doctrine of the Holy Spirit," in *Basil of Caesarea: Christian Humanist, Ascetic*, ed. Paul J. Fedwick (Toronto: Pontifical Institute of Medieval Studies, 1981), part 1, 342.

17 J.H. Newman, *The Arians of the Fourth Century*, 3rd ed. (London: 1871), 217.

will they push Him to a creature's place?"[18] Does the Holy Spirit belong to the created order? Does he have his being with the Son on the divine side of that line of demarcation between the Creator and the creature? Given that the deity of the Son was the central issue at the Council of Nicaea, we encounter there only the phrase, "We believe in the Holy Spirit," without elaboration. The church recognized "such vagueness would not do, that the Church of Christ was disintegrating into a jumble of warring factions, and that…words adequate for God, were necessary to define the catholic faith."[19] It was only in subsequent years, between A.D. 325 and 381, that profound reflection on the personal nature of the Holy Spirit emerged, which eventually led to a matured understanding of it. Basil the Great, bishop of Caesarea, was instrumental in helping the church find the linguistic and conceptual models for understanding the Spirit.

Athanasius has Christology as his theological prolegomena, the starting point for his pneumatology. Statements about the Spirit are to be derived from the Christological formulation. To deny the essence of the Son with the Father is to deny the essence of the Spirit. He stated, "from our knowledge of the Son we may be able to have true knowledge of the Spirit. For we shall find that the Spirit has to the Son the same proper relationship as we have known the Son to have to the Father."[20] The language of the Spirit's relationship to the Son as the Son is to the Father frequently occurs throughout his correspondence with Serapion. To cite one:

> For as the Son, who is in the Father and the Father in him, is not
> a creature but pertains to the essence of the Father (for this you
> also profess to say); so also it is not lawful to rank with the crea-
> tures the Spirit, who is in the Son, and the Son in him, nor to divide
> him from the Word and reduce the Triad to imperfection.[21]

---

18 *On the Spirit* 16.37. See Leslie Prestige, *God in Patristic Thought* (London: S.P.C.K., 1952), 80–86.

19 Anderson's introduction to *On the Holy Spirit*, 7.

20 Letter III.1; quotations of Athanasius' *Letters to Serapion* are from C.R.B. Shapland's translation, *The Letters of Saint Athanasius Concerning the Holy Spirit* (London: The Epworth Press, 1951).

21 Letter I.21.

Similarly evident in Basil's treatise is the movement from the confession of the Son's deity to that of the Spirit's deity.[22] Asserting the full deity of the Son, as in the Nicene Creed, was the basis for asserting the full deity of the Spirit. Basil declared, in regard to the baptismal statements with reference to Christ: "To address Christ in this way is a complete profession of faith, because it clearly reveals that God anoints the Son (the Anointed One) with the unction of the Spirit."[23] To speak of Christ is to speak of the entire Godhead. Thus Christology is the abiding presupposition of trinitarian theology. Against those who subordinate the Spirit, Basil argued that the Spirit is united through the Son to the Father, and that belief in three persons upholds the orthodox doctrine of divine unity:

We do not divide divine knowledge and scatter the pieces to the winds; we behold one Form [so to speak] united by the invariableness of the Godhead, present in God the Father and God the Only-Begotten. The Son is in the Father and the Father in the Son; what the Father is, the Son is likewise and vice versa—such is the unity. As unique Persons [eg. the Father and the Son], they are one and one; as sharing a common nature, both are one. How does one and one not equal two Gods? Because we speak of the emperor, and the emperor's image—but not two emperors…and since the divine nature is not composed of parts, union of the persons is accomplished by partaking of the whole. The Holy Spirit is one, and we speak of Him as unique, since through the one Son He is joined to the Father. He completes the all-praised blessed Trinity.… He does not share created nature. He is united to the Father and the Son.[24]

Latent in the baptismal formula of Matthew 28:19–20 is the confession of the Spirit's deity on account of Jesus' own words. "This passage," Pelikan stated, "became the cornerstone of Basil's case" for the Spirit's

---

22 Kei Yamamura, "The Development of the Doctrine of the Holy Spirit in Patristic Philosophy: St. Basil and Gregory of Nyssa," *St. Vladimir's Theological Quarterly* 18 (1974), 14–15.

23 *On the Spirit* 12.28.

24 *On the Spirit* 18.45.

deity.[25] The great importance Basil attached to this passage was obvious in the way he framed his own question: "But before the great tribunal, what have I prepared to say on the great day of judgment?" With reverence, he then answered with these words: "This: that I was in the first place led to the glory of the Spirit by the honor conferred by the Lord in associating Him with Himself and with His Father at baptism."[26] Jesus' command in baptism reveals his delight in his communion with the Spirit, and in being ranked with him. Thus it is impious of us not to obey Jesus' own words (Acts 5:29). The arrangement of the name of Father, Son and Spirit in "the baptism of salvation" testifies to their union and communion within God's own life.[27] The Matthean text does not establish conumeration nor subnumeration, but rather the co-ordination between the Father, Son and Spirit—the three persons conspire together in perfecting baptism. This solves the problem of subordinationism. Hence Basil challenged his opponents: "Their names are mentioned in one and the same series, how can you speak of numbering *with* or numbering *under*?"[28] If we must count, he wrote, we do so not by arithmetic adding, implying three separate deities. Citing Isaiah 44:6, "I am the first, and I am the last," Basil concluded that there is one supreme God and three distinct persons of equal dignity. As unique persons [Father, Son and Spirit], they are one, one and one; as sharing a common nature, all are one.[29] This order established by the Lord is not the order of rank, but of relationship, in which the Spirit's relation to the Son "equals" to that of the Son with the Father.[30] The Spirit is to be glorified with the Father and the Son because he is the same in nature and not inferior in dignity from them.

---

25 Pelikan, "The 'Spiritual Sense' of Scripture," 346.

26 *De Spiritu Sancto* 29.75.

27 *On the Spirit* 10.24.

28 *On the Spirit* 17.43. See Henry B. Swete, *The Holy Spirit in the Ancient Church* (Grand Rapids: Baker, 1912), 232ff.

29 *On the Spirit* 18.45. Basil Studer, *The Trinity and Incarnation of the Early Church*, trans. Matthias Westerhoff, ed. Andrew Louth (Collegeville: The Liturgical Press, 1993), 142, where he states that Basil was the first to distinguish between *hypostasis* and *ousia*.

30 *On the Spirit* 17.43.

Through the baptismal formula, we are initiated into the knowledge of the triune God.[31] The invocation of the trinitarian formula is essential to making baptism "complete and perfect."[32] The invocation of any single person alone is never alone, but always in proximity and unity with the other two. Scripture speaks of being baptized into Christ (Galatians 3:27), yet no one would say that the invocation of Christ's name alone renders baptism efficacious. Likewise, when Scripture speaks of being baptized with the Spirit (Acts 1:5), it does not intend to say the invocation of the Spirit's name alone suffices. To speak of Christ is to speak of the triune God, even when Scripture may omit the names of the Father and the Spirit; likewise to speak of baptism by the Spirit alone does not exclude the other two. The three persons are inseparably united in being, communion and agency, without which baptism is divested of its saving reality.

Basil's opponents refused to accept his position that baptism in the Spirit suffices for the Spirit to be ranked with God. Based on 1 Corinthians 10:2, "They were baptized into Moses in the *cloud* and in the *sea*," they denied the Spirit's consubstantiality with God. They argued that it was common of the old to profess faith "in the Lord *and* in his servant Moses" (Exodus 14:31) without magnifying either. Thus, baptism in the Spirit is no basis for ranking him with God, just as baptism in Moses is no basis for exalting him above others. As a response, Basil undertook a typological exegesis of 1 Corinthians 10:2, conceiving of Moses' exodus event as a shadow or type of the grace which was yet to come.[33] The order in which he discussed these two types is not the same as they actually appear in the text. Here Basil transposed the order of the text, beginning with type "sea" instead of type "cloud." This transposition parallels Basil's understanding of what happens in baptism.[34] In the sea, the enemies are swallowed up by its killing waves; in baptism, the enmity between us and God is swallowed up in victory. The old self dies in the waves, as typified by the "sea," and the new self rises from the water imbued with the Spirit, as foreshadowed by the "cloud."

---

31 *On the Spirit* 29.75.

32 *On the Spirit* 12.28.

33 *On the Spirit* 14.31.

34 Michael A.G. Haykin, "'In the Cloud and In the Sea': Basil of Caesarea and the Exegesis of 1 Cor. 10:2," *Vigiliae Christianae* 40 (1986): 142.

The people emerged from the sea unharmed, and we come up from the water as alive from the dead, saved by the grace of Him who has called us. The cloud is a shadow of the Spirit's gifts, for He cools the flames of our passions through the mortification of our bodies.[35]

If the separation of the Spirit from the first two persons renders baptism ineffectual, Basil reasoned, the same holds true for the confession of faith. Should the confession of the deity of the Spirit be wanting, Christ and all his redeeming benefits are devoid of any saving efficacy:

He who redeemed our life from corruption gave us the power to be renewed, and the source of this power is hidden in an indescribable mystery. It brings great salvation to our souls, but to add or to take anything away from it is to forfeit eternal life. The position of the baptizer who separates the Spirit from the Father and the Son is precarious indeed, since the baptism received from him is useless. How can we be safe if we tear the Spirit away from the Father and the Son? Faith and baptism are two inseparably united means of salvation. Faith is perfected through baptism; the foundation of baptism is faith, and both are fulfilled through the same names. First we believe in the Father, Son and Holy Spirit; then we are baptized in the name of the Father, the Son and the Holy Spirit. The profession of faith leads us salvation, and then baptism follows, sealing our affirmation.[36]

The knowledge by which Christ is known as our redeemer is the domain of the Spirit. The Spirit's deity is necessary for the confession of Christ, otherwise nothing remains of faith, baptism and salvation. "For he who does not believe the Spirit," Basil declared, "does not believe the Son, for none can say that Jesus is Lord but by the Holy

---

35 *On the Spirit* 14.31.

36 *On the Spirit* 12.28. Also cited in Michael A.G. Haykin, *The Spirit of God. The Exegesis of 1 & 2 Corinthians in the Pneumatomachian Controversy of the Fourth Century* (Leiden: E.J. Brill, 1994), 130.

Spirit."[37] All three persons work together as One God *ad extra*, achieving salvation for us. Christ, the Spirit and salvation are so closely bound that none can be viewed independently of the other. Basil thus exhorted his people to preserve the Spirit's deity in the profession of faith, and sing him doxology together with the Father and the Son at baptism.

Correspondence theory: Spirit's titles, operations and gifts

Procedurally, Basil moved from Christological titles, works and blessings to discern the proper nature and dignity of Christ. Titles perform the task of identifying the nature and grace of Christ. Titles such as Son, Only-Begotten, Power and Wisdom of God and Word are reflective of his supreme dignity, exalting him as "the name which is above every name" (Philippians 2:9). It is with these titles that Christ is glorified as God and Son together *with* the Father. The phrase *with him* denotes the Son's communion with his Father. Basil dealt with this Christological question: In what way does the Son come *after* the Father? Does it refer to a later in time, or in rank, or in dignity? In God, he argued, there is no before, nor after. An *after* in time is senseless, for how could "the Maker of the ages" hold "a second place; no interval could possibly divide the natural union of Father and Son."[38] Basil elaborated:

> Even limited human thought demonstrates that it is impossible for the Son to be younger than the Father; first, we cannot conceive of either apart from their relationship with each other, and second, the very idea of "coming after" is applied to something separated from the present by a smaller interval of time than something else which "came earlier."...In addition to being impious, is it really not the height of folly to measure the life of Him who transcends all times and ages, whose existence is incalculably remote from the present? Things subject to birth and corruption are described as prior to one another; are we therefore to compare God the Father as superior to God the Son, who exists before the ages?[39]

---

37 *On the Spirit* 11.27.
38 *On the Spirit* 6.14.
39 *On the Spirit* 6.14.

For Athanasius, as was for Basil, the begetting of the Son is not a temporal begetting, involving procreation, separation or creation. "The supreme eminence of the Father is inconceivable; thought and reflection are utterly unable to penetrate the begetting of the Lord."[40] Basil maintained the concept of the Son's begetting within the "tangible boundaries" of the two words of St. John: "In the *beginning was* the Word" (John 1:1). He wrote: "No matter how far your thoughts travel backward, you cannot get beyond the *was*. No matter how hard you strain to see what is beyond the Son, you will find it impossible to pass outside the confines of the *beginning*."[41] Therefore the preposition *with* is rightly attached to the doxology of the church, which speaks of the Son and the Father as inseparably one in name and nature, as the radiance and its source (glory) are inseparably joined.

Basil continued: an *after* in place, which relegates the Son as subordinate to the Father, also does not make sense because the Father cannot be separated from the Son spatially. There is no partition in the being of God, for God is indivisibly one. God permeates all things, and cannot be confined in defined places. Both the Father and Son are incorporeal beings who, in their own rights, cannot be conceived in the same manner as corporeal beings. The opponents' error, Basil contended, lies in their misunderstanding of biblical metaphors. "In a fallen, fleshly sense," they wrongly applied form, shape and bodily position to a being like God, confining the absolute, the infinite, the incorporeal, within prescribed boundaries of the creaturely world. This is tantamount to collapsing the distinction between the uncreated order and created order. When Hebrews 1:3 spoke of the Son as sitting at the Father's *right hand*, the writer did not intend a creaturely meaning, referring to "a lower place as they contend, but a relationship of equality" he has with his Father. By such expression, the writer extols "the magnificence of the Son's great dignity."[42] Basil rebutted: "How is it not reckless to rob the Son of His position of equality in the doxology as if He deserved to be ranked in a lower place?"[43] He exhorted his opponents to learn that the phrase *right hand* refers to Christ as "the

---

40 *On the Spirit* 6.14.

41 *On the Spirit* 6.14.

42 *On the Spirit* 6.15.

43 *On the Spirit* 6.15.

power of God and wisdom of God, and the image of the invisible God, and the brightness of His glory, and the one whom God the Father has sealed, whom the Father stamped with the image of His Person."[44]

Other titles such as Shepherd, King, Physician, Bridegroom, Way, Door, Fountain, Bread, Axe and Rock reveal the grace of Christ, not his nature.[45] Most appropriate to these titles is the phrase *through whom*, which expresses our relationship with him, or the way in which he works grace in us. Since both the Father and the Son are involved in creation, the act of creating from the Father *through* the Son substantiates "their unity of will."[46] The "commandment" the Father gave to the Son is not one that proceeds from a superior to an inferior; nor does a "transmission of will" from the Father to the Son occur temporally in a created order, with an interval of time in between but, like a reflection of an object in a mirror, occurs eternally within the Godhead "without passage of time."[47] Therefore the phrase "*through whom* admits of a principal [antecedent] cause, but cannot be used as an objection against the efficient cause."[48] Basil listed a treasury of blessings which reaches us from the Father *through* the Son: revelation, sanctification, illumination, guidance, healing, providence, etc. The preposition *through* reflects an order in the Godhead, which God keeps in its proper place without attributive diminutive inferiority or slavish obedience to a being like God. For the order has nothing to do with the order of importance or value, but with *relationship* between the Father and the Son. Thus it is godlike glory for the Son to obey the Father who commands, as is proper to the relationship between them. From this, Basil derived his conclusion concerning the nature and work of the Son whose origin is the Father:

> We must not be so dazzled by the greatness of the Lord's works that we imagine that He has no origin. What does the self-existent One say about this? "I live through the Father," (Jn. 6:57) and concerning the divine power He says that "the Son can do

---

44 *On the Spirit* 6.15.
45 *On the Spirit* 8.17.
46 *On the Spirit* 8.21.
47 *On the Spirit* 8.20.
48 *On the Spirit* 8.21.

nothing of His own accord" (Jn. 5:19). Where is the source of His perfect wisdom? "The Father...has Himself given me command-ment what to say and what to speak" (Jn. 12:49). Through all these words...He directs our amazement at everything that He has made so that we may know the Father through Him....[T]he Word was full of His Father's grace; He shines forth from the Father, and accomplishes everything to His parent's plan. He is not different in essence, nor is He different in power from the Father, and if their power is equal, then their works are the same. Christ is the power of God, and the wisdom of God. All things were made through Him, and all things were created through Him and for Him, not as if He were discharging the service of a slave, but instead He creatively fulfills the will of His Father.[49]

Consequently, the church accepted both forms of worship, on the one hand ascribing glory to the Son with the Father, and on the other hand affirming the way God's grace reaches us from the Father through the Son in a differentiated unity between them. The form *with* was most appropriate for adoration offered to the immanent Godhead, while the form *through* was best for giving thanks for the way God deals with humans in the economy of salvation.

Whenever we reflect on the majesty of the nature of the Only-Begotten, and the excellence of His dignity, we ascribe the glory to Him *with* the Father. On the other hand, when we consider the abundant blessings He has given us, and how He has admit-ted us as co-heirs into God's household, we acknowledge that this grace works for us *through* Him and *in* Him. Therefore the best phrase when giving Him glory is *with whom* and the most appro-priate for giving thanks is *through whom*.[50]

The same procedure emerges in Basil's apprehension of the Spirit's dignity. The justification of his liturgical practice is to be sought in three sets of biblical passages that deal with titles, activities and gifts.

---

49 *On the Spirit* 8.19.

50 *On the Spirit* 7.16. Also cited in Christopher A. Hall, *Learning Theology with the Church Fathers* (Downers Grove: InterVarsity Press, 2002), 106.

The theological implications for the nature of the Spirit, and its causal connection with worship, can be drawn from the same. Not by discursive exercise, but by contemplation, Basil proceeded from the Spirit's titles, operations and gifts to an assertion of the supreme nature of the Spirit. In so doing, he accentuates a correspondence between God's nature and God's names, God's immanent being and God's economic actions, divine attributes and the various gifts. Arguably, he claimed, it is possible to "arrive to a certain extent at intelligent apprehension of the sublimity of His nature and of His approachable power" by pondering upon the meaning of his name, the greatness of his works and the bountiful blessings of his gifts.[51]

Basil asked, "First of all, who can listen to the Spirit's titles and not be lifted up in his soul? Whose thoughts would not be raised to contemplate the supreme nature?"[52] He began listing the different titles for the Spirit in the Bible: "He is called the Spirit of God (Matthew 3:16), the Spirit of truth who proceeds from the Father, the right Spirit, willing Spirit. His first and most proper title is Holy Spirit, a name most especially appropriate to everything which is incorporeal, purely immaterial, and indivisible."[53] While nowhere did Basil say that the Spirit is God, he saw a correspondence between these titles and the Spirit's supreme nature. The biblical language for the Spirit reflects the very nature of the Spirit. For instance, the incorporeal being such the Spirit "cannot be circumscribed. When we hear of the word 'Spirit' it is impossible for us to conceive of something whose nature can be circumscribed or is subject to change or variation, or is like a creature in any way."[54] All his titles are his by right and nature, not by exaltation.

The Spirit is called holy, as the Father is holy and the Son is holy. For creatures, holiness comes from without; for the Spirit, holiness fills His very nature. He is not sanctified, but sanctifies. He is called good, as the Father is good; the essence of the Spirit embraces the goodness of the Father.... He shares the name

---

51 *De Spiritu Sancto* 19.48.
52 *On the Spirit* 9.22.
53 *On the Spirit* 9.22.
54 *On the Spirit* 9.22.

Paraclete with the Only-Begotten, who said, "I will ask the Father, and He will give you another Paraclete." The Spirit shares these titles held in common by the Father and the Son; He receives these titles due to His natural and intimate relationship with them.[55]

As a solution to the Tropici's problem[56] about the origin of the Spirit, Basil wrote: the Spirit is "from God," not in the way creaturely things are from him, but as "proceeding" from the Father, "not by generation, like the Son, but as breath of his mouth."[57] Constitutive of the Godhead is a relational dynamism, in which the three persons mutually relate to each other. The Spirit is called "the Spirit of Christ, since he is naturally related to Him" (Romans 8:9); as "the Paraclete, he reflects the goodness of the Paraclete (Father) who sent Him, and His own dignity reveals the majesty of Him from Whom He proceeded," just as the Son's dignity reveals the majesty of him from whom he came.[58] The testimony of mutual glory of the Father, Son and Spirit is in the fourth Gospel, where the Son glorifies the Father (John 17:4), the Spirit glorifies the Son (John 16:14) and the Father glorifies the Son (John 13:28). The glory that they share is not a servile kind, offered by a creature to his superior. It is a kind of glory shared by "intimates, and it is this which the Spirit fulfills."[59] The Spirit, who is "from God," never exists outside God, but is eternally related to the Father and the Son within the Godhead, and hence is to be glorified with them

Scripture also testifies that the Spirit is called *Lord*. Basil wrote: "Our opponents place the Holy Spirit among the ministering spirits sent forth to serve.... Let them listen to even more testimony of the Spirit's lordship: 'Now the Lord is the Spirit' (2 Corinthians 3:17), and 'this comes from the Lord who is the Spirit' (2 Corinthians 3:18)."[60] As proof, Basil quoted the apostle's words at length: "To this day, when they read the Old Testament, that same veil remains unlifted, because

---

55 *On the Spirit* 19.48.

56 The Tropici were a group in Alexandria who taught the heresy that the Spirit was created out of nothing and was not God but a superior angel.

57 *On the Spirit* 18.46.

58 *On the Spirit* 18.46.

59 *On the Spirit* 18.46.

60 *On the Spirit* 21.52.

only through Christ is it taken away...when a man turns to the Lord the veil is removed. Now the Lord is the Spirit" (2 Corinthians 3:14, 16–17).[61] Basil's identification of the Spirit as Lord is later incorporated into the Constantinopolitan Creed: "And in the Holy Spirit, the Lord and life-giver, Who proceeds from the Father, Who is worshipped and glorified together with the Father and Son, Who spoke through the prophets."[62] The creedal declaration that the Spirit is Lord, as Thomas Torrance states, possesses "the effect of affirming full belief in the unqualified Deity of the Holy Spirit along with the Father and the Son."[63] The same effect may be predicated of Basil's attribution of the Spirit as Lord, a title specifically reserved in the biblical tradition for God himself.[64]

The Spirit's operations are the ground of his being God, neither an intermediary nor a creature. By the Christological method, Basil justified a theology of worship proper to the Spirit on the basis of the works he performs. Just as "the recital of [Christ's] benefits is an appropriate argument in favor of the doxology [addressed to] him,"[65] so also "the enumeration of the wondrous works that [the Spirit] has done" is the legitimate basis of glorifying him.[66] Concerning the Spirit's deeds, Basil wrote: "His works are ineffable in majesty, and innumerable in quantity."[67]

Because the Spirit performs various works which are exclusively divine, he must share the divine nature. For instance, if sanctification is exclusively a divine work, and if it is the Spirit who sanctifies (1 Corinthians 6:11), then the Spirit must be God. We know of the loftiness of the Spirit's nature because the Spirit works as the Father and the Son. Basil illustrated this by considering creation. Based on Psalm 33:6, "By the Word of the Lord the heavens are made, and all their hosts by the Spirit of His mouth," Basil asserted that while three persons are named: the Lord, his Word and his Spirit, yet David did

---

61 On the Spirit 21.52.

62 John H. Leith, ed., Creeds of the Churches: A Reader in Christian Doctrine from the Bible to the Present, 3rd ed. (Atlanta: John Knox Press, 1982), 33.

63 Torrance, The Christian Doctrine of God, 96.

64 Larson, "A Re-examination of De Spiritu Sancto," 71.

65 De Spiritu Sancto 8.17.

66 On the Spirit 23.54.

67 On the Spirit 19.49.

not acknowledge more than one Creator. The Lord does not act separately, nor does the Word act separately, nor does the Breath act separately. All three persons work *ad extra* in full unity with himself as one God in creation, as in salvation. Creation is a work performed exclusively by God, but because Scripture attributes the operations of creation to the Spirit, then the Spirit's deity is affirmed. The Spirit cannot be separated in being and act from the Father and the Son. He is united with them in being the cause of everything that exists. So when thinking of creation, he advised:

> [F]irst think of Him who is the first cause of everything that exists: namely, the Father, and then of the Son, who is the creator, and then the Holy Spirit, the perfector…. The Originator of all things is One: He creates through the Son and perfects through the Spirit. The Father's work is in no way imperfect, since He accomplishes all in all, nor is the Son's work deficient if it is not completed by the Spirit. The Father creates through His will alone and does not need the Son, yet chooses to work through the Son. Like the Son works as the Father's likeness, and needs no other cooperation, but He chooses to have His work completed through the Spirit.[68]

Basil cited Isaiah 48:16, "The Lord God and His Spirit have sent me," and "the Spirit came down from the Lord and led them," to deduce an identification of the Spirit and God. To him, "this 'leading' by the Spirit is [not] some lowly service. Scripture testifies that this is the work of God: 'He led forth His people like sheep.'"[69] Also, 1 Corinthians 2:11 adds to the support of the dignity of the Spirit. Here, Basil adopted a form of argument from human personality to divine personality. Analogously, the Spirit is to God just as the spirit of man is to man. The Spirit cannot be a creature, for he searches the deep things of God, a work which is beyond human possibility and solely Divine. Therefore the Spirit is not of a nature alien to God, just as the human person is

---

68 *On the Spirit* 16.38. See Thomas F. Torrance, *The Trinitarian Faith* (Edinburgh: T & T Clark, 1988), 228; Lewis Ayres, *Nicaea and Its Legacy: An Approach to Fourth-Century Trinitarian Theology* (Oxford: Oxford University Press, 2004), 196.

69 *On the Spirit* 19.49.

not of a nature alien to him. "The greatest proof that the Spirit is one with the Father and the Son," he explained, "is that he is said to have the same relationship to God as the spirit within us has to us: 'For what person knows a man's thoughts except the spirit of the man which is in him? So no one comprehends the thoughts of God except the Spirit of God.'"[70] That the Spirit is the revealer of the mysteries of God is an indication of his deity.

For Athanasius, Psalm 36:9, "In Thy light do we see light," was a proof for the Son's deity. "Inasmuch as the Father is eternal, his Radiance, who is his Logos, is eternal."[71] To rephrase the words of the psalm: "In Thy light [that is, in the Radiance or the Son] we see the light [that is, the light of the Father]." The same text became instead a proof for the Spirit's deity in Basil's treatise. So the light in which the saint sees the light of God was not the light of Christ as the revealer, but "the illumination of the Spirit, the true light that enlightens every man that comes into the world."[72] It was Athanasius' position, and the consensus of tradition, that the Johannine phrase in John 1:9, "the true light that enlightens every man," is exclusively a reference to the unique status of the Second Person of the Trinity. However, by applying the Christological phrase to the Third Person, Basil attributed the same unique status to the Spirit. As true light, the Spirit works as the Son does in revelation, this very work that rightly belongs to God. Thus, the Spirit and the Son mutually cohere in being and in the external indivisible work of revelation. The Spirit enables the saint to behold the glory of the Only-Begotten, the true light. He does this not from "outside sources," but from himself "personally."[73]

Just as what is done by one person is done by all three in a differentiated unity, so conversely what is done by us to one person is done to the same Godhead. So, to sin against the Spirit is to sin against God. Underlying Acts 5:3–4 is Basil's identification of the Spirit as essentially one with God.

---

70 *On the Spirit* 16.40.

71 Athanasius, *Contra Arians* 1.7.25 as cited in Pelikan, "The 'Spiritual Sense' of Scripture," 342.

72 *On the Spirit* 18.47.

73 *On the Spirit* 18.47.

Let our opponents determine what place they will give to the Holy Spirit. Will they rank him with God, or will they push him down to a creature's place? Peter said to Sapphira, "How is it that you have agreed together to tempt the Spirit of the Lord? You have not lied to men but to God," and this shows that to sin against the Holy Spirit is to sin against God. Understanding from this that in every operation, the Holy Spirit is indivisibly united with the Father and the Son.[74]

The common rejection by the world of the Father, Son and Holy Spirit adds to the evidence of their natural communion and essential unity. The world, conceived as "life enslaved by carnal passions," does not know the Spirit (John 14:17); nor does it know the Father (John 17:25); and nor does it see the Son (John 14:19). As indicated earlier, glorification of one person is predicated of all three in the one Godhead. Likewise, rejection of the Spirit alone is predicated of all three, thus of the same Godhead. This shows that the Spirit cannot be separated from the Godhead. He derives glory from his association with the Father and the Son, and Jesus' own testimony in Matthew 12:32: "Every sin and blasphemy will be forgiven men; but the blasphemy against the Holy Spirit will not be forgiven."[75]

There is an overlap between the Spirit's deeds and his gifts, the latter also forming a distinct argument for the Spirit's deity. The principal gift is salvation, along with numerous blessings including "knowledge of the future, understanding of the mysteries, apprehension of hidden things, distribution of wonderful gifts, heavenly citizenship, a place in a choir of angels [worship], endless joy in the presence, becoming like God, and, the highest of all desires, becoming God."[76] The Spirit fashions the soul into a temple for God to dwell so that it could partake of what he lavishly bestows. The Spirit sanctifies the soul, the temple in which he dwells, and illuminates its eyes so that it might behold in him both the Son and Father.

Like the sun, He will show you in Himself the image of the invisible, and with purified eyes you will see in this blessed image the

---

74 *On the Spirit* 16.37.
75 *On the Spirit* 18.46.
76 *On the Spirit* 9.23.

unspeakable beauty of its prototype. *Through* Him hearts are lifted up, the infirm are held by the hand, and those who progress are brought to perfection. He shines upon those who are cleansed from every spot, and makes them spiritual men through fellowship with Himself.[77]

The Spirit is of God, the breath of his mouth; he possesses the power to sanctify, so how could he be a mere creature? Being sanctified by the Spirit, the soul is enabled to fulfill the goal of his existence: deification. Basil's deification doctrine has its root in the Alexandrian theology of Athanasius, whose definition was moral and ethical, not essential.[78] Only by the Spirit, is God's sanctification accomplished and can we partake of the heavenly blessings: our ascension to the Kingdom of heaven, our adoption as God's children, our freedom to call God our Father and sharing in eternal glory.[79] For instance, to adopt as children of God cannot be the work of any other than God. The Spirit is the causative agency of our adoption, as says the apostle in Romans 8. Therefore the Spirit cannot be a creature but God.

Based on 1 Corinthians 14:24–25, "But if all prophesy, and an unbeliever or outsider enters, he is convicted by all, he is called to account by all, the secrets of his heart are disclosed; and so, falling on his face, he will worship God and declare that God is really among you," Basil drew out the implications of Paul's teaching concerning the Spirit: "If God is recognized to be present among prophets because their prophesying is a gift of the Spirit, let our opponents determine what place they will give to the Holy Spirit. Will they rank Him with God, or will they push Him down to a creature's place?"[80]

In respect to the distribution of gifts in the Corinthian congregation, Paul offered a trinitarian interpretation:

---

77 *On the Spirit* 9.23.

78 Athanasius, *On the Incarnation*. The Treatise *De Carnatione Verbi Dei*, trans. and ed. Penelope Lawson (New York: MacMillan Publishing Co, 1946), VIII.54. Cf. Gregory of Nazianzus, "The Fifth Theological Oration—*On the Spirit*," in *Christology of the Later Fathers*, ed. Edward R. Handy (Philadelphia: Westminster Press, 1954), 31.10, 199.

79 *On the Spirit* 15.36.

80 *On the Spirit* 16.37.

Now there are varieties of gifts, but the same Spirit; and there are varieties of services, but the same Lord; and there are varieties of workings, but it is the same God who inspires them all in everyone.... All these are inspired by one and the same Spirit, who apportions to each one individually just as he wills (1 Corinthians 12:4–6, 11).

By ruminating on this passage, Basil deduced his conclusion that the Spirit is not separated from the Father and the Son, and that all three conspire together in the dispensation of gifts. It is the Father who originates the gifts, the Son who sends them and the Spirit who inspires in us an appropriation of them. Priority, not superiority, is due to the Spirit, who brings into perfection the gifts of the one and same God. This passage evinces an order, not of essence (*ordo essendi*) but of experience (*ordo cognoscendi*), in which gratitude is offered, first to the Spirit, then the Son and finally the Father.

God works in various ways, and the Lord serves in various capacities, but the Holy Spirit is also present of his own will, dispensing gifts to everyone according to each man's worth.... Just because the Apostle in the above passage mentions the Spirit first, and the Son second, and God the Father third, do not assume that he has reversed their rank. Notice that he [Paul] is speaking the same way we do when we receive gifts: first we thank the messenger [Spirit] who brought the gift; next we remember him [Son] who sent it, and finally we raise our thoughts to the fountain and source of all gifts [Father].[81]

Additionally, in the distribution of these gifts, the Spirit's activity was understood as that of one who is "is simple in being; his powers are manifold: they are wholly present everywhere and in everything. He is distributed but does not change. He is shared, yet remains whole."[82] The divine attributes of simplicity, omnipotence, omnipresence, immutability and indivisibility are predicated of the Spirit. Thus the being of the Spirit is consubstantial with God.

---

81 *On the Spirit* 16.37.
82 *On the Spirit* 9.22.

Therefore, the same glory attributed to the God and Father of our Lord Christ and the Only-Begotten Son is attributed to the Spirit: "He is divine in nature, infinite in greatness, mighty in His works, good in His blessings; shall we not exalt Him; shall we not glorify Him? I reckon that this 'glorifying' is nothing else but the recounting of His own wonders."[83] Grasping, even partially, the major works of the Spirit in creation, sanctification, revelation, illumination and adoption inevitably leads us to exalt and praise the Spirit's unapproachable nature. Basil unequivocally declared: "Understanding all this, how can we be afraid of giving the Spirit too much honor? We should fear that even though we ascribe to Him the highest titles we can devise or our tongues pronounce, our ideas about Him might still fall short."[84]

Prepositional uses in Scripture and tradition

The customary form for Greek Christian worship was "Glory to the Father through (*dia*) the Son in (*en*) the Holy Spirit."[85] The form, "Glory to the Father with (*meta*) the Son together with (*syn*) the Holy Spirit," is the point at which Basil was attacked for being nontraditional and innovative.[86] In his rebuttal, Basil saw the importance of the different prepositional uses in Scripture. Warning against an intellectual idleness that counts theological terminology as secondary, he wrote:

> Instruction begins with the proper use of speech, and syllables and words are the elements of speech. Therefore to scrutinize syllables is not a superfluous task.... Hunting truth is no easy task; we must look everywhere for its tracks.... If a man spurns fundamental elements as insignificant trifles, he will never embrace the fullness of wisdom.[87]

The prepositions used in doxologies contain deeper meaning than at first glance. More crucially, Basil saw behind the attack of the Pneumatomachians a greater theological opposition:

---

83 *On the Spirit* 15.36.
84 *On the Spirit* 19.49.
85 Anderson's introduction to *On the Spirit* 11.
86 *On the Spirit* 6.13.
87 *On the Spirit* 7.16.

These are the reasons for their vexation: they say that the Son is not equal with the Father, but comes after the Father. Therefore it follows that glory should be ascribed to the Father *through* Him, but not *with* Him. *With* Him expresses equality but *through* Him indicates subordination.[88]

The immediate implication of this prepositional reticence on the part of his opponents becomes apparent in relation to the third person of the Trinity: if the Son is subordinate to the Father, then the Spirit is placed on an even lower plane. The main feature of this heresy concerns its ontological subordination of the Spirit, according to which the Spirit cannot be "ranked with the Father or the Son, but under the Father and the Son, not in the same order of things as they are, but beneath them, not numbered with them."[89] As a result, the heretics "divide and tear away the Spirit from the Father, transforming His nature to that of a ministering spirit."[90]

The dissimilar prepositions, according to the Pneumatomachians, are "made to indicate a corresponding nature."[91] Based on 1 Corinthians 8:6, "there is but one God, the Father, from whom all things came and from whom we live, and there is but one Lord, Jesus Christ, through whom all things came and through whom we live," they argued that *from* refers to the Father, *through* refers to the Son, *in which* would most appropriately refer to the Spirit.[92] And these prepositions were teleologically designed to describe the differences of nature between the Father, Son and Spirit, since each corresponds to his specific nature, totally alien from the others. Contrarily, Basil considered such reasoning unbiblical, but philosophically based on the four Aristotelian causes: formal, material, efficient and final.[93] He spoke of the disastrous result of this technical discussion of prepositions: "Cause (*from*) has one nature, an instrument (*through*) has another, and place (*in*) yet another. So the Son's nature is alien to the Father's, since

---

88 *On the Spirit* 7.16.
89 *On the Spirit* 6.13.
90 *On the Spirit* 10.25.
91 *On the Spirit* 2.4.
92 *On the Spirit* 2.4.
93 *On the Spirit* 3.5.

Basil of Caesarea

c. A.D. 330–379

the tool is by nature different from the craftsman, and the nature of the Spirit is foreign to both, since place and time are different from tools or those who handle them."[94] These temporal aspects of causality, Basil argued, are inapplicable to an uncreated being like God. He then went on to demonstrate the wide variety of prepositional usages as description of the essence and activity of the three persons. *From which* can refer to the Father as well as inanimate objects as wood and clay. Its use is not restricted to the Father, and cannot be used to support a distinction of natures. Differences in prepositions were meant to distinguish between the Persons and to describe the union of one identical nature that interpenetrates among the three Persons without confusion. His position is enhanced by resorting to Romans 11:36, "for *from* him and *through* him and *to* him are all things." This reveals the errors of his opponents' exegesis, for these dissimilar prepositions predicated of the Son do not support a distinction, but an identity of nature. He continued: *from whom* can refer to the Son (Ephesians 4:15-16; Colossians 2:19; John 1:16; Luke 8:46) and also to the Spirit (Galatians 6:8; 1 John 3:24; Luke 1:20). The same preposition used of three persons does not support three alien natures. *Through whom* or *by whom* can refer to the Father (1 Corinthians 1:9,11; Romans 6:4; Isaiah 19:15) and also the Spirit (2 Timothy 1:14; 1 Corinthians 12:8). The preposition *in* is used in relation to the Father (Psalm 108:13; 89:16; 2 Thessalonians 1:1; Romans 1:10; 2:17), and also to the Son and the Spirit, of whom biblical instances are plentiful. This inevitably leads Basil to conclude: "But I cannot refrain from remarking that the 'wise hearer' may easily discover that if terminological differences indicate differences in nature, then our opponents must shamefully agree that identical terminology is used for identical natures."[95]

His prepositional definition lends support to the Spirit's immanental relationship with the Father and the Son within the same Godhead. The doxological language, "Glory to the Father *with* the Son, together *with* the Holy Spirit," points to the union of identical nature between the three persons. Basil knew far too well that his *with* doxology was not contained in Scripture. Even so, it cannot be established from Scripture that prepositions must be confined to a particular person of

---

94 *On the Spirit* 4.6.
95 *On the Spirit* 5.11.

the Trinity. The various prepositions in Scripture which were used for the persons of the Trinity support Basil's specific use of *with* to accentuate the unity of the Son and the Spirit with the Father.

Basil knew of no place in Scripture where the doxology championed by the Pneumatomachians was found. The doxological phrases beginning with *through* and *in* are found in Scripture, he argued, yet not one instance that conforms precisely to their championed doxology, "Glory to the Father *through* the Son *in* the Holy Spirit," can be found in Scripture.[96] Basil's point was that his opponents also appealed to custom or tradition to justify their doxology. They, in their insistence that *with* is alien, while *through* is biblical, are themselves guilty of being a theological innovator. Rather, the church endorses both Christological usages, for there is no contradiction between them. As stated earlier, the phrase *with him* denotes the Son's relationship with his Father; the phrase *through him* denotes our relationship with him, in which his grace comes to us. Correspondingly, the same pattern transpires in Basil's pneumatology. The phrase *with them* denotes the communion of the Spirit within the Trinity, and thus justifies a doxology proper to the Spirit, who is inseparably united with the Father and the Son; the phrase *in us* expresses our relationship with the Spirit, or the situations where the Spirit works grace in us. These two sets of theological terminology complement each other: one describes God as God—the one living Being equally shared by the Father, Son and Spirit—the proper object of our worship, and another describes God's work of salvation *in us* through the Son by the Spirit, the befitting cause of our gratitude.

> As far as His relationship to the Father and the Son is concerned, it is more appropriate to say that He dwells *with* them rather than *in* them.... Whenever the union between things is intimate, natural and inseparable, it is more appropriate to use *with* since this word suggests an indivisible union. On the other hand, in situations where the grace of the Spirit comes and goes, it is more proper to say that the Spirit exists *in* someone, even in the case of well-disposed persons with whom He abides continually. Therefore, when we consider the Spirit's rank, we think of Him

---

96 *On the Spirit* 25.58.

as present *with* the Father and the Son, but when we consider the working of His grace on its recipients, we say that the Spirit is *in* us.[97]

There is another approach in Basil's use of the distinction between *with* and *in*.[98] He observed in certain texts that when the preposition *in* was used, *with* is actually intended. This is not his innovation, but is borne out by the context which determines its definition. For instance, Psalm 65:13 reads, "I will go into thine house *in* burnt offerings," in which the preposition *in* actually signifies *with*. Similarly Psalm 104:37 reads, "He brought them out *in* silver and gold," or Psalm 43:9, "Thou wilt not go forth *in* our armies." All these verses indicate that the preposition *in* carries the same force as *with*. While his enemies preferred the expression *in the Spirit*, which to them designates degrees of dignity, Basil used both *with the Spirit* and *in the Spirit* as interchangeable expressions of a dignity just as lofty. This approach strengthens the theological presupposition that the Spirit is ranked permanently equal with the Father and the Son, not under or outside them. Basil's use of the preposition *with* in his doxology spells the absolute death of any subordinationism and Sabellianism, for the preposition affirms both "eternal communion [of one essence] and unceasing cooperation [of distinct persons]."[99]

Basil's criticism of his opponents springs from his love of both Scripture and tradition. The phrase *with whom* has been preserved unchanged as the tradition of the church fathers. Basil esteemed the traditions of the fathers so highly that he stated, "If we attacked unwritten customs, claiming them to be of little importance, we would fatally mutilate the Gospel."[100] It was Basil's concession that without the unwritten tradition (liturgical or doctrinal), the true meaning of the written Scriptures might escape our grasping. He enumerated well-known fathers in the church who have used the doxological form

---

97 *On the Spirit* 26.63.

98 David Rainey, "The Argument for the Deity of the Holy Spirit according to St. Basil the Great, Bishop of Caesarea" (M.Th. dissertation, Vancouver: Vancouver School of Theology, 1991), 38.

99   *On the Spirit* 25.59.

100   *On the Spirit* 27.66.

"*with* the Spirit." For instance, Dionysius of Alexandria, in his second letter, on *Conviction and Defence*, concluded with these words: "Since we have received a form and a rule from the presbyters who have gone before us, we offer thanksgiving in harmony with them, and following everything they have taught us, we conclude our letter to you. To God the Father, and the Son our Lord Jesus Christ, *with* the Holy Spirit be glory and dominion unto ages of ages. Amen."[101] Eusebius of Caesarea, too, invoked "the holy God of the prophets, the Giver of Light, through our Savior Jesus Christ, *with* the Holy Spirit."[102] The notable Origen (*c.* A.D. 185–*c.* 254), in the "eighth" chapter of his *Commentary on the Gospel according to John*, clearly declared that the Spirit is to be worshipped:

> The washing with water is a symbol of spiritual washing, when the filth of wickedness is washed away from the soul. Nevertheless, if a man submits himself to the Godhead of the adorable Trinity, this washing will become the source and fountain of graces for him, through the power of the invocation.[103]

And again, Basil quotes Origen's *Commentary on the Epistle of Romans*: "The holy powers are able to reflect the Only-Begotten, and the divinity of the Holy Spirit."[104] This form of doxology was not unknown even to the historian Julius Africanus who, in his *Epitome of the Times*, wrote: "We who are acquainted with the meaning of prophecy, and are not ignorant of the grace of faith, offer thanks to the Father, who gave Jesus Christ, the Savior of all and our Lord, to us, His own creatures. Glory and majesty be to Him, *with* the Holy Spirit, unto all ages."[105]

These churchmen apprehended the power of the unwritten tradition in true religion. Basil held in high regard this "familiar and dear" word *with* of the saints: "From the day when the Gospel was first preached even until now, it has been welcomed by the churches, and, most importantly of all, has been defined in conformity to righteous-

---

101 *On the Spirit* 29.72.
102 *On the Spirit* 29.72.
103 *On the Spirit* 29.73. Basil mistakenly put "sixth" chapter. See note 359.
104 *On the Spirit* 29.73.
105 *On the Spirit* 29.73.

ness and true religion."[106] Both Scripture and tradition "have equal force in true religion. No one would deny either source—no one, at any rate, who is even slightly familiar with the ordinances of the Church."[107] Did Basil propound a double authority? No. His point was that the validity of the tradition hinges on whether its teaching concurs with the meaning of Scripture. Scripture is the prior norm, to which tradition is subservient. Thus, he stated his task: "It remains for me to describe the origin and force of the word 'with' and to show that its usage is in accord with Scripture."[108] What was important was not what was acclaimed as tradition, but that the church fathers followed the sense of Scripture, with the evidence which he had just extracted from the Scriptures and presented as above.[109]

The Spirit within the Godhead: Necessity for worship

To place the Spirit outside the Godhead, as the Pneumatomachians did, is tantamount to committing an unpardonable sin of blasphemy against the Spirit, and thus suffers eternal consequences:

> How can we separate the Spirit from his life-giving power and associate him with things which by nature are lifeless? Who is so perverse; who is so devoid of the heavenly gift, so unnourished by God's good words; who is so empty of sharing eternal hopes, that he would separate the Spirit from the Godhead, and number him among creatures?[110]

The doctrine of the deity of the Spirit has to be believed for one's salvation: "The Lord has delivered to us a necessary and saving dogma: the

---

106   *On the Spirit* 29.75.

107   *On the Spirit* 27.66.

108   *On the Spirit* 27.65.

109   *On the Spirit* 7.16. See de Mendieta, *The "Unwritten" and "Secret" Apostolic Tradition in the Theological Thought of St. Basil of Caesarea*, 27: "Putting a tremendous emphasis on the moment of the 'unwritten' tradition coming from the Apostles and the Fathers, Basil seems to place it on the same level as the 'written' and canonical tradition of the Church, namely the biblical books, and in particular the New Testament. But, according to Basil himself, the genuine 'unwritten' tradition of the Apostles and Fathers ought in fact to be in harmony with the sense of Scriptures."

110   *On the Spirit* 24.56.

Holy Spirit is to be ranked with the Father."[111] Basil warned that those who deny that the Spirit rightly belongs to the Godhead, as the Father and the Son, are deprived of both salvation and true worship:

> I swear to every man who confesses Christ but denies the Father: Christ will profit him nothing. If a man calls upon God, but rejects the Son, his faith is empty. If someone rejects the Spirit, his faith in the Father and the Son is made useless; it is impossible to believe in the Father and the Son without the presence of the Spirit. He who rejects the Spirit rejects the Son, and he who rejects the Son rejects the Father. "No one can say that "Jesus is Lord" except in the Holy Spirit," (1 Cor. 12:3), and "no one has ever seen God; the only begotten God, who is in the bosom of the Father, He has made Him known" (Jn. 1:18). Such a person has no part in true worship. It is impossible to worship the Son except in the Holy Spirit; it is impossible to call upon the Father except in the Spirit of adoption.[112]

As declared in the Constantinopolitan Creed, the Holy Spirit is Lord and Giver of Life, thus is in no sense a creature, but in every sense essentially God as the first two persons. If the Spirit who unites us to Christ is no more than a creature, and not fully and perfectly God, then our participation in Christ and all that he has done and continues to do for us is devoid of divine efficacy and saving reality.[113] The Spirit subsists in God, and his activity is not apart from nor outside of God but from within God. His activity is God's immediate activity, which draws us through Christ into the presence of God. In the language of causality, Basil spoke of "the original cause of all things that are made,

---

111   *On the Spirit* 10.25.

112   *On the Spirit* 11.27. For Calvin, the twin truths—salvation and worship—truly constitute the substance of Christianity. Calvin's is traceable to Basil's. See John Calvin "The Necessity of Reforming the Church," in Calvin, *Tracts Relating to the Reformation*, trans. Henry Beveridge (Edinburgh: Calvin Translation Society, 1844), 1:126–127: "a knowledge, first, of the right way to worship God; and secondly of the source from which salvation is to be sought. When these are kept out of view, though we may glory in the name of Christians, our profession is empty and vain."

113   Cf. Thomas F. Torrance, *The Trinitarian Faith* (Edinburgh: T & T Clark, 1995), 5.

the Father; ...the creative cause, the Son; ...the perfecting cause, the Spirit."[114] Here we are distinguishing, not separating, what the three persons do, for they mutually coinhere in being and act. "To say that the Spirit is the perfecting cause of creation," Gunton wrote, "is to make the Spirit the eschatological person of the Trinity: the one who directs the creatures to where the creator wishes them to go, to their destiny as creatures."[115] In other words, the Spirit constitutes us as a new creation who would freely worship God through Christ as the proper end. By the perfecting causality of the Spirit, we are drawn through the Son into the heavenly sanctuary of divine grace and the intimacy of divine communion. The Spirit communicates to our hearts the gospel about a God who summons us into being, and includes us as his beloved in his inner life in which we partake of all the riches of God's being. The Spirit is the efficacy of God's work *in nobis* so that all the benefits Christ won are ours, if only we believe:

> Through the Holy Spirit comes our restoration to Paradise, our ascension to the Kingdom of heaven, our adoption as God's sons, our freedom to call God our Father, our becoming partakers of the grace of Christ, being called children of light, sharing in eternal glory and, in a word, our inheritance of the fullness of blessing, both in this world and the world to come. Even while we wait for the full enjoyment of the good things in store for us, by the Holy Spirit we are able to rejoice through faith in the promise of the graces to come.[116]

The focus point of the doxological form, "Glory to the Father through the Son *in* (*by*) the Holy Spirit," is the confession of the Spirit's deity as the dynamic of true worship. In confessing this doxology, we are not describing the Spirit's proximate relationship within the God-

---

114 *De Spiritu Sancto* 16.38. Cf. Calvin's *Institutes* 1.13.18. Following Basil, Calvin noted a distinctive action attributed to each person: "To the Father is the beginning of activity, and the fountain and wellspring of all things; to the Son, wisdom, counsel, and the ordered disposition of all things; but to the Spirit is assigned the power and efficacy of that activity."

115 Cf. Colin Gunton, *Father, Son and Holy Spirit: Essays Toward a Fully Trinitarian Theology* (London: T & T Clark, 2003), 81–82.

116 *On the Spirit* 15.36.

head, but confessing our own weaknesses and inability to glorify God on our own. Basil's understanding resonates with the position of Hilary of Poitiers (c. A.D. 300–c. 368) who stated: "God cannot be comprehended except through God himself, and likewise God accepts no worship from us except through God himself…it is by God that we are initiated into the worship of God."[117] Through the Spirit, we share in the incarnate Son's communion with the Father, as Paul said in Galatians 4:6, "God has sent the Spirit of his Son into our hearts, crying 'Abba! Father!'" Only in the Spirit is our worship and access to God made efficacious:

> In Him we are able to thank God for the blessings we have received. To the extent that we are purified from evil, each receives a smaller or a larger portion of the Spirit's help, that each may offer the sacrifice of praise to God. If we offer glory to God in the Spirit, we mean that the Spirit enables us to fulfill the requirements of true religion. According to this usage, then, we say that we are in the Spirit, but it is not objectionable for some-one to testify, "the Spirit of God is in me, and I offer glory because His grace has given me the wisdom to do so." The words of Paul are appropriate: "I think that I have the Spirit of God" (1 Cor. 7:40), and "guard the truth that has been entrusted to you by the Holy Spirit who dwells within us" (2 Tim. 1:14).[118]

In the life of worship, John 4:24—"God is Spirit, and his worshippers must worship him in spirit and in truth"—was of great importance to Basil.[119] For him, the text is a reference to Christ ("truth") and the Spirit, constituting both the manner and basis of worship. Just as the Father is made known in the Son, so also the Son is recognized in the Spirit. Likewise the worship of the Father in the Son is made possible in (by) the Spirit. The Father moves toward us in Christ, whose presence is felt in worship that we might share with him in his own communion

---

117 Cf. Hilary, *De Trinitate*, 4:20, as cited in Philip W. Butin, *Reformed Ecclesiology: Trinitarian Grace According to Calvin Studies in Reformed Theology and History* (Princeton: Princeton Theological Seminary, 1994), 26 n. 81.

118 Hilary, *De Trinitate*, 26.63.

119 Pelikan, "The 'Spiritual Sense' of Scripture," 345.

with the Father. This cannot happen without the Spirit's help. To put it in another way: the Spirit reveals Christ to us in worship and, through him, enables us to offer to God both our being and act [worship] in thanksgiving and praise. To worship *in* the Spirit means that

> [O]ur intelligence has been enlightened.... If we say that worship offered *in* the Son (the Truth) is worship *in* the Father's Image, we can say the same about worship offered *in* the Spirit since the Spirit in Himself reveals the divinity of the Lord. The Holy Spirit cannot be divided from the Father and the Son in worship. If you remain outside the Spirit, you cannot worship at all, and if you are *in* Him you cannot separate Him from God. Light cannot be separated from what it makes visible, and it is impossible for you to recognize Christ, the Image of the invisible God, unless the Spirit enlightens you. Once you see the Image, you cannot ignore the light; you see the Light and Image simultaneously. It is fitting that when we see Christ, the Brightness of God's glory, it is always through the illumination of the Spirit.[120]

Basil found such understanding of worship in the Spirit in the Old Testament. Juxtaposed with the Johannine text were Old Testament passages in which the Spirit is understood not spatially, but figuratively as a "place" in which people are sanctified to participate in the holy of holies.[121] Words that carry a physical meaning are often transposed to a spiritual plane, for the sake of clarifying the truth behind. Thus, the figurative language (place) used of the Spirit does not downgrade but rather glorifies him. For instance, when God says to Moses in Exodus 33:21, "Behold, there is a place by Me: thou shalt stand upon the rock," Basil understood the "place" as a reference to the Spirit, in whom God became recognizable by Moses. "Only in this 'special' place can true worship be offered."[122] In addition, Basil interpreted the sacrifice indicated in Deuteronomy 12:13–14 as the sacrifice of praise offered by the church to God. For the sacrifice of praise to be efficacious, as prescribed in the Law, it must be offered *in* the

---

120 *On the Spirit* 26.64.

121 *On the Spirit* 26.62.

122 *On the Spirit* 26.62.

Spirit, "a place which the Lord shall choose."[123] It is *in* the Spirit, "the place of the saints," that the church can offer doxology to God. This teaching, Basil claimed, came from the Lord himself, who taught us to worship God *in* Spirit and *in* Christ (Truth). For Basil, the Spirit is the dwelling place of the saint; conversely, the saint is a suitable habitation of the Spirit, as the allusion to 1 Corinthians 3:16 shows.[124] Just as Paul speaks *in* Christ, so also Christ speaks *in* Paul (2 Corinthians 2:17; 3:13). The same pattern occurs in reference to the Spirit: just as Paul utters mysteries *in* the Spirit, the Spirit does the same *in* Paul (1 Corinthians 14:2). Only *in the Spirit* does our worship offered *in the Son* reach the Fatherly sanctuary; conversely, the Spirit *in* us enables us, those whom he sanctifies, to engage in the contemplation and worship of the Godhead. In any case, the Spirit's deity is the power of efficacy of the church's worship.

The double movements of the Trinity: divine descent and human ascent

Athanasius summed up the double movement of the Trinity in a statement which became normative in the patristic church: "God became human so that human beings could be deified."[125] The first part points to divine descent (*katabasis*), whilst the second points to human ascent (*anabasis*). The divine descent presupposes the role of the sending of the Son; the human ascent presupposes the homecoming of the Son to glory, but with our humanity eternally attached. The Spirit is the power of efficacy of both movements in us. Basil also talked about these two movements, but with an emphasis on the second:

> When, in a power that illumines us, we look unswervingly upon the beauty of the image of the invisible God, and through that image are led upwards to the vision of that Primal Image which is beyond all measure lovely, then the Spirit of knowledge is inseparably present.... Just as no man knoweth the Father save the Son (Matt. 11:27), so no one can say Lord except in the Holy

---

123 *On the Spirit* 26.62.

124 *On the Spirit* 26.62.

125 Athanasius, *De Incarnatione*, ch. 54, as cited in Jurgen Moltmann, *The Spirit of Life: A Universal Affirmation* (Minneapolis: Fortress, 1993), 299.

Spirit (1 Cor. 12:3).... The way to the knowledge of God, therefore, proceeds from the one Spirit through the one Son to the one Father. Conversely, essential goodness and holiness and royal dignity proceed from the Father through the Only Begotten One to the Spirit. Thus we confess the *hypostases* without infringing that article of faith which speaks of the monarchy.[126]

The descending movement is *from* the Father *through* the Son *in* the Spirit; the ascending movement is *from* the Spirit *through* the Son *to* the Father. The economic actions of the Trinity sum up the two sides of salvation history, which proceeds "from God" and leads "to God." On the one hand, there is God's activity from above to below, concerning which Basil wrote, "[N]atural goodness, inherent holiness and royal dignity reaches from the Father through the Only-Begotten to the Spirit."[127] On the other hand, there is God's activity from below to above, of which Basil wrote, "The Spirit reveals the true glory of the Only-Begotten in Himself, and He gives true worshippers the knowledge of God in Himself. The way to divine knowledge ascends from the one Spirit through the one Son to the one Father."[128] The implication of this double movement for worship is that, on the one hand, it is God who comes to us as human, revealing himself as the object of worship in the dynamic of the Spirit, who is of the same being with the first two persons; on the other hand, by the Spirit we are led to participate in the incarnate Son's ascending movement to the Father, which includes access to the holy of holies. By the Spirit, who is not numbered with any creaturely beings, but with the Father and Son, we are drawn into his intimacy with them in the same uncreated Deity. The Spirit's proximity with the first two persons enables our communion with God, in which we enjoy the benefits of the Son's ascension to the right hand of the Father.

While the Father, Son and Spirit are personally distinct, they are inseparably united in the uncompounded nature and communion of the Godhead, and in the three-fold activity toward us. The unity of the monarchy is maintained along with the indivisible operations of three

---

126   Basil of Caesarea, *De Spiritu Sancto* 39, d and e. Also cited in Moltmann, *Spirit of Life*, 300; Hanson, *The Christian Doctrine of God*, 777.

127   *On the Spirit* 18.47.

128   *On the Spirit* 18.47.

persons. Without an interval of time, the grace that reaches us *from* the Father *through* the Son *in* the Spirit is the same which leads us home, *through* the Son *to* the Father *in* the Spirit. This constituted what Basil called the "true" doctrine: "Their oneness consists in the communion of the Godhead."[129] The two-way activity of God in revelation and worship does not compromise the oneness of being, for it is the same God who acts in a differentiated unity of his economic and immanent self-communication as the undivided and ever-blessed Trinity. The double-movement is a tripersonal activity *ad extra* of the one God in a differentiated unity with himself.[130] With clarity, Basil asserted: "We worship God from God, confessing the uniqueness of the persons, while maintaining the unity of the monarchy."[131] Just as God cannot be known except through God himself, so it is with our worship, that God deems no worship except through God himself.

Basil's doctrine of the union of divine operations grounds worship as a trinitarian activity, originated from the Father, effected through the Son and perfected in the Spirit. There is no work of God in which the members of the Trinity are not jointly operative. This is true of creation, redemption and worship. It is by the perfecting causality of the Spirit that the church's worship offered in the Son reaches the Father. As a perfector, the Spirit leads us to the Son, through whom our being and our act [worship] have free access to the Fatherly sanctuary in the same Godhead. Only Spirit-perfected worship is true worship. Not only is the Spirit joined through the Son to the Father the proper *object* but also the causative *agency* of worship, the one who exalts the community in Christ to the heavenly throne of the Father. Or, to put it differently, as Gunton did: "we worship the Spirit, the one through whom we worship."[132] The unitive movement of the Spirit in which we participate is the presupposition of an efficacious worship, which is through the Son to the Father. As such, worship is a gift of grace: what God begins in us he shall complete. God is the *alpha* and the *omega* of worship. The reverential knowledge of God in

---

129 *De Spiritu Sancto* 45, as cited in Torrance, *The Christian Doctrine of God*, 127; *On the Spirit* 18.47.
130 *On the Spirit* 18.47.
131 *On the Spirit* 18.45.
132 Gunton, *Father, Son & Holy Spirit*, 84.

Christ by faith is the action of the Holy Spirit, the completion of the all-praised blessed Trinity.

Conclusion

It is primarily as a theologian of the Spirit that Basil stands out.[133] Despite his restraint in the usage of the word *homoousios*, he contributed to what was later affirmed in the Council of Constantinople (A.D. 381) concerning the Spirit. His attempt to show the necessity of the Spirit's deity as the effective agency of salvation and worship is praiseworthy. Contemplating the meaning of the Spirit's names, acts and gifts directs our thoughts on high, and thus necessarily leads to the proper conclusion that the Spirit is God. Hence, doxology is proper to the Spirit, whose ineffable dignity is an ontological derivative of his eternal relationship with the Father and the Son. With his insistence on the third person, which was characteristic of all the main theologians of his time against the Pneumatomachians, Basil succeeded in turning the Arian question into a fully trinitarian one.[134] Since then, the place of the Spirit in the Trinity had begun to be given lawful attention. This was in no way his invention. The Council of Nicaea had already affirmed its faith in the Spirit, and Athanasius, in learning of the subordination doctrine of the opponents, was intransigent in condemning it. But Basil's treatise, *On the Spirit,* represents a significant landmark for the definitive introduction of the Holy Spirit in the Arian controversy, and his pneumatological insights continued to shape subsequent thinking, including that of the Protestant reformers.[135] Most significantly, it was with this celebrated work that communion as an ontological category subsequently gained much attention. The Spirit himself, in being consubstantial with God, is in ever living, two-way communion between the Father and the Son. God's being as communion excludes any unipersonal view of God or tritheistic conception of the Holy Trinity, but magnifies the onto-relational dynamism of the Father, Son and Spirit in the one living Being of God.

---

133   Cf. Anthony Meredith, *The Cappadocians* (Crestwood: Geoffrey Chapman, 1995), 30.

134   González, *A History of Christian Thought*, 318.

135   Cf. David F. Wright, "Basil the Great in the Protestant Reformers," *Studia Patristica* 17 (1982): 1149–1155.

04

Gregory's doxological theology

By Keith Goad

GREGORY OF NAZIANZUS (A.D. 329/330–389/390) was given the title "The Theologian" because his theology defined the lasting legacy of doctrine and spirituality for the Eastern Church. John McGuckin observes that for Gregory, "theology (and particularly Trinitarian theology) is wholly confessional, that is, doxological, in character and soteriological in its import."[1] The goal of his theology was to provide a vision of God that allowed the church to draw near to him and to do so according to how God designed salvation as a Triune event.[2] A proper vision of God must be accomplished through the appropriate means. When addressing bishops in their consecration, he challenged them to draw near according to God's means, saying, "I fear that we may not draw near in the right way—that, like a straw before a fire, we may not be able to endure the flame."[3]

---

1   John A. McGuckin, "'Perceiving Light from Light in Light': The Trinitarian Theology of St. Gregory the Theologian," *Greek Orthodox Theological Review* 39, no. 1 (1994): 18.

2   Brian Daley recognizes that Gregory's intent was to provide a way for the church to profess God in a way "consistent with Scripture and the Church's tradition of faith"; Brian Daley, *Gregory of Nazianzus* (New York: Routledge, 2006), 41.

3   *Oration* 26 in *Sources Chrétiennes* (Paris: Éditions du Cerf, 1942–), 250.87; *Patrologia Graeca* (Paris: J.P. Migne, 1857–1866), 36.16, English translation from Daley,

Gregory did not attempt to describe God in tight syllogistic formulas as had his neo-Arian opponents. He maintained that man could only know God as he revealed himself. A doctrine of the knowledge of God that makes a distinction between *theologia* and *oikonomia* is fundamental to Gregory's spirituality. *Theologia* denotes God's nature that man does not have access to and, therefore, remains in the sphere of either speculative theology or mystery.[4] *Oikonomia* refers to God's work, particularly his plan of salvation. This means that God cannot be fully comprehended and explained. For Gregory, the purpose of doctrine was to affirm and guard what God had revealed about himself, while protecting the mystery of God.

Just as God is not meant to be known in syllogisms, the spirituality of the church does not fit into a clear, simple formula. Gregory employs a number of metaphors and analogies to describe Christian spirituality, and there are three major aspects that permeate his sermons: illumination, purity and ascension. They are often mentioned together because they are interrelated: the light purifies the believer and the believer sees more light as he ascends to God by purifying himself.

Gregory's spirituality of illumination

Gregory refers to God as the great and perfect Light throughout his sermons and poems, providing clarity by contrasting the eternal light, which provides the stability man needs, to the other lights that bring a world of chaos, changing shadows and temporary radiances.[5] In *Oration* 44.3, *On New Sunday*, he expounds,

---

Gregory of Nazianzus, 106. Daley's translation will be used for *Orations* 8, 14, 26, 38, 39 and 42. Hereafter cited as *Oration* [no.] (SC [no.]; PG [no.]), Daley [page].

4   *Oration* 6.22 (SC 405.174-76; PG 35.752), *St. Gregory of Nazianzus: Select Orations* in *The Fathers of the Church*, trans. Martha Vinson, vol. 107 (Washington: The Catholic University of America Press, 2004), 20. Vinson's translation will be used for *Orations* 6, 10, 11, 15, 17, 19, 20, 22, 23, 24, 25, 32 and 44. Hereafter cited as Vinson [page]. The internal ordering is behind the first veil that man cannot pass, but God's actions are revealed behind the second veil. Gregory guards against a complete knowledge, but demands enough knowledge for worship, "its internal ordering known only to itself, but for us equally the object of reverence and adoration."

5   *Oration* 17.4 (PG 35.969), Vinson 107:88.

There was light, unapproachable and everlasting, God, light without beginning, without end, without limit, ever shining with triple splendor, light whose magnitude can be envisioned by few, no, not even them. And there were lights of the second order, effulgences of the first, the powers that surround him and ministering spirits.... Indeed, it is fitting that the great light should have begun his creation with light, by which he disperses the darkness and the chaos and disorder that formerly prevailed.[6]

The angels draw "from the first light and are illumined by the word of truth," but are not perfect light because perfect light alone has the characteristic of lacking "conflict and faction."[7] Gregory demanded that God alone is perfect light because nothing can be greater than God or before God.

The metaphor of light is particularly important to Gregory because the light of God shines into the darkness of the mind and soul, enabling one to think about God. This is why Gregory's spirituality is primarily defined as a life of contemplation. The light looses the mind that is bound by the material and the senses so that the mind can contemplate God in his illuminations.[8] In *Oration 39, On The Holy Lights*, he equates divine light with divine knowledge, which comes down as a gift from above, that man must have because he is "darkened and confused by sin."[9] Man is naturally in a state of complete darkness, and it is not until God illuminates him that he is able to overcome the complete veil of darkness. Even after the Christian receives the gift of illumination, he still has a veil and only sees the light in a mirror dimly.

The goal of the theologian then is to remove as much sin from his soul as possible so that he might see God more purely.

---

6 *Oration* 44.3 (PG 36.609), Vinson 107:232.

7 *Oration* 6.12 (SC 405.150–152; PG 35.737), Vinson 107:12.

8 *Oration* 8.23: "a higher illumination, purer and more perfect than that of this world, the light of the Trinity, which no longer eludes a mind bound and diffused by the senses, but is contemplated as a whole by the whole mind, grasping us now and letting its radiance illumine our souls with the full light of the godhead. Now you all enjoy these things, while yet on earth, you possessed only in distant distillations, through the clarity of your instinct for them" (SC 107.75; PG 35.793).

9 *Oration* 39.1 (SC 358.150; PG 36.336), Daley 128.

Illumination is the splendor of souls, the conversion of the life, the question put to the Godward conscience. It is the aid of our weakness, the renunciation of the flesh, the following of the Spirit, the fellowship of the Word, the improvement of the creature, the overwhelming of sin, the participation of light, the dissolution of darkness. It is the carriage to God, the dying with Christ, the perfecting of the mind, the bulwark of the Faith, the key of the Kingdom of heaven, the change of life, the removal of slavery, the loosing of chains, the remodeling of the whole man.[10]

Illumination is a return to God where man reasons with the incomprehensible light of God and is purified; it is the process of God opening the eyes of man, and man properly responding to the divine light by casting off carnal and sinful thinking. Reason is seen as the "god-like, divine thing" that "mingles with its kin the copy and returns to the pattern it now longs after."[11] The soul is the light of man that is able to intermingle with the light and the mirror that is able to reflect the light. In becoming more and more purified of false images, the theologian is able to see "light with light and the more brighter through the more dim."[12]

God is "light the most sublime" which one is only able to see as "a momentary emanation or radiance penetrating the regions below."[13]

---

10 *Oration* 40.2 (SC 358.200–202; PG 36.361) in Gregory of Nazianzus, *Select Orations*, trans. Charles Gordon Browne and James Edward Swallow, NPNF², vol. 7 (Peabody: Hendrickson, 1994), 7:352.

11 *Oration* 28.7 (SC 250.112–114; PG 36.33) in Gregory of Nazianzus, *On God and Christ: The Five Theological Orations and Two Letters to Cledonius*, trans. Lionel Wickham and Frederick Williams (Crestwood: St. Vladimir's Seminary Press, 2002), 41–42.

12 *Oration* 20.1. In this way, one is always becoming a spotless mirror of God and divine things, assimilating light to light, and aligning clarity to indistinct beginnings, until we come to the source of the light that radiates in this world and lay hold of our blessed end, where mirrors are dissolved in true reality. One can scarcely achieve this, except either by training oneself in the discipline of philosophy for a long time, and so detaching the noble and luminous elements of the soul, little by little, from what is base and mingled with darkness, or else by obtaining God's mercy—or by a combination of the two" (SC 270.56–58; PG 35.1065), Vinson 107:107.

13 *Oration* 32.15 "God is light, light the most sublime, of which all our light is but a momentary emanation or radiance penetrating the regions below, dazzling though it may appear" (SC 318.116–118; PG 36.192), Vinson 107:107.

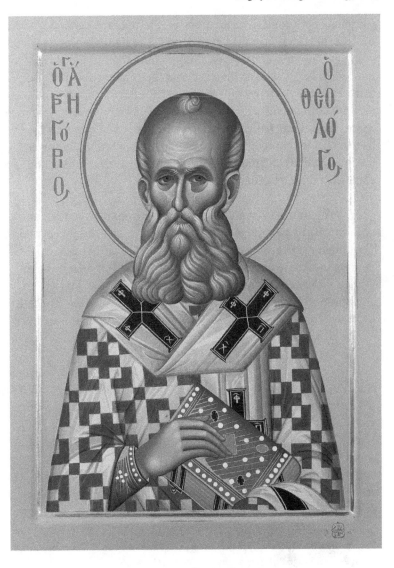

Gregory of Nazianzus
A.D. 329/330–389/390

God has only provided emulations and temporary radiances of his perfect light, not absolute knowledge. The light God provides for creation gives men and women glimpses of the divine and places a veil or shadow of gloom over them so that they cannot see the light perfectly.[14] Gregory's spirituality is constantly reflecting upon God's greatness and humankind's limitations. God, being too great to be known while humankind, being too dark to see, sets boundaries on what can be known and said about God. Humankind's limitations, however, are used to instill in the believer a sense of wonder and mystery. The Light shines, according to Gregory,

> on our guiding reason...that it might stir up our wonder, and through our wonder might be yearned for all the more, and through our yearning might purify us, and in purifying us might make us like God; and when we have become thus, that he might then associate with us intimately as friends—my words here are rash and daring!—uniting himself with us, making himself known to us, as God to gods, perhaps to the same extent that he already knows those that are known by him.[15]

A key passage for Gregory throughout his work is 1 Corinthians 13:12, "Now we see but a poor reflection as in a mirror; then we shall see face to face. Now I know in part; then I shall know fully, even as I am fully known." The light is set within a gloom, "like the veil of Moses," so that the illumination is only a partial knowledge of the perfect light that is yet to be seen.

Gregory also likens God to the sun to argue that just as man's eyes are too weak to look at the sun, so man's soul is too weak to look at God.[16] His radiance is too bright for man's feeble and sinful nature.[17]

---

14 *Oration* 6.22 (SC 405.174–176; PG 35.752), Vinson 107:20 and *Oration* 29.11 (SC 250.198–200; PG 36.89), Nazianzus, *On God and Christ*, 78.

15 *Oration* 38.7 (SC 357.114–116; PG 36.317), Daley 120.

16 *Oration* 44.3 (PG 36.109), Vinson 107:232.

17 *Oration* 23.11. "Our minds and our human condition are such that a knowledge of the relationship and disposition of these members with regard to one another is reserved for the Holy Trinity itself alone and those purified souls to whom the Trinity may make revelation either now or in the future. We, on the other hand, may know that the nature of divinity is one and the same characterized by lack of source,

Man will only have eyes to see the perfect light in heaven. This is clear in Gregory's rules for theological discussion in *Oration* 27.10, *Against the Eunomians*, where he writes, "of God himself the knowledge we shall have in this life will be little, though soon after it will perhaps be more perfect, in the same Jesus Christ our Lord to whom be glory for ever and ever. Amen."[18] The promise of seeing him perfectly is used by Gregory as motivation for the believer to draw near to God. The hope is that "we shall come into the joy of the same Lord and shall be illumined more brightly and more purely. I know it well, by light of the blessed and sovereign Trinity in which we have put our faith."[19] The believer is to long for a perfect vision by pursuing it in this life and hoping for it in the life to come. He is called to pursue a partial participation in the illuminating work of God and to wait upon the promise for full participation. Gregory looks forward to the day when we will see the full light of God, "the radiance of the Holy Trinity... which we worship, which we glorify, whose existence is intimately bound up with our own through our worship of the Father in the Son, and of the Son in the Holy Spirit."[20]

Gregory presents a dynamic vision of God to his church by making God the focal point of his preaching. His desire was for the church to be illuminated so that they too might see the radiance of God's pure light in the three persons of the Trinity.[21] By seeing these three more

---

generation, and procession (these correspond to mind, word and spirit in humans, at least insofar as one can compare things spiritual with things perceptible and things that are very great with those that are small, for no comparison ever represents the true picture exactly)" (SC 270. 302–304; PG 35.1164), Vinson 107:139.

18 *Oration* 27.10 (SC 250.96–98; PG 36.25), Nazianzus, *On God and Christ*, 33–34.

19 *Oration* 11.6 (PG 35.840), Vinson 107:34.

20 *Oration* 24.19 (SC 107.155; SC 284.152–154; PG 35.1191).

21 McGuckin recognizes the different approach to God in Gregory: "Gregory's general theme that theology is not a speculative *theoria* that produces knowledge from deduction, rather a personal communion with God which initiates by intimation or sanctification" (McGuckin, "'Perceiving Light from Light in Light,'" 16). In *Oration* 39.20, Gregory calls the church to celebrate Christ's baptism, "Be completely purified, and you shall be pure, since God rejoices in nothing so much as in the correction and salvation of a human being, on whose behalf is all our speech, and all this Mystery. It is so that 'you may become as lights in this world,' a living force for other men and women, so that as perfect lights you may stand with the great light, and in his presence be initiated in the Mystery of light, illuminated yet more purely and clearly by the

clearly in contemplation, the light of man's ability to reason becomes brighter. Christopher Beeley rightly places the Trinity at the centre of Gregory's theology when he states, "for Gregory the doctrine of the Trinity is not only the essential expression of the Christian life; in an important sense, it is that life."[22] God is not a static light because the three lights are always seen as emanating from the one sun. He argues that in order to achieve a proper vision of God, "you must be illuminated at once by one flash and by three."[23] Gregory argues that "each one [is] God, if contemplated separately, because the mind can divide the three God if contemplated collectively, because their activity and nature are the same."[24] The three reveal themselves in distinct ways but as the same divine light. Here, the first and greatest blessing is "to be more perfectly and purely enlightened, by [his] grace, to see how the same Mystery can be understood as one, yet discovered to be three."[25]

In *Oration* 28, *On The Doctrine of God*, Gregory begins with a dedication that shows how the three work inseparably, but distinctly.

Trinity, of which you have now received, in modest measure, this one ray of the one divinity, in Christ Jesus our Lord, to whom be glory for the ages of ages. Amen" (SC 358.194–196; PG 36.360), Daley 138.

22 Christopher Beeley, *Gregory of Nazianzus on the Trinity and the Knowledge of God: In Your Light We Shall See Light* (Oxford: Oxford University Press, 2008), 187.

23 *Oration* 39.11 (SC 250.171; PG 36.345–347), Daley 132. See also *Oration* 6.12 (SC 405.150–152; PG 35.737), Vinson 107:12.

24 *Oration* 23.11 (SC 270.302–304; PG 35.1164), Vinson 107:138–139. This argument is working from Eunomius' (d. A.D. 394) own assertion that "the energies follow their being," and "sameness of energy produces sameness of work" (quotation of Eunomius found in Gregory of Nyssa, *Contra Eunomius* 1.13 (NPNF² 5:50). The Cappadocians responded by showing that the three persons worked inseparable and accomplished the same work in order to show they were the same essence.

Gregory of Nyssa (c. A.D. 330–395) made the sameness of activity the basis of his work, *On Not Three Gods*. He argues that all three persons see and that this is the operation referred to in the term Godhead. The argument is that Godhead cannot be a name for the unknowable substance. Lewis Ayres has highlighted the proper emphasis of the Gregory's argument on the sameness of operation rather than the generic essence. Lewis Ayres, "On Not People: The Fundamental Themes of Nyssa's Trinitarian Theology as Seen in *To Ablabius: On Not Three Gods*," in *Re-thinking Gregory of Nyssa*, Sarah Coakley, ed. (Oxford: Blackwell, 2003), 15–44.

25 *Oration* 26.19 (SC 284.232; PG 35.1252), Vinson 107:190.

Well now let us go forward to discuss the doctrine of God, dedicating our sermon to our sermon's subjects, the Father, the Son, and the Holy Spirit, that the Father may approve, the Son aid, and the Holy Spirit inspire it—or rather that the single Godhead's single radiance, by mysterious paradox one in its distinctions and distinct in its connectedness, may enlighten it.[26]

The subject of the sermon is the one God, but the one God is seen through the unique work of the three persons. Each person plays a distinct role in helping the believer apprehend what is revealed. In *Oration* 31, *On The Holy Spirit*, Gregory demonstrates that each of the three persons, sharing the identical expression of being light, shows that they have an identical nature. Gregory begins with the text, "He was the true light that enlightens every man coming into the world," applying it to the Father, Son and Holy Spirit.[27] He explains the three identical expressions as follows:

These are three subjects and three verbs—he was and he was and he was. But a single reality was. There are three predicates—light and light and light. But the light is one, God is one. This is the meaning of David's prophetic vision: "In your light shall we see light." We receive the Son's light from the Father's light in the Spirit: that is what we ourselves have seen and what we now proclaim—it is the plain and simple explanation of the Trinity.[28]

The quoted verse from Psalm 36:9 is interpreted from a Trinitarian hermeneutic so that the three lights are understood to be incorporated into the one light.[29]

---

26 *Oration* 28.1 (SC 250.100; PG 36.25), Nazianzus, *On God and Christ*, 37.

27 *Oration* 31.3 (SC 250. 278; PG 36.136), Nazianzus, *On God and Christ*, 118–119.

28 *Oration* 31.3 (SC 250. 278; PG 36.136), Nazianzus, *On God and Christ*, 118–119.

29 *Carmina* 1.1.3.3, "let us quake before the great Spirit, who is my God, who made me know God," (PG 37.410), Nazianzus, *On God and Christ*, 43. *Carmina* 1.1.3.71, "in threefold lights the one nature is established, not a numberless unity, since it subsists in three excellencies, nor a threesome worshipped severally, since the nature is inseparable" (PG 37.410), Nazianzus, *On God and Christ*, 46.

Gregory's unique contribution of arguing for the Spirit's deity is proven to be significant within his spirituality.[30] If the Spirit is not divine, there is no true spirituality because the Spirit illuminates the soul so that the believer can see the Son and the Father.

Were not the Spirit to be worshipped, how could he deify me through baptism? If he is to be worshipped, why not adored? And if to be adored, how can he fail to be God? One links with the other, a truly golden chain of salvation. From the Spirit comes our rebirth, from rebirth comes a new creating, from new creating a recognition of the worth of him who affected it.[31]

The Spirit is the internal witness that illuminates the believer to see Christ whose light was caused by the Father.[32]

In his three sermons on the Theophony (*Orations* 38 to 40), Gregory emphasizes the role of Christ as the Light that must come to purify man so that he might see God. Worship begins with the baptism of Christ because he is "the true light which enlightens every man and woman coming into the world...which we darkened and confused by sin."[33] In order for man to rise above the material world and his own sin, the Son had to come and provide purification. Gregory articulates the purpose of the incarnation with great clarity, "He came to his own proper image and bore flesh for the sake of flesh, and mingled with a rational soul for my soul's sake, wholly cleansing like by like.[34]

---

30 The uniqueness is in his applying *homoousios*. Basil of Caesarea (c. A.D. 330–379) and Gregory of Nyssa clearly view the Spirit as God, but use reserved language.

31 *Oration* 31.28 (SC 250.330–332; PG 36.165), Nazianzus, *On God and Christ*, 138–139. See Everett Ferguson, *Baptism in the Early Church* (Downers Grove: Eerdman's Publishing, 2009), 592–602.

32 *Oration* 31.3 (SC 250.278; PG 36.136), Nazianzus, *On God and Christ*, 118–119.

33 *Oration* 39.1 (SC 358.150; PG 36.336), Daley 128.

34 *Oration* 38.13, "He came to his own proper image and bore flesh for the sake of flesh, and mingled with a rational soul for my soul's sake, wholly cleansing like by like. In every respect save that of sin, he became human: conceived from the Virgin, who had first been purified in soul and flesh by the Spirit (for it was right both that the childbirth be honored and that virginity be honored still more highly); coming forth as God, along with what he had taken on; one from two opposites, flesh and Spirit—the one of which shared divinity, the other of which was divinized. O new mixture! O unexpected blending! He has come to be, the uncreated one is created, the limitless

He shows how the Eastern doctrine of *theosis* functions with the spiritual metaphor of God as light in the theophany *Orations*: "Christ is full of light, let us shine with him! Christ is baptized: let us go down with him, so that we may rise up with him!"[35] The believer is to follow the model of Christ who was also baptized, and by doing so the believer participates in his death and resurrection. The believer grows in spirituality as he contemplates the life and death of Christ so that he is "taught to be purified first, to be lowly in [his] thinking, to proclaim the Gospel in the fullness of [his] spiritual and bodily maturity."[36]

Gregory's spirituality of purification and ascension

One of the key texts for Gregory and many of the church fathers concerning spirituality and the purpose of theology is Matthew 5:8, "Blessed are the pure in heart for they shall see God."[37] The themes of illumination and purity come together in this text as God illuminates the mind in order to be seen, and the believer is called to purify himself in order to see God.[38] The call to purity begins with rightly understanding God according to his revelation and is complete when one casts off his carnal thinking and living.[39] By participating in the light that God reveals, the believer "improves" by following the Spirit and fellowshipping in the Word. His life is changed as the chains of sin are loosed and he is able to contemplate that which is above the material and sinful. The spiritual life that seeks a pure vision of God focuses upon the "way of living and contemplation."[40] The light comes

---

one is contained through the mediation of a rational soul standing between divinity and the coarseness of flesh" (SC 358.130–134; PG 36.325), Daley 123.

35 *Oration* 38.14 (SC 358.134–136; PG 328), Daley 124.

36 *Oration* 38.14 (SC 358.134-36; PG 328), Daley 124.

37 *Oration* 22.15 (SC 270.276–278; PG 35.1147), Vinson 107:128–129.

38 *Oration* 20.1-3, "Must purify the ears and intelligence before taking spiritual leadership" and "only when they had very thoroughly purified themselves" (SC 270.56–64; PG 35.1065–1068), Vinson 107:107–109. There are two ways to live. One is "they drive themselves to every transgression, rejoice in evil, love their own doom." The others behold God with the pure eye of the mind" *Carmina* 2.1.1.37–62 (PG 37.973–974), [St. Gregory of Nazianzus, *Three Poems*, trans. Dennis Meehan, vol. 75 of *The Fathers of the Church: A New Translation* (Washington: The Catholic University of America Press, 1987), 75:26–27].

39 *Oration* 28.2–3 (SC 250.100–102; PG 36.25), Nazianzus, *On God and Christ*, 37–39.

40 *Oration* 26.19 (SC 284.232; PG 35.1252), Vinson 107:190. Beginning of wisdom

down and "penetrates the regions below" so that it might "draw [man] ever upward with desire, and a mind made pure might approach the most pure."[41]

Gregory shows the connection in many passages where illumination either leads to purification or purification to illumination. The two are interdependent, "where there is [purification], there is illumination; and illumination is the fulfillment of desire for those eager to share in the greatest things—or in the Greatest Thing, or in that which is beyond the Great."[42]

Gregory emphasizes the importance of purity by stating that it is the beginning point of theology in a number of texts, many of which are addressed to the consecration of bishops.[43] He reasons that "one must first purify oneself, and then draw near to the pure."[44] True theology is not simply right thoughts about God, but a mystical experience

---

is fear, therefore, "one ought not to begin with contemplation and then finish in fear—after all, a free-wheeling kind of contemplation might push you over the cliff! Rather, being instructed in fear, cleansed and (one might even say) lightened by it, one should then be lifted on high. Where there is fear, there is observation for the commandments; where the commandments are observed, there is a cleansing of the flesh, that cloud that blocks the soul's vision and keeps it from seeing clearly the rays of divine illumination; but where there is cleansing, there is also illumination, and illumination is the fulfillment of desire for those eager to share in the greatest things— or in the greatest thing, or in that which is beyond the great!" *Oration* 38.8 (SC 358.118–120; PG 36.320), Daley 131.

Carmina 2.1.1. 262, "Fleeing this world, this way of life and the anxieties of the flesh, I could have filled my mind totally with Christ. I could have lived apart from others, elevating a pure spirit to God alone until the day when, in a buoyant hope, I should attain my final goal. Would to God indeed" (PG 37.989), Meehan, *Three Poems,* 75:33. See Donald F. Winslow, *Dynamics Of Salvation: A Study In Gregory Of Nazianzus* (Macon: Mercer University Press, 1979), 151.

41 *Oration* 32.15 (SC 318.116; PG 36. 192), Vinson 107:201–202.

42 *Oration* 39.8 (SC 358.164–166; PG 36. 344), Daley 131. Daley's translation has "cleansing" and I have replaced it with "purification." See also *Oration* 23.11, "Our minds and our human condition are such that a knowledge of the relationship and disposition of these members with regard to one another is reserved for the Holy Trinity itself alone and those purified souls to whom the Trinity may make revelation either now or in the future" (SC 270.302–304; PG 35.1164), Vinson 107:138–139.

43 *Oration* 19.8 (PG 35.1052), Vinson 107:99. "First requirement is to purify oneself, then to associate oneself with the One who is pure."

44 *Oration* 20.4 (SC 270.62–64; PG 35.1069), Vinson 107:109.

with the dynamic revelation of God. The worship service is an event where the church participates in the divine, and therefore the church must be purified to truly experience it.[45] McGuckin explains this mystical aspect of worship in Gregory's theology, "Worship is a dynamic and soteriological experience, the beauty of God experienced in liturgy or prayer expressed in the Church's confession of praise."[46]

Man's eyes have been darkened by sin and corruption so that they cannot see the light of God perfectly. [47] This is why Gregory limits the conversation about theology to include only those who have purified themselves and are seeking a pure vision of God.[48]

> Discussion of theology is not for everyone...nor is it for every occasion, or every audience.... It must be reserved for certain occasions, for certain audiences, and certain limits must be observed. It is not for all people, but only for those who have been tested and have found a sound footing in study, and, more importantly, have undergone, or at least are undergoing, purification of body and soul, just as it is for weak eyes to look at the sun's brightness.[49]

If a man desires to lead others in seeing God, he must first draw near to God himself in the right way by desiring the highest goal of a philosophical life. The talkativeness of most bishops makes him long for the "philosophy that comes from above."[50] Gregory says that theology

---

45 *Oration* 38.11, "since we have cleansed this theatre of ours by the Word, come, let us speculate now about the feast" (SC 358.124–126; PG 324), Daley 132.

46 See McGuckin, "Perceiving Light from Light in Light," 18.

47 *Oration* 28.4, "For language may show the known if not adequately, at least faintly, to a person not totally deaf and dull of mind" (SC 250.106–108; PG 36.32), Nazianzus, *On God and Christ*, 132.

48 The crowds in Constantinople had been discussing the controversy over the Trinity as casually as amusement and entertaining small talk. See *Oration* 27.3 (SC 250.80; PG 36.14), Nazianzus, *On God and Christ*, 27.

49 *Oration* 27.3 (SC 250.80; PG 36.14), Nazianzus, *On God and Christ*, 27.

50 *Oration* 20.1 (SC 270.56–58; PG 35.1065), Vinson 107:107. Gregory takes the term philosophy in its truest sense: a pursuit of the happiest life. He believes Christianity is the only philosophy that provides true happiness.

properly done spurs the theologian to listen more than to speak.[51] He serves as an extreme example of emphasizing purity by taking a vow of silence until he can first purify himself.[52] His monastic conviction is that a life of contemplation must precede teaching and preaching. The need for purity is seen throughout his sermons on the pastoral ministry and summed up well in *Oration* 20, "but before we rise above [the world of matter that drags me down] as far as possible and sufficiently purify our ears and minds, I think it is dangerous either to accept the responsibility for other souls or to take up theology."[53]

One of Gregory's most common and powerful metaphors for spirituality is drawing near to God like Moses approached the holy mountain.[54] This is important for the pastor because he must be closer to God in order to pull others closer with him. Before one can teach others about God, he must first purify himself so that he might see the light of God. The purer the theologian, the closer he is drawn to God, "his place matching his purity."[55] McGuckin argues that Gregory "defines the nature of theology as an invitation to ascent given by God

---

51 *Oration* 32.21 (SC 318.128–130; PG 36.200), Vinson 107:206–207.

52 *Oration* 6.1, "It was then I set a bridle on my lips, which were not in any case inclined to speak, because I thought that the priorities of the Spirit were first to purify myself through the philosophy that resides in action; next, to open the mouth of my mind and draw in the Spirit; then to utter a godly theme and to speak of God's perfect wisdom among them that are perfect" (SC 405.120–121; PG 35.721), Vinson 107:3. See also *Oration* 19.1–3: "When I realized that nothing I said was able to curb popular talk or the current all-pervasive passion to speak and lecture on the things of the Spirit without the inspiration of the Spirit, I embarked on another course—a better one" (PG 35.1044), Vinson 107:95–96.

53 *Oration* 20.1. His desire was "to block out his senses, severing all ties with the flesh and the world…to live the life that transcends visible nature…and be and ever come to be a spotless mirror, as it were, of God and the divine, capturing light with light…and finally attain the blessed goal, our mirrors shattered by the reality of the truth" (SC 270.56–58; PG 35.1065), Vinson 107:107.

54 *Oration* 20.2. "It was truly a great thing for them simply to hear God's voice, and this only after they had been thoroughly purified" (SC 270.58–60; PG 35.1065), Vinson 107:108. See *Oration* 38.7 (SC 357.114–116; PG 36.317), Daley 120. McGuckin says this is an *idée maitresse* of Gregory's work to which he returns time and again." See McGuckin, "Perceiving Light from Light in Light," 13.

55 *Oration* 28.2 (SC 250.100; PG 36.25), Nazianzus, *On God and Christ*, 38–39.

only to the purified and elected souls."[56] This ascent is further defined by "moral fidelity, and a life of prayer and reflection."[57]

The spirituality of Gregory that focuses on purity and ascension insists that the believer must strive for virtue. He argues that the pastor "must not only wipe out the traces of vice from his soul, but also inscribe better [virtues]."[58] Gregory exhorts his church, "Seek to keep the commandments, walk in his statutes. Conduct is the stepping stone of contemplation."[59] He explains the necessity of a virtuous life in relation to worshipping the true God,

> If one has nurtured some good qualities that has molded his character, transgression becomes more difficult than becoming good in the first place, for every virtue that is firmly rooted by time and reason becomes second nature, as does the love within us too, with which we worship the true love and which we have folded to our hearts in love and adopted as the guiding principle for all our existence.[60]

Virtue is a conduct learned from discipline that not only leads to a pious life but, more importantly, to true worship and love for God. Virtue is what makes someone a true theologian.[61]

Conclusion

Gregory's definition of spirituality is built upon the theological rules that God is incomprehensible in his revelation. He must be pursued according to his works and not our reason. The sinful mind cannot grasp the whole of the boundless Being of God, but it can recognize the light of God in his work. Gregory's theology is also built upon the

---

56 McGuckin, "Perceiving Light from Light in Light," 13. This is in contrast with Horton who dismisses the idea of ascent as a modernistic concept.

57 See McGuckin on how this ascent demands man overcoming his "materially based consciousness" in order to "transcend material limitations, when the soul is invited back to God, to its true spiritual nature and destiny in communion with God" "Perceiving Light from Light in Light," 13.

58 *Oration* 2.14 (PG 35.424), NPNF² 7:208.

59 *Oration* 20.12 (SC 270.80–82; PG 35.1080), Vinson 107:115–116.

60 *Oration* 23.1 (SC 270.260; PG 35.1152), Vinson 107:131–132.

61 *Oration* 23.1 (SC 270.260; PG 35.1152), Vinson 107:131–132.

mystery of God being partially revealed with the hope of seeing the whole in heaven. His theology consistently draws man closer to God by articulating the vision of God as seen in Scripture. So how should we benefit from Gregory as a pastor? I have three recommendations for pastors to consider.

First, pastors should be intentional about presenting a vision of God that draws people to him. Every sermon should be about God: his care, love, power, wisdom, holiness and justice. The Father loves us by sending his Son to us. The Father and Son love us by sending the Spirit to keep and empower us until the day of his return. This essential doctrine must be presented as part of the believer's hope, power and spiritual growth. Preaching from texts such as Romans 8:11, Matthew 3 and 28 and Ephesians 2 will give pastors opportunities to help the church see that all three persons of the Godhead are at work for their salvation and sanctification.

Second, the pastor must seek personal purification and counsel others toward that end. Wrestling with one's own sin, maintaining the discipline of personal confession and being refreshed by the gospel will help lead others to a life of contemplation that recognizes the corruption and fallen nature of their souls and help others draw closer to God. The church must see the pastor model what it means to be purified so that they can follow in their own purity and worship. This is what it means to be a worship leader after the model of Christ: be the first to lay down your life by humbly confessing sin. This is how Christ will be exalted.

Third, pastors should constantly be reminding their church of the hope set before them. The circumstances that hinder believers in a fallen world and the frustration of constantly wrestling with corrupt desires can discourage the believer. The church needs to be reminded of the hope that Christ will perfectly restore us when we are drawn into his presence. While we wait for this, the church needs to be reminded that they can find relief from their suffering and struggles by drawing near to God now, getting a taste of the blessings that are still to come.

05

PATRISTICS · MEDIEVAL

The Christological centre of piety in the prayers of Anselm of Canterbury

By David S. Hogg

WHEN CHRISTIANS STUDY the Bible, the presupposition that undergirds their reading is that the content of divine revelation is everlasting. We read Scripture understanding that there may be more than one hermeneutical horizon, but also recognizing that despite the separation of space and time between author and reader, the truth presented is as applicable now as it was then. But what of other texts? Do texts written by pastors, theologians and apologists reflecting on the Word of God transmit or emulate its inspired character? How far does inspiration go?

That Scripture was inspired by the Holy Spirit is clear from texts such as 2 Timothy 3:16 and 2 Peter 1:21, to say nothing of myriad other evidences found throughout the Old and New Testaments alike. Moreover, the history of interpretation and theology is replete with affirmations and arguments that support inspiration. Within the tradition of the orthodox faith, the question of inspiration has rarely been an issue; nevertheless, the question of the nature of inspiration beyond the text has proven more provocative.

John Calvin (1509–1564) is helpful here when he reminds us that due to our sinful state, "without the illumination of the Holy Spirit, the word has no effect."[1] Elsewhere, Calvin argues along similar lines when he explains that, "the word is the instrument by which the illumination of the Spirit is dispensed."[2] The doctrine of inspiration cannot stand alone or apart from a robust pneumatology that takes into account the continuing work of the Spirit in the heart and mind of the reader. In other words, the Spirit's inspiration of Scripture does not end with the *autographa* or the final form of the text; rather, it continues in the activity of illumination.

This distinction is what both unites and distinguishes divine revelation with human reflection on that deposit. It is the Holy Spirit himself who unites the two, yet the specific manner in which the Spirit is working is also what distinguishes them. That is to say, a work of theology is not inspired in the same way as the Bible, but it is, nevertheless, a work of illumination that carries weight insofar as it reflects Scripture. The Spirit who guarantees the original is the same Spirit who guides what is derived.

Turning to Anselm

As we turn to Anselm of Canterbury's (1033–1109) prayers and meditations, we must bear in mind that he was not composing prayers in an extemporaneous fashion. It was neither the practice of the day to pray without forethought, nor the desire of spiritual directors to encourage such prayer among their disciples. When Anselm replied to the request for written prayers that could be used in personal worship and for the development of piety, he took the opportunity to write out of the overflow of his extensive theological learning.[3] Thus, it would be a mistake to think that these prayers and meditations are simplistic, superficial or, worse, not theologically grounded. They are, in fact, deeply theological or, more accurately, profoundly Christological. What Anselm presents to us is a form of Christology that is rooted in the practice of piety.

---

1   John Calvin, *Institutes of the Christian Religion*, 2 vols., ed. John T. McNeill, trans. Ford Lewis Battles (Philadelphia: Westminster Press, 1960), 3.2.33.

2   Calvin, *Institutes*, 1.9.3

3   It is important to note here that we do not know the dates for all the prayers, and that they were written and revised at different points in his career. Even so, he did not begin writing them until he was at least prior of the monastery at Bec.

After all, "Christocentrism is the *Leitmotiv* of Anselm's spirituality" such that his prayers are, "Christology *in actu*."[4]

Insofar as Anselm's prayers are steeped in Christology, they reflect something of the character and quality of the Scriptures from which they are derived. This means that while Anselm's works are by no means inspired, they are the product of the illumination of the Spirit which is an extension of his work of inspiration. This being the case, we understand that Anselm's prayers are not infallible or inerrant, to be sure, but this does raise the question of the context of their interpretation. Do we apply the same hermeneutic to the prayers and meditations as we would to Scripture?

The answer to this is surely both yes and no. No, we do not interpret Anselm as though he speaks infallibly or inerrantly. The foundation is not the same for both texts. We can, however, apply biblical hermeneutics to theological texts in two different ways. First, as with so much biblical interpretation in the last century or so, we can seek to understand as much of the historical context and background to Anselm's life and writing, in the hopes of using that information to inform our own interpretation of this notable archbishop. Second, as with so much biblical interpretation throughout the history of the church, we can seek to read the texts as they stand. This would be analogous to the Augustinian concept of Scripture interpreting Scripture.

Ideally, both history and the text, on their own terms and in their own right, are used as guides to understanding. When it comes to Anselm, however, the preponderant emphasis has been on his historical context and not on the abiding character of his theology as pneumatological illumination. This is why commentators of the calibre of John McIntyre, for instance, can simultaneously have so much of value to contribute to our appreciation of Anselm's thought, yet miss the mark in maintaining that decidedly unscriptural cultural influences predominate in his work.[5] It is for this reason that in what follows I will

---

4   Dániel Deme, *The Christology of Anselm of Canterbury* (Aldershot: Ashgate, 2003), 30–31. Thanks are also due to Nathan Tarr's fine unpublished paper on the canonical and creedal roots of Anselm's Christology where this point is developed more thoroughly.

5   John McIntyre, *St. Anselm and His Critics: a Re-Interpretation of the* Cur Deus Homo (Edinburgh: Oliver and Boyd, 1954).

examine some of Anselm's prayers and meditations in their own right. This is my attempt to begin to redress both the lack of sensitivity to the pneumatologically illuminated character of Anselm's Christology in his prayers, and also this widely recognized lacuna in Anselmian studies.[6]

Our common faith: modern and medieval unity

The purpose of Anselm's prayers is to propel the reader's thoughts toward loving and fearing God even as, or perhaps because, they realize the state of their own heart. In a letter to the Countess Matilda of Tuscany (c. 1045–1115), Anselm reminded her that the prayers he sent to her are not an end in themselves, but the beginning.[7] Here, of course, is the danger of devotional literature. Some will assume that in reading such well formed prose and following whatever other activities are prescribed, they have done well. This not good, and Anselm knew it. Devotional literature, at its best, is intended only as an aid to the believer in focusing and concentrating one's thoughts on worship in its many facets. There is a fine line between worshipping through liturgy and worshipping liturgy. Jesus' words in John 5:39 are applicable, "You search the Scriptures because you think that in them you have eternal life; and it is they that bear witness about me." If the Bible itself can become an idolatrous stumbling block to piety and spiritual growth, how much more what we write and create for ourselves?

To avoid this idolatrous confusion between his prayers and prayer, Anselm cautions the reader against believing they need to get through the whole of any one prayer, "but [need] only [read] as much as will stir up the affections of prayer," for, it is sufficient that these prayers should stir up affections and thoughts appropriate to the nature and

---

6   "But the prayers and meditations, which were the most popular of his works in his own time, and continued to be read widely for several centuries, have received less attention by modern scholars than his other works, although they are of great interest as works of what might be called popular culture, and it is to be hoped that they will receive more study as works of this genre." Sally Vaughn, *Archbishop Anselm 1093–1109, Bec Missionary, Canterbury Primate, Patriarch of Another World* (Aldershot: Ashgate, 2012), 8.

7   Benedicta Ward, trans., *The Prayers and Meditations of Saint Anselm with the Proslogion* (London: Penguin, 1973), 90. All quotes from Anselm's prayers in what follows are taken from her translation, rather than my own, in order to better serve the reader who wishes to find a reference easily.

work of prayer.[8] In fact, it is worth noting that prayer in the monastic context was a matter of work; not as an independent requirement for salvation, but as an outpouring of love and thanksgiving. Medieval monasticism at its best appreciated that *orare est laborare*, to pray is to work or, more colloquially yet more precisely, *prayer is the work*. What matters is that the soul is stirred. What matters is that the mind is moved. What matters is that the heart is roused. The aim of all prayer is that we become greater lovers of God, and as all lovers know, love comes through sacrifice and activity. Those who claim to love God greatly have, we might say, the knees to prove it. If Anselm had set himself to no other task, he would still have left us a feast.

Even at a feast, however, there is always something a guest does not like. Although Anselm's prayers have been embraced as models of piety and adopted as exhibits of spiritual formation, they have also been disdained as relics of misguided medieval musings and eyed with suspicious curiosity. Anyone who takes the time to read through Anselm's nineteen prayers will soon discover why. The order in which they are presented in Benedicta Ward's fine translation, begins with Anselm's prayer to God, followed by a prayer to Christ, then on to a prayer before receiving the body and blood of Christ. So far so good, though the third title might make a few Protestants nervous. The fourth prayer is to the Holy Cross and most of the remainder are prayers to saints, with the exception of the final two prayers which are offered for friends and enemies. Anselm serves us some wonderful morsels on which to feed, but he also supplies us with some fare that particular segments of the church find less palatable, even disagreeable. This is the danger of praying one's theology.

Does a theological disagreement negate the value of another's insights? Can an evangelical Protestant read Anselm's prayers, especially those offered to saints, with profit? If, as we noted above, Anselm's prayers are fundamentally Christological, even when dressed in the garb of communion with saints in heaven, perhaps civil conversation is still possible, fruitful dialogue remains conceivable and mutual edification and education attainable. Without releasing a firm grip on our own convictions, let us be quick to listen and slow to speak, humble in spirit and jealous for truth.

---

8 Ward, *Prayers and Meditations*, 90.

"Prayer to God"

Reading through the Psalms on a weekly basis is enough to give a man or woman occupying any social strata in society a profound sense of their own measure against the holiness and majesty of God. This is what Anselm wants to pass on to his readers. In the midst of the busyness that makes up their lives, he wants them to benefit from what he has learned and inculcated in the quiet solemnity of the monastery. He desires to impart a vision of the Almighty that stresses his transcendent sovereignty, but not to the exclusion of knowing his immanence. He desires to impart an understanding of human frailty and sinfulness, but never apart from the grace and forgiveness available from Christ. These themes run throughout Anselm's prayers, and are clearly laid out in his short but powerful "Prayer to God."

Anselm opens with the petition, "Almighty God, merciful Father, and my good Lord, have mercy on me, a sinner. Grant me forgiveness of my sins."[9] Anyone conversant with the Gospels may be forgiven for thinking that they have read this before. These words are remarkably similar to those found on the lips of the tax collector in Jesus' parable in Luke 18. This connection is no accident. Like the master painter who thinks of everything from brush strokes to focal point, the master writer thinks of allusions and analogies. Anselm is calling us to our knees amidst a world that would beat its breast and turn God's good grace on its head through a kind of perverted spiritual alchemy. The time for rebellion and self assurance, the time for striking out on our own, the time for making our own way in the world is past. The time for repentance, obedience and humility has come.

Strange though it may seem, it would behoove us here to recall the methodology that lies behind all good writing. Whereas the popular conception is often that writers stare at a blank screen and wait for inspiration to hit them as they flail about for direction and ideas, the truth is that any good writer knows where they are headed (even when the words do not come so easily!). Put another way, the beginning is written in light of the end. This means that even though what is written at the beginning might lead the reader to the end, the opposite is the case for the author. For the author, the end is what dictates and drives the beginning. Why does this matter here? It matters because

---

9   Anselm, "Prayer to God," in Ward, *Prayers and Meditations*, lines 1–3.

the end to which Anselm is driving his readers, and which has deeply informed his own writing, is the joy that can be known only through salvation in Jesus Christ. To get there, however, we must recognize our sin and seek mercy and forgiveness from God. Much like Psalm 123, echoes of which are also present in this prayer, Anselm leads us to cry out from our lowly estate to the one who is enthroned in the heavens. Our end is to dwell undisturbed and at rest in the heavenlies, even though now we struggle on earth. With the psalmist, Anselm urges us in every prayer to lift up our eyes, but always to do so in conjunction with looking clearly at our own situation.

There should be no doubt that our lot is to be continually in dangers of "snares, temptations, and harmful pleasures;"[10] even so, it is our purpose to "hope, love and live, according to your purpose and your will…purely, soberly, devoutly, and with a true and effective mind."[11] What we see in a rhythmic, almost poetic fashion in these prayers, is the same truth made so concisely by John Calvin that nearly all sound wisdom we possess consists both of the knowledge of God and the knowledge of ourselves.[12] What was foundational for piety and wisdom throughout the Reformation was no less foundational during the Middle Ages.

In addition to the allusions to Luke 18 and Psalm 123, there is another Scriptural resonance that becomes evident if we look at the structure of the whole. As we noted above, Anselm begins by addressing God as Father from whom he pleads help to, "make me guard against and overcome all snares, temptations, and harmful pleasures."[13] Lead us not into temptation. A little further on, we read, "Let me believe and hope, love and live, according to your purpose and your will."[14] Your will be done on earth as it is in heaven. The prayer ends with the simple request, "Deliver me from all evil and lead me to eternal life through the Lord."[15] In so many ways, this prayer has been modelled on the Lord's Prayer of Matthew 6. The astute reader will note that while

---

10 Anselm, "Prayer to God," line 5.

11 Anselm, "Prayer to God," lines 9–10, 16–17.

12 Calvin, *Institutes*, 1.1.1

13 Anselm, "Prayer to God," lines 4–5.

14 Anselm, "Prayer to God," lines 9–10.

15 Anselm, "Prayer to God," lines 30–32.

Anselm has drawn on Scripture as a model for this prayer, he has not followed it slavishly or simply restated it. He has interwoven his own reflections and thoughts, yet not so as to blur our view of God and his revelation, but like a master weaver, he has worked in the threads of human devising as a backdrop against which the glory of the divine threads of truth and revelation are clearly and brightly displayed.

But what does all this assume? What makes Anselm think that modelling his prayers on Scripture, and infusing them with biblical allusions, will be effective? What undergirds a prayer that addresses the Father, requires the work of the Son and relies on the indwelling of the Spirit? Faith. These prayers are not for the unbeliever, but for those who come with a vibrant and living faith in the application of redemption accomplished and applied. This is what guards the reader against spiralling ever downward into a pit of despair. For Anselm and his contemporaries, the knowledge of God that gives us a true knowledge of ourselves is both negative, insofar as it highlights our sin along with our moral and spiritual impotence, and positive, insofar as it provides us with hope that cannot disappoint. This faith and hope is repeatedly grounded in love—not our love of God so much as his love for us. This is what we see so clearly in Anselm's "Prayer to Christ."

"Prayer to Christ"

To read through Anselm's "Prayer to Christ" is to be reminded that prayer may be a characteristic of spirituality, but this characteristic cannot be glibly equated with maturity or genuine piety. A robust theology of prayer is founded on, or perhaps embedded within, a sound doctrine of God. Do you wish for improvement in some aspect of your praying? Attend to God. Anselm began this in his prayer to God, but here, now, he uncovers the depths of his Christology, surely guided by the ancient principle, *opera ad extra trinitatis indivisa sunt.*[16] The doctrine of Christ, for all its specialized treatment, is part of the doctrine of God, and as such, is indissolubly linked to the theology and practice of prayer. And how does Christology inform prayer? Most concretely, it becomes the meeting point of divine and human love.

---

16 *Latin*, meaning: all the works of the triune God are indivisibly the works of the Father, the Son, and the Holy Spirit.

As the reader wends her way through this prayer,[17] it might appear that Anselm is concentrating more on his own love and its subjective experience than on the love of God. A closer reading, however, makes it clear that while there is a strong element of the subjective experience, the subjective is grounded in the objective truth of God's prevenient love. This is why Anselm opens the prayer bemoaning the fact that Christ "deserves a better return of love" than what Anselm has so far been able to offer. The presupposition that undergirds this prayer is the "sweet riches of your love" that place his soul in debt.[18]

In fact, it is this very principle of the riches of Christ's grace lavished on sinners, leading to an insurmountable debt that the redeemed owe their Saviour, that puts one in mind of the *Cur Deus Homo* (1097–1098). Since this prayer is not known prior to 1104, and that is the time by which the *Cur Deus Homo* was finished, it is not surprising that we should see a theological connection between the two. Anselm's *Meditation on Human Redemption* (1099–1100) is another practical outworking of his emerging Christology. Here, though, Anselm is making a concrete effort to take his theology of the atonement and apply it to himself and to all who would read and use his prayer as a guide to personal devotion. Without a theology of the person and work of Christ, without a theology of the cross and empty tomb, without a theology that wrestles with the application of grace, there can be no genuinely Christian piety. It is by grace that we know the depth of our sin because we see it displayed at Golgotha, but it is also by grace that we experience the love and mercy that is deeper yet, made known in the empty tomb, so that we can pray to the living God who gives life.

A well known criticism about Anselm's theology of the atonement is that he borrowed from his medieval culture. His notion of satisfaction owed to the God who saves us and the need to repay a debt equivalent to the greatness and majesty of the one who accomplished our redemption is said to be inextricably bound to the medieval context.[19] This, in other words, is a theology for a time rather than timeless

---

17 Ward, *Prayers and Meditations*, 60. Ward notes this prayer is first found in the collection of the Countess Mathilda in 1104.

18 Anselm, "Prayer to Christ," line 7.

19 For a good, brief introduction to this debate, see D. Bentley Hart, "A Gift Exceeding Every Debt: an Eastern Orthodox Appreciation of Anselm's *Cur Deus Homo*," *Pro Ecclesia* 7, no. 3 (Summer 1994): 333–349.

theology. And yet, we should wonder, how can anyone hold the passion narratives in the Gospels along with their further explication in the New Testament epistles in one hand, while holding Anselm's Christology as displayed in the *Cur Deus Homo, Meditation on Human Redemption* and "Prayer to Christ" in the other, all the while contending that a medieval monk has muddled the truth? What is anachronistic to the revelation of the person and work of Christ is failing to see what a great debt the redeemed do, in fact, owe, to say nothing of the poverty of our gratitude to the one who deserves "a better return of love."[20] After all, it is the divine kindness that first came to us, and because of that, "if my soul wills any good, you gave it to me."[21]

In addition to recognizing the foundation upon which this prayer stands, its overall structure also helps us to appreciate how Scripture and theology inform prayer. After Anselm has spent some time orienting us to the depths of the riches of Christ's love, he moves on to summarize Christ's redemption more broadly conceived. He recalls Jesus' passion with the "buffeting" and "scourging," "cross" and "wounds." He speaks of the burial, but then recalls "your glorious Resurrection, and wonderful Ascension." But what does the ascension mean but exile, were it not for the promised second coming when we all shall see his face?[22] Yet it is not enough for Anselm to recount these facts; like a good preacher, he invites us into the narrative of Scripture.

One of the chief characteristics of Anselm's prayers, and many medieval prayers, is that the reader is drawn out of their own world and into the biblical world. What is real is contained in divine revelation. The world in which we live from day to day is full of darkness and shadows.[23] Consequently, in this prayer, Anselm elaborates on the details of Christ's work to encourage the reader to take stock of what is real, what matters and the sphere in which life is possible. This is the effect Anselm seeks to achieve by interspersing interrogatives throughout his prayer.

An effective writer never uses just one mood. The indicative is certainly prominent since facts, truths and information must be conveyed. The subjunctive can also be used to good effect as possibilities are

---

20 Anselm, "Prayer to Christ," line 5.
21 Anselm, "Prayer to Christ," line 22.
22 Anselm, "Prayer to Christ," lines 64–68.
23 Cf. Psalm 73, especially verses 16–20.

explored and suggested. The imperative arrests our attention and requires us to give an answer. The interrogative, however, though not a mood, *per se*, may not convey truth, but does require it in order to be effective. The interrogative searches out possibilities, but in a much more personal way than the subjunctive. And as for the imperative, while it demands an answer, the interrogative invites reflection. When, therefore, Anselm asks his questions, they are well placed because they build on the indicatives and personalize the searching questions that invoke the passions as much as the intellect. Surely in Anselm's prayers we find "no romantic opposition of sensation to intellect or of imagination to the rational capacities of human beings; likewise there is no gulf of thought between thought and life."[24]

What is Anselm doing when he asks, "Why, O my soul, were you not there to be pierced by a sword of bitter sorrow when you could not bear the piercing of the side of your Saviour with a lance?" What is he getting at when he asks, "Why did you not see with horror the blood that poured out of the side of your Redeemer?"[25] Why should Anselm ask the impossible? Why should he regret his absence from an event that occurred over a thousand years before? The answer lies in this statement:

> I am like an orphan deprived of the presence of a very kind father, who, weeping and wailing, does not cease to cling to the dear face with his whole heart. So, as much as I can, though not as much as I ought, I am mindful of your passion...."[26]

Anselm wants to place us in the position of orphans. This analogy does not work on the level of what has been lost, but on the very emotional level of hope and imagination. The orphan who is old enough to have known the kindness of his father, stares into the picture or memory of that man and dreams of living life with him again. So too, in this prayer, the believer is ushered out of his comfort into the realization that his experience of Christ is not entirely proper. Jesus is not an abstract idea or person who lived long ago and to whom we pray and about whom

---

24 Thomas S. Hibbs, "Iris Murdoch, Spiritual Exercises and Anselm's *Proslogion* and Prayers," *The Saint Anselm Journal* 3, no. 1 (Fall 2005): 64.

25 Anselm, "Prayer to Christ," lines 79–86.

26 Anselm, "Prayer to Christ," lines 58–63.

we speak. Jesus is the Man whose kindness we have received, but with whom we have never physically walked or lived. It is certainly true that those who have believed even though they have not seen the risen Lord are blessed, but that does not make his presence inconsequential. To put this another way, our separation from Christ is abnormal, and Anselm wishes to awaken us to this by making us feel our absence from our Saviour at the very moment he should not have been left alone.

Among other things, this highlights the way in which we have all failed Christ. And if we have failed Christ in this monumental manner, should there be any surprise at the way we all too often treat our friends? Christ is certainly not just another friend, but he is the archetypal example to which friendship should aspire. When he was abandoned, he did not hold a grudge. When a mocking thief eventually recognized who Jesus was, he did not pronounce divine judgement, but eternal life. While we were his enemies, Christ died for us (see Romans 5:10). This is the ground of salvation, and for this reason, it is also the ground of Anselm's "Prayer for Friends."

"Prayer for Friends"

In an eroticized culture, the first casualty is friendship. This helps to explain why, in recent decades, attempts have been made to redefine our perception of Anselm. John Boswell was, notoriously, the first to categorize Anselm as a homosexual, along with countless other medieval figures.[27] The grounds upon which he made his case have been shown as spurious at best and self-serving at worst;[28] nevertheless, the language Anselm used when writing to his friends is most definitely not the way we relate to our friends in contemporary society.[29] Then again, Anselm's view of friendship is theologically informed, even Christologically informed, which is rather uncommon.[30]

---

27 Cf. John Boswell, *Christianity, Social Tolerance and Homosexuality: Gay People in Western Europe from the Beginning of the Christian Era to the Fourteenth Century* (Chicago: Chicago University Press, 1980).

28 Cf. Richard Southern, *Saint Anselm: a Portrait in a Landscape* (Cambridge: Cambridge University Press, 1990), 148–153.

29 Cf. Anselm's expression of longing and love, embracing and kissing in, for instance, Epistles 117 and 120 in Walter Fröhlich, trans., *The Letters of Saint Anselm of Canterbury*, vol. 1 (Kalamazoo: Cistercian Publications, 1990).

30 Southern, *Saint Anselm*, 155. Southern rightly identifies Anselm's concept of friendship as theological, but fails to appreciate its more specifically Christological character.

Anselm of Canterbury
1033–1109

While there is no direct evidence that Anselm had Romans 5 in mind when he wrote this brief prayer, the first quarter of it is suffused with the logic of divine love as presented by Paul. It is possible that someone might die for a good person, even an outside chance that someone might give their life for a righteous person, but what has Christ done? While we were sinners and enemies and weak and disobedient and demonstrating everything except love toward God, he loved us by sending his Son to die in our place (Romans 5:8–10).

> Jesus Christ, my dear and gracious Lord, you have shown a love greater than that of any man and which no one can equal, for you in no way deserved to die, yet you laid down your dear life for those who served you and sinned against you. You prayed for those who were killing you that you might make them just men and your brothers and restore them to your merciful Father and to yourself.[31]

This raises the question for the believer of how we should love one another. In one sense, Anselm's answer is obvious insofar as we should love others as Christ has loved us; but in another sense, his answer is unexpected. He conceives of our love for others as, in some way, a return on God's love originally bestowed on us.[32] In other words, I may love a friend in the way that approximates the way Christ has loved me, but the reason I love my friend in this way is because I owe it to Christ to love him so. I do not love my friend because he deserves to be loved, but because Christ's love demands that I love him. Clearly, the manner and reason for loving my friend overlap, but this is so because Christ's command to love one another entails it. This is why Anselm says that, "insofar as I have already received the sweet alms you freely give, I love all men, in you and for your sake."[33]

Seen in this light, Anselm's almost embarrassingly passionate expressions for others in his letters and prayers are not hints of suppressed eroticism and perverted passions. They are instead expressions of love that seek to emulate what he sees at Calvary. If God, in Christ,

---

31 Anselm, "Prayer for Friends," lines 1–9.

32 Anselm, "Prayer for Friends," line 15.

33 Anselm, "Prayer for Friends," lines 38–40.

can speak of his love for the church as he does in the Song of Solomon, who are we to shrink back from loving those God has called his bride?[34]

It is this deep love that propels Anselm onward to become an intercessor for his friends, as well. Despite the majority of his prayers being addressed to saints for help in different times of need, Anselm recognizes that intercessory prayer is also required of the members of the church militant. In characteristic humility, Anselm feels unsuited for this task because of his own sin, but is able to overcome this obstacle on the strength of three realizations. First, God has commanded that we pray for one another. Second, his love for his friends prompts him. Third, his "conscience cries out" against him.[35] As we shall now see, this imperative to pray and intercede was not limited to friends, but extended even to enemies.

"Prayer for Enemies"

It is in the nature of sinful humanity to expect others to give us the benefit of the doubt, but not to return the favour so willingly. This comes from self-righteousness and pride. The centre of the sinful soul is the self, and left to our own devices, we are pleased with this state of affairs. Anselm, thankfully, is not content to leave us to our own devices. This is why he begins his prayer for enemies, ironically, not with them, but with himself. Not unlike Richard Baxter (1615–1691) of centuries later, Anselm recognized that the Christian who does not take stock of himself in light of the gospel will not live the gospel well.[36] It may, therefore, first appear to be selfish and self serving to begin praying for one's self in a prayer for enemies, but what turns this irony on its head is its Christological orientation.

By now it will come as no surprise that Anselm begins this prayer with a keen sense of his own sin. What is different here is the recognition that sin is not only committed against God, but against others, and in the most hideously self-righteous manner. What is the greatest

---

34 As is evident, for example, in Bernard of Clairvaux's (1090–1153) exposition of the Song of Songs, the prevailing medieval view was that the book was written as an allegory of Christ and the church. Cf. *On the Song of Songs* (Kalamazoo: Cistercian Publications, 1991).

35 Anselm, "Prayer for Friends," lines 57–61.

36 Cf. Richard Baxter, *The Reformed Pastor* (Edinburgh: The Banner of Truth Trust, 1974).

temptation when thinking about and dealing with an enemy? At the top of the list is usually blame. One of the great sinful habits of the heart, as old as the first sin itself, is to blame others for our sin. Anselm is acutely aware of the temptation to compound sin by justifying it, rationalizing it or otherwise identifying the cause as something external to our own heart. "The devil made me do it." This is what Anselm will not allow. This is why Anselm begins this prayer by bringing before the Lord what is, "in my heart" along with "the secrets of my mind."[37]

Although it would be difficult to prove definitively, I am deeply suspicious that Anselm is most reliant on the Psalms at this stage in his prayers. Throughout the Psalms, the psalmists give voice to pleas for deliverance from enemies, but always with reference to their own righteousness. In other words, a psalmist dare not utter a prayer unless he knows he acted in a manner consistent with God's character and will. Here, it is as though Anselm recognizes the tendency of the uninspired heart to vindicate itself unjustly. The prayers and cries in the Psalms cannot be thoughtlessly applied to our own situation without first applying the balm of mercy so sorely needed. This is where Anselm helps us most.

In fact, the one place where Anselm is almost certainly drawing on the Psalms in this prayer is most intriguing in this regard. In the middle of the opening stanza, Anselm prays, "Merciful God, do not judge me according to that which displeases you in me."[38] Does this not resonate powerfully with Psalm 103:10, that God does not deal with us according to our sins or repay us according to our iniquities? The steadfast love of the Lord is the guiding principle of divine interaction with humanity. If faith seeking understanding is the leading thought in Anselm's theological method, surely the steadfast love and mercy of God is the leading thought of his prayers. This is what makes his prayer so thoroughly Christological. Anselm intuitively recognizes that he must be forgiven by God in a way that he is unable to forgive his enemies. Sin against another is hurtful and harmful, but all sin is also against God. This is perhaps no more evident than in Anselm's *Cur Deus Homo* where he defines sin as injustice toward God, as not

---

37 Anselm, "Prayer for Enemies," lines 3, 6.
38 Anselm, "Prayer for Enemies," lines 19–20.

giving to God what is owed, which is obedience.[39] Anselm's enemy may sin grievously against him, but he does not use that to heap condemnation upon his foe, but as a reminder that he himself is a sinner in grave need of mercy before a holy God.

If we look at Anselm's prayer in this way, and keep the *Cur Deus Homo* in mind as providing deeper insight into Anselm's way of thinking, we can also begin to appreciate how closely he is following 1 Peter 2:19–25. There Peter, one of only two disciples who dared to stay close to Jesus while he was tried and beaten, reminds us that the one who was perfectly righteous and just was reviled and suffered silently because he entrusted himself to him who judges justly. This is where responding to enemies and those who sin against us begins. The servant is never greater than the master. It is for this reason that Anselm is able to pray of his enemies only what he should pray of himself. There is something profoundly impressive about praying,

> You alone, Lord, are mighty; you alone are merciful; whatever you make me desire for my enemies, give it to them and give the same back to me, and if what I ask for them at any time is outside the rule of charity, whether through weakness, ignorance, or malice, good Lord, do not give it to them and do not give it back to me.[40]

Jesus' death brought life, and while that was a unique act and work of God, those who claim union with Christ can bring about, in however small a measure, the possibility of life when they act and pray after the example of their Saviour (1 Peter 2:21). This also means, though, that a response to being sinned against that does not follow the example of Christ and is therefore not redemptive, brings the shadow of death rather than the hope of life. Again, Anselm's insight is remarkable.

> Tender Lord Jesus, let me not be the cause of the death of my brothers, let me not be to them a stone of stumbling and a rock

---

39 Anselm, Cur Deus Homo in *Anselm of Canterbury, the Major Works*, ed. Brian Davies and G.R. Evans (Oxford: Oxford University Press, 1998), 1.11–21.

40 Anselm, "Prayer for Enemies," lines 28–36.

of offence. For it is more than enough, Lord, that I should be a scandal to myself, my sin is sufficient to me.[41]

If the ground of Christian piety is a correct assessment of ourselves in the light of the holiness of God, then Anselm has laid a firm foundation. What gives his spiritual direction substance is that he has turned his theology into prayer, and more than that, prayer that presumes and expects change supremely in the petitioner. To refer dispassionately to "the reader" of these prayers is to belie misunderstanding. There can be no mere reader, only participants. Thomas Hibbs has rightfully noted that Anselm seeks, "to move the reader from the distant encounter with the text of an author to adopting the place of the author, as suppliant, sinner, pilgrim."[42]

We noted in our examination of Anselm's "Prayer for Friends" that friendship is the first casualty of an eroticized culture. As we consider his prayer for enemies, I would argue that in our litigious society, the first casualty is forgiveness. Medieval Europe was not without its lawsuits, so we should take care not to idolize the past. Still, the penchant to seek revenge or satisfaction in the modern Western world is alarmingly high. In the face of his own culture, and in the face of ours, Anselm calls us again to live in the light of Jesus' words, "Forgive me all my debts as I before you forgive all those indebted to me."[43] In what follows, Anselm penetrates to our deepest need and desire: "that you may perfectly forgive my sins and deal with me as gently as you can."[44] Who of us could stand were it not for mercy? Who of us can ask it from God who will not offer it to others? If God did not deal with us gently, we would be crushed. As it is, we who receive a gentle treatment out of all proportion to what our sin deserves, are not in a position to demand revenge or satisfaction, but to offer only what we have received. We are no more worthy of mercy and gentleness than our enemies.

---

41 Anselm, "Prayer for Enemies," lines 46–52.
42 Hibbs, "Iris Murdoch, Spiritual Exercises and Anselm's *Proslogion* and Prayers": 66.
43 Anselm, "Prayer for Enemies," lines 76–77.
44 Anselm, "Prayer for Enemies," lines 83–84.

Assessment

There is much that Anselm has already taught us, it goes without saying, and there is much more we can stand to learn from him. Even so, how ought we to assess what we have seen of Anselm's piety, his theology in practice? The first point of consideration we must appraise is his view of sin. If, in reading Anselm's prayers, we come away with nothing else, we cannot help but recognize his tremendous emphasis on sin. Anselm was consumed by his own sinfulness, and this has caused a number of theologians over the last century either to reject him or at least hold him in suspicion.[45] After all, this must be a relic of monastic life, a consequence of a medieval mindset, a culturally bound expression of a less enlightened mind.

The answer Anselm gives to this charge is riddled throughout his prayers because it is ubiquitous throughout Scripture. Most succinctly, Anselm said, "You have not considered how heavy is the weight of sin."[46] Anselm's prayers are meant to make us feel the weight of our own sin. Why? Because there is no piety without awareness of sin. Piety is not about adjusting our situation a little bit. Piety is not about fixing a few things that have gone wrong. Only when we realize the weight of our sin are we set to begin a life of godliness, because only then will we appreciate the necessity of the cross. Jesus did not pray that, if at all possible, the cup of divine wrath could pass because basically good people just need an extra infusion of grace. The spotless Lamb of God was not crucified by mistake—as though the Lion of Judah were helpless. No, "he himself bore our sins in his body on the tree, that we might die to sin and live to righteousness." (1 Peter 2:24) The Lord dwells with the contrite of heart, and the contrite of heart are wise to sin.

The second note that rings throughout Anselm's prayers is God's mercy. For the believer, this goes hand in hand with the emphasis on sin because, in Christ, mercy is the answer to sin. This is where a delicate balance must always be kept, and it is one that Anselm may be judged to have failed in keeping from time to time. The truth of Christian living is that we who trust in Christ live under his dominion even

---

45 Cf. Timothy Gorringe, *God's Just Vengeance* (Cambridge: Cambridge University Press, 1996), 85–103.

46 Anselm, *Cur Deus Homo*, 1.21.

while the presence of sin remains. Sometimes Anselm's evocative language for the presence of sin crosses the line and gives the impression that even the believer is still labouring under the dominion of sin. On the one hand, this resonates with some of what the writer to the Hebrews says when he speaks of the church still longing for rest[47]; on the other hand, Anselm is in danger of neglecting the truth that Paul is so eager to accentuate, that we are "in Christ" and that changes everything.[48] There is a tension here, but a tension that must be carefully tended. Consequently, it may be that for Christians who have lost their wonder at the mercy of God, Anselm still provides a needed corrective, even if he oversteps the bounds sometimes.

The final point, and perhaps the one most worthy of continued reflection, is that Anselm took the time to write prayers. What could be more obvious, yet what has been least emulated? Those within traditions that use prayer books or other set liturgies might claim immunity from this charge, but when was the last time prayers were written for the church? If tradition is the living faith of the dead, what are we leaving to those who will come after we die? The great cry from the Reformation that keeps much theological discourse moving forward is *semper reformandum*—always reforming. Ought not this to be applied to teaching others how to pray? In a world that esteems, values and looks up to giants of various kinds, Anselm reminds us that "we become taller when we bow."[49]

---

47 Cf. Hebrews 4.

48 Cf. Ephesians. 1.

49 This quote is from G.K. Chesterton, as cited without reference by C.S. Lewis in C.S. Lewis, "Membership" in *Fern-seed and Elephants*, ed. Walter Hooper (London: Harper Collins, 1998), 10.

06

PATRISTICS · MEDIEVAL

Apocalyptic spirituality in the early Middle Ages: hope for escaping the fire of doomsday through a pre-conflagration rapture

By Francis X. Gumerlock

THE COLLAPSE OF the Western portion of the Roman Empire in the fifth century had a profound impact on the eschatology of early medieval Christians. The eschatological optimism that followed the conversion of Constantine in the previous century gave way to increasing focus on the destruction of the present world and speculation about the cataclysmic events associated with it as they are revealed in the Bible. Hesychius, bishop of Salona (d. *c.* A.D. 429) in Dalmatia interpreted an eclipse and a drought as signs of the nearness of the Second Coming, and Sulpicius Severus (*c.* A.D. 360—*c.* 430) wrote that the coming of Antichrist was at hand.[1] The invasions of the Goths, Vandals, Huns and Arabs were viewed as fulfillments of prophecy about Gog and Magog; and there was a general feeling that the end of the world

---

1 Hesychius of Salona, "Letter to Augustine," in Saint Augustine, *Letters IV* (165–203), trans. Wilfrid Parsons (Washington: Catholic University of America Press, 1955), 354; Suplicius Severus, *Life of Martin*, 24, in *The Nicene and Post-Nicene Fathers*, Second Series, ed., Philip Schaff and Henry Wace (Grand Rapids: Wm. B. Eerdmans, 1989), 11:15 (hereafter cited as *NPNF*[2]). See Francis X. Gumerlock, *The Day and the Hour: Christianity's Perennial Fascination with the End of the World* (Powder Springs: American Vision, 2000), 28–29.

was at the door.[2] In fact, some early medieval leaders throughout Europe—like Caesarius of Arles (A.D. 470–542) in Gaul (modern France), Apringius of Beja on the Iberian peninsula, Beatus of Liebana (d. A.D. 798) in northern Spain and Ambrose Autpert (d. A.D. 784) in Italy—wrote only one biblical commentary, and that was on the book of Revelation.[3]

In their attention to the details of the end time, early medieval speculation about the fire of doomsday loomed large. For example, Gregory the Great (c. A.D. 540–604), who described his own day as a "time when the End of the world is drawing nigh," warned his readers in the year 593: "For lo! there will be no delay: the heavens on fire, the earth on fire, the elements blazing, with angels and archangels, thrones and dominions, principalities and powers, the tremendous Judge will appear."[4]

This essay, after discussing the biblical basis for early medieval belief in the fire of doomsday and examining several descriptions of it in early medieval literature, explores how early medieval Christians thought the elect will be saved from that grand conflagration.

The biblical basis for the fire of doomsday

The Old Testament contains many passages about the Lord coming with fire. They include Daniel 7:10: "A river of fire was flowing and coming out from before Him"; Psalm 50:3: "Fire devours before Him"; Psalm 97:3: "Fire goes before Him"; Isaiah 66:15: "For, behold, the Lord will come with fire"; and Malachi 4:1: "For, behold, the day is coming, burning like a furnace." The New Testament also talks about the conflagration associated with the end of the world in passages like 2 Thessalonians 1:7–8: "The Lord Jesus shall be revealed from heaven with his mighty angels in flaming fire"; 2 Peter 3:12: "The heavens being on

---

2   Richard K. Emmerson and Bernard McGinn, ed., *The Apocalypse in the Middle Ages* (Ithaca: Cornell University Press, 1992), 35.

3   The commentaries of Caesarius and Apringius are translated in *Latin Commentaries on Revelation,* trans. William Weinrich (Downers Grove: InterVarsity Press, 2011); Ambrose Autpert, *Expositio in Apocalypsin,* in *Ambrosii Autperti opera. Corpus Christianorum Continuatio Mediaevalis,* ed. Robert Weber (Turnhout: Brepols, 1975), 27; Beatus of Liebana, *Commentarius in Apocalypsin,* Eugenio Romero-Pose, ed., 2 vol. (Rome: Typis Officinae Polygraphicae, 1985).

4   Gregory the Great, *Epistles,* Bk. 3, Ep. 65. NPNF[2], 12:141.

fire shall be dissolved, and the elements shall melt with fervent heat";
and Revelation 20:9: "Fire came down from God out of heaven."

Based upon these, early medieval Christians believed that the Last
Judgement will be preceded by a great conflagration through which
"heaven and earth will pass away" (Luke 21:33).[5] This burning up of
the heaven and earth differed from the lake of fire, i.e. hell, and from
their as yet undeveloped concept of purgatorial fire for souls after
death but before the Last Judgement. For early medieval Christians,
the fire of doomsday referred to that burning up of the present heaven
and earth, with its corruption and moral pollution, in preparation for
the creation of "a new heaven and earth wherein righteousness dwells"
(2 Peter 3:13).

Descriptions of the fire of doomsday

The literature of the early medieval period is replete with descriptions
of the fire of doomsday, of which the following three are fairly representative. The *Second Apocalypse of John*, written by a Greek author
sometime between the sixth through eighth century, records that the
Lord told John that before he appears from heaven

> I will send my angels over all the earth's surface. They will burn
> up the earth to a depth of 4,250 metres; the great mountains will
> be burnt up; all the rocks will be melted down and turn to dust.
> Every tree will be burnt up, and all livestock and reptiles on the
> earth, everything swarming on the earth's surface, and every-
> thing flying in the air; there will no longer be anything on the
> earth's surface that depends on it.[6]

The anonymous writer above, when describing the depth or height
of the fire of doomsday, was probably carrying on the Petrine tradition of comparing the fire of doomsday to the great flood of Noah

---

5   In a chart prepared as part of his conference paper, "The Darker Side of the
Millennium Revisited," prepared for the 57th annual meeting of the Evangelical Theological Society (Valley Forge: November 2005) Earl L. Brown Jr. analyzed forty Scripture passages that speak of eschatological fire.

6   The English translation of the *Second Apocalypse of John* used here is in John M.
Court, *The Book of Revelation and the Johannine Apocalyptic Tradition* (Sheffield: Sheffield Academic Press, 2000), 39.

(cf. 2 Peter 3:5–12), even with regard to its extent.[7] The author also depicted the effects of the conflagration on the mountains, rocks, trees, animals and birds.

Haimo of Auxerre (d. A.D. 875) continued the tradition of comparing the fire of doomsday to the waters of the great flood, writing that when the Lord comes and "fire will precede him," the fire will fill "as much space in the air as water did in the Flood."[8]

An early medieval English poem described the horrors of the fire of doomsday in this manner:

> [T]he ravaging flame will raze tall buildings to the ground by the terror of fire, and the holocaust, notorious afar, hot and ravening for gore will raze the world withal. The shattered walls of cities will collapse outright. Mountains will melt and lofty cliffs…. The deadly flame will catch every creature then, beast and bird; the fiery sooty flame, a turbulent warrior, will travel across the land…. Then the fishes of the ocean will scorch in a sea of fire, stopped from swimming; every beast of the wave will perish in misery; the water will burn like wax.[9]

That poem depicted the effect of the conflagration upon buildings, city walls, mountains, animals, birds, water, fish and sea creatures.

Such descriptions beg the question: What did they believe will happen to the righteous when that terrible conflagration occurs? The early medieval writers were not silent on this issue.

Salvation from the fire of doomsday

In the early Middle Ages, Christians generally believed that God would save his elect from the fire of doomsday. This is reflected in the prayer of Theodorus Studios: "When the stream of fire will usher forth…then

---

7   Francis X. Murphy, "Conflagration: The Eschatological Perspective from Origen to John Chrysostom," *Studia Patristica* 18, no. 1 (1985): 179–185.

8   Haimo of Auxerre, "Commentary on 2 Thessalonians," in *Second Thessalonians: Two Early Medieval Apocalyptic Commentaries,* trans. Steven R. Cartwright and Kevin L. Hughes (Kalamazoo: Medieval Institute Publications, 2001), 23.

9   *Christ III*, lines 972–985. The poem, preserved in the *Exeter Book* from about A.D. 900, was translated into modern English by S.A.J. Bardley, and is available at http://www.apocalyptic-theories.com; accessed November 29, 2010.

save me from these flames that can never be cooled."[10] But exactly how God would save his people from that fire varied from writer to writer. Their explanations can be divided into two manners. Some believed that the saints will be miraculously preserved through the fire, while others taught that the saints will be miraculously removed from it.

Advocating the former position, Thietland of Einsiedeln explained that God would miraculously protect the saints through the fire of doomsday by the same miraculous power with which he protected the three Hebrew boys in the midst of the fiery furnace (cf. Daniel 3).[11] Similarly, the anonymous *Tidings of the Resurrection* stated that just like the "fire did not burn the holy children," so also the fire of doomsday "will do no harm to the bodies of the righteous, for that fire will be like a soothing rain to the saints."[12] This idea of the righteous being saved through the fire can be traced back to the *Sibylline Oracles* of the earliest centuries of Christianity which state that when Christ comes in glory for judgement "then shall all pass through the burning river and unquenchable flame; and the righteous shall be saved, but the impious shall perish."[13]

Removal from the fire by rising above it

A more common way that Christians of the early Middle Ages understood how believers living at in the end time would be delivered from the fire of doomsday is through a miraculous rapture of the saints above the fire. Their explanation of salvation in this manner seems dependent upon popular writers of late antiquity like Hilary of Poitiers (c. A.D. 315–367/368) and Augustine of Hippo (A.D. 354–430).

Hilary of Poitiers, in his comments on Matthew 24:40–41, described the rapture as a separation between believers and unbelievers, which "when God's wrath is kindled, the saints shall be gathered into his garner, and the unbelievers shall be left as fuel for the fire from

---

10 Cited in Desanka Milosevic, *The Last Judgment* (New York: Taplinger, 1964), 72.

11 Thietland of Einsiedeln, "Commentary on 2 Thessalonians," in Cartwright and Hughes, *Second Thessalonians*, 46.

12 An English translation of the eleventh century *Tidings of the Resurrection* is available at http://www.ucc.ie/celt/published/T207001.html; accessed June 10, 2008.

13 *Sibylline Oracles*, 2:252–254, Edgar Hennecke, *New Testament Apocrypha* (Philadelphia: Westminster, 1965), 2:716.

heaven."[14] Or in another English version: "When the wrath of God rises, the saints will be hidden in God's chambers but the faithless will be left exposed to celestial fire."[15] In other words, when the fire of doomsday comes, unbelievers will left on earth to be burned by the fire, but the saints will be gathered into God's granary. Paschasius Radbertus (d. A.D. 865), commenting upon the same verses, carried Hilary's thought into the Carolingian era. At the rapture, he wrote, "the one who seeks the things that are of God will be taken, but the one who seeks the things that are of the world will be left in the fire."[16] However, neither Hilary nor Radbertus explained exactly where the righteous will be taken, or what exactly God's "garner" is; but Augustine was more specific.

Concerning the protection that God will provide from the fire of doomsday, Augustine wrote in his *City of God* that the Lord will keep his people unharmed by changing their locality. "Someone will perhaps put the question...where shall the saints be during the conflagration, and before it is replaced by a new heavens and a new earth, since somewhere they must be, because they have material bodies?" His answer is as follows: "We may reply that they shall be in the upper regions into which the flame of that conflagration shall not ascend, as neither did the water of the flood."[17] For Augustine, the saints will be preserved in the "upper regions" above the flames of that great fire. In the early Middle Ages, Julian of Toledo (d. A.D. 690), in his work on eschatology entitled, *Foreknowledge of the World to Come*, repeated verbatim those words of Augustine.[18]

---

14 Hilary of Poitiers, *Commentary on Matthew*. Cited in Newman, *Catena Aurea*, vol. 1, 834. Cf. Latin and French text in Jean Doignon, ed., *Hilaire de Poitiers Sur Mathieu Sources Chrétiennes* 258 (Paris: Les Éditions du Cerf, 1979), 2:198–199.

15 Hilary of Poitiers, *Commentary on Matthew*. Cited in Manlio Simonetti, ed., *Matthew 14–28*. Ancient Christian Commentary on Scripture. New Testament Ib (Downers Grove: InterVarsity, 2002), 209.

16 Paschasius Radbertus, *Expositio in Matheo Libri XII*. On Matt. 24:40–41. CCCM 56B:1200.

17 Augustine, *The City of God*, 20.18, trans. Marcus Dods (New York: Random House, 1950), 738.

18 Julian of Toledo, *Prognosticorum futuri saeculi libri tres*, 3.49. J.N. Hillgarth, ed., *Sancti Iuliani Toletanae sedis episcopi opera, pars I*. CCSL 115 (Turnhout: Brepols, 1976), 117. Cf. ACW 63:457.

The Venerable Bede (A.D. 673–735) provided more detail about how believers will be transported from earth to these upper regions during the grand conflagration, associating salvation from the conflagration with the rapture of the saints in 1 Thessalonians 4. Contrasting those who will be left behind on earth to be surrounded by fire with those who will be caught up above the earth to meet Christ, Bede wrote:

For it stands that when the Lord descends for the judgment "in the twinkling of an eye" (1 Cor. 15:52), and the celebrated judgment of all of the dead will take place, the saints are immediately caught up to meet him in the air. For this is understood, as the Apostle indicates when he says, "Then the Lord himself with a command and with the voice of the archangel and the trumpet of God will descend from heaven, and the dead who are in Christ will rise first; then we who are alive, who remain, will be caught up together with them in the clouds to meet the Lord in the air" (1 Thess. 4:15–16). However, it is asked whether the reprobate will then be sublimely lifted up to meet the coming Judge, or whether they will be weighed down with the merits of sins, so that although having immortal bodies, they will be unable to be elevated to higher places.... But then if that greatest and highest fire will cover the whole surface of the earth, and the unjust, raised from the dead, will be unable to be caught up into heaven, it stands that those positioned on earth will await the sentence of the Judge surrounded by fire.[19]

In other words, the unrighteous will remain on the earth when the fire of doomsday envelops it, but the righteous will be elevated or caught up over the fire "to higher places."

The Revelation commentary of pseudo-Alcuin, written in the eighth or ninth century, said that believers will be raptured into the cloud in which Christ would return, and that cloud would act as a protective barrier, defending the saints from being harmed by the conflagration. On Revelation 1:7: "Behold He comes with clouds," the commentary reads: "If we should understand this literally, when the Lord comes

19 Bede, *De Temporum Ratione*, 70. CCSL 123B:541.

for judgment, there will be a white cloud which, screening the saints, should protect them from the fire burning the world."[20]

The tenth- or eleventh-century Lismore version of the *Life of St. Brendan* also recorded the concept of divine protection from the conflagration through bodily rapture. It said that as the ark of Noah was lifted over the waves, so during the conflagration Brendan's monks and household will be raised "on high over the Fire of Doom, so that neither smoke nor mist nor spark will hurt them."[21] Like Augustine and others, this author also believed that when the fire of doomsday arrives, God will lift up his saints over the fire to protect them from being burned by it.

The idea that God will preserve his people from the fire of doomsday by means of the rapture was carried into later centuries. Bruno the Carthusian (d. 1101) in his commentary on the Psalms wrote about how the faithful will be preserved unharmed through and from the fire of doomsday by being caught up in the clouds. He wrote on Psalm 50:3:

> He will take vengeance upon those who neglect his first coming in humility. But how He will take vengeance is explained in this way: truly *He will not be silent; for fire will burn* the elements *in His sight* (Ps. 50:3), that is, in His presence.
>
> However, it should be noted that this fire will not be the eternal fire, in which afterward the impious will be tortured without end. But, as blessed Peter affirms, in that resurrection of the dead, that fire will reach the same height in the air as the waves of the Flood ascended (cf. 2 Pet. 3:10–12). By that fire the pollution of all the air will be expiated, through which fire the bodies of the faithful along with their souls joined together with them, just as they are now, will hasten with the greatest swiftness and without any harm to meet the Lord in the air for judgment. Accord-

---

20 pseudo-Alcuin, *Commentarius in Apocalypsin*, I, on Revelation 1:7, *Patrologia Latina* (Paris: J.P. Migne, 1862–1865) 100:1094 (hereafter cited as PL). My translation of *Ecce venit cum nubibus. Si juxta litteram intelligamus, veniente Domino ad judicium, erit nubes candida, quae sanctos obumbrans ab igne saeculum cremante defendat.*

21 Cited in John D. Seymour, "The Eschatology of the Early Irish Church," *Zeitschrift für celtische Philologie* 14 (1923):179–211 at 198. The full text of the Lismore version of the *Life of St. Brendan* is available at http://www.lamp.ac.uk/celtic/bblismore.htm; accessed June 3, 2008.

ingly Paul [wrote]: *We shall be caught up to meet the Lord in the air* (1 Thess. 4:17). But the impious, with the bulk of the weight of their sins bringing much harm upon themselves, will go forth to judgment and be sent into the torment of eternal fire.[22]

Bruno believed that the fire of doomsday would purify the earth from its pollutions, and would rise in height to the same height as the waters of the flood of Noah. Also, those faithful to Christ will hasten through the fire "to meet the Lord in the air" (1 Thessalonians 4:17) where they, above that fire, will be safe from its flames.

In summary, the fire of doomsday that immediately precedes Christ's Second Coming pervaded early medieval eschatology. Moreover, Christians of the early Middle Ages believed that God would preserve the godly from that burning up of the world. Key theologians and biblical commentators of that time period held that God's means of protecting his people from that great fire would be by being miraculously raised or raptured, over the fire. Thus they would be completely unharmed by its flames.

Similar views among Protestants

Most of the Protestant reformers of the sixteenth and seventeenth centuries were students of the church fathers, and as such accepted much of their teaching as authentically biblical and apostolic, eg. the Trinity and deity of Christ. But they rejected some teachings of medieval Catholicism as human tradition. Apparently the Protestants, at least those of later centuries, did not view the pre-conflagration view of the rapture as unbiblical; for many of the luminaries of seventeenth- and eighteenth-century England and the New World articulated a similar view. These included Joseph Mede (1586–1638), Increase Mather (1639–1723), Cotton Mather (1663–1728) and John Gill (1697–1771).

Joseph Mede, a teacher at Cambridge in Protestant England, taught that the rapture might be God's way of granting escape from the grand conflagration and claimed to have come upon the idea not in medieval authors but Jewish rabbinic tradition, citing and translating *Gemara Sanhedrin*. In *Epistle XXII: Mr. Mede's Answer to the Tenth Quere, about*

---

22 Bruno the Carthusian, *Expositio in Psalmos-Psal. XLIX*, PL 152:854.

the 1000 years Regnum Sanctorum, Mede wrote (I have retained his italics and capitalization):

> I will add this more, namely, what may be conceived to be the cause of this *Rapture* of the Saints on high to meet the Lord in the Clouds, rather then [sic] to wait his coming to the Earth. What if it be, that they may be preserved during the *Conflagration of the earth and the works thereof,* 2 Pet. 3:10, that as *Noah* and his family were preserved from the Deluge by being lift up above the waters in the *Ark*; so should the Saints at the *Conflagration* be lift up in the Clouds unto their *Ark, Christ,* to be preserved there from the *deluge of fire,* when the wicked shall be consumed. There is a Tradition of the *Jews* found this way, which they ascribe unto one *Elias a Jewish* Doctor...I will transcribe it...
>
> The Hebrew words are in *Gemara Sanhedrin.... The Tradition of the house of Elias. The just whom God shall raise up* (viz. in the First Resurrection) *shall not be turned again to dust. Now if you ask, How it shall be with the just in those Thousand years wherein the Holy Blessed God shall renew his world, whereof it is said* (Isa. 2:11). *And the Lord alone shall be exalted in that day; you must know, that the Holy Blessed God will give them the wings, as it were of Eagles, to fly upon the face of the waters: whence it is said* (Psalm 46:3). Therefore shall we not fear, when the Earth shall be changed. *But perhaps you will say, it shall be a pain and affliction to them. Not at all, for it is said* (Isa. 40:31), They that wait upon the Lord, shall renew their strength, they shall mount up with wings as Eagles.[23]

Mede clearly believed that the purpose of the rapture might be to preserve the saints from the fire of doomsday, and cited a Jewish rabbinic teaching in support of the concept. Interestingly the *Apocalypse of Elijah,* a third-century Christian text with a Jewish substratum, taught that in the last days God would save his people from the persecution of Antichrist by bearing them up to paradise on angels' wings.[24]

---

23 Joseph Mede, "Letter 32," in The Works of the Pious and Profoundly Learned Joseph Mede, B.D., 2 Vols. (London: James Flesher, 1664), 2:950–951.

24 Francis Gumerlock, "The Rapture in the Apocalypse of Elijah," *Bibliotheca Sacra* (October 2013, forthcoming).

However, the relationship between this *Apocalypse of Elijah* and Mede's citation of a Jewish tradition ascribed to Elias has not been established and deserves further research.

In 1710, Increase Mather, a Puritan in Boston, wrote a *Dissertation Concerning the Future Conversion of the Jewish Nation*. Speaking about the grand conflagration, Increase believed that "Where the fires did ravage, living saints would 'be caught up into the Air' and thus escape the fate of ungodly men."[25] Thus, similar to Mede and the many early medieval Christian authors cited earlier, Increase saw the rapture in terms of escape from the grand conflagration at the end of the world.

Cotton Mather, the son of Increase, wrote likewise of a pre-conflagration rapture of the saints in his treatise, *The Third Paradise*. He explained:

> But our Glorious Lord making His Descent in *Flaming Fire*, and the *Conflagration* going to begin, among the *Christians* that cry unto Him to be *delivered from the Wrath to come*, under the General and Horrible Consternation the World shall then be filled withal, our Lord will distinguish the *Righteous*, and those *Humble Walkers* with GOD, which will be found with his *Marks* upon them; and by the Assistance of His *Angels*, they shall be *caught up to meet the Lord, & the Raised*, whom shall be Consigned over to the *Flames*, and Perish as *Bundles of Tares*, in the tremendous *Conflagration*, which will then bring about the *Perdition of Ungodly Men*.[26]

Mather pictures the righteous as being "caught up to meet the Lord" in the air (1 Thessalonians 4:17) or raptured above the fire of doomsday while the unrighteous remain on earth and are burned by its flames.

John Gill, a Baptist preacher in London of whose church the famous Charles Spurgeon was later the pastor, wrote on 1 Thessalonians 4:17:

---

25 The quotation is a summary of Increase Mather's teaching by James West Davidson, *The Logic of Millennial Thought: Eighteenth Century New England* (New Haven: Yale University Press, 1977), 61.

26 Cotton Mather, "The Threefold Paradise," in *The Threefold Paradise of Cotton Mather: An Edition of "Triparadisus,"* ed. Reiner Smolinski (Athens: University of Georgia Press, 1995), 225.

> To meet the Lord in the air; whither he'll descend, and will then
> clear the regions of the air of Satan and his posse of devils, which
> now rove about there; …as yet he will not descend on earth,
> because not fit to receive him; but when that and its works are
> burnt up, and it is purged and purified by fire, and become a new
> earth, he'll desend [sic] upon it, and dwell with his saints in it:
> and this suggests another reason why he'll stay in the air, and his
> saints shall meet him there, and whom he'll take up with him
> into the third heaven, till the general conflagration and burning
> up the world is over, and to preserve them from it; and then shall
> all of the elect descend from heaven as a bride adorned for her
> husband, and he with them, and the tabernacle of God shall be
> with men.[27]

According to Gill the reason that the Lord will stay in the air when he
returns is because the world with its spiritual pollutions will not be fit
to receive him. When Jesus descends from heaven the saints will rise
and meet him in the air. He will then take them to the third heaven
until after the burning of the world. After the Lord purifies the earth
by fire, he will once again descend upon it with the saints. Hence, the
purpose of the rapture is to protect the saints from the conflagration.

In a sermon preached on December 27, 1752, entitled, "The Glory
of the Church in the Latter Day," Gill said:

> This being done, these living saints, changed, shall be caught up
> together with the raised ones, to meet the Lord in the air; where
> it seems as if he and they should stop awhile, until an after-event
> is accomplished…. The precious dust of the saints being collected
> out of the earth, and their bodies raised and united to their souls,
> and living ones changed, and both taken up from hence, and with
> the Lord, the general conflagration will begin; the heavens shall
> pass away with a great noise, and the elements shall melt with
> fervent heat; the earth also, and the works that are therein, shall
> be burnt up, with all the wicked in it; for the heavens and the
> earth that now are, that is, the earth with its surrounding atmo-

---

27 John Gill, "Commentary on 1 Thessalonians," in *Expositions of the New Testament
by John Gill* (1809; reprint, Paris, Arkansas: Baptist Standard Bearer, 1989), 3:238–239.

sphere, are kept in store, reserved unto fire, for the perdition of ungodly men, when.... There will succeed new heavens, and a new earth, which God has promised; and which, the apostle Peter says, saints look for according to his promise; and which the Apostle John had a vision of. In this new earth Christ will descend and dwell; here the tabernacle of God will be with men; and he shall dwell with them.[28]

In that sermon, Gill described the fire of doomsday in the language of the passage in Peter's epistle. Before the conflagration, he preached, the Lord will raise and rapture his elect to a place above the earth where they will not be harmed by its flames. After the conflagration, God renews the earth onto which Christ and his saints descend and dwell.

The pre-conflagration rapture: a common medieval hope

Some of the current literature on the history of the rapture discusses the rapture views of Mede, the Mathers and Gill; and their views are even referred to as a "pre-conflagration" rapture.[29] But, in reality, these Protestant authors, consciously or otherwise, were giving voice to a view of the rapture that was very popular in the early Middle Ages. It held that when the Lord comes, fire will precede him. That fire will burn up the present heaven and earth and rise as high as the waters of the ancient flood. However, God will protect his followers from that conflagration by means of the rapture of 1 Thessalonians 4, which takes them high above the flames and preserves them unharmed.

Fire was a continual threat for medieval Europeans for a variety of reasons. Candles, an easy source for ignition of fires, were often used for lighting. Their houses, mainly constructed of flammable wood, were arranged very closely to one another in cities and towns, increas-

---

28 John Gill, "The Glory of the Church in the Latter Days." Quoted in John L. Bray, *The Second Coming of Christ and Related Events* (Lakeland: John L. Bray Ministry, 1985), 49, who cited Gill's *Sermons and Tracts*, Vol. 1.111.

29 Thomas Ice, "The History of the Doctrine of the Rapture. Part II: A History of the Pre-Conflagration Rapture," Eighteenth Annual Barndollar Lecture Series, September 10, 2010; http://www.bbc.edu/barndollar; available in audio sermon form at www.sermonaudio.com; Roy A. Huebner, *John Nelson Darby: Precious Truths Revived and Defended*, 2nd ed. (Jackson: Present Truth Publishers, 2004), 1:117–118.

ing the risk for a fire to spread from one structure to another. Also, many of the tradesmen like bakers and smiths in their work used open fires from which a single spark could easily set an inferno; and fire brigades were almost non-existent.[30] Furthermore, there was the constant threat of war, whose tactics at the time included setting fire to a besieged city or town. Medieval historian Norman Pounds noted that "medieval people took it for granted that their town might some day be consumed" by fire.[31] In the countryside and forests, the threat of fire was no less present. The years between A.D. 800 and 1300 experienced the climatic change dubbed the "Medieval Warm Period." This resulted in prolonged droughts and more frequent fires.[32]

Also looming large in the consciousness of medieval Christians was the biblical promise of destruction by the greatest fire that would ever occur, a fire which would destroy not only their towns and fields but the entire world. Its flames, they believed, would reach as high as the tallest mountains of the world. And from its blaze there could be only one means of escape: the other biblical promise that when Jesus returns "those who are His at His coming" (1 Corinthians 15:23) will rise to meet Christ in the air (cf. 1 Thessalonians 4:17). In this rapture, reserved only for the righteous, the faithful will be elevated high above the flames and there their Lord protector will preserve them from the dreaded fire of doomsday.

---

30 "Life in Medieval Cities and Towns," http://www.public.iastate.edu; "Why was fire a major threat in medieval cities?" http://wiki.answers.com; "Top 10 Most Famous Fires in History," http://www.toptenz.net; all sites accessed August 7, 2012.

31 Norman Pounds, *The Medieval City* (Westport: Greenwood Press, 2005), 39.

32 "Medieval Droughts of Northern Europe and Beyond," http://www.co2science. org; "Giant Redwood Trees Endured Frequent Fires Centuries Ago," http://www. livescience.com; "Medieval Warming Period 'Mega-Droughts': 20th/21st Century Droughts are Pimples in Comparison," http://www.c3headlines.com; all sites accessed August 7, 2012.

REFORMATION · PURITAN

Martin Luther: preaching and Protestant spirituality

By Carl R. Trueman

Introduction

For several decades now, we in the West have been living in a world which is increasingly enamoured of images and aesthetics and less and less verbal in its orientation.[1] In such a context, Protestantism faces an acute question: Can its spirituality continue to exist, given its ineradicably verbal nature?[2] Given that the verbal form is also part of the content, of the essence, of Protestantism, what future can it have at this point? Given the importance of Protestantism to the life and work of Michael Haykin, and given his well-known concern with that vital, existential engagement with God which Protestant spirituality embodies, it seems appropriate to address the question in a volume dedicated to honouring his work.

Of course, a question like this cannot be answered in a brief essay; but one can make a start. Indeed, the question of the importance of Protestantism's verbal nature is also the question about its origins: Was it verbal by mere cultural happenstance? Or was it driven in its origin

---

1   See Neil Postman, *Amusing Ourselves To Death* (London: Penguin, 2005), originally published in 1985.

2   On the verbal nature of specifically Reformed Protestant spirituality, see Peter Adam, *Hearing God's Words: Exploring Biblical Spirituality* (Leicester: Apollos, 2004).

by a theological commitment to words? And there can be no better way of starting to address that question than an examination of Martin Luther's (1483–1546) own thinking on that most central of Protestantism spiritual acts: the preaching of the Word. Luther is important because good preaching, upon which Protestantism depends for its existence, is not simply an act of technical proficiency; it is also a theological act; and only as preachers and congregations understand the theology of which it represents and, indeed, embodies will they come to perform and appreciate preaching for what it is.

The late medieval background

Ever since the groundbreaking work of the Jesuit scholar Joseph Lortz, in the 1940s, students of Luther have been aware of the positive connection between late medieval theology and Luther's Reformation thought.[3] Indeed, in many ways, Luther remained a man of the Middle Ages: his politically conservative feudalism and his acute sense of the physical presence of the Devil are just two examples of things that separate him from the other reformers, with their Renaissance humanist sympathies.[4]

On the theological front, it was the critical philosophy of language, connected to the radical application of the dialectic of God's two powers, which gripped Luther's theological imagination and remained with him from the monastic cloister to the day of his death. To summarize these late medieval approaches, the dialectic of the two powers was in origin an attempt to safeguard both God's infinite omnipotence and the stability of the finite created order. According to God's absolute power, he could do anything, subject only to the law of non-contradiction. Thus, he could not, for example create a world where Herod both existed and did not exist at the same time. According to his ordained power, however, he has realized a finite set of possibilities. Thus, he has made human beings with two legs, rather than with three, and apples that, when ripe, are green, yellow or red, not black or silver.

---

3   Joseph Lortz, *The Reformation in Germany*, trans. Ronald Walls (New York: Herder and Herder, 1968).

4   On Luther as medieval man, see Heiko A. Oberman, *Luther: Man Between God and Devil*, trans. Eileen Walliser-Scharzbart (New Haven: Yale University Press, 1989).

As confidence in human reason declined from the twelfth century onwards, the dialectic between the two powers was used in an increasingly sharp and critical way to articulate this growing epistemological modesty with regard to God. Reason became less and less competent and thus theologians focused increasingly on revelation as the source of knowledge of God. This revelation was, of course, not identified with Scripture so much as with the teaching of the church's *Magisterium*.

The distinction also fed into and strengthened a perennial linguistic debate about the nature and function of words. For example, does the word "dog" refer to something real, a universal "dogginess" in which all dogs participate, in order to have the word legitimately applied to them? Or does it simply refer to lots and lots of individual dogs, with no ideal "dogginess" out there in which they participate? Taken to its extreme, this became an anti-essentialist ontology which effectively made words themselves the determiners of reality. This is what is known as late medieval nominalism and it was this linguistic school in which Luther was trained and whose basic assumptions remained with him throughout his career.

As critics of postmodernism such as Terry Eagleton have pointed out, there are potent similarities between late medieval nominalism and certain schools of postmodern linguistic theory. We might summarize these similarities by saying that both envisage the world as a linguistic construct. Words, not essences, become determinative and constitutive of reality. I suspect that Luther would have little time for the excesses of postmodern anti-essentialism, with the kind of vertiginous anarchy it has created with regard to gender, sexuality and even the notion of human nature. Nevertheless, we should note that Luther would not object to postmodernism by reasserting a kind of essentialist ontology. Rather, Luther's rejection of today's postmodern anarchy would be based on his belief that God is the supreme reality and that he is ultimately the one who speaks and whose speech is therefore the ground of existence and of difference. Reality is not determined by the linguistic proclivities of any human individual or community but by the Word of God.

The theological implications of this are obvious. For example, consider the theology of the cross: the empiricist or essentialist looks at the cross and sees weakness, agony, suffering and defeat—and no more. That is what the outward aesthetics of the cross would seem to indicate; and it is what the social and philosophical conventions of Jews and Greeks would also lead one to believe. But neither the empirical aesthetics, nor their interpretation through the grid of constructed social conventions is any guide to the reality of what is actually taking place. God has extrinsically declared the cross to be powerful, a victory, a moment of triumph; and God's Word trumps everything in determining what the reality is. Thus, only those Christians who reject the evidence of their senses and the established logics and expectations of their culture, and instead trust in the counter-intuitive truth of God's Word, can truly understand the reality.

The same applies in justification. Older medieval approaches to justification required the individual actually to be somewhat righteous before God could declare the person to be justified. Late medieval theologians, such as Gabriel Biel (d. 1495), had broken with this, arguing instead that God could set his own criteria for the declaration of justification. For Biel, God had entered into a *pactum* with human beings and had agreed, according to his ordained power, to accept an individual's best efforts at righteousness as meeting the condition for God to declare that person in a state of grace. Once in such a state of grace, the individual could then benefit from sacramental grace and do works of real righteousness and intrinsic merit.

Luther came to reject the theology of Biel as a form of semi-Pelagianism. The very idea that one could do one's best and meet any condition became anathema to him. If human beings are morally dead, then the only thing they can do is acknowledge this in all humility, despair of self and look to God for unmerited mercy. Yet in breaking with Biel, Luther remained indebted to one of Biel's most important conceptual moves. For Biel, as later for Luther, the justified person was not necessarily *actually* righteous; they were simply *declared to be* righteous by God. By making entry into a state of grace something that was not based on intrinsic merit but rather on merit determined by the extrinsic *pactum*, Biel shattered the link between essential reality and divinely determined reality. This is something for which conservative Catholic historians of dogma, such as Lortz, have never forgiven him and which, indeed, shapes how modern historians like Brad

Gregory of Notre Dame view the Reformation: the evil fruit of anti-essentialist late medieval nominalism.[5]

The practical significance of this linguistic philosophy for Luther is that words become absolutely foundational to everything the pastor does. If words determine reality, then, of all things the pastor does, the words he speaks are the most important. Reading the Bible in public, preaching the Word from the pulpit, applying the Word individually in the confessional: each of these things determines the reality of the church. This linguistic emphasis also helps explain to those of us with less sacramental proclivities than Luther, why he holds such high views of baptism and the Lord's Supper that, on the latter point at least, he is willing to divide Protestant Christendom over the issue. If God says it is Christ's body and blood, given for you, then that is what it becomes at that moment, whatever your physical sense might tell you.

The theological foundation

It would be remiss of me, however, simply to reduce Luther's Reformation theology to a particularly radical application of late medieval linguistic theory as a means of solving his own personal issues with angst and despair. If one wants to reduce Reformation theology to cultural factors, one might just as easily point to the increasing prominence of words in a culture which, for the time, has access to relatively cheap print and was seeing the start of slowly increasing literacy rates. This, too, would be true. Luther's thinking, however, is not simply driven by his philosophical and cultural context; it is also theological.

There is, of course, a happy coincidence or, perhaps better, an elective affinity between such critical linguistic philosophy of Luther's teachers and what Luther saw as the Bible's own teaching about the nature of God. For Luther, God in himself was utterly unknowable in any positive sense. He dwelt in deep darkness; he rode on the wings of the storm; like the God described by Job, he was invisible, unaccountable, infinitely powerful and utterly incommensurable with anything or anyone else. Like a good late medieval theologian, Luther considered that God could only be known to be a certain kind of God on the basis of how he had revealed himself to be. In short, only as he

---

5   See Brad Gregory, *The Unintended Reformation: How a Religious Revolution Secularized Society* (Cambridge: Belknap Press, 2012).

spoke could he be known. Further, consistent with late medieval nominalism, only as God spoke could there actually be a reality external to himself. Material reality exists external to God because God has chosen to speak it. We might perhaps say that the Creator-creature distinction in Luther is that between the one who speaks and that which is itself spoken.

In his 1535 *Lectures on Genesis*, Luther says this when he comes to the work of the fifth day:

> Who could conceive of the possibility of bringing forth from the water a being which clearly could not continue to exist in water? But God speaks a mere Word, and immediately the birds are brought forth from the water. If the Word is spoken, all things are possible, so that out of the water are made either fish or birds. Therefore, any bird whatever and any fish whatever are nothing but nouns in the divine rule of language; through this rule of language those things that are impossible become very easy, while those that are clearly opposite become very much alike, and vice versa.[6]

The particular point he is making has general theological significance: when God speaks, that speech determines reality; it is, to use late medieval terminology, both the expression and the actualization of his ordained power. The substance of water, by every law of physics, both in Luther's day and in our own, should lead to the conclusion that it is impossible to make from such fish, birds or any other creature. Yet when God speaks, these creatures are created and possess existence. Essentialism is trumped by the greater determining reality of God's Word.

For Luther, however, this emphasis on word is not simply a philosophical commitment but one that carries with it deep moral implications precisely because it is God who speaks these words and this reality into existence. This is clear from his account of the temptation and sin of Adam and Eve in the Garden. In Luther's mind it is no

---

6   Martin Luther, *Luther's Works, Vol. 1: Lectures on Genesis: Chapters 1–5*, ed. J.J. Pelikan, H.C. Oswald and H.T. Lehmann (Saint Louis: Concordia Publishing House, 1999).

Martin Luther
1483–1546

coincidence that the serpent chooses to attack God's Word as the means of his assault upon Eden. Commenting on Genesis 3:1, he says:

> Moses expresses himself very carefully and says: "The serpent said," that is, with a word it attacks the Word. The Word which the Lord had spoken to Adam was: "Do not eat from the tree of the knowledge of good and evil." For Adam this Word was Gospel and Law; it was his worship; it was his service and the obedience he could offer God in this state of innocence. These Satan attacks and tries to destroy. Nor is it only his intention, as those who lack knowledge think, to point out the tree and issue an invitation to pick its fruit. He points it out indeed; but then he adds another and a new statement, as he still does in the church.[7]

What the serpent does in Eden is attempt to create a new reality—an alternative to that established by God himself—by attacking the words God has spoken. In casting doubt upon God's trustworthiness, and thus upon the reality of the words he had spoken, Satan casts doubt upon the nature of the reality in which Adam and Eve find themselves. When Adam and Eve eat the fruit, they are rejecting God's words and the reality he established and choosing instead to accept that of the serpent. The problem is, of course, that the reality they accept is no reality at all. What they have done is reject God.

In short, we can see from Luther's *Lectures on Genesis* that the linguistic philosophy of late medieval nominalism possesses elective affinities with his understanding of how God's speech is itself determinative of reality. In addition, we can also see the connection of this speech to God's person. For Luther, the rejection of this speech is a rejection of God himself and not simply a matter of epistemological significance. It is also of serious moral significance.

One final theological observation is that an obvious inference of God's speech as constitutive of reality is that God's speech is also the *mode* of his presence. Human beings can only have to do with God as he reveals himself to them; and that means they can only have to do with him as he *speaks* to them. Thus, the absence of God's speech is

---

7   Luther, *Lectures on Genesis*, Genesis 3:1.

for Luther the same as the absence of God himself, a very terrible situation to contemplate. Commenting on Amos 8:11, he observes:

I shall send a famine on the land. This is the last blow. It is the worst, the most wretched, of all. All the rest of the blows would be bearable, but this is absolutely horrible. He is threatening to take away the genuine prophets and the true Word of God, so that there is no one to preach, even if men were most eager to wish to hear the Word and would run here and there to hear it. This happened to the Jews in the Assyrian captivity and in that last one.[8]

The absence of God's Word is the absence of God. More significant from the point of view of understanding pastoral ministry, the absence of the prophets who speak God's words is the absence of God. And as Luther will later make clear in this same passage, the modern preacher is the successor of the ancient prophet and thus central to the notion of God's presence within the New Testament church.

God's Word in the church

Moving from a theology of God's speech to Luther's Reformation church, we need to reflect for a moment on the broader context. Westminster Theological Seminary students will confirm that one of my classroom mantras is "certain social and economic conditions must apply." What I mean by this is that Christian practice, the Christian form of life, cannot stand apart from the social and economic limitations of the time. To take a simple example, one cannot have a "quiet time" if one cannot read, has no access to cheap print and does not have a private space. That means, of course, that most Christians throughout most of church history have not had "quiet times" as conceived of by modern evangelicalism.

Luther's context imposed a natural corporate emphasis on church life in general. Travel was difficult and the rural population of Wittenberg and its environs would have been generally tied to a fairly small

---

8 Martin Luther, *Luther's Works, Vol. 18: Minor Prophets I: Hosea-Malachi*, ed. J.J. Pelikan, H.C. Oswald and H.T. Lehmann (Saint Louis: Concordia Publishing House, 1999), Amos 8:11.

geographical area. While the Reformation was certainly a movement of printed words, literacy rates were low so for most people it was a movement of exclusively spoken words. They did not read the Bible for themselves; they heard it read and they heard it explained in sermons and homilies. That was how they encountered the Word of God.

This meant that literate preachers of God's Word were singularly important in the life of the church in the sixteenth century. Indeed, they were the only source of reliable Christian teaching in the early Reformation. Pamphlets played a very significant role but it was the pictures, the woodcuts, which had the most impact on most people— ironic for a movement which taught the primacy of words over images! A picture of the pope being excreted from the rectum of the devil was surely more powerful than tens of thousands of words establishing the papacy as the Antichrist.

Given the dependence on preachers for popular knowledge of God's Word, there is once again a happy elective affinity between the wider world in which Luther lived and the theology he formulated. For Luther, the modern preacher was the successor of the Old Testament prophet, the one who brings God's Word into the present. Commenting on Amos 8:11, Luther makes the point that the loss of preachers in the modern world would be functionally the same as the loss of prophets in the ancient world: it would mean the disappearance of God and leave only the darkness of divine absence in its wake.[9] Indeed, the preaching of the Word was for Luther the most basic and the most non-negotiable mark of the church. This is why he lists it as the first of the seven marks in *On the Councils of the Church*:

> Now, wherever you hear or see this Word preached, believed, professed, and lived, do not doubt that the true *ecclesia sancta*

---

9   "We must watch and pray lest that same famine be sent on us, too. Now we are by the grace of God overwhelmed with a manifold abundance of God's Word. But we must watch and pray that it may not be taken away again and that palpable darkness and the foulest errors may not be sent upon us, so that even if we wanted to hear the Word, there would be no one to preach it, as happened to the Jews, Greeks, and Romans, who once abounded in the Word of God. For when the Word has been taken away, what else remains but the most terrible darkness of human reason which wants to be our mistress and which can teach nothing else than the doctrines of the demons?" Luther, *Minor Prophets*, Amos 8:11.

catholica, "a Christian holy people" must be there, even though their number is very small. For God's Word "shall not return empty," Isaiah 55 [:11], but must have at least a fourth or a fraction of the field. And even if there were no other sign than this alone, it would still suffice to prove that a Christian holy people must exist there, for God's Word cannot be without God's people, and conversely, God's people cannot be without God's Word. Otherwise, who would preach or hear it preached, if there were no people of God? And what could or would God's people believe, if there were no Word of God?[10]

And so the connection between God's speech as defining reality and the preacher is crucial. If the most basic element of the church is the presence of God mediated by his Word, then the most important person in the church in terms of function is the preacher and, at the risk of tautology, the most important task he performs is that of preaching. The preacher is the one, under God, who makes reality in the church.

For this reason, Luther does not allow his early emphasis on the general priesthood of all believers to ultimately undermine his high view of the ordained ministry. Certainly his early Reformation writings contain a certain democratic exuberance which might point toward a purely pragmatic view of ordination. However, the struggles with Andreas Karlstadt (c. 1477–1541) and the Zwickau Prophets in 1522 and then, more dramatically, the violence of the Peasants' War of 1525, served to crystallize a much clearer understanding of the ordained ministry in Luther's mind. Indeed, the use of Reformation rhetoric by peasant radicals in the uprisings of 1525 virtually killed the language of general priesthood in the subsequent discourse of magisterial Protestantism. For the post-1525 Luther, the preacher of God's words must explicitly be someone who is competent for the task by both calling and training; and the presence of properly called and ordained men is the fifth mark of the church, after the Word, baptism, the Lord's Supper and confession.[11]

---

10 Martin Luther, *Luther's Works, Vol. 41: Church and Ministry*, ed. J.J. Pelikan, H.C. Oswald and H.T. Lehmann (Philadelphia: Fortress Press, 1999), 150.

11 *Luther's Works, Vol. 41*, 154.

At this point we should note how Luther's most basic theological commitments lead directly to this very practical reality. Luther's overwhelming religious concern was his desire to find a gracious God and how he found that gracious God only in the crucified flesh of the incarnate Lord Jesus Christ. Gospel ministry, therefore, is defined on a foundational level by the crucified Christ. Preaching connects to this in at least two ways. First, Luther understood the empirical reality of the cross to hide the reality of God's grace from the rational mind and to reveal it only to the eye of faith as it grasps the Word of God. Thus, the Word preached, the Word which explained the counterintuitive glory of the cross, was the means by which the reality of the cross could be grasped by the congregation.

Second, the practical question is always: Where is this crucified Christ to be found today? And the answer to that is: the crucified Christ is made present through the Word preached. It has always been through his speech that God has made himself present; and now in the church that presence is mediated through the Word preached. Again, the preached Word is central.

This represents a distinct shift from the late medieval piety with which Luther would have grown up. There, God is present primarily through the sacramental action of the church, especially as focused in the performance of the Mass. Yes, there was certainly preaching, sometimes great preaching, in the medieval church; and, despite popular Protestant myths to the contrary, biblical exposition was extremely important in the theological curriculum of the Middle Ages. Thomas Aquinas, for example, before he was considered even remotely qualified to be a teacher of the church, had to exegete and lecture his way through more of the Bible than any current faculty member in any Protestant seminary in the United States had to do before receiving a teaching post. Yet there is a difference between Reformation Protestantism and medieval Catholicism that is not only of emphasis—of Word taking priority over sacrament—but of theological significance as well. For Luther, the Word preached is the basic means by which God is present with his people; presence in the sacrament is dependent upon, and thus subordinate to, that in the Word. Take away the Word preached and there is nothing left. And that makes perfect sense, given the theology and philosophy of language to which Luther is committed.

For this reason, the supreme and central task of the Lutheran pastor is proclaiming the Word. That is the medium or the tool which connects the congregation to the crucified Christ. We should also note in this context that this refers to a proclamation of the Word, not a conversation or a debate. The precursor of the New Testament church pastor is the Old Testament prophet. The prophet brings a word from God; he reveals future realities; and, more often, he creates present realities by unmasking the false masks of current reality and penetrating to the counter-intuitive reality which lies beneath. The golden calves may look like aesthetically appropriate representations of Jehovah; a king like the nations around might look like a beneficial change to the constitution; Egypt might look like a useful ally in holding a foreign invader at bay; but the prophets of the Lord unmask the deceptive appearances and force the people to stare reality in the face.

Thus, the New Testament preacher is to show people that all their righteousness is as filthy rags and as unreliable a leaning post as a spider's web. And, counter-intuitive and counter-cultural as it may be, it is in the filthy and broken corpse of a man condemned as a criminal to hang on a cross that true righteousness, mercy and grace are to be found.

We must remember, as well, that this is not simply a descriptive task: the preacher is not merely correcting a wrong description of the world. The reorientation brought about by the preacher is moral and existential at the deepest possible level because it involves a confrontation between God's Word and sinful human beings. One becomes a theologian of the cross, Luther would say, by death through the law and resurrection through the gospel.

Luther brings out the moral power of the Word preached perhaps most nicely in *On the Bondage of the Will*:

> It is thus that he hardens Pharaoh, when he presents to his ungodly and evil will a word and work which that will hates—owing of course to its inborn defect and natural corruption. And since God does not change it inwardly by his Spirit, but keeps on presenting and obtruding his words and works from without, while Pharaoh keeps his eye on his own strength, wealth, and power, in which by the same natural defect he puts his trust, the result is that Pharaoh is puffed up and exalted by his own imag-

ined greatness on the one hand, and moved to proud contempt on the other by the lowliness of Moses and the abject form in which the word of God comes, and is thus hardened and then more and more provoked and exasperated the more Moses presses and threatens him.[12]

The Word of God is intrinsically powerful. If God does not free the hearer to believe the gospel, the hearer's fallen will causes him to be hardened and to deepen in his opposition to the God who confronts him in the Word. Thus, as Isaiah declares, the Word of God cannot return to him empty (Isaiah 55:11). Indifference to the Word is impossible because it is a moral force, not a simple redescription of reality. The Word of God transforms the reality of the world. That is the power of preaching; that is the power of the pulpit.

Conclusion

First, we must note that there are other aspects of the creative act of preaching beyond the mere principles outlined here. For example, Robert Kolb has recently demonstrated how modern narrative theory helps to elucidate the importance of the form of Luther's preaching.[13] Yet even on the basis of what I have outlined, it should be clear that understanding preaching as a *theological* act is crucial to understand why Luther—and Protestantism after him—placed pulpit ministry at the centre of the pastor's calling.

Thus, I am convinced that, while much time is spent at seminaries teaching the technical aspects of preaching—exegesis, the move to doctrinal synthesis and then to application and exhortation—it is equally, if not more, important that preachers understand the nature of the theological action they perform when they stand in a pulpit. How we perform any task is determined, to some extent, by what we understand the task to be doing. Such knowledge makes our actions more intentional in execution. There is a fundamental difference between, for example, lecturing and preaching. The connection between the

---

12 Martin Luther, *Luther's Works, Vol. 33: Career of the Reformer III*, ed. J.J. Pelikan, H.C. Oswald and H.T. Lehmann (Philadelphia: Fortress Press, 1999), 179.

13 Robert Kolb, *Luther and the Stories of God: Biblical Narratives as a Foundation for Christian Living* (Grand Rapids: Baker Academic, 2012).

speech of God and the speech of those who declare his Word in his name is perhaps one of Luther's greatest pastoral insights. It is at once something that should humble the preacher—how can finite, sinful man speak the words of God?—and something that should give him supreme confidence—he speaks God's words and therefore their ultimate power does not depend upon the knowledge, eloquence or righteousness of the pastor. His task is to exegete, proclaim and apply to the best of his ability; whether the Word looses or binds those who hear is not within the sphere of the preacher's competence.

Second, this insight should also temper preoccupation with the technicalities of preaching. It disturbs me when I read of those who claim that stand-up comics are the best models for preachers today. That is not a comment on the use of humour in the pulpit. I am a great believer in the pedagogical usefulness of humour. The problem with saying that stand-up comedy is the best model for preaching is that you are assuming two things: first, that the most important key to preaching after a good grasp of the Bible's message is the issue of communication. You are assuming the issue is primarily a technical one. Second, you are saying that the conversational style of stand-up comedy is the best model (and that, presumably, because you see communication as the key issue). Neither are true. Clear communication is important; but far more important is the self-conscious understanding that preaching is confrontation—that it brings a word from outside, to use Lutheran terminology.

Third, preaching must remain central to Protestantism. It cannot be moved from that position without theological and ecclesiastical consequences. Lecturing has its place; but when the man in the pulpit merely lectures, merely exegetes the Word, merely finds Christ there and considers his task done, without impressing on the people the existential urgency and the transformative nature of what he is doing— that is not preaching and that will kill churches. In the same way, the conversational approach of the counsellor's couch has its place; but to displace the general proclamation of the pulpit with the particularities of the one-on-one represents either a lack of confidence (and of theological understanding) of proclamation or an unnecessary preoccupation with the personal uniqueness of the individual rather than the universality of the underlying problem. Put simply, the answer to the failure of preaching is better preaching.

Finally, for all of the criticism of the passé nature of pulpit ministry, it is surely true that we live in a profoundly linguistic age. What do I mean by that? Simply this: we live in an age where the power of words is recognized perhaps as never before. Most of the battles in the culture wars are battles over words: racist words, sexist words, homophobic words, hate speech. Battles over words are all around us. And underlying these battles is the understanding that words are, in an important sense, constitutive of reality. For all the problems that deconstruction embodies, it has served us well in drawing attention to the importance of the verbal aspect of what constitutes reality. When you call me an idiot, I can shrug my shoulders and outwardly ignore you; but deep down inside, I am affected by those words. My reality has been shaped by it. Certainly my relation to you has been shaped by it.

Thus, on the grounds that every setback should be an opportunity, I will conclude by saying that we live in an age, like Luther's, where anti-essentialist philosophies and nominalist linguistic theories rule the day; and in such a climate, the preacher is really acknowledged by all to be very powerful. Indeed, the secular authorities acknowledge this in the way they try to squeeze Christian speech from the public square and the way that legislation is slowly but surely redefining freedom of religion as freedom of worship, and pushing religious language and religious claims about language into private space. If religious language were not powerful, it would be a matter of indifference to all. That it stirs such passionate emotions illustrates that friends and foes alike acknowledge its potency. Luther offers theological insight into why words are so powerful and why preaching is more than mere technique. We might do a lot worse in our seminary training than spending time reading and reflecting not simply on the great preachers and preaching of the past but on the theology of the preached Word—the real power behind their pulpit strategies. Our world acknowledges the creative power of words, for good and for evil; let us not be blind to the significance of this cultural moment nor slow to capitalize on it.

Calvin and his Puritan heirs on Christ's humanity in Hebrews

By Mark Jones

Introduction

Nobody disputes that John Calvin (1509–1564) played a significant role during the time of the Reformation. As a demonstration of his significance there are literally hundreds of studies devoted to his life and theology. What more can really be said of the Genevan reformer's life, theology and influence? Still a great deal, no doubt—a testimony to Calvin's massive output of writing during his years in Geneva. Still, even if every area of Calvin's thought had been analyzed, the fact remains that scholars will still find themselves disagreeing with each other over what Calvin said and why he said this or that, as well as debating his enduring influence (or lack thereof) upon later Christian theologians.

In the secondary literature, a major area of inquiry in Calvin studies over the past several decades has focused on Calvin's relation to the Reformed tradition, particularly his heirs in the Post-Reformation era.[1]

Author's note: Professor Michael Haykin co-supervised my Ph.D. thesis at Leiden Universiteit, which was later published as *Why Heaven Kissed Earth: The Christology of the Puritan Reformed Orthodox Theologian, Thomas Goodwin (1600–1680)* (Göttingen: Vandenhoeck & Ruprecht, 2010). When we initially discussed a Ph.D. topic he suggested looking at Christology in Hebrews. My study took on a different focus, and so

The well-known phrase, "Calvin against the Calvinists," refers to the idea promoted by a number of scholars that Calvin's heirs departed from Calvin's theology in various ways, some of which are not insignificant. The "Calvin against the Calvinists" thesis has suffered a number of blows in the last decade or so, but the final death-blow to that thesis came with the publication of Richard Muller's most recent work, *Calvin and the Reformed Tradition*.[2]

This essay attempts to analyze Calvin's understanding of Christ's humanity in the book of Hebrews in comparison to how several Puritan theologians spoke of the humanity of the God-man in their writings on certain passages in Hebrews. The idea that Calvin's heirs somehow lost or jettisoned the "Christocentricity" of Calvin has been adequately refuted in various ways, either by questioning the usefulness of the term "Christocentricity"[3] or by showing that scholars have sometimes not adequately analyzed the primary sources of those theologians who allegedly departed from Calvin's Christological focus.[4]

This essay contends that while Calvin's 1549 commentary on Hebrews certainly demonstrates an understanding of the benefit of Christ's humanity for his people, his Christology is in fact not as developed as the Christology of later Reformed theologians. There are clear areas of agreement between Calvin and his heirs, but there are also places where they ventured to speak on the benefit of Christ's humanity

---

I am glad to be able to revisit a subject that appears to be of great interest to Professor Haykin. I was also privileged to co-edit a book with him: *Drawn into Controversie: Reformed Theological Diversity and Debates Within Seventeenth-Century British Puritanism* (Göttingen: Vandenhoeck & Ruprecht, 2011).

1　See Andreas J. Beck & William den Boer, ed., "The Reception of John Calvin and His Theology in Reformed Orthodoxy," *Church History and Religious Culture* 91.1–2 (2011).

2　Richard Muller, *Calvin and the Reformed Tradition: On the Work of Christ and the Order of Salvation* (Baker Academic: Grand Rapids, 2012).

3　See Richard A. Muller, "A Note on 'Christocentrism' and the Imprudent Use of Such Terminology," *Westminster Theological Journal* 68, no. 2 (2006): 253–260.

4　For example, Julie Canlis speaks about the Reformed tradition's decreased emphasis and inadequate understanding of Calvin's doctrine of union with Christ, but she does not really marshal any evidence to support her claim from the primary sources of Reformed orthodox theologians. See "Calvin, Osiander and Participation in God," *International Journal of Systematic Theology* 6, no. 2 (2004): 177–182. See Muller's response in *Calvin and the Reformed Tradition*, passim.

that Calvin did not address with the same degree of sophistication or, some might argue, speculation.

This can be partly explained by the fact that Calvin was a second-generation codifier of Reformation theology, and for that reason was, as Richard Muller notes, "seldom highly original, and frequently not as detailed or carefully defined in his arguments as would eventually become necessary to resolve the debates of subsequent generations."[5] This point by Muller may surprise many, particularly in the broader Reformed community, who have come to revere Calvin as the greatest theologian of the Reformed church; but the evidence below shows that Calvin's well-known penchant for lucid brevity kept him from making the types of contributions to Christology that one finds among his Puritan heirs in the seventeenth century.

In terms of biblical spirituality, a further aim of this essay is to show that one of the most rewarding studies for anyone wishing to come to a deeper love and appreciation of the Christian faith is to study the man, Christ Jesus, and precisely what it means for him to be not only *homoousios* with God, but also *homoousios* with man.

Reformed Christologies?

The Chalcedonian Creed (A.D. 451) provides an orthodox statement of the person of Christ. But anyone familiar with the Christological debates leading to Chalcedon knows full well that the creed lends itself to various interpretations.[6] Scholars continue to debate which side— the Antiochene's or the Alexandrian's—came out victorious.[7] In the

---

5   Richard Muller, "The 'Reception of Calvin' in Later Reformed Theology: Concluding Thoughts," *Church History and Religious Culture* 91.2 (2011): 256.

6   Two relatively recent studies stand out in terms of analyzing the Christology of Cyril of Alexandria (c. A.D. 376–444) and Nestorius (A.D. 386–451): Susan Wessel, *Cyril of Alexandria and the Nestorian Controversy: The Making of a Saint and of a Heretic* (Oxford: Oxford University Press, 2004); and John McGuckin, *Saint Cyril of Alexandria and the Christological Controversy* (Crestwood: St. Vladimir's Seminary Press, 2004). McGuckin's analysis, which is deeply sympathetic to Cyril, paints a remarkably fair picture of Nestorius's Christology. Wessel shows that Nestorius was in fact prepared to refer to Mary as *theotokos*!

7   Among the studies that argue for a Cyrilline victory, see H. Diepen, *Les Trois Chapitres au Concile de Chalcédoine* (Oosterhout, 1953); John Meyendorff, *Christ in Eastern Christian Thought* (Washington: Corpus Books, 1969). Conversely, Robert

Western tradition, Roman Catholic, Lutheran, and Reformed theologians have developed Christologies that differ significantly. Of the three aforementioned traditions, only the Reformed tradition is able to do justice to the humanity of Christ. For example, John McGuckin shows that Cyril explained Christ's prayer life "as an economic exercise done largely for our instruction and edification."[8] This is wholly unacceptable for Reformed theologians. Contrary to this position, they believed that Christ, as a true man, needed to pray; which is to say, of course, that he did not pray merely for our instruction. Moreover, in relation to this point, Herman Bavinck correctly notes that Reformed theologians "had fundamentally overcome the Greek-Roman and Lutheran commingling of the divine and the human" in understanding how the two natures related to one another in the one person, Christ Jesus.[9] Because of the well-known Reformed axiom, *finitum non capax infiniti*, the human nature of Christ retained its integrity in both his state of humiliation and his state of exaltation.

There were a number of important implications that resulted from this premise. However, even in the Reformed tradition, there has not been entire unanimity on the *communicatio idiomatum*.[10] The difference

---

Jenson has argued that Chalcedon leans in an Antiochene direction. See *Systematic Theology, 1: The Triune God* (New York: Oxford University Press, 1997), ch. 8. Before Jenson, Jaroslav Pelikan also argued for an Antiochene victory: "Even though it may be statistically accurate to say that 'the majority of the quotations come from the letters of St. Cyril,' the contributions of Leo's *Tome* were the decisive ones." *The Emergence of the Catholic Tradition (100–600)* (Chicago: University of Chicago Press, 1992), 264.

8   McGuckin, *Saint Cyril of Alexandria*, 133. Related to this point, Susan Wessel makes the comment that Luke 2:52 "presented Cyril with something of a challenge, for it clearly stated that Jesus advanced in stature, wisdom, and grace.... Cyril could say only that Christ's advance and increase were merely apparent." *Cyril of Alexandria and the Nestorian Controversy*, 133.

9   Herman Bavinck, *Reformed Dogmatics: Sin and Salvation in Christ*, vol. 3 (Grand Rapids: Baker, 2006), 258.

10 See Stephen Holmes, "Reformed Varieties of the Communicatio Idiomatum" in *The Person of Christ*, ed. Stephen Holmes and Murray Rae (London: T & T Clark International, 2005), 70–86.

Calvin describes the *communicatio idiomatum* thus: "[The Scriptures] sometimes attribute to [Christ] what must be referred solely to his humanity, sometimes what belongs uniquely to his divinity; and sometimes what embraces both natures but fits neither alone. And they so earnestly express the union of the two natures that is in

between how Calvin and John Owen (1616–1683) understand the relationship between the two natures of Christ are rather remarkable. Calvin has been described as the theologian of the Holy Spirit; but it was actually Owen who gave the most erudite and sophisticated account of the relationship between the Holy Spirit and Christ, which enabled him to explain to readers the precise relationship between Christ's two natures.[11] Not all agree with Owen; but there is very little in Calvin's writings that provide an adequate explanation for why there is such a decided emphasis upon the role of the Holy Spirit in Christ's ministry. For these reasons, and others, the topic of Christ's humanity was an area where a great deal of advancement took place less than a century after Calvin.

Like his brothers

Of all the epistles in the New Testament, the book of Hebrews provides the most fascinating insights into the human nature of Jesus Christ. The first chapter has made readers inescapably aware that Jesus is divine (1:8–12); chapter two makes his humanity equally clear, as verses 14 to 18 speak of Christ sharing in "flesh and blood," being made "like his brothers in every respect" in order to be a merciful high priest. Commenting on these verses, Calvin states that in Christ's human nature there are two things to be considered, "the essence of the flesh and the affections."[12] But then he claims that the Son did not need to experience misfortunes "to become accustomed to the emotion of mercy."[13] According to Calvin, Christ's life experience and qualification for being a merciful high priest was not, then, for himself, but for us. We are assured of his merciful disposition toward us only because he was acquainted with our miseries.[14] The emphasis on Christ's *learning* to be merciful is missing in Calvin.

Christ as sometimes to interchange them. This figure of speech is called by the ancient writers 'the communication of properties.'" *Institutes of the Christian Religion* (Louisville: Westminster John Knox, 2006), 2.14.1.

11 See Alan Spence, *Incarnation and Inspiration: John Owen and the Coherence of Christology* (London: T & T Clark International, 2007).

12 John Calvin, *The Epistle of Paul the Apostle to the Hebrews and the First and Second Epistles of St. Peter*, trans. William B. Johnston (Grand Rapids: Wm. B. Eerdmans, 1963), 32.

13 Calvin, *Epistle to the Hebrews*, 33.

14 Calvin, *Epistle to the Hebrews*, 33.

In the seventeenth century, John Owen wrote the most extensive commentary ever on the book of Hebrews. Owen's commentary dwarfs Calvin's in point of length; but more germane to the present discussion, Owen also provides occasion to look at certain points of Christology in a lot more detail than Calvin. Calvin speaks of Christ's mercy and assures believers that Jesus is indeed merciful. But Owen goes farther by distinguishing between God's mercy, which is "but a naked, simple apprehension of misery, made effective by an act of his holy will to relieve," and Christ's mercy, which is "a compassion, a condolency, and hath a moving of pity and sorrow joined with it."[15] This is one example of several where Calvin seems content to give a basic, albeit accurate (in my opinion) answer, whereas Owen draws a great deal more out of the text for his readers.

The issue is not whether Christ is merciful, but whether he is a merciful high priest. God is merciful; but God is not a merciful high priest—it is an ontological impossibility. To be a merciful high priest, the Son had not only to assume a human nature and be called to the priesthood, but he also had to experience miseries, sufferings and temptations. According to Owen, Christ "had particular experience thereby of the weakness, sorrows, and miseries of human nature under the assaults of temptations; he tried it, felt it, and will never forget it."[16] For these reasons, Christ will relieve, favour and comfort his people by his grace. Christ's experiences did not "add" to his mercifulness, but made him more ready to dispose grace to those who require it. Owen observes that Christ "bears still in his holy mind the sense he had of his sorrows wherewith he was pressed in the time of his temptations, and thereon seeing his brethren conflicting with the like difficulties is ready to help them."[17] There is much agreement between Calvin and Owen on this matter, but it seems as though for Owen there is a sense in which Christ's human experiences on earth were as beneficial for him as they are for us. Calvin has an almost exclusive emphasis on the latter.

---

15 John Owen, *Epistle to the Hebrews*, 7 vols. (Edinburgh: The Banner of Truth Trust, 1991), 3:469.

16 Owen, *Epistle to the Hebrews*, 3:470.

17 Owen, *Epistle to the Hebrews*, 3:485.

John Owen

1616–1683

Affections in heaven

Having previously spoken of Christ's human nature in relation to the priesthood (2:17–18), in chapter four the author of Hebrews brings into distinct focus the role of Christ's humanity in his current high priestly ministry in heaven. Calvin again explains how Christ's life and trials persuade his people that he is merciful toward them. But Calvin also notes that Christ's humanity in heaven has the added benefit of assuring believers that there is no reason to fear him since he is our brother as well as our Lord. His heavenly majesty might cause some to shrink back from seeking him; but his humanity gives us confidence that he is more inclined to take care of us. In this context, Calvin raises the "frivolous" question of whether the exalted Christ is still subject to our sorrows.[18] Answering this question would be, to Calvin, nothing more than an "idle speculation."[19] Nonetheless, in his comments on Matthew 9:36, written in 1555, he claims that in heaven Christ "does not retain the same feelings to which he chose to be liable in this moral life."[20] What Calvin was apparently unwilling to discuss in 1549, he now answers, albeit modestly, several years later.

Among the Reformed orthodox theologians in the seventeenth century, Thomas Goodwin (1600–1680) wrote one of the most sophisticated and penetrating treatises on Christ's humanity in the context of his heavenly ministry. Goodwin ventures to discuss Christ's human affections in his state of glory in the type of detail nowhere found in Calvin's *corpus*. Indeed, Goodwin raises the question concerning how to distinguish between Christ's affections in his time of weakness and frailty and his remaining affections in his state of glory. He candidly admits this is a difficult question and, judging by his opening discussion, one might be persuaded that Calvin's relative simplicity is the best course of action.

Christ's resurrected body is termed a "spiritual" body (1 Corinthians 15:44). This does not mean, of course, that he somehow shed his human nature in heaven, but that his body is now "powerful" (Romans 1:4). Not only Christ's body, but also his affections are "spiritual."

---

18 Calvin, *Epistle to the Hebrews*, 55.

19 Calvin, *Epistle to the Hebrews*, 55.

20 John Calvin, *Commentary on a Harmony of the Evangelists, Matthew Mark, and Luke*, trans. William Pringle (Grand Rapids: Baker Books, 2003), 1:421.

Thomas Goodwin
1600–1680

According to Goodwin, Christ's affections do not work in his soul only, but also in his body, "as their seat and instrument."[21] However, the body is "so framed to the soul that both itself and all the operations of all the powers in it are immediately and entirely at the arbitrary *imperium* and dominion of the soul."[22] In other words, the infirmities in Christ's human nature on earth, experienced in terms of hunger and weakness, do not now affect his soul in heaven because his body is raised in power. Following from this, Goodwin notes that the affections of pity and sympathy move his "bowels and affect his bodily heart" both in his states of humiliation and exaltation.[23] But there is this difference: his affections in heaven "do not afflict and perturb him in the least, nor become a burden and a load unto his Spirit, so as to make him sorrowful or heavy."[24] This is so because Christ's human nature is "impassible" insofar as he cannot experience any hurt now that he is in his glorified state. Jesus is still compassionate and merciful, and thus his perfection does not destroy his affections, "but only corrects and amends the imperfection of them."[25] Echoing the "best of the schoolmen", Goodwin adds, "*Passiones perfectivas* to be now in him."[26]

Like Calvin, Goodwin aims to address the benefits of Christ's human nature toward believers. In addressing the abovementioned question, Goodwin states that man has certain affections that are natural, and not the result of sin. In the Garden of Eden, Adam possessed natural affections that were governed not by sin, but by reason. Thus Christ's affections of pity and compassion in his state of glory "quicken and provoke him to our help and succour."[27] That is to say, Christ is no longer a "man of sorrows," but rather a "man of succours" to his people! There is no doubt that the members of Jesus' bride who remain on earth are living in a world of sin and misery. Christ must necessarily

---

21 Thomas Goodwin, *The Heart of Christ in Heaven Towards Sinners on Earth* in *The Works of Thomas Goodwin, D.D.*, 12 vols. (Edinburgh: James Nichol, 1861–1866), 4:144.

22 Goodwin, *Heart of Christ in Heaven*, 4:144.

23 Goodwin, *Heart of Christ in Heaven*, 4:145.

24 Goodwin, *Heart of Christ in Heaven*, 4:145.

25 Goodwin, *Heart of Christ in Heaven*, 4:145.

26 Goodwin, *Heart of Christ in Heaven*, 4:145.

27 Goodwin, *Heart of Christ in Heaven*, 4:145. To "succour" is to give help, especially in times of difficulty.

possess affections suitable to their condition while he is in heaven. If heaven was suited only for Christ's personal happiness then there is no need for Christ to possess the affections of sympathy and mercy. But, as Goodwin observes, Christ's relationship to his people is a part of his glory. Therefore, these types of affections are required to be in him if he is to be a good husband to his bride. Moreover, far from being a weakness, Christ's affections of pity and mercy are his strength: "it is his glory to be truly and really, even as a man, sensible of all our miseries, yea, it were his imperfection if he were not."[28]

The beauty of Goodwin's theology emerges precisely at this point. Though Christ has shed affections that were once a burden to him, and are thus not compatible or suitable to his state in heaven, there are nonetheless other affections that possess a "greater capaciousness, vastness" that more than makes up for his lack of the former affections. In fact, Goodwin argues that just as Christ's knowledge was "enlarged" in heaven, "so his human affections of love and pity are enlarged in solidity, strength, and reality…Christ's affections of love are as large as his knowledge or his power."[29] Another way to look at this would be to argue that since Christ is freed from oppressive affections it actually gives greater scope to his effective affections—being free from grief actually lets you be more compassionate. So, for example, when you yourself are desperately hungry, other people's problems don't receive your best attention. This can be applied to Christ based on the theology that Goodwin sets forth.

Whereas Goodwin uses Hebrews 4:15 to discuss what affections are now in Christ in his heavenly state, Calvin actually claims that the author "does not discuss the nature of Christ in Himself, but His nature as He shows Himself to us."[30] So while both Calvin and Goodwin are concerned to highlight the pastoral value of Christ's humanity in heaven, Goodwin ventures into territory that Calvin does not. Some might argue that Calvin is less "speculative" than his heirs on certain questions; others might contend, however, that Calvin simply is not as sophisticated as later Reformed theologians—after all, he was not a trained theologian in the same manner as Reformed theologians in

28 Goodwin, *Heart of Christ in Heaven*, 4:146.
29 Goodwin, *Heart of Christ in Heaven*, 4:146.
30 Calvin, *Epistle to the Hebrews*, 55.

the period of high orthodoxy. Goodwin's example might show that his Christological concerns enabled him to draw more out of Hebrews 4:15 than Calvin. As a result, the question between Calvin and a later "Calvinist" is not one so much of divergence, but rather one of heightened clarity and greater spiritual value.

Another example of the value of good Christology in relation to a believer's personal frailties comes from Stephen Charnock (1628–1680). Looking at Hebrews 4:15, Charnock argues that because of the incarnation "an experimental compassion" was gained which the divine nature was not capable of because of divine impassibility.[31] As our sympathetic high priest, Christ "reflects" back on his experiences in the world and so the "greatest pity must reside in him" because the "greatest misery was endured by him." Christ is unable to forget above what he experienced below.[32] Charnock does not intend to say that Christ's human nature suffers in any way, which would contradict Goodwin. Instead, he is speaking about Christ's knowledge and memory of his sufferings as the means by which Christ is able to be sympathetic to his people in a way that would otherwise be impossible if the Son did not assume a human nature. Consequently, the value of an elaborate Reformed Christology for the advancement of biblical spirituality cannot be overstated.

Learning obedience

The idea that the God-man, Jesus Christ, learned obedience (Hebrews 5:8) has been a perplexing thought to some, both for laypeople and for many pastors as well. Calvin constantly aims to draw out the benefits of Christ's humanity to his people. It is a constant refrain in his exegesis of Hebrews. Calvin's focus may even cause him to miss the point of Hebrews 5:8. He notes that Christ was "more than willing" to obey the Father; but he obeyed "for our own benefit, to give us the instance and pattern of His own submission even to death itself."[33] Moving to a more decidedly Christological focus, Calvin does affirm that Christ, by suffering, including his death, learned what it was to obey God.

---

31 Stephen Charnock, *A Discourse of Christ's Intercession* in *The Complete Works of Stephen Charnock*, 5 vols. (Edinburgh: James Nichol, 1864), 5:106.

32 Charnock, *A Discourse of Christ's Intercession*, 5:106.

33 Calvin, *Epistle to the Hebrews*, 65–66.

John Calvin
1509–1564

However, his analysis of what it means for Christ to "learn obedience" is rather anemic in his comments on Hebrews 5:8.

In discussing the obedience spoken of in Hebrews 5:8, Owen distinguishes between Christ's *general* obedience, which refers to the whole pattern of his life on earth, and Christ's *peculiar* obedience, which refers specifically to his obedience unto death.[34] This verse in question has in view the latter understanding of obedience. Following from that, to learn obedience has a threefold sense:

1. To learn it *materially*, that is, to be taught by God to obey him, which we were at some time ignorant of. This does not apply to Christ, for he knew what was required of him.

2. To learn it *formally*, which has in view God's instruction, help, and direction of us in our acts of obedience because we are weak and unskillful. Again, this could not be true of Christ since he always had a fullness of grace, and so constantly knew what he had to do and was perfectly willing to do what was required of him.

3. To learn it *through experience*. By undergoing such severe trials of hardship, even death on a cross, Christ learned suffering-obedience. This type of obedience required suffering so that his knowledge of suffering might be of great value to the church.[35] All of Christ's life was one of suffering. In his sufferings he "had occasion to exercise those graces of humility, self-denial, meekness, patience, faith, which were habitually present in his holy nature, but were not capable of the peculiar exercise intended but by reason of his sufferings."[36] Owen makes a pastoral note that should not go unnoticed. He claims that in God's dealing with men, those who have been most afflicted have also been the "most humble, most holy, fruitful, and wise among them"— no doubt this applies to Christ himself.[37]

---

34 Owen, *Epistle to the Hebrews*, 4:523.
35 Owen, *Epistle to the Hebrews*, 4:524.
36 Owen, *Epistle to the Hebrews*, 4:525.
37 Owen, *Epistle to the Hebrews*, 4:530.

By the use of various distinctions, Owen gives his readers a lot more to think about concerning Christ's obedience than Calvin. Calvin aims to help his readers with his remarks on Christ's humanity, but Owen helps his readers more because his exegesis is more elaborate and detailed than Calvin's.

A body prepared

Hebrews 10:5 draws on Psalm 40:6 to address the body that was prepared for Christ by the Father. Instead of explaining what this verse means relative to the incarnation and Christ's human nature, Calvin spends his time explaining why "the Apostle" used Psalm 40:6 the way he did. After all, Calvin rightly notes that Psalm 40:6 reads "you have given me an open ear." The Septuagint translation (Psalm 39:7–9) understands this phrase to indicate the creation of a person's body, which the author of Hebrews picks up on rather than quoting the Masoretic text. Calvin comments that the apostles were "not over-scrupulous in quoting words provided that they did not misuse Scripture for their convenience."[38] Calvin's "lucid brevity" on this verse is inexcusable, for his readers are not given any hint of what it means for Christ that a body was prepared for him. This verse addresses directly the humanity of Christ, and an important detail of who "prepared" the body the Son was to assume.

In his learned commentary on Hebrews, the Puritan theologian William Gouge (1575–1653) notes that "body" is meant by way of synecdoche to refer to the soul as well.[39] In the context of Hebrews 10, the human nature of Christ is necessary for Christ to be able to offer a sacrifice. Gouge understands the word "prepared" in Hebrews 10:5 as a compound which signifies "to make perfect."[40] The Father "ordained, formed, made fit and able Christ's human nature to undergo, and fulfill that for which he was sent into the world."[41] Following from this, Gouge contends that God enables men in specific ways to do the work for which they have been set apart. In other

---

38 Calvin, *Epistle to the Hebrews*, 136.

39 William Gouge, *A learned and very useful commentary on the whole epistle to the Hebrews* (London, 1655), 436.

40 Gouge, *Epistle to the Hebrews*, 436

41 Gouge, *Epistle to the Hebrews*, 436.

words, God does not "send forth dumb Orators...lame messengers. Such are not prepared of God."[42]

God prepared a sinless body, and fitted Christ with the requisite gifts and graces to perform the work of Mediator. Owen picks up on this very theme, and notes that the body prepared for Christ by the Father was "the effect of the mutual counsel of the Father and the Son."[43] According to the terms of the covenant of redemption, the Father was required to provide the Son with all things needed to be able to fulfill the will of the Father. According to Owen, "Among those the principal was, that the Son should have a body prepared for him, that so he might have somewhat of his own to offer."[44] Two of Owen's "observations" are worth noting. They are beautiful instructions to believers on how they ought to respond to the idea that the Father prepared a body for the Son. First, that we should praise the Father for the "holy properties" of Christ's human nature.[45] Second, in connection with the first point, it was the Father who not only "prepared" the Son's body, but also "filled it with grace...strengthened, acted, and supported it in [Christ's] whole course of obedience."[46]

After that, Owen claims that a more particular inquiry is required into the nature of this preparation of a body by the Father for Christ. He highlights ten points for consideration: (1) That the body should come from the loins of Abraham; (2) That the body should be free from sin; (3) That the body should consist of real flesh and blood; (4) That the body should have a rational soul; (5) That the body should be able to undergo sorrows and sufferings; (6) That this body could be tempted by outward temptations; (7) That the body could physically die; (8) That the same body could be raised again from the dead; (9) That his soul could be with God in heaven while his body lay in the grave; and (10) That his body was visibly taken to heaven, and there resides.[47]

Gouge's explanation is no doubt sufficient, and he pulls something out of the text that not only explains what the verse means, but also

---

42 Gouge, *Epistle to the Hebrews*, 437.
43 Owen, *Epistle to the Hebrews*, 6:460.
44 Owen, *Epistle to the Hebrews*, 6:461.
45 Owen, *Epistle to the Hebrews*, 6:461.
46 Owen, *Epistle to the Hebrews*, 6:461.
47 Owen, *Epistle to the Hebrews*, 6:462–464.

some practical application for his readers. Owen, true to form, takes verse 5 and draws out many important truths about Christ's humanity along with several applications that should cause believers to marvel at the wonder of the Father's preparation of Christ's body. Calvin does not commit any sins of commission, so to speak, but his apparent reluctance to be too prolix in his commentaries essentially robs his readers of insights into Christ's humanity.

Conclusion

What conclusions can be drawn from this brief analysis of how Calvin and the "Calvinists" understood the humanity of Christ in the book of Hebrews? First, there is little doubt that Calvin's Christology is not nearly as developed as what we find in many later Reformed theologians. His *Institutes*, which were not analyzed in this essay, were a manual for ministers. Despite the fact that the *Institutes* are one of Christ's greatest gifts to the church, the theology contained in that work is not nearly as intricate and refined as the writings of later Reformed Protestant scholars, such as Petrus van Mastricht (1630–1706) and Francis Turretin (1623–1687). This is not to minimize Calvin's obvious genius and importance; but it seems to me that there is a sort of existential crisis among many Reformed churchmen, and indeed even some scholars, who feel the need to make too much out of Calvin—as if getting the reformer to agree with our position is the ace in the pack. Perhaps if the Latin writings of other theologians had been translated, as Calvin's have, the typical view of Calvin would be slightly modified.

Second, as this essay has shown, Calvin's commentary on Hebrews was less than detailed, sometimes even neglecting to actually comment on the passage in question. The specific details that would need to be answered by Calvin's heirs did not appear to occur to Calvin to answer at the time, though it is interesting that Peter Martyr Vermigli (1500–1562) did in fact answer certain questions with a great deal more clarity than Calvin.

Third, Calvin's omissions and absences of detail may reflect an "anti-speculative" bent on his part, which some find appealing. But the precision and clarity of later theologians such as Owen, Goodwin and Charnock on the humanity of Christ actually fosters a richer, deeper spirituality. Knowledge of the person and work of Christ is the chief part of Christian growth. Calvin paved the way—he pioneered the threefold office of Christ—and his heirs have done much to improve on his own contributions. This is precisely how theology ought to function in the Reformed church. And, I have little doubt that a Calvinistic Baptist such as Professor Haykin would heartily agree with that sentiment.

Anabaptist spirituality

By Malcolm B. Yarnell

IN THE YEAR 1539, one sister Apollonia, wife of Leonhard Seyle, having been with him in the upper country, was apprehended in the Earldom of Tyrol, and brought to Brixen; but, through the immutable grace and power of God, who valiantly aided her womanly heart, she constantly and firmly continued in the true faith, and in what she had promised God in Christian baptism, and would depart neither to the right nor to the left. Hence she was then sentenced to death, and drowned, thus receiving the martyrs' crown.[1]

This is one of the many accounts of martyrdom in the history of the sixteenth-century Anabaptists and it serves to encapsulates their spirituality. The grace of God transformed the hearts of these common people through the inner work of the Holy Spirit and the outer work of the Word of God. However, the grace of God did not end with initial faith, but compelled them by true faith into a visible witness to Christ as Lord. This visible witness was made first in the church to God

---

1 *The Bloody Theater or Martyrs Mirror of the Defenseless Christians*, ed. Thieleman J. van Braght, trans. Joseph F. Sohm, 2nd English ed. (1886; reprint, Scottdale: Herald Press, 2004), 450.

through conscientious obedience to the Lord's ordinance of believers' baptism. And this visible witness continued into the world, where it refused to compromise the faith even in the face of death. The Anabaptists held to a *cruciform spirituality*, believing that the cross of Christ both saved them and provided the paradigm for their own journey through the darkness of this world and into the light of eternity.

In this essay, we are seeking to describe the spirituality of the evangelical Anabaptists in continental Europe during the sixteenth century. In light of the interesting, yet potentially distracting, contemporary debates in which both Michael Haykin and I have staked out periodically divergent, yet always friendly, positions, three delimitations of purpose must be stated. First, this essay is not interested in defining the Anabaptists with regard to historical origins, systematic theology or polemical confessionalism. Second, we do not intend to survey the spirituality of the entire Radical Reformation of the sixteenth century, which would lead to lengthy considerations of spiritualist, violent and other positions tangential to the evangelical Anabaptists. Nor are we interested in extending the conversation into the subsequent history of the Anabaptists as they moved both east, ultimately into Russia, and west, ultimately into the Americas. Finally, we are not primarily concerned with the relationship of the Anabaptists to the Roman Catholic Church, to the other Reformation traditions or to modern Baptists. Although these important conversations are related to our interests, and thus may be momentarily touched upon in this essay, the reader seeking answers to those complex issues should consult elsewhere.

Again, our concern is a description of the early continental evangelical Anabaptists in their presentation of Christian spirituality. This objective will entail the consultation of original sources and secondary scholarly conversations concerning the three major interrelated evangelical Anabaptist movements generally located in: Switzerland, which includes the seminal contributions of Felix Manz (c. 1498–1527), Conrad Grebel (c. 1498–1526) and Michael Sattler (c. 1490–1527); south Germany and Austria, which includes the works of Balthasar Hubmaier (c. 1480–1528), Hans Hut (c. 1490–1527), Hans Denck (c. 1495–1527), Leonhard Schiemer (c. 1500–1528), Hans Schlaffer (d. 1528) and Pilgram Marpeck (c. 1495–1556); and, the Netherlands and northern Germany, which includes Dirk Philips (1504–1568) and Menno Simons (1496–1561). After a review of the various origin theories of Anabaptist spirituality, we shall explore the Anabaptist understanding of spirituality as being deeply rooted in the divine encounter of transforming grace with sinful humanity and visibly expressed through external evidences of transformed spirituality in church and society. The contemporary significance of Anabaptist spirituality will conclude this essay.

The origins of Anabaptist spirituality

Three major positions have been proposed for the origins of Anabaptist spirituality, though other influences must also be taken into account. The oldest position was put forward in standard hagiographical texts like the *Martyrs' Mirror*, which begins by tracing the origins of Anabaptist piety from the biblical martyrs through the persecution of Christian dissenters during the Middle Ages before arriving with the sixteenth-century Anabaptists.[2] While such a theory of succession may have a certain valuable apologetic appeal, it should be noted that descent through especially late medieval dissent could ground similar claims for the existence of coercive magisterial churches, as in John Foxe's monumental work, which argued the Reformed Church of England was the chosen nation.[3] Moreover, as I have argued elsewhere, little can be said about the exact beliefs of most medieval dissenters as we have few literary artifacts from them that were not filtered through the charged categories of the persecuting church authorities.

In a second theory, Dennis Martin, Arnold Snyder and Peter Erb have opined that Anabaptists derived much of their spirituality from medieval monasticism.[4] This proposal relies heavily on the similarities

---

2   Donald F. Durnbaugh, *The Believers' Church: The History and Character of Radical Protestantism* (New York: Macmillan, 1968), 9–16; Timothy George, "The Spirituality of the Radical Reformation," *Southwestern Journal of Theology* 45 (2003): 28–32.

3   V. Norskov Olsen, *John Foxe and the Elizabethan Church* (Los Angeles: University of California Press, 1973), ch. 2.

4   Dennis D. Martin, "Catholic Spirituality and Anabaptist and Mennonite Discipleship," *Mennonite Quarterly Review* [hereinafter *MQR*] 62 (1988): 5–25; C. Arnold Snyder, "The Monastic Origins of Swiss Anabaptist Sectarianism," *MQR* 57 (1983): 5–26; Peter C. Erb, "Anabaptist Spirituality," in *Protestant Spiritual Traditions*, ed. Franc C. Senn (New York: Paulist Press, 1986), 80–124. Cf. C. Arnold Snyder, *Following in the Footsteps of Christ: The Anabaptist Tradition*, Traditions of Christian Spirituality Series (Maryknoll: Orbis Books, 2004), 111–116.

between the language of the monks and the Anabaptists, especially the monastic concern for "rules," which utilized Matthew 18:15–20 as the basis for disciplined communal spirituality, and the Anabaptist concern to follow the "rule of Christ," which also refers to the Lord's disciplinary instruction in Matthew 18. However, similarity does not entail dependence, for the Anabaptists were quite adamant about their rejection of medieval theology and religious authority. Moreover, a similar method of correlation, especially with regard to the affirmation of discipline in Matthew 18, has been used to argue a continuity of spirituality between John Calvin (1509–1564) and his Anabaptist opponents.[5] Yet, while one might ingeniously close the loop of speculation and thereby correlate Calvinist spirituality with medieval monastic spirituality, I am not aware that anyone has cared to say such simply on the basis of similar concerns for discipline as taught in Matthew 18. Similarities in biblical citation and linguistic usage indicate neither dependence nor convergence, for the contextual dynamics of language and Scripture may just as well indicate interpretive independence and opposition.

In a third theory, some scholars have argued for a similarity between various expressions of medieval mysticism and Anabaptist spirituality. Comparisons have been made to the Rhineland Mystics of the fourteenth and fifteenth centuries and to the mysticism of Benedict in the early sixth century. Thomas Finger believes that the mystical tradition that began with Meister Eckhart (c. 1260–c. 1328) and continued with an emphasis on *Gelassenheit* in Tauler and the *Theologia Deutsch* mirrored the Anabaptist teaching to yield to Christ and embrace the life of the cross.[6] In a related move, Andrew Martin claims that Benedict's emphasis on humility was carried into the spirituality of the *Martyrs' Mirror* through similar use of "fear" toward God.[7] While Martin and Finger make highly suggestive connections,

---

5   Richard C. Gamble, "Calvin and Sixteenth-Century Spirituality: Comparison with the Anabaptists," *Calvin Theological Journal* 31 (1996): 335–358.

6   Thomas Finger, "A Sixteenth-Century Anabaptist Social Spirituality," *Conrad Grebel Review* 22 (2004), 93–104; idem, "Sources for Contemporary Spirituality: Anabaptist and Pietist Contributions," *Brethren Life & Thought* 51 (2006): 28–53.

7   Andrew C. Martin, "Toward an Anabaptist Spirituality: An Investigation of the Martyrs Mirror in Light of the Theme of Humility in the Monastic Tradition," *Brethren Life & Thought* 56 (2011): 39–45.

both are subject to the same criticisms as the monastic sectarian thesis of the second theory. As Ralf Schowalter of Bonn, Germany, demonstrated in a recent dissertation, the similarities between Hans Denck and both medieval mysticism and the violent apocalypticism of Thomas Müntzer (c. 1489–1525) do not justify the ascription of dependence but merely "conversation."[8]

There are a number of other influences that should be taken into account when speaking about the origins of Anabaptist spirituality. These include the emphasis on a return to and simple reading of Scripture in concert with humanists such as Erasmus, from whose commentary on Scripture Abraham Friesen argues the Anabaptists garnered their distinctive and fundamental understanding of the Great Commission.[9] One must also account for the influence of the evangelical spirituality of the major reformers. Martin Luther's doctrine of the spiritual liberation that faith in Christ bestowed was not lost on the evangelical Anabaptists, even as they rejected any hint of Lutheran antinomianism.[10] Ulrich Zwingli's (1484–1531) practice in the Zürich disputations of judging all religious practice according to the careful reading of Scripture was joined heartily by the progenitors of the Swiss Brethren; indeed, their deepening scriptural piety is what led to their subsequent decisive break with Zwingli.[11] One theory of spiritual origins that must be dismissed summarily is Heinrich Bullinger's (1504–1575) misanthropic claim that the Anabaptists originated territorially in Saxony and spiritually with the devil.[12]

---

8 Ralf Schowalter, "Neither Mystic Nor Müntzerite: The Conversational Theology of Hans Denck" (Ph.D. dissertation, Southwestern Baptist Theological Seminary, 2012).

9 Abraham Friesen, *Erasmus, the Anabaptists, and the Great Commission* (Grand Rapids: Wm. B. Eerdmans, 1998).

10 On Pilgram Marpeck's embrace and then departure from Luther, see Malcolm B. Yarnell III, *The Formation of Christian Doctrine* (Nashville: B&H Academic, 2007), 74.

11 For more on the Anabaptists and their theological similarities yet advancement beyond the magisterial reformers, see Malcolm B. Yarnell III, ed., *The Anabaptists and Contemporary Baptists: Restoring New Testament Christianity* (Nashville: B&H Academic, 2013).

12 Heinrich Bullinger, *Widertäufer Ursprung* (Zürich, 1560). The baleful influence of Bullinger's history upon subsequent Reformed historiography is discussed in George Huntston Williams, *The Radical Reformation*, 3rd ed., Sixteenth Century Essays & Studies (Kirksville: Sixteenth Century Journal Publishers, 1992), 1292–1296.

What becomes clear in any discussion of the origins of Anabaptist spirituality is that the Anabaptists shared commonalities with, yet diverged sharply from, the other Christian spiritualities of the late medieval and early modern period, whether traditional Catholic or magisterial Protestant.

The transformative grace of God through Word and Spirit

Three aspects of spiritual conversion to Christ as Lord come to the fore in the writings of the earliest Anabaptists. First, the evangelical Anabaptists believed that salvation comes to human beings entirely as a work of divine grace. Second, they believed that salvation came to the believer inwardly, as a work of the Holy Spirit, even as it came outwardly, through the means of the proclamation of the Word. Finally, the Anabaptists believed that the divine gift of salvation necessarily entails a transformation of the human heart that evidences itself externally in the church and the world.

1. THE PRIORITY OF TRINITARIAN GRACE

"For Anabaptists, God was totally free." So Garry Schmidt began his discussion of Anabaptist spiritual theology.[13] While Anabaptist writers were primarily interested in obeying Christ thoroughly rather than crafting academic theological treatises, when they did speak about the origin of salvation, they inevitably ascribed it to God. To a question about how Anabaptist conversion "fit together," Hans Denck responded in the first full year after the Anabaptist movement began, "No one comes of himself to Christ except the Father draw him, which he truly does, of course, according to his goodness." In order to forestall Pelagian misinterpretations, he followed that positive proposal with a denunciation: "Whoever on his own initiative, however, undrawn, wishes to come on his own, presumes to give God something which he has not received from him. He wishes to be deserving from God in order that he need not thank him for his grace."[14]

---

13 Garry Schmidt, "Early Anabaptist Spirituality: History and Response," *Direction* 34 (2005): 31. Schmidt then proceeds to argue that this freedom meant that God was not bound by any theological system.

14 Hans Denck, *Whether God is the Cause of Evil* (Augsburg, 1526), in *Spiritual and*

Michael Sattler, who exercised foundational influence on the Swiss Brethren, independently concurred with Denck's affirmation of the priority of divine grace, even as he focused on the necessity of the transformed life. Sattler often began and/or ended his works with the Trinitarian movement of divine grace or glory. Thus, his treatise on the theological interpretation of Scripture begins with this blessing: "Grace, peace and salvation from God the Father, through the redemption of Christ His beloved Son, through the power and working of His Holy Spirit, Amen."[15] The orthodox Trinitarian form of this blessing indicates that grace begins with the Father and flows through the Son and the Spirit toward humanity. Working among the south German Anabaptists, Pilgram Marpeck made comparable moves. While affirming both *erbsund* (original sin) and *erbgnad* (original grace), "Marpeck could also claim that even the desire to want to be saved is the product of God's grace."[16]

The Dutch Anabaptist leader, Dirk Philips, wrote more at length about the Trinitarian grace of God that engenders regeneration. Citing the apostle James, he began his explanation of the origin of regeneration with the claim that "every good and perfect gift is from above, coming down from the Father of the heavenly lights, who does not change like shifting shadows. He chose to give us birth" (James 1:17–18). Dirk went on to demonstrate repeatedly from Scripture that the Father sends his grace to humanity through the Word of truth and by the Holy Spirit. "From all this it is absolutely clear that the new birth is actually a work of God in human beings by which one is born again from God through faith in Jesus Christ in the Holy Spirit."[17] While

Anabaptist Writers: Documents Illustrative of the Radical Reformation, ed. George Huntston Williams and Angel M. Mergal, The Library of Christian Classics (Philadelphia: Westminster Press, 1957), 107.

15 Michael Sattler, *How Scripture Should Be Discerningly Exposited* (circa 1527), in *The Legacy of Michael Sattler*, ed. John Howard Yoder, Classics of the Radical Reformation (Scottdale: Herald Press, 1973), 152.

16 Neal Blough, *Christ in Our Midst: Incarnation, Church and Discipleship in the Theology of Pilgram Marpeck* (Kitchener: Pandora Press, 2007), 163.

17 Dirk Philips, *Concerning the New Birth and the New Creature: Brief Admonition and Teaching from the Holy Bible* (1556), in *Early Anabaptist Spirituality: Selected Writings*, ed. Daniel Liechty, The Classics of Western Spirituality (New York: Paulist Press, 1994), 202–203.

there are disagreements about whether the evangelical Anabaptists held to a Protestant position on justification,[18] there seems little doubt that the Anabaptists ascribed salvation to the divine initiative of grace.

2. THE CORRELATION OF THE INNER SPIRIT WITH THE OUTER WORD

Complementing the Anabaptist claim that salvation begins with divine grace was their contention that salvation came to the believer inwardly as a work of the Holy Spirit even as it came externally through the means of the proclamation of the Word. In a contradictory manner, the Anabaptists have been accused of both literalism and spiritualism by their magisterial opponents and by subsequent historical scholarship. A more careful study of the Anabaptist view of the way grace comes to humanity indicates that the wide centre of the movement correlated the inner work of the Holy Spirit with the outer preaching of the Word of God.

In concert with state church evangelicals, free church evangelicals decried the various medieval Roman ascriptions of *ex opere operato* grace to the sacraments distributed through the sacerdotal hierarchy. And like the magisterial reformers, the Anabaptists turned to the Word of God as the mediator of grace and truth. For instance, one Roman priest, Menno Simons, admitted he was administering the mass faithfully yet with questions about whether transubstantiation was true. At first, he feared that if he should read Scripture, "I might be misled." However, "helped by Luther" and "through the illumination of the grace of the Lord," he increased in scriptural knowledge. Later, he took up both Scripture and the writings of Luther, Martin Bucer and Heinrich Bullinger, in order to reevaluate the sacrament of baptism as well. Menno became convinced that the reformers' conflicting individual answers furthered the deception of infant baptism. He was subsequently converted to true faith and called to minister as an Anabaptist elder. Menno describes his profound spiritual shift as

---

18 Michael Whitlock has surveyed the secondary arguments, constructed a fourfold evangelical measure from the writings of the reformers, and concluded from an analysis of major Anabaptist theologians that the early Anabaptists did indeed hold to an orthodox doctrine of justification. Michael Whitlock, "Justification by Grace and Early Sixteenth Century Anabaptism" (Ph.D. dissertation, Southwestern Baptist Theological Seminary, 2013).

a triune work: "I obtained a view of baptism and the Lord's Supper through the illumination of the Holy Ghost, through much reading and pondering of the Scriptures, and by the gracious favor and gift of God."[19] What is interesting about Simons' description of his spiritual transformation is that while it emphasizes fidelity to the Word, it stresses just as much the illuminating work of the Holy Spirit.

Stuart Murray detects a spectrum of views regarding the relation of the Word with the Spirit among the Anabaptists. The spectrum points to a large centre ground that appears diverse due to the fact that "Anabaptist leaders were fighting on two fronts—against reformers and spiritualists. In debates with the former they often stressed the Spirit, whereas in debates with the latter they concentrated on the Word."[20] On the literalist side of the common ground of Anabaptism could be grouped the major Swiss Brethren, Hutterite and Dutch Anabaptist leaders. On the spiritualist side of Anabaptism were leading lights among the south Germans, including Hans Denck and Hans Hut, and the Dutch, including Obbe Philips. Occupying the centre were the more systematic theologians, such as Balthasar Hubmaier, Pilgram Marpeck and Leopold Scharnschlager.[21] However, while Hans Denck has been presented as the major representative of a spiritualist Anabaptism, scholars have begun to question that classification as an overstatement. "Denck's concern...was not to oppose Scripture and the Spirit but to show how the two worked together."[22]

Marpeck utilized the coordinate terms of *eusserlich* (outward) and *innerlich* (inward) to describe the concurrent working of the Word and the Spirit with one another. Maintaining a distinction between the inner work of the Spirit and the outer work of the Word, while simultaneously holding to the need for the presence of both, helped Marpeck in conflicts with a variety of opponents. Against the Roman understanding, Marpeck objected to the idea that the sacraments confer

19 Menno Simons, "Reply to Gellius Faber (1554)," in *The Complete Writings of Menno Simons c.1496–1561*, trans. Leonard Verduin, ed. J.C. Wenger (Scottdale: Herald Press, 1984), 669.

20 Stuart Murray, *Biblical Interpretation in the Anabaptist Tradition*, Studies in the Believers Church Tradition (Kitchener: Pandora Press, 2000), 127.

21 Murray, *Biblical Interpretation*, 129–130.

22 Murray, *Biblical Interpretation*, 150–152. Cf. Schowalter, "Neither Mystic Nor Müntzerite," ch. 2–3.

grace merely through the working of the priest. It is necessary for people to hear the Word and believe through the gracious work of the Spirit. "Indeed, even today, God will reveal His art and wisdom only through the Holy Spirit."[23] And against the spiritualist understanding of theologians like Caspar Schwenckfeld, Marpeck objected to the idea that, because some have unduly limited the work of the Spirit, the church with its preaching and sacraments may be considered redundant. "Only by means of the Word of truth does the Holy Spirit generate faith, even in all truly believing hearts."[24] For Marpeck, as for the evangelical Anabaptists in general, true spirituality began with the Spirit working upon the heart as the Word worked upon the ear. The outer Word, which indicated Christ—and by extension the Bible, and by further extension the church with its proclamation and ordinances— was necessary, just as the inner Spirit was necessary.

3. SPIRITUAL REGENERATION

Thirdly, for the early evangelical Anabaptists, the divine gift of salvation necessarily entails a transformation of the human heart that evidences itself externally in the church and the world. While the Anabaptists agreed with evangelicals on the priority of divine grace, as well as on the correlative work of the Holy Spirit with the preaching of the Word in generating faith, they registered stark disagreement concerning the definition of true faith. For the Anabaptists, if a person had truly been born again by faith, then it would necessarily result in visible manifestations in church and society. Part and parcel of the Anabaptist concept of true faith is a more vibrant anthropology,[25] along with a singular stress upon discipleship, than is typical among the leading Protestant theologians, who mimicked the dour anthropology of Augustine of Hippo.

---

23 Pilgram Marpeck, "Letter to Caspar Schwenckfeld (1544)," in *The Writings of Pilgram Marpeck*, trans. and ed. William Klassen and Walter Klaassen, Classics of the Radical Reformation (Scottdale: Herald Press, 1978), 372.

24 Marpeck, "Letter to Caspar Schwenckfeld," 370.

25 "Anabaptism was preoccupied with the human response to the Gospel." John Rempel, *The Lord's Supper in Anabaptism: A Study in the Christology of Balthasar Hubmaier, Pilgram Marpeck, and Dirk Philips*, Studies in Anabaptist and Mennonite History (Scottdale: Herald Press, 1993), 26.

From the earliest days of the Anabaptist movement, the distinction between true faith and false faith drove their complaint against both Roman and Protestant Christianity. The highly successful evangelist and martyr Hans Hut stated it negatively, "their false and worthless faith [is] a faith which brings no betterment of life." More positively, he said, "no one may obtain the truth except he follow in the footsteps of Christ and his elect in the school of affliction."[26] Balthasar Hubmaier, who exercised leadership among the Swiss, south German and Austrian Anabaptists, and was perhaps their most educated theologian, believed that true discipleship required the commitment of the human will under the leadership of divine grace. "Hubmaier was striking a balance between the tendency toward determinism in the Magisterial Reformers and the works-righteousness approach of the Roman Church."[27] He agreed with the reformers in these two truths: "Faith saves us," and, "We can do nothing of ourselves." However, Hubmaier argued that to stop there would not be saying enough. "But under the mantle of these half truths, all kinds of iniquity, unfaithfulness, and injustice have completely taken over, and fraternal love has meanwhile become colder among many."[28] If a person is truly born again, he will live a transformed life. "Accordingly, after the restoration the soul is now made healthy and truly free through the sent Word. Now it can will and do good, as much as depends on it, for it can command the flesh in such a way that it tames and masters it."[29]

Even as stress was laid upon human response in discipleship, the priority of divine grace was not forgotten. Leonhard Schiemer, a former Franciscan monk who converted to Anabaptism, wrote a treatise explaining the Anabaptist order of salvation in its comprehensively transformative effect on the convert. He spoke of three kinds of grace by which the triune God brings a person into relation with himself. The first grace is the general light that comes from the Father

26 Hans Hut, *On the Mystery of Baptism* (1526), in *Early Anabaptist Spirituality*, 65.

27 Michael McDill, "Balthasar Hubmaier and Free Will," in *The Anabaptists and Contemporary Baptists*, 140.

28 Balthasar Hubmaier, *On Fraternal Admonition* (1527), in *Balthasar Hubmaier: Theologian of Anabaptism*, trans. and ed. H. Wayne Pipkin and John H. Yoder, Classics of the Radical Reformation (Scottdale: Herald Press, 1989), 375.

29 Hubmaier, *On the Freedom of the Will*, I (1527), in Pipkin and Yoder, ed., *Balthasar Hubmaier*, 441.

to every human being through the law. "Now this light does nothing other in people than to show them what is good and what is evil."[30] There are three types of response that people, who are all sinners, can make to this first grace: they can strive against God; they can react lukewarmly to the light by saying they believe, though they reject the cross when it comes; or, they can humble themselves and hear the Word of God that leads to the second grace.

The second grace is the righteousness that comes through the cross of the Son of God. The justification of a sinful person "cannot take place outside of Christ, who through his conception, birth, death and resurrection in us, when that happens, is our righteousness."[31] The Holy Spirit comes to dwell in those who accept the cross of Christ and take it up to follow the Lord. Schiemer perceives that true justification by faith in Christ and the embrace of the cross by the disciple occur simultaneously. Those who know God by faith will love God and hold to him above all things, including suffering. Out of love for Christ, the disciple will gather with other disciples, separate from the world, and submit to brotherly discipline.

The third grace is the joy that sustains the disciple as he or she carries the cross of suffering. The "oil of joy" is the Holy Spirit who anoints the church in the name of the Son from the Father. The Holy Spirit brings us "inexpressible joy" even as we temporarily experience sorrow in this world. The Holy Spirit also grants such joy externally through the congregation, for "each Christian can comfort another and speak words of comfort to those in tribulation."[32] The Austrian authorities repeatedly questioned Schiemer under torture regarding his beliefs and the progress of his missionary tours. After seven weeks of such imprisonment, he was beheaded in January 1528. Schiemer's inner spirituality, built on a theology of suffering grace, sustained his external witness to the Lord through the very end of his earthly life.[33]

---

30 Leonhard Schiemer, *Three Kinds of Grace Found in the Scriptures, the Old and New Testaments* (1527), in *Early Anabaptist Spirituality*, 84–87.

31 Schiemer, *Three Kinds of Grace*, 90.

32 Schiemer, *Three Kinds of Grace*, 94.

33 Michael D. Wilkinson, "Suffering the Cross: The Life, Theology, and Significance of Leonhard Schiemer," in *The Anabaptists and Contemporary Baptists*, 49–64.

The external nature of Anabaptist spirituality

Within the context of Anabaptist scholarship regarding spiritual principles, Dale Stofer argued thus in response to Norman Kraus:

> One cannot read the writings of major representatives of any of the main Anabaptist groups during the sixteenth century without being aware of a principle woven like a thread through these writings.... The principle is that there is an intimate and necessary connection between the inner, spiritual life of the individual or church and their outward actions.[34]

Stated a second way, the classical Catholic division between the *vita contemplativa* and the *vita activa* was dissolved in the Anabaptist understanding of the holistic Christian life. Stated a third way, the Protestant division between the soteriological graces of justification and sanctification was enfolded within the Anabaptist emphasis on the grace of the disciplined life in Christ. The Anabaptists taught that the grace of true faith must engender real change in the human being and result in a holy life dedicated to taking up the cross and following Christ. It is to the external manifestations of Anabaptist spirituality in church and society that we now turn.

1. MANIFESTATIONS IN THE CHURCH

The first place that this vibrant inner spirituality of Anabaptism displayed itself externally was in the worship of the church. The descriptions of worship in Anabaptism indicate the centrality of the Word of God, including Bible instruction and memorization,[35] along with heartfelt response to the Spirit of God's movement within the fellowship. The Anabaptist conduct of worship was formed around the idea that the Word could be perceived best when made the centre and authority over Christian thought and practice. Following the *lex sedentium* or *Sitzerrecht* (law of sitting) of 1 Corinthians 14:29–33 and in

---

34 C. Norman Kraus, "An Anabaptist Spirituality for the Twenty-first Century," *Conrad Grebel Review* 13 (1995): 23–32; Dale Stofer, "A Response," *Conrad Grebel Review* 13 (1995): 197.

35 On Anabaptist Bible memory and the centrality of Scripture in Anabaptist worship, see Snyder, *Following in the Footsteps of Christ*, 117–126.

concert with the priesthood of all believers taught by 1 Peter 2:5–9, the whole congregation patiently and orderly listened to the prophets speak in turn before passing judgement upon the teaching.[36] Was the teaching based in Scripture as interpreted by the Holy Spirit? Did it properly incorporate the historical progress of Scripture from the old covenant to the new fulfilled in the Lord Jesus Christ? Did it recognize and remain centred upon the Lord and his cross? What was the congregation's sense of the Lord's will?

Regarding the first believers' baptism that took place in Zürich on January 21, 1525, the Hutterite *Chronicle* left a paradigmatic description of it. Reading Scripture as a community and coming to one mind, a fear (*Angst*) from God compelled them to recognize that true faith requires lifelong worshipful obedience to the Lord, which begins in the practice of believers' baptism. The transitions between paired truths—the external reading of Scripture and the internal movement of the Spirit, divine grace and human response, faith and love, conscience and covenant, individual and community, divine command and human obedience beginning in baptism, initial conversion and continuing service—form a nearly seamless movement. The Father's grace through Word and Spirit, which carries sinners from *Angst* (repentance-inducing fear) to *Gelassenheit* (internal yieldedness to God) to *Mitzeugnis* (the co-witness of making a covenant with a good conscience toward God, internally through baptism by the Spirit and externally through the practice of water baptism) to *Nachfolge Christi* (a committed life of following Christ) to a potential "third baptism" (perseverance in martyrdom), profoundly shaped these early Anabaptists:

They came to one mind in these things, and in the pure fear of God they recognized that a person must learn from the divine Word and preaching a true faith which manifests itself in love, and receive the true Christian baptism on the basis of the recognized and confessed faith, in the union with God of a good conscience, henceforth to serve God in a holy Christian life with all godliness, also to be steadfast to the end. And it came to pass that they were together until fear began to come over them, yea, they were pressed in their hearts.... After the prayer,

---

36 Williams, *The Radical Reformation*, 405, 415, 518–521, 1256–1257.

George Cajacob arose and asked Conrad to baptize him, for the
sake of God, with the true Christian baptism upon his faith and
knowledge. And when he knelt down with that request and
desire, Conrad baptized him.[37]

The holistic transformation that makes its initial external manifestation in believers' baptism subsequently became the given norm in
evangelical Anabaptism, even as different groups sometimes stressed
various aspects of the spiritual life in its external manifestations.

Within the covenanted church, baptism did not stand alone as a
binding ordinance from the Lord. Balthasar Hubmaier identified two
regular congregational practices that arise from "the Rule of Christ"—
water baptism and Christ's Supper—while two other congregational
practices—fraternal admonition and the ban—might be necessary
in certain cases. In concurrent treatises, Hubmaier created congregational forms for water baptism and Christ's Supper and addressed
the practices of fraternal admonition and the ban. For Sattler and
the Swiss Brethren at Schleitheim, as for Hubmaier at Nikolsburg,
Christ intended his ordinances to be integrated into congregational
life. True believers "are of one mind to abide in the Lord as God's
obedient children," which requires being "separated from the world"
as well as from "certain false brethren," who believe spiritual freedom
allows them to dismiss Christ's ordinances for the church. Sattler,
too, went on to correlate baptism, church discipline and the Lord's
Supper by addressing them in the first three articles of his highly
influential confession.[38]

The practice of water baptism was to be reserved for believers who
make a credible profession of faith. While they were falsely accused
of "rebaptizing," thus the name "Anabaptist," which means "baptize
again" (cf. German *Wiedertäufer*), many preferred to call themselves
"Brethren." As one persecuted baptized woman explained to those who
tortured and eventually drowned her: "No, my Lords, I have not been
rebaptized. I have been baptized once upon my faith; for it is written

---

37 An Excerpt from the Hutterite *Chronicle*, in *Spiritual and Anabaptist Writers*, 43.
38 *Brotherly Union of a Number of Children of God concerning Seven Articles* (1527),
in *Baptist Confessions of Faith*, ed. William L. Lumpkin (Valley Forge: Judson Press,
1969), 24–25.

that baptism belongs to believers." When accused of holding to baptismal regeneration, she denied that misunderstanding, too: "No, my lords, all the water in the sea could not save me; but salvation is in Christ."[39] Hubmaier agreed, and in the most significant defense of believers' baptism written in the sixteenth century, he demonstrated at length from Scripture both the proper meaning and order of baptism. The preaching of the Word and personal cognition of and commitment to the faith must precede water baptism.[40] In his *A Form for Water Baptism*, he also argued that the proper church order is for baptism to precede and make available the breaking of bread.[41]

The restoration of the New Testament practice of the Lord's Supper was just as important for the Anabaptists as was baptism. Gay Lynn Voth has argued that the early Anabaptists "supported the liturgical centrality of the Supper."[42] Hans-Jürgen Goertz said it was "the most important symbol of their fellowship."[43] However, before explaining their own views of communion, the Anabaptists had to clear away the errors of the Catholic mass. In general agreement with Zwingli, Grebel said that the Lord's Supper, like baptism, contained no sacramental power within itself. "They are signs (*significatum*) which point to Christ, the cross event, and resurrection."[44] The Lord's Supper was a truly communal practice, which involved the uniting participation of all congregants; indeed, it could be presided over by laity.[45] In a helpful article, Timothy George summarized Simons' four-part view of the Lord's Supper: it is a memorial; it is a pledge of Christ's love; it is a

---

39 *Martyrs' Mirror*, 482, cited in Timothy George, "Early Anabaptist Spirituality in the Low Countries," *MQR* 62 (1988), 266. George prefers to call this understanding of baptism "repenters' baptism."

40 *On the Christian Baptism of Believers* (Waldshut, 1525), in *Balthasar Hubmaier*, 95–149.

41 *A Form for Water Baptism* (Nikolsburg, 1527), in *Balthasar Hubmaier*, 390. For more on the Anabaptists and baptism, see Rollin Stely Armour, *Anabaptist Baptism: A Representative Study Studies in Anabaptist and Mennonite History* (Scottdale: Herald Press, 1998).

42 Gay Lynn Voth, "Anabaptist Liturgical Spirituality and the Supper of Christ," *Direction* 34 (2005): 10.

43 Foreword to Rempel, *The Lord's Supper in Anabaptism*, 13.

44 William Estep, *The Anabaptist Story* (Grand Rapids: Wm. B. Eerdmans, 1963), 175.

45 Wally Kroeker, "The Element of Unity in the Anabaptist Practice of the Lord's Supper," *Direction* 12 (1983): 33–34.

symbol of the bond of Christian unity; and, it is "the communion of the body and the blood of Christ."[46] To keep the ordinances properly related, Hubmaier pointed out that "the power and the right to admonish another" arises "from the baptismal commitment, which a person gave before receiving water baptism, in which he subjected himself to the order of Christ, to the church and all her members."[47] In other words, baptism opened the door to communion and obligated the maintenance of communion through fraternal admonition and occasionally the ban. Yet for Hubmaier, the integration and privileging of the ordinances was not intended in a legalistic manner, for he "placed an emphasis on the role of the Holy Spirit in shaping the church and her worship practices."[48] His A Form for Christ's Supper offers an eleven-part worship service that encourages dependence upon the Word, gentle and probing catechesis by the elder, and sensitivity to the movement of the Spirit. Hubmaier's Form still speaks persuasively to students of the Lord's Supper today.[49]

The Anabaptist communities were also shaped by the loving practice of church discipline. Simon Goncharenko has argued that for Hubmaier individual spirituality was formed within the context of church discipline. While he rejected the works-righteousness of the Romanists and affirmed salvation by grace through faith, Hubmaier also believed that sanctification must become a part of individual spirituality. Personal sanctification was aided by the integration of church discipline with the Lord's Supper as authorized through baptism. "Hubmaier guarded against lax living, which often characterized the churches and societies of the Magisterial Reformers, with his usage of church discipline as an integral part of the salvation process."[50]

Church discipline was divided into two major parts: fraternal admonition, which involved verbal warning, and the ban or excommunication, which was ultimately intended for redemption rather than

---

46 George, "Early Anabaptist Spirituality," 268–269.

47 On Fraternal Admonition (Nikolsburg, 1527), in Balthasar Hubmaier, 383.

48 Voth, "Anabaptist Liturgical Spirituality," 12. Rempel argues that baptism in Hubmaier was related to faith, while the Lord's Supper was related to love. Rempel, The Lord's Supper in Anabaptism, 22, 56–57.

49 A Form for Christ's Supper (Nikolsburg, 1527), in Balthasar Hubmaier, 393–408.

50 Simon Goncharenko, Wounds that Heal: The Importance of Church Discipline within Balthasar Hubmaier's Theology (Eugene: Pickwick, 2012), 78.

punishment. While some Anabaptists, especially in the Swiss and Mennonite traditions, tipped into legalistic attitudes with the ban,[51] Pilgram Marpeck, among others, argued for the granting of sufficient time to people so that the Holy Spirit might work upon them and demonstrate his fruit in their lives. Love, patience and the avoidance of hasty judgements were key to redemptive church discipline.[52]

The Anabaptists were drawn to worship together by dominical command and for mutual benefit. Upon visiting their unusual gathering places, one is still struck with how incredibly effective their community-forming spiritual practices are. Menno Simons reported,

> ...we preach, as much as is possible, both by day and by night, in houses and in fields, in forests and wastes, hither and yon, at home or abroad, in prisons and in dungeons, in water and in fire, on the scaffold and on the wheel, before lords and princes, through mouth and pen, with possessions and blood, with life and death. We have done this these many years, and we are not ashamed of the Gospel of the glory of Christ.[53]

While one visits court and cathedral in all their human glory to survey Catholic and Protestant architectural history, it is outside the homes from which they were driven, and into the cold prisons where they were tortured, beyond the remote mountainous caves where they gathered for worship and, finally, to the public squares and riversides where they were executed, that one must travel to survey Anabaptist church "architecture."

2. MANIFESTATIONS IN THE WORLD

The second place that this vibrant inner spirituality of Anabaptism displayed itself externally was in witness to the world. On the one hand, the Great Commission of the Lord drove the Anabaptists into the world as witnesses, but the harshness of their persecutors turned

---

51 George, "Early Anabaptist Spirituality," 270–271.

52 *Judgment and Decision* (circa 1531), in *The Writings of Pilgram Marpeck*, 309–361; C. Arnold Snyder, "An Anabaptist Vision for Peace: Spirituality and Peace in Pilgram Marpeck," *Conrad Grebel Review* 10 (1992): 189–193.

53 *Reply to Gellius Faber*, in *Complete Writings of Menno Simons*, 633.

that world into a dark and dangerous wilderness. On the other hand, the Lord also commanded them to find spiritual refuge and comfort in the body of Christ, and their churches were kept on the way to purity through his ordinances of fearful baptism and joyous communion. Yet even the church was sometimes removed from individual Anabaptists through persecution. And when the church was not available, the Anabaptist martyrs left witness that God showed his presence personally.

The relationship of the Anabaptists to the world has suffered misrepresentation since the appearance of Richard Niebuhr's *Christ and Culture* in the mid-twentieth century. In that little lecture, which became a key text in subsequent theological discourse, the sixteenth-century sectarians are dismissed as being summarily "against culture" in a Tolstoyan sense, and proof is offered by referring to contemporary Mennonites, who themselves are grossly caricatured as having "renounced all participation" in the world.[54] It is true that separation from the world was strictly maintained among the Anabaptists as an act of obedience to their Lord. However, early Anabaptist separation was not intended for reclusive antagonism to the world but to prepare faithful witnesses to carry the Word of God back into the world.

A hymn of discipleship attributed to Michael Sattler tracks the origin, progress and end of the Christian life in relation to God and the world. The first verse states,

As Jesus with his true teaching
Gathered to himself a small flock,
He told them that each with patience
Should daily carry his cross.

The origin of the disciple's life, therefore, is in the calling of Christ. The next verse indicates that the disciple must have as his or her single desire the love of Christ and obedience to his teaching. Verses three through six then explain that the result of following Christ will lead to persecution. This is not a cause for concern, but for rejoicing, for Christ was also killed in spite of the fact that he is "God's son," had

---

54 H. Richard Niebuhr, *Christ and Culture* (San Francisco: Harper & Row, 1951), 40–41, 56–57.

"always done well" and was "the best of all." The self-sacrificial goodness of Christ in his life, suffering and death is the model for the lives
of his disciples. However, while Christ's suffering and death are central
to the parallel life of the Christian, the Christian should also think
eschatologically, not fearing man but God, "Who has the power to
judge." God will ultimately transform "your misery, fear, anxiety, need
and pain" into "joy," "praise," and "honor" (verses 7, 10). In the mean-
time, there is the continuing presence of Christ and his promise of
eternal life to comfort the disciples: "For I am yours and you are mine;
Where I am, there you should be" (verse 9). The example of the
apostles, who likewise followed Christ, and the continuing intercession of Christ himself will see the disciples "through your bitter death"
and into eternal life (verses 11–12). Sattler ends the hymn with his
characteristic appeal to Trinitarian blessing.[55] This hymn is highly
instructive, for much of Anabaptist piety was transmitted through and
is still available in their hymnody.[56] It also traces the historical progress
of the Anabaptist spirituality of discipleship in the world.

  Gelassenheit, Nachfolge Christi, Märtyrertheologie, "the Anabaptist
vision"[57]—each term has been used to describe the Anabaptist belief
that God intends the earthly Christian life to begin and end in the Christian's cross, which is carried in emulation of Christ and his cross. I have
demonstrated elsewhere that the Anabaptists rejected speculative
philosophical theology in favour of a theology garnered from the biblical
order of history.[58] Ethelbert Stauffer contends furthermore, "The Anabaptist theology of history is from the very outset centred in Christ; that
is, the Son who in obedience to his Father takes the Cross upon himself,
is the very hub of world and history."[59] The priority of Christ's cross is
maintained, yet it also serves as a paradigm for the Christian life. Again,
Stauffer writes, "The Anabaptists understood the Cross in a twofold
way: (1) as the event which centres all history, and (2) as the principle

55 Ausbund, Song #7, in Early Anabaptist Spirituality, 54–56.

56 Preston Atwood, "The Martyrs' Song: The Hymnody of the Early Swiss Brethren,"
The Artistic Theologian 2 (forthcoming 2013); Harold S. Bender, "The Hymnology of
the Anabaptists," MQR 31 (1957): 5–10.

57 Harold S. Bender, The Anabaptist Vision (Scottdale: Herald Press, 1944), 20–26.

58 Yarnell, The Formation of Christian Doctrine, 95–98.

59 Ethelbert Stauffer, "The Anabaptist Theology of Martyrdom," trans. Robert
Friedmann, MQR 19 (1945): 190.

that guides the way of God's people through history."[60] Or, as Conrad Grebel wrote, "Christ must suffer still more in his members."[61]

Similarly, Hans Hut appealed to Paul against the Protestant theologians, "The whole Christ suffers in all members.... Paul gives witness to this when he said, 'I rejoice in my suffering for in this I restore what is lacking of Christ's suffering on my own body.'"[62] Hut developed his theology of suffering both from general revelation and the New Testament, and encapsulated it in what he called "the gospel of all creatures." He went on to demonstrate that water baptism is where the Christian's spiritual commitment to suffering and death begins. The baptism of the new birth, wrought by the Holy Spirit, "is not an external symbol but rather a bath of the soul which washes and cleanses the heart of all lust and carnal appetites." The world rejects this baptism, even as it accepts the error of infant baptism, because true baptism involves suffering, but this suffering is intended to purify us and will be temporary.[63] Hans Schlaffer agreed and traced baptism through three related stages, according to 1 John 5:7–8. First is the baptism of the Holy Spirit in personal spiritual regeneration. Second is the baptism of water in the church. Finally, there is the baptism of blood in the world.[64]

The Anabaptists believed that the history of the world involves a continuing warfare between the violent city of the devil and the persecuted people of God. It is this warfare into which new Christians are inducted by baptism and preserved by the joy of obedient trust in God. While they disagreed over such things as communal goods and the extent to which the ban might be used, the Anabaptists agreed that they must demonstrate love toward their enemies and faithfulness toward Christ. Indeed, the battle in which Christians are engaged is of apocalyptic proportions. For the evangelical Anabaptists, the Christian knight's battle is directed against one's own flesh and the cross is

---

60 Stauffer, "Anabaptist Theology of Martyrdom," 197.

61 Conrad Grebel et al., to Thomas Müntzer, September 5, 1524, in *Spiritual and Anabaptist Writers*, 84.

62 Hut, *On the Mystery of Baptism*, in *Early Anabaptist Spirituality*, 67–68. See Colossians 1:24.

63 Hut, *On the Mystery of Baptism*, in *Early Anabaptist Spirituality*, 77–81.

64 Hans Schlaffer, *Instruction on Beginning a True Christian Life* (1527), in *Early Anabaptist Spirituality*, 108–109.

the means of victory over one's sin.[65] In opposition to the diabolical coercions of Rome, Wittenberg, Zürich and Münster, the evangelical Anabaptists embraced what George called a "peaceful apocalypticism."[66] Martyrdom was the ultimate act of sacrifice, a sacrifice of love, to which God might call a Christian, though it was not, of course, typically sought.[67] Because it stood at the pinnacle of the Christian life, Snyder could classify martyrdom as "the very essence of the Anabaptist spiritual tradition."[68]

Martyrdom was also a seed of witness leading to converts.[69] As Tripp York has argued in his wide-ranging discussion of Christian martyrdom, "The shaping of the body by liturgical formation and the witnessing of Christ through martyrdom are part of what it means to simultaneously praise God and reveal to the world who God is."[70] The Anabaptists understood, from their earliest days, the price that witness to Christ in a hostile world may exact. A synod of the brethren gathered in several Augsburg homes in August 1527, in order to clarify Anabaptist preaching and send missionaries of the gospel. The Lord blessed both intentions, but Protestant and Catholic persecution resulted in the deaths of most of those who had been ordained for missions, thus earning it the name of "Martyrs' Synod."[71]

The Anabaptists believed the Lord himself would sustain them through the cross of persecution and even a martyr's death. "The living presence of God, experienced in the heart, lay at the centre of Anabaptist spirituality."[72] In 1572, Jan Wouters was tortured brutally through hanging, deprivation and beating, but he refused to betray his fellow believers. He was able to describe in a letter to his family, triumphantly, "I had drunk that bitter cup...I prayed within myself, that the Lord should not suffer me to be tempted above that I was

---

65 Stauffer, "The Anabaptist Theology of Martyrdom," 200.

66 George, "Early Anabaptist Spirituality in the Low Countries," 271–272.

67 Stauffer, "The Anabaptist Theology of Martyrdom," 199; George, "Early Anabaptist Spirituality in the Low Countries," 272–273.

68 Snyder, *Following in the Footsteps of Christ*, 161.

69 Stauffer, "The Anabaptist Theology of Martyrdom," 199.

70 Tripp York, *The Purple Crown: The Politics of Martyrdom* (Scottdale: Herald Press, 2007), 52.

71 Williams, *The Radical Reformation*, 282–286.

72 Snyder, *Following in the Footsteps of Christ*, 174.

able." And in preparation for another torture session, he prayed for more strength. He reported afterwards, "I bear witness of Him, that He is a faithful helper in distress."[73] The Anabaptists understood death as part of the journey into life, so they did not fear it. Stauffer summarized the martyrs' spiritual journey in pithy Latin: *per crucem ad lucem* (through the cross to the light).[74]

These courageous Christ-followers often encouraged one another to see that even the most excruciating death could be withstood through genuine faith. In one early case, after having had his tongue split and strips of flesh torn from his body, Michael Sattler raised two fingers on each hand as the flames consumed his body to indicate that God would strengthen the steadfast believer. They took courage from such displays, because they saw a martyr's death as itself opportunity for a powerful confession of faith to the world.[75] The authorities also discovered that steadfast martyrdom was a dynamic witness to the gathered crowds, so some resorted to secret executions in order to dampen their effectiveness.[76] However, the authorities simply could not keep the witness of the martyrs silent. After she was delivered a death sentence, Maeyken Wens wrote to her son in 1573 that he should not fear the temporary suffering of this life, but consider eternity. The report and related woodcut showing her son digging through the ashes of his mother at her execution looking for the only remaining memento of her life, the tongue screw by which she was bound from speaking, indicate her hope was not in vain.[77]

Contemporary significance

Four aspects of Anabaptist spirituality immediately suggest means for enhancing the contemporary understanding of life in the Spirit. First, the Anabaptists provide a deterrent against the ever-present temptation to spiritual antinomianism, the confidence (often unacknowledged) that faith is largely an internal matter. By categorically linking justification with regeneration in the gracious movement of

---

73 Snyder, *Following in the Footsteps of Christ*, 174–175.
74 Stauffer, "The Anabaptist Theology of Martyrdom," 202.
75 Stauffer, "The Anabaptist Theology of Martyrdom," 208–211.
76 Snyder, *Following in the Footsteps of Christ*, 179.
77 Schmidt, "Early Anabaptist Spirituality," 41–42.

God in salvation under the rubric of discipleship, the Anabaptists ensured that "faith" includes not only cognitive belief but also living trust. While many contemporary evangelical free church theologians, including the present writer,[78] would maintain a distinction between justification as imputed righteousness and sanctification as imparted righteousness, the Anabaptist witness properly maintains a necessary transition between the two.

Second, Dietrich Bonhoeffer (1906–1945) famously called for "costly grace" and denounced the practice of "cheap grace." This dualism, which teaches that the call of Christ to become a disciple is itself a movement of divine grace, has continuing relevance for those tempted to succumb to the popular viewpoints of a fallen world. It is instructive that Bonhoeffer, a Lutheran church-state theologian, found himself somewhat uncomfortably dealing with Luther's followers in order to describe what discipleship to Christ truly means.[79] While our twenty-first-century context is not parallel to that of either the sixteenth century or the twentieth century, the problem of "cheap grace" is a recurring temptation. To put it more provocatively, many today speak of "the doctrines of grace," which is a good thing, but if such language is not accompanied with transformed lives it manifests a human betrayal of the divine grace it claims to hold.

Third, Robert Friedmann has pointed out that around the turn of the eighteenth century, the lineal descendants of the Swiss Brethren began to adopt a pietist spirituality from the Lutheran and Reformed traditions that stressed emotive transformation and downplayed the flesh's bearing of the cross.[80] Where the Anabaptists of the sixteenth century taught the "bitterness" of suffering must be expected in the Christian life, the pietistic tradition focused on the "sweetness" of life with Christ. Today, it is instructive that Christians primarily think of crosses as

---

78 Yarnell, "Christian Justification: A Reformation and Baptist View," *Criswell Theological Review*, n.s. 2 (2005): 71–89.

79 Dietrich Bonhoeffer, *Discipleship*, trans. Barbara Green and Reinhard Krauss, Dietrich Bonhoeffer Works (Minneapolis: Fortress Press, 2001), 47–54; Abram John Klassen, "Discipleship in Anabaptism and Bonhoeffer" (Ph.D. dissertation, Claremont Graduate School, 1970).

80 Robert Friedmann, "The Devotional Literature of the Swiss Brethren 1600–1800," *MQR* 16 (1942): 207–211. Cf. Stauffer, "The Anabaptist Theology of Martyrdom," 203–204; George, "Early Anabaptist Spirituality in the Low Countries," 274–275.

beautiful pieces of jewellery. The brutality and harshness of the cross of Christ, a brutality and harshness that Christ himself warned us would be part of our own experience as Christians (John 15:20), has been downplayed in an effort to sweeten our lives. The Anabaptist martyrs remind us that the cross hurts, in daily suffering and in final martyrdom. We must seriously ask whether our therapeutic culture is propagating a deception of painlessness that is keeping Christians from seeing that all of life, including suffering and death, is part of becoming all that God intends us to be in worship and witness.

Fourth, Anabaptist spirituality is characterized by a sense of seamlessness between the individual and the community. As a result of *inter alia* the Enlightenment, which defined the human being in a solipsist manner as a "self," many Christians have come to view themselves almost exclusively as individuals in their spiritual life. The Anabaptists remind us that there is a form of Christianity that correlates an intense sense of the personal presence of God by means of Word and Spirit with a commitment to the comforting presence of Christ in the congregation covenanted to obey him. The Anabaptist doctrine of baptism brings together the covenant of the individual conscience in faith through a vertical covenant with God and a horizontal covenant with other believers. Paul Fiddes has detected a similar correlation among the early English Baptists.[81] The reintegration of isolated individuals to become persons in community is a desperate need for many modern and postmodern Christians, and the Anabaptists offer a solution through the Lord's gifts of baptism, the Lord's Supper and church discipline.

For these and other reasons, may Anabaptism's *cruciform spirituality* see a revival in our day.

---

81 Paul S. Fiddes, *Tracks and Traces: Baptist Identity in Church and Theology,* Studies in Baptist History and Thought (Carlisle: Paternoster, 2004), ch. 2.

William Perkins

1558–1602

REFORMATION · PURITAN

William Perkins: application in preaching

By Erroll Hulse

WILLIAM PERKINS (1558–1602) laboured at Cambridge, the leading centre of training Puritan divines, with remarkable success. In him was combined unusual spiritual qualities and ministerial skills. His youth was given to recklessness, profanity and drunkenness, but, while a student, Perkins experienced a powerful conversion. This, it is believed, began when he overheard a woman in the street, while chiding her naughty child, threatening to hand him over for punishment to "drunken Perkins"! He experienced a deep conviction and gave up his evil life. He also gave up the study of mathematics and his fascination with black magic and the occult, and took up theology. He joined Laurence Chaderton (1536–1640), his personal tutor and lifelong friend, who was called "the pope of Cambridge Puritanism," and became part of the spiritual brotherhood which was the essence out of which Puritanism developed during the reign of Queen Elizabeth (1558–1602). He has unity with the well-known Puritan leaders Richard Greenham (c. 1540–c. 1594) and Richard Rogers (1551–1618). He earned a bachelor's degree in 1581 and a master's degree in 1584.

From 1584 until his death, Perkins served as lecturer, or preacher, at Great St. Andrew's Church, Cambridge. This most influential church was situated just across the street from Christ's College. St. Andrews was regularly packed with eager hearers many of whom were converted under Perkins' ministry. He also served as a Fellow at Christ's College from 1584 to 1595. Fellows were required to preach, lecture and tutor students and also work as "guides to learning as well as guardians of finances, morals, and manners." Perkins served the university in several capacities. He was Dean of Christ's College from 1590 to 1591. He catechized the students at Corpus Christi College on Thursday afternoons, lecturing on the Ten Commandments in a manner that deeply impressed the students. On Sunday afternoons, he worked as an adviser, counselling the spiritually distressed.

Perkins was a powerful preacher. His aim was to reach and minister to the spiritual needs of a wide range of hearers. He spent as much time on exegesis of the text as he did prayerfully considering the spiritual state of his hearers. He ministered to the prisoners in the Cambridge jail, including those who were on death row. Samuel Clarke (1599–1682) provides a striking example of Perkins' pastoral care. He says a condemned prisoner was climbing the gallows, looking "half-dead," when Perkins said to him, "What man! What is the matter with thee? Art thou afraid of death?" The prisoner confessed that he was less afraid of death than of what would follow it. "Sayest thou so," said Perkins. "Come down again man and thou shalt see what God's grace will do to strengthen thee." When the prisoner came down, they knelt together, hand in hand, and Perkins offered "such an effectual prayer in confession of sins...as made the poor prisoner burst out into abundance of tears." Convinced the prisoner was brought "low enough, even to hell's gates," Perkins showed him the freeness of the gospel in prayer.[1] Clarke writes that the prisoner's eyes were opened "to see how the black lines of all his sins were crossed and cancelled with the red lines of his crucified Saviour's precious blood; so graciously applying it to his wounded conscience, as made him break out into new showers of tears for joy of the inward consolation which he found." The prisoner rose from his knees, went cheerfully up the ladder, testified of salvation in Christ's blood and bore his death with patience, "as if he actually saw himself delivered from the Hell which he feared before, and heaven opened for the receiving of his soul, to the great rejoicing of the beholders."[2]

---

1   This biographical sketch is dependent on Joel R. Beeke and Randall J. Pederson, *Meet the Puritans: With a Guide to Modern Reprints* (Grand Rapids: Reformation Heritage Books, 2006), 469–472.

2   Samuel Clarke, *The Marrow of Ecclesiastical History: Contained in the lives of one*

Thomas Fuller writes that Perkins' sermons were of many colours: "They seemed to be 'all Law and all gospel, all cordials and all corrosives, as the different necessities of people apprehended' them."[3] He was able to reach many types of people in various classes, being systematic, scholarly, solid and simple at the same time. Most important is the fact that he lived his sermons. What he declared in the pulpit he was in daily life.

Perkins pioneered Puritan casuistry—the art of dealing with "cases of conscience" by self-examination and scriptural diagnosis.

It is no exaggeration to say that William Perkins, as a theologian and pastor, became the main architect of the Puritan movement in his generation. He was handicapped in his right hand and so wrote with his left. Thomas Fuller said of him, "This Ehud, with a left-handed pen did stab the Romish cause!"[4]

As an author, he was used to an astonishing degree. Joel R. Beeke, in his paper on Perkins at the Westminster conference at Westminster Chapel in London in 2004, asserted that "Perkins was the first theologian to be more widely published in England than Calvin, and the first English Protestant theologian to have a major impact in the British Isles, on the European continent, and in North America. Many Puritan scholars marvel that Perkins' rare works have been largely unavailable until now."[5]

After his death his works were published eleven times up to 1635. These contained nearly fifty treatises. Beeke and Randall Pederson researched the fact that at least fifty editions of Perkins' works were printed in Switzerland and in various parts of Germany. "His writings were also translated into Spanish, French, Italian, Irish, Welsh, Hungarian and Czech."[6] Beeke researched that in New England, nearly

---

hundred forty eight fathers, schoolmen, first reformers and modern divines which have flourished in the Church since Christ's time to this present age (London: Printed for T.V., 1654), 852–853.

3 Thomas Fuller, Abel Redevivus, Or, The Dead Yet Speaking: The Lives and Deaths of the Modern Divines (London: William Tegg, 1867), 148.

4 Thomas Fuller, The Holy State and the Profane State (London: Thomas Tegg, 1841), 83.

5 Joel R. Beeke, "William Perkins and 'How a Man May Know Whether He Be a Child of God or No," in The Faith That Saves: Papers Read at he Westminster Conference Papers (London: Westminster Conference, 2004), 7–32.

6 Beeke and Pederson, Meet the Puritans, 475.

100 Cambridge men who led early migrations to the New World, including William Brewster of Plymouth, Thomas Hooker of Connecticut, John Winthrop of Massachusetts Bay and Roger Williams of Rhode Island, grew up in Perkins's shadow. Richard Mather was converted while reading Perkins books. A century later, Jonathan Edwards was fond of reading Perkins.[7]

Perkins died from kidney stones at the relatively young age of forty-four, in 1602. His wife of seven years was pregnant at the time and caring for three small children. His major writings include expositions of Galatians 1–5, Matthew 5–7, Hebrews 11, Jude and Revelation 1–3, as well as treatises on predestination, the order of salvation, assurance of faith, the Apostles' Creed, the Lord's Prayer, the worship of God, the Christian life and vocation, ministry and preaching, the errors of Roman Catholicism and various cases of conscience.

I am going to concentrate on Perkins book on preaching. It is called *The Art of Prophesying* and it is the first English Puritan work on that subject.[8]

Perkins book: The Art of Prophesying

As far as I can tell, this was the first book on preaching within the three generations of English Puritans in the period 1558 to 1662. *The Art of Prophesying* was first published in Latin in 1592 and translated into English in 1606, four years after Perkins' death. In 1996, The Banner of Truth Trust published a revised edition in modern English.[9] In the twenty-first century the title is likely to convey the idea of a special charismatic gift of prophesying. That is not what Perkins meant. All the Puritan ministers believed that the apostolic period was unique and were cessationists. That is, they believed that charismatic gifts of tongues and prophesying direct from God had ceased and that churches are to be built up mainly through preaching and teaching. Perkins took prophesying to mean the declaration of the Word of God through preaching. He also took it to mean praying on behalf of the congrega-

---

7   Beeke and Pederson, *Meet the Puritans*, 475.

8   William Perkins, *The Arte of Prophesying: Or, A Treatise Concerning the Sacred and Onely True Manner and Methode of Preaching* (London: Felix Kyngston, 1607).

9   William Perkins, *The Art of Prophesying and the Calling of the Ministry* (1996; reprint, Edinburgh: The Banner of Truth Trust, 2011).

tion. It is the norm to understand a prophet to be one who speaks to the people *from* God and a priest is one who prays *to* God on behalf of the people. Believers are all priests in the sense that they pray to God for each other. This difference is really one of minor importance. Perkins included public prayer in the remit of the pastor as he desired that the public prayer be of the highest order. He suggested that the public prayer be taken by the pastor or by a leader or officer in the church who was spiritually equipped for that responsibility. He advocated that public prayer should begin with confession of sin. He summarizes as follows: "There are three elements in praying: (i) Carefully thinking about appropriate content in prayer; (ii) Setting the themes in an appropriate order; (iii) Expressing the prayer so that it is made in public in a way that is edifying for the congregation."[10]

Helpful guidelines for pastors

In *The Art of Prophesying*, Perkins proceeds from the general to the particular. He begins with explaining the nature of the Bible as the Word of God. He outlines the canon of Scripture. Perkins explains the principles for expounding Scripture. For instance, he addresses the subject of the physical body of Christ, which is just as relevant today as it was then since it is a subject that continues to divide Protestants from Roman Catholics.

How do we understand the words, "This is my body which is broken for you" (1 Corinthians 11:24). Various interpretations have been given to this statement including: the bread in the communion is actually the body of Christ, becoming so by conversion (the Roman Catholic view); or that the body of Christ is in, under or with the bread (the Lutheran view). But to expound these words in either of these senses would be to disagree with a fundamental article of the faith—Christ "ascended into heaven"—and also with the nature of the sacrament, as a memorial of the absent body of Christ. Consequently another interpretation must be sought.

Another different interpretation is that in this context the bread is a sign of the body. In this case the figure of speech known as metonymy is being employed—the name of one thing is used

---

10 Perkins, *Arte of Prophesying*, 147.

for something else which is related to it. This is an appropriate exposition for the following reasons: First of all, it agrees with the analogy of faith in two ways: 1. 'He ascended into heaven;' he was taken up locally and visibly from the earth into heaven. Consequently his body is not to be received with the mouth at the communion, but by faith apprehending it in heaven. 2. He was 'born of the virgin Mary;' Christ had a true and natural body which was long, broad, firm, and seated and circumscribed in one particular place. If this is so, the bread in the Supper cannot be his actual body but must be only a sign or pledge of it.[11]

ON MEMORIZING THE SERMON

The subject of preparation, the writing out of a sermon and whether the preacher should preach from rough notes or read his manuscript is often discussed. Perkins was clearly in favour of the discipline of writing out material but once the preparation was made he was in favour of freedom, "There is no need to be overly anxious about the precise words we will use. As Horace says, words 'will not unwillingly follow the matter that is premeditated.'"[12] Perkins was clearly in favour of using a rough outline and proceeding extempore from there for the sake of gaining Spirit-given unction. He warns against the preacher losing his way in a discourse, which is embarrassing for both preacher and congregation. When men start off in the ministry they find it needful to write out their materials and then follow an outline but, with more experience and a trained memory, they are able freely to preach with just a rough outline. Very few have the confidence and an able memory so as to discard notes altogether and remember a fully structured outline of exposition and application.

ON AVOIDING UNNECESSARY CONTROVERSY

In the area of unnessary controversy, Perkins exhorts as follows:

> Reprove only the errors which currently trouble the church. Leave others alone if they lie dead in past history, or they are not relevant to the people, unless you know that spiritual danger may still arise

---

11 Perkins, *Arte of Prophesying*, 48.
12 Perkins, *Arte of Prophesying*, 131.

from them. This is the situation described in Revelation chapter two when the church at Pergamos was warned to beware of the Nicolaitans whose teaching had already influenced some of them.[13]

The necessity of a calling to the ministry

Perkins held firmly to the necessity of a call to the ministry. Over a third of his book is devoted to this call. He opens up the subject by expounding Isaiah 6. The manner in which Perkins divides the text is typical of the Puritans. The spiritual application which follows goes to the very heart of the calling of a pastor. Here is how Perkins hits the mark:

Isaiah's fear and amazement are described in two ways.
1. By two signs: (i) A note of exclamation, "Woe is me." (ii) A note of extreme dejection about himself, "I am undone."
2. By its two causes: (i) He was an unclean man, and dwelt among unclean people. (ii) He had seen the Lord. "So I said: 'Woe is me, for I am undone!'"[14]

Perkins is careful to explain that Isaiah's confession of sin is referring not to some scandalous or outrageous sin but rather general unworthiness felt in the presence of the perfect holiness and majesty of God and suggests that "small fault in other men is a great one in ministers, and what may be to a certain extent pardonable in other men is not so in them."[15]

The exposition runs like this:

The first point to note is the fear and sense of ecstasy into which the Lord drove his holy prophet, not in his anger against him but in his love for him; not as a punishment for his sin, but as an evidence of his further love. For the purpose of God in striking this fear into him was to enable him to be a true prophet, and a suitable messenger for himself.

This may seem to be an unusual course for God to take in order to conform and energize his servant in zeal and courage: to strike

13 Perkins, *Arte of Prophesying*, 123.
14 William Perkins, *Of the Calling of the Ministrie, Two Treatises. Describing the Duties and Dignities of that calling* (London: Thomas Creede, 1606), 16.
15 Perkins, *Of the Calling of the Ministrie*, 18.

him with extreme fear, indeed to astonish and amaze him. Yet it is clear that this is the way the Lord takes. It teaches us that all true ministers, especially those appointed to speak the greatest words in his church, must be first of all marked by a great sense of fear in the consciousness of the greatness. They represent him and bring his message. The more they shrink under the contemplation of God's majesty and their own weakness, the more likely it is that they are truly called of God and appointed for worthy purposes in his church. Anyone who steps into this function without fear puts himself forward, but it is doubtful whether he is called by God as the prophet Isaiah clearly was.

Nor is such fear limited to Isaiah. Whenever God called any of his servants to any great work, he first drove them into this sense of fear and amazement. That is evident in Moses (Exodus 3:11), Jeremiah (Jeremiah 1:6), Paul (Acts 9:5), and others. The reason for this is clear: man's nature is always ready to take too much upon itself. God therefore, in his wisdom, puts a bridle into the corrupt nature of man and stuns him, lest he presume too much and trust himself too much.

In addition, a minister must teach his people to fear and reverence the Lord. But how can he teach others when he had not tied that bond in his own conscience and has never been cast down in admiration of God's glory and majesty?[16]

Perkins concludes with the observation that "if ever you aim to be an instrument of God's glory in saving souls, then at the outset set before your eyes not the honour but the danger of your calling, and 'humble yourself under the mighty hand of God that he may exalt you in due time' (1 Peter 5:6)."[17]

The importance of calling is related to two principal issues, that of perseverance and that of steadfastness in holy living. Isaiah, Jeremiah and Ezekiel were called in a way which impressed indelibly upon them the awesome holiness of God as well as the high nature of their calling. In the face of rebellion and constant resis-

---

16 Perkins, *Of the Calling of the Ministrie*, 16.
17 Perkins, *Of the Calling of the Ministrie*, 17.

tance by the people and paucity of results, these prophets required remarkable perseverance. The glory of God kept them on course. Pastors often have to persevere through lean times when dogged perseverance is required. An absolute assurance of calling to the ministry will keep a pastor on course. Furthermore, a pastor who is always mindful of the glory and holiness of God and is diligent in his disciplines will never fall (2 Peter 1:5–10).

In his exposition of Isaiah's calling, Perkins probes deep into the realm of spiritual experience. "When by the sight and sense of our sins and our misery because of sin, God has driven us out of ourselves so that we find nothing in ourselves but reasons for fear and horror; then he pours the oil of grace and of sweet comfort into our hearts, and refreshes our weary souls with the dew of his mercy."[18] He suggests that, "If we look into the Scriptures we shall find God never called people into the state of grace or to any notable work or function in his church without first humbling them."[19] Further, he asks the question,

Does God bring some great affliction on you? It may be he has some mighty work of grace to do in you, or some great work of mercy to be wrought by you in his church, and is preparing you for it. Learn to say with the holy prophet, "I was mute, I did not open my mouth because it was you who did it" (Psalm 39:9). Although he does not refer to Jeremiah it is that prophet who records his extreme anguish even to saying he would prefer to be dead than alive (Jeremiah 15:10) and at one point suggesting that he would not speak any more in God's name (Jeremiah 20:9).

A call to the ministry must be endorsed by the church. "If the church of God does not recognize your sufficiency, God is not sending you." Perkins goes on to give a timely warning against academic pride,

This doctrine is relevant to all ministers, but particularly for those of us who live in the university. We live as it were in a seminary; many of us are by God's grace to be directed to the ministry,

---

18 Perkins, *Art of Prophesying and Calling to Ministry*, 151.
19 Perkins, *Art of Prophesying and Calling to Ministry*, 151.

as some of us already have been. We have many occasions to be puffed up in self-conceit. We see ourselves grow in age, in degrees, in learning, in honour, in reputation and estimation. To many of us God gives an abundant supply of his gifts. But there are many temptations to allure us to pride and over-inflated opinions of our own value. So let us remember that the goal we aim at is not human or carnal. Since our purpose is to save souls, the weapons of our war must not be carnal ones (2 Corinthians 10:4)—such as pride, vanity and conceit.

Application in preaching

Perkins' emphasis on application in preaching is vital. He proceeds along the lines that the pastor should be sensitive to the spiritual state of all the individual members of the congregation. He explores the effect of the application of the Word to all the individual needs. In the chapter on Christ as chief Shepherd of the sheep who will not allow the bruised reed to be broken, he describes a variety of special needs such as orphans, widows and those struggling with appalling affliction or travelling through desperately difficult times. However, while Christ is compassionate to human suffering of all kinds as illustrated by his healing ten lepers with only one returning to give thanks, suffering does not mean spiritual progress. Suffering may open individuals to spiritual issues but suffering never *guarantees* spiritual awakening or spiritual hunger. Perkins suggests that the pastor/preacher must think and pray his way through the spiritual conditions of his people.

It is nearly always been the case that congregations consist both of believers and unbelievers. In former generations, in countries nominally Christian like England, the proportion of unbelievers would be quite high. Perkins stated that such was the case in the congregations of his time.

In preparing to preach, Perkins evidently thought through and prayed through the issues of application very carefully. There is a danger, particularly with pastors who are diligent in exposition, of spending nearly all their preparation time in producing well-ordered teaching materials while neglecting equally diligent application to the wide variety of individuals before them.

In addressing the subject, Perkins defines application as

the skill by which the doctrine which has been properly drawn from Scripture is handled in ways which are appropriate to the circumstances of the place and time and to the people in the congregation. This is the biblical approach to exposition: "I will feed My flock, and I will make them lie down," says the Lord God. "I will seek what was lost and will bring back what was driven away, bind up the broken and strengthen what was sick" (Ezekiel 34:15,16). "And on some have compassion, making a distinction, but others save with fear, pulling them out of the fire" (Jude 22, 23).[20]

Perkins insists that

the basic principle in application is to know whether the passage is a statement of the law or of the gospel. For when the Word is preached the law and the gospel operate differently. The law exposes the disease of sin and as a side-effect stimulates and stirs it up. But it provides no remedy for it. However, the gospel not only teaches us what is to be done, it also has the power of the Holy Spirit joined to it. When we are regenerated by him we receive the strength we need both to believe the gospel and to do what it commands. The law is, therefore, first in the order of teaching; then comes the gospel.[21]

In this emphasis, Perkins is typical of Puritan preachers. In the cameo of his life there was that comment about Perkins' preaching, "The sermons seemed to be 'all law and all gospel, all cordials and all corrosives, as the different necessities of people apprehended' them."[22] If there is no sense of need and no conviction of sin there will never be any progress. Christ came not to call the righteous but sinners to repentance. What is sin? Sin is the transgression of the law. Jesus promised that the Holy Spirit would convince the world of sin, righ-

---

20 Perkins, *Arte of Prophecying*, 99–100.
21 Perkins, *Of the Calling of the Ministrie*, 100.
22 Fuller, *Abel Redevivus*, 148.

teousness and judgement. The gospel is irrelevant if these subjects are not preached. I must feel my need of Christ otherwise I will not seek him.

Perkins writes,

> A statement of the law indicates the need for perfect inherent righteousness, of eternal life given through the works of the law, of the sins which are contrary to the law and the curse that is due them. "For as many as are of the works of the law are under the curse; as it is written, 'Cursed is everyone who does not continue in all things which are written in the book of the law, to do them.'" "But that no one is justified by the law in the sight of God is evident, for the just shall live by faith" (Galatians 3:10). "Brood of vipers, who warned you to flee from the wrath to come.... And even now the axe is laid at the root of the trees. Therefore every tree that does not bear good fruit is cut down and thrown into the fire" (Matthew 3:7,10). By contrast, a statement of the gospel speaks of Christ and his benefits, and of faith being fruitful in good works. For example, "For God so loved the world that he gave His only begotten Son, that whoever believes in Him should not perish but have everlasting life" (John 3:16).[23]

For Perkins application consisted not only of an astute awareness of law and gospel, the law to convict and the gospel to heal, but preparation in preaching was to think about and pray about and prepare to preach to a variety of people with differing needs.

Categories of hearers

Perkins outlined the different kinds of hearers as follows:

1. Those who are unbelievers and are both ignorant and unteachable. These must first be prepared to receive the doctrine of the Word. Jehoshaphat sent Levites throughout the cities of Judah to teach the people, and to draw them away from idolatry (2 Chronicles 17:9). This preparation should be partly by discussing or reasoning with them, in order to become aware of

---

23 Perkins, *Arte of Prophecying*, 100–101.

their attitude and disposition, and partly by reproving any obvious sin, so that their consciences may be aroused and touched with fear and they may become teachable (see Acts 9:3–5; 16:27–31; 17:17; 17:22–24).

When there is some hope that they have become teachable and prepared, the message of God is to be given to them, usually in basic terms concentrating on general points (as, for example, Paul at Athens, Acts 17:30–31). If there is no positive response to such teaching, then it should be explained in a more detailed way. But if they remain unteachable and there is no real hope of winning them, they should be simply be left (Proverbs 9:8; Matthew 7:6; Acts 19:9).

2. Those who are teachable, but ignorant. We should instruct such people by means of a catechism (cf. Luke 1:4; Acts 18:25–26). A catechism is a brief explanation of the foundational teaching of the Christian faith given in the form of questions and answers. This helps both the understanding and the memory. The content of a catechism, therefore, should be the fundamentals of the Christian faith, a summary of its basic principles (Hebrews 5:12).

He continues:

Here it is important to recognize the difference between "milk" and "strong meat." These categories refer to the same truth; the difference between them lies in the manner and style of the teaching. "Milk" is a brief, plain and general explanation of the principles of the faith: that we must believe in one God, and in three persons, Father, Son and Holy Spirit; that we must rely only upon the grace of God in Christ; that we ought to believe in the forgiveness of sins; and when we are taught that we ought to repent, to abstain from evil and to do good.

"Strong meat", on the other hand, is a detailed, full, illuminating and clear handling of the doctrines of faith. It includes careful and lucid exposition of man before the Fall, the Fall, original and actual sin, human guilt, free-will; the mysteries of the Trinity, the two natures of Christ, their union in one person, the office of Christ as Mediator, the imputation of righteousness; faith, grace, and the use of the law. "Milk must be set before babes, that is those who are immature or weak in knowledge; strong meat should be given to those who are more mature, that is to those who are better instructed (1 Corinthians 3:1–2; Hebrews 5:13).

3. There are those who have knowledge, but have never been humbled. Here we need to see the foundation of repentance stirred up in what Paul calls godly sorrow (1 Corinthians 7:8–10). Godly sorrow is grief for sin simply because it is sin. To stir up this affection, the ministry of the law is necessary. This may give birth to a real sense of contrition in the heart, or to terror in the conscience. Although this is not wholesome and profitable on its own, it provides a necessary remedy for subduing sinful stubbornness, and for preparing the mind to become teachable.

   In order to arouse this legal sorrow it is appropriate to use some choice section of the law, which may reprove any obvious sin in those who have not yet been humbled. Sorrow for and repentance from even one sin is in substance repentance for all sin (Psalm 32:5; Acts 2:23; 8:22).

   Further, if someone who is afflicted with the cross and with outward tragedies has only a worldly sorrow—that is if he does not mourn for sin as sin, but only for the punishment of sin—he is not to be given immediate comfort. Such sorrow must first be transformed into godly sorrow. Think about the analogy of medical healing. If a man's life is in danger because of the amount of blood he is losing from a nose-bleed, his physicians may prescribe that blood be let out of his arm, or from some other suitable place, in order to staunch the flow of blood from his nose. The motive, of course, is to save someone who is in danger of death.

   Then let the gospel be preached in such a way that the Holy Spirit effectually works salvation. For in renewing men so that they may begin to will and to do what is pleasing to God, the Spirit really and truly produces in them godly sorrow and repentance to salvation.

To the hard-hearted the law must be stressed, and its curse stated clearly along with its threats. The difficulty of obtaining deliverance until people are pricked in their heart should also be taught (Matthew 3:7; 19:16–17; 23:13,33). But when the beginning of genuine sorrow appears, they are to be comforted with the gospel.

4. Those who have already been humbled. Here we must carefully consider whether the humbling that has already taken place is complete and sound or only just begun and still light and superficial. It is important that people do not receive comfort sooner than is appropriate. If they do they may become hardened in the same way iron which has been cast into the furnace becomes exceptionally hard when it is cold.

Here are some guidelines for dealing with those who are partially humbled. Expound the law to them carefully tempered with the gospel, so that being terrified by their sins and the judgement of God they may at the same time find comfort in the gospel (Genesis 3:9–15; 2 Samuel 12; Acts 8:20–23). Nathan gives us an example here. He recalled David to an awareness of his true condition through a parable, and then pronounced him pardoned when his repentance was certain.

In this was faith and repentance and the comforts of the gospel ought to be taught and offered to those who have been fully humbled (Matthew 9:13; Luke 4:18; Acts 2:37–38).

5. Those who already believe. We must teach them:

(i) The gospel: the biblical teaching on justification, sanctification and perseverance.
(ii) The law: but as it applies to those who are no longer under its curse, so that they may be taught how to bear the fruit of a new obedience in keeping with their repentance (Romans 8:1; 1 Timothy 1:9). Here Paul's teaching in Romans serves as a model.

Although someone who is righteous and holy in the sight of God should not be threatened with the curse of the law, their remaining sin should still be stressed. As a father may show his sons what he will do as punishment to induce a proper sense of fear of doing wrong, so meditation on the curse of the law should be frequently encouraged in true believers, to discourage abusing the mercy of God by sinful living, and to increase humility. Our sanctification is partial as yet. In order that the remnants of sin may be destroyed, we must always begin with meditation on the law, and with a sense of our sin, in order to be brought to rest in the gospel.

6. Those who have fallen back. Some may have partly departed from the state of grace, either in faith or in lifestyle. Failure in faith is either in the knowledge of the doctrine of the gospel or in apprehending Christ. Failure in knowledge involves declining into error, whether in a secondary or fundamental doctrine. In this situation the specific doctrine which counteracts their error should be expounded and taught. We need to stress the importance to them, along with the doctrine of repentance. But we must do this with a brotherly affection, as Paul says in Galatians 6:1 (cf. 2 Timothy 2:25).

A fall from apprehending Christ leads to despair. In order to restore such we need to diagnose their condition and then prescribe the remedy. We must analyse either the cause of their temptation or their condition. The diagnosis of the cause can be done appropriately by confession (cf. James 5:17). But to prevent such a confession being turned into an instrument of torture it must be governed by these principles:

(i) It ought to be done freely and not under any compulsion. Salvation does not depend on it.
(ii) It must not be a confession of all sins, but only of those which eat at the conscience and may lead to even greater spiritual danger if they are not dealt with.
(iii) Such confession should chiefly be made to pastors, but with the understanding that it may be confidentially shared with other reliable men in the church.

The diagnosis of a person's spiritual status involves investigating whether they are under the law or under grace. In order to clarify this, we must probe and question to discover from them whether they are displeased with themselves because they have displeased God? Do they hate sin as sin? This is the foundation of the repentance which brings salvation. Then, secondly, we must ask whether they have or feel in their heart a desire to be reconciled with God. This is the groundwork for a living faith.

When the diagnosis is complete, the remedy must be prescribed and applied from the gospel....

(i) That their sin is pardonable
(ii) That the promises of grace are made generally to all who believe. They are not made to specific individuals; they therefore exclude no one.
(iii) That the will to believe is itself faith (Psalm 145:19; Revelation 21:6)
(iv) That sin does not abolish grace but rather (since God turns everything to the good of those who are his) can lead to further illustrations of it.
(v) That in this fallen and sinful world, all of God's works are done by means which are contrary to him![24]

I have quoted Perkins at length to illustrate the thoroughness of his practice with regard to application.

His book, *The Art of Prophesying*, ends on positive notes of encouragement. Subsequent generations of preachers suffered intensely. Soon after Perkins death, a number of pastors resolved to sail for New England in search of freedom from persecution. Following the Great Ejection of 1662 came a time of severe suffering for about 2,000 mostly Puritan ministers who were ejected from the Established Church. Much comfort would be administered to these pastors through Perkins' books, especially in such words as these:

If he sends them he will defend and protect them, so that not even one of their hairs is able to perish. If he sends them he will provide for them and reward them adequately. He will honor them in the

---

24 Perkins, *Arte of Prophecying*, 102ff.

heart of his own people and magnify them in the faces of their enemies. And lastly, if he sends them he will pay their wages; an eternal weight of comfort here and of glory in heaven.[25]

He concludes with the text from Daniel 12:3:

Those who are wise shall shine
  Like the brightness of the firmament,
And those who turn many to righteousness,
  Like the stars for ever and ever.

---

25 Perkins, *Of the Calling of the Ministrie*, 44.

REFORMATION · PURITAN

Poetry and piety: John Owen, Faithful Teate and communion with God
By Crawford Gribben

SPIRITUALITY, THE POET and historian of piety Michael Haykin has observed, lay at the "very core" of English Puritanism, and John Owen (1616–1683), he has elsewhere continued, was a "marvellous exemplar" of the concern for authentic spiritual experience that lay at the heart of so much of the movement's thinking.[1] Haykin's identification of the importance of these subjects reflects their recent move from the periphery to the centre of the study of early modern English religion. It is particularly evident that scholarly interest in Owen is accelerating as we approach the four-hundredth anniversary of his birth.

Much of this recent work has focused on Owen's ideas. These studies have come to reflect the concern of Richard A. Muller, and others, to take seriously the intellectual claims of the writers of post-Reformation

---

1 On the significance of Puritan spirituality, see Michael A.G. Haykin ed., "To Honour God": The spirituality of Oliver Cromwell, Classics of Reformed Spirituality (Dundas: Joshua Press, 1999), 14. Haykin has expanded upon this comment in "'Drawn nigh unto my soul': English Baptist piety and the means of grace in the seventeenth and eighteenth centuries," The Southern Baptist Journal of Theology 10, no. 4 (Winter 2006): 54–73. On the significance of Owen, see Michael A.G. Haykin, "The Calvin of England: Some aspects of the life of John Owen (1616–1683) and his teaching on Biblical piety," Reformed Baptist Theological Review 1, no. 2 (2004): 169–183.

Reformed dogma.[2] Thus a spate of publications has considered Owen as a high Calvinist theologian, presenting detailed accounts of his theology proper, Christology, soteriology, ecclesiology and eschatology.[3] A much smaller body of work has considered his role as preacher to the Long Parliament, as chaplain to the Cromwellian invasions of Ireland and Scotland, as dean of Christ Church, Oxford, as vice-chancellor of the University of Oxford, as architect of the Cromwellian religious settlement, as defender of the toleration of Dissenters after the Restoration and the author of over eight million words of theological polemic and biblical commentary.[4] Thorough as they may be, many of these recent studies seem oddly disinterested in the historical contingencies of Owen's thought, and seem uninfluenced by the broader concern in contemporary intellectual history, often influenced by Quentin Skinner, to locate ideas in social and cultural spaces.[5] A

---

2   Owen is a significant figure in the tradition represented in Richard A. Muller, *Post-Reformation Reformed Dogmatics: The Rise and Development of Reformed Orthodoxy, ca. 1520 to ca. 1725*, 4 vols. (Grand Rapids: Baker Academic, 2003).

3   See, for example, Sinclair B. Ferguson, *John Owen on the Christian Life* (Edinburgh: The Banner of Truth Trust, 1987); Steve Griffiths, *Redeem the Time: Sin in the Writings of John Owen* (Fearn, Ross-shire: Mentor, 2001); Richard W. Daniels, *The Christology of John Owen* (Grand Rapids: Reformed Heritage Books, 2004); Brian K. Kay, *Trinitarian Spirituality: John Owen and the Doctrine of God in Western Devotion*, Studies in Christian History and Thought (Milton Keynes: Paternoster, 2007); Alan Spence, *Incarnation and Inspiration: John Owen and the Coherence of Christology* (London: T & T Clark, 2007); Lee Gatiss, *From Life's First Cry: John Owen on Infant Baptism and Infant Salvation*, St. Antholin's Lecture 2008 (London: Latimer Trust, 2008); material in Kelly M. Kapic and Mark Jones ed., *The Ashgate Research Companion to John Owen's Theology* (Aldershot: Ashgate, 2012); and Christopher Cleveland, *Thomism in John Owen* (Aldershot: Ashgate, 2013).

4   See, for example, Crawford Gribben, "Apocalyptic, polemic and print culture in the Cromwellian invasion of Scotland," *Literature & History* (forthcoming); Crawford Gribben, "John Owen, Renaissance man? The evidence of Edward Millington's *Bibliotheca Oweniana* (1684)," *Westminster Theological Journal* 72, no. 2 (2010): 321–332, reprinted in Kapic and Jones ed., *The Ashgate Research Companion to John Owen's Theology*, 97–109.

5   The approach outlined by Quentin Skinner has been usefully applied to the study of Owen in, among others, Barry H. Howson, "The Puritan Hermeneutics of John Owen: A Recommendation," *Westminster Theological Journal* 63, no. 2 (2001): 351–376; Kelly M. Kapic, *Communion with God: The Divine and the Human in the Theology of John Owen* (Grand Rapids: Baker Academic, 2007); and Tim Cooper, *John Owen, Richard Baxter, and the Formation of Nonconformity* (Aldershot: Ashgate, 2011).

"social history of ideas" would offer new resources to a great deal of modern Owen scholarship, and would call attention to the changing contexts in which Owen's thought was articulated, to the theological and political debates which provoked his interventions, and to the broader set of cultural trends in which his work was invested. And, perhaps most surprisingly, it would allow scholars to consider Owen's interest in, and his influence upon, poetry.

Owen's interest in classical and contemporary poetry does not appear to have been noticed by many of his readers. And yet Owen may have been the Reformed scholastic theologian with the greatest interest in and enthusiasm for the genre. He appears to have read widely in poetry. His early theological work is particularly interested in quoting classical writers, from *Salus Electorum, Sanguis Jesu; or the death of death in the death of Christ* (1648) to *Theologoumena Pantodapa* (1661); in the latter text he often takes the claims of classical writers to inspiration at face value, recognizing their articulation of demonic voices. *Bibliotheca Oweniana* (1684), the auction catalogue of what was purported to be the contents of Owen's library, cannot be used without qualification as a guide to his ownership of consumption of books, but it does suggest that Owen had extensive interests in contemporary English verse.[6] The catalogue represents his library as including a volume of works by Edmund Spenser, which included both *The Faerie Queene* and *The Shepheardes Calender* (1613); the works of Fulke Greville, the Lord Brooke (1633); George Herbert's *The Temple* (1633), as well as *Herbert's Remains, or, Sundry Pieces of that Sweet Singer of the Temple, Mr George Herbert* (1652); poems by Edmund Waller (1645); Sir John Suckling's *Fragmenta aurea*, a "Collection of … Incomparable pieces" (1646); Henry More's *Philosophical Poems of the Soul* (1647); Sir William D'Avenant's *Gondibert an Heroick Poem* (1651); John Milton's *Paradise Lost* (1667); the works of Abraham Cowley (third edition, 1672); *Poems by the most Deservedly Admired Mrs. Katherine Philips, the Matchless Orinda* (1678); and *Poems and Songs* by Thomas Flatman (third edition, 1682).

Owen appears to have been a collector of those writers who, with the exception of Flatman, would go on to enjoy greatest prestige in the emerging canon of English literature. But there are many sur-

---

6 Gribben, "John Owen, Renaissance man?" *passim.*

prises in this list of publications. A number of the writers were vocal critics of the political and religious values which Owen endorsed: D'Avenant, Cowley, Suckling and Waller were each committed royalists, and Milton had attacked Owen in his sonnet to Oliver Cromwell. And there are surprising gaps: Owen appears not to have owned anything by the royalist soldier and courtier Richard Lovelace (1617–1657), though around 1642 he had served as chaplain in the household of Anne Lovelace, a relative of the poet and the dedicatee of his *Lucasta* (1649).

In fact, Owen's connection with the Lovelace family had first taught him the dangers of civil war, and the ability of poetry to refer beyond the published page. When his patron joined the Royalist army, Owen left the Lovelace household, moved to London, and appears to have been staying in the household of Sir Edward Scot in April 1642 when Richard Lovelace led as many as 500 supporters on a march from Blackheath to London, in order to present a petition to the House of Commons. The rising, which Owen later described as a "horrid insurrection of a rude, godless multitude," resulted in Richard Lovelace's imprisonment in the Tower, as well as some of the finest writing of the seventeenth century: for "Stone Walls doe not a Prison make, / Nor Iron bars a Cage."[7]

Of course, we can know nothing of Owen's response to this collection of poetic material. His personal acquaintance with Andrew Marvell and John Bunyan provides no evidence that he was aware of their poetry, much of which he might have found more conducive to his political and religious commitments. But the evidence of his library's auction catalogue does suggest that Owen was an enthusiastic consumer of a wide range of contemporary verse.

---

7   Sarah Gibbard Cook, "A political biography of a Religious Independent John Owen, 1616-83" (Ph.D. dissertation, Harvard University, 1972), 40; Raymond A. Anselment, "Lovelace, Richard (1617–1657)," *Oxford Dictionary of National Biography*, Oxford University Press, 2004; online ed., January 2010 (http://www.oxforddnb.com/view/article/17056; accessed September 21, 2011). It is interesting that Andrew Marvell refers to this event in his commendatory poem to Richard Lovelace's *Lucasta*, though he later comes to Owen's side. John Owen, *The Works of John Owen*, ed. William Goold, 24 vols. (London: Johnstone and Hunter, 1850–1853), 13:3; Richard Lovelace, *Lucasta* (1649), 98.

Owen was also a writer of poetry.[8] In 1654, his poem "Ad Protec-torem" opened *Musarum Oxoniensium* (1654), an anthology of poems praising Cromwell on his successes in the Dutch wars and on his election as Protector.[9] The anthology was continuing a tradition in the English and Irish universities, stretching back over several decades, of publishing volumes of poetry to praise or commemorate important institutional patrons, and having "Ad Protectorem" open the work was signalling the obligations of the vice-chancellor to the chancellor of the University of Oxford. *Musarum Oxoniensium* included poetry in Latin, Greek and Hebrew by a number of staff and students in the university, including the young John Locke.[10] But Owen's contribution may have been more nuanced than we might expect. A number of literary critics have recently commented on the suggestive ambiguity of its adulation of the Proctector,[11] supporting Laura Lunger Knopper's claim that "in the very act of representing Cromwell, print made Cromwell vulnerable to misrepresentation and rejection."[12] Whatever the nuance of his own contribution, it appears that Owen also influ-enced one of the most important long poems of the Cromwellian period, published in the immediate aftermath of Owen's ground-breaking account, *Of communion with God the Father, Sonne, and Holy Ghost, each person distinctly in love, grace, and consolation, or, The saints fellowship with the Father, Sonne, and Holy Ghost* (1657).

As this literary relationship suggests, Owen, man of many parts, was a significant figure in the evolution of Western spirituality, and *Of*

---

8   His work should be distinguished from that of the Roman Catholic poet of the same name; D.K. Money, 'Owen, John (1563/4–1622?)', *Oxford Dictionary of National Biography*, Oxford University Press, 2004 (http://www.oxforddnb.com/view/article/21013; accessed January 10, 2013); *Ioannis Audoeni epigrammatum*, ed. John R.C. Martyn, 2 vols. (Leiden: Brill, 1976).

9   Anonymous, *Musarum Oxoniensium* (1654), 1.

10 *Musarum Oxoniensium*, 45.

11 Edward Holberton, *Poetry and the Cromwellian Protectorate: Culture, Politics and Institutions* (Oxford: Oxford University Press, 2008), 61–86; Gráinne McLaughlin, "The idolater John Owen? Linguistic hegemony in Cromwell's Oxford" in Richard Kirwan, ed., *Scholarly Self-Fashioning and Community in the Early Modern University* (Aldershot: Ashgate, 2013), 145–166.

12 Laura Lunger Knoppers, *Constructing Cromwell: Ceremony, Portrait, and Print, 1645–1661* (Cambridge: Cambridge University Press, 2000), 5.

communion with God has become one of his best known and most frequently cited works, being frequently reprinted and occasionally popularized in "modern English."[13] Among theologians, Owen is now widely regarded for his contribution to Trinitarian thought.[14] But in a great deal of the scholarship that has established this reputation, as well as in scholarship on the development of Western spirituality, the significance of his work on the believer's experience of the Trinity has perhaps been underplayed. Haykin has explored to very good effect the innovations proposed in Owen's *PNEUMATOLOGIA, or, a discourse concerning the Holy Spirit* (1676): he uses Owen's famous claim that "I know not any who ever went before me in this design of representing the whole economy of the Holy Spirit" to open up the breadth of his engagement with late medieval and early modern pneumatology.[15] But it was *Of communion with God* (1657)—an earlier text—that first attempted to cultivate a devotional revolution among English Puritans.

The character and effect of this devotional revolution—and especially its brief duration—has not been widely noticed by scholars of Owen's work. This oversight, as we noted above, can be explained by the fact that a great deal of scholarship on Owen's theology has advanced without sufficient regard for its early modern contexts and, as we will see, with undue regard for the accuracy of the nineteenth-century edition prepared by William H. Goold (1850–1855). Building on Haykin's contribution to recent Owen scholarship, this chapter will argue that the nature and effect of Owen's intervention in the

---

13 See, for recent editions of the text, John Owen, *Communion with God*, ed. R.J.K. Law (Edinburgh: The Banner of Truth Trust, 1991), and John Owen, *Communion with the Triune God*, ed. Kelly M. Kapic and Justin Taylor (Wheaton: Crossway, 2007); and, more generally, on the text's significance in the revival of Owen's spirituality, Reginald Kirby, *The Threefold Bond: A study of John Owen's Of the Communion with God the Father, God the Son and God the Holy Spirit* (London: Marshall, Morgan and Scott, [1936]); Ferguson, *John Owen on the Christian Life*, 74–98; David M. King, "The Affective Spirituality of John Owen," *Evangelical Quarterly* 68 (1996): 223–233; Haykin, "The Calvin of England"; Kapic, *Communion with God*; and Kay, *Trinitarian Spirituality*.

14 Carl R. Trueman, *The Claims of Truth: John Owen's Trinitarian Theology* (Carlisle: Paternoster, 1998); Daniels, *The Christology of John Owen*; Carl R. Trueman, *John Owen: Reformed Catholic, Renaissance Man* (Aldershot: Ashgate, 2007); Spence, *Incarnation and Inspiration*; Cleveland, *Thomism in John Owen*; see also the essays in Robert W. Oliver ed., *John Owen: The Man and his Theology* (Phillipsburg: Presbyterian & Reformed, 2002).

15 Owen, *Works*, 3:7; Haykin, "The Calvin of England," 169–183.

conceptual development of Western spirituality can be seen in one of the most important and most recently recovered poems from the period. Owen does not appear to have owned a copy of *Ter Tria* (1658), by Faithful Teate (1626–1666), an Irish Independent pastor then ministering in England, and neither does the poem admit to its being influenced by him. Nevertheless, the form and content of *Ter Tria* reflect the ideological legacy of Owen's treatise on communion with God, while also suggesting reasons why the devotional revolution prompted by Owen's treatise proved to be so short-lived.[16]

Of communion with God

John Owen published *Of communion with God* (1657) shortly before he ended his term as vice-chancellor of the University of Oxford. The book itself, he claimed in his preface, was based on sermons that he had preached to undergraduates in St Mary's, Oxford, in 1651, which he had promised to publish, but which he had preferred to improve.[17] There were certainly good reasons for his delay. The influence of the Independent party had risen and fallen through the middle 1650s, and Owen's public fortunes had risen and fallen accordingly. His colleagues in the Independent party, with others committed to political and theological principles, were now often regarded as a "sorry company of seditious, factious persons."[18] (The judgement was perhaps not unreasonable, as rumours of Owen's involvement in the collapse of the Richard Cromwell administration would later suggest). By the middle part of the decade, Trinitarian theology had become thoroughly politicized, with the effort to clamp down upon the tiny Socinian party demanding substantial government resources, as well as the large amount of Owen's time required for the production of such texts as

---

16 *Ter Tria* has not received a great deal of critical attention. For a recent discussion, see Angelina Lynch, "To 'truck for trade with darksome things': Faithful Teate's 'Epithalamium' (1655) and Cromwell's 'Western Design,'" *Early Modern Literary Studies* 14, no. 3 (2009): 1–32 (http://purl.oclc.org/emls/14-3/Lyncteat.html; accessed January 17, 2013); Crawford Gribben, "English poetry in Cromwellian Ireland," *The Seventeenth Century* 25, no. 2 (2010): 281–299; Aisling Byrne, "Faithful Teate's *Ter Tria* as an influence on Edward Taylor," *Notes and Queries* 59, no. 2 (2012): 206–209.

17 Owen, *Works*, 2:2–3; Cook, "A political biography," 240–241.

18 Owen, *Works*, 2:38.

Vindicae Evangelicae (1655).[19] In the summer of 1657, when not engaged in university business, and with the wider political environment turning slowly but surely against him, Owen spent much of his free time responding to an attack made on his earlier study *Of Schism* (1656) in Daniel Cawdrey's *Independency a Great Schism* (1657). Finding "the spare hours of four or five days" to defend the Independent churches, Owen signed the preface to his response to Cawdrey on July 9 and the preface to his book on communion with God one day later.[20]

Owen's account, *Of communion with God*, lifted his spiritual interests above his responsibility to govern a restless and uneasy university community and to manage its affairs under a government in political decline. The book outlined an experiment in spirituality. Owen, who had spent the previous few years articulating his own and his government's concern at the spread of Socinian ideas, did something which few of his readers would have expected, and which has puzzled later historians. His move, to radically distinguish the operations of the divine persons, was made in the context of the Socinian advance, and could easily be misconstrued as reflecting Socinian influence.[21] For *Of communion with God* drew upon Owen's massive biblical and theological learning to expand upon the Western Trinitarian consensus by arguing that Christians could and should cultivate distinct relationships with each of the divine persons. Brian Kay has correctly argued that Owen's language "exploited underdeveloped and latent allowances in the tradition" even as it "stretched the limits of then current Augustinian assumptions about the unity of the Godhead."[22] But Owen placed this keen theological intervention at the centre of the devotional revolution he hoped to lead. He drew upon the famous opening of Calvin's *Institutes* (1559) to reflect upon the character of the theological task: "the sum of all true wisdom and knowledge" could, he argued, "be reduced to these three heads": "the knowledge of God, his nature and his properties," "the knowledge of ourselves in reference to the will of God

---

19 Philip Dixon, *Nice and Hot Disputes: The Doctrine of the Trinity in the Seventeenth Century* (London: T & T Clark, 2003), 34–65; Sarah Mortimer, *Reason and Religion in the English Revolution: The Challenge of Socinianism* (Cambridge: Cambridge University Press, 2010), 196–212.

20 Owen, *Works*, 2:3; 13:209–210, 267.

21 Mortimer, *Reason and Religion in the English Revolution*, passim.

22 Kay, *Trinitarian Spirituality*, 6–7.

concerning us," and, he added, "skill to walk in communion with God."[23]

The third emphasis was vital to Owen's project. The scholastic bent of much mid-seventeenth century preaching and writing was not producing the godliness that Owen believed it should—and Owen was not uncritical of the theological tradition in which he participated. He identified in his peers a deficient spirituality, an expectation of Christian life that was insufficiently interested in spiritual experience. Of course, he assumed, unregenerate persons who can think of God as "hard, austere, severe, almost implacable, and fierce,"[24] cannot be expected to "abide with God in spiritual meditations," for they "fix their thoughts only on his terrible majesty, severity and greatness; and so their spirits are not endeared."[25] But Owen feared that the situation was not much better among believers. "How few of the saints are experimentally acquainted with this privilege of holding immediate communion with the Father in love," he lamented.[26] Even "saints" were "afraid to have good thoughts of God. They think it a boldness to eye God as good, gracious, tender, kind, loving."[27] Owen believed that a fuller grasp of divine revelation would change these opinions: "Would a soul continually eye [God's] everlasting tenderness and compassion, his thoughts of kindness that have been from of old, his present gracious acceptance, it could not bear an hour's absence from him; whereas now, perhaps, it cannot watch with him one hour."[28]

Owen's discussion of "skill to walk in communion with God" built upon his presuppositions about "the knowledge of God, his nature and his properties" and "the knowledge of ourselves in reference to the will of God concerning us"—as well as his interest in poetry.[29] He was quick to note the redemptive-historical particularity of his theme: "By nature, since the entrance of sin, no man hath any communion with God," he insisted, so that "this communion and fellowship with God is not in express terms mentioned in the Old Testament. The thing itself is found there; but the clear light of it, and the boldness of faith

---

23 Owen, *Works*, 2:80.

24 Owen, *Works*, 2:35.

25 Owen, *Works*, 2:32.

26 Owen, *Works*, 2:32.

27 Owen, *Works*, 2:35.

28 Owen, *Works*, 2:32.

29 Owen, *Works*, 2:80.

in it, is discovered in the gospel, and by the Spirit administered therein."[30] The specifically new covenant character of the Christian experience of communion with God was highlighted in the roles Owen identified in its cultivation for Jesus Christ and the Holy Spirit. This new covenant spirituality was necessarily and distinctively Trinitarian. But it was Trinitarian in a unique sense, as we have noticed, and decidedly Christological. Owen insisted that Jesus Christ was the mediator who made possible the believer's communion with God.[31] He defined "communion" as

> the mutual communication of such good things as wherein the persons holding the communion are delighted, bottomed upon some union between them…. Our communion, then, with God consisteth in his communication of himself unto us, with our returnal unto him of that which he requireth and accepteth, flowing from that union which in Jesus Christ we have with him.[32]

Borrowing an analogy frequently employed by medieval mystics, Owen described Jesus Christ as the "beam" and the "stream" of the "love of the Father…wherein though actually all our light, our refreshment lies, yet by him we are led to the fountain, the sun of eternal love itself."[33] The trope insisted that the Son's incarnation was central to the establishing of the believer's communion with the triune God: for had Christ "not been man, he could not have suffered;—had he not been God, his suffering could not have availed either himself or us,—he had not satisfied; the suffering of a mere man could not bear any proportion to that which in any respect was infinite."[34] The work of Christ was key to the illustration of the new revelation of divine mercy in the administration of the new covenant: "Had not God set forth the Lord Christ, all the angels in heaven and men on earth could not have apprehended that there had been any such thing in the nature of God

---

30 Owen, *Works*, 2:6.

31 Daniels, *Christology of John Owen*, 499–514.

32 Owen, *Works*, 2:8.

33 Owen, *Works*, 2:23.

34 Owen, *Works*, 2:67.

as this grace of pardoning mercy."[35] And this Christological focus inspires some of the most evocative language in Owen's extraordinary literary corpus:

> To see, indeed, a world made good and beautiful, wrapped up in wrath and curses, clothed with thorns and briers; to see the whole beautiful creation made subject to vanity, given up to the bondage of corruption; to hear it groan in pain under that burden; to consider legions of angels, most glorious and immortal creatures, cast down into hell, bound with chains of darkness, and reserved for a more dreadful judgment for one sin; to view the ocean of the blood of souls spilt to eternity on this account,—will give some insight into this thing. But what is all this to that view of it which may be had by a spiritual eye in the Lord Christ? All these things are worms, and of no value in comparison of him. To see him who is the wisdom of God, and the power of God, always beloved of the Father; to see him, I say, fear, and tremble, and bow, and sweat, and pray, and die; to see him lifted up upon the cross, the earth trembling under him, as if unable to bear his weight; and the heavens darkened over him, as if shut against his cry; and himself hanging between both, as if refused by both; and all this because our sins did meet upon him;—this of all things doth most abundantly manifest the severity of God's vindictive justice. Here, or nowhere, is it to be learned.[36]

While a number of scholars have published monographs on Owen's Christology, they have paid more attention to the content than the form of his writing.[37] Yet there was more than a vein of poetry running through Owen's imaginative and pious response to the mercy of God as revealed in the gospel of Jesus Christ.

Owen's inclination to the poetic was not only reflected in his response to the gospel—for the argument in *Of communion with God* was also developed on his reading of poetry. Owen established his

---

35 Owen, *Works*, 2:83.

36 Owen, *Works*, 2:85.

37 See insightful work by Daniels, *Christology of John Owen*; Kay, *Trinitarian Spirituality*; Spence, *Incarnation and Inspiration*.

novel doctrine of communion with God on the basis of an extended allegorical exegesis of the Song of Solomon. Although an hermeneutically chastened reader, Owen wanted to maximize the potential of his response to the Song, and pushed beyond the conservatism of earlier commentators on the book, arguing that "the allegory is not to be straitened, whilst we keep to the analogy of faith"—that is, that his reading of the Song could make any point that was not contradicted elsewhere in Scripture.[38] And so, as Owen's poetic temperament responded to the inspired poetic text, his exploration of the theme of communion with God prompted outbursts of rhapsodic language and, at times, an almost mystical literary style.[39] "Few can carry up their hearts and minds to this height by faith, as to rest their souls in the love of the Father; they live below it, in the troublesome region of hopes and fears, storms and clouds," he argued. But "all here is serene and quiet...the love of the Father is the only rest of the soul."[40] And when the believing soul identifies its longing for that rest, Owen continued, it "gathers itself from all its wanderings, from all other beloveds, to rest in God alone,—to satiate and content itself in him... and this also with delight."[41]

Of course, this focus on the Song of Solomon, and this method of reading the text, was no novelty in Western spirituality.[42] Owen's novelty was rather his insistence that Christians could have communion with the individual persons of the Trinity. But recent scholarship on Owen has not noticed the radical quality of this claim—perhaps because much of this scholarship continues to access Owen through the Goold edition (1850–1855), and because Goold's edition of the text includes, without explanation or date, Daniel Burgess's preface to the second edition of the work (1700). Goold's decision to use the Burgess preface is significant—and particularly so in light of the largely ahistorical quality of much Owen scholarship. This scholarship, which often evacuates Owen of his contexts, and fails to consult early modern

---

38 Owen, *Works*, 2:72.

39 Dixon, *Nice and Hot Disputes*, 61.

40 Owen, *Works*, 2:23.

41 Owen, *Works*, 2:26.

42 Owen's reading of the Song, and the context of controversy, is discussed in Elizabeth Clarke, *Politics, Religion and the Song of Songs in Seventeenth-Century England* (Basingstoke: Palgrave Macmillan, 2011), 177—181.

editions of his work, has, ironically, missed the innovative quality of this aspect of his thinking. Burgess' preface defends Owen from the charge of novelty, reminding his audience that while "this treatise… is the only one extant upon its great and necessary subject," the "doctrine of distinct communion with the Divine Persons" was not "new-fangled" or "uncouth."[43] Nevertheless, Burgess seemed to struggle to find earlier examples of its use. He referred to recent work by Lewis Stucley, who identified himself as a "soul friend," but is otherwise unknown (1667), and by the biblical annotator Samuel Clarke (1626–1701), in a sermon on 1 John 1:7 which was undated and possibly unpublished, in that it is not recorded in the Short Title Catalogue.[44] The important thing to note is that Burgess defends *Of communion with God* from the charge of novelty by referring the reader to only two texts, at least one of which was published after the first edition of Owen's work. In fact, as we shall see, Burgess missed the opportunity to refer to one of the most immediate and most interesting evidences of Owen's influence upon the Independent party—Faithful Teate's poem on the Trinity, recently recovered, republished and beginning to attract critical interest, *Ter Tria* (1658).[45]

Faithful Teate's Ter Tria (1658)

Owen's often rhapsodic reading of the Song of Solomon perhaps suggests something of the possible appeal of his ideas to the poetic imagination of Faithful Teate. Teate, son of a father of the same name, had been born into a Puritan clerical family in County Cavan, Ireland, around 1626. The family had suffered considerably during the 1641 rebellion. Around October 23, 1641, in unusually cold and snowy weather, Teate senior, having heard of the troubles, prepared to take his family, and £300 in gold and silver, to Dublin. The party was set upon by around 300 rebels, who robbed Teate of his monies and stripped the refugee party of its valuables. The party could find no accommodation:

---

43 Owen, *Works*, 2:4.

44 Lewis Stucley, "To the Reader," in Theophilus Polwheile, *Of quencing the spirit the evill of it, in respect both of its causes and effects* (1667), sig. A3.

45 Faithful Teate, *Ter Tria*, ed. Angelina Lynch (Dublin: Four Courts, 2007).

they & many scores more of their neighbours beeing deprived
both of victuals & Clothes they were *all* enforced to lodge all that
night under a snowie rock, where…my sucking babe had
perished (the mother hauing then noe milk in her brests had not
the lord of his mercie under the rock where they lay provided a
bottle of clabber or buttermilk, which preserved the childs life
till the next day when as they came to Virginia [County Cavan].

Teate's losses were exceptional: "since my comming to towne two of
my foresaid children are dead: myself, my wife & the rest of my children & most of my servants haue been extreamly sick & neare to death,
through this ill usage."[46] The suffering of the refugee party was only
beginning, but the popular press identified the provision of the
buttermilk as the miraculous intervention of an angel, and the family
was represented in a haze of unusual spiritual experience.[47] But the
contingences of the civil wars once again interrupted their life. In
Dublin, Teate senior was appointed vice-provost of Trinity College,
but had to leave the city when it came under Royalist control. His
son fled to England in 1646, was ordained in 1649, graduated from
Cambridge in 1650, and, in 1651, began seven years of pastoral ministry
in Suffolk, during which he published a number of texts and established himself as a writer of devotional prose in the literary culture
of Independents.

Teate's poem, *Ter Tria* (1658), may have been composed as part of
the family's interest in returning to Ireland. If such a strategy did exist,
it was successful: his father had been invited to return to Ireland by
Henry Cromwell in 1657, and two years later the poet was appointed
to a clerical position in Limerick, though it is uncertain whether he
ever took it up.[48] Teate dedicated *Ter Tria* to Henry Cromwell, then
lord deputy of Ireland, and his poem epitomizes the increasingly conservative mood of the Irish administration in appealing for reconciliation between Presbyterians and Independents, and in disavowing the

---

46 Trinity College Dublin, MS 833, fols 061r-062v.

47 Raymond Gillespie, "Imagining angels in early modern Ireland," in Peter Marshall and Alexandra Walsham, ed., *Angels in the Early Modern World* (Cambridge:
Cambridge University Press, 2006), 225–226.

48 "Introduction," in Teate, *Ter Tria*, 14.

appeal of radical theologies.[49] Teate adopted a moderate position on the ecclesiastical and political issues to which he alluded, and, like Owen in his vice-chancellor's oration to the University of Oxford in the same year, identified the dangers of radical opposition to education, condemning those who would "Antichrist in *Law* and *Learning* find."[50] Of course, as we have noted, Teate's interest in Trinitarian theology was politically expedient in the theological climate of the late 1650s, in which public discussion on the nature of the Godhead had become thoroughly politicized. It is therefore significant that he dedicated his poem to Henry Cromwell as *PRÆFECTO SACROSANCIÆ INDIVISÆQ, TRINITATIS CULTOLRI INDIVISO.*[51]

Perhaps unsurprisingly, the little scholarship that has been published on the poem has argued that its purpose is political. But this reading of the poem has been established in the absence of any substantial reflection on the theological import of its content and contexts, a scholarly gap made all the more ironic by the fact that the poem's form and content suggest that its purpose is pietistic. Formally, *Ter Tria* is arranged in three divisions of three themes: sections on the three persons of the Trinity, "Father," "Son" and "Spirit," are followed by sections on the three graces, "Faith," "Hope" and "Love," and these in turn are followed by sections on the three duties, "Prayer," "Hearing" and "Meditation."[52] And in terms of form, *Ter Tria* defends the task of sacred poetry within a Puritan milieu:

Oft have I seen Luxuriant Vicious Wit
A wanton Rape on a fair Muse commit:

At once distaining, by leud Poetrie,
The Writers Paper-sheets, and Readers Eye.

And may I not oblige the thrice three Muses
Chastly to serve so Sacred thrice three Uses?

---

49 See Toby Barnard, *Cromwellian Ireland: English Government and Reform in Ireland* (Oxford: Oxford University Press, 2000).

50 Teate, *Ter Tria*, "Son," 130; Peter Toon ed., *The Oxford Orations of Dr John Owen* (Callington: Gospel Communication, 1971), 30–46.

51 Teate, *Ter Tria*, 39.

52 Teate, *Ter Tria*, 5.

Is the grave Body of Divinity
Less Currant for the feet of Poetry?[53]

Teate's argument plays on the ambiguity of "feet" as a metrical as well as a metaphorical device. For his poem was to advance the "grave Body of Divinity" by exemplifying the new Trinitarian devotion. Of course, earlier poems, such as John Donne's "A Hymn to God the Father," had addressed individual persons of the deity. But Teate was the first English writer to address this theme systematically, and to expand upon Owen's novel idea that Christian believers could commune with individual members of the Trinity. By making this move, Teate was positioning himself with a theological approach advanced by the most senior of the Independent ministers, one of the most politically useful of the period's theologians, whose work was well known to the dedicatee of his poem, Henry Cromwell.[54]

The ideas represented in *Of communion with God* do not appear to have been the only literary influence on the poet. *Ter Tria* seems to reflect the formal influence of George Herbert, of whom both Teate and Owen appear to have been aware. Owen's library, as we noticed, seems to have included Herbert's work in two separate volumes. And Teate was certainly aware of Herbert's contribution. He would refer to "Holy Herbert" in the preface to *The Thoughts of the Righteous are Right* (1666), and, in a commendatory poem to a later edition of *Ter Tria* (1669), John Chishull would associate work by Herbert and Teate as having the ability to "inspire / *Randals* and *Davenants* with Poetick fire"—rather pointedly contrasting Teate with other, less spiritual, poets represented in Owen's collection.[55] Herbert, although a conservative conformist, had attracted a wide readership among radicals in the civil wars period. Nehemiah Rogers, in a dedicatory poem to *Ohel or Bethshemesh* (1653), by John Rogers, a minister in Dublin and London who described Owen as "my honoured friend,"[56] had alluded to

---

53 "The author to the reader," Teate, *Ter Tria*, 40.

54 See, for example, Thomas Harrison to Henry Cromwell, [June or July 1656], in *The Correspondence of Henry Cromwell*, ed. Peter Gaunt, Camden fifth series (London: Royal Historical Society, 2007), 151–152.

55 "To the WITS of this AGE, Pretended or Real," in Teate, *Ter Tria*, 250.

56 John Rogers, *Ohel or Bethshemesh* (1653), 77; Rogers cites Owen's essay on church government, 175.

Herbert's "Easter Wings" when stating that he would not "imp my wings with foreign borrowed Plumes."[57] Similarly, Walter Gostello, a self-identified prophet in county Cork, regarded Herbert's *Country Parson* as indispensable, believing that the faces of those who took its advice to heart "shall shine with glory."[58]

Teate's debts to Herbert are more public than are his debts to Owen. Teate does not appear to have referred to Owen's work in any of his earlier writing, which does occasionally refer to other writers in the literary culture of English Puritanism: *A Scripture-map of the Wildernesse of Sin, and Way to Canaan* (1655), for example, refers to work by the Presbyterian Richard Baxter and by the Independents John Cotton and Jeremiah Burroughs.[59] It is impossible to know the route by which the ideas advanced in *Of communion with God* came to Teate's attention. But Teate does anticipate the difficulty with which the new spirituality would be sustained. *Ter Tria* reflected upon the difficulties of maintaining its innovative Trinitarian style: "how hard a thing is this believing?"[60]

Conclusion

Owen's intervention in Western spirituality was unprecedented, but although demand for his work pushed his text into multiple editions, its significance was ultimately eclipsed. *Of communion with God* went through two printings in quarto in 1657, and was republished in a second edition in octavo, with a new preface defending it from the charge of novelty, in 1700. Teate's work also went into eclipse. *Ter Tria*, first published in 1658, came out in a second edition in 1669, and a third edition was printed in Leipzig in 1700. The fates of these texts were illustrated in the *Catalogus librorum ex bibliotheca nobilis cujusdam Angli qui ante paucos annos in humanis esse desiit accesserunt libri eximii theologi D. Gabrielis Sangar, adjectis theologi alterius magni, dum vixt, nominis libris selectioribus* (1678), an auction catalogue of the library of the Baron Brooke, which listed *Ter Tria* and the poems of George

---

57 Rogers, *Ohel*, 90.

58 Walter Gostello, *Charls Stuart and Oliver Cromwell United* (1654), 311–312.

59 Faithful Teate, *A Scripture-map of the Wildernesse of Sin, and Way to Canaan* (1655), sig. A3, ar.

60 Teate, *Ter Tria*, "Son," 140.

Herbert among its examples of "English divinity" without referring at all to the prodigious dogmatic works of Owen.[61] Owen's devotional revolution had failed to make an enduring impact on the piety of popular Protestantism; Teate's contribution was only remembered in the short term, and perhaps then only because of its genre.

The reason for the eclipse of Owen's innovative approach may be partly political, in that "the suspicion of 'enthusiasm' that became endemic in English life after the Restoration was to prove the death knell for pneumatology," as the aristocratic provenance of the auction catalogue may suggest.[62] And, among the godly, the expiration of Owen's devotional revolution may have owed something to the lack of robust exegetical support for important parts of his argument, especially in relation to the believer's communion with the Spirit, which Owen defended on the rather slight basis that prayers to the Spirit were implied by the inclusion of the third person of the Trinity in the New Testament benedictions;[63] too much of his argument depended on unchecked allegory. Even Goold hinted that Owen "carries out the idea of distinct communion between the believer and each of the persons of the Godhead to an extent for which there is no scriptural precedent."[64] Owen replied to his principal critic in *A vindication of some passages in a discourse concerning communion with God from the exceptions of William Sherlock* (1674), but his approach was ultimately to be ignored.

If Teate's descent into obscurity was less rapid, it was to be more enduring, continuing long after the recovery of interest in Owen in the mid-nineteenth century. The New England Puritan poet Edward Taylor may have been influenced by *Ter Tria*, but thereafter Teate's work was almost entirely ignored until the republication of a critical edition in 2007.[65] The family's poetic reputation would be secured by Teate's son, Nahum Tate, who in 1692, almost thirty years after his

---

61 *Catalogus librorum ex bibliotheca nobilis cujusdam Angli* [i.e. Baron Brooke] *qui ante paucos annos in humanis esse desiit accesserunt libri eximii theologi D. Gabrielis Sangar, adjectis theologi alterius magni, dum vixt, nominis libris selectioribus : quorum omnium auctio habebitur Londini 2 die Decembris proxime sequenti* (1678), 41, 42, 44.

62 Dixon, *Nice and Hot Disputes*, 60.

63 Owen, *Works*, 2:14.

64 Owen, *Works*, 1:lxxii.

65 Byrne, "Faithful Teate's *Ter Tria* as an influence on Edward Taylor," 206–209.

father's death, became poet laureate, producing a bulk of writing which literary scholars now read only for its historical value. Yet Owen appears to have owned a copy of his first published work, a commendatory verse in the *Poems and Songs* by the similarly talented Thomas Flatman.

Perhaps a new and contextually wealthier approach to the study of Owen's writing could better explain his poetic impulses and influences. It might also identify some of the causes for the failure of his experiment in spirituality. And it might modify some of the enthusiasms of the current renaissance in scholarship on Owen's theology and in the repackaging of his ideas and the rewriting of his books, including *Of communion with God*, for the general evangelical public. Owen would surely have welcomed the rising reputation of his work. "What poor, low, perishing things do we spend our contemplations on!" he exclaimed, wondering why believers chose not to pursue the remarkable opportunities of communion with the triune God.[66]

---

66 Owen, *Works*, 2:69.

Engraved by J. Grattre from a picture supposed to be by Copley in possession of Mrs. Elizabeth Edwards, Hartford, Ct.

Jonathan Edwards
1703–1758

A resolved piety: living in light of eternity with Jonathan Edwards

By Peter Beck

THREE HUNDRED YEARS after his birth, Jonathan Edwards (1703–1758) continues to loom large over the Christian landscape. His legacy casts a long shadow across church history. Considered by many to be America's greatest theologian, Edwards simply cannot be ignored. Sereno Dwight, an early Edwards biographer and descendant of his subject, rightly recognized this.

> The number of those men, who have produced great and permanent changes in the character and condition of mankind, and stamped their own image on the minds of succeeding generations, is comparatively small; and, even of this small number, the great body have been indebted for their superior efficiency, at least in part, to extraneous circumstances, while very few can ascribe it to the simple strength of their own intellect. Yet here and there an individual can be found, who, by his mere mental energy, has changed the course of human thought and feeling, and led mankind onward in that new and better path which he had opened to their view. Such an individual was JONATHAN EDWARDS.[1]

---

1   Sereno E. Dwight, *Life of Edwards* (New York: G. & C. & H. Carvill, 1830), 2.

Thus, Jonathan Edwards continues to influence the church through his writings and sermons. Pastors and theologians turn to him for guidance and support on a host issues ranging from cosmology to eschatology and everything in between. Yet, if the church, so desperate to rediscover what it perceives to be the purity and passion of an earlier era, wishes to honour Edwards aright, it must rediscover that which moved his spirit and shaped his thought: the desire for unbroken communion with his great God.

Edwards' piety is the stuff of legend. Stories of his childhood prayer booth in the wilderness amaze readers who lack the spiritual discipline of that precocious boy. Hours spent alone with God, whether on horseback or cutting firewood, shaped his preaching and challenge modern sensibilities and schedules. Letters to his children reveal Edwards' pious concern for the well-being of their souls and convict a new generation of parents of their spiritual apathy. What may be his most widely-read work, *The Life of David Brainerd*, shines a bright light on the darkness of the evangelical soul as the reader confronts a model of Christian devotion that seems so unobtainable and, dare we say, perhaps undesirable. Yet, just as we cannot seem to take our eyes off the grisly carnage of a fatal accident, Christians cannot turn their eyes away from Edwards even here, as he directs our attention to those areas of our own walk with God that we'd rather ignore. Jonathan Edwards' vision for the Christian life, the life he determined to live, cannot and must not be ignored any longer.

"Resolutions" for life

The quest for godliness began early for Edwards. Speaking of those nascent attempts to pray in the woods, Edwards recalled, "I seemed to be in my element when engaged in religious duties."[2] Yet, in short order, he later lamented, the affections wore off and his efforts petered out. Years later, while a student at Yale, Edwards enjoyed the saving favour of God and experienced regeneration. New life brought him new interest in the exercise of piety. Of this change, he wrote, "I kept saying, as it were singing these words of Scripture [1 Timothy 1:17] to

---

2   Jonathan Edwards, "Personal Narrative," in *Letters and Personal Writings*, Vol. 16 of *The Works of Jonathan Edwards*, ed. George S. Claghorn (New Haven: Yale University Press, 1998), 791.

myself; and went to prayer, to pray to God that I might enjoy him; and prayed in a manner quite different from what I used to do; with a new sort of affection."[3] These new affections drew Edwards toward God.

> My mind was greatly fixed on divine things; I was almost perpetually in the contemplation of them. Spent most of my time in thinking of divine things, year after year. And used to spend abundance of my time, in walking alone in the woods, and solitary places, for meditation, soliloquy and prayer, and converse with God.[4]

Edwards' desires only intensified when he moved to New York to take over the pastorate of a small, splinter congregation of Presbyterians, recently removed from their mother church.

> My longings after God and holiness, were much increased. Pure and humble, holy and heavenly Christianity, appeared exceeding amiable to me. I felt in me a burning desire to be in everything a complete Christian; and conformed to the blessed image of Christ: and that I might live in all things, according to the pure, sweet and blessed rules of the gospel. I had an eager thirsting after progress in these things. My longings after it, put me upon pursuing and pressing after them. It was my continual strife day and night, and constant inquiry, how I should be more holy, and live more holily, and more becoming a child of God, and disciple of Christ.[5]

Now a son of God, Edwards longed to live with the Father and for the Father.

In terms of personal piety, the eight months Edwards spent in New York proved to be both fulfilling and formative. It was here that he began his ministry and it was here that he charted the course of his spiritual life. Sometime in the fall of 1722, the young pastor, only nineteen years old, determined to live his life in the pursuit of holiness. To

---

3   Edwards, "Personal Narrative," 792–793.
4   Edwards, "Personal Narrative," 794.
5   Edwards, "Personal Narrative," 795.

that end, he penned his now famous "Resolutions." The first of these seventy "Resolutions" spells out his desire and reveals his commitment to the joyous task before him.

> Resolved, that I will do whatsoever I think to be most to God's glory and to my own good, profit, and pleasure, in the whole of my duration, without any consideration of the time, whether now or never so many myriad of ages hence. Resolved to do whatever I think to be my duty, and most for the good and advantage of mankind in general. Resolved to do this, whatever difficulties I meet with, how ever so many and how ever so great.[6]

Edwards acknowledged the path he had set for himself would be difficult. Yet it was to this great end that he dedicated himself. To a life of genuine piety he was resolved.

As he knew from earlier attempts at godliness, strong desires alone are insufficient. One needs proper motivation to stay the course. Numerous "Resolutions" point to that which motivated Edwards: eternity. The first of the "Resolutions" looked to the "myriad of ages" to come. "Resolutions" No. 6 points to his understanding of his own mortality: "Resolved, to live with all my might, while I do live." The next resolution continues the theme: "Resolved, never to do anything that I should be afraid to do if it were the last hour of my life." Again, later in "Resolutions" No. 17, Edwards determined, "I will live so as I shall wish I had done when I come to die." Edwards sought to live a life worthy of eternity.[7]

Contrary to many modern attempts to offer the Christian life as the means for the removal of the consequences of sin in the hereafter, it was the promise of heaven that moved Edwards. He set his other-worldly focus on knowing God and enjoying him now and forevermore. This is the theme of the "Resolutions." As Edwards explained in "Resolutions" No. 18: "Resolved, to live so at all times as I think is best in my devout frames, and when I have clearest notions of things of the

---

6 Jonathan Edwards, "Resolutions," in *Letters and Personal Writings*, vol. 16 of *The Works of Jonathan Edwards*, ed. George S. Claghorn (New Haven: Yale University Press, 1998), 753.

7 Edwards, "Resolutions," 753–754.

gospel and another world." Or, as he determined in "Resolutions" No. 22: "Resolved, to endeavor to obtain for myself (as much happiness, in the other world,) as I possibly can, with all the power, might, vigor, and vehemence, yea violence, I am capable of, or can bring myself to exert, in any way that can be thought of."

Thus, for Edwards, a resolved piety looked both at the present for its immediate expression and toward heaven for its eternal goal. In this way Edwards' "Resolutions" offer more than a spiritual self-examination as one might think or a self-help manual as one might hope. Instead, they put before each new generation of readers the opportunity to join Edwards on a quest to be like God that we might live with God.[8]

To aid him on his journey, Edwards looked to the various duties of the Christian life. These duties, many of which are considered among the spiritual disciplines written of today, can be found scattered throughout Edwards' works. They find their way into his sermons and his "miscellanies." They're explained in his *Religious Affections*. They're on display in his accounts of the First Great Awakening. They're found first, however, in his "Resolutions." Those included there provide a glimpse into their author's resolve. Among other duties mentioned are learning, charity, and, to no surprise for the informed Edwards reader, fasting. Two such duties, however, provided the heartbeat of Edwards' vision for spirituality cast in the "Resolutions"—Bible reading and prayer.

Believing Edwards' theocentric vision of piety and spirituality worthy of emulation, those duties he thought most important, those he resolved to pursue and practice with godly "violence," will be considered here. After all, these things, he believed, promoted the great concerns of his first resolution: "God's glory" and "my own good, profit, and pleasure."[9]

"Study the Scriptures"

That Jonathan Edwards loved and honoured the Bible is beyond question. Twelve-hundred extant sermons bear witness to this fact, each and every one of them given over to the exposition of Scripture and its application. This commitment, too, began to take shape during his time in New York. As Edwards recounted in his "Personal Narrative,"

---

8   Edwards, "Resolutions," 754.
9   Edwards, "Resolutions," 753.

I had then, and at other times, the greatest delight in the holy Scriptures, of any book whatsoever. Oftentimes in reading it, every word seemed to touch my heart. I felt an harmony between something in my heart, and those sweet and powerful words. I seemed often to see so much light, exhibited by every sentence, and such a refreshing ravishing food communicated, that I could not get along in reading. Used oftentimes to dwell long on one sentence, to see the wonders contained in it; and yet almost every sentence seemed to be full of wonders.[10]

He explored the source of those wonders in "Miscellanies" 204, written about the same time as the "Resolutions" and the period described in the "Personal Narrative." God, he reasoned, created man with a spirit for the purpose of communicating with him. He continued, "They are made for this very end, to meditate on him and to love [him]."[11] For that reason Edwards believed that all men, but particularly Christians, should set their hearts and minds to the studying of God's Word wherein God clearly revealed his will and his way. Hence, he added number twenty-eight to his "Resolutions": "Resolved, to study the Scriptures so steadily, constantly, and frequently that I may find, and plainly perceive myself to grow in the knowledge of them."[12]

Preached just one year later in the fall of 1723 or the winter of 1724, Edwards' sermon, "A Spiritual Understanding," foreshadowed the theological content of his more famous sermon, "A Divine and Supernatural Light" (1733). In this early sermon, the young preacher emphasized the important role of the Holy Spirit in conversion as he brings to light spiritual mysteries once misunderstood or overlooked by men while unregenerate. The same can be said, he argued, of their understanding of Scripture. Yet, he added, the lost as well as the found must be urged to read the Bible. "We must be much in reading Scripture," he observed, "if we would get spiritual and saving knowledge." Unless one "diligently and frequently read the Scriptures," Edwards

---

10 Edwards, "Personal Narrative," 797.

11 Jonathan Edwards, "Miscellanies" 204, in *The "Miscellanies" (Entries Nos. a—z, aa—zz, 1–500)*, vol. 13 of *The Works of Jonathan Edwards*, ed. Thomas A. Schafer (New Haven: Yale University Press, 1994), 339.

12 Edwards, "Resolutions," 755.

continued, he enjoyed no hope of being so enlightened.[13] Because of the sinfulness of the heart, this discipline requires great effort and persistence as the reader awaits the fruit of his labour.

> The reason why multitudes read the Scriptures no more, is because 'tis so insipid to them, they don't find that they gain knowledge by it. But the light of Scripture will not break forth at once. Our hearts are naturally contrary to the things contained therein, we are quite blind when we first take the Bible in hand.[14]

However, great reward comes to those who persevere. "But if we follow it diligently, light will begin to break forth by degrees," Edwards continued. "Instruction will come, if we search for it in the Bible as silver and as hidden treasures." To find his prize, the Christian must be resolute, ever focused on the task before him. As Edwards remarked, "The law of God should be a constant companion to converse with, lying down and rising up, and wherever we are."[15]

A similar theme echoes through another sermon from the same decade. Preached in late 1728 or early 1729, during Edwards' early years in Northampton, "Profitable Hearers of the Word" offers three doctrinal statements, versus the Puritan norm of one, in which the preacher connected the faithful attendance to God's Word with fruitful living. Explaining the parable of the sower and the seed, Edwards commented that the defining mark of a Christian over against that of an unbeliever is his ability to understand the Bible. Proper understanding, he posited, "consists in the apprehension and judgment," or discernment, of the Bible.[16] Apprehension and judgement, Edwards knew, require diligent effort.

Those matters that are to be apprehended, or grasped, by the hearer and the reader of the Word are "the glory of God, the excellency and

---

13 Jonathan Edwards, "A Spiritual Understanding," in *Sermons and Discourses 1723–1729*, vol. 14 of *The Works of Jonathan Edwards*, ed. Kenneth P. Minkema (New Haven: Yale University Press, 1997), 94.

14 Edwards, "A Spiritual Understanding," 94–95.

15 Edwards, "A Spiritual Understanding," 95.

16 Jonathan Edwards, "Profitable Hearers of the Word," in *Letters and Personal Writings*, vol. 16 of *The Works of Jonathan Edwards*, ed. George S. Claghorn (New Haven: Yale University Press, 1998), 249.

fullness of Jesus Christ, the nature of holiness, the reason and foundation of duty." Pointing to conclusions he would draw nearly thirty years
later in *The End for Which God Created* (published posthumously in
1765), Edwards argued, "it is not only the end of the Scriptures, but
'tis the end of the works of creation and providence to show forth God's
glory." Such conclusions make the Bible a worthy object of study, be
it in reading or listening. Edwards would explain his understanding of
the excellency of Christ at length in the sermon of the same name a
decade later (preached in 1736; published 1738). The holiness to which
he pointed was the doctrine of salvation.[17]

Key to the present study, Edwards dedicated as much space to the
foundation of duty, the reason or reasons for faithfulness, as he did to
the aforementioned doctrines. "The godly," he said, "are distinguished
from others in that they understand the foundation of duty." The Scriptures, he explained, are "a revelation of the will of God as directing our
actions and behavior,"[18] the foundation of which is "God's greatness
and worthiness."[19] Without a proper understanding of these things
man will never live in the way that God intended or even understand
why he should. If one did understand these matters correctly, Edwards
proposed, "They would practice it."[20] Thus, properly understanding
the Bible proves foundational for living in light of eternity.

Laden with practical application, "Profitable Hearers" offered much
encouragement to Edwards' early audience to dedicate themselves to
the study of God's Word. "With all your gettings," he preached, "get
this understanding."[21] Edwards exhorted the hearer and the reader to:

> Make much use of the Word of God. That is God's own teachings
> and instructions, and it is there only that we have the knowledge
> of things that pertain to our salvation originally taught. 'Tis there
> only that we have an invaluable guide, a sure rule, which, if we
> follow, we cannot err.[22]

---

17 Edwards, "Profitable Hearers of the Word," 249.
18 Edwards, "Profitable Hearers of the Word," 249.
19 Edwards, "Profitable Hearers of the Word," 251.
20 Edwards, "Profitable Hearers of the Word," 251.
21 Edwards, "Profitable Hearers of the Word," 264.
22 Edwards, "Profitable Hearers of the Word," 265.

The Word brings good news to the lost and perfect tutelage to the saved. To this Edwards appended, "How can we ever hope that we shall understand the Word, if we won't so much as read it, nor attend to it when it is preached to us?" Hence, Edwards concluded, "we must often go to him whose Word it is and beg him to teach."[23]

Preaching from 2 Peter 1:19 in 1737, Edwards once again connected a thorough understanding of Scripture with godly living. Of this text he understood the apostle to be "exhorting" the church "to give all diligence to grow in grace, and to live an holy life, and in this way make their calling and election sure."[24] Believing the world to be a darkened place because of sin, Edwards saw the Bible as the light by which God reveals both man's sinfulness and his own goodness. For that man must be grateful. More than that, however, believers should treat the Bible as the great treasure that it is. Echoing themes from "A Spiritual Understanding," Edwards pled with his audience,

Since we have this light in our hands, let us prize it, and make use of [it]. O! what a precious treasure have we, in that we have this very revelation [of God's will]. Let us therefore not neglect, and let it lie by, as if it were good for nothing, a thing of no use. Let us consider it something sent from heaven to enlighten a dark world, and what a blessing it has been made to the world. And we may hope it will be a blessing to us, if we improve it.

The key to such improvement, Edwards explained, is for Christians to "read and search it, and diligently use it from day to day." Christians who rightly understands the value of the gift, Edwards concluded, would be "stirred up to converse more with our Bibles," to "read, and labor to understand what we read, and apply it to ourselves, that it may be a light to our feet, and a lamp to our paths."[25] The Bible, Edwards reasoned, was a jewel to be enjoyed daily not a trinket to be marvelled at once and then cast aside.

---

23 Edwards, "Profitable Hearers of the Word," 266.

24 Jonathan Edwards, "Light in a Dark World, a Dark Heart," in *Sermons and Discourses 1734–1738*, vol. 19 of *The Works of Jonathan Edwards*, ed. M.X. Lesser (New Haven: Yale University Press, 2001), 707.

25 Edwards, "Light in a Dark World, a Dark Heart," 722.

In the appropriately named sermon, "The Importance and Advantage of a Thorough Knowledge of Divine Truth" (1739), preached during the spiritual lull between the outbreak of revival in Northampton and the beginnings of the broader First Great Awakening, Edwards offered a much needed call to the spiritual discipline of Bible reading. "Every Christian," the sermon's doctrine declares, "should make a business of endeavoring to grow in knowledge in divinity."[26] Here Edwards spoke from experience, as he had resolved to do this very thing nearly twenty years earlier with his eleventh resolution: "Resolved, when I think of any theorem in divinity to be solved, immediately to do what I can toward solving it, if circumstances don't hinder."[27] Now he expected the same of his congregation.

As Edwards saw it, "Divinity comprehends all that is taught in the Scriptures." "All that we need know, or is to be known, concerning God and Jesus Christ, concerning our duty to God, and our happiness in God," he proffered, is found there. Thus, he challenged his hearers to dedicate all of their energy and "diligence" to the task before them. To aid his congregation on their journey, this sermon offered further encouragement to bolster their resolve. Christians, he announced, "Consider yourselves as scholars or disciples, put into the school of Christ" to become proficient in the things of Christ.[28] "Therefore," he counselled them, "be not contented in possessing but little of this treasure." Instead, he added, "Let it be very much your business to search for it, and that with the same diligence and labor with which men are wont to dig in mines of silver and gold."[29]

The sermon also offered much in the way of practical application. To reach their goal, to seize the prize, Edwards told them, would require unremitting dedication to the task of reading the Bible. "This is the fountain whence all knowledge in divinity must be derived," he

---

26 Jonathan Edwards, "The Importance and Advantage of a Thorough Knowledge of Divine Truth," in *Sermons and Discourses 1739–1742*, vol. 22 of *The Works of Jonathan Edwards*, ed. Harry S. Stout and Nathan O. Hatch (New Haven: Yale University Press, 2003), 85.

27 Edwards, "Resolutions," 754.

28 Edwards, "The Importance and Advantage of a Thorough Knowledge of Divine Truth," 86.

29 Edwards, "The Importance and Advantage of a Thorough Knowledge of Divine Truth," 97–98.

reminded them. Though hard work would be needed, he promised, the goal is attainable for those who are pleased to try. Likewise, the dedicated reader should not "content" himself "with only a cursory reading" of Scripture. That, Edwards said, "is an ill way of reading" all too common in the church. Such an approach, he was concerned, neglects the true meaning of the author for the shallow victory of simply reading the words. Instead, the committed reader will search out the meaning, making observations of the text, and resorting to Bible study tools as necessary.[30] Christians should encourage others in the process as well, he added, learning from those further along in the process and giving help to those who struggle. He warned them, however, that they should seek to grow in this knowledge not for the "sake of applause" or to equip themselves to "dispute with others." Ultimately, Edwards concluded, the best resource available to the "student of Christ" is God. "Seek to God," Edwards suggested, "that he would direct you, and bless you, in this pursuit after knowledge." Finally, the disciple must exercise that which he has learned. This, said Edwards, is "the way to know more."[31]

Just as Edwards had begun his ministry in the early 1720s with the recognition of the importance of and need for Scripture, so he began his final years in the pulpit in the 1750s. Preaching a trial sermon before the mixed congregation at the Stockbridge mission outpost, Edwards outlined those "things that belong to true religion" (1751). Mindful of the unconverted Native Americans in the audience, Edwards simplified his homiletical method and his message. Yet, his concern for their spiritual well-being was in no wise lessened. The first of "these things" that Edwards mentioned that day was "to be instructed [to] understand what the true God is, to know and understand Christ and the way how God saves men by Christ, and to know about another world." These things, he said, are what the "Bible teaches," enabling believers "to taste the sweetness of 'em and have those things sink down into the heart."[32]

---

30 Edwards, "The Importance and Advantage of a Thorough Knowledge of Divine Truth," 101.

31 Edwards, "The Importance and Advantage of a Thorough Knowledge of Divine Truth," 102.

32 Jonathan Edwards, "The Things that Belong to True Religion," in *Sermons and Discourses 1743–1758*, vol. 25 of *The Works of Jonathan Edwards*, ed. Wilson H. Kimnach (New Haven: Yale University Press, 2006), 572.

After listing a number of other matters belonging to true religion, the preacher turned their attention to the Bible once more in the sermon's application. He told his audience to pursue "the religion that the Bible teaches." Salvation, he argued, could be found nowhere else. Moreover, he said, the Mohawk and Mohican parents should see to it that their children "learn English that they may read the Bible and there learn this religion" for themselves. Those that have this religion, he promised, "need not be afraid to die."[33]

From beginning to end, from resolution to dissolution, Jonathan Edwards' life and ministry were dedicated to understanding Scripture better and teaching others to do the same. Just as he had once desired to grow in the knowledge of the Bible, he finished his course encouraging his last flock to follow his example. After all, a resolute desire to know the God of the Bible and to live accordingly is the hallmark of true religion.

"Prayer or a Petition of a Prayer"

Years before his conversion, Edwards exercised an almost singular focus on spirituality, albeit intermittently. As he noted in his "Personal Narrative," during a time of religious upheaval among his father's congregants, "I was then very much affected for many months, and concerned about the things of religion, and my soul's salvation." He was, Edwards recalled, "abundant in duties." The duty to which Edwards felt most strongly called was prayer. "I used to pray five times a day in secret," he remembered.[34] In addition to that, he and his childhood friends would often pray together, retiring to their prayer booth in the swamps alongside the Connecticut River. Even that was not enough for Edwards. He would retreat to his own secret places to pray even more. Lacking the true key to spirituality, the indwelling of the Holy Spirit, Edwards soon left off his exercises and chased after childish pursuits once more.

His heart waxed hot and cold for years until Edwards finally acquiesced and acknowledged God's sovereignty one day while reading 1 Timothy 1:17. Upon his reading of that text, Edwards recognized God as the "King eternal, immortal, invisible, the only wise God." In

---

33 Edwards, "The Things that Belong to True Religion," 574.
34 Edwards, "Personal Narrative," 790.

response, he confessed, "I thought with myself, how excellent a Being that was; and how happy I should be, if I might enjoy that God, and be wrapt up to God in heaven, and be as it were swallowed up in him." The change in him was immediate. He began to sing and "to pray to God that I might enjoy him."[35] Once again, Edwards retired to the woods with great frequency to commune with God.

> And it was always my manner, at such times, to sing forth my contemplations. And was almost constantly in ejaculatory prayer, wherever I was. Prayer seemed to be natural to me; as the breath, by which the inward burnings of my heart had vent.[36]

New affections were at work in his soul.

These feelings continued as Edwards moved to New York in 1722. Of this, he wrote,

> My longings after God and holiness were much increased. Pure and humble, holy and heavenly Christianity, appeared exceeding amiable to me. I felt in me a burning desire to be in everything a complete Christian; and conformed to the blessed image of Christ: and that I might live in all things, according to the pure, sweet and blessed rules of the gospel.[37]

While there, he maintained his practice of going to solitary places for extended periods of prayer. And, it was there that Edwards committed himself to a life of prayer. "Resolved, never to count that a prayer, nor to let that pass as a prayer or as a petition of a prayer, which is so made that I cannot hope that God will answer it; nor that as a confession, which I cannot hope God will accept."[38]

As with his concern for the importance of faithful Bible reading, Edwards preached often of the need for faithful prayer as well. "Christian Happiness" (1720/1721), perhaps Edwards' first sermon, speaks of "the pleasures of [the] communion of the Holy Ghost in conversing

---

35 Edwards, "Personal Narrative," 792.
36 Edwards, "Personal Narrative," 794.
37 Edwards, "Personal Narrative," 795.
38 Edwards, "Resolutions," 755.

with God" and "the pleasure that results from the doing of our duty."[39]
He encouraged that first audience to persevere in their duties no matter
the hindrance. "Go on in those excellent ways in which you have
begun," he said. "Let nothing in the world discourage you." Here, too,
one hears Edwards' heart for the things of heaven:

> Go on, therefore, and forgetting the things which are behind, be
> pressing forward toward those which are before, even toward the
> mark for the prize of the high calling of God; and those afflictions
> will seem less and less to you, and your path will shine brighter
> and brighter, even till at length the night of this life shall be
> turned into perfect day, when God shall wipe away all tears from
> your eyes and there shall be no more death; neither sorrow nor
> crying, neither shall there be any more pain, for the former
> things will then be passed away [Revelation 21:4].[40]

Thus, even with this first sermon, Edwards cast a vision for the resolved
piety to which he would commit himself.

Though none address prayer exclusively or extensively, a number of
other sermons from the early 1720s, years which would include Edwards'
time in New York and his brief foray to Bolton, Connecticut, speak often
of prayer. Explaining matters of eschatological significance in "Importance of a Future State" (1721/1722), Edwards advised his audience to
remain steadfast in their prayers while they await their final state.

> Wherefore, let nobody put off their great work to a further opportunity, but set about it this minute, and go on in it with all our
> might and vigor till we perpetrate the same. Let us look continually unto God for his help and assistance; pray earnestly in all
> prayers and supplications, without ceasing. Let us not only seek,
> but strive in the great work, knowing that there are many that
> seek that shall not be able.[41]

---

39 Jonathan Edwards, "Christian Happiness," in *Sermons and Discourses 1720–1723*,
vol. 10 of *The Works of Jonathan Edwards*, ed. Wilson H. Kimnach (New Haven: Yale
University Press, 1992), 305.

40 Edwards, "Christian Happiness," 306–307.

41 Jonathan Edwards, "Importance of a Future State," in *Sermons and Discourses*

Seeking God in prayer demanded Edwards' attention in another sermon that year as well. In "Fragment: On Seeking," Edwards reminded his audience of the importance of prayer to the finding of God.

There must not only be public and family prayer, but secret prayer; that is what is particularly commanded and urged in the gospel. He that would find God must frequently retire from all the world, and secretly make his application to him who seeth and heareth in secret, and earnestly cry after that God whom we have lost, and wait for an answer from him, that we may find him and enjoy him.[42]

As he argued in "Living to Christ" (1722/1723), having found God, Christians are to continue to dedicate themselves to prayer in their quest for holiness. "For this end, be more prayerful, more frequent and more earnest in your approaches to the throne of grace."[43] Such prayers, he added, can be lifted both in times of scheduled intercession and in the course of everyday activities.

Edwards' final sermon of this era ends as he began his preaching ministry, calling people to prayer, this time for the great pleasure it brings. "The external duties of religion are made easy and pleasant by true love to God," he explained in "True Love to God." "Duties toward God, such as prayer, singing God's praises, hearing the Word and the like, are his delight."[44] Christians, Edwards believed, are the most happy when they are engaged in communion with the greatest love of their life.

Just as Edwards admitted the need for divine intervention in one's quest for godliness in his "Resolutions," he did the same in his sermons.

1720–1723, vol. 10 of *The Works of Jonathan Edwards*, ed. Wilson H. Kimnach (New Haven: Yale University Press, 1992), 375.

42 Jonathan Edwards, "Fragment: On Seeking," in *Sermons and Discourses 1720–1723*, vol. 10 of *The Works of Jonathan Edwards*, ed. Wilson H. Kimnach (New Haven: Yale University Press, 1992), 381.

43 Jonathan Edwards, "Living to Christ," in *Sermons and Discourses 1720–1723*, vol. 10 of *The Works of Jonathan Edwards*, ed. Wilson H. Kimnach (New Haven: Yale University Press, 1992), 576.

44 Jonathan Edwards, "True Love to God," in *Sermons and Discourses 1720–1723*, vol. 10 of *The Works of Jonathan Edwards*, ed. Wilson H. Kimnach (New Haven: Yale University Press, 1992), 639.

In his prefatory remarks to the "Resolutions," Edwards owned, "I am unable to do anything without God's help." To resolve his spiritual ineptitude, he prayed: "I do humbly entreat him by his grace to enable me to keep these resolutions."[45] Just a couple of years later, in "A Spiritual Understanding," mentioned earlier in relation to Bible reading, Edwards commended prayer to his congregation. This, he said, is vital to the acquisition of said knowledge. "We must be often praying to God that he would give us wisdom." To that command Edwards attached a promise: "They that come to God for instruction are most likely to be instructed by him."[46] Having gained such knowledge, he would say nearly a decade later, the believer's prayers are changed as they "make much use of those things, that you have heard [and learned], in prayer."[47]

Revealing Edwards' conviction that revival and prayer are intimately related, the subject of prayer came up often during the season of awakening in Northampton in the mid-1730s. He spoke of prayer as the means to continue spiritual growth in the face of opposition when his Uncle Hawley unexpectedly killed himself.[48] He addressed the question of the prayers of the lost in "All That Natural Men Do Is Wrong."[49] He encouraged his church to pray for the spread of God's Word among the "heathen nations."[50] It was during this time also that Edwards preached his most significant sermon to date on the doctrine of prayer: "The Terms of Prayer."

By May 1738, the renewal of spiritual interests in Northampton had waned. As he struggled to rekindle the revival fires of three years earlier, Edwards called his people to prayer once more. The doctrinal

---

45   Edwards, "Resolutions," 753.

46   Edwards, "A Spiritual Understanding," 95.

47   Jonathan Edwards, "Heeding the Word, and Losing It," in *Sermons and Discourses 1734–1738*, vol. 19 of *The Works of Jonathan Edwards*, ed. M.X. Lesser (New Haven: Yale University Press, 2001), 51.

48   Jonathan Edwards, "Continuing God's Presence," in Sermons and Discourses 1734–1738, vol. 19 of The Works of Jonathan Edwards, ed. M.X. Lesser (New Haven: Yale University Press, 2001), 403.

49   Jonathan Edwards, "All That Natural Men Do Is Wrong," in *Sermons and Discourses 1734–1738*, vol. 19 of *The Works of Jonathan Edwards*, ed. M.X. Lesser (New Haven: Yale University Press, 2001), 527–529.

50   Edwards, "Light in a Dark World, a Dark Heart," 722–723.

statement of "The Terms of Prayer" offers Christians reasonable cause to approach the throne of God. "God never begrutches his people anything they desire, or are capable of," Edwards promised them, "as being too good for 'em."[51] He was not offering them false hope with the temptation of having their every whim fulfilled by a God who awaits their merry requests. Instead, Edwards maintained, God desires to give his people what is best for them, "his own fullness," if only they'd ask.[52] Moreover, as Christ serves as the Christian's mediator, even in prayer, "[God] begrutches nothing as too good for his own son."[53] In other words, as Christ intercedes on the behalf of the prayer, God responds graciously to the believer through his own Son.

Because "God's goodness is without bounds," Edwards prodded them, Christians should go boldly before God with their requests.[54] As he concluded the doctrinal section of this sermon,

And therefore nothing that they need, nothing that they ask of God, nothing that their desires can extend themselves to, nothing that their capacity can contain, no good that can be enjoyed by them, is so great, so excellent that God begrutches it to them.[55]

As God himself is the greatest good that man can aspire to, he should pray confidently to that end.

Therefore let the godly take encouragement from hence in their prayers to come boldly to the throne of grace, and come frequently. It may well be your delight to you to come to a God that is so ready at all times to hear and to grant you whatever you desire that tends to your happiness.[56]

Pray, Edwards said, because God wants you to be eternally happy in him.

---

51 Jonathan Edwards, "The Terms of Prayer," in *Sermons and Discourses 1734–1738*, vol. 19 of *The Works of Jonathan Edwards*, ed. M.X. Lesser (New Haven: Yale University Press, 2001), 772.

52 Edwards, "The Terms of Prayer," 776.

53 Edwards, "The Terms of Prayer," 779.

54 Edwards, "The Terms of Prayer," 780.

55 Edwards, "The Terms of Prayer," 781.

56 Edwards, "The Terms of Prayer," 785.

Edwards concluded "The Terms of Prayer" with this powerful observation: "All real and true prayer is the voice of faith."[57] That is, as Edwards discovered in his own personal experience and said in a later sermon, "Prayer is as natural an expression of faith as breathing is of life."[58] According to this later sermon, "Hypocrites Deficient in the Duty of Prayer" (1740), real Christians pray. The failure to pray proves inconsistent with one's claims to love God most supremely. "If you live in the neglect of secret prayer," Edwards warned his people, "you show your good will to neglect all the worship of God." Worse, "he that casts off the worship of God, in effect casts off God himself."[59] How can such a person reasonably expect to dwell with God forever when he fails to walk with him here? Edwards asked.

Edwards devoted the remainder of "Hypocrites Deficient" to the means of keeping oneself in the way of prayer. One will find in Scripture committed perseverance in prayer commanded and ample motive to that end, he argued. Perseverance, he added, is "a necessary prerequisite to eternal life."[60] Perseverance requires continued watchfulness and diligence. The final motive to perseverance that Edwards offered spoke directly to his own resolve on this point.

Consider the great benefit of a constant, diligent, and persevering attendance on this duty. It is one of the greatest and most excellent means of nourishing the new nature, and of the causing the soul to flourish and prosper. It is an excellent means of keeping up an acquaintance with God, and of growing in knowledge of God. It is the way to a life of communion with God.[61]

To that end, wise Christians will be vigilant against the beginnings of any neglect of this duty. They will be aware of temptations and excuses to forsake prayer that might creep into their lives. They will

57 Edwards, "The Terms of Prayer," 787. See also, Peter Beck, *The Voice of Faith: Jonathan Edwards's Theology of Prayer* (Guelph: Joshua Press, 2010)

58 Jonathan Edwards, "Hypocrites Deficient in the Duty of Prayer," in *Seeking God: Jonathan Edwards' Evangelism Contrasted with Modern Methodologies*, ed. William C. Nichols (Ames: International Outreach, 2001), 365.

59 Edwards, "Hypocrites Deficient in the Duty of Prayer," 365.

60 Edwards, "Hypocrites Deficient in the Duty of Prayer," 369.

61 Edwards, "Hypocrites Deficient in the Duty of Prayer," 371–372.

"be watchful to keep up the duty in the height of it" so as to not let it "begin to sink."[62]

Prayer continued as a recurring Edwardsean theme during the years leading up to the First Great Awakening. In 1740, Edwards once again reminded his church members that God longs to hear their prayers. As he had preached in "The Most High a Prayer-Hearing God" (1736), Edwards reminded them again in his sermon "Praying for the Spirit" (1740): "God is a prayer hearing God."[63] In the latter message he called on his congregants once more to seek greater blessings. "Those desires that are expressed in prayers for the most excellent blessings are the most excellent desires, and therefore God will be most ready to gratify 'em."[64] The Holy Spirit, the very indwelling of God, he told them, is the blessing they should seek vehemently. That prayer request, he told the church, God longs to answer. He "is more ready to bestow it in answer to prayer than any other blessing."[65]

Though not a sermon, Edwards kept appealing for others to pray for the coming of the Spirit in his tract promoting the idea of a concert of prayer amongst Christians in English-speaking lands. In what has come to be known as *An Humble Attempt* (1747), Edwards called for God's people to come together in "extraordinary prayer." Here, too, he informed his audience that the Spirit is the greatest gift to be asked of God. "The sum of the blessings Christ sought, by what he did and suffered in the work of redemption, was the Holy Spirit." Other superlatives given by Edwards to speak of this gift include "the grand blessing," "that great benefit" and "the chief subject of the promises of the New Testament." Christ's church, then, should constantly pray for more of the Spirit, for themselves and for the world. All that stands between spiritual remission and revival is the want of prayer.[66]

---

62 Edwards, "Hypocrites Deficient in the Duty of Prayer," 373.

63 Jonathan Edwards, "The Most High a Prayer-Hearing God," in *The Works of Jonathan Edwards* (Peabody: Hendrickson, 1998), 2:113; Jonathan Edwards, "Praying for the Spirit," in *Sermons and Discourses 1739–1742*, vol. 22 of *The Works of Jonathan Edwards*, ed. Harry S. Stout and Nathan O. Hatch (New Haven: Yale University Press, 2003), 215.

64 Edwards, "Praying for the Spirit," 216.

65 Edwards, "Praying for the Spirit," 220.

66 Jonathan Edwards, *An Humble Attempt to Promote Explicit Agreement and Visible Union of God's People in Extraordinary Prayer*, in *Apocalyptic Writings*, vol. 5 of *The*

Edwards told those gathered to hear him preach for the first time in Stockbridge in 1751 that the Bible reading was central to "true religion." With that, he included prayer among those things that marked true believers. Christians "must go alone and pray to him every day." Moreover, they are "to pray to him with the heart."[67] They must pray, he concluded, "to the great God that he will enlighten your minds and give you new hearts, that you may have true religion."[68] He wished for them the same thing he had experienced so long ago when he came to faith.

Just as he pointed to the centrality of prayer in his very first sermon, "Christian Happiness," Edwards closed his ministerial career with a call to prayer. He preached his final sermon on January 15, 1758, to his church of Indians and settlers in Stockbridge. That sermon, aptly named "Watch and Pray Always," returned one last time to the matter to which Edwards had dedicated his life. Coloured by his desire to live and die for God's glory, Edwards cautioned those assembled that day to "watch and pray always that we may be thought worthy [to stand before Christ]."[69] The application of the short remaining outline shows that Edwards ended his ministry as he had begun it, teaching others how to pray.

Thirty-six years earlier, Edwards determined to pray for only that worth asking, to seek in prayer only that worth seeking. Throughout his ministry he called others to join him in his resolve. In the end, he had stayed the course. He had kept "Resolutions" No. 65: "Resolved, very much to exercise myself in this [open and honest prayer before God] all my life long."[70]

Conclusion

It has been said of the spiritual disciplines that they are a way to experience God. Jonathan Edwards knew this truth well. He committed his life and ministry to this lofty goal from the start. His youthful "Resolutions" mark the beginning of a lifelong quest to be like God for the

---

Works of Jonathan Edwards, ed. Stephen J. Stein (New Haven: Yale University Press, 1977), 341.

67 Edwards, "The Things That Belong to True Religion," 573.

68 Edwards, "The Things That Belong to True Religion," 574.

69 Jonathan Edwards, "Watch and Pray Always," in *Sermons and Discourses 1743–1758*, vol. 25 of *The Works of Jonathan Edwards*, ed. Wilson H. Kimnach (New Haven: Yale University Press, 2006), 716.

70 Edwards, "Resolutions," 758.

purpose of being with God. Samuel Hopkins, a close friend and personal disciple of Edwards, remarked in his biographical sketch of Edwards' life that the "Resolutions" "may justly be considered as the foundation and plan of his whole life."[71] To that end, Edwards resolved to examine his heart and actions nightly to ensure that he stayed the course for the duration of his life beginning in 1722.

With God's help, Edwards sought God's glory and the promise of his own. "Resolutions" No. 63, first affirmed on January 14, 1723, and then recommitted to on July 13 of the same year, reveal his longing to be the model Christian, a shining example of piety for all to see.

> On the supposition, that there never was to be but one individual in the world at any one time who was properly a complete Christian, in all respects of a right stamp, having Christianity always shining in its true luster, and appearing excellent and lovely from whatever part and under whatever character viewed: Resolved, to act just as I would if I strove with all my might to be that one who should live in my time.[72]

While his own critical self-evaluations produced frequent bouts of doubt and disappointment with his spiritual progress expressed in his "diary," history suggests instead that Edwards faithfully completed the course set before him. As Hopkins explained hopefully,

> And no one perhaps, has been in our day more universally esteemed and acknowledged to be a bright Christian, an eminently good man. His love to God and man; his zeal for God and his cause; his uprightness, humility, self-denial, and weanedness from the world; his close walk with God; his conscientious, constant, and universal obedience, in all exact and holy ways of living: in one word, the goodness, the holiness of his heart, has been as evident and conspicuous, as the uncommon greatness and strength of his understanding.[73]

---

71 Samuel Hopkins, *The Life and Character of the Late Reverend, Learned and Pious Mr. Jonathan Edwards* (Northampton: Andrew Wright, 1804), 5.

72 Edwards, "Resolutions," 758.

73 Hopkins, *The Life and Character of Jonathan Edwards*, iii.

To that assessment Hopkins appended,

> And there is reason to hope, that though he is now dead, he will yet speak for a great while to come, to the great comfort and advantage of the church of Christ; that his publications will produce yet a greater harvest, as an addition to his joy and crown of rejoicing in the day of the Lord.[74]

Thus, today Jonathan Edwards calls another generation of Christians to follow his example, to see the joys of those alive given over to God, and join him in his resolve.

---

74 Hopkins, *The Life and Character of Jonathan Edwards*, iv.

13

Response to nineteenth-century holiness teaching: two case studies

By Sharon James

EVANGELICALS IN THE nineteenth century divided over the subject of holiness.[1] The lives and ministries of Elizabeth Prentiss (American) and Frances Ridley Havergal (British) were both impacted by this controversy. Their writings were enormously popular, because, ministering in a context of spiritual renewal, both spoke directly to the yearning of so many at that time for total consecration.

Elizabeth Prentiss (1818–1878) was best-known as the author of *Stepping Heavenward* (1879), and she authored a number of other books for both children and adults. Frances Ridley Havergal (1836–

---

1 A wide spectrum of views was believed and debated. Some believed that a Christian could reach sinless perfection in this life; others that there is always indwelling sin. Some believed that 'entire sanctification' is a "one-off" experience; others that sanctification is a lifelong process. There were numerous variations of these views. During the 1830s, partly due to the ministries of the revivalist Charles Finney (1792–1875), and the president of Oberlin College, Asa Mahan (1799–1889), the teaching that entire sanctification is possible in this life began to gain popularity. The early 1840s saw the growth of the influence of Phoebe Palmer (1807–1874) and others who taught a popularized version of John Wesley's teaching on "entire sanctification." Palmer believed she had an experience of "entire sanctification" on July 27, 1837, and taught that any believer who surrendered all to God would experience the same. Robert Boardman wrote *The Higher Christian Life* in 1858 which popularized the idea of a "two tier" Christianity.

1879) became a spokeswoman for the evangelical movement through her phenomenally popular hymns, poems, devotional booklets, stories for children and daily devotional notes. This chapter will outline the lives of these two women, and offer some reflections on their responses to the claims of the "perfectionists."

Elizabeth Prentiss

Elizabeth Prentiss, best known as the author of the novel *Stepping Heavenward*, was born in 1818 in Portland, Maine. Her father, Edward Payson, was a well-known preacher in New England. Edward and his wife Louisa had six children, and the Payson home was close-knit and loving. Elizabeth was just nine years old when her father died of tuberculosis at the age of forty-four. This tragedy affected her deeply.

Career options for women were limited, and being in her late teens, Elizabeth began teaching in order to help support her family. She taught in Maine and Virginia until the age of twenty-seven.

In 1845, she married George Prentiss, who was then minister of a Presbyterian church in Bedford, Massachusetts. In 1851, they moved to New York where George served a leading church there until 1873. From her marriage until her death at the age of fifty-nine, Elizabeth saw her role primarily as a wife and mother. For twenty-eight years she also worked to support her husband in pastoral ministry, apart from a break of two years in Europe from 1858 to 1860, where George sought recovery from a breakdown in health.

While her husband was in the ministry, Elizabeth counted it a privilege to be the first on the scene of human tragedy or need. She was a naturally lively person, and her brightness brought human comfort as well as spiritual consolation in such circumstances. She wrote to her eldest daughter Annie: "If I were you, I wouldn't marry anybody but a minister; it gives one such lots of people to love and care for."[2] And to a friend she wrote:

> You can't think how sweet it is to be a pastor's wife; to feel the *right* to sympathise with those who mourn, to fly to them at once, and join them in their prayers and tears. It would be pleasant to

---

2 George Lewis Prentiss, *More Love to Thee: Life and Letters of Elizabeth Prentiss* (1882; reprint, Amityville: Calvary Press, 1993), 330.

spend one's whole time among sufferers, and to keep testifying to them what Christ can and will become to them if only they will let Him.[3]

In 1873, her husband accepted an invitation to teach at Union Theological Seminary, New York. Elizabeth bitterly regretted leaving the pastoral role which she had always fulfilled alongside him.

Along with many women at this time, Elizabeth's life after marriage had followed a predictable pattern: youthful health shattered by a succession of pregnancies and the demands of sick children. In thirteen years she bore six children: Annie (1846), Eddie (1848), Elizabeth (1852), Minnie (1854), George (1857) and Henry (1859).

Childbirth and nursing sick infants sapped Elizabeth's strength, leaving her weighing less than ninety-eight pounds, and with her sleep pattern broken permanently. When Eddie was nineteen months she wrote to a friend:

I have written very few letters and not a line of anything else the past winter, owing to the confusion my mind is in most of the time from distress in my head. Three days out of every seven I am as sick as I well can be—the rest of the time languid, feeble, and exhausted by frequent faint turns, so that I can't do the smallest thing for my family…everything is going to destruction under my face and eyes, while I dare not lift a finger to remedy it. I live in constant alternations of hope and despondency about my health.[4]

And to her husband:

It seems to me I can never recover my spirits and be as I have been in my best days, but what I lose in one way perhaps I shall gain in another. Just think how my ambition has been crushed at every point by my ill-health, and even the ambition to be useful and a comfort to those about me is trampled underfoot, to teach me what I could not have learned in any other school![5]

---

3   Prentiss, *More Love to Thee*, 295.
4   Prentiss, *More Love to Thee*, 121.
5   Prentiss, *More Love to Thee*, 122.

Eddie died during their first winter in New York, at the age of three. Elizabeth was submissive, writing the well-known words in her journal:

> "Oh," said the gardener, as he passed down the garden-walk, "who plucked that flower?" His fellow-servants answered, "The Master!" And the gardener held his peace.[6]

But the grief further affected her health. Four months after Eddie's death, a baby girl was born. Elizabeth was left so dangerously ill that she was not even allowed to hold her daughter, and the doctor only allowed her to see her once a day. The infant died aged one month, and Elizabeth was haunted by her inability to nurse and comfort her. Now left with only her daughter Annie, Lizzie penned the following:

> One child and two green graves are mine,
>   This is God's gift to me;
> A bleeding, fainting, broken heart—
>   This is my gift to Thee.[7]

In 1854 she gave birth to another baby girl who suffered months of critical illness, and it seemed that they would lose her too. Elizabeth's experience equipped her to empathize with others. That year she received news that her childhood friend, Carrie, had also lost two children. Now she wrote from her own experience:

> Is it possible, is it possible that you are made childless? I feel distressed for you, my dear friend; I long to fly to you and weep with you; it seems as if I *must* say or do something to comfort you.... Dear Carrie, I trust that in this hour of sorrow you have with you that Presence, before which alone sorrow and sighing flee away. God is left; Christ is left; sickness, accident, death cannot touch you here. Is this not a blissful thought?...May sorrow bring us both nearer to Christ!... How strange our children,

---

6   Prentiss, *More Love to Thee*, 132.
7   Prentiss, *More Love to Thee*, 138.

Elizabeth Prentiss
1818–1878

our own little infants, have seen Him in his glory, whom we are only yet longing for and struggling towards![8]

Twenty-nine years later, Carrie remembered that after the death of her second child she had collapsed with grief. For days she lay on her bed wanting to die. Then Elizabeth's letter had arrived: "I was fairly aroused, lifted up, placed upon my feet, and by the grace of God have continued to this day."[9]

Elizabeth initially began writing as a means to distract her from her grief over the death of her two children. It was also a way in which she could feel useful, even at times when ill health meant she was unable to engage fully in all the activities of the church, and she viewed her writing as a natural offshoot of her husband's pastoral ministry.

As a teenager she had been a regular contributor to *The Youth's Companion*, a magazine which circulated widely among the children of New England. During the 1850s, she produced a popular series of didactic children's books, called the *Little Susie* books, as well as other books for children. In 1869, *Stepping Heavenward* was published, a full length adult novel which quickly became very successful. It had a wide circulation in the U.S.A., Britain, Canada and Australia, and was translated into French and German. The success of *Stepping Heavenward* encouraged Elizabeth to continue writing, including novels (effectively, advice books for women on themes such as marriage and parenting) and religious poetry. She died after a short illness at the family summer home in Dorset, Vermont, on August 13, 1878.

While the most widely read works in America during much of the eighteenth century were theological, the sale of novels overtook the sale of theological books during the nineteenth century. For many, it seems that reading religious novels took the place of reading narrowly theological works. The popularity of Prentiss' works (didactic in tone and intent) during the nineteenth century (in America, Great Britain and further afield) needs to be understood within this context. With the passing of the nineteenth century her books fell out of fashion.

---

8 Prentiss, *More Love to Thee*, 141–142.

9 Elizabeth Prentiss, *How Sorrow was changed into Sympathy: Words of Cheer for Mothers bereft of Little Children* (London: Hodder & Stoughton, 1884), 136. This was published after Elizabeth's death, compiled by her husband.

Some of her works were reprinted in the late twentieth century. Since being reprinted in the 1990s, over 100,000 copies of *Stepping Heavenward* have been sold. One of Elizabeth's poems, "More Love to Thee" became a well-known hymn, and is still sung in some churches today.

HOLINESS THROUGH SURRENDER

Marriage and childbearing were the inevitable destiny for the majority of women in the nineteenth century. All too often, the joy of having children was overshadowed by the danger posed by the medical challenges of the day. Many infants were stillborn, childhood disease carried off others and many mothers found their health destroyed, if not by the trauma of mismanaged labour, then by the constant anxiety of nursing critically ill children. Elizabeth had experienced this herself, and as a minister's wife she was constantly called on to visit women whose babies had died, or whose children were critically ill. The number of funerals of infants she attended probably ran into hundreds. Every year brought the inevitable death toll of children carried away by infectious disease. Whenever possible, Elizabeth went to comfort the bereaved parents. The death of her own children equipped her with an instinctive empathy, which was a great comfort to those she visited.

As far as she could see, the biological destiny of the women around her was not going to change: they would go on having babies, they would go on losing their health, and many of their babies would die. But she felt compelled to share the life-changing comfort which her knowledge of Christ had brought to her. She regarded her own ill-health as the means God used to make her depend on him more. She regarded the death of her children as drawing her closer to heaven, as she longed to be with Christ, where they had gone ahead. Merely stating these truths in a bald way to sick and grieving mothers would seem so crass, so she wrote her first full-length novel, aiming to entertain, and hold and move, at the same time as communicating the spiritual lessons which had gripped her.

Stepping Heavenward is written in the form of a journal, beginning when the protagonist, Katy, is sixteen. Self-willed and impetuous, she cannot see any appeal in the godliness displayed by her mother. Gradually, she realizes that real happiness is only found in knowing God. Marriage and motherhood pose real challenges: she struggles with exhaustion, irritability, sleeplessness and the feeling that she is failing as a mother and a wife. There is the strain of difficult in-laws living with the family, and the trauma of bereavement, poverty and ill-health. In the midst of constant family demands she has to fight to maintain any form of devotional life, and worries that she is failing spiritually. The truth that despite all this, she is in reality "stepping heavenward" brought in much of Elizabeth's own experience, and proved to be a real encouragement to many others.

Her friend Eliza Warner wrote:

> Believing in Christ was to her not so much a duty as the deepest joy of her life, heightening all other joys, and she was not satisfied until her friends shared with her in this experience. She believed it to be attainable by all, founded on a complete submitting of the human to the Divine will in all things, great and small.[10]

This was what drove Elizabeth to write so prolifically. She wanted to bring the joy and comfort of the love of Christ into the lives of others. In particular, she wrote for women: showing them that surrender to the will of God can provide strength for mundane tasks, and grace for the various challenges of family relationships.

Perhaps the commonest complaint of young mothers is "I'm just too busy to pray!" Katy is no exception. But she learns:

> I have made prayer too much of a luxury, and have often inwardly chafed and fretted when the care of my children at times, made it utterly impossible to leave them for private devotion—when they have been sick, for instance, or in other similar emergencies. I reasoned this way: "Here is a special demand on my patience, and I am naturally impatient. I must have time to go away and entreat the Lord to equip me for this conflict." But I see now that the simple act of cheerful acceptance of the duty imposed and the solace and support withdrawn would have united me more fully to Christ than the highest enjoyment of His presence in prayer could.[11]

---

10 Prentiss, *More Love to Thee*, 285.

11 Elizabeth Prentiss, *Stepping Heavenward* (1869; reprint, Amityville: Calvary Press, 1993), 246.

The novel thus urged women to view every act of obedience, however humble, as an act of worship. This gave significance to everyday life. Women with a sense of purpose and dignity were less likely to succumb to depression and all the physical problems associated with that. "*Not my will! But Thine!*" This motif runs through the novel. There are allusions throughout to the teachings of François Fénelon (1616–1715, author of *Letters of Spiritual Counsel*) and Thomas à Kempis (1380–1471, author of *The Imitation of Christ*). Both writers emphasize submission to God. Katy learns submission, most particularly in being willing to "give her children back to God." While, ultimately, accepting God's sovereignty in such tragedies, Katy finds it harder to submit patiently in the smallest details of life:

What grieves me is that I am constantly forgetting to recognise God's hand in the little everyday trials of life, and instead of receiving them as from Him, find fault with the instruments by which He sends them. I can give up my child, my only brother, my darling mother without a word; but to receive every tiresome visitor as sent directly and expressly to weary me by the Master Himself...all this I have not fully learned.[12]

At the close of the novel, Katy reflects on a leap forward in her spiritual life that had occurred seven years previously:

If I die it will be to leave a wearied and worn body, and a sinful soul, to go joyfully to be with Christ, to be weary and sin no more. If I live, I shall find much blessed work to do for Him. So living or dying, I will be the Lord's. But I wish, oh, how earnestly, that whether I go or stay, I could inspire some lives with the joy that is now mine. For many years I have been rich in faith; rich in an unfaltering confidence that I was beloved of my God and Saviour. But something was missing; I was always groping for a mysterious grace the lack of which made me often sorrowful in the very midst of my most sacred joy, imperfect when I longed most for perfection. It was that *personal love of Christ* of which my precious mother so often spoke to me, which she often urged

12 Prentiss, *Stepping Heavenward*, 230–231.

me to seek upon my knees. If I had known then, as I know now, what this priceless treasure could be to a sinful human soul, I would have sold all that I had to buy the field in which it lay hidden. But not till I was shut up to prayer and the study of God's word by the loss of earthly joys, sickness destroying the flavour of them all, did I begin to penetrate the mystery that is learned under the cross. And wondrous as it is, how simple is that mystery! To love Christ, and to know that I love Him—this is all![13]

It has been suggested that this episode demonstrates, at the least, an equivocation about the validity of the "perfection" that the "higher life" movement was advocating at this time.[14] But the focus of Katy's testimony here is two-fold: first a deep awareness of love for and from Christ—which had arisen from her years of suffering, and second, a longing to be with Christ. She says clearly that she longs to leave "a sinful soul" and "sin no more." Prentiss believed that sin would remain with a Christian until death.

REJECTION OF PERFECTIONISM

Before Elizabeth's marriage, her older sister Louisa became attracted to the views of the "perfectionists." The two sisters had many long discussions on this point. Elizabeth was unconvinced by the perfectionist arguments: she was too aware of the deep-seated sinfulness of her own life and believed that the battle against sin would be a reality throughout this life.

The year after the publication of *Stepping Heavenward*, the controversy over "Christian perfection" resurfaced with the publication and subsequent popularity of Robert Pearsall Smith's *Holiness through Faith* (Boston, 1870). Elizabeth read it, rejected it, then read it again, and found it more convincing.[15] In the end, she again found herself compelled to reject the notion of "holiness through faith."

She could sometimes write about the perfectionists humorously.

---

13 Prentiss, *Stepping Heavenward,* 270–271.

14 Miho Yamaguchi, "Elizabeth Prentiss' Faith in Suffering and Perplexity about the Wesleyan and the Higher Life Doctrines: On *Stepping Heavenward*," *Literature and Theology* 18.4 (2004): 415–426.

15 Prentiss, *More Love to Thee,* 378, 396, 427, 431–436, 480.

It seems almost incredible that a wholly sanctified character could publish such a book, made up as it is of the author's own letters and journal and most sacred joys and sorrows; but perhaps when I get sanctified I shall go to printing mine—it really seems to be a way they have.[16]

In a letter to a friend in October 1871, she delivered a devastating critique of their thinking. Perfectionists, she observed, pour scorn on the vast majority of Christians as "ordinary" and "miserable doubters."[17] They deny the truth that God chastizes those he loves. They say that true religion is rapture, not conflict. They claim exclusive knowledge of truth, and accuse anyone who doubts perfectionist claims to be doubting God himself.[18] Such claims made Elizabeth really angry: "Imagine soldiers getting ready for warfare, being told by their commander that they had no need to drill, and had nothing to do but drink nectar!"[19]

She was also sad to see the stress that this teaching placed on tender consciences: "A worthy young woman in our church has been driven into hysterics by reading 'Holiness through Faith.' I went to see her as soon as I got home…, but she was asleep under the influence of an opiate."[20] And subsequently: "Poor M— has gone crazy on 'Holiness through Faith,' and will probably have to go to an asylum."[21]

In 1872, she wrote: "I have read and re-read the books that treat on this subject, and cannot believe in that instantaneous sanctification that looks so plausible, but which thus far I have vainly sought on my knees and in my Bible."[22] And later still, in 1877, to another friend:

My friend Miss —, reproached me for not having preached perfection in it [*Urbane and His Friends*]; but I told her I could not find perfection in the Bible, had never seen it in my life, and

16 Prentiss, *More Love to Thee*, 286.

17 Prentiss, *More Love to Thee*, 477.

18 Prentiss, *More Love to Thee*, 478.

19 Prentiss, *More Love to Thee*, 479.

20 Prentiss, *More Love to Thee*, 392.

21 Prentiss, *More Love to Thee*, 395.

22 Elizabeth Prentiss, "Letter to George Prentiss, March 25, 1872," in Elizabeth Prentiss, *Urbane and His Friends* (Surrey: AB Publishing, 1999), 303.

had observed that those who claimed that they attained it, usually ended by running into spiritualism or antinomianism, and made shipwreck of their faith. One, who assured me he had not sinned for twenty-five years, talked and behaved (in the one interview I had with him) in such a manner that for days I was so staggered I could not pray.... If this had been a common man I should not have been so upset; but he was a leader in the church and had been a great light.... I had a perfectionist in my house a month, during which, though she rose hours before breakfast, she never once came to prayers, thereby bidding defiance to our habits as a family. The idea appeared to be that she could not join in confession of sins. But that we may be kept from wilful sin I do not doubt.[23]

Prentiss' settled conviction for most of her life (including the period when *Stepping Heavenward* was written) was that their claims of perfection were spurious and dangerous. Having said that, she was willing to concede that she respected their great desire for holiness, and that one could learn from some, not all, of their teaching. She agreed with them that sometimes Christians do experience a "sudden and extraordinary experience" which transforms their lives, but she argued that this is normally preceded by much prayer and disciplined obedience.[24]

Elizabeth's own experience had matured by going through a long "dark night" experience, in which all felt sense of peace had gone. As a younger Christian she believed that whatever the circumstances, a Christian could know peace, through submitting to the will of God. She herself had experienced this; she wanted to help others to know this peace too. But, during 1871 and 1872, she was plunged into a "dark night of the soul" experience, when she lost all conscious sense of the presence of God. Through church history, there have been those who testify that such a terrible sense of desertion can serve to wean a Christian away from excessive reliance on feeling. Afterwards Elizabeth was able to write:

---

23 Elizabeth Prentiss, "Letter to Mrs A. B. H., April 27, 1877," in Prentiss, *Urbane and His Friends*, 313–315.

24 See her husband's comments on this, Prentiss, *More Love to Thee*, 433–434.

Mere delight in Him, sweet as it is, is not to be our pursuit on earth. Let us go on seeking Him if it leads to death itself, and spare neither the right hand or the right hand when they offend us.[25]

At the time, it seems that only her husband was aware of the inner conflict of these years. Elizabeth kept as busy as ever, with the family, with writing, and with pastoral visiting. But as she began to emerge from what seemed to be a dark tunnel, she did write about it to a few trusted friends.[26] Elizabeth told her cousin George Prentiss in a letter in March 1872 that she had been "buffeted by a messenger of Satan" for more than a year in a way that she had never before known. This was giving her a new sympathy for those afflicted with doubt and despair. She was not talking much about this loss of the sense of God's presence, for fear of discouraging others, but believed that this "baptism of fire" might be needed to consume remaining selfishness.[27] Then, in May, she described something of the desolation caused by the loss of the felt sense of the presence of God:

I knew, for years, the sweetest peace and rest, with periods of joy that was [sic] almost insupportable. At the same time I never thought myself sinless. I only knew that I had a perfect Saviour, and the instant I fell into inadvertent sin, I asked Him to forgive me, and He did.... But whether I was exalted by the abundance of revelations, or whatever else might be the reason, I was suddenly cast down from heaven to hell—yes, to hell; for the loss of the Presence, in which I had lived so long, is nothing less; and I have been in this valley of humiliation eighteen months, or somewhere near that, and it has been precisely like that described by Bunyan. I used to preach, in season and out of season, the doctrine that anybody could live in perfect peace;

---

25 Elizabeth Prentiss, "Letter to 'a young friend', April 11, 1872," in Prentiss, *Urbane and His Friends*, 302.

26 As with her other correspondence, after her death in 1878 her husband went through and edited some for publication. Some letters relating to the holiness controversy were included in the 1887 edition of *Urbane and His Friends*, as they clarified her views on this hotly disputed topic.

27 Prentiss, "Letter to George Prentiss, March 25, 1872," in Prentiss, *Urbane and His Friends*, 304.

but now I have come to an *experience* wholly new, and I know other Christians in the same condition.... Now you may never need and so never have such an awful affliction, but as I have learned it through personal experience, I cannot doubt that God has permitted it for some wise, some kind reason, for which I shall bless Him in the next life, if I never know enough to do it in this. As He could not severely hurt me by taking away any beloved earthly object, since if He were left, enough would be left to make life perfectly sweet, He has come nearer, and inflicted blows of tenfold severity. Madame Guyon had nearly seven years of such desolation, and it completed the work God was resolved to do in her.... Certainly I could not have endured, in my youth, the anguish of the last months.[28]

The allusion to Madame Guyon (1648–1717) is telling. During the first part of 1870, Elizabeth had spent a lot more time studying the writings of this French mystic. The two central emphases in Guyon's writings are the need to accept the will of God in all the sufferings of life, and the need to die to self. These were the very themes that had become so central to Elizabeth's spiritual life. Her husband George wrote: "Madam Guyon for several years exerted a decided influence on her views of the Christian life."[29] The highly introspective elements of Guyon's thought may have exacerbated the difficult experience Elizabeth went through during this time.

While Elizabeth denied that "sinless perfection" can be reached in this life, or that sanctification could be achieved by means of an instantaneous experience, she yet insisted that the quest for absolute holiness was one that every Christian should be engaged in. "I think if I knew I should never say or do or feel anything sinful, I should be too happy to live."[30]

---

28 Elizabeth Prentiss, "Letter to George Prentiss, May 23, 1872," in Prentiss, *Urbane and His Friends*, 306–307.

29 Prentiss, *More Love to Thee*, 293.

30 Prentiss, "Letter to George Prentiss, March 25, 1872," in Prentiss, *Urbane and His Friends*, 305.

I had a talk with Mrs — the other day. She said I was aiming too high, trying to be as perfect as God is. But is not this the Scriptural command? Whatever I aim at, I am far enough below, at any rate.[31]

Her own life was always characterized by an ongoing quest for holiness. She never thought she had "arrived," to the end she was always concerned about the state of her own heart: not what others thought about her but what God thought. This desire for single-minded integrity is reflected in this seemingly trivial incident, remembered by a friend:

She was honest, truthful, *genuine* to the highest degree. It may have sometimes led her into seeming lack of courtesy, but even this was a failing which "leaned to virtue's side." I chanced to know of her once calling with a friend on a country neighbor, and finding the good housewife busy over a rag-carpet. Mrs Prentiss...was full of questions and interest, thereby quite evidently pleasing the unassuming artist.... When the visitors were safely outside the door, Mrs Prentiss' friend turned to her with the exclamation, "What tact you have! She really thought you were interested in her work!" The quick blood sprang into Mrs Prentiss' face, and she turned upon her friend a look of amazement and rebuke. "Tact!" she said, "I despise such tact!—do you think *I would look or act a lie?*"[32]

After her death, her husband wrote at length about her convictions on the subject of holiness, and concluded:

The finer and more exalted the sentiment of of purity and honour, the more sensitive will one be to what is impure or dishonourable in one's own character and conduct. Such is substantially her ground of dissent from the "Higher Life" theory. Her own sense of sin was so profound and vivid that she shuddered at the

31 Prentiss, "Letter to George Prentiss, May 23, 1872," in Prentiss, *Urbane and His Friends,* 308.

32 Prentiss, *More Love to Thee,* 358–359

thought of claiming it for herself, and it seemed to her a very sad delusion for anybody else to claim it. True holiness is never self-conscious; it does not look at itself in the glass; and if it did, it would see only Christ, not itself, reflected there…. [S]he came to regard all theories, still more all professions, of entire sanctification as fallacious, and full of peril.[33]

Although *Stepping Heavenward* does not endorse the teaching of the perfectionists, it was published at a time when there was widespread interest in the quest for holiness. The transparent sincerity of Katy's pursuit of godliness struck a chord with Christians from many different traditions, which partly accounted for its success. Prentiss managed to communicate how a life lived close to God could be grounded in the everyday reality of routine mundane responsibilities—she showed how "real" holiness was possible in "real" life.

A letter written in December 1870 contained the following words on the work of the Spirit:

I have been led, during the last month or two, to a new love of the Holy Spirit, or perhaps to more consciousness of the silent, blessed work He is doing in and for us…. The more I reflect and the more I pray, the more life narrows down to one point—What am I being for Christ, what am I doing for Him?[34]

As Elizabeth reflected on "what am I doing for Him," she was always grounded in the daily reality of family and church life. Spirituality, for her, was not some esoteric experience. It was being patient with a tired and grumpy child, serving the needs of her husband when she was exhausted herself and listening patiently to the complaints of a discontented church member. It was about cheerful homemaking, always trying to make family and guests happy. Her own hospitality was legendary. One grateful guest wrote:

What a delightful home she made! The "good cheer" she furnished for the minds, hearts, and bodies of her guests was something

---

33 Prentiss, *More Love to Thee*, 434.
34 Prentiss, *More Love to Thee*, 319.

remarkable. I shall never forget my visits; I was in a state of high entertainment from beginning to end. What entertaining stories she told! What practical wisdom she gave out in the most natural and incidental way! And what housekeeping! Common articles of food seemed to possess new virtues and new zest. I always went away full of the marvels of the visit, as well as loaded down with many little tokens of her kindness and thoughtfulness.[35]

Elizabeth Prentiss' writing reflected the cultural assumptions of the nineteenth century.[36] But her works communicated exalted truth about God in a style that was grounded in everyday life. Writing to a young friend in 1873, she said:

To love Christ more—this is the deepest need, the constant cry of my soul. Down in the bowling ally, and out in the woods, and on my bed, and out driving, when I am happy and busy, and when I am sad and idle, the whisper keeps going up for more love, more love, more love![37]

Frances Ridley Havergal

Frances Ridley Havergal was born in 1836 in a large vicarage in a tiny hamlet, Astley, in the depths of the English countryside. Her father, William Havergal, was an evangelical, and a distinguished church musician and composer. When Frances was born, her five older siblings were aged nineteen down to seven. She soon displayed unusual gifts: she could read at the age of three and quickly learned French and German. When she was nine, her father became a rector in the city of Worcester. Little Frances found the wrench away from the

---

35 Prentiss, *More Love to Thee*, 461.

36 Elizabeth Prentiss is named in Ann Douglas' seminal work *The Feminization of American Culture* as one of the female writers who exemplified the shift to a more sentimental approach to religion. Douglas argues that the nineteenth century marked a shift in American theology and culture, and that the growing influence of female writers (many of them daughters and wives of clergymen) played a significant part in this. She names thirty key women writers including Elizabeth Prentiss. For discussion of this point, see Sharon James, *Elizabeth Prentiss: More Love to Thee* (Edinburgh: The Banner of Truth Trust, 2006), 214–216.

37 Prentiss, *More Love to Thee*, 411–412.

country fields to the narrow streets very hard. Far worse, two years later, her mother died.

As a little girl, and right into her teens, Frances was deeply aware of her own sinfulness. In her quest for assurance, she set herself to read the Bible for an hour daily. It was not until 1851, when she was fifteen, that she was certain that she herself was saved. "I could and did trust the Lord Jesus...for the first time my Bible was sweet to me."[38] In 1852 she was able to attend a school in Germany for a while, and despite all the studies being conducted in German she gained top place in all her subjects. She was also enabled to make a clear profession of faith, even though none of the other students were Christians, and she came in for a fair deal of opposition. She then went to stay with a German pastor and his family for a while, in order to further her studies. The pastor wrote:

> She showed from the first, such application, such rare talent, such depth of comprehension, that I can only speak of her progress as extraordinary. She acquired such a knowledge of our most celebrated authors in such a short time as even German ladies attain after much longer study.... What imprinted the stamp of nobility upon her whole being, and influenced all her opinions, was her true piety, and the deep reverence she had for her Lord and Saviour, whose example penetrated her young life through and through.[39]

At the age of seventeen, back in Worcester, she was confirmed. During the service she had a powerful sense of being loved by all three persons of the Trinity:

> On reaching our seat, I sunk on my knees and the thought of "whose I am" burst upon me and I prayed "My God, oh, my *own* Father, Thou blessed Jesus my *own* Saviour, Thou Holy Spirit my *own* comforter."[40]

---

38 Maria V.G. Havergal, *Memorials of Frances Ridley Havergal* (London: J. Nisbet, 1884), 39.

39 Janet Grierson, *Frances Ridley Havergal: Worcestershire Hymnwriter* (Worcestershire: FRH Society, 1979), 11.

40 Havergal, *Memorials*, 53.

Having finished her schooling, she spent her time continuing her private studies. By the age of twenty, she had committed large portions of the Bible to memory, many sections in the Greek; later she learned Hebrew. She was fully involved in the spiritual and benevolent aspects of parish work alongside her father and new stepmother. She loved teaching Sunday school, took a detailed interest in her pupils and offered them weekly opportunities for one-to-one times of Bible reading and prayer. She excelled in this kind of personal work. Her Sunday School register served as a daily prayer diary for her scholars, and she noted in the last page of the register:

It has been to my own soul a means of grace. Often, when cold and lifeless in prayer, my nightly intercession for them has unsealed the frozen fountain, and the blessing sought for them seemed to fall on myself. Often and often have my own words to them been as a message to myself of warning or peace...seldom have Bible truths seemed to reach and touch me more than when seeking to arrange and simplify them for my children.[41]

In 1860, when she was twenty-three, her father moved to a much smaller parish near Litchfield, a hamlet with less than 400 inhabitants—there simply wouldn't be work for Frances there. Her father, stepmother and older unmarried sister Maria could cover the needs.

Frances was hugely gifted, intellectually and musically, and had considerable experience in all kinds of Christian work. But there was no way that she could enter into an independent vocation or career. It was assumed at this time that middle class women would not go out to paid employment. There were all sorts of useful philanthropic things they could do, as long as it was voluntary work. If they did not marry, they were always dependent on relatives. The only occupation thought to be "respectable" was that of governess. So, for approximately the next six years, Frances went to live with her older sister Miriam and her family, to act as governess to her two little girls until they were ready for boarding school. Oakhampton, the family home, was a beautiful estate, near the parish of Astley where Frances had spent her early years. Frances loved the children, her life was pleasant

---

41 Havergal, *Memorials*, 67.

enough, she used every spare moment for Bible study, developing her music, or leading Bible studies for people in the nearby village. But teaching two little girls was not an ideal use of her gifts, and she never had the freedom of having a home of her own. After the girls went to boarding school, Frances moved to another older married sister, Ellen, to act as governess for her four children for a short period.

In 1867, Frances' father and stepmother moved to Leamington Spa. She was no longer needed as a governess, so she moved to Leamington with them. Again, she became involved in a whole variety of voluntary ministries. She was fully involved in raising funds for missions, she led the choir in her church, using it as a discipleship class, she started Bible classes for young working women in Leamington and she was involved in the early years of the Young Women's Christian Association (YWCA).

After just a year, her father died, and Frances had little option but to continue living with her stepmother Caroline. Frances was by now thirty-three. She had received several proposals of marriage, but had declined them. She would not have considered marrying anyone who was not a really committed Christian. But the next eight years were very difficult. Caroline was a difficult and demanding woman who never allowed Frances any real freedom. She didn't allow Frances to have visitors in her room, or even to have a fire there, which meant that during the day Frances had to be downstairs in the general living area with no privacy for writing. Frances believed it her duty to remain with her stepmother and submit to her, but her life was very restricted.

In the summer, Caroline closed up the house to go travelling, and Frances had to leave also. So Frances travelled during the summers: sometimes staying with her various married siblings, sometimes travelling with them or with a friend to Wales, the Lake District or to the Continent. The introduction of railways had opened up continental travel for British tourists, and large numbers of the middle classes began taking trips to France, Switzerland and Italy. Frances visited the continent five times between 1869 and 1876. Each time she recorded her daily experiences in "circular" letters to her family members, and after her death they were edited and published.[42] They make

---

42 Frances Ridley Havergal, *Swiss Letters*, ed. Jane Miriam Crane (London: James Nisbet, 1881). Her letters found a ready audience. Just as an appreciative American public pounced on Harriet Beecher Stowe's *Sunny Memories of Foreign Lands* (1854),

delightful reading. Frances loved meeting different people, and she was able to converse fluently in German and French. She had an eye for the humour in any situation, and her vivid descriptions are lively, funny and show her love of beauty. Woven through her letters are numerous anecdotes of personal witness. She made friends effortlessly with fellow travellers, hotel maids, workers in the fields and mountain guides. She constantly shared the gospel and gave out tracts. For example, when she and her friend Elizabeth passed through Paris, which had been recently torn apart by war, they spent nearly three hours giving out tracts:

> Such eagerness for the little books, such gratitude, such attentive listening as we tried to talk of Jesus, such tears as we touched the chord of suffering, still vibrating among these poor people, to whom war had been an awful reality! Surely God sent us!... We went into a large room where several wounded soldiers lay... here again all was earnest attention and gratitude.... As we returned through the town we found many waylaying us. At one point...at least thirty persons were waiting, and pressed around us begging for more tracts.[43]

In every inn they stayed, they spoke to the maids, and gave out Gospels in the appropriate language with key texts marked up. While out walking they went to groups of haymakers, spoke to them and gave tracts. They memorized verses in French and German, to share with others. Frances graphically described the spiritual darkness of the Catholic cantons of Switzerland, and appealed for others to go and share the gospel with them.

It was during the Leamington years that Frances saw her first book published. *The Ministry of Song* (1869) was to be the first of many published works: some poetry, some devotional, some for children. She seems to have caught the mood of the time in style and content.

---

using Stowe's holiday diaries almost as a guidebook for the new pastime of visiting Europe, so Havergal's admirers were able to learn about the new possibilities of continental travel from her *Swiss Letters*, and pick up tips as to where to go, what to do and even what to wear.

43 Havergal, *Swiss Letters*, 194.

Seventeen publications appeared during the period 1871 to her death in 1879, and then thirteen appeared after 1880. Many of them achieved wide circulation. There were also three musical works, and countless articles and poems in religious periodicals, equally numerous writings appeared in leaflet or tract form, or printed out on small gift cards: "After her death, her popularity was so great that the market was flooded with small booklets containing selections from her prose and verse, often illustrated."[44] Her writing had to take place on what she said were the "margins" of her time, as her life was pretty full with all sorts of other ministries.

In 1878 her stepmother died, and Frances had to close up the home in Leamington. She moved to Wales, to set up house with her older sister Maria. The next months were incredibly productive, in terms of writing and also local evangelism. She continued to be heavily involved in raising support for Irish mission work, and was about to travel over to Ireland when she herself died at the early age of forty-two, from acute peritonitis.

THE KESWICK MOVEMENT

Frances' name became linked with the Keswick Movement, as her hymns became a staple component of the Keswick Convention (an annual meeting of evangelicals in the Lake District, first held in 1875 with the aim of the promotion of "practical holiness"). Keswick teaching could be summed up as "sanctification by faith." This emphasis had been a feature of the annual Mildmay conferences, organized by William Pennefather (a few of which Frances had attended).

Frances never attended Keswick. Her teaching and experience was, she said, the result of private Bible study and prayer, not conferences or conventions. She did not believe that a Christian could ever achieve sinless perfection in this life. Unlike many Keswick leaders, she was not pre-millennial in her view of the last things, rather holding to one final return of Christ. It would be unfair to associate her with all Keswick teaching, just because her hymns became so popular with convention goers.

Having said that, her experience and writings did seem to endorse one aspect of Keswick teaching. Frances enjoyed a one-off and intense

---

44 Grierson, *Frances Ridley Havergal*, 190.

spiritual experience, and then attributed to this experience a change of life: peace replacing worry; perfect assurance replacing insecurity. Arguably the peace and enjoyment which she enjoyed in her last years cannot be separated from her deliberate, careful, obedient discipleship over preceding years, her prayer, meditation, Bible memorization and study, witnessing and worship. The danger of putting her experience in writing was that Christians who could not be bothered with all of that painful discipline might then attend a Keswick Convention and expect a consecration experience that would lift them onto the same "higher plain" of peace and assurance. Keswick teaching could become a short cut for the lazy. Consecration and surrender could be misread as passivity. Frances would not have endorsed the unhealthier extreme of Keswick teaching, but some of her hymns and poems could be hijacked by advocates of that extreme.

On Advent Sunday 1873, just six years before her death, Frances had an experience that was to affect her profoundly. It was a powerful awareness, such as she had never had before, of the cleansing blood of Jesus, and that having cleansed her, Christ had the power to keep her, "so I just utterly yielded myself to Him, and utterly trusted Him to keep me."[45]

By nature Frances was a perfectionist, and constantly disappointed with her own spiritual performance. But on this day, the text 1 John 1:7 seemed to speak to her in a new way. She suddenly grasped the significance of the present tense: "the blood of Jesus cleanses us from all sin." As she wrote to her sister Maria:

I saw it as a flash of electric light, and what you see, you can never unsee. There must be full surrender before there can be true blessedness. God admits you by the one into the other…. First, I was shown that "the blood of Jesus Christ his Son cleanseth us from all sin," and then that it was made plain to me that He who had thus cleansed me had power to keep me clean, so I utterly yielded myself to Him, and utterly trusted Him to keep me…. It was that one word "cleanseth" which opened the door of a very glory of hope and joy to me. I had never seen the force of the tense before, a continual present, always a present tense, not a

---

45 Grierson, *Frances Ridley Havergal*, 139.

present which the next moment becomes a past. It goes on cleansing, and I have no words to tell how my heart rejoices in it. Not a coming to be cleansed in the fountain only, but a remaining in the fountain, so that it may and can go on cleansing.[46]

While other Christians at the time claimed to have attained sinless perfection, it was precisely *because* Frances was so aware of her ongoing sin that she revelled in the certainty of ongoing forgiveness. While some misread her experience, and suggested that she had joined those who claimed sinless perfection, she fiercely denied it.[47] Rather, this renewed experience of consecration was the culmination of her prayer "take my will…my heart…my self." She wrote on Easter Sunday the next year:

Oh, it was so sweet, so glorious to see something of that, the being His own, the serving Him and pleasing Him, the being utterly at His disposal, and with Him, and in Him, and all for Him, on and on through ages and ages of eternity. My whole heart said, "Whom have I in heaven but Thee? and there is none upon earth that I desire beside Thee!" It has been such a special day, that I cannot help hoping it may have been given, not for myself only, but to prepare me for some special message bearing, perhaps only one-to-one, perhaps to many while I am away. But I never feel eager even for that now; it is so much happier to leave it all with him, and I always pray, "Use me Lord, or do not use me, just as Thou wilt. Oh, he is so good to me, I really did not know six months ago that such unvarying peace was possible here…. Only I wish everybody had it, and I wish good people would not think it their duty to stay in Romans vii, as I always conscientiously believed till of late! I cannot imagine how they can think that Rom. vii 25 and Rom. viii 2 could both describe St Paul's experience at the same moment. They seem so clearly consecutive and not contemporaneous. So "Thanks be to God which giveth us the victory, through our Lord Jesus Christ!"[48]

46 Havergal, *Memorials*, 126–127, 129.
47 Havergal, *Memorials*, 128.
48 Havergal, *Swiss Letters*, 140–141.

Frances Ridley Havergal
1836–1879

She wrote in May 1874:

The wonderful and glorious blessing which so many Christians are testifying to having found, was suddenly, marvellously sent to me last winter; and life is now what I never imagined life on earth could be, though I knew much of peace and joy in believing.... It seems as if a call were going forth to His own children to make a more complete surrender of their whole selves and lives, and to enter into a fullness of consecration, which I for one had not realised before.[49]

And in October 1874:

So you too are being stirred up by the "loving Spirit" to seek holiness and rest beyond that you have as yet found! Thank God! And I know not how to thank him enough that though only a year ago I knew absolutely nothing of this blessed life—had not read one word about it,—I can now tell you joyously that His own hand has led me into it, and that for nearly a year I have not known what it is to have a shadow of care in things temporal or spiritual, all is cast on Him and He gives me the victory and gladness in response to the utter trust (which is no less His gift); so that it is living a new life, and one which I really did not even suppose to be possible on earth.[50]

This was not merely an emotional experience but was rooted in the objective truth of the doctrine of union with Christ. She was now less dependent on her emotional ups and downs. This powerful sense of union with Christ seemed to liberate Frances, she felt as if a new life had begun. It was in the following year that she wrote her most famous hymn:

Take my life, and let it be
  Consecrated, Lord, to Thee,
Take my moments and my days,
  Let them flow in ceaseless praise.

---

49 Quoted in T.H. Darlow, *Frances Ridley Havergal: A Saint of God* (London: 1927), 39.
50 Havergal, *Swiss Letters*, 217.

Take my hands and let them move
   At the impulse of Thy love;
Take my feet and let them be
   Swift and beautiful for Thee.

Take my voice and let me sing
   Always, only for my King;
Take my lips and let them be
   Filled with messages from Thee.

Take my silver and my gold,
   Not a mite would I withhold;
Take my intellect and use
   Every power as Thou shalt choose.

Take my will and make it Thine;
   It shall be no longer mine:
Take my heart, it is Thine own;
   It shall be Thy royal throne.

Take my love; my Lord I pour
   At Thy feet its treasure store:
Take myself and I will be
   Ever, only, all for Thee.

She explained the circumstances in which it was written:

I went for a little visit of five days [to friends at Areley House,
outside Stouport]. There were ten persons in the house, some
unconverted and long prayed for, some converted but not rejoicing Christians. He gave me the prayer, "Lord, give me *all* in this
house!" And He just *did*! Before I left the house everyone had got
a blessing. The last night of my visit I was too happy to sleep, and
passed most of the night in praise and renewal of my own consecration, and these little couplets formed themselves and
chimed in my heart one after another until they finished with
Ever, only, ALL for Thee![51]

---

51 Havergal, *Memorials*, 132–133.

Scribbled out at the end of that night of praise, Frances did not at first think the verses worthy of publication. But they soon became well loved. When invited to speak at meetings, Frances began taking supplies of cards with the hymn printed out and a blank space for a signature. After explaining its meaning she would invite all who could sincerely sign to do so. She also wrote a companion devotional book *Kept for the Master's Use*, which was packed with practical advice on living a consecrated life. The book focused on the love of Christ and how the only fitting response is total devotion. Here is an extract:

Himself for thee. "Christ also has loved us, and given himself for us." "The Son of God loved me, and gave himself for me." Yes, himself! What is the Bride's true and central treasure? What calls forth the deepest, brightest, sweetest thrill of love and praise? Not the Bridegroom's priceless gifts, not the robe of his resplendent righteousness, not the dowry of unsearchable riches, not the magnificence of the palace home to which he is bringing her, not the glory which she shall share with him, but himself, Jesus Christ, "who his own self bare our sins in his own body on the tree;" this same Jesus, "whom having not seen, ye love;" the Son of God and the Man of Sorrows; my Saviour, my Friend, my Master, my King, my Priest, my Lord, and my God—he says, "I also for thee." What an "I"! What power and sweetness we feel in it, so different from any human! For all his Godhead and all his manhood are concentrated on it—and all for thee. *And not only all but ever for thee*! His unchangeableness is the seal upon every attribute; he will be this same Jesus forever. How can mortal mind estimate this enormous promise? How can mortal heart conceive what is enfolded in these words, "I also for thee"? One glimpse of its fullness and glory, and we feel that henceforth it must be, shall be, and by this grace will be our true-hearted, whole-hearted cry—"Take myself, and I will be, ever, only, all for thee!"[52]

She was gripped by the simple truth "all for Jesus," and shared it with as many as possible, whenever she could. While on holiday in

---

52 Frances Ridley Havergal, *Kept for the Master's Use* (Grand Rapids: Baker Book House, 1977), 127–128.

Europe in 1875 she organized an impromptu French gospel service for the locals at her hotel that afternoon, for which she wrote the hymn *Seulemont pour Toi*. She also spoke to fellow tourists whenever possible. One of these later wrote to her sister:

> God led us to Champery that we might meet your dear sister, Frances.... She was so happy and whole-hearted, and she spoke to me of the Lord Jesus, and the joy of being altogether and only his. Yes, it was on the balcony at Champery that a new life and love seemed lighted up in my soul. Even as she was speaking to me I felt that with God's grace, I must take the same step as she had, and henceforth live "only for Jesus."

Empowered by her Advent Sunday experience, Frances produced a rapid succession of enormously popular booklets, books, poems and hymns. Publishers vied with each other for her writings, she received an average of 600 letters a week from appreciative readers. After her premature death in 1879, at the early age of forty-two, her writings continued in popularity, and several of her hymns are still used today.

In March 1879 (the year of her death), she noted "H – converted; and O P – consecrated." Her sister Maria explained this journal entry as follows:

> [Frances] had promised to take most needed rest from her desk-work on the breezy cliffs that afternoon. The hour passed by, and still her door was shut. Then she came, beaming of course: "Marie, I've had such a tussle with Satan! I had my hat on and was going to the cliffs with you when I saw O.P. on a ladder painting my study windows. I was so tired, that it was quite a battle to talk to him *then*, but I threw the window open to ask how he was getting on. Directly he said, 'O, Miss Frances, I've been longing for weeks for a chance to speak to you.' Then came such an out-pour of his desire to be quite out and out on the Lord's side; so I saw the time was come, as I expected it would from our last conversation. So I told him to come in through the window; and after reading and prayer, I asked if he would *now* in his own words say to Jesus himself, 'Thou art my King.' And so he did, fully and really, and the answer 'I will be thy King' seemed to fall with

hushing power as we knelt. And afterwards he told me how differently he left my study than when he came in, so glad that Jesus was henceforth his King as well as his Saviour."[53]

This terminology certainly meshed with the "two-tier" emphasis increasingly adopted by proponents of Keswick teaching, and could be read in such a way as to encourage the idea that consecration can be reached by a one-off experience.[54]

EVERYDAY HOLINESS

The main impact of Frances Ridley Havergal's ministry, however, did not lie in promoting a "two-tier" Christianity, so much as in urging all Christians to life of complete consecration. The great popularity of Frances' writing, like Prentiss arose from her ability to communicate how holiness could be translated into everyday life.

Also, like Prentiss, she was an attractive role model. Those who knew her, spoke of her warmth, charm, cheerfulness, affection and genuinely outgoing personality. There was a radiance and glow about her that could not be captured in any picture.[55] Her brother-in-law commented that wherever she went, numerous individuals wanted to make appointments to see her. When she visited a large household, many, whether family, friends, mere acquaintances or servants, would seek her out to speak "one to one" about their spiritual lives.

Frances set herself to "live for the moment": to serve others cheerfully in little ways and regard the trivial duties of each day as sent from God. This gave significance to what would otherwise have been a disjointed existence. She seized every opportunity for "personal work," whether sharing the gospel message with non-Christians, or encouraging Christians to trust Christ more fully. A large portion of her writings treat this theme, and her letters give many examples of her willingness

---

53 Havergal, *Swiss Letters*, 324–325.

54 It should be noted that in recent years, the teaching at the Keswick Convention has moved away from the "higher life" emphasis, and now represents a broader section of conservative evangelicalism.

55 Havergal, *Memorials*, 202. "In one instance, at a garden party, my sister's happy face attracted a young stranger, so that she sought conversation with her. Often have I been told: 'FRH looks so really happy, she must have something we have not.' With the utmost skill, no artist or photograph gives a real idea of her lighted up expression."

to engage others, whether friends, contacts or strangers, in spiritual conversation. She filled her "spare" time with correspondence, wanting friends and relatives to "go on" with the Lord.

In an address to Christian workers, she explained her passion for "speaking for Jesus" and urged her listeners to take every opportunity to do the same:

> We meet with those who have not "like precious faith," and we are content to speak only of what is nothing worth. Yet each is in the danger from which we have fled, each has the same soul-needs. If we believed that she with whom we are lightly exchanging pleasant or necessary remarks, must perish for ever unless Jesus saves her, should we not "therefore speak"? Let us try to realise, the young friend or stranger at my side, if she does not know Jesus, has no Friend, no Comforter…nothing to fill an aching void within. But more. This very one, if she does not know Jesus, must be shut out from Him for ever, and endure the unknown terrors of God's wrath for ever, and ever, and ever. There is but a step between her and death, and this may be her last opportunity to hear of the Saviour's love. Can I believe these truths, and part from her with smiling nothings, without one word to arouse, to win, to save?
>
> WHAT shall we speak? Say that to God. He will give us words. With our highest skill, we can but draw the bow at a venture…. Let us trust in Him Who can and will both give and guide the arrow. An imperceptible pause in conversation is time enough for an unworded prayer, a heart-glance up to Him for the right words, and for those words to be flashed into our minds, in swift and gracious answer. Let our hearts be filled with Christ and His salvation, and out of their abundance our mouths will speak.[56]

Frances used her musical ability in this cause too. She got involved in several city missions: singing, giving testimony, and speaking about the meaning of the songs she sang. At society parties, where it was customary for ladies to play and sing, she would invariably sing a Christian song, even if an embarrassed silence fell afterwards.[57]

---

56 Address to Christian workers based on the text: "We believe, and therefore speak." 2 Corinthians 4:13.

57 Havergal, *Memorials*, 133–134.

She wrote numbers of tracts, both for Christians and non-Christians, which she gave out whenever possible. When staying in France, in one typical instance, she wrote a hymn in French for an impromptu evangelistic service held by herself and sister Maria, and the indomitable Maria then took a copy of the hymn to the local priest as a pretext to engage him in conversation about the gospel.[58]

Frances was a woman who lived all out for God. In her everyday life she wanted to "bring a blessing" to everyone she encountered. She wrote her hymns, poems, books and letters because she wanted to bring that same blessing to a wider audience. Her life and writings represent and express the best elements of Victorian evangelicalism. She was a child of her times, and certainly suffered the limitations so cruelly placed on single women during that era. But the struggles she went through resulted in deeper dependence on God. The theme of her life was consecration, summed up in her verse:

> Take my love; my Lord I pour
>> At Thy feet its treasure store:
> Take myself and I will be
>> Ever, only, all for Thee!

Conclusion

Prentiss and Havergal were both very much children of their time.[59] This chapter has focused on just one aspect of their lives and teaching.

---

58 Havergal, *Memorials*, 209.

59 The many ways in which they were both influenced by their time and culture cannot be mentioned in the confines of this chapter. Both were clearly influenced by the Romantic Movement, both took full advantage of the newly opened opportunities for travel in Europe, both were accomplished linguists and translated lengthy works from German to English. By the end of their lives, both had been enlisted in the cause of temperance. Neither of them engaged in overt political campaigning against social injustice but they did take every opportunity to sacrificially do good to others on a practical level. Both were active in evangelism: Prentiss helping with enquirers at the great 1875/6 Moody Campaign in New York and Havergal speaking and singing and doing personal work at many City Missions in Britain. Many have pointed out that the nineteenth century saw a greater feminization of the church, with an increasing trend toward sentimentality and a greater emphasis on childhood piety. For further discussion, see James, *Elizabeth Prentiss* (2006) and Sharon James, *In Trouble and in Joy: Four Women Who Lived for God; with Selections from Their Writings* (Darlington: Evangelical Press, 2003).

During the second half of the nineteenth century, "the evangelical movement was a dominant force in the English-speaking world."[60] While the movement divided over the issue of how holiness could be attained, it was united on the vital importance of the subject. In this context, Elizabeth Prentiss and Frances Ridley Havergal both articulated the longing so many felt for progress in sanctification. In their teaching on holiness, both stressed the necessity of complete surrender to the will of God.[61]

Frances Ridley Havergal's Advent Sunday experience led her to move in the direction of a "two-tier" spirituality. She claimed, after that, to enjoy unbroken awareness of the love of Christ. However, had she not died at the early age of forty-two, perhaps her experience might have been further tempered and nuanced. Earlier in her life, Elizabeth Prentiss, too, had believed that a continual sense of peace could be attained by every Christian. But, when she was in her fifties, her own "dark night of the soul" experience caused her to modify that expectation. During her final years, she was more aware of the positive role of ongoing struggle in the life of the Christian, even after many years of obedience and trust.

In their response to the great controversy of their day, both Prentiss and Havergal used their influence to urge fellow-Christians to repudiate any boast of having attained complete perfection, while also, and always, encouraging them to long for and work toward complete consecration and holiness.

---

60 David W. Bebbington, *The Dominance of Evangelicalism: The Age of Spurgeon and Moody* (Leicester: IVP, 2005), 249.

61 This was a popular theme at the time. Submissiveness was a motif in 223 out of 638 hymns in the influential *Hymns: Ancient and Modern* [Ian Bradley, *Abide With Me: The World of Victorian Hymns* (London: SCM Press, 1997), 124].

14.

"Gentlemen, I like the supernatural!": the spirituality of B.B. Warfield

By Fred G. Zaspel

ONE OF THE best kept secrets about Benjamin Breckinridge—"B.B."—Warfield (1851–1921) is that the weighty scholarship of this theological giant is matched only by his fervent heart, a heart inflamed by a deep sense of rescue and marked by utter dependence upon divine grace in Christ. He is deservedly recognized as the theologian of the doctrine of inspiration, having given that doctrine a more careful and thorough statement and defense than any before or after him. And this degree of learned theology is evident in his writings on Christology also, for example, and on perfectionism. His published works—his only legacy, really—remain influential and continue to be held universally in highest regard, demonstrating a depth and breadth of learning that is rarely achieved. This giant of Old Princeton was indeed a uniquely equipped

---

Author's note: Michael Haykin is a friend whom I hold in the highest regard. His knowledge of Christian history increasingly strikes me as encyclopedic, and his heart for Christ and for truth and for genuine experiential faith is as evident. He is also a good friend, and he has modelled for me what a good friend is, happily providing needed advice and practical help on many occasions. Still further, Michael willingly served as one of my readers and advisors throughout the years I prepared my dissertation on the theology of B.B. Warfield. And so it is with great pleasure that I contribute this chapter in his honour for his sixtieth birthday. We love you, Michael, and we thank the Lord for you.

theologian, and in our day his writings remain important for the treasure of biblical and theological learning they afford. But what has not been given due recognition is the fact that pulsing through virtually all his works is an unmistakable fervency of spirit that reflects a deep and lively heart of love for and thankfulness to God his Saviour. This, in brief, is the spirituality of B.B. Warfield. And we do not understand him until we recognize that it was this heart—may I say his *spirituality?*—that drove and shaped not just his sermons and devotional writings but his scholarly works also.

Warfield in context

It goes (almost) without saying that the significance of a given historical figure is not truly appreciated unless we understand him within the context of his times, and this truism is particularly pronounced in a study of the life and work of B.B. Warfield. Names such as Schleiermacher, Wellhausen, Darwin, Harnack, and Ritschl stand as symbols of the era—an era Warfield frequently characterized as decidedly anti-supernaturalistic. Human society now could boast of previously unimaginable achievements. The very world in which we live could be explained in naturalistic terms. Do we need, then, to explain the origin of the Bible in terms of the supernatural? And is it necessary to understand Jesus as something more than a man? Is it not the obligation of "historical scholarship" to peel back these layers of myth in order to discover the "historical Jesus"? And when we do, is there need any longer for the "biblical Christ," "the Christ of faith"? And for that matter, what is the source of religious truth? Must we look to a centuries-old book? If human intellect can bring about such scientific and technological progress, is it not also a sufficient authority for ethics and religious ideals? Moreover, considering all these academic, social, cultural, scientific and technological advances, what need is there for a "saving Jesus"? Just what is that salvation? And what is its need? Is humanity so bad, or so bad off, that it actually needs redemption? And are notions such as Trinity and incarnation even tenable in such a scientifically advanced age?

In such an "enlightened" age there is little place for the supernatural. And where naturalism reigns there is no place for religious dogma at all, particularly such mysterious concepts as Trinity, incarnation, virgin birth, atonement and resurrection. And, as Warfield repeatedly noted, neither is there room for external authority. Whatever "inspiration" means as it applies to the biblical authors, it cannot connote divine origin, and we must now relocate religious authority to the human psyche. And once we have said all this, Christianity itself has been relegated to a mere historical religion. It may be the best yet, but it is of the same class as all others and may be explained and understood in naturalistic terms.

Now the age in which we live is anything but supernaturalistic: it is distinctly hostile to supernaturalism. Its most striking characteristic is precisely its deeply rooted and wide-reaching rationalism of thought and sentiment.... It has invaded with its solvent every form of thought and every activity of life. It has given us a naturalistic philosophy (in which all "being" is evaporated into "becoming"), a naturalistic science (the single-minded zeal of which is to eliminate design from the universe); a naturalistic politics (whose first fruits was the French Revolution, and whose last may well be an atheistic socialism); a naturalistic history (which can scarcely find place for even human personality among the causes of events); and a naturalistic religion, which says, "Hands off" to God—if indeed it troubles itself to consider whether there be a God, if there be a God, whether He be a person, or if He be a person, whether He can or will concern Himself with men.[1]

Warfield's career lay in the heyday of this theological "liberalism." The face and the very soul of Christianity were changing. It was no longer a supernatural religion. Many conservatives still felt the pressure to concede or else risk seeing Christianity become marginalized to complete irrelevance. And yielding to this pressure, many within the professing church were yielding over virtually all the metaphysical and the supernaturalistic elements of the faith in order to preserve Christianity, they thought, from complete collapse.

Warfield, however, felt no pressure at all. Rather, he was supremely confident that the supernaturalistic faith of the church was the only Christianity that would endure and that no historical-critical scholar-

---

1   Benjamin B. Warfield, *Calvin and Augustine* (Phillipsburg: Presbyterian and Reformed, 1956), 504.

ship or anti-supernaturalistic bias would ever overthrow the faith once for all delivered to the saints. To be sure, he continuously affirmed that this supernaturalistic Christianity would more than endure—it would finally prevail universally. "I fall back gladly" on the assurances of the biblical writers, he says,

> that God will not permit his truth to perish out of the earth.... It is one thing to say that the current theologizing is in the direction of Rationalism, Naturalism, Socinianism; and another thing to say that Christianity is to sink in that slough. After all, the divine Christ is not abolished because men bid us cease to reverence him, or the Christian system of truth destroyed because men ask us no longer to believe it, or the divine Word robbed of its power because we are warned no longer to bow to its authority. Men may come and men may go, but these are things that abide forever.[2]

The very earliest piece of work we have from Warfield is a transcription of a sermon from 1876 in which, taking Romans 3:4 as his text, he passionately exhorted his hearers to calm confidence in all biblical truth, no matter how they may be under assault—"Let God be true, and every man a liar." It is not without significance that the utter confidence in revealed truth that stands today as the legacy of this giant Princetonian marks his ministry from the very beginning.

Traits of Warfield's spirituality

Basic as this is to understanding the spirituality of B.B. Warfield, to say that he was persuaded of Scripture's teaching, or even that he was fully persuaded of it, is only the first step. It is a necessary first step to understanding Warfield's piety, for it is foundational. But it is only the first step. These convictions so vigorously maintained had reached his affections also, and with deeply shaping influence. Here we will trace out the leading features of Warfield's piety and spirituality—his own religious experience—narrowing our focus as we proceed.

---

2   John E. Meeter, ed., *Selected Shorter Writings of B.B. Warfield*, 2 vols. (Phillipsburg: Presbyterian and Reformed, 1970, 1973), 2:103, 298–299.

Benjamin Breckinridge Warfield
1851–1921

1. Appreciation of the supernatural

A former student of Warfield's recalls that in his classroom Warfield would affirm with hearty enthusiasm, "Gentlemen, I like the supernatural!"[3] This remark—made, we are told, with an evident twinkle in his eye—is quite revealing. Warfield not only embraced the supernatural claims of the Christian faith: they were for him a source of joy. That is to say, this sense of the supernatural character of Christianity was for Warfield no mere abstract doctrine detached from Christian living. His appreciation of it was larger than that. Supernaturalism was for him foundational to Christian theology *and to Christian experience also*. We will not go too far if we say that Warfield's *lively sense* of Christian supernaturalism was a fundamental shaping factor of his entire spiritual experience. Here and there throughout Warfield's works we find glimpses into his thinking that drive us to this conclusion. This thinking is best examined in the logical stages as he seemed to understand them.

SUPERNATURALISM AS FUNDAMENTAL

First, and foundationally, it is important to see that for Warfield Christianity is supernaturalism. He argued extensively that without supernaturalism Christianity is evacuated of all meaning and relevance.

In his 1906 "The Supernatural Birth of Jesus" Warfield provides a clear summary of his perception of the Christian faith.

> Were I asked to name the three pillars on which the structure of Christianity, as taught in the New Testament in its entirety, especially rests, I do not know that I could do better than point to these three things: the supernatural, the incarnation, redemption.[4]

In his comments that follow, he clarifies that of these three supernaturalism is the general, all-inclusive factor that characterizes the other two—and, indeed, all other—aspects of Christianity. This is basic. As he insists elsewhere, "Christianity, in its very essence, is supernatural-

---

3   Oswald T. Allis, "Personal Impressions of Dr Warfield," *Banner of Truth* 89 (Fall 1971): 11.

4   Benjamin B. Warfield, *The Works of Benjamin B. Warfield*, 10 vols. (Grand Rapids: Baker Books, 1991), 3:450.

ism," "the supernatural is the very breath of Christianity's nostrils," and in this debate over supernaturalism what is at stake is nothing less than Christianity itself.[5]

Such is the issue of the day and Warfield addresses it often in his works and expounds it at length in his 1896 address, "Christian Supernaturalism."[6] Beginning with the biblical teaching regarding God, "the supernatural fact," the Creator, Warfield highlights the supernaturalness of all the strands of biblical teaching—revelation, the incarnation, birth, life, atonement and resurrection of Christ, and salvation itself in all its dimensions. As he asserts elsewhere, in brief,

> The religion of the Bible is a frankly supernatural religion. By this is not meant merely that, according to it, all men, as creatures, live, move and have their being in God. It is meant that, according to it, God has intervened extraordinarily, in the course of the sinful world's development, for the salvation of men otherwise lost.[7]

This sense of the foundational significance of Christian supernaturalism pervades Warfield's works, most prominently in reference to Christology and to revelation and inspiration. Popular at the time were the various kenotic theories of Christ's incarnation. Taking the "emptying" language of Philippians 2:7 (*ekenosin*) these theologians sought to establish a naturalistic Jesus, one who perhaps had been God but in his incarnate state was no longer. Against all this, Warfield published hundreds of pages of rebuttal and critique,[8] expounding and defending the proposition that Jesus Christ is the supernatural Saviour who, coming from heaven, entered supernaturally in to this world to accomplish his supernatural work. The liberal's non-supernatural Jesus, he argued, is but a figment of the modern imagination that finds no warrant either in Scripture or in history. In passionate tones he insisted tirelessly that neither Scripture nor history know of any Jesus

---

5   Meeter, ed., *Selected Shorter Writings*, 2:680–684; Warfield, *Works*, 9:29.

6   Warfield, *Works*, 9:25–46.

7   Warfield, *Works*, 1:3.

8   See, for example, volume 3 of his *Works* and Benjamin B. Warfield, *The Person and Work of Christ* (Phillipsburg: Presbyterian & Reformed, 1950).

but a supernatural one, and that a naturalistic Jesus is neither capable of accomplishing human redemption nor worthy of our worship.

Although he published more pages on the person and work of Christ, Warfield is best known, of course, for his extensive and tireless championing of the doctrines of revelation and inspiration. And in a real sense, for him this was fundamental. He frequently referred to Christianity as *the revealed religion*. This is its distinctive. Distinguishing Christianity from all other religions is its revelatory character. It is not the product of human reflection or imagination, and it is not simply the most developed religion history has witnessed. It is distinctly a revealed religion, resulting from God's own self-disclosure climaxing in Scripture, the Word of God written.[9]

It was this conviction that Scripture is in fact God's very Word that led Warfield to champion the doctrine of inerrancy: God cannot err! And it was this conviction that led him to emphasize Scripture's authority for life. At several points he cites the lines from Kipling—

The heathen in his blindness bows down to wood and stone.
He don't obey no orders, except they is his own.[10]

That is, as Warfield explained, the heathen's religion rises from his own imagination. It is a natural religion. The Christian, by contrast, is "under orders." He has heard from God and is obligated accordingly. Likewise, in the ancient world, religion and ethics were separate categories of thought, and in our contemporary society also there are increasing claims of "spiritual but not religious." But these are distinctions Warfield could never have recognized. Ethical norms are impossible apart from divine revelation, and non-theological spirituality is a self-contradiction. It was this conviction that shaped Warfield's sustained opposition to mysticism also.[11] In all its various forms, mysticism is but a natural, non-revealed religion. True knowledge of God and direction from God is not found in our "inner lights" but in

---

9 Warfield's famous definition of inspiration: "a supernatural influence exerted on the sacred writers by the Spirit of God, by virtue of which their writings are given Divine trustworthiness" (Warfield, *Works*, 1:77–78).

10 Warfield, *Works*, 9:650.

11 See, for example, Warfield, *Works*, 9:649–666.

his objective Word. Accordingly, genuine Christian piety is founded on and specifically shaped by the revealed Word of God.

Samples of Warfield's emphasis on the foundational significance of supernaturalism for genuine Christianity could be multiplied at great length, and we will see more as we move along. Our point here is simply to note this major factor in Warfield's own thinking and religious outlook. He was keenly aware that supernaturalism is essential to the objective claims of Christianity. This is a Christian fundamental. Apart from a full confession of this robust supernaturalism, he insists, there is no claim to the name Christian. The Christian worldview, "incumbent on every Christian," is a frank confession of the "absolute supernatural" that pervades the Christian faith at virtually every point—a supernatural God, a supernatural redemption, accomplished by a supernatural Saviour, interpreted by a supernatural revelation and applied by the supernatural operations of his Spirit.

> This confession constitutes the core of the Christian profession. Only he who holds this faith whole and entire has a full right to the Christian name: only he can hope to conserve the fullness of Christian truth…and witness a good confession in the midst of its most insidious attacks." Supernaturalism is, in short, "the very heart of the Christian religion."[12]

A supernatural gospel

This reference to supernaturalism as "the very heart of the Christian religion" moves us to the next step in Warfield's thinking. When Warfield says that supernaturalism is "the very heart of the Christian religion" he does not have in mind its foundational significance only. Whenever Warfield speaks of "the very heart" of the Christian religion he means, specifically, *redemption*—redemption in all that it entails. For Warfield, this—redemption—is what Christianity is all about, its purpose and reason for being. And this redemption, he insists, is a supernatural redemption supernaturally accomplished and supernaturally applied. In short, for Warfield supernaturalism is essential not only to the objective claims of Christianity; it is essential to its very *raison d'être*.

---

12 Warfield, *Works*, 9:45–46.

Warfield pointed out that we perceive Christianity rightly only as we understand its reason for being, the purpose for which God brought it into the world. Christianity has come into the world to address the problem of sin and bring redemption to fallen humanity. Warfield insisted repeatedly and at length that it is fundamental to the very conception of Christianity that it is a remedial scheme.

> By "the fundamental theology of the Church" is meant especially the Church's confession of that series of the redemptive acts of God, by which he has supernaturally intervened in human history for the salvation of sinful man.... The message of Christianity concerns, not "the values of human life," but the grace of the saving God in Christ Jesus. And in proportion as the grace of the saving God in Christ Jesus is obscured or passes into the background, in that proportion does Christianity slip from our grasp. Christianity is summed up in the phrase: "God was in Christ, reconciling the world with himself." Where this great confession is contradicted or neglected, there is no Christianity.[13]

> It belongs to the very essence of the type of Christianity propagated by the Reformation that the believer should feel himself continuously unworthy of the grace by which he lives. At the center of this type of Christianity lies the contrast of sin and grace; and about this center everything else revolves.[14]

Again, he says crisply in summary, "A Christianity without redemption—redemption in the blood of Jesus Christ as a sacrifice for sin—is nothing less than a contradiction in terms. Precisely what Christianity *means* is redemption in the blood of Jesus."[15]

Further, for Warfield it was not enough to say simply that Christianity is a redemptive religion, generally. Not just in whole but in its constituent teachings and elements also, Christianity has a specifically redemptive focus. For example, he describes the incarnation as "the very core of Christianity," because it is the means to the accomplish-

---

13 Meeter, ed., *Selected Shorter Writings*, 1:50.

14 Warfield, *Works*, 7:113.

15 Warfield, *Works*, 3:357–358.

ment of redemption. Christianity is first and foremost a redemptive religion, and thus we are not surprised to read that the incarnation has "sin as its occasion" and "salvation as its end"—"Christ came into the world to save sinners" (1 Timothy 1:15). Similarly, Warfield emphasizes that the study of the Trinity is but a study of God's self-revelation *in the outworking of his redemptive purpose.* That is to say, the revelation of the three-in-oneness of God is itself a gospel revelation made known only in the unfolding of his saving plan. Indeed, revelation itself is a distinctly redemptive act, given as it is to restore fallen sinners "otherwise lost" to the knowledge and favour of God.[16] And because of all this, the systematic theologian is, simply, a preacher of the gospel.[17]

These kinds of examples from Warfield could continue at length—it seems he could not say it enough. It was for him a regular point of emphasis that Christianity is in its very essence and meaning a redemptive religion, a religion for sinners. The saving love of God for sinners is not only "the main theme of the Bible," and not only does God's self-revelation climax in the revelation of his saving grace, and not only does Christianity provide the only rescue for sinners, but Christianity is by definition a redemptive scheme divinely wrought. This is why for Warfield supernaturalism must be maintained at all costs, because anything less deteriorates the redemptive character of the faith.[18]

If we can know anything about Warfield it is that his was a gospel-centred Christianity. Indeed, we can say with equal certainty that he himself was a gospel-centred Christian. If we can judge by the frequency and the lively vigour with which Warfield repeats this emphasis, we may say that he not only understood Christianity as a redemptive religion—he revelled joyfully in that fact.

All of this is uppermost in Warfield's mind and heart, and these are the factors that, self-consciously, give his piety its distinctly Christian shape. Yet underlying all this gospel centredness is a robust sense and awareness of supernaturalism. The salvation that Christianity came to proclaim is no mere human accomplishment, and the gospel in

---

16 Warfield, *Works*, 1:3, 11–13, 42, 45; Meeter, ed., *Selected Shorter Writings,* 1:69–70.

17 Warfield, *Works*, 9:86.

18 Meeter, ed., *Selected Shorter Writings,* 2:718; 1:82–87; Warfield, *Works*, 2:144.

which Warfield gloried was a distinctly supernatural gospel, proclaiming a supernatural salvation.

EXPERIENCING THE SUPERNATURAL

All this allows us to narrow our focus further. Warfield understood and embraced a distinctly supernatural Christianity, and he understood Christianity as given by God to provide a salvation supernaturally accomplished. Finally, he understood salvation itself in supernatural terms also. Seeing the trees as well as the forest, Warfield insisted that supernaturalism is essential to any and all genuinely *Christian* religious experience.

Of course, on one level, Warfield understood this in an objective sense. As we have already seen, Christianity for him is thoroughly grounded in divine revelation, and thus Christian guidance is rooted in the supernatural. So also our salvation is accomplished by a supernatural, i.e., divine, Saviour who in his death reconciled us to God. Warfield would emphasize this to his students, insisting very simply that "all theologies divide at one point—does God save men or do they save themselves?"[19] It is a point of common emphasis in Warfield that salvation is a work of God from start to finish—the Father who chose, the Son who became incarnate and redeemed us to God by his sacrificial death and rose from the dead, and the Spirit who united us to Christ, liberating us from the bondage of sin, and who will raise us from the dead to share in the glory of Christ. Ours is a supernatural salvation through and through.

But for Warfield the supernaturalness of Christian salvation is not to be understood in objective terms only. There is a more subjective, experiential dimension of salvation that is thoroughly supernaturalistic also. That is, as in its accomplishment so also in its application, reception and experience, salvation cannot be understood or explained apart from a thorough-going supernaturalism.

This is not the place for a complete exposition of Warfield's thinking here, but we can at least highlight its various dimensions. In its broadest application, Warfield would point out the supernatural effects of the Christian message as witnessed in its global advance, for

---

19 Thomas Chafer Rollin, "A Syllabus of Studies in Hermeneutics Part 1," *Bibliotheca Sacra* 91.364 (1934): 460.

example, in his 1882 "The Divine Origin of the Bible."[20] Wherever Christianity has gone, he observes, there has been an improvement of society. Religious rituals of sacrifice forever embedded in the consciousness of men and societies suddenly fell into neglect when brought into contact with the Christian gospel. Religion and morals, in their practice and in their very theory, have been revolutionized. Moreover, its influence has always been beneficent. This is not to deny the many abuses of professing Christians, but it is an unchallenged fact that where the Bible has gone society has improved. Love has replaced hate and horror, and new ideals have been established. And all this has been accomplished without the commendation of royalty, against the most determined and violent opposition and by means of the efforts of a dozen unlearned men bringing a message considered foolish by all who heard it. And, Warfield concludes, there is simply no explanation for all this apart from the supernatural—the working of God himself.

Not only in his extensive treatments of Augustine and Pelagius particularly but throughout his works, Warfield opposes Pelagianism precisely on the ground that it strips Christian salvation of the supernatural. It is a scheme of self-salvation that has no need of the supernatural workings of the Spirit of God in the human heart. But what is required for men and women lost and under the dominion of sin is nothing less than divine quickening, a grace that looses us from sin's power. So also in his treatment of the doctrine of the *testimonium Spiritus Sancti,* Warfield presses the conviction that the Christian who has come to faith is one whose mind has been "repaired" by the supernatural workings of divine grace. Warfield considers irresistible grace necessary to a purely supernatural salvation and "the very heart of the doctrine of 'renewal.'" It is "the hinge" and "distinguishing principle" of the Calvinistic soteriology, which, at its very heart, is concerned to exclude all creaturely elements in the initiation of the saving process so as to magnify the pure grace of God.[21] Every Christian, by very definition, Warfield would argue, is a living, walking miracle.

---

20 Warfield, *Works,* 1:429–447.
21 Warfield, *Works,* 2:461; 5:359; Meeter, ed., *Selected Shorter Writings,* 2:415.

It is upon a field of the dead that the Sun of righteousness has risen, and the shouts that announce His advent fall on deaf ears: yea, even though the morning stars should again sing for joy and the air be palpitant with the echo of the great proclamation, their voice could not penetrate the ears of the dead. As we sweep our eyes over the world lying in its wickedness, it is the valley of the prophet's vision which we see before us: a valley that is filled with bones, and lo! they are very dry. What benefit is there in proclaiming to dry bones even the greatest of redemptions? How shall we stand and cry, "O ye dry bones, hear ye the word of the Lord!" In vain the redemption, in vain its proclamation, unless there come a breath from heaven to breathe upon these slain that they may live. The redemption of Christ is therefore no more central to the Christian hope than the creative operations of the Holy Spirit upon the heart: and the supernatural redemption itself would remain a mere name outside of us and beyond our reach, were it not realized in the subjective life by an equally supernatural application.[22]

Still further, the Christian life itself is one extended experience of the supernatural influence of the Holy Spirit. Warfield treats this vividly in his "The Leading of the Spirit."[23] Here he expounds the assertion of the apostle Paul in Romans 8:14, that "all who are led by the Spirit of God are sons of God." This "leading of the Spirit," he demonstrates at great length, is to be understood in terms of the dominating influence of the Spirit of God in every believer. Every child of God, by definition, is one in whom the Spirit of God has become the new controlling factor, leading us away from sin and to faithfulness. We are no longer people dominated by the flesh and sin, but supernaturally delivered from sin's dominion we now live under the supernatural direction of God's Spirit. The Christian is one who has undergone a transforming work initially in regeneration, continually in sanctification and then finally in glorification. Once again, every Christian is a living miracle, one whose life cannot be explained apart from the supernatural.

---

22 Warfield, *Works*, 9:43–44.

23 Benjamin B. Warfield, *The Power of God Unto Salvation* (1903; reprint, Grand Rapids: Wm. B. Eerdmans, 1930), 151–179.

These samples are sufficient to illustrate the point at hand. When Warfield would say to his students, "Gentlemen, I love the supernatural," he was expressing not only his decided opposition to the naturalism of the age and his settled belief in the objective, supernatural elements of the Christian faith, he was expressing his own self-conscious appreciation of the supernatural salvation that he experienced. Warfield's own spirituality was one of experiencing the supernatural and a conscious enjoyment of a supernatural salvation.

All this will help us move to a sharper focus. Warfield's appreciation of the supernatural is foundational, and it provides the framework for concerns that are more central.

2. Helpless dependence

For Warfield, the notion of rightly *appreciating* the supernatural shows itself in a keen sense of helpless dependence. These two thoughts are of course very closely related, the latter naturally growing out of the former. But this sense of helpless dependence in Warfield is so pronounced that it warrants specific mention.

Here and there in his works, Warfield shows a familiar acquaintance with the teachings and influence Friedrich Schleiermacher, and, predictably, he is consistently critical of them. He argued that Schleiermacher's concern to rescue Christianity from cold German rationalism, however justified, merely replaced a subjective intellect with a subjective "feeling," which Warfield saw as no improvement at all. But he does seem to appreciate Schleiermacher's language of "feeling of dependence." Virtually all religion, no less Christianity itself, must be understood at the very least in terms of dependence. And Warfield reminds us frankly that "we do not need Schleiermacher to teach us that there is no human self-consciousness which is destitute of the God-consciousness."[24]

Warfield's sense of dependence has two major aspects: we are utterly dependent on God as creatures, and as *fallen* creatures. It is a point of regular emphasis in Warfield that, created in the image of God, humankind cannot escape a sense of dependence on God. We can no more escape our sense of dependence than we can escape our humanity. We are creatures, and we know it. This is a frequent theme in

---

24 Warfield, *Works*, 10:368.

Warfield, and it leads him to a robust awareness of divine providence. Further, it is also a regular point of his emphasis that this feeling of dependence is fostered in the Christian gospel. The gospel message comes to us promising grace for our helplessness and demanding trust for our inability. Warfield understand that as creatures, and especially as fallen creatures, we are utterly dependent on God, and the biblical teaching of creation and redemption alike declare it. This second emphasis in Warfield is seen in his frequent insistence that the salvation needed by utterly dependent, fallen creatures, and the salvation offered in the gospel, is not adequately understood except in its Augustinian expression. That is, simply, the character of Christian supernaturalism drives us to a Calvinistic soteriology. I will cite a few examples from Warfield to illustrate.

> Is it not that sense of absolute dependence on God which, conditioning all the life and echoing through all the thought, produces the type of religion we call "evangelical" and the type of theology we call "Augustinian"?[25]

> In Calvinism, then, objectively speaking, theism comes to its rights; subjectively speaking, the religious relation attains its purity; soteriologically speaking, evangelical religion finds at length its full expression and its secure stability. Theism comes to its rights only in a teleological conception of the universe, which perceives in the entire course of events the orderly outworking of the plan of God, who is the author, preserver, and governor of all things, whose will is consequently the ultimate cause of all. The religious relation attains its purity only when an attitude of absolute dependence on God is not merely temporarily assumed in the act, say, of prayer, but is sustained through all the activities of life, intellectual, emotional, executive. And evangelical religion reaches stability only when the sinful soul rests in humble, self-emptying trust purely on the God of grace as the immediate and sole source of all the efficiency which enters into its salvation. And these things are the formative principles of Calvinism.[26]

---

25 Warfield, *Works*, 4:274.
26 Warfield, *Works*, 5:355.

The evangelical note is formally sounded by the entirety of orga-nized Protestantism. That is to say, all the great Protestant bodies, in their formal official confessions, agree in confessing the utter dependence of sinful man upon the grace of God alone for salva-tion, and in conceiving this dependence as immediate and direct upon the Holy Spirit, acting as a person and operating directly on the heart of the sinner. It is this evangelical note which deter-mines the peculiarity of the piety of the Protestant Churches. The characteristic feature of this piety is a profound consciousness of intimate personal communion with God the Saviour, on whom the soul rests with immediate love and trust. Obviously this piety is individualistic to the core, and depends for its support on an intense conviction that God the Lord deals with each sinful soul directly and for itself.[27]

Whoever believes in God; whoever recognizes in the recesses of his soul his utter dependence on God; whoever in all his thought of salvation hears in his heart of hearts the echo of the *soli Deo gloria* of the evangelical profession—by whatever name he may call himself, or by whatever intellectual puzzles his logical under-standing may be confused—Calvinism recognizes as implicitly a Calvinist, and as only requiring to permit these fundamental principles—which underlie and give its body to all true religion— to work themselves freely and fully out in thought and feeling and action, to become explicitly a Calvinist.[28]

Elsewhere he argues that the "central truth" of Calvinism is not predestination but something deeper—a "complete dependence upon the free mercy of a saving God."[29] In this same vein he says of the reformers that, "to them the doctrine of predestination was given directly in their consciousness of dependence as sinners on the free mercy of a saving God."[30] So also Reformed theology is that which has

---

27 Benjamin B. Warfield, *The Plan of Salvation* (Grand Rapids: Wm. B. Eerdmans, 1977), 69.

28 Warfield, *Works*, 5:356.

29 Warfield, *Works*, 5:357.

30 Warfield, *Works*, 9:117–118.

"left men dependent for salvation on nothing but the infinite love and free grace of God."[31] This Calvinistic theology is one

> in which, in place of the alternations of hope and fear which vex the lives of those who, in whatever degree, hang their hopes on their own merits, a mood of assured trust in the mercy of a gracious God is substituted as the spring of Christian life. And a new theology corresponding to this new type of piety dates from him; a theology which, recalling man from all dependence on his own powers or merits, casts him decisively on the grace of God alone for his salvation.[32]

Warfield describes Calvinistic theology in reference to Calvin himself similarly:

> What was suffusing his heart and flowing in full flood into all the chambers of his soul was a profound sense of his indebtedness as a lost sinner to the free grace of God his Saviour.[33]

And again,

> Now, Calvinism means just the preservation, in all our thinking and feeling and action, of the attitude of utter dependence on God which we assume in prayer. It is the mood of religion made determinative of all our thinking and feeling and willing.[34]

These kinds of quotes could continue at length, but these suffice to illustrate that a keen sense of dependence upon God is a prominent aspect of Warfield's spirituality.

Warfield is widely noted as a champion of Reformed theology, but what is not often noted is that along with this theological commitment, or, rather, *underlying* this theological commitment, is a heart that can find satisfaction nowhere else. Warfield felt himself to be, first of all,

---

31 Warfield, *Works*, 9:430.

32 Warfield, *Works*, 4:128–129.

33 Warfield, *Calvin and Augustine*, 484.

34 Warfield, *Calvin and Augustine*, 499.

a sinner rescued by divine grace, and he gives joyful expression of this at seemingly every turn.

> Because he [Jesus] is man he is able to pour out his blood, and because he is God his blood is of infinite value to save; and that it is only because he is both God and Man in one person, that we can speak of God purchasing his Church with his own blood (Acts 20:28). And unless God has purchased his Church with his own blood, in what shall his Church find a ground for its hope?[35]

> The sinful soul, in throes of self-condemnation, is concerned with the law of righteousness ingrained in his very nature as a moral being, and cannot be satisfied with goodness, or love, or mercy, or pardon. He cries out for expiation.[36]

> It is in the hands of such love we have fallen.[37]

He also observes that the importance of the doctrine of justification by faith lies in its renunciation of human merit and its confession of "dependence on the grace of God alone for salvation."[38] Again, these kinds of expressions of utter dependence upon divine grace pervade Warfield's works. He seemingly cannot speak enough of dependence, even "entire dependence" and "utter dependence" upon God and upon the grace of God. This manifestly reflects a dominant note of Warfield's own spirituality.

Samuel Craig, a man who was well acquainted with both Warfield himself and his writings, mentions this in passing:

> What most impresses the student of Warfield's writings apart from his deeply religious spirit, his sense of complete dependence on God for all things including especially his sense of

---

35 Meeter, ed., *Selected Shorter Writings*, 1:166.
36 Warfield, *Works*, 3:340.
37 Warfield, *The Power of God Unto Salvation*, 144.
38 Warfield, *Works*, 9:465.

indebtedness as a lost sinner to His free grace—is the breadth of his learning and the exactness of his scholarship.[39]

This sense of dependence, for Warfield, reflects the reality of the sinful creature's status before the sovereign God. But it is important for him on another level also: it is of the essence of saving faith. Just as grace is the fundamental element of religion on the divine side, so faith—faith as trust, faith as "a confident entrusting of ourselves to Christ," a "looking to God for blessing," a "casting" of oneself upon God, "utter dependence" or "resting" or "reposing" on God—is the very essence of true religion on the human side.[40]

On several occasions Warfield finds opportunity to stress this understanding of saving faith in his exposition of the "childlikeness" that Jesus requires of all who would enter the kingdom. We must come, he says, as helpless babes, utterly dependent upon his mercy. In this context, and in several others, he quotes a favourite revival hymn that was popular in the day—

Cast your deadly doing down,
   Down at Jesus' feet.
Stand in him, in him alone
   Gloriously complete.

This attitude of complete dependence upon Christ is for Warfield the mark of the Christian—at the outset and throughout the Christian experience. Indeed, one of his major criticisms of higher life teachings is that for all its talk of dependence on the Holy Spirit or on Christ, at the end of the day it suspends success on so much human effort—the act of depending! And in connection with Augustinianism, Calvinism, the Westminster Confession of Faith and expositions of related doctrines and biblical passages Warfield points out repeatedly that notions of the supernatural, sovereign, immediate and individual-particular workings of God in the human heart cannot fail

---

39 "Introduction" to Benjamin B. Warfield, *Biblical and Theological Studies* (Phillipsburg: Presbyterian & Reformed, 1968), xvii.

40 Warfield, *Works*, 2:506; 9:332; 10:460; Benjamin B. Warfield, *Faith and Life* (1916; reprint, Edinburgh: The Banner of Truth Trust, 1974), 155, 170–171, 213, 397.

to produce a distinctive piety that is marked by a keen and lively sense of joyful dependence on God our Saviour. Faith, he affirms, finds its object in the God who makes himself known, becomes incarnate, sovereignly chooses, rescues by sacrifice of himself, renews and effectually draws us to our Redeemer, assumes control of our life (Romans 8:14), promises the brightest of hope—in short, in the God who does for us all that he requires of us.

This is the mark of Warfield's spirituality—a joyful resting in divine provision and a gospel explained wholly in terms of supernatural rescue. His gleeful, "Gentlemen, I like the supernatural" is an expression of his a piety, a piety that is marked by joyful dependence.

3. Worshipful adoration

Warfield's spirituality, then, was confessedly of the traditional Reformed model. It is consciously founded on God's own Word, in a redemption of divine accomplishment and a divine initiative from first to last. Central to it is the cross of Christ, where reconciliation with God was secured by the divine mediator. And essential to its success is the powerful and ongoing work of the Spirit of God in the lives of God's people. His was, simply, a gospel-shaped spirituality.

On one level, of course, this is not surprising. It is what we would expect from a Reformed theologian of Warfield's stature. Indeed, Warfield would be—and often was—severely critical of any other professed breed of spirituality. And so, in one sense, there is nothing unique here. What is noteworthy, however, is Warfield's grasp of it all and its evident effects in his own experience. This in two senses. First, there is no evidence in any of Warfieldiana that he struggled with troubling thoughts of needed self-attainment. There is no hint of legalism: he understood the gospel in its implications for the Christian life, and his faith seems from all accounts to have been one of genuine, "utter dependence" on the God of supernatural redemption. He appears to have seen the forest and the trees—the big picture of the gospel and its applications to life. Faults he no doubt had, and struggles. But it seems from all the evidence that the Reformed model of spirituality is one that found healthy expression in this Princetonian giant.

Second, and now to our point here, Warfield's grasp of the gospel and its implications for life shows itself in a heart lively with joyful, worshipful adoration of the God who had saved him. There is throughout Warfield's works a doxological note that resounds continuously in all dimensions of Christian praise. But it is not a praise merely, dutifully performed—it is a praise marked by a fervent love kindled by a deep sense of divine rescue. To state our point again, Warfield's piety was not marked by worship, simply, but worshipful *adoration*.

Again, expressions of this could be multiplied. A few samples will do for now.

The blood of Jesus,—O, the blood of Jesus!—when we have reached it, we have attained not merely the heart, but the heart of the heart of the Gospel.[41]

For you and me, sinners, He is most glorious and most precious, as a Saviour. Let others make elaborate inquisition into the possible reasons which led Him to come into this sinful world of ours. He Himself tells us that there were but two reasons which could have brought Him into the world—to judge the world, or to save the world. And, blessed be His name, He has further told us that it was actually to save the world that He came. This is the only reason that can satisfy our hearts, or even our reason,—that Jesus Christ came into the world to save sinners. It is only as the Lamb of God that has been slain, to purchase unto God by His blood of every tribe and tongue and people and nation, and to make them unto God a kingdom and priests who shall reign on the earth,—that the heavenly hosts in the apocalyptic vision hymn Him; and it is only as we catch a glimpse of this His true glory that we can worthily add our voices to His praise. It is only when we see in Him a slaughtered lamb, lying on a smoking altar, from which ascends the sweet savour of an acceptable sacrifice to God for sin, that we can rise to anything like a true sense of the glory of Jesus Christ, or in any degree give a sufficing account to our souls of His presence in the world.

There is no one of the titles of Christ which is more precious to Christian hearts than "Redeemer." There are others, it is true,

---

41 Benjamin B. Warfield, *The Saviour of the World*, (1914; reprint, Edinburgh: The Banner of Truth Trust, 1991), 88.

which are more often on the lips of Christians. The acknowledg-
ment of our submission to Christ as our Lord, the recognition of
what we owe to Him as our Saviour,—these things, naturally,
are most frequently expressed in the names we call Him by.
"Redeemer," however, is a title of more intimate revelation than
either "Lord" or "Saviour." It gives expression not merely to our
sense that we have received salvation from Him, but also to our
appreciation of what it cost Him to procure this salvation for us.
It is the name specifically of the Christ of the cross. Whenever
we pronounce it, the cross is placarded before our eyes and our
hearts are filled with loving remembrance not only that Christ
has given us salvation, but that He paid a mighty price for it. It
is a name, therefore, which is charged with deep emotion, and is
to be found particularly in the language of devotion. Christian
song is vocal with it.[42]

Christianity did not come into the world to proclaim a new
morality and, sweeping away all the supernatural props by which
men were wont to support their trembling, guilt-stricken souls,
to throw them back on their own strong right arms to conquer a
standing before God for themselves. It came to proclaim the real
sacrifice for sin which God had provided in order to supersede
all the poor fumbling efforts which men had made and were
making to provide a sacrifice for sin for themselves; and, planting
men's feet on this, to bid them go forward.[43]

The glory of the Incarnation is that it presents to our adoring gaze,
not a humanized God or a deified man, but a true God-man one
who is all that God is and at the same time all that man is: on
whose mighty arm we can rest, and to whose human sympathy
we can appeal. We cannot afford to lose either the God in the
man or the man in the God; our hearts cry out for the complete
God-man whom the Scriptures offer us.[44]

---

42 Warfield, Works, 2:375.
43 Meeter, ed., Selected Shorter Writings, 2:435.
44 Meeter, ed., Selected Shorter Writings, 1:166.

In very fact not only does the unvarying voice of Scripture commend this doctrine of the principle of the Incarnation to us, but
so do also the ineradicable demands of the Christian soul. Only
so is the distance between God and man recognized with due
poignancy. Only so is the "blood of Christ" given its proper place
in the saving process and in the plan of God. Only so is the
amazing love of God made to stand out in its full wonderfulness.
And only so is the answering love of the saved sinner drawn out
to its full height.[45]

This sense of dependent adoration pervades Warfield's works, in
language of deep devotion and delight, and crops up often even in
articles polemically designed. He does not understand providence
simply in terms of sovereignty and the divine decree—although he
does that, very clearly—but in terms of the Father's tender care for his
children and of Christ's watchful eye over "his little ones." He sees the
incarnation not as merely an object of faith but of wonder and adoration that seeks to grasp the infinite condescension of our great Saviour.
He understands the atoning work of Christ, first and foremost, in
terms of a great transaction by which our Redeemer reconciled us to
God by the sacrifice of himself. He does not understand conversion
simply in terms of our activity of faith and repentance, necessary as
these are, but in terms of the supernatural workings of divine grace,
the renewal of the Holy Spirit, liberating the soul from sin and drawing
us to Christ in faith and repentance. The Christian, by definition, he
senses, is a living miracle. Similarly, Warfield understands the Christian life itself not simply in terms of so much Christian activity or
behaviour but in the work of the Spirit assuring our hearts of our
childship to God, leading us in holiness, pursuing us in love even when
we sin, causing us to persevere and finally bringing us to glory. Likewise, Christian piety for him is not found simply in religious exercises
but in the Spirit's work drawing our hearts to God, prompting us to
and aiding us in prayer, strengthening us in the love of Christ and
enlarging our hearts for him. So also prayer—at once a confession of
weakness, "the sanctuary where the soul meets habitually with its God,"
and "the foundation-stone of your piety"—is born of need and prac-

---

45 Meeter, ed., *Selected Shorter Writings*, 1:147.

ticed in the expectation of divine response.[46] Prayer as well as Bible reading and attendance to the corporate ministry of the Word are not simply Christian exercises but the means of communion with God and of his working in us to strengthen us for life for him.

This is the leading mark of Warfield's piety. His mind and heart were caught up with the saving work of the Triune God, and, stemming from this, he manifests continually a keen sense of helpless yet adoring dependence upon his glorious Redeemer. He revels in the love of God displayed in the incarnation and in the cross. His expositions of these themes are characterized not merely by precise theological definitions. He does provide marvelously precise definitions, of course, and he views this exercise as essential and basic—basic to genuine, heartfelt worship. But all throughout, his expositions are marked by the language of humble and grateful adoration. Here is the great Saviour, eminently qualified, glorious in his condescension and mighty in his saving virtues. This is the One in whom we rest, the great Redeemer from heaven who has lovingly come to our rescue and in whose blessed person and work we are forever safe. He is the One by whom and in whom we live. And he is the One *for* whom we live.

Conclusion

In brief, for Warfield, supernaturalism is not a mere abstract item of doctrinal affirmation—it is the joyful life experience of every child of God. And for him a spirituality that is distinctly Christian is gospel-centred, certainly, and it is a spirituality that is robustly informed by, and that remains, keenly aware of this gospel-centred supernaturalism at work in us and for us.

---

46 Meeter, ed., *Selected Shorter Writings*, 1:422; 2:481–482.

15

EVANGELICALISM · MODERN

Accelerating the rhythm: two eighteenth-century Presbyterians on the frequency of the Lord's Supper

By Kenneth J. Stewart

The situation since 1930

DURING THE LAST century, more and more evangelical Protestants came to accept what they had not previously accepted: that the Lord's Supper is the "central act of Christian worship." Such an assertion entails more than an affirmation that the Lord's Supper should be frequently observed; it in fact holds this rite to be so indispensable that it must be central in the service. This conviction spread under a number of influences, the chief of which was the Oxford or Tractarian Movement. This early nineteenth-century movement influenced first Anglicans, then Presbyterians, Methodists and Baptists in the direction of heightened frequency of administration of the Supper and the recovery of pre-Reformation ideas about worship and ministry.[1] Yet,

---

1   The young Oxford Movement's plea for frequent communion was the thrust of "Tract 26: Bishop Beveridge on the Necessity and Advantage of Frequent Communion" in *Tracts for the Times*, vol. 1 (London: Rivingtons, 1834). The best short history of this movement is that of S.L. Ollard, *A Short History of the Oxford Movement* (1915; reprint, London: Faith Press, 1963). For the repercussions of this movement beyond England, see for example, the evidence of this in nineteenth century Scotland in J.R. Fleming, *The Church in Scotland, 1843–1874*, 2 vols. (Edinburgh: T & T Clark, 1927), 1:116–123, and A.L. Drummond and James Bulloch, *The Church in Victorian Scotland 1843–1874* (Edinburgh: St. Andrew Press, 1975), ch. 7, "Changing Worship." The reach of this

200 years ago, even Anglicans—known today for their weekly observance of "Holy Communion"—would have maintained this rite
between two or four times annually. David Bebbington has argued in
his *Holiness in Nineteenth-Century England*, that the Oxford movement
had a more pervasive influence in the English-speaking world in the
reign of Queen Elizabeth II (of our time) than it did in the reign of
Victoria.[2] The relaying of these impulses to wider Protestantism was
accomplished nowhere as effectively as through W.D. Maxwell's manual of 1936, *An Outline of Christian Worship*.[3]

It is important to grant that this renewed emphasis has also come
in the wake of nineteenth-century "restorationist" Christianity. Rooted
in the small Glasite/Sandemanian movement of eighteenth-century
Scotland and continuing into the Churches of Christ and the Plymouth
Brethren Movement, this stream also championed the idea that the
Lord's Supper—if not the *central* act of Christian worship—was at least
an essential part, such that it ought to be a weekly observance.[4]

The aim of this paper is to show that responsible evangelical theologians of the eighteenth century had begun to review the question of
the frequency of observance of the Lord's Supper quite in advance of
these two "stimuli," for quite distinct reasons and that they reached
distinct conclusions—worthy of our current consideration.

---

movement into the twentieth century is explored in Stewart J. Brown and Peter B.
Nockles, ed., *The Oxford Movement: Europe and the Wider World* (Cambridge: Cambridge
University Press, 2012).

2   David W. Bebbington, *Holiness in Nineteenth-Century England* (Carlisle: Paternoster, 2000), 28.

3   W.D. Maxwell, *An Outline of Christian Worship* (Oxford: Oxford University Press,
1936). Maxwell (1901–1971), Canadian by birth, received his theological education in
Scotland and served churches there before becoming a theological professor in South
Africa. See D.H. Murray, "Maxwell, W.D.," in *Dictionary of Scottish Church History and
Theology*, ed. Nigel M. de. S. Cameron (Downers Grove, InterVarsity, 1993), 554–555.

4   John Glas (1695–1773) was ordained as a Church of Scotland minister in 1719
and proceeded into Independency in 1730. While he had upheld a monthly practice
of communion as a Presbyterian (a high frequency given the 'status quo' in that time),
he introduced weekly communion in the 1730's. Robert Sandeman (1718–1771) became
Glas' son-in-law and transmitted his ideas into England and America. See entries for
each in Cameron, ed., *Dictionary of Scottish Church History and Theology*. For the early
roots of the Churches of Christ movement, see David M. Thompson, *Let Sects and
Parties Fall* (London: Berean Press, 1980), ch. 1.

Ambitious early Reformation practice gives way to seasonal observance

In both Reformation Europe and Reformation Scotland, the expectation was that each believer would participate in the Lord's Supper between four and twelve times per year.[5] But this standard was hard to achieve both because of the initial shortage of pastors (only a fraction of pre-Reformation priests and monks had entered the ministry of the Reformed churches) and because of the low expectations regarding the holy meal that rank-and-file Protestants (all former Roman Catholics) brought with them in the first generations after the Reformation.[6] It was hard to explain to such "novice" Protestants that their minimalist expectation of participating only once-annually in communion (though masses had been celebrated at least weekly) suggested a lack of spiritual vitality.

A further complication was that pre-Reformation Catholicism had often linked this prevailing infrequent participation in communion with seasonal festivals and pageantry such as the feast of Corpus Christi and especially of Easter. These festivals had served to glamorize the rite, by associating it with pageantry. The multi-generational "project" of working to uproot and displace a lingering Catholic mythology surrounding the administration of the Lord's Supper entailed seventeenth-century Presbyterians in Scotland and Northern Ireland taking over the Catholic practice of such seasonal communion festivals and turning them into large-scale public events involving gospel preaching

---

5   James K. Cameron, ed., *The First Book of Discipline* (1560) (Edinburgh: St. Andrew Press, 1972), ninth head, 183. The book of service forms produced by John Knox, while still at Geneva (1556) and formally adopted by the Church of Scotland in 1564, assumed a cycle of monthly Lord's Suppers [*The Liturgy of John Knox* (Glasgow: The University Press, 1886), 138]. The wider practice of the European Reformed churches in mid-sixteenth century is admirably surveyed in W.D. Maxwell, ed., *John Knox's Genevan Service Book* (Edinburgh: Oliver and Boyd, 1931), Appendix E.

6   The acuteness of the ministerial shortage, lasting decades after 1560 is highlighted in George B. Burnet, *The Holy Communion in the Reformed Church of Scotland 1560–1960* (Edinburgh: Oliver and Boyd, 1960), 14. The ways in which seventeenth-century Presbyterians continued to fall short of the expectations of their Reformation regarding the Lord's Supper are helpfully detailed in Gordon Donaldson, "From Covenant to Revolution," in Duncan Forrester and Douglas Murray, ed. *Studies in the History of Worship in Scotland* (Edinburgh: T & T Clark, 1984), 55, 59.

and administration of the Supper.[7] This interesting adaptation carried with it certain unforeseen ripple effects, among which were these:

1. Communion festivals tied to particular seasons required multiple preachers drawn from a wide region for a long weekend. The staging of a communion festival in one place meant that church services (and the availability of the Lord's Supper) in other places took a back seat. Peter was robbed to pay Paul, as we would say.

2. Communion seasons promoted on this scale could not be staged even the four times yearly mandated in light of distances travelled, personnel required and the expectation that communicants be free from a Thursday through a Monday.

3. By the early 1700s, there was a growing sense of unease over the negative effects of these practices. While communion festivals had "morphed" into evangelistic events, they had, for the two reasons just named, made the Lord's Supper less accessible as an ordinary means of grace. Communion festivals were, by definition, only periodic and seasonal. And against this, protests began in earnest. We read that already by 1708 at Glasgow, the regional Synod (a regional aggregate of presbyteries) commended to its churches a somewhat more energetic practice of four times yearly communion. The commendation was renewed in 1748.

We will look at two men, one from each side of the Atlantic, who protested against the prevailing infrequency of the Lord's Supper: John Erskine (Church of Scotland) and John Mitchell Mason (Associate Reformed Presbyterian Church in America).

---

7   This adaptation of Reformation principle regarding the Supper to long-established Scottish Catholic custom is detailed in Leigh Eric Schmidt, *Holy Fairs: Scotland and the Making of American Revivalism*, 2nd ed. (Grand Rapids: Wm. B. Eerdmans, 2001), chap. 1. An important alteration introduced with these Protestant festivals was the change of season (usually summer or autumn) so that there would be clear differentiation between the old and the new festivals.

John Erskine

John Erskine (1721–1803) was a well-born Edinburgh native who had been encouraged by his family to prepare for a career in law, a discipline of which his father was a professor at Edinburgh University. Nevertheless, young Erskine was redirected toward theological studies and the Christian ministry. After theological studies at Edinburgh University where he had earlier pursued studies in law, Erskine entered the pastoral ministry in 1743 at Kirkintilloch, some ten miles east of Glasgow. This placed him in the vicinity of the earliest Scottish venues where George Whitefield (1714–1770) had, in the year previous, preached in conjunction with outdoor communion festivals. Erskine made it his business to defend the Anglican evangelist's reputation against some criticisms which were levelled.[8]

In that same decade, however, and in a manner unrelated to Whitefield's activity, there began to be a fresh attempt (just as in 1708) to encourage congregations of the Church of Scotland to celebrate more frequent communions. Kirkintilloch was within the Synod of Glasgow and Ayr and, in 1748, that body went on record as urging its churches to aim at recovering the Reformation-era standard of communion four times yearly, in the face of lackadaisical practice which had seen frequency decline to once or twice per year. Young Erskine went into print in 1749 to add such arguments as he could muster in support of this stance.

Especially of note is the fact that this treatise, *Dissertation on Frequent Communicating*, was composed in his twenty-seventh year, the fifth year of his pastoral ministry at Kirkintilloch and at, what was by the standards of that time, an inconvenient distance from theological libraries at Glasgow or Edinburgh.[9] In the treatise of seventy pages are displayed the considerable theological skills which would eventually secure for him the Doctor of Divinity degree from Glasgow University in 1766.[10]

---

8 Moncreiff Wellwood, *Account of the Life and Writings of John Erskine* (Edinburgh: Archibald Constable, 1818), 114; Jonathan Yeager, *Enlightened Evangelicalism: The Life and Thought of John Erskine* (New York: Oxford University Press, 2011), 35–36

9 We cannot rule out that Erskine went, at intervals, to draw on the theological holdings of Glasgow or Edinburgh Universities.

10 N.R. Needham, "John Erskine," in Cameron, ed., *Scottish Dictionary of Church History and Theology*, 300–301. The doctorate was conferred in the aftermath of the publication, in two volumes, of Erskine's *Theological Dissertations* in the year preceding.

THE ARGUMENT IN OUTLINE

Erskine began by addressing two important preliminary issues related to the frequency of communion. He insisted that: (1) The motivation behind the determination to see communion frequency increased to four times annually was wholesome and commendable, and (2) There was no denying that the means designated for securing more frequent observance (simpler, less-extended weekends, not requiring extra visiting preachers, and with all congregations observing on the same Sundays) were proper and unexceptionable.[11] With these fundamentals in place, he posed the searching question: "And are there any whose faith is so lively and vigorous, that they seldom need the help of this ordinance to strengthen and increase it?"[12]

But he knew better than to leave matters there, at the level of reckoning up of practical benefits; he understood that his case would be made or broken by his supplying biblical and theological reasoning in support of communion frequency, and to that he next turned.

THE NEW TESTAMENT EVIDENCE

Like a good number of evangelical Christians in the eighteenth century, Erskine took the view that the church in the apostolic and post-apostolic age had enjoyed the Lord's Supper at least weekly. He believed this to be supported by the "as often" language of 1 Corinthians 11:26 and still more certainly by Acts 2:42, 46 (where he took the "breaking of bread" language to be an unambiguous reference to the Supper). While acknowledging that we have no apostolic command to uphold weekly observance, he reminded his readers that we do not have a command from the apostles regarding the alteration of our day of rest from the seventh to the first day either.[13] He showed himself familiar with the rejoinder of those, like Daniel Whitby (a standard commentator of that era), that the "breaking of bread" language of the New Testament has a much wider usage than references to the Lord's Supper;[14] however

---

11 John Erskine, "Dissertation on Frequent Communicating," in *Theological Dissertations*, vol. 2 (London: Edward and Charles Dilly, 1765), 244.

12 Erskine, "Dissertation on Frequent Communicating," 248.

13 Erskine, "Dissertation on Frequent Communicating," 256–257, 265.

14 Whitby's well-founded caution about the range of occurrences of New Testament "breaking of bread language" came in his commentary on Acts 2:42; mysteriously, he took the opposite view when treating the same phrase in his comment on Acts 20:7.

he believed that the "scope" or context of the passages he cited required this meaning. He also found strong New Testament support for weekly communion in Acts 20:7 and 11.[15]

From this New Testament material, he passed naturally to the period of the church fathers, and showed by appeals to Ignatius, Justin Martyr, Tertullian, Cyprian, Jerome and Augustine that frequent and even weekly communion was widespread in the second through fourth-century church.[16] In order to undergird this historical-theological point, he then showed how such Protestant authorities as John Calvin, Johann Franz Buddæus and Daniel Waterland had cited these same church fathers in their own descriptions of the early church's practice of frequent communion.

SEEDS OF DECLINE

Yet, having done so, Erskine needed to deal with the evident fact that this frequency of observance in the early Christian centuries had disappeared.[17] Where did he lay the blame for this decline? Erskine proposed that it was the official toleration opening the way for the eventual adoption of Christianity as the religion of the Roman Empire:

> The most probable cause I can assign for this, is, that till then the religion of Christ being persecuted, few professed it who had not felt the power of it on their hearts. But soon after, Christianity became the established religion of the Roman empire, a greater

His *Critical Commentary and Paraphrases on the New Testament* (1710) has been accessed through the expanded, multi-author *A Critical Commentary and Paraphrase on the Old and New Testaments and Apocrypha*, 4 vols. (New York: Wiley and Putnam, 1845), 4:430, 487.

15 Appeals to this passage in favour of weekly observance suppose that the "breaking of bread" (which itself may only indicate a common meal) was a Lord's Supper and that this constituted the central purpose of this assembly. Given the range of usage of this terminology across the New Testament, it is not possible to be dogmatic in upholding the interpretation which Erskine favoured. That second century writers understood these passages in such a sense was evident to Erskine, and this may have coloured his interpretation of this New Testament language.

16 Erskine, "Dissertation on Frequent Communicating," 258. His access to these church fathers in Greek editions, while a pastor in a country town, either implies an impressive private library or regular visits to Glasgow University.

17 Erskine, "Dissertation on Frequent Communicating," 266.

number of hypocrites, from views of worldly interest, inter-
mingled themselves with the true disciples of Christ. And in a
century or two more, this little leaven leavened the whole
lump.... Such nominal Christians could have no just sense of the
use and benefits of the Lord's Supper and the obligation to frequent it.... Their example would soon be followed by lukewarm
Christians who had fallen from their first love.[18]

Erskine is asserting more here than that the Imperial toleration and
eventual recognition of the early church contributed to a decline in
frequency of communion; it is that this toleration and eventual recognition contributed to a decay of piety, and the decay of piety showed
itself in indifference to the holy meal. He cited conciliar decisions
from Elibris (Spain) in A.D. 324 that forbade monetary contributions
to the church from those who declined to participate in the Supper.
Another council, held at Antioch in A.D. 341, agreed that those who
came to services only to hear the Scripture read and then departed
before the administration of the Supper were to be "cast out of the
church, till such time as they gave public proof of their repentance."
He noted that this problem only intensified over time; by the late
fourth century, Chrysostom had lamented that at the administration
of the holy meal "we stand in vain at the altar and none care to receive."
The Council of Toledo in A.D. 400 had needed to depose clergy who
absented themselves from "daily prayers and communion."[19]

Thus far, Erskine had sketched a trajectory depicting a weekly
administration of the Lord's Supper from apostolic times to A.D. 450,
yet with a steadily diminishing regular participation of the bulk of
professed Christians. In reliance on the early Christian historian,
Socrates (born A.D. 380), he took the view that the first church to
abandon this weekly standard was Rome, followed by Alexandria. By
A.D. 506, he found that in the West the stated expectation for a professed Christian's participation in the Lord's Supper had been lowered
to three times per year; for a further two centuries the principle of

---

18 Erskine, "Dissertation on Frequent Communicating," 267.

19 Erskine, "Dissertation on Frequent Communicating," 268. Such a policy indicates
the existence of a widely-divergent dual policy, with very lofty expectations on the
clergy in comparison with those laid on ordinary believers.

weekly communion was upheld in the churches of the East. The process of decline had gone on, almost unchecked, so that by the time of the Council of Trent (1546–1560), the Church of Rome had stipulated that a once-annual participation in the Supper was sufficient.[20]

REFORMATION SEEDS OF RECOVERY

Erskine took special pains in demonstrating that the reformers and Puritans, while determined to distance themselves from the errors of the Roman Mass, were united in zeal to far surpass the actual frequency of participation insisted on by Rome. In Erskine's day, the Church of Rome, despite its many Eucharistic services (offered even on behalf of the dead), still upheld the minimalist expectation that once-annual participation was sufficient.

Situated in the west of Scotland, Erskine lamented that he did not have at his fingertips all the information about Europe's Protestant churches that he desired. He entered into correspondence with European pastors to try to fill lacunae in his understanding. On this basis, he could tell his readers that the Bohemian Brethren and the French Reformed were insisting on four celebrations of the Supper per year and the Church of England three. Lutherans, he understood to be still maintaining a weekly Lord's Supper. Erskine knew of Puritans in Old and New England upholding the practice of the Lord's Supper on the first Sunday of each month, or eight times per year.[21] It was his understanding that Calvin, who personally had preferred the early church practice of weekly communion, had settled for a monthly administration, as had the English congregation at Geneva led by John Knox during the persecuting reign of Queen Mary Tudor.[22]

Now, having reached the career and example of Knox, Erskine had his opportunity to detail the expectations regarding administration of the Supper, set out at the enactment of the Scottish Reformation in 1560. The First Book of Discipline (1560) had set out the expectation that each congregation would celebrate the Supper four times annually.[23] This policy had been modified only slightly, two years later.

---

20 Erskine, "Dissertation on Frequent Communicating," 271.
21 Erskine, "Dissertation on Frequent Communicating," 273–274.
22 Erskine, "Dissertation on Frequent Communicating," 275. See also footnote 5.
23 See footnote 4.

Given the shortage of ministers, it was agreed that rural congregations might have the Supper twice annually and that those in towns
would be expected to maintain quarterly administration.[24] But the
combination of shortage of ministers, political turmoil pitting the
young King James VI against the General Assembly, and the long-
established medieval pattern of neglect of regular participation,
meant that these Reformation expectations were as often honoured
in the breach as in the observance. The whole question needed to be
revisited in 1638 and 1641.[25]

As to why, even in the second half of that century, the problem of
infrequent communion seemed so intractable, Erskine pinpointed
issues already mentioned in passing. First was political and religious
turmoil with the Stuart monarchy which, both before and after the
Commonwealth period (when there was no monarch), meddled too
much in the government and liturgy of the Scottish Church and
which polarized churches and ministers by these efforts.[26] Second
was the practice (alluded to in our introduction) adopted by pastors
who sought to capitalize on the evangelistic possibilities of regional
communion festivals, stretching from a Thursday through a Monday
and involving as many as ten preachers. Whatever these festivals
achieved in exposing vast crowds to the preaching of the gospel and
admitting many hundreds in attendance to participation in the Lord's
Supper, came at the expense of other nearby congregations which
lost their preachers and people to the mass rallies. Whatever these
communion festivals were, they were not an effective method of
instilling stated, frequent congregational communions, community
by community. Erskine noted that the General Assembly of 1701,
surveying the ongoing popularity of these festivals, recommended
that congregations and pastors give higher priority to the administration of the Supper "in their bounds."[27] He concluded his historical
survey by pressing the question:

---

24 Erskine, "Dissertation on Frequent Communicating," 278.

25 Erskine, "Dissertation on Frequent Communicating," 280.

26 Erskine, "Dissertation on Frequent Communicating," 282.

27 Erskine, "Dissertation on Frequent Communicating," 284. This stance was reiterated once more in 1712 and 1724

Are our times better than the Reformation and covenanting periods, when our church approached much nearer to the primitive simplicity in dispensing the Supper of the Lord? Has our church gained anything, has practical religion been increased by the change of the old for our present way? Does it not deserve inquiry, if our neglect of frequently communicating be not one cause why "the love of many has waxed cold"?[28]

ANSWERS TO OBJECTIONS

Erskine could not leave his subject without dealing with objections that his support for more frequent communion provoked. One, which will strike us as rather "from the blue," insisted that Christian believers in primitive times had lived at a higher plane and could benefit from frequent participation in the Supper without the more extensive preparations which had grown customary of late. Erskine turned this aside by insisting that this argument failed to reckon with how more frequent communion could elevate rank-and-file Christians of modern times.[29] A second argued that as the Jewish Passover was observed but once a year, the Lord's Supper might be administered appropriately on that same plan. In reply, Erskine, relying on the late Puritan, Stephen Charnock (1628–1680), maintained that Passover did not stand so solitarily as this objection maintained, inasmuch as the Jewish sacrificial system was ongoing: weekly, monthly and annually. Thus, the Passover as an offering of sacrifice was not utterly solitary in the cycle of the Jewish calendar.[30]

A third argument insisted that too-frequent participation in the Supper lessened its solemnity, whereas participation at long intervals preserved this. Erskine responded by warning against trying to be wiser than God: if it was God's will that we participate frequently, then the question of hypothetical ill effects was his to deal with. Other means of grace, such as prayer, and hearing the Word did not suffer from frequent use; why suggest this of the Supper?[31] Fourth, and as we can imagine, Erskine needed to respond to the insistence that more

---

28 Erskine, "Dissertation on Frequent Communicating," 287.
29 Erskine, "Dissertation on Frequent Communicating," 287.
30 Erskine, "Dissertation on Frequent Communicating," 288.
31 Erskine, "Dissertation on Frequent Communicating," 291–292.

frequent communion—even if it be quarterly—represented a clear innovation. This he turned aside with the reminder that the eighteenth-century practice fell *below* that recommended at the Reformation, and before it in the primitive church.[32]

Fifth, he needed to address the insistence that the Christian population of Scotland did not favour the recommended frequency. This objection, which may have been very well-founded, he turned aside with a proper insistence that the church is to decide such matters on biblical grounds, not on the basis of popular sentiment. That great Christian pastors and writers in previous days had argued for frequent participation in the Supper, Erskine demonstrated by providing details regarding the biblical arguments of John Calvin and Richard Baxter (1615–1691), and his own contemporaries John Willison (1680–1750) and Jonathan Edwards (1703–1758).[33]

There was, last of all, the veiled threat that the General Assembly's policy of proposing not less than quarterly communions might drive people out of the Church of Scotland and into the breakaway Secession movement (begun in 1733), where the administration of the Supper was also still following the "festival" pattern. To this, Erskine calmly replied that as the reason for the Secession two decades earlier had nothing to do with communion practice and, as its leaders were very reasonable people who could not find fault with the Church of Scotland's determination to address this problem, this threat was exaggerated.[34]

John Mitchell Mason

Our second eighteenth-century Presbyterian to press the case for more frequent communion was a full generation younger than our first— and clearly in his debt. John Mitchell Mason (1770–1829) was born in New York City and was the son of a prominent immigrant Presbyterian minister (also named John Mason). Educated in his native city's

---

32 Erskine, "Dissertation on Frequent Communicating," 295.

33 Erskine, "Dissertation on Frequent Communicating," 296–301. John Willison, long the minister of Brechin and Dundee South, had himself been an advocate of more frequent communion in his *Sacramental Directory* (1716) and *Sacramental Companion* (1720). His significance has been highlighted in recent times by Kimberly Bracken Long, *The Eucharistic Theology of the American Holy Fairs* (Louisville: Westminster John Knox, 2011), ch. 6.

34 Erskine, "Dissertation on Frequent Communicating," 302.

Columbia College (now University) as well as Edinburgh University, he was, from 1793, successor to his late father as pastor of the city's Associate Reformed Presbyterian congregation.[35] It is clear from correspondence between father and son, conducted while young John matriculated at Edinburgh, that John Erskine, by then a minister of Old Greyfriars Church, very near the university, was familiar to them.[36]

Though John M. Mason (like his deceased father) served a congregation of the Associate Reformed Presbyterian Church (the American denomination descended from a division in the Scottish Church in 1733), it is evident that in the matter of the administration of the Lord's Supper, there was little or no distinction between the mother church and the congregations which had stood apart from her since 1733. The frequency of communion was, in neither, in excess of once or twice annually. And the crossing of the Atlantic by the various branches of the Scottish Presbyterian family had, if anything exacerbated this infrequency due to the ongoing shortage of ministers. It was in his first decade of pastoral ministry at New York and while not yet thirty years old that Mason took up his pen to write *Letters on Frequent Communion*.[37]

THE ARGUMENT IN OUTLINE

Mason's approach to the question of communion frequency could be described as pastoral and practical. He maintained that Holy Communion as practiced (especially) in the Associate Reformed Presbyterian Church was embraced by the people with neither "that frequency nor simplicity which were the delight and ornament of the primitive churches." He described a current communion practice of "once in twelve months or once in six"; moreover, this practice was

35 The outlines of Mason's life are provided in Philip W. Butin, "John Mitchell Mason," in *Dictionary of the Presbyterian and Reformed Tradition in America*, ed. D.G. Hart (1999; reprint, Phillipsburg: Presbyterian and Reformed, 2005), 150; Jacob Van Vechten, *Memoirs of John M. Mason* (New York: Carter, 1856); and Cornelius van Santvoord, "John Mitchell Mason," in *The Presbyterian Review* (1882): 264–277.

36 Van Vechten, *Memoirs of John M. Mason*, 47–48.

37 The publication of 1798 was issued by T. & J. Swords, Pearl Street, New York. An Edinburgh edition, published by J. Ritchie was issued in the same year. I have consulted the work as it is printed in volume 1 of Ebenezer Mason, ed., *Complete Works of John M. Mason, D.D.*, 4 vols. (New York: Baker and Scribner, 1849).

also "loaded with encumbrances which lack scriptural warrant."[38] He was focusing, in late-eighteenth-century New York, on the identical practices which had motivated Erskine to write almost half-a-century before. Mason would take the two issues in turn.

THE NEW TESTAMENT EVIDENCE

Mason was very quick to admit that Jesus himself had left no explicit indication in the Gospels of the frequency he intended his followers to remember him in the Lord's Supper. "Something is, no doubt, to be left to Christian prudence."[39] This restraint on Jesus' part, he took to be the basis for a reasonable flexibility on the church's part. "Incidental hindrances" could, in this way, be honestly accommodated.

Yet with this admission in place, Mason went on to lament the fact that the Presbyterian churches of his time—far from simply dealing with the question of frequency in light of Jesus' reserve—had fallen into carelessness. He attributed to many an attitude which supposed that "whether we communicate twice in a year, or once; or only every other year is…indifferent." At root, this casual attitude toward the frequency of the Supper sidestepped the expectation of *frequent* communion services. The apostle Paul had instructed, "as often as you eat and drink" (1 Corinthians 11:26).[40] Pressing the issue further, he asked:

> And does not the tenor of this command teach thee, that the frequency of thy sacramental commemorations of him will be in proportion to the ardor of thy love? Alas, brethren, if this is a criterion of love to our Lord, the pretentions of most of us are low indeed.[41]

OBJECTIONS NEEDING ANSWERS

a) *What is advocated represents innovation over common practice*
Having acknowledged, initially, the fact that Jesus himself left us with no firm policy on frequency of communion, and then personally advocated a heightened frequency of administration as an expression of

---

38 "Letters on Frequent Communion," in *Works of Mason*, 1:377.
39 "Letters on Frequent Communion," in *Works of Mason*, 1:379.
40 "Letters on Frequent Communion," in *Works of Mason*, 1:380.
41 "Letters on Frequent Communion," in *Works of Mason*, 1:383.

love to him, Mason first faced an objection that represents his proposal as an unwarranted innovation. In response, he will only allow that if innovation is found in his argument, it is of a kind which challenges recent rather than ancient custom. In sum, Mason argues that the infant church practiced a frequent communion which was only lost because of the advance of the carnality in the church after Rome's decree of toleration of Christianity in the year A.D. 312.[42]

He found evidence of this frequency of observance in New Testament Scriptures now familiar to us. They are "proofs" still being cited: Acts 20:7,11 where "breaking bread" is named as a central purpose of the assembly in which Paul preached until nearly midnight. He found similar support in 1 Corinthians 11:20; there also he claimed to find that participation in the communion meal was central to the assembling of the believers of that city.[43] Explicitly following an earlier author, Erskine, he went on to claim that the weekly communion associated with Paul and his churches continued as the practice of the early churches for "above two centuries" and as universal practice.[44] Declension from this uniformity was observable "toward the close of the fourth century." By A.D. 506, he found that the expectation of the early church had been lowered; believers were by then expected to participate in the Lord's Supper at "Christmas, Easter, and Whitsunday." By the time of the Fourth Lateran Council of 1215, this expectation had been lowered to a mere once-annual participation in the Supper.[45]

It was this shrunken conception of participation in the Lord's Supper which had confronted the reformers of the sixteenth century. John Calvin had denounced such a practice as "a contrivance of the

---

42 "Letters on Frequent Communion," in *Works of Mason*, 1:389.

43 "Letters on Frequent Communion," in *Works of Mason*, 1:400, 402. This interpretation of the signification of the verb "*sunerchomai,*" still remarkably widespread in the Christian world, does not properly take into account that even in 1 Corinthians 11–14, the verb and its cognates need imply no more than an assembling for religious purposes. Thus, for example, in 1 Corinthians 14:26, the verb is used to introduce the idea of a highly participatory church service which will include numerous elements. There is no mention of the Lord's Supper occurring in the church service Paul describes there.

44 "Letters on Frequent Communion," in *Works of Mason*, 1:403.

45 "Letters, on Frequent Communion," in *Works of Mason*, 1:405–406.

devil."[46] Mason was aware that Calvin's own preference would have been to institute a weekly observance of the Supper; he also found that Calvin's contemporary, the Lutheran theologian Martin Chemnitz, was of the same mind.[47] He reported that the Belgic Confession of the Reformed Churches of the Netherlands had stipulated a six-times-yearly cycle for the Supper, while the Reformed Churches of France had set a minimum number of observances at four. Scotland's own Reformed Church had set a similar standard at the enactment of her Reformation in 1560.[48] As for the seventeenth century, he reported that a monthly communion had been the practice of many of the ministers who participated in the sessions of the Westminster Assembly (1643–1647).[49] With all this in place, Mason could confidently plead that "the facts will convince every honest inquirer that frequent communion is not an innovation.... Let us return to the old way in which the first confessors of the cross have walked before us."[50]

b) *The proposal encourages irreverence*

Mason knew that he must also deal with the protest that the consequence of very frequent participation in the Lord's Supper would "deaden affection, destroy solemnity, banish reverence and thus be injurious."[51] He was utterly unimpressed by such an objection inasmuch as he judged it to be the sentiment *not* of the person who was truly seeking to advance reverence for God but "of the formalist, who goes to the communion table only once or twice a year to save appearances, or to quiet conscience.... That such (an opinion) should ever be proposed by a living Christian is truly astonishing."

To this seemingly perennial line of reasoning, Mason countered with another question: "Do *other* duties grow contemptible by their frequency? Is the Sabbath vile because of its weekly return? The

---

46 John Calvin, *Institutes of the Christian Religion*, IV.17.46, quoted in "Letters on Frequent Communion," in *Works of Mason*, 1:407.

47 "Letters on Frequent Communion," in *Works of Mason*, 1:408.

48 "Letters," 410. Mason here cites the Scottish church's *First Book of Discipline*, Article XIII. I have searched in vain for any reference to frequency of communion in Belgic Confession Article 35, which pertains to the Holy Meal.

49 "Letters on Frequent Communion," in *Works of Mason*, 1:412.

50 "Letters on Frequent Communion," in *Works of Mason*, 1:412.

51 "Letters on Frequent Communion," in *Works of Mason*, 1:413.

Divine Scriptures, family religion, secret prayer?" No. Believers, entrusted with the Lord's Supper for their spiritual nourishment "should not refuse, and justify their refusal by pleading that it would (if frequent) diminish their reverence." Could it really be possible that "the seldomer we communicate the better?"[52]

c) *The proposal would disturb long-established "fasts" and "thanksgivings"*
Both in Scotland and early America, annual or semi-annual Presbyterian communion festivals had incorporated into their extended weekend formats a preliminary day of fasting and a concluding day of thanksgiving. Mason could well anticipate that the proposal for more frequent communion would encounter a serious objection that more frequent communions would threaten these now-hallowed days which were like prelude and postlude to the main event. It would do so by making unsustainable (through a quarterly or still more frequent communion schedule) that extended Thursday through Monday program, which had come to be considered inseparable from the communion itself. People could simply not be away from their daily toil (Thursday through Monday) *multiple* times during the yearly round. And any argument for frequency of communion (such as made by Mason) thus threatened to strip away these revered practices associated with the ordinance.

To this considerable objection, Mason abruptly emphasized, "They have no warrant in the book of God." Neither Jesus or the apostles had done anything to encumber the Lord's Supper with these *additional* practices. To this he added, "They are contrary to the judgment of almost the whole Christian church." However venerated these fasts and thanksgivings had come to be regarded among seventeenth- and eighteenth-century Protestants, they were not part of the practice of the church of the ages.

He went on to add, that though days of fasting and of thanksgiving are innocent enough in and of themselves, "the question is whether (these) are divine ordinances *with* the holy supper."[53] By extending the number of days necessary to be spent in attending the established communion festivals, these fasts and thanksgivings in effect served as

---

52 "Letters on Frequent Communion," in *Works of Mason*, 1:415–420.
53 "Letters on Frequent Communion," in *Works of Mason*, 1:430.

barriers to the frequent observance of the Supper provided for by Jesus and the apostles. The multiplying of services in which sermons needed to be preached necessitated the calling away from their congregations of additional ministers who, by their assisting in communion festivals away from home, deprived whole congregations of their regular diet of the preached Word on given Lord's Days.[54]

Analysis

Though both treatises were written by young pastor-theologians not yet thirty years of age, and in overwhelming agreement, it is not difficult, at the same time, to draw distinctions between them. The treatises differed as to setting, depth of investigation and form of argument. Erskine had written in open support of his denomination's repeated appeals for greater frequency of administration. Mason dealt with the same practical realities, yet had no existing denominational initiative to strengthen by his writing. The treatise of Mason deserves to be seen as the less original work, when compared with the writing of Erskine on this subject; Mason showed a clear literary dependency on that work of 1749 (as recirculated in Erskine's *Theological Dissertations* of 1765).[55] Erskine was one of the two near-contemporary theological writers on whom Mason leaned most heavily. Thus, when Mason referred to Patristic writers, he seems only to have cited these opinions to the extent that they were provided in the named authors.[56] Yet while the "laurels" for depth of research would fall to Erskine, it can honestly be said that it was Mason who took the fruits of the research of others and set them out in the compelling way which was more likely to be consulted by laymen and church officers. His answers to potential

---

54 Mason's treatise, though written in North America was read on both sides of the Atlantic. A reply was composed by a Glasgow minister of his denomination, John Thomson, entitled *Letters Addressed to the Rev. John Mason M.A. of New York*. Of this, an American edition was prepared at Troy, N.Y. in 1801.

55 Note that Erskine's treatise is explicitly cited in *Works of Mason*, 1: 404, 406, 412.

56 The other authority was that of Joseph Bingham (1668–1723), *Origines Ecclesiasticae* (Halle, 1738). Intriguingly, both the Bingham and the Erskine volumes are among the holdings of the Burke Theological Library associated with today's Columbia University, New York. John Mitchell Mason was founding professor of theology in the first American theological seminary of his denomination, begun at New York in 1805 and enduring until 1821.

objections came earlier in his treatise and were more extensive than comparable material offered by the earlier writer.

If the two treatises on frequency of communion can be contrasted in these ways, they may also be viewed aggregately (since of largely overlapping sentiments). The following commonalities can be observed:

1. Each writer granted, from the outset, that neither Jesus nor his apostles left to the church any actual pronouncement on the subject of frequency of communion. At best, there are inferences which may be drawn from the New Testament.

2. Each agreed that a primitive high frequency of communion in the first Christian centuries had gradually given way in medieval Catholicism to a minimalist expectation of once-annual participation.

3. Each accepted that the now-hallowed practice of annual or semi-annual communion festivals represented an innovation of the early seventeenth century, and as such represented a departure from the original Reformation expectation of an at least quarterly administration.

4. The annual or semi-annual communion festival—whatever might be said about its evangelistic potentialities for preaching the gospel to the mixed multitudes which gathered—was inadequate to the spiritual needs of ordinary Christians and provided to these insufficient opportunities for communing with their Lord.

5. The annual or semi-annual communion festival was not only inadequate to the needs of the ordinary Christian believer, it was also injurious to the health of neighbouring congregations which—forfeiting their preachers who went to assist in these weekend events—had no Sunday services of any kind.

6. While each writer was personally convinced that the primitive church had enjoyed the Lord's Supper weekly and knew that the restoration of that primitive frequency had been the

desire of John Calvin, they also accepted that, from the time of Constantine, the church had declined from its original purity and cohesiveness. The mixed nature of the church from Constantine forward rendered it less capable of delighting in the frequency of practice enjoyed in earlier times. Sadly, that mixed character continued to their own day, two-and-a-half centuries after the Reformation.

7. The common position of Erskine and Mason, therefore, was that evangelical churches and believers needed to resort to the Lord's Supper more frequently than the communion festival practice had allowed—while not attempting to recover precisely the practices they believed were characteristic of apostolic times. A quarterly, six-times-yearly or monthly communion all represented a giant step in the desired direction, and they asked for no more at that time.

No one will suggest that our ecclesiastical situation is identical to that faced by Erskine and Mason. Since their times, the case for weekly administration of the Supper has been forcefully made twice by the dawning of nineteenth-century "restorationist" initiatives, such as the Plymouth Brethren and the Stone-Campbell movements, and by the percolation into evangelical Protestantism of ideas whose genesis lay in the nineteenth-century Oxford movement.[57] In our own time, one also regularly hears appeal being made to the preference of John Calvin for weekly communion.

To this writer, the literary efforts of Erskine and Mason are salutary in three respects. First, we should note that both men were renowned for their evangelical zeal and pan-denominational interests. No one could charge either with a love of ritual or liturgical embroidery at the expense of gospel proclamation.[58] Let those who want to contend for

---

57 The contemporary influence of these two nineteenth-century movements has been alluded to in the introduction to this paper.

58 The biographers of Erskine, Moncreiff-Wellwood and Yeager, make it plain that Erskine was the forthright leader of the rising "popular" or evangelical party in the Church of Scotland in the period up to his death and, as well, an evangelical leader of trans-Atlantic significance. He had been the means of the publication of most of the works of Jonathan Edwards in Edinburgh and was the benefactor of numerous American

heightened frequency of administration of the Supper in our time demonstrate the same multiple zeal, lest heightened sacramental observance be brought in at the expense of the proclamation of the gospel which is so necessary for encouraging the pious hunger and aspiration which the Lord's Supper presupposes to exist.

Second, they show themselves to be vitally concerned that evangelical practice surrounding the Lord's Supper be at least *informed* by early church practice. That is not the same thing as to say that evangelical practice must be *only* that of the early church. Our evangelical Protestant tradition is being faulted in our day for having shown itself to be so utterly unconcerned with conformity to the early church as to be "threadbare." Erskine and Mason stand as important examples of how ancient Christian practice was consulted with care in the very period when our evangelical movement is alleged to have slipped from its moorings. Yet their consultation of Christian antiquity did not lead them to endorse wooden conformity to it.

Third, Erskine and Mason are important examples of how the study of early Christian practice by Christians in a later age must involve more than simple imitation of the practices of an earlier time. They illustrate an understanding that the early church's communion practices had been seriously compromised by the transformation of the church begun in Constantine's time. By this transformation, which cost the fourth-century church much of its zeal and purity, the existing high frequency of administration of the Supper came to be perceived as burdensome and intrusive. It followed (for Erskine and Mason) that unless this loss of zeal and purity was addressed, an increase of frequency of the Supper (in and of itself) would face opposition all over again for similar reasons. They sensed a reciprocal relationship between two factors which modern Christians are perhaps more likely

---

college libraries. Similarly, Mason was a minister and seminary professor in New York City, president of Dickinson College, Carlisle, PA, known for his pan-evangelical sympathiesm and efforts at collaboration with Presbyterian bodies beyond his own. He had been a founding member of the New York Missionary Society (1790) and the American Bible Society (1816). Even more influential than his *Letters on Frequent Communion* (1798) was his written advocacy of inter-communion between various Presbyterian bodies which, to that point, would neither open their pulpits or communion tables to ministers and members of the other denominations. This was his *A Plea for Holy Communion on Catholic Principles* (1816), published in *Works of Mason*, vol. 2.

to take separately. A survey of the current practices of the various denominations on the question of frequency of administration of the Lord's Supper will illustrate that weekly administration, does not *itself* engender health and zeal. The Supper presupposes at least a measure of spiritual hunger and some desire to grow in grace in those who partake. Where these spiritual appetites are present, good can result from a more frequent resort to the Supper; but where they are lacking it is not so much these symbols of Christ that are needed, but Christ *himself*—available to us now through the Word preached and applied. The infrequent communion festivals which both Erskine and Mason sought to curtail had at least upheld this important priority: the gospel itself was first preached to gathered multitudes present and the Supper subsequently administered to that portion of hearers who demonstrated the requisite faith and zeal.

16

Bunyan's perseverance
By Joel R. Beeke

WHEN MEN DO come to see the things of another world, what a God, what a Christ, what a heaven, and what an eternal glory there is to be enjoyed; also, when they see that it is possible for them to have a share in it, I tell you it will make them run through thick and thin to enjoy it.—John Bunyan[1]

Author's note: I am one of hundreds who can say that Michael Haykin has been a great friend for many years. I am grateful to him for that treasured friendship, for teaching a variety of courses at our Puritan Reformed Theological Seminary over the years, and for being my assistant editor of our *Puritan Reformed Journal*. The great talks we've had when he was in our home and his deep voice reverberating through our classrooms and hallways (he's the only professor I can hear lecture when I am in my study!) are alike unforgettable. I have deeply enjoyed co-labouring with him on various projects, including a forthcoming book we are presently coauthoring on Calvin's theology. My respect is nearly unparalleled for Dr. Haykin and for his perseverance in both his own life and in his multifaceted projects. Being a Baptist and a prolific workhorse, he reminds me of John Bunyan, particularly in terms of his perseverance—hence the theme of this chapter.

1   *The Works of John Bunyan*, ed. George Offor, 3 vols. (Glasgow: Blackie and Son, 1854), 3:388. This chapter is an expansion of an address I gave at the West Cannon Baptist Church Conference, Belmont, Michigan, on September 20, 2011; portions of it have been adapted from Joel R. Beeke and Randall J. Pederson, *Meet the Puritans: With a Guide to Modern Reprints* (Grand Rapids: Reformation Heritage Books, 2006), 101–108. I wish to thank Paul Smalley for his valuable input on this chapter.

John Bunyan (1628–1688) was a powerful preacher and the best-known of all Puritan writers. John Owen (1616—1683), another great Puritan preacher, said he would gladly exchange all his learning for Bunyan's power of touching men's hearts. While we are thankful to God that Owen retained his learning, we are also thankful that Bunyan had the remarkable gift of communicating sound doctrine in imaginative, heart-stirring ways. His book, *The Pilgrim's Progress*, has strengthened countless Christians through the centuries. But Bunyan was no one-title wonder. He wrote more than sixty books in his sixty years of life, many of which continue to feed the souls of men and women today.

Saturated with Scripture and deeply influenced by Reformed theology, Bunyan believed in the doctrine of the perseverance of the saints. On the one hand, he taught that perseverance in faith was necessary for salvation. On the other hand, he taught that such perseverance was guaranteed to believers by the electing grace and preserving power of God. He said,

> To be saved is to be preserved in the faith to the end. "He that shall endure unto the end, the same shall be saved" (Matt. 24:13). Not that perseverance is an accident in Christianity, or a thing performed by human industry; they that are saved "are kept by the power of God, through faith unto salvation" (1 Peter 1:3–6). But perseverance is absolutely necessary to the complete saving of the soul.... He that goeth to sea with a purpose to arrive at Spain, cannot arrive there if he be drowned by the way; wherefore perseverance is absolutely necessary to the saving of the soul.[2]

Bunyan also wrote,

> The Father's grace provideth and layeth up in Christ, for those that he hath chosen, a sufficiency of all spiritual blessings, to be communicated to them at their need, for their preservation in the faith, and faithful perseverance through this life; "not according to our works, but according to his own purpose and

---

2   Bunyan, *Works*, 1:339.

grace, which was given us in Christ Jesus before the world began" (2 Tim. 1:9; Eph. 1:3–4).[3]

David Calhoun writes, "Most English Puritans were Calvinists, and Bunyan was no exception.... Someone has called *The Pilgrim's Progress* 'the Westminster Confession of Faith with people in it.'"[4] While Bunyan, as a Baptist, did not subscribe to all the doctrines of Westminster, in his book, indeed "under the similitude of a Dream," the Westminster teachings on Christian experience come to life, take on names and faces and walk before our eyes.

Rather than offering a systematic analysis of Bunyan's doctrine of perseverance, I will walk through his life, drawing seven lessons we can learn from this man. For Bunyan not only taught perseverance; he also persevered, through many sore trials, across many years. His life, like those of the saints mentioned in Hebrews 11, is an illustration of the faith that does not "draw back unto perdition" but perseveres "to the saving of the soul" (Hebrews 10:39). His life likewise reveals that such perseverance is not rooted in mere human strength, but results from God's mighty grace at work in us.

Young John Bunyan: rebellious blasphemer and convicted sinner

John Bunyan was born in 1628, at Elstow, near Bedford, to Thomas Bunyan and Margaret Bentley. Thomas Bunyan, who was a brazier or tinker, was poor but not destitute. John Bunyan was not highly educated. As he grew up, he became rebellious, living for pleasure and frequently indulging in cursing. He later wrote, "It was my delight to be taken captive by the devil at his will: being filled with all unrighteousness; that from a child I had but few equals, both for cursing, swearing, lying, and blaspheming the holy name of God."[5] Sporadic convictions of sin helped restrain some of that rebellion, however.

When Bunyan was sixteen, his mother and sister died just a month apart. His father remarried soon after. Young Bunyan joined Oliver

---

3   Bunyan, *Works*, 1:344.

4   David B. Calhoun, *Grace Abounding: The Life, Books, & Influence of John Bunyan* (Ross-shire: Christian Focus Publications, 2005), 170.

5   Bunyan, *Works*, 1:6.

Cromwell's (1599–1658) New Model Army, where he continued in his rebellious ways. Fighting in the Civil War sobered him, however. On one occasion, his life was wonderfully spared. He wrote later,

> When I was a soldier, I with others, was drawn out to go to such a place to besiege it. But when I was just ready to go, one of the company desired to go in my room; to which when I consented, he took my place, and coming to the siege, as he stood sentinel, he was shot in the head with a musket bullet and died.[6]

Bunyan was discharged from the army in 1646 or 1647. His military experience was later recounted in his book about spiritual conflicts of the soul, *The Holy War*. He returned to his father's trade as a tinker or metalworker, carrying tools and a sixty-pound portable anvil on his back from farm to farm to find work. In 1905, his anvil was discovered in a pile of scrap metal, still engraved with his name and his hometown.[7]

In 1648, Bunyan married a God-fearing woman whose name remains unknown, and whose only dowry was two books: Arthur Dent's (1571–1607) *The Plain Man's Pathway to Heaven* and Lewis Bayly's (d. 1631) *The Practice of Piety*. When Bunyan read those books, he was once more convicted of sin. He started attending the parish church, stopped swearing (when rebuked by a dissolute woman of the town), gave up sports and dancing and observed the Sabbath. After some months, Bunyan came into contact with some women whose joyous conversation about the new birth and faith in Christ deeply affected him. He mourned his joyless existence as he realized that he was lost outside of Christ. "I cannot now express with what longings and breakings in my soul I cried to Christ to call me," he wrote. He believed that he had the worst heart in all England. He said he was jealous of the animals because as brute beasts they did not have a soul to account for before God.

---

6 Bunyan, *Works*, 1:6.

7 Faith Cook, *Fearless Pilgrim: The Life and Times of John Bunyan* (Darlington: Evangelical Press, 2008), 64.

LESSON 1: PERSEVERANCE DEMANDS REGENERATION AND FAITH IN CHRIST, NOT MERE CONVICTION OF SIN.

At this stage of his life, Bunyan might have convinced many people that he was a Christian. His conscience was active, his conduct clean, his church attendance regular and he even read the works of Puritan writers. If such a man falls away from the faith, that is no argument against the doctrine of perseverance of the saints. Men can perform outward religious duties without being born again into the family of God. There is no promise of preservation to those who merely practice the outward forms of godliness. Bunyan himself warned that there are many ways to get rid of the conviction of sin, including busying oneself in religious matters.[8] He decried "a formal customary coming to [God's] ordinances and ways of worship, which availeth not anything."[9]

Apart from God's gift of life in regeneration and true faith, we have nothing in which to persevere. Bunyan thus wrote,

> Wherefore sinners, before faith, are compared to the wilderness, whose fruits are briars and thorns.... They are said to be Godless, Christless, Spiritless, faithless, hopeless.... Now, these things being thus, it is impossible that all the men under heaven, that are unconverted, should be able to bring forth one work rightly good.... Good works must come from a good heart.[10]

However, once God begins the good work of grace within the soul, we may confess with Paul in Philippians 1:6 that we are "confident of this very thing, that he which hath begun a good work in you will perform it until the day of Jesus Christ." Those in whom the Father "hath begotten...again unto a lively hope by the resurrection of Jesus Christ from the dead...are kept by the power of God through faith unto salvation ready to be revealed in the last time" (1 Peter 1:3, 5). A firm foundation of perseverance is regeneration, a new birth.

Jesus said in John 6:37–39, "All that the Father gives me will come to me, and whoever comes to me I will never cast out. For I have come down from heaven, not to do my own will but the will of him who sent

---

8 Bunyan, *Works*, 1:350–351.
9 Bunyan, *Works*, 1:247.
10 Bunyan, *Works*, 2:551.

me. And this is the will of him who sent me, that I should lose nothing of all that he has given me, but raise it up on the last day." The unbreakable chain forged in heaven is that the Father gives regeneration, the soul comes to this by faith and Christ saves the believer to the end. Bunyan thus wrote, "Christ is as full in his resolution to save those given to him as is the Father in giving of them. Christ prizeth the gift of his Father; he will lose nothing of it."[11]

Bunyan's conversion and justification

In 1651, the godly women who impressed Bunyan with their joyful conversation introduced Bunyan to John Gifford, their pastor in Bedford. God used Gifford to lead Bunyan to repentance and faith. Bunyan was particularly influenced by a sermon that Gifford preached on Song of Solomon 4:1, "Behold thou art fair, my love, behold thou art fair." He was also influenced by Luther's commentary on Galatians, in which Bunyan found his own experience "largely and profoundly handled, as if [Luther's] book had been written out of my own heart."[12] While walking through a field one day, Christ's righteousness was revealed to Bunyan's soul. Bunyan wrote of that unforgettable experience:

> But one day, as I was passing in the field…this sentence fell upon my soul: Thy righteousness is in heaven; and methought withal I saw, with the eyes of my soul, Jesus Christ, at God's right hand; there, I say, as my righteousness; so that wherever I was, or whatever I was a-doing, God could not say of me, he wants [lacks] my righteousness, for that was just before him. I also saw, moreover, that it was not my good frame of heart that made my righteousness better, nor yet my bad frame that made my righteousness worse; for my righteousness was Jesus Christ himself, the same yesterday, today, and forever. Now did my chains fall off my legs indeed, I was loosed from my afflictions and irons; my temptations also fled away…now I went home rejoicing, for the grace and love of God.[13]

---

11 Bunyan, *Works*, 1:254.

12 Quoted in Richard L. Greaves, *John Bunyan*, Courtenay Studies in Reformation Theology 2 (Grand Rapids: Wm. B. Eerdmans, 1969), 18.

13 Bunyan, *Works*, 1:35–36.

John Bunyan
1628–1688

This encounter with Christ's righteousness had a profound and lasting effect upon Bunyan. It captured his heart for Christ. He said,

> I lived for some time, very sweetly at peace with God through Christ; Oh! methought, Christ! Christ! there was nothing but Christ that was before my eyes, I was not now only looking upon this and the other benefits of Christ apart, as of his blood, burial, and resurrection, but considered him as a whole Christ!... It was glorious to me to see his exaltation, and the worth and prevalency of all his benefits, and that because of this: now I could look from myself to him, and would reckon that all those graces of God that now were green in me, were yet but like those cracked groats and fourpence-halfpennies that rich men carry in their purses, when their gold is in their trunk at home! Oh, I saw that my gold was in my trunk at home! In Christ my Lord and Saviour! Now Christ was all.[14]

LESSON 2: PERSEVERANCE IS GROUNDED UPON CHRIST'S RIGHTEOUSNESS, NOT OURS.

We must cling to justification by faith in Christ alone and the imputation of Christ's righteousness to believers. Otherwise, our constant imperfections and daily ups and downs will threaten our sense of assurance. We will end up plucking the petals from a daisy, saying, "He loves me, he loves me not." The doctrine of perseverance will then degenerate into legalism, guilt and fear. This was true of Bunyan's condition in all his religious strivings before he trusted Christ as his righteousness.

Our status with God is grounded not on our righteousness but on Christ's. Our covenant with God is ratified by his blood, not our obedience. Thus in Romans 8:33–34 Paul exclaimed, "Who shall lay any thing to the charge of God's elect? It is God that justifieth. Who is he that condemneth? It is Christ that died, yea rather, that is risen again, who is even at the right hand of God, who also maketh intercession for us." Bunyan thus wrote, "I believe then, that the righteousness that saveth the sinner from the wrath to come, is properly and personally Christ's, and ours but as we have union with him; God by grace imputing it to us."[15]

---

14 Bunyan, *Works*, 1:36.
15 Bunyan, *Works*, 2:596.

Hebrews 7:25–26 says, "Wherefore he is able also to save them to the uttermost that come unto God by him, seeing he ever liveth to make intercession for them. For such an high priest became us, who is holy, harmless, undefiled, separate from sinners, and made higher than the heavens." Bunyan wrote in response, "The durableness of his intercession proves that the covenant in which those who come to God by him as concerned and wrapped up is not shaken, broken, or made invalid by all their weaknesses and infirmities."[16] It is not shaken because the covenant stands upon Christ's work, not ours. Bunyan said, "He is the Lord our righteousness, and he is the Saviour of the body, so that my sins break not the covenant; but them notwithstanding, God's covenant stands fast with him, with him forevermore."[17] Just as the personal foundation of perseverance is true faith in Jesus Christ, so the legal or covenantal foundation of perseverance is righteousness in Christ.

Without the unchangeablity of God's covenant promise, sealed with the blood of Christ, the perfection of Christ's righteousness and the irrevocability of God's sentence of justification, neither Bunyan nor any other Christian could persevere to the end.

Bunyan's first steps as a preacher and writer

The year 1654 was momentous for Bunyan. He moved to Bedford with his wife and four children under the age of six, one of whom, his first-born, Mary, was blind from birth. That same year, Bunyan became a member of Gifford's church and was soon appointed deacon. His testimony became the talk of the town. It helped lead several people to conversion. By the end of the year, Bunyan lost his beloved pastor to death.

In 1655, Bunyan began preaching to various congregations in Bedford. Hundreds came to hear him. He published his first book the following year, *Some Gospel Truths Opened*, which was written to protect believers from being misled by Quaker and Ranter[18] teachings about Christ's person and work. Two years later, Bunyan published

---

16 Bunyan, *Works*, 1:231.

17 Bunyan, *Works*, 1:232.

18 In Bunyan's time, a Ranter was "a member of a 17th century pantheistic, antinomian, and highly individualistic religious group in England" (Webster).

A Few Sighs from Hell, an exposition of Luke 16:19–31 about the rich man and Lazarus. The book attacks the professional clergy and wealthy people who promote carnality. It sold well and helped establish Bunyan as a reputable Puritan writer. About that time, his wife passed away, leaving him four young children.

In 1659, Bunyan published *The Doctrine of the Law and Grace Unfolded*, which explains his view of covenant theology, stressing the promissory nature of the covenant of grace and the dichotomy between law and grace. This helped establish him as a thorough Calvinist, though it led to false charges of antinomianism by Richard Baxter.

In 1660, while preaching in a farmhouse at Lower Samsell, Bunyan was arrested under the terms of the newly-revived Act of Uniformity, requiring attendance upon the services and ministry of the Church of England. When told that he would be freed if he no longer preached, he replied, "If I am freed today, I will preach tomorrow." He was thrown into prison, where he wrote many books and made shoelaces for more than twelve years.

LESSON 3: PERSEVERANCE INVOLVES A WILLINGNESS TO SUFFER FOR CHRIST.

Jesus Christ said, "He that shall endure unto the end, the same shall be saved" (Matthew 24:13). In running, the word *endure* means to go the distance to the finish line, despite hardship. Bunyan wrote,

> It is an easy matter for a man to run hard for a spurt, for a furlong [an eighth of a mile], for a mile or two: Oh, but to hold out for a hundred, for a thousand, for ten thousand miles!—that man that doth this, he must look to meet with cross, pain, and wearisomeness to the flesh, especially if, as he goeth, he meeteth with briers and quagmires, and other encumbrances that make his journey so much the more painful.[19]

Acts 14:22 reports that Paul and Barnabas visited their latest converts, "confirming the souls of the disciples, and exhorting them to continue in the faith, and that we must through much tribulation enter into the kingdom of God." Surely one lesson Bunyan intended

---

19 Bunyan, *Works*, 3:387.

to teach in *The Pilgrim's Progress* is that our path to heaven is full of trials in the form of crosses to be borne and dangers to be faced, and that we must endure all these things for the sake of the King of the Celestial City.

Bunyan's experience of outward injustice and inward pain

Prior to his arrest, Bunyan married again, this time to a godly young woman named Elizabeth. She pleaded repeatedly for her husband's release from prison, but judges such as Sir Matthew Hale (1609–1676) and Thomas Twisden (1602–1683) rejected her plea. Her boldness is a wonder to behold; she was very young (perhaps nineteen or twenty) at the time and very pregnant. When she heard about the arrest of her husband, she went into premature labour and lost the baby, but she stood up to her husband's accusers with courage. One justice told Bunyan's wife that he was "a pestilent fellow." Another asked, "Will your husband leave off preaching? If he will do so, then send for him." Elizabeth responded, "My Lord, he dares not leave preaching, as long as he can speak."

His accusers then said he was a "breaker of the peace." But Elizabeth said her husband only wanted to live peacefully, pursue his calling and provide for his family of four small children, one of whom was blind. When asked what her husband's calling was, she said, "a tinker," meaning a worker who mended pots, pans, and other metal household objects.

Another justice accused Bunyan, saying, "He will preach and do what he lists [whatever he wants]." Elizabeth's response was, "He preacheth nothing but the Word of God."

Another judge became so angry that Elizabeth feared he would hit her. He said Bunyan preached the doctrine of the devil. She replied, "My Lord, when the righteous Judge shall appear, it will be known that his doctrine is not the doctrine of the devil."[20] John Brown commented, "Elizabeth Bunyan was simply an English peasant woman: could she have spoken with more dignity had she been a crowned queen?"[21]

---

20 Bunyan, *Works*, 1:61.

21 John Brown, *John Bunyan: His Life Times and Work* (Boston: Houghton, Mifflin, and Co., 1888), 159.

Bunyan remained in prison without any formal charge and without a legal sentence, in defiance of the *habeas corpus* provisions of the Magna Carta. Bunyan steadfastly refused to give up preaching the gospel and would not promise to attend worship in the local parish church.

In 1661 and from 1668 to 1672, some jailers permitted Bunyan to leave prison at times to preach. George Offer notes, "It is said that many of the Baptist congregations in Bedfordshire owe their origins to his midnight preaching."[22]

Those prison years were not easy, however. Bunyan experienced what his characters Christian and Faithful, in *The Pilgrim's Progress* would later suffer at the hands of Giant Despair, who thrust pilgrims "into a very dark dungeon, nasty and stinking."[23] Bunyan particularly felt the pain of separation from his wife and children, including "blind Mary," describing it as a "pulling of the flesh from my bones."[24]

LESSON 4: PERSEVERANCE DOES NOT PRECLUDE TIMES OF DOUBT AND DEPRESSION.

Let us not be foolishly optimistic. God's promise of preserving grace does not include walking in unbroken sunshine. Regarding one occasion when he was in prison, Bunyan wrote, "I was once above all the rest in a very sad and low condition for many weeks, sometimes lasting for weeks at a time.... For indeed at that time all the things of God were hid from my soul."[25] Sometimes the thought of his death by execution obsessed Bunyan. Did he know for sure he would go to heaven? At other times his heart broke when he imagined how his children, especially his blind daughter, would become destitute beggars because of his imprisonment. During this period he learned how, in his words, "to live upon God that is invisible" (Hebrews 11:27).[26]

Even the apostle Paul was brought low by sorrows. He writes in 2 Corinthians 1:8–9, "For we would not, brethren, have you ignorant of our trouble which came to us in Asia, that we were pressed out of measure, above strength, insomuch that we despaired even of life: but

---

22 George Offor, "Introduction" to Bunyan, *Works*, 1:lix.
23 Bunyan, *Works*, 3:140.
24 Bunyan, *Works*, 1:48.
25 Bunyan, *Works*, 1:49.
26 Bunyan, *Works*, 1:48.

we had the sentence of death in ourselves, that we should not trust in ourselves, but in God which raiseth the dead."

Bunyan recalled his struggles in the image of a fire burning against a wall in *The Pilgrim's Progress*. A man poured water on the fire, showing how the devil tries to extinguish the work of grace that God produces in the heart. But the fire kept burning, indeed, grew hotter. How could that be? Hidden behind the wall, the pilgrim saw another man pouring oil on the fire, showing how Christ sustains grace in the heart of a believer. Bunyan said the reason the man remained hidden was to show "that it is hard for the tempted to see how this work of grace is maintained in the soul."[27] In the darkness of depression, we sometimes cannot sense God's presence. But he is there, in fulfillment of his promise never to leave us or forsake us (Hebrews 13:5).

This image of the fire by the wall is perhaps Bunyan's most insightful metaphor for the struggle and triumph of perseverance. Robert Richey notes that Bunyan not only captured the doctrine of perseverance in 200 words but did so in a way that emphasized the sustaining grace of God. He says, "Grace was the motif of Bunyan's heart."[28] Perseverance does not mean that believers march triumphantly through life like heroes in a victory parade; rather, it means that we battle our way through temptations, trials and deep discouragements, all the while discovering the truth of the Lord's promise, "My grace is sufficient for thee, for my strength is made perfect in weakness" (2 Corinthians 12:9).

Bunyan's productivity behind bars

Bunyan's years in prison years were difficult, yet they were also productive. In the mid-1660s, he wrote extensively, with only the Bible and *Foxe's Book of Martyrs* at his side. In 1663, he wrote *Christian Behaviour*, a handbook for Christian living and a reply to charges of antinomianism. It was also intended as a kind of last will and testament, since Bunyan expected to die in prison. He also finished *I Will Pray with the Spirit*, which expounds the truths of 1 Corinthians 14:15 and focuses on the Spirit's inner work in prayer.

---

27 Bunyan, *Works*, 3:100.

28 Robert A. Richey, "The Puritan Doctrine of Sanctification: Constructions of the Saints' Final and Complete Perseverance as Mirrored in Bunyan's '*The Pilgrim's Progress*'" (Th.D. dissertation, Mid-America Baptist Theological Seminary, 1990), 150.

In 1664, Bunyan published *Profitable Meditations*, and in 1665, three more works, *One Thing Needful*, *The Holy City*, an exposition of church history and the end times and *The Resurrection of the Dead*. The latter work is a sequel to *The Holy City*, in which Bunyan explains the resurrection from Acts 24:14–15, then draws on his prison hardships to illustrate the horrors that await the damned after the final judgement.

In 1666, Bunyan wrote *Grace Abounding to the Chief of Sinners*, to describe how God had converted him and brought him to peace through Christ. During the last part of his imprisonment, he finished *A Confession of My Faith*, *A Reason for My Practice* and *A Defence of the Doctrine of Justification*, an uncompromising criticism of Pelagianism among the Nonconformists and latitudinarianism among the Anglicans.

LESSON 5: PERSEVERANCE REQUIRES BEING ACTIVE IN THE SERVICE OF THE LORD.

Bunyan was prolific in writing books during his time in jail, despite the hardships of lacking a comfortable chair, a desk, a library of books and a fine pen—much less a laptop computer with Internet access! Faith Cook writes, "How he managed to write at all amidst those overcrowded, filthy, rat-infested surroundings, with the groans of the prisoners resounding in his ears and the ever present clank of chains reminding him of the death sentence imposed on many inmates, is astonishing."[29] Under such conditions, it took great discipline to produce books. The world is much better for it. But Bunyan was also the better for it. The discipline of work helped him to endure his harsh surroundings.

Moreover, it should also be noted that, in God's wise, sovereign purposes, Bunyan was shut up in prison for this very thing, that he might produce these great works of Christian literature for the generations that followed him. God's ways and thoughts are truly above ours (Isaiah 55:8–9).

Notice the connection between serving the Lord and perseverance in 1 Corinthians 15:58, "Therefore, my beloved brethren, be ye steadfast, unmovable, always abounding in the work of the Lord, forasmuch as ye know that your labour is not in vain in the Lord." Working for

---

29 Cook, *Fearless Pilgrim*, 225.

the Lord strengthens us because it exercises our hope, while laziness weakens us. Proverbs 15:19 says, "The way of the slothful man is as an hedge of thorns: but the way of the righteous is made plain." Idleness goes hand in hand with sinful fear, for Proverbs 22:13 says, "The slothful man saith, There is a lion without, I shall be slain in the streets." By contrast, Daniel 11:32 tells us, "The people that do know their God shall be strong, and do exploits."

Bunyan was convinced of this. He wrote, "Slothfulness is usually accompanied with carelessness, and carelessness is for the most part begotten by senselessness; and senselessness doth again put fresh strength into slothfulness, and by this means the soul is left remediless."[30]

Bunyan out of jail and back again

When the Bedford congregation sensed that magistrates were lessening their resistance to Puritan preaching, they appointed Bunyan as their pastor on January 21, 1672. Bunyan was not released until May, however. He remained firm in his principles, saying, "I have determined, the Almighty God being my help and shield, yet to suffer, if frail life might continue so long, even till the moss shall grow on mine eyebrows, rather than thus violate my faith and principles."[31] He was the first to suffer under Charles II, and the last to be released. His years in Bedford's county prison made him a martyr in the eyes of many people.

Bunyan enjoyed only a few years of freedom when he was again arrested for preaching and put in the town jail. Here he wrote *Instruction for the Ignorant* (a catechism for the saved and unsaved that emphasizes the need for self-denial), *Saved by Grace* (an exposition of Ephesians 2:5 that encourages the godly to persevere in the faith despite persecution), *The Strait Gate* (an exposition of Luke 13:24 to awaken sinners to the gospel message) and *Light for Them That Sit in Darkness* (a polemical work against those who oppose atonement by Christ's satisfaction and justification by his imputed righteousness, especially Quakers and Latitudinarians).

He also wrote the first part of *The Pilgrim's Progress*. This book, which sold more than 100,000 copies during its first decade in print, has since been reprinted in at least 1,500 editions and translated into

---

30 Bunyan, *Works*, 3:378.
31 Bunyan, *Works*, 2:594.

more than 200 languages. Some scholars say that, with the exception of the Bible and perhaps Thomas à Kempis's (c. 1380–1471) *The Imitation of Christ*, *The Pilgrim's Progress* has sold more copies than any other book. It forever etches upon our minds the image of the Christian as a pilgrim journeying through this world on his way to another.

LESSON 6: PERSEVERANCE NECESSITATES A PILGRIM MINDSET.
The life of faith is a pilgrimage through this world to heaven. Hebrews 11:13–16 says,

> These all died in faith, not having received the promises, but having seen them afar off, and were persuaded of them, and embraced them, and confessed that they were strangers and pilgrims on the earth. For they that say such things declare plainly that they seek a country. And truly, if they had been mindful of that country from whence they came out, they might have had opportunity to have returned. But now they desire a better country, that is, an heavenly: wherefore God is not ashamed to be called their God: for he hath prepared for them a city.

We should not love this world or count it as our home, or it will own our hearts and our souls.

In *The Pilgrim's Progress*, pilgrims had to pass through the town of Vanity, which keeps up its Vanity Fair all year long. George Cheever said, "Vanity Fair is the City of Destruction in its gala dress, in its most seductive allurements."[32] The world dons its best clothes to seduce Christians away from the right way. But the pilgrims remained faithful, which aroused the ire of people at the fair. When asked what they would buy, the pilgrims said, "We buy the truth" (cf. Proverbs 23:23). This caused a riot and led to the arrest of Christian and his friend. But the pilgrims told the authorities "that they were pilgrims and strangers in the world, and that they were going to their own country, which was the heavenly Jerusalem."[33] So too we must resist the world if we

---

32 George B. Cheever, *Lectures on the Pilgrim's Progress and on the Life and Times of Bunyan* (New York: Edward Walker, 1846), 47.
33 Bunyan, *Works*, 3:128.

are to persevere in faith. If we do not, we will abandon the faith out of love for the world, as did Demas (2 Timothy 4:10).

Bunyan's final days

John Owen, minister of an Independent congregation at Leadenhall Street, in London, appealed to Thomas Barlow (1607–1691), bishop of London, on behalf of Bunyan. Bunyan was released from prison on June 21, 1677. He spent his last years ministering to the Nonconformists and continued to write. In 1678, he published *Come and Welcome to Jesus Christ*, an exposition of John 6:37 that proclaims the offer of grace to sinners and urges them to fly to Jesus Christ and be saved. This book went through six editions in the last decade of Bunyan's life. In 1680, he wrote *The Life and Death of Mr. Badman*, which has been described as "a series of snapshots depicting the commonplace attitudes and practices against which Bunyan regularly preached."[34] Two years later, Bunyan published *The Greatness of the Soul* and *The Holy War*. In 1685, he published the second part of *The Pilgrim's Progress* dealing with Christian's wife, Christiana, and her pilgrimage to the Celestial City. He also wrote *A Caution to Stir Up to Watch Against Sin* and *Questions About the Nature and the Perpetuity of the Seventh-day Sabbath*. In the final three years of his life, Bunyan wrote ten more books, of which the best-known are *The Pharisee and the Publican*, *The Jerusalem Sinner Saved*, *The Work of Jesus Christ as an Advocate*, *The Water of Life*, *Solomon's Temple Spiritualized* and *The Acceptable Sacrifice*.

In 1688, Bunyan died from a fever he caught while travelling in cold weather. On his deathbed, he said to those who gathered around him, "Weep not for me, but for yourselves. I go to the Father of our Lord Jesus Christ, who will, no doubt, through the mediation of his blessed Son, receive me, though a sinner; where I hope we ere long shall meet, to sing the new song, and remain everlastingly happy, world without end."[35] To the end, his heart was filled with the wonder of God's grace to sinners. After telling his friends that his greatest desire was to be with Christ, he raised his hands to heaven, and cried, "Take me, for I come to Thee!"—and then died. He was buried in London's Bunhill Fields cemetery, close to Thomas Goodwin and John Owen.

---

34 *Oxford Dictionary of National Biography*, 8:707.
35 Bunyan, *Works*, 1:lxxviii.

LESSON 7: PERSEVERANCE IS DRIVEN BY THE HOPE OF GLORY.

In dark times, whether we are in prison, on a sick bed, or at death's door, God's Word shines brighter to us. Bunyan wrote that during his prison years, certain Scriptures that had previously meant little to him before now became very real to him. Specific Bible verses gave him "great refreshment." Like Christian, he escaped from the dungeon of Giant Despair with the key called "promise." Bunyan said he especially found strength in the promises of John 14:1–4; 16:33; Colossians 3:3–4 and Hebrews 12:22–24.[36] Reflect on the hope presented by these texts:

John 14:1–4: "Let not your heart be troubled: ye believe in God, believe also in me. In my Father's house are many mansions: if it were not so, I would have told you. I go to prepare a place for you. And if I go and prepare a place for you, I will come again, and receive you unto myself; that where I am, there ye may be also. And whither I go ye know, and the way ye know."

John 16:33: "These things I have spoken unto you, that in me ye might have peace. In the world ye shall have tribulation: but be of good cheer; I have overcome the world."

Colossians 3:3–4: "For ye are dead, and your life is hid with Christ in God. When Christ, who is our life, shall appear, then shall ye also appear with him in glory."

Hebrews 12:22–24: "But ye are come unto Mount Sion, and unto the city of the living God, the heavenly Jerusalem, and to an innumerable company of angels, To the general assembly and church of the firstborn, which are written in heaven, and to God the Judge of all, and to the spirits of just men made perfect, and to Jesus the mediator of the new covenant, and to the blood of sprinkling, that speaketh better things than that of Abel."

The hope of glory is not just the *goal* of perseverance—it is its *daily* bread and butter. If you want to persevere in this race, feed your soul with a view of the One who is seated at God's right hand, and those who gather around him in shining garments. This will fill you with a longing to see God's glory fully revealed in Christ.

---

36 Bunyan, *Works*, 1:47.

One Lord's Day, when he was in jail, Bunyan was supposed to preach to his fellow prisoners. He found himself "empty, spiritless, and barren." Looking through his Bible, he came upon the description of the heavenly Jerusalem at the end of Revelation. He was so dazzled by the splendour of God among his heavenly people that he took up the text with prayer, then preached it with such power that he later enlarged it into his book, *The Holy City; or, the New Jerusalem*.[37]

The hope of glory will strengthen you to press on to the end. Bunyan said,

> For when men do come to see the things of another world, what a God, what a Christ, what a heaven, and what an eternal glory there is to be enjoyed; also, when they see that it is possible for them to have a share in it, I tell you it will make them run through thick and thin to enjoy it.[38]

Conclusion

Pilgrims must travel a long and difficult road to glory. Yet their steps are certain because God is faithful (1 Corinthians 1:8–9). Bunyan described the battle of perseverance in painful detail. He did not minimize the intense struggles, the doubts and even the backslidings of the true believer. He himself had experienced these things in the Bedford jail.

Yet he confidently portrayed the perseverance of true saints because of the unchangeable decree and sovereign power of God. He wrote, "I believe, that there is not any impediment attending the election of God that can hinder their conversion, and eternal salvation."[39] Just as God infallibly ordains the conversion of his chosen ones, so he infallibly carries them through every trial to eternal glory. Nothing can separate us from the eternal love of God that is in Christ Jesus (Romans 8:30–39).

Bunyan's life exemplified what his doctrine teaches: perseverance is a battle, but it is a battle already won for us by Christ upon the cross. Let us take courage from that, and press on in the way, trusting in God, looking to Christ, praying in the Spirit and hoping for glory.

---

37 Bunyan, *Works*, 3:395. See Calhoun, *Grace Abounding*, 32.

38 Bunyan, *Works*, 3:388.

39 Bunyan, *Works*, 2:598.

The spirituality of Edmund Ludlow: the religious convictions of a regicide

By Robert W. Oliver

THE EXECUTION OF Charles I in 1649 remains one of the most controversial events in English history. For the defeated Royalists it was a bitter ending to the two civil wars in which they had expended wealth and blood to maintain what they saw as the lawful authority of the monarchy. In the opposing camp, the Scots, whose armies had contributed so much to the Parliamentary victory, were generally angry because they were not consulted about the treatment of their king. Charles' father, James, had been king of Scotland long before he inherited the English crown in 1603. Support for the royal house of Stuart was to divide Scotland for years to come in spite of the savage treatment of the Presbyterian church after the Restoration, and the Jacobite cause continued to attract considerable support until well into the next century. In England, the trial and execution of the king sharply divided both the Parliamentarians and the Puritans and was only possible after the army purged the House of Commons of many of the objectors. Support for the monarchy and the Stuart dynasty continued from many of the Presbyterians and one of their ministers, Christopher Love (1618–1651), paid for his loyalty with his life. Richard Baxter (1615–1691) was more cautious, but he was convinced that lasting damage had been inflicted on the cause of Christ by the execution of the king. He wrote of:

the infamous effects of error, pride, and selfishness, prepared by Satan, to be charged hereafter upon reformation and godliness, to the unspeakable injury of the Christian name and Protestant cause, the rejoicing and advantage of the Papists, the hardening of thousands against the means of their own salvation, and the confusion of the actors when their day should come.[1]

Parliamentarians who supported the execution of the king were described as the Commonwealth Party. They promoted a form of government in which Parliament should legislate and a Council of state without a single head would administer the realm. But the need for resolute leadership became urgent and, in 1653, Oliver Cromwell was proclaimed Lord Protector to the dismay of the convinced Commonwealth men who distrusted the concentration of power in a single person.

Cromwell's rule secured respect abroad and a considerable measure of prosperity at home, but his death in September 1658 ushered in a period of instability. The leadership qualities of Cromwell and his ideals are now more widely acknowledged than in the period immediately after his death. By that time, Puritans and Parliamentarians were hopelessly divided. Betrayed by the treachery of General George Monck, they were outwitted by the Royalists who were able to secure the restoration of the Stuart monarchy in the person of Charles II, eldest son of Charles I.

Many sincerely hoped for a fresh start with old scores forgotten. Some Puritans, led by Baxter, Thomas Manton (1620–1677) and Edmund Calamy (1600–1666), hoped to negotiate a church settlement broad enough to include moderate Presbyterians. Politicians of various opinions scrambled for favours. There were promises of an act of indemnity and oblivion to cover past divisions. It soon became apparent that one group that could expect no mercy was the men who had been involved in the trial and execution of Charles I. These were described as the regicides. These were to be charged with treason. In a preliminary address to a grand jury in 1660 to establish that there was a case to hear, Sir Orlando Bridgeman claimed, "*The King can do no wrong*:

---

1   Richard Baxter, *Autobiography*, ed. J.M. Lloyd-Thomas (1925; reprint, London: J. Dent and Sons, 1931), 64.

that is a rule of law, it is frequently found in our law books.... If he can do no wrong, he cannot be punished for any wrong."[2] These sinister words were reflected in the revenge that was exacted. Some two dozen of the regicides were seized and after show trials presided over by Bridgeman were butchered to death. Others who had already died were disinterred and their corpses subjected to mock trials and infamous treatment. These included Oliver Cromwell. At the same time, the bodies of Cromwell's deceased mother and sister, neither of whom had played any part in these affairs, were used in the same vile fashion.

By 1660, the cause of the regicides was clearly lost and generally history has not treated them kindly. A partial exception has been the case of Oliver Cromwell who has been more widely appreciated since the nineteenth century. More recently, the research of Geoffrey Robertson, QC, has shown that, by seventeenth-century standards, the trial of the king was fair and that the prosecutors were careful to proceed by rule of law—in marked contrast to the manner in which they themselves were to be treated by Bridgeman and his cronies. What has gone unmarked is the spirituality of some of these men who suffered in 1660.

One of the few to escape from the revenge of the king and his court was Edmund Ludlow, Member of Parliament for the county of Wiltshire at the time of Charles' execution. Ludlow had attended the court that tried the king and was a signatory to the death warrant. Recent research suggests that he was a Baptist by conviction, although at present it is not known whether he was ever a member of a Baptist church.

A brief history

In 1617, Edmund Ludlow was born into a family of Wiltshire landed gentry who had farmed an estate near Maiden Bradley for some 200 years. Over that period, members of the Ludlow family had often represented their county at Westminster. After schooling at Blandford in the neighbouring county of Dorset, Edmund proceeded to Trinity College, Oxford, from where he graduated as Bachelor of Arts in 1636. In 1638 he enrolled in the Inner Temple to gain the legal knowledge

---

2 Quoted in Geoffrey Robertson, *The Tyrannicide Brief: The Story of the Man Who Sent Charles I to the Scaffold* (London: Chatto & Windus, 2005), 295.

requisite for a county landowner who could expect to become a justice of the peace.

Edmund grew up at a time when Charles I was governing without Parliaments, a period that was to be described by Parliamentarians as "the Eleven Years Tyranny." A rising in Scotland forced Charles I to turn back to Parliament for money. Parliament was in no mood to grant money until its grievances were redressed. The increasingly bitter disputes led to Civil War. Edmund's father, Sir Henry Ludlow, was a zealous Parliamentarian. Not surprisingly, Edmund enrolled in the Parliamentary army as an officer under the Earl of Essex. On his father's death in 1646, he was elected Member of Parliament for Wiltshire. He was at the centre of affairs for some years, serving eventually as second in command of the army in Ireland.

At the Restoration, Ludlow found himself in danger. Charles II declared himself ready to forgive all his enemies, except those closely involved in the death of his father. Ludlow had been a member of the Court that had tried the king and was a signatory of the death warrant. Charles could not act immediately, but arrests began and Ludlow felt the net closing round him. Like many of his associates he considered that he had acted in he best interests of the country. He went into exile in Switzerland, where, in spite of attempts by the English government to extradite exiled regicides or in some cases to assassinate them, he survived until his death in 1692. There he wrote his *Memoirs*.

To appreciate the significance of his written account, it is necessary to review the events surrounding the collapse of the Commonwealth. Richard Cromwell, who succeeded his father as Lord Protector, proved incapable of exercising leadership and was persuaded to resign in the spring of 1659. In the confusion and uncertainty which followed, General George Monck (1608–1670), commander of the Commonwealth army in Scotland, marched south with his troops. Although Monck professed loyalty to the Commonwealth, acting as a double agent, he negotiated with both the Parliamentarians and the exiled Charles Stuart, who agreed to a settlement that promised an amnesty for all apart from any who might be "excepted by Parliament."

The Long Parliament dissolved itself in 1660 and Ludlow was elected for the borough of Hindon, Wiltshire, in the Convention Parliament that succeeded it and was to agree to the restoration of the monarchy. Almost immediately, Ludlow found himself in danger.

Some arrests were made, but for the present Ludlow was still free and, as a Member of Parliament, would remain so until Parliament lifted his immunity. Ludlow was warned that the authorities viewed him with suspicion and he left the country just before any serious attempt was made to arrest him. He explained:

> I am satisfyed, as well from the example as precept of Christ, that it is the duty of the people of God when persecuted in one city to flee to another, Mat. 10. 23, and not to expose themselves to the mercyless cruelty of their bloody enemyes when they can secure themselves without the use of sinfull meanes; it being properly a denying of the cause when we shall disowne it to save our lives, not when in a warrantable way we seek to save our lives to promote God's cause.[3]

The publication of Ludlow's Memoirs

Until he lost favour with Oliver Cromwell, Ludlow had been at the centre of affairs and remained a keen observer of events. The *Memoirs* were first published some six years after his death, but much was written close to the time described. Several editions were published before the definitive two volume edition edited by Sir Charles Firth appeared in 1894.[4] From the time of their first appearance, there were questions about the authenticity of Ludlow's *Memoirs*. Firth was convinced that these were genuine, although extracts copied by the philosopher John Locke were found among his papers after his death in 1704. These included details missing from the already published *Memoirs*. Firth restored these to his edition.

More recently, a considerable handwritten section of the *Memoirs* was discovered in the library of Warwick Castle. The writing is that of a scribe, but there are numerous corrections in Ludlow's own hand. It was obvious that the first printed edition of the *Memoirs* had been subjected to considerable revision before they first appeared in 1698.

---

3   Edmund Ludlow, *A Voyce from the Watch Tower, Part Five: 1660–1662*, ed. A.B. Worden (London: Royal Historical Society, 1978), 126. In the quotes from this work, original spelling and punctuation have been retained.

4   C.H. Firth, ed., *The Memoirs of Edmund Ludlow, 1625–1672*, 2 vols. (Oxford: The Clarendon Press, 1894).

For further light, we are indebted to the research of Professor A.B. Worden. Professor Worden has transcribed and published a section of the Warwick Castle manuscript under the original title, *A Voyce from the Watch Tower, 1660–1662*. Whoever edited the original carefully removed most of the religious content of the work in which Ludlow continually appeals to Scriptures and seeks to see the hand of God in events. Worden explains:

> The contrast between the Ludlow of the *Memoirs* and the Ludlow of the manuscript is nowhere more vividly displayed than in the treatment by the two documents of the execution of Charles I's judges in 1660 and 1662. In the *Memoirs*, the regicides die like Romans: in the manuscript, "those poor innocent lambs of Christ" meet their deaths like early Christian martyrs.[5]

Professor Worden considered that the most likely seventeenth-century editor was the Deist John Toland (1670–1722). Toland was a bitter critic of orthodox Christianity, but a Whig pamphleteer who would have found useful material in Ludlow to support the Whig cause at the end of the century. Geoffrey Robertson has commented on the Whig-Liberal mindset:

> Whigs were liberals, entranced by the Civil War and the victory of Parliament but embarrassed by the execution of the King, which was put down to "cruel necessity" and quickly passed over—as, in consequence, was the trial of the regicides.[6]

Ludlow, on the other hand, had a Nonconformist readership in view and Worden states that among the Dissenters that "Ludlow held in admiration and affection were Vavasour Powell, Nicolas Lockyer, Ralph Venning, Thomas Brooks, William Bridge, Edward Bagshaw, Henry Jessey, Henry Wilkinson, Praisegod Barebone and Walter Thimelton."[7] This list includes some significant Puritan names.

---

5   Ludlow, *A Voyce from the Watch Tower*, 6.
6   Robertson, *The Tyrannicide Brief*, 357.
7   Ludlow, *A Voyce from the Watch Tower*, 10.

Ludlow's spirituality

We do not know when Ludlow became a believer, but it is likely that this happened while he was still a young man. Certainly before he became an Member of Parliament, he was already identified with the Puritan party. His political development is a little clearer. As tension between king and Parliament built up, his father emerged as a supporter of the Parliamentary cause. His legal training would have taught him that no citizen was above the law. By the time King Charles I surrendered to the Scots in 1646, Ludlow was convinced that the king must also be subject to the law. He seems to have been among the Members of Parliament who, at that time, hoped for a settlement between king and Parliament—a settlement in which both king and Parliament could agree on their respective roles in the life of the nation.

It was the outbreak of the short but bloody Second Civil War in 1648 that convinced Ludlow that the king must be brought to trial. It became clear that while Charles was negotiating with Parliament, he was writing to tell the Queen in France that he had no intention of reaching an agreement with Parliament, but was in fact playing for time. At this point, Ludlow's theological understanding came into play.

[T]he Lord having hardened his [the king's] heart as Pharaoh's, that he might make his power to be knowne upon him, he refuset to consent to the Propositions that were sent to him by the Scotch, the army and the Parliament; the latter having applyed themselves to him to that end severall tymes, which yet prevayled not with him, but caused him to be more high and proud; the consequence of which was sad and dangerous, for it occationed a second warr.[8]

After the second war, a powerful group of Parliamentarians backed by the army determined that the king should be brought to trial. Ludlow explained events:

[T]hose of the Parliament and army who minded the welfare of the publique interest, and had respected the blood that had bin shedd both of their freinds and enemies, looked upon it as their

---

8 Ludlow, *A Voyce from the Watch Tower*, 130.

duty to hearken unto this and other loud voyces of the Lord's providences, so as to bring the authour of so much blood the King to justice, as a tyrant, traytor, murderer, and enemy to the Comonwealth of England; wherein the Lord was pleased to strengthen the hearts and hands of all that acted therein, who thought that it best that as he sinned openly, so he should be tryed, sentenced and executed in the face of the world, and not secretly made away by poysinings and other private deaths (as in Scotland, and other partes of the world, other kings, farr less offenders, had bin treated).[9]

After the execution of Charles I, Ludlow was convinced that it was dangerous for the country to be ruled by a single person. For that reason, he later opposed the appointment of Oliver Cromwell as Lord Protector in 1653. Understandably, he was no longer in favour with Cromwell. After the fall of Richard Cromwell, Ludlow was appointed a member of the Council of State which was directing affairs in the country. He was asked to take command of the army in Ireland, where he had previously served. He accepted because the Committee of Safety "declared their intentions to be, that the nation should be governed by way of a Commonwealth, without a King, single person, or House of Lords."[10]

While he was in Ireland, the confusion in England gave an opportunity for General Monck to intervene with his army—intent to restore order. This led to the restoration of the Long Parliament, the election of the Convention and, eventually, the resolve to restore the monarchy, events regarded by Ludlow as a fatal betrayal. He returned to discover the old Parliamentarians so deeply divided that Monck was able to exploit the situation in his own interest.

It is at the time of his exile that Ludlow writes more about his religious convictions, although throughout this extract from the *Voyce* his strong Christian convictions emerge. Ludlow's escape route to safety in Switzerland took him through Roman Catholic France, where the government of Louis XIV was sympathetic to the Stuart cause and where the English authorities had agents. His experiences

---

9 Ludlow, *A Voyce from the Watch Tower*, 131.
10 Firth, ed., *The Memoirs of Edmund Ludlow*, 2:82–83.

strengthened his Protestant convictions, although on one occasion he had some difficulty in avoiding bowing to the host when facing a religious procession.

Leaving Paris without serious problems, he joined a group of French and German travellers.

[A]ll of them, as farr as I could ghess by their discourse, of the popish religion, at least not of the Reformed, and pressing me very earnestly to discover of what judgement I was, and finding that I was not of theirs were no less desirous to know whether I were a Lutheran or Calvinist; I telling them I was for both as farr as they were agreed with the word of God, and for neither any further. This gentleman, whom I took to be a Frenchman...presently cryed out, He is a Quaker, a Quaker; to whom I replyed, "I was one who desired to tremble at God's word."[11]

By this time, Ludlow was fearful that one of his fellow travellers, whom he suspected was a Jesuit, would report him to the French authorities. As they approached Lyons, he was told that the names of all travellers had to be reported to the governor. Passing into the city in a crowd, he was able to avoid detection and from Lyons to Geneva he enjoyed the company of "two of the Reformed Religion to ballance that young man whome I tooke for a Jesuite." Soon in Genevan territory, he was filled with gratitude to God "in that I had a great love and inclynation to the ayre of a Commonwealth [a republic], but for that I hoped to enjoy the society of mankind, and above all the servants, and ordinances, of Christ."[12] Reflecting later on his safe arrival in Geneva, he wrote: "the Lord hid me in the hollow of his hand. O that I might be so affected therewith as to sacrifice the remainder of my life entirely to his praise and service."[13]

Ludlow's feelings were intensified as reports of the trials and executions of his former colleagues began to filter through to Switzerland. He was in correspondence with his wife, who joined him in 1663, but other friends kept him in touch with English affairs. He

---

11 Ludlow, *A Voyce from the Watch Tower*, 194.
12 Ludlow, *A Voyce from the Watch Tower*, 195.
13 Ludlow, *A Voyce from the Watch Tower*, 195.

collected information about the trials and executions, writing detailed accounts, which indicate something of his own understanding of experimental religion.

He recorded in detail the testimony of Major General Harrison who suffered many indignities during his trial. "[B]lessed be the Lord his soule was above their reach, being carryed above the feare of death, as it is recorded of the martyrs of old, Heb. 11.34."[14] In Harrison's final speech, Ludlow recorded that he said:

> [H]e...had found the way of God to be a perfect way, his word a perfect word, and he a buckler to those that trust in him; assuring them, that though the people of God might suffer hard thinges, yet the end would be for his glory, and his people's good; and therefore encouraged them to be cheerefull in the Lord, and to hold fast that which they had, and not to be affrayd of sufferings, for God would make bitter thinges sweete, and hard thinges easy, to those that trusted in him; and that notwithstanding the clowd that was now upon them, the sun would shine, and God would give a testimony to what he had bin doing in a short tyme.[15]

It would be impossible to examine all the testimonies recorded by Ludlow. That of John Cooke merits special attention, as among the regicides he was probably the closest associate of Edmund Ludlow. Cooke was the lawyer who had drawn up the legal case against Charles. The two men had served in Ireland together and there are frequent references to Cooke throughout this fragment of the *Voyce*. Ludlow paid tribute to Cooke's firm Protestantism:

> This person, Chief Justice Cooke, in his younger dayes travayled through France and Italy; and being at Rome, spake freely *on the behalfe* of the Reformed Religion, and so farr discovered his zeale and abillityes therein that no endeavours were wanting for the drawing him to owne the popish interest. But he, as enlightned from above, was not the least shaken by their tentations. Residing for some monthes at Geneve, at the house of Mr. Deodat, he was

---

14 Ludlow, *A Voyce from the Watch Tower*, 214.
15 Ludlow, *A Voyce from the Watch Tower*, 216.

observed to live a very strict and pious life, and to be a constant
frequenter of publique ordinances. He was appointed Sollicitour
by and to the High Court of Justice for tryal of the King, without
any knowledge or seeking of his; and was taken by Leiftenant
Generall Cromwell with him into Ireland, and by him appointed
Chiefe Justice of Mounster.[16]

Ludlow's report of Cooke' speech at the scaffold gives insight into
his convictions:

The Most Glorious Sight That Ever Was Seene In The World Was
Our Lord Jesus Christ Upon The Cross; and next to that it's the
most glorious sight to see any poore creature suffer in his cause. He
blessed the Lord for the peace that he found in his soule, through
the application of the blood of Christ, for sanctification; professing
himselfe ready to beare a testimony unto God, and to Jesus Christ,
for justice, and truth, and righteousness, and holyness. He cleared
himselfe from having any mallice, against jury, Court, or King, or
any man living. But, said he, poore we have bin bought and sold
by our brethren as Joseph was. Brother hath betrayed brother to
death, and that scripture is in a great measure fulfilled, Mat. 10.2.
However (saith he), I desire to kiss the rodd. He professed that his
faith was founded on the Rock Christ, and that he expected not
salvation for anythinge that ever he did, but that he layd hold on
Christ as a naked Christ, and there bottomed his soule. He professed further, that he had through grace endeavoured to doe that
which might be to God's glory, according to the best of his understanding.... He professed himselfe to be (as to fellowshipp in the
gospell) of the congregationall way, and for liberty of conscience
to all who walke humbly and holily before the Lord.[17]

The last martyr to be mentioned in the recently published extract
from the *Voyce* was that of John James, an obscure London Baptist
pastor who had played no part in the events surrounding the execution
of Charles I. James was pastor of a poor congregation; he supported

---

16 Ludlow, *A Voyce from the Watch Tower*, 229.
17 Ludlow, *A Voyce from the Watch Tower*, 238.

himself as a weaver and would probably be completely forgotten today, but for the events leading to his death. Ludlow described him as "a precious servant of the Lord" and "this poore innocent lamb."[18] James was arrested while preaching at a meeting in Whitechapel, London, in October 1661. He was charged with treason because he had said that "Jesus Christ, the Son of God was King of England, Scotland and Ireland and all the kingdoms of this world." His wife secured an interview with Charles II to plead that these words were not treasonable. Charles contemptuously "threw the petition over his shoulder, saying, 'He is a rogue and shall be hanged.'"[19] The sentence of hanging, drawing and quartering took place at Tyburn in November 1661. Unlike the regicides, John James was given a decent burial and his grave can still be seen in Bunhill Fields, London. Ludlow described him as "a preaching and a praying Saint."[20] His references to John Cooke's churchmanship and the esteem he obviously had for John James are some indication of his own ecclesiology.

Unfortunately, the extract so far published does not include further elaboration of Ludlow's convictions, but Professor Worden has supplied more information in his introduction. Although Geneva offered religious freedom, Ludlow was disappointed with state of religion in the city.

> [T]hough I dare not as guiltless cast a stone against this citty, yet... neither in doctrine or discipline, principle or practice, they have made such progress since the tyme of the first Reformation as might have been hoped for...but...have rather gone backward, and brought forth sower grapes.[21]

He elaborates, explaining that he could not take part in the communion of the Swiss churches:

> [A] freedome to communicate with any in that holy ordinance of the Lord's Supper, of whom we had not a particcular satisfac-

---

18 Ludlow, A Voyce from the Watch Tower, 315.

19 Ludlow, A Voyce from the Watch Tower, 316.

20 Ludlow, A Voyce from the Watch Tower, 316. A fuller account of the trial and execution of John James can be found in Thomas Crosby, The History of the English Baptists, vol. 2 (London, 1739), 165–172.

21 Ludlow, A Voyce from the Watch Tower, 7–8.

tion of a worke of grace in their hearts, and that their conversation was suitable thereto, a vissible church consisting of living stones, to wit of beleevers.... By communicating with such in this ordinance who in our judgement eate or drinke unworthily, we should contribute to their sin and consequently to their punishment, such eating and drinking their own damnation.[22]

Worden associates these sentiments with the influence of Jean de Labadie who was ministering in Geneva at this time. De Labadie was a former Roman Catholic priest who spent a few years in Switzerland before moving to the United Provinces. He caused disturbance in the Reformed churches by setting up home Bible study groups and prayer meetings and pressing for clear evidence of regeneration in the hearts of would-be communicants. Ludlow certainly refers to Labadie as "our true and sincere freind,"[23] but as far as is known, Labadie was a paedobaptist. Both in Geneva and in the United Provinces de Labadie was recognized as a minister of the Reformed Church, whereas Ludlow writes that "nothing bee more express in Scripture then that none but believers were subjects of water baptisme."[24] Ludlow's views coincide with those expounded in the *First London Baptist Confession* (1646):

Jesus Christ has here on earth a spiritual kingdom, which is his Church, which he has purchased to himself as a peculiar inheritance; which Church is a company of visible saints, called and separated from the world by the word and Spirit of God, to the visible profession of faith of the gospel, being baptized into that faith, and joined to the Lord, and each other by mutual agreement in the practical enjoyment of the ordinances commanded by Christ their head and king.[25]

Throughout these troubled times, Edmund Ludlow continued to trust God. He demonstrated a confidence that God had worked

---

22 Ludlow, *A Voyce from the Watch Tower*, 8.
23 Ludlow, *A Voyce from the Watch Tower*, 304.
24 Ludlow, *A Voyce from the Watch Tower*, 8.
25 James M. Renihan, ed., *True Confessions: Baptist Documents in the Reformed Family* (Owensboro: Reformed Baptist Academic Press, 2004), 34–35.

mightily to bring great privileges to the people of England, but these had been abused, especially by fruitless divisions and strivings for power, even among the godly.

> The Lord hath appeared in our dayes to doe great thinges, such as our fathers had not seene, nor eares scarse heard of. He raysed up the poore, foolish, unexperienced and weake ones of the earth, to confound the rich, the wise, and the mighty thereof, speaking clearly, as well by his providence as by his word, that his designe is to advance himselfe, and the riches of his grace in his sonne, and to give him the necks of all his enemyes who would not that he should reigne over them. And as in all ages he hath bin making way for this glorious reigne of his, so did the wheele hasten to that end in our dayes. But the Tobias and Sanballats, having an enmity thereunto, did what they could to obstruct the same.... Yet was the Lord so mercyfull to us that he made those mountaines plaine before him, and put a prize into our hands, which had we wise-dome we might have made a wounderfull improvement of.[26]

The "prize," which should have been wonderfully improved, was *religious freedom* on a scale never before enjoyed. This had been secured by the victory of the Parliamentary armies and was enjoyed for a few years. Ludlow believed in freedom of conscience and rejected the notion that any Puritan group should try to enforce religious uniformity. His sentiments echoed those of his contemporary, John Milton, Latin Secretary to the Commonwealth, who addressed the Long Parliament:

> Because you have thrown off your Prelate lord,
> And with stiff vows renounc'd his liturgy,
> To seize the widowed whore Plurality
> From them whose sin ye envied, not abhorr'd,
> Dare ye for this adjure the civil sword
> To force our consciences that Christ set free,
> And ride us with a classic hierarchy.
>
> ...

---

26 Ludlow, *A Voyce from the Watch Tower,* 307.

When they shall read this clearly in your charge,
New *Presbyter* is but Old *Priest* writ large.[27]

Sadly, freedom of conscience was not widely appreciated during the Commonwealth. Maybe men like Ludlow were themselves partly to blame. It was Cromwell who strove to maintain freedom of conscience, but for political reasons Ludlow and his associates could never give him the support that the wider interests of the gospel needed. Independents suspected Independents and both suspected Presbyterians, who tried so hard but unsuccessfully to negotiate a deal with the Laudians at the Restoration. Failures and divisions meant that the settlement made between 1660 and 1662 was very painful for the Puritans:

[H]aving through the assistance of the Lord subdued all those enemyes who publiquely opposed the liberty due to us as men and Christians, our enemyes began to be those of our owne howse; amongst whom the lust of power and domination prevayling, much art was used by them for the drawing in of many zealous, well-meaning and pious Christians (who earnestly desired to see those good thinges which the Lord had promised, and their soules thirsted after, accomplished) to joyne in destroying the civill authority of the nation.[28]

Ludlow saw the sufferings brought by the Restoration as the judgement of God upon a divided people of God, writing: "I became more and more convinced of the hand of the Lord in this confusion of languages amongst us, seeing that those whose interest it was to unite had still such principles of division raigning in them."[29]

In spite of the disappointments of these years Ludlow did not abandon hope, but seems increasingly to have looked to spiritual weapons to win victories in the cause of Christ. Writing of his situation in Switzerland, he wrote:

27 John Milton, "On the New Forcers of Conscience under the Long Parliament," in *Selected Poems*, ed. John Leonard (London: Penguin Books, 2007), 67.

28 Ludlow, *A Voyce from the Watch Tower*, 307.

29 Ludlow, *A Voyce from the Watch Tower*, 89.

As well therefore from the consideration of prudence, as of duty and conscience (which tells us that we ought to obey the higher powers, and content ourselves with our share in government relating to the outward man, submitting to, or at least not opposing, those in whom the Lord by his providence declares the power to be, who though it may be are not so righteous and just as were to be wisshed, yet by praying *for them* we may lead *quiet and peaceable lives, in all godlynesse and honesty,* and blessing the Lord for the libertyes and priviledges they permit us to enjoy, and by *accompanying the* preaching *the word* with an holy and righteous conversation), let us endeavour to wynne them to be of the same perswation in spirituall thinges with ourselves. In the meanetyme let us not impose our beleefe on them, as we desire not to be imposed on by them, it being no less reasonable that the majestrate should enjoy the liberty of his conscience as we that of ours. Now therefore, seeing such a righteous government is aggreable to the word of God and the rule of right reason, the true interest of men and Christians (who understand not of what spirit they are, if they would lord it over their brethren, and have fire from men to consume those who differ from them), let us learne to doe to others, as we would they should doe to us, with plaine trueth.[30]

Conclusion

Edmund Ludlow's political convictions commanded the support of only a small minority of his fellow citizens and it would be easy to dismiss him as one of the failures of history. The Commonwealth he idealized was never a practical possibility. His doctrine of the church, although during his lifetime was that of a persecuted minority, was to be widely accepted in the centuries after his death. Against so many of his corrupt contemporaries, he stands out as a man of integrity. That integrity was sustained by his Christian convictions. He feared God and desired to be guided by his infallible Word. Ludlow was a keen observer of providence, but the Scripture was his ultimate guide and surely he deserves that Scriptural commendation, "he was a faithful man and feared God more than many" (Nehemiah 7:2).

---

30 Ludlow, *A Voyce from the Watch Tower*, 309.

18

Benjamin Keach: cultivating corporate spirituality and church covenants

By Austin R. Walker

BENJAMIN KEACH (1640–1704) prefaced the church covenant which he published in 1697 with the following paragraph:

> We who desire to walk together in the Fear of the Lord, do, through the Assistance of the Holy Spirit, profess our deep and serious Humiliation for all our Transgressions. And we do also solemnly, in the Presence of God, of each other, in the Sense of our own Unworthiness, give up ourselves to the Lord, in a Church State according to the Apostolic Constitution that he may be our God, and we may be his People, through the Everlasting Covenant of his Free grace, in which alone we hope to be accepted by him, through his blessed Son Jesus Christ, whom we take to be our High Priest, to justify and sanctify us, and our Prophet to teach us; and to subject to him as our Law-Giver, and the King of Saints; and to conform to all his Holy Laws and Ordinances, for our growth, Establishment, and Consolation; that we may be as a Holy Spouse unto him, and serve him in our Generation, and wait for his second Appearance, as our glorious Bridegroom.[1]

---

1 Benjamin Keach, *The Glory of a True Church, And its Discipline Display'd* (London, 1697), 71–74, (hereafter *The Glory of a True Church*). An identical statement is found

When Keach published *The Glory of a True Church, And its Discipline Display'd* in 1697, he concluded it by incorporating his church covenant into its pages. He wrote it for the "Baptized Churches, particularly to that under my care."[2] It was the direct result of earnest requests from his church members and from one other pastor (perhaps his son Elias Keach).[3]

By the 1690s, Benjamin Keach was a prominent, if not the most prominent, leader among London Particular Baptists. He had been pastor of his Southwark congregation in London for almost thirty years. He had come from his native Buckinghamshire to London in 1668 and soon after identified himself with the London Particular Baptists churches and their distinctive Calvinistic theology, abandoning his previously held General Baptist persuasions. The publication of *The Glory of a True Church* was the result of his more mature reflections and convictions about the ordered life and discipline of a local church of Christ.

Following his introductory statement, eight solemn promises were then stated, each promise clearly reflecting that corporate spirituality lay at the heart of Keach's understanding of the life of the gathered church. The promises were introduced in the following way:

> Being fully satisfied in the way of Church-communion, and the Truth of Grace in some good measure upon one another's spirits, we do solemnly join ourselves together in A Holy Union and Fellowship, humbly submitting to the Discipline of the Gospel, and all Holy Duties, required of a People in such a spiritual relation.

---

in Elias Keach, *The Glory and Ornament of a true Gospel-constituted Church* (London, 1697), 71–72. Father and son clearly collaborated in the production of these books and the church covenant which concludes each volume. The original is the work of the father as Elias Keach acknowledged in his *Epistle*. Benjamin Keach's title for the church covenant includes the date, *The Solemn Covenant of the Church Meeting in White-Street, at its Constitution: June 5, 1696*. This church was not Keach's congregation but was located in Southwark and established under the influence of Keach. See Walter Wilson, *The History and Antiquities of Dissenting Churches and Meeting Houses in London, Westminster and Southwark; including the Lives of their Ministers, from the Rise of Non-Conformity to the present Time*, 4 vols. (London, 1808), 4:329.

2   Keach, *The Glory of a True Church*, Epistle, [iii].

3   Similarly, Elias Keach's book produced for the church meeting at Tallow-Chandlers Hall, Dowgate Hill, London, where he had functioned as pastor.

The eight promises are as follows:

1. We do promise and engage to walk in all Holiness, Godliness, Humility, and Brotherly Love, as much as in us lieth to render our Communion delightful to God, comfortable to ourselves, and lovely to the rest of the Lord's people.

2. We do promise to watch over each others Conversations, and not to suffer sin upon one another, so far as God shall discover it to us, or any of us; and to stir up one another to Love and good Works; to warn, rebuke, and admonish one another with meekness, according to the Rules left to us of Christ in that behalf.

3. We do promise in an especial manner to pray for one another, and for the Glory and Increase of this church, and for the presence of God in it, and the pouring forth of his Spirit on it, and his Protection over it to his Glory.

4. We do promise to bear one another's burdens, to cleave to one another, and to have a fellow-feeling with one another, in all conditions both outward and inward, as God in his Providence shall cast any of us into.

5. We do promise to bear with one anothers weaknesses, failings and infirmities, with much tenderness, not discovering to any without the Church, not any within, unless according to Christ's rule, and order of the Gospel provided in that case.

6. We do promise to strive together for the truths of the Gospel, and purity of God's ways and ordinances, to avoid causes, and causers of division, endeavouring to keep the unity of the Spirit in the bond of peace.

7. We do promise to meet together on Lord's Days, and at other times, as the Lord shall give us opportunities, to serve and glorify God in the way of his worship, to edify one another, and to contrive the good of his Church.

8. We do promise according to our ability (or as God shall bless us with the good things of this world) to communicate to our Pastor or Minister, God having ordained that they that preach the Gospel should live of the Gospel. (And how can anything lay a greater obligation upon the conscience than this covenant, what then is the sin of such who violate it?)

Keach then concludes that

> these and all other Gospel duties we humbly submit unto, prom-
> ising and purposing to perform, nor in our own strength, being
> conscious of our own weakness, but in the power and strength
> of the blessed God, whose we are, and whom we desire to serve.
> To whom be glory now and evermore. Amen.[4]

Keach's concern for corporate spirituality

Keach's covenant was replete with the use of "each other" and "one
another" and occasionally "together." The godliness reflected in the
promises each church member undertook to fulfil was a godliness that
was to be expressed not only in the life of one individual Christian but
in the life of the people of God as they interacted with one another in
the local church to which they belonged.

Like the godliness of each individual, corporate godliness is the
result of the work of the Holy Spirit. As such, it reflects the unity of
the church and the love that each member has one for another. Furthermore, it reflects that togetherness, that being of one mind, heart
and purpose, as expressed by Luke in his use of the adverb ὁμοθυμαδόν
(first used in Acts 1:15). Any concept of corporate spirituality must
also embrace those passages in the New Testament epistles which
speak of our responsibilities as Christians to each other. The nearly
fifty biblical references used by Keach to validate the content of the
church covenant contain a number of those passages (though for the
sake of space they have been omitted here).

Whatever conclusions anyone draws about the warrant for or usefulness of such a church covenant, there can be little doubt that Keach
and his church were aspiring to put into practice what they were
persuaded were the teachings of the New Testament Scriptures. Godliness must be expressed in the life of the local church. Without a regular and orderly discipline, reflected in the church covenant, Keach
believed that a church "will soon lose its beauty, and be polluted."[5] The
church was to be a godly community, bound together by a common
understanding of their corporate biblical responsibilities. It is those

---

4   Keach, *The Glory of a True Church*, 74.
5   Keach, *The Glory of a True Church*, Epistle, [iii].

responsibilities which came to expression in the church covenant published by Keach in 1697. Our purpose is to examine this church covenant as a genuine expression of corporate spirituality.

Martin Bucer's attempts to cultivate corporate spirituality

Keach stood in a long line of sixteenth- and seventeenth-century church leaders who were concerned for the corporate spirituality of the church of Christ. Such concerns were expressed in the early days of the European Reformation. The magisterial reformers retained the assumptions of the medieval church, holding "that the Church must be a comprehensive society, embracing and supervising both the elect and the reprobate."[6] The practice of infant baptism was upheld despite the objections of the Anabaptists to both infant baptism and the idea of a state or territorial church. By retaining those assumptions and the practice of infant baptism, tensions in the church were inevitably created, especially in the area of church discipline, not least because of the intervention (some would say, unwarranted meddling) of the magistrate or other civil authorities in the affairs of the church. However, the possibility of "an 'inner ring' of devout believers who exceeded the average Christian in evangelical enthusiasm and activity" was actively considered by a number of the leaders of the reformation.[7]

Among the magisterial reformers, perhaps no one felt the tensions of working within a comprehensive church system more than Martin Bucer (1491–1551). For over twenty-five years, Bucer—based in Strasbourg—was an undisputed leader of the Protestant Reformation. He longed to see a congregation of truly believing, practicing Christians. The longer he stayed in the city, the more disturbed he became because of the conduct of many of the citizens of Strasbourg, in particular their lack of personal commitment to Christ and their failure to walk with God. In 1538, Bucer published a book whose title has been translated as *Concerning the True Care of Souls and Genuine Pastoral Ministry.*[8] It

---

6   Euan Cameron, "The 'Godly Community' in the Theory and Practice of the European Reformation," in W.J. Sheils and Diana Wood, ed., *Voluntary Religion*, Studies in Church History 23 (Oxford: Basil Blackwell, 1986), 132.

7   Cameron, *Voluntary Religion*, 132.

8   Martin Bucer, *Concerning the True Care of Souls and Genuine Pastoral Ministry,*

was, in effect, a Reformation handbook of pastoral theology, intended to be a blueprint for the way the church of Jesus Christ is to be ruled by him. Bucer and his colleagues regarded church discipline as nothing less than the exercise of Christian love over and among the members and believed it was of supreme importance.

Throughout his ministry in Strasbourg, Bucer faced opposition. Those who stood in the way included the civil authorities, who were opposed to a full ban (excommunication); the Anabaptists, who criticized the church because they said it was effectively a church of sinners; and the citizens, who had long memories of the perverted "papist ban."[9] It appears that by the mid-1540s Bucer became disillusioned by the lack of progress. Had he now become disenchanted because of the failure of the "state church" system to produce real Christians, or was he wearied by the resistance against his plans? Perhaps both factors were responsible.

Bucer's goal was simple: he wanted to see a community of *real* Christians—people who trusted Christ and displayed a sincere obedience to Christ. To accomplish this he organized *Christlichen Gemeinschaften* (Christian associations) within the state church.[10] Those who joined them submitted themselves to precisely the kind of life and discipline that Bucer wanted to apply to all, and took a voluntary vow to live an exemplary Christian life before others. In effect, he was seeking to cultivate genuine corporate spirituality among the members of the church; he was striving after unity, holiness and faithful-

---

trans. Peter Beale (Carlisle: The Banner of Truth Trust, 2009). This is probably the first time Bucer's work has been translated from German into English.

9   Lorna Jane Abray, *The People's Reformation: Magistrates, Clergy, and Commons in Strasbourg, 1500–1598* (Oxford: Basil Blackwell, 1985), 196–197. Abray points out that the ban, or excommunication, had been misused for temporal ends, e.g. for compelling debtors to make repayment. The citizens of Strasbourg feared that a pastor with power to excommunicate was a threat to lay supremacy and would create a situation little different from the tyranny of papal power.

10 For the details of the *Christlichen Gemeinschaften,* I have drawn extensively on David Lawrence, *Martin Bucer: Unsung Hero of the Reformation* (Nashville: Westview Publishing Co., 2008), 141–145. He refers us to Amy Nelson Burnett, *The Yoke of Christ: Martin Bucer and Christian Discipline* (Kirksville: Sixteenth Century Journal Publishers, 1999); and D.F. Wright, *Martin Bucer: Reforming Church and Community* (Cambridge: Cambridge University Press, 2002). I have also consulted Abray, *The People's Reformation,* 186–208.

ness among them. Pastors set the example, followed by other leaders who made their commitment, confessed their theology and pledged their households. Their names were then entered in a register. Potential members and families were interviewed concerning their doctrine, the sacraments, their conduct and their repentance. If a member proved ready to make a further commitment then the pastor would extend the right hand of fellowship and the applicant's name would be entered in the register as a member of the *Christliche Gemeinschaft*.

Some have interpreted these steps as a forerunner to the twentieth-century practice of small groups within a large church. But might it not also be seen as an indication of the failure to produce a godly community within a territorial church because such are built on a shaky foundation, namely, the comprehensive model of church and state established on the practice of infant baptism? Not surprisingly, Bucer was accused of forming separatist church groups. This was one reason why, in 1549, he left Strasbourg, taking up an invitation from Thomas Cranmer to become a professor at Cambridge University.

Anabaptists

A similar desire for corporate spirituality characterized the Anabaptists, who—unlike the magisterial reformers—rejected outright both infant baptism and the notion of a territorial church. The Schleitheim Confession was produced by Swiss Anabaptists in 1527. They maintained that infant baptism was "the highest and chief abomination of the pope." It was their conviction that the church should be comprised of believers "who have learned repentance and amendment of life."[11] Champlin Burrage provides clear evidence that these churches also used church covenants and described those associated with early sixteenth-century Anabaptists: Michael Sattler, Hans Hut, Balthasar Hubmaier and Melchior Hoffmann, among others.[12]

Anabaptists suffered intensely for their convictions. In the seventeenth century, the first generation of Particular Baptists, together

---

11 Article I, *The Schleitheim Confession*, Adopted by a Swiss Brethren Conference, February 24, 1527. See William L. Lumpkin, *Baptist Confessions of Faith* (Valley Forge: Judson Press, 1969), 25.

12 Champlin Burrage, *The Church Covenant Idea: Its Origin and Development* (Philadelphia: American Baptist Publication Society, 1904), 15–22.

with those—like Keach—who followed them, wanted to distance themselves from Anabaptists and did so with understandable reasons. Nevertheless, they were seeking to return to what they all regarded as apostolic practice and doctrine regarding the identification of those who constituted the true church of Christ. Whatever other differences existed—and there were many—they were of one mind in rejecting the model of a territorial church with its inbuilt practice of infant baptism.

The direction taken by the Anabaptists was significant because it led to a radical change in the theology of church membership, not only for them but for others who separated from the territorial church system after them. It was in this new environment of a gathered church of believers (among paedobaptists it included their children) that the idea of church covenants arose as they set out the marks of their distinctive corporate identity.

Church covenants and the English and Welsh Separatists

The Reformation in England took on a distinctive character after the turmoil of Henry VIII's reign and the brief reigns of Edward VI and Mary I. An established or national Church of England was created with the Thirty-Nine Articles as the doctrinal basis, early in the reign of Elizabeth I. The tensions mentioned before still existed and were addressed both by Puritans within the national church and by Separatists whose consciences no longer allowed them to remain within the un-Reformed national church. Both parties were concerned for the godliness of the church. Nothing was resolved satisfactorily during the long reign of Elizabeth and those same tensions continued to be evident in the seventeenth century. Separatists began to express their convictions clearly during the early years of Elizabeth (although there had been a congregation with similar convictions meeting in London in the days of Mary).[13] There is evidence that suggests that a congregation, whose members made a definite covenant with each other, existed as early as 1568.[14]

---

13 See B.R. White, *The English Separatist Tradition: from the Marian Martyrs to the Pilgrim Fathers* (London: Oxford University Press, 1971), 20–43.

14 Albert Peel, *The First Congregational Churches: New Light on Separatist Congregations*

According to Michael Mullett, such early church covenants were regarded as

> a solemn, recorded, renewable foundation document of a gathered community of worship, a binding indenture pledging its subscribers' exclusive allegiance to the church and to acceptance of its discipline; ultimately, a covenant was also a written agreement between the members and God, committing them to "walk in his ways," to "walk in the Faith and Order of the Gospel," in return for his blessings.[15]

Among those who formed separatist churches with a form of church covenant were Robert Browne (c. 1550–1633) in Norwich around 1580 or 1581, John Greenwood (d. 1593) and Henry Barrowe (c. 1550–1593) in London in the 1580s and Francis Johnson (1568–1618) in the English congregation at Middelburg in 1591. The church covenant of the latter congregation is fairly typical:

> ...wee doe willingly ioyne together to live as the Churche of Christe, watching over one another, and submittinge ourselves vnto them, to whom the Lorde Jesus commiteth the oversight of his Churche, guiding and censuring vs according to the rule of the worde of God.[16]

In either 1606 or 1607, a congregation of English Separatists in Gainsborough made a covenant together. John Smyth (c. 1570–c. 1612) was the architect of this covenant though he had been closely associated with Francis Johnson. Smyth's group was not yet a Baptist church but within a year they were in exile in Amsterdam, and within two years they had adopted believer's baptism and had identified themselves with Dutch Anabaptists. In 1611, some members of that group

---

in London 1567–81 (London: Cambridge University Press, 1920), 23. Further details of these churches together with actual documents can be found in Champlin Burrage, *The Early English Dissenters in the light of recent research (1550–1641)*, 2 vols. (Cambridge: Cambridge University Press, 1912).

15 Michael Mullett, *Sources for the History of English Nonconformity, 1660–1830* (British Records Association, 1991), 46.

16 Burrage, *The Church Covenant Idea*, 50. Original spelling retained.

returned to England and, under Thomas Helwys (c. 1575–c. 1616), became the first General Baptist church in England. A third part of the original covenanting group had worshipped in Scrooby but they also went to Holland—to Leiden—but did not become Baptists. With John Robinson (1576–1625) as their pastor, many of them sailed for America on the *Mayflower* and became one of the roots of New England Congregationalism. They also adopted a church covenant.

Helwys did not agree with Smyth about formal church covenants; rather, he was persuaded that believer's baptism was the key. For him, the right form of a church resulted from baptism and not from a covenant. Smyth had written, "the true form of a true visible church is partly inward, partly outward." He described the outward part as "a vowe, promise, oath or covenant betwixt God and the faithful." This covenant itself had two parts, respecting firstly, God and the faithful and secondly, the faithful to one another. He concluded that the latter "conteyneth all the duties of love whatsoever. Levit 19:17, Mat 18:15,16, 1 Thes 5:14, Mat 22:39, 2 Thes 3:14,15, Heb 3:13, 10:24–25."[17]

In Southwark, London, the Independent (or Congregational) church, which became known as the Jacob-Lathrop-Jessey Church (named after its first three pastors), also adopted a church covenant. It was out of this congregation that the Particular Baptists were to emerge in the late 1630s. In 1616, Henry Jacob (1563–1624) returned to England from Holland. Realizing that there was no prospect of a national reformation in the Church of England, he laid the foundation for this important London church. Having openly confessed their faith in the Lord Jesus Christ, "…standing together they joined hands and solemnly covenanted with each other in the presence of Almighty God, to walk together in all God's ways and ordinances, according as he had already revealed, or should further make known to them."[18] Lathrop renewed the covenant when he became pastor in 1630.[19]

---

17 John Smyth, "Principles and Inferences Concerning the Visible Church," in *The Works of John Smyth, Fellow of Christ's College, 1594–8*, 2 vols. (Cambridge University Press, 1915), 1:253–254.

18 Congregational Library, CUEW/CCEW Archives, IX.3.588 'Notes towards a study of Covenants' (compiled by William Gordon Robinson). Permission to cite them is given by the Library Committee of the Congregational Memorial Hall Trust. Robinson's invaluable notes provide nearly sixty Congregational church covenants from the sixteenth and seventeenth centuries.

19 Burrage, *The Early English Dissenters*, 1:301–302.

In Wales the first gathered church was established in 1639. It was founded with the help of Henry Jessey (1603–1663) and was formed on the basis of a church covenant. Other churches followed suit. Baptists first in Gwent in 1652 and then in Carmarthenshire in 1668, made use of church covenants.[20]

For Smyth and the early Independents, a key element in their understanding of a church covenant was the formulation of the kind of conduct that was required of church members. This clearly indicates their concern for both the corporate identity and the spirituality of the gathered church.

Church covenants and the English Baptists

The use of a church covenant, adopted by Smyth while he was in England, did not become the uniform practice among churches which separated from the Church of England. However, no one should conclude that, by not adopting a church covenant, churches and ministers were therefore less concerned for the corporate spirituality of their members.

Covenants were employed by some General and Particular Baptist churches as well as Independent churches. Charles W. Deweese has written extensively on church covenants that some Baptists accepted.[21] He provides evidence of their use among both Baptist groupings and also points out that these covenants had an influence on successive generations of Baptists both in England and America. His suggestion that "English Separatist, Independent, and Congregationalist influence upon the emergence of the Baptist church covenant idea was probably wider than that of the Anabaptists" is the correct one.[22]

According to Deweese these church covenants were "intended to produce a voluntary commitment to particular ways of practicing one's faith."[23] He concludes that Particular Baptists used church covenants more widely than General Baptists and suggests that both the major confessions of faith reflect "an implicit covenantal concern."[24]

---

20 Gwyn Davies, *Covenanting with God: the story of personal & church covenants & their lessons for today* (Bridgend: Evangelical Library of Wales, 1994), 41–43.

21 Charles W. Deweese, *Baptist Church Covenants* (Nashville: Broadman Press, 1990).

22 Deweese, *Baptist Church Covenants*, 28.

23 Deweese, *Baptist Church Covenants*, 24.

24 Deweese, *Baptist Church Covenants*, 27.

Thus, the 1644 *London Confession* speaks of those who were "baptized into that faith, and joined to the Lord, and each other, by mutual agreement, in the practical enjoyment of the Ordinances, commanded by Christ their head and king."[25] The 1689 *Second London Baptist Confession of Faith* speaks of those who "do willingly consent to walk together according to the appointment of Christ, giving up themselves to the Lord & to one another by the will of God, in professed subjection to the Ordinances of the Gospel."[26]

This clearly suggests that church covenants were in use before Keach produced a church covenant at the request of his members. Deweese provides specific examples from different Baptist churches— the Broadmead Church in Bristol (1640), Leominster (1656), Amersham (1675), Hitchin (1681), Pinners Hall Seventh Day Baptist Church, London (1686), Great Ellingham Baptist Church, Norfolk (1699)—as well as those covenants produced by Benjamin and Elias Keach in 1697 for their London congregations.[27]

None of these church covenants appear to have provided a model for Keach. He was writing *The Glory of a True Church* as a Baptist and, as far as he was aware, no one among the Baptists had written before on the subject. However, he freely acknowledged in his own day that "reverend divines of the Congregational way have written most excellently...on church discipline."[28] It may well be that Keach drew his inspiration for his work on the nature of the true church, and for the

---

25 William L. Lumpkin, *Baptist Confessions of Faith* (Valley Forge: Judson Press, 1969), 165.

26 Lumpkin, *Baptist Confessions of Faith*, 286.

27 Some of these church covenants are also included in Timothy and Denise George, ed., *Baptist Confessions, Covenants, and Catechisms* (Nashville: Broadman and Holman, 1996), 173–183. They include the covenants of Benjamin and Elias Keach.

28 Keach, *The Glory of a True Church*, Epistle, [iii]. He was probably thinking of Independents such as John Owen and Isaac Chauncy. See John Owen, *The Nature of a Gospel Church*, vol. 16 of *The Works of John Owen* (London: The Banner of Truth Trust, 1968), 1–208. See also Isaac Chauncy, *Ecclesia Enucleata: The Temple Opened: Or a clear Demonstration of the True Gospel Church in its Nature and Constitution, According to the Doctrine and Practice of Christ and the Apostles* (London, 1684). In the same year as Keach published his book, Chauncy also published another book, *The Divine Institution of Congregational Churches, Ministry and Ordination [As has bin Professed by those of that Persuasion] Asserted and Proved from the Word of God* (London, 1697). Keach refers his readers to Chauncy in various notes throughout *The Glory of a True Church*.

church covenant he published, from English Independents. John Owen (1616–1683) speaks of "the special consent and agreement of all the members of it to walk together in the observation of the same ordinances numerically," and describes that agreement as a "covenant" in the following paragraph.[29] There is no doubt from reading both Owen and Isaac Chauncy (1632–1712) that they were both concerned for the corporate godliness of the congregations to which they ministered. Keach shared their concerns but he provides us with no clues as to the precise sources for his church covenant.

Keach's church covenant

Keach's use of a church covenant was therefore not a new idea. In effect, it crystallized much of what he had written in *The Glory of a True Church*. The church covenant is brief, certainly briefer than that compiled by a near neighbour of Keach's in Southwark. In 1699 an Independent pastor, Joseph Jacob (1667–1722), published *The Covenant and Catechism of the Church of Christ meeting at Horsly-Down in South-wark*.[30] It provides a very thorough and detailed covenant agreement which was signed by the elders, the deacons and the members of the church. Keach's church covenant was much briefer and more focussed on specific corporate responsibilities of the members.

Keach did not use the word "voluntary" in his church covenant. Earlier, we drew attention to the fact that Deweese believed church covenants were "intended to produce a voluntary commitment to particular ways of practicing one's faith." Would Keach have been happy with that definition? Obviously, in one sense, it was voluntary— it was something the members of the church desired and something with which they were in complete agreement. Yet, on the other hand, Keach's Calvinistic theology recognized the everlasting covenant of

---

29 John Owen, *A Brief Instruction in the Worship of God and Discipline of the Churches of the New Testament*, vol. 15 of *The Works of John Owen* (London: The Banner of Truth Trust, 1968), 528.

30 Joseph Jacob, *The Covenant and Catechism of the Church of Christ meeting at Horsly-Down in Southwark* (London, 1700). The title page provides no author and both Wing and W.T. Whitley ascribe authorship to Keach. However, the contents soon reveal this cannot be the case. The copy in Dr. Williams's Library in London has a note to the effect that Joseph Jacob is the author. He was pastor of this Independent church in Southwark from 1698 until 1702.

free grace and the church's desire was to "be as a Holy Spouse unto him [Christ], and serve him in our Generation, and wait for his second Appearance, as our glorious Bridegroom."[31] The term "voluntary" is misleading because it does not convey the idea of a gracious constraint which naturally flows from God's initiative in salvation. It is possible to see the church covenant as the only true response to that divine initiative and Keach might well have asked whether any church had any other option if they properly understood the purpose of God in sending Jesus Christ. Christ was their king and they desired to "conform to all his Holy Laws and Ordinances, for our growth, Establishment, and Consolation."[32]

Several features relating to the content of Keach's church covenant are worthy of comment.

THE FOUNDATION—NAMELY, THAT OF BEING "IN A CHURCH STATE ACCORDING TO THE INSTITUTION OF CHRIST IN THE GOSPEL"[33]

Being a convinced Particular Baptist meant at least three things for Keach. First, the church was built with living stones, converted persons, who then became part of a congregation of godly Christians. Second, these were persons who had become Christians and who had been baptized by immersion upon profession of their faith. Third, it was those, and only those, who belonged to the church of Christ who covenanted together to walk together with God. In the opening section of *The Glory of a True Church*, he explains how members are to be admitted into a true and orderly Gospel-Church:

> before the church they must solemnly enter into a covenant, to walk in the fellowship of that particular congregation, and to submit themselves to the care and discipline thereof, and to walk faithfully with God in all his holy ordinances, and there to be fed and have communion, and worship God there, when the church meets (if possible) and give themselves up to the watch and charge of the pastor and the ministry thereof: the pastor then also signifying in the name of the church their acceptance

---

31 Keach, *The Glory of a True Church*, 71–72.
32 Keach, *The Glory of a True Church*, 71.
33 Keach, *The Glory of a True Church*, 5.

Benjamin Keach
1640–1704

of each person, and endeavour to take care of them; and to watch over them in the Lord, (the members being first satisfied to receive them, and to have communion with them). And so the pastor is to give them the right hand of fellowship of the church, or church organical.[34]

Thus, there is a firm rejection not only of infant baptism but also of any notion that the church of Christ is a national or state church, modelled on the typical Old Testament church of the Jews which included their physical seed. He cut through the tensions that Bucer felt so acutely 150 years before. The idea of a national church was still cherished by the Church of England, even after the Act of Toleration in 1689. In the 1680s and 1690s, Richard Baxter, reckoned among the Dissenters, was still arguing for a national church. On the one hand, he rejected popery because it profaned the sacred offices of kings and magistrates and, on the other hand, he rejected the Nonconformists because of the separation and division which they caused.[35] The accusation against the Nonconformists was firmly resisted by Keach and repeatedly received extended treatment in his sermons and writings. For example, in expounding Matthew 15:13, "Every plant which My heavenly Father has not planted will be uprooted," he states his conviction forcefully:

the carnal seed of believers, as such, I mean little babes, according to the constitution of the gospel church ought not to be admitted as members thereof; though some of the children of believers are in the election of grace, and of such belongs the kingdom of heaven; yet it is not known which of the children of believers are elected to salvation; besides baptism and the Lord's Supper are ordinances of mere positive right, and none but such who do believe, and make a profession of their faith, being regenerate persons, ought to be received or admitted to either of these ordinances, or be members of the church of Christ. Faith and repentance being required of all that ought to be baptized and

---

34 Keach, *The Glory of a True Church*, 7.

35 Richard Baxter, *Of National Churches: Their Description, Institution, Use, Preservation, Danger, Maladies and Cure: Partly applied to England* (London, 1691), 4–5.

planted in gospel congregations, by virtue of Christ's great commission, and the practice of apostolical churches.[36]

Baptists like Keach were persuaded that infant baptism was a serious error that hindered the thorough reformation of the church of Christ. Keach reserved some of his severest criticisms for infant baptism as practiced in the national church (in his case, the Church of England). He affirmed that

> I look upon Infant-Baptism to be one of the chief Pillars of the Romish Church, and of all National Churches and Constitutions in the European World.... Thus the inhabitants of the Earth are cheated, and deluded with a Shadow and empty Name that signifies nothing; and certain I am, until Christendom (as it is called) is Unchristianed of this pretended Rite, or Christendom, there will never be a thorough Reformation.... 'Tis Infant-Baptism that tends to uphold all National Churches, and deceives poor People who think they were hereby made Christians.[37]

IT TOOK CHURCH MEMBERSHIP SERIOUSLY

Remember that Bucer had organized *Christlichen Gemeinschaften* within the territorial church. Those who joined them submitted themselves to a particular pattern of life and discipline and took a vow to live an exemplary Christian life before others. Keach's church covenant was based on the same principle. They gave themselves to the Lord and to one another "by mutual agreement and consent."[38] Furthermore, each agreement undertaken was expressed in the form of a solemn promise. Feeling the weight of such an undertaking— "how can anything lay a greater obligation on the conscience?"—led Keach to also reflect on the sin of violating such a covenant.[39] Some

---

36 Benjamin Keach, "Every plant God has not planted," in *Expositions of the Parables,* Series Two (Grand Rapids: Kregel, 1991), 364.

37 Benjamin Keach, *Light broke forth in Wales expelling darkness; or the Englishman's Love to the Ancient Britains. Being an Answer to a Book, Intituled, Children's Baptism from Heaven; published in the Welsh tongue, by Mr. James Owen* (London, 1696), 234.

38 Keach, *The Glory of a True Church,* 5.

39 Keach, *The Glory of a True Church,* 45.

see such church covenants as restricting the freedom of the individual, even perhaps as an imposition. Keach would probably have replied to such objections by pointing out that undertaking such promises was warranted by specific New Testament teaching. Even a cursory glance through the eight promises demonstrates that Keach was only spelling out the biblical conduct required of church members if corporate spirituality was to be maintained in the life of the church.

IT TOOK CHURCH DISCIPLINE SERIOUSLY

"Discipline" has a pejorative connotation in the minds of most of our twenty-first century peers. Keach's church covenant does not employ that term but discipline did not mean only *corrective* discipline for offences. There was also *formative* discipline which was, among other things, intended to be preventative. Thus, in the first two promises, members undertook to "walk in all holiness, godliness, humility, and brotherly love," and to stir one another into action "to love and good works." At the same time, members were to act in a responsible and caring manner for one another so that when sin became evident among any of them appropriate action would be taken. This might take the form of warning, rebuke or admonishment, carried out in a spirit of meekness following the rules given by Christ. Keach had written extensively in *The Glory of a True Church* about church discipline in a section entitled, "The Power of the Keyes, with Church-Discipline, and Members Duties one to another."[40]

IT EMPHASIZED THAT THE CHURCH SHOULD BE CENTRAL IN THE PRAYERS OF THE MEMBERS

Corporate spirituality can only be maintained if each member has a high regard and prays regularly for the church of Christ. The third promise undertakes to pray "in an especial manner." Five things are mentioned: (i) prayer for one another; (ii) prayer for the glory and increase of the church; (iii) prayer for the presence of God in the church; (iv) prayer for the pouring out of his Spirit on the church; and, finally, (v) prayer for his protection over the church for his glory. None of these emphases was intended to undermine prayer for individual or family needs but rather to underline that members of a corporate

---

40 Keach, *The Glory of a True Church*, 19.

body should be primarily concerned for the well-being and prosperity of that body. Therefore, they undertook to pray to God accordingly.

IT RECOGNIZED THE REALITIES INVOLVED IN WALKING TOGETHER

The precise tensions created by the comprehensive view of the church adopted by the reformers and the Church of England were not present among Baptists. However, that did not mean that they were free from other tensions and problems. Keach's covenant recognized the reality of living together in a world where there was still human sin and human weakness. The fourth promise involved an undertaking to share one another's burdens, to show sympathy and compassion for one another's particular needs. The fifth promise faced the fact that each of the members had various "weaknesses, failings, and infirmities." These were to be faced by each member with patience, and integrity was to be shown by not making such things the subject matter of conversation, either among the members or among outsiders. In addition, a sixth promise recognized the need to stand together for the gospel, to maintain the purity of the church, and—above all—to avoid division and strife. In *The Glory of a True Church* there are more detailed sections on this subject.[41]

IT UNDERLINED THE IMPORTANCE OF THE LORD'S DAY AND THE NEED TO MEET TOGETHER

Meeting together on a regular basis was an essential expression of corporate spirituality. Worshipping together, edification of the body and the good of the church were therefore the concerns of the seventh promise. Keach's congregation were firmly persuaded of the warrant for observing the Lord's Day and Keach himself wrote specifically on the subject.[42] A part of this worship would have included the regular observance of the Lord's Supper. Members, therefore, undertook to meet for worship on the Lord's Day and to take other opportunities to meet together in order to serve and glorify God.

---

41 "Of such that cause divisions; or unduly Separate themselves from the Church," and "Of Disorders, or causes of Discords, and how to be prevented, corrected, and removed," in Keach, *The Glory of a True Church*, 24–33.

42 Benjamin Keach, *The Articles of the Faith of the congregation of Horseley-down [Back Street], as asserted this 10th of the sixth month, 1697* (London, 1697), XXVIII. Also, Benjamin Keach, *The Jewish Sabbath Abrogated: or the Saturday Sabbatarians confuted* (London, 1700).

IT UPHELD THE DUTY OF PROVIDING A COMFORTABLE
MAINTENANCE FOR THE PASTOR OF THE CHURCH

The final promise concerned the members responsibilities toward their pastors, especially in providing for their living in keeping with the principle laid down in 1 Corinthians 9:14: "the Lord has commanded that those who preach the gospel should live from the gospel." This had been a matter of concern for Keach and other Particular Baptists for some years. This becomes clear from a book he wrote in 1689. He wrote it because he was asked to address the issue by his ministerial colleagues.[43] Some congregations were delinquent in their duty but Keach ensured that this practice was included in the duties of church members.

IT COULD ONLY BE UNDERTAKEN IN COMPLETE DEPENDENCE ON GOD

The final paragraph of the church covenant mentioned the eight specific duties and promises, as well as other gospel duties. Keach stressed that such promises cannot be made and such responsibilities cannot possibly be fulfilled as a mere human undertaking. Only in the power and strength of Lord can they be performed. In his concluding words, there is also a heightened sense of devotion and commitment to God, "whose we are, and whom we desire to serve: To whom be glory now and evermore. Amen."[44] That same spirit permeates everything Keach wrote in *The Glory of a True Church*, and is expressed again in the church covenant. Those who covenanted together as a church wanted to walk together in the fear of the Lord.

Some lessons for today

During the last decade or so, there appears to be something of a revival of interest in the idea of church covenants and an awareness of the importance of corporate spirituality. The books written by Gwyn Davies, Charles Deweese and also one edited by Timothy and Denise

---

43 Benjamin Keach, *The Gospel Minister's Maintenance Vindicated. Wherein, a regular Ministry in the Churches is first asserted, and the objections against Gospel maintenance for ministers answered* (London, 1689). Keach used material already partly prepared by Nehemiah Coxe who had died in 1689. Otherwise Coxe would probably have produced the book.

44 Keach, *The Glory of a True Church*, 74.

George are indications of this. Furthermore, the practice of using a church covenant has been revived by Mark Dever and those associated with 9Marks Ministries in Washington, D.C. In an article available on the page of their online journal, Matt Schmucker wrote that a church covenant can be described in five different ways. It is a promise, it describes how members of the church live, it is a sign of commitment, it is an ethical statement that provides accountability and, finally, it provides the church with a biblical standard of conduct.[45]

In 2003, in the United Kingdom, Paul S. Fiddes included a chapter in his *Tracks and Traces* entitled, "'Walking Together': The place of covenant theology in Baptist life yesterday and today."[46] Fiddes provides a brief and helpful historical survey before concluding with a chapter concerning confessions of faith and covenants. Writing with the concern of "communicating our faith to others and ecumenical relationships" he has significant reservations about the place of confessions of faith and suggests "that a theological and practical distance should be kept between confessions and covenants."[47] 9Marks, while not addressing the issue of the relationship between confessions of faith and covenants, would not appear to share Fiddes conclusion. The covenant they provide is preceded by sections covering the importance of expository preaching, biblical theology, of understanding the good news, conversion and evangelism. Their concerns for corporate godliness are further expressed by sections covering church membership, church discipline and also for promoting Christian discipleship and growth.

Keach would certainly not have approved of keeping a "theological and practical distance" between confessions and covenants. *The Glory of a True Church* reflects that conviction. The idea of a church covenant is inseparably linked to that of a confession of faith in Keach's understanding. Even though not all of Keach's Particular Baptist contemporaries who signed the *1689 Second London Baptist Confession of Faith*

---

45 Matt Schmucker, "Membership Matters—What is Our Church Covenant?" (http://www.9marks.org/journal/membership-matters-what-our-church-covenant; accessed December 8, 2012).

46 Paul S. Fiddes, *Tracks and Traces: Baptist Identity in Church and Theology*, Studies in Baptist History and Thought 13 (Milton Keynes: Paternoster, 2003), 21–47.

47 Fiddes, *Tracks and Traces*, 47.

would have agreed with him about the necessity of a church covenant, there was agreement among them about the vital importance of a confession of faith.[48] Speaking in the context of being instructed and established in the great truths of the gospel, they were all persuaded that "the clear understanding, and steady belief of which, *our comfortable walking with God, and fruitfulness before him*, in all our ways, is most nearly concerned."[49] The corporate godliness of the church was thus bound up with, and inseparable from, the great truths of the gospel expressed in their confession of faith. Martin Bucer, the Puritans in the Church of England, and the various groups of Separatists outside her walls, all shared that concern. The question was: How was it best to be accomplished?

The same question faces every generation of Christians and every church. There are many Baptist churches—and other Christian communities—each of which hold fast to the doctrines of historic biblical Christianity. They take confessions of faith and church membership seriously and require of each church member a clear undertaking to fulfil their responsibilities. By such a practice, they are stressing that they are persuaded that corporate spirituality must not only be expressed but also upheld. To do otherwise would result in a loss of both the identity and the integrity of the church of Jesus Christ.

However, we live in a day when others question the validity of church membership. Many Baptist churches have an open membership with a minimal number of requirements for their members; membership of the church is sometimes expressed by little more than a nod of the head by the pastor. In the ecumenical climate, the plea is for openness, with a firm rejection of the implied narrowness imposed by church confessions and the covenants flowing from them. Some professing Christians have a very low view of the place of the church in Christ's purpose; regular attendance at church is no longer seen as required; a Christian's loyalties are often divided between church and

---

48 Deweese notes that Keach's close friend, Hanserd Knollys, was opposed to church covenants, believing they did not reflect a New Testament practice. See Deweese, *Baptist Church Covenants*, 24.

49 "To the Judicious and Impartial Reader," in *A Confession of Faith put forth by the Elders and Brethren of many Congregations of Christians (baptized upon Profession of their Faith) in London and the Country* (London, 1677), italics mine.

parachurch organizations; church discipline is frowned upon and often ignored; and, worldliness threatens to engulf parts of the professing church. What then happens to the corporate godliness of the church, so essential to her life and ministry, and repeatedly stressed throughout the New Testament epistles?

If what Keach and others believed and practiced is a reflection of what the New Testament teaches, then the situation just described is a crisis that will only continue to undermine the corporate life of the church of Christ. In the light of these trends and practices, Benjamin Keach has something positive to say to this generation by drawing attention to what Christ expects of those who profess to belong to his church. In an age of individualism and anti-authoritarianism, today's church needs to recapture the vision of men like Keach for the godliness and corporate spirituality of the body of Christ. Submission to Christ's Word lies at the heart of that spirituality, together with promises to obey those directives in dependence on the power of the Holy Spirit. Only then can we serve our Redeemer and his church faithfully in this generation.

A positive reappraisal of Keach's fundamental convictions and concerns would, I believe, lead to a spiritual renewal among God's people, a renewed appreciation of God's everlasting covenant love and a renewed commitment to the Lord Jesus Christ and to his church as that commitment comes to expression in the corporate life, ministry and godliness of each local church.

Writing in 1785, a century after Keach, Andrew Fuller (1754–1815), in a Circular Letter of the Northamptonshire Baptist Association, challenged his readers to live with a much greater zeal for Christ.

It is to be feared the old puritanical way of devoting ourselves wholly to be the Lord's, resigning up our bodies, souls, gifts, time, property, with all we have and are to serve him, and frequently renewing these covenants before him, is now awfully neglected. This was to make a business of religion, a life's work, and not merely an accidental affair, occurring but now and then, and what must be attended to only when we can spare time from other engagements. Few seem to aim, pray, and strive after eminent love to God and one another. Many appear to be contented if they can but remember the time when they had such love in exercise, and then, tacking to it the notion of perseverance without the thing, they go on and on, satisfied, it seems, if they do but make shift just to get to heaven at last, without much caring how. If we were in a proper spirit, the question with us would not so much be, "What must I do for God?" as, "What can I do for God?" A servant that heartily loves his master counts it a privilege to be employed by him, yea, an honour to be entrusted with any of his concerns.[50]

---

50 Andrew Fuller, "Causes of Declension in Religion, and Means of Revival," in *The Complete Works of Andrew Fuller*, 3 vols. (Harrisonburg: Sprinkle Publications, 1988), 3:320.

19

BAPTISTS

Andrew Fuller's Edwardsean spirituality

By Nathan A. Finn

IN 2001, MICHAEL HAYKIN edited a book titled, *The Armies of the Lamb: The Spirituality of Andrew Fuller,* as part of Joshua Press's Classics of Reformed Spirituality series.[1] In many ways, this short volume perfectly encapsulates the heart of Haykin's scholarly vision. He has been interested in the doctrine of the Holy Spirit since his dissertation work on the fourth-century Pneumatomachian controversy at Wycliffe College and the University of Toronto in the early 1980s.[2] Beginning in the late 1980s, he became increasingly interested in British Particular Baptist history and theology, particularly during the so-called long eighteenth century. As a development of that emphasis, Haykin has emerged as arguably the key scholar associated with the renaissance in Andrew Fuller (1754–1815) studies over the past thirty years.[3] He has also become

---

1 Michael A.G. Haykin, ed., *The Armies of the Lamb: The Spirituality of Andrew Fuller,* Classics of Reformed Spirituality (Dundas: Joshua Press, 2001).

2 The dissertation was subsequently revised and published. See Michael A.G. Haykin, *The Spirit of God: The Exegesis of 1 and 2 Corinthians in the Pneumatomachian Controversy of the Fourth Century* (Leiden: Brill, 1994).

3 See Nathan A. Finn, "The Renaissance in Andrew Fuller Studies: A Bibliographic Essay," *The Southern Baptist Journal of Theology* 17, no. 2 (Summer 2013): 44–61. Haykin has made numerous contributions to Fuller studies. His most important contribution thus far is serving as the general editor of the forthcoming critical edition of the *Works*

one of the leading evangelical scholars of spirituality, even helping to launch the first Protestant doctoral program in spirituality at The Southern Baptist Theological Seminary in Louisville, Kentucky.[4] Each of these scholarly emphases are evident in *The Armies of the Lamb*.

The text of *The Armies of the Lamb* is comprised primarily of annotated selections from Fuller's correspondence, along with a couple of other short primary source documents in the appendices. But for the purposes of this chapter, the key section of the book is Haykin's opening essay, which serves as a thirty-page introduction to Fuller's life and thought. Like most scholars who have studied Fuller, Haykin highlights the influence of Jonathan Edwards (1703–1758) upon Fuller's theology and ministry. As Haykin notes, "Indeed, after the Scriptures, Edwards' writings exerted the strongest theological influence on Fuller."[5] Furthermore, Edwards' theological vision

> was devoted to a scholarly and contemporary defence of Calvinistic convictions, and to tracing the work of the Spirit in corporate revival and spirituality. This twin commitment of Edwards' theological reflection provided both the shape and substance for Fuller's own theology and piety.[6]

Haykin is undoubtedly correct that Jonathan Edwards exercised a signal influence upon Andrew Fuller's theology and piety. Yet, while much has been written on Edwards' impact upon Fuller's theology, few scholars have overtly addressed the influence of Edwards upon Fuller's piety or spirituality.[7]

---

of Andrew Fuller, a multi-volume project that will be published by Walter de Gruyter.

4   Garrett Wishall, "SBTS Introduces First Protestant Ph.D. Degree in Spirituality in United States," *Towers* (December 8, 2008); available online at http://news.sbts.edu/2008/12/08/sbts-introduces-first-protestant-phd-degree-in-spirituality-in-united-states/; accessed February 21, 2013. His noteworthy books on spirituality include Michael A.G. Haykin, *The God Who Draws Near: An Introduction to Biblical Spirituality* (Darlington: Evangelical Press, 2007) and Michael A.G. Haykin, *The Reformers and Puritans as Spiritual Mentors: "Hope is kindled"* (Kitchener: Joshua Press, 2012). Haykin has also served as the series editor for Classics of Reformed Spirituality, published by Joshua Press, and Profiles in Reformed Spirituality, published by Reformation Heritage Press.

5   Haykin, *Armies of the Lamb*, 27.

6   Haykin, *Armies of the Lamb*, 27, 29.

7   For an excellent treatment of Edwards' influence upon Fuller's theology, see

According to Alister McGrath, "Christian spirituality concerns the quest for a fulfilled and authentic Christian existence, involving the bringing together of the fundamental ideas of Christianity and the whole experience of living on the basis of and within the scope of the Christian faith."[8] While this is a fine basic definition, several varieties of Christian spirituality have been influential throughout church history. Since the mid-eighteenth century, a uniquely Edwardsean spirituality has been prevalent among many evangelicals in the English-speaking world, often providing resources for spiritual renewal.[9] This essay argues for a distinctively Edwardsean shape to Andrew Fuller's spirituality. Like other Edwardseans of the era, Fuller's piety focused on authentic religious affections, was missions-minded and was committed to disinterested benevolence. This chapter proceeds with a brief introduction to Jonathan Edwards' spirituality and its legacy in North America. It then looks at Fuller's spirituality, emphasizing Edwardsean echoes in his thought. It will become clear that Fuller was not only shaped by Edwards' theology, but as with Edwards, theology was closely tied to spirituality.

Jonathan Edwards' spirituality

Jonathan Edwards' personal piety was influenced by at least two key tributaries. He stood in continuity with a Puritan tradition that, though declining by Edwards' time, had for a century and a half been a vibrant spiritual renewal movement within the Reformed tradition

---

Chris Chun, *The Legacy of Jonathan Edwards in the Theology of Andrew Fuller*, Studies in the History of Christian Traditions, vol. 162 (Leiden and Boston: Brill, 2012). For other recent studies of this topic, see also Peter Beck, "The Gospel According to Jonathan Edwards: Andrew Fuller's appropriation of Jonathan Edwards' Justification by Faith Alone," *Eusebeia: The Bulletin of The Jonathan Edwards Centre for Reformed Spirituality* (Spring 2005): 53–76; Thomas J. Nettles, "The Influence of Jonathan Edwards on Andrew Fuller," *Eusebia: The Bulletin for the Andrew Fuller Center for Baptist Studies* 9 (Spring 2008): 91–116; Michael A.G. Haykin, "Great Admirers of the Transatlantic Divinity: Some Chapters in the Story of Baptist Edwardseanism," in *After Jonathan Edwards: The Courses of the New England Theology*, ed. Oliver D. Crisp and Douglas A. Sweeney (New York: Oxford University Press, 2012), 197–207.

    8   Alister McGrath, *Christian Spirituality* (Oxford: Blackwell, 1999), 2.

    9   Richard Lovelace, *Dynamics of Spiritual Life: An Evangelical Theology of Renewal* (Downers Grove: InterVarsity, 1979), 12.

in the English-speaking world.[10] He also inherited a revival tradition from his grandfather and pastoral predecessor, Solomon Stoddard, who had led his church in Northampton through five different seasons of spiritual awakening between 1670 and 1729. In Edwards, these two traditions intersected in one of the greatest theological minds of the modern era. Over the course of his career, Edwards reframed these two streams, always in dialog with challenges raised by the Enlightenment, thus casting a vision of Christian spirituality that was forged in revival experience, longed for the global spread of Christianity and promoted an ethics of benevolence that encouraged evangelical activism.

Edwards' spirituality was rooted in revival, particularly as it related to authentic Christian experience. According to Stuart Piggin, "Edwards identified 'true religion,' we might say 'genuine spirituality,' with the affections."[11] Gerald McDermott defines affections in Edwards' thinking as "strong inclinations of the soul that are manifested in thinking, feeling, and acting."[12] Individuals possess both good and bad affections which lead us either toward God or away from him. Edwards believed that affections "are at the root of all spiritual experience, both true and false. Holy affections are the source of true spirituality, while other kinds of affections lie at the root of false spiritualities."[13] He makes this case in his classic work, *A Treatise Concerning Religious Affections*, first published in 1746. In *Religious Affections*, Haykin contends that "we find Edwards' most exhaustive and penetrating expositions of the nature of true Christian spirituality."[14]

---

10 The relationship between Edwards and the Puritans has been the source of considerable scholarly debate. Most recent scholars have emphasized continuity rather than discontinuity. For example, see Harry S. Stout, "The Puritans and Edwards," in *Jonathan Edwards and the American Experience*, ed. Nathan O. Hatch and Harry S. Stout (New York: Oxford University Press, 1988), 142–159.

11 Stuart Piggin, "'Sweet Burning in My Heart': The Spirituality of Jonathan Edwards," Address given at the Launch of the Jonathan Edwards Centre, Ridley College, (April 29, 2010), 8. This paper is available online at www.cte.mq.edu.au/public/download.jsp?id=11408; accessed February 21, 2013.

12 Gerald McDermott, *Seeing God: Jonathan Edwards and Spiritual Discernment* (1995; reprint, Vancouver: Regents College Press, 2000), 31.

13 McDermott, *Seeing God*, 31.

14 Michael A.G. Haykin, "The Life and Legacy of Jonathan Edwards: A Tercentennial Appreciation," 15. Unpublished paper in the author's possession.

Edwards wrote *Religious Affections* at a time when the revival was being threatened by conservatives, such as Charles Chauncey, and radicals, such as James Davenport. In carving out a more moderate approach, Edwards made a distinction between those affections that are evidence of true religion and those that are not.[15] He argued that true religious affections were at the core of biblical Christianity.

For although to true religion, there must indeed be something else besides affection; yet true religion consists so much in the affections, that there can be no true religion without them. He who has no religious affection, is in a state of spiritual death, and is wholly destitute of the powerful, quickening, saving influences of the Spirit of God upon his heart. As there is no true religion, where there is nothing else but affection; so there is no true religion where there is no religious affection.... If the great things of religion are rightly understood, they will affect the heart. The reason why men are not affected by such infinitely great, important, glorious, and wonderful things, as they often hear and read of, in the Word of God, is undoubtedly because they are blind; if they were not so, it would be impossible, and utterly inconsistent with human nature, that their hearts should be otherwise, than strongly impressed, and greatly moved by such things.[16]

For Edwards, authentic religious affections are foundational to true Christianity, and thus biblical spirituality.[17]

---

15 In his history of the Great Awakening, Thomas Kidd argues against a "two-party" reading of the revivals and contends for three positions: anti-revivalists, moderate evangelicals and radical evangelicals. He places Edwards in the middle category by the 1740s. See Thomas S. Kidd, *The Great Awakening: The Roots of Evangelical Christianity in Colonial America* (New Haven: Yale University Press, 2004), 117–173.

16 Jonathan Edwards, *Religious Affections*, in *The Works of Jonathan Edwards*, vol. 2, ed. John E. Smith (New Haven: Yale University Press, 1959), 120–121. Hereafter *WJE*.

17 Many modern evangelicals agree with his assessment, as evidenced in the enduring appreciation for *Religious Affections*. In addition to McDermott's *Seeing God,* see also Sam Storms, *Signs of the Spirit: An Interpretation of Jonathan Edwards' Religious Affections* (Wheaton: Crossway, 2007), and Iain D. Campbell, "Jonathan Edwards' Religious Affections as a Paradigm fro Evangelical Spirituality," *Scottish Bulletin of Evangelical Theology* 21.2 (Autumn 2003): 166–186.

Edwards' personal Christian experience was defined by his attempts to cultivate his own affections for the glory of God. He advanced a vision of experiential piety that McDermott and Michael McClymond argue centred around three themes: discipline, enjoyment and consummation.[18] He pursued a number of personal disciplines for the sake of directing his affections Godward. As Sean Lucas notes, Edwards "desired to raise his 'religious affections' to a holy ardor through Scripture reading and prayer, attendance upon the means of grace, and encountering the spiritual relations of others."[19] Donald Whitney notes that Edwards cultivated his piety by pursuing eight different spiritual disciplines, including Bible intake, prayer, solitude, fasting and keeping a personal spiritual journal.[20]

Enjoyment and consummation were closely related in Edwards' spirituality. He delighted in God and urged his parishioners to do so as well. God desires for us to be happy and to be holy. Our holy happiness is evidenced in authentic religious affections. Edwards believed that God is glorified when he is enjoyed by his people— indeed, that he has ultimately created the world for this very purpose. As Owen Strachan and Doug Sweeney argue, "Edwards's answer to the question of why God created the world is this: to emanate the fullness of his glory for his people to know, praise, and enjoy."[21] But experiential spirituality is not only for the here and now. God-centred enjoyment of the Christian life is an anticipation of heaven, which is characterized by perfect happiness and holiness. Spirituality is

---

18 Michael J. McClymond and Gerald R. McDermott, *The Theology of Jonathan Edwards* (New York: Oxford University Press, 2011), 60–76.

19 Sean Michael Lucas, *God's Grand Design: The Theological Vision of Jonathan Edwards* (Wheaton: Crossway, 2011), 13.

20 Donald S. Whitney, "Pursuing a Passion for God Through Spiritual Disciplines: Learning from Jonathan Edwards," in *A God-Entranced Vision of All Things: The Legacy of Jonathan Edwards*, ed. John Piper and Justin Taylor (Wheaton: Crossway, 2004), 112–125.

21 Owen Strachan and Doug Sweeney, *Jonathan Edwards on the Good Life*, The Essential Edwards Collection (Chicago: Moody, 2010), 17. This is a theme that Edwards' most famous contemporary protégé, John Piper, has attempted to echo through his many writings and the work of Desiring God Ministries. See John Piper, *Desiring God: Meditations of a Christian Hedonist*, 3rd. ed. (Eugene: Multnomah, 2011). Sam Storms has also sounded this Edwardsean theme. See Sam Storms, *Pleasures Evermore: The Life-Changing Power of Enjoying God* (Colorado Springs: NavPress, 2000).

ultimately eschatological in that it is a foretaste of, and is ultimately fulfilled in, the next life.[22]

In his writings, Edwards provided several examples of authentic religious affections in the context of revival. In *A Faithful Narrative of the Surprising Work of God in the Conversion of Many Hundred Souls in Northampton* (1737), Edwards held up Abigail Hutchinson and six-year-old Phoebe Bartlett as examples of true revival piety. But by far his most famous case study was his wife, Sarah Pierpont Edwards, whose experiences he recounted anonymously in *Some Thoughts Concerning the Present Revival of Religion* (1742).[23] Sarah's own revival testimony validated her husband's arguments about authentic spiritual experiences and became part of his apologetic for Edwardsean spirituality.[24] Because of Sarah's personal piety, Jonathan was convinced that they had an "uncommon," even spiritual union that would survive their deaths and be transformed into something even greater in heaven.[25]

While Edwards' spirituality began with authentic religious affections, frequently spurred on by revival, his piety was not merely inwardly focused. Edwardsean spirituality was also missional, committed to the global diffusion of the gospel to all the peoples of the world. Edwards, of course, spent seven years as a missionary to the Native Americans in and around Stockbridge, Massachusetts.[26] But he also promoted a

---

22 McClymond and McDermott, *Theology of Jonathan Edwards*, 69–70, 74–75. See also Stephen J. Nichols, *Heaven on Earth: Capturing Jonathan Edwards's Vision of Living in Between* (Wheaton: Crossway, 2006).

23 Jonathan Edwards, *Some Thoughts Concerning the Revival*, in *The Great Awakening*, WJE 4:331–341.

24 See George M. Marsden, *Jonathan Edwards: A Life* (New Haven: Yale University Press, 2003), 240–249.

25 Piggin, "Sweet Burning in My Heart," 8. See also Elisabeth D. Dodds, *Marriage to a Difficult Man: The Uncommon Union of Jonathan and Sarah Edwards* (Philadelphia: Westminster, 1971) and James Wm. McClendon Jr., *Ethics: Systematic Theology*, vol. 1, 2nd ed. (Nashville: Abingdon, 2002), 119–138.

26 See Stephen J. Nichols, "Last of the Mohican Missionaries: Jonathan Edwards at Stockbridge," in *The Legacy of Jonathan Edwards: American Religion and the Evangelical Tradition*, ed. D.G. Hart, Sean Michael Lucas and Stephen J. Nichols (Grand Rapids: Baker Academic, 2003), 47–63; Rachel Wheeler, "Edwards as Missionary," in *The Cambridge Companion to Jonathan Edwards*, ed. Stephen J. Stein (New York: Cambridge University Press, 2007), 196–216; Jonathan Gibson, "Jonathan Edwards: A Missionary?" *Themelios* 36.3 (November 2011): 380–402.

missionary spirituality through his writings. Ronald Davies suggests that Edwards should even be called the "grandfather of modern Protestant missions."[27] The two classic works that demonstrate the relationship between religious affections and missionary zeal are *Humble Attempt to Promote Explicit Agreement and Visible Union of God's People in Extraordinary Prayer for the Revival of Religion and the Advancement of Christ's Kingdom on Earth* (1747) and *The Life of David Brainerd* (1749). The purpose of *Humble Attempt* was to promote a "concert of prayer" in the English-speaking world that would help bring about a global revival, ultimately ushering in Christ's millennial reign. According to McClymond and McDermott, this work "stirred enthusiasm for foreign missions among nineteenth-century Anglo-American Protestants."[28]

The Life of David Brainerd, an edited version of Brainerd's personal diary, was even more influential than *Humble Attempt*. The book became Edwards' bestselling work and remains a classic in missions history and spiritual biography. It also made Brainerd one of the most well-known evangelicals of the eighteenth century, even though he died of tuberculosis at age twenty-nine. As Doug Sweeney argues, "Although Brainerd served for less than five years on the mission field, Edwards' *Life* transformed him into a Christian hero."[29] For Edwards, Brainerd was also an example of one who wed together true religious affections and missionary zeal. As David Weddle argues, "Edwards edited the diary in order to present Brainerd as an example of the sort of mature spirituality he himself achieved, or at least described with persuasive eloquence in his extensive writings on religious experience."[30]

---

27 Ronald E. Davies, "Jonathan Edwards: Missionary Biographer, Theologian, Strategist, Administrator, Advocate—and Missionary," *International Bulletin of Missionary Research* 21.2 (April 1997): 60.

28 McClymond and McDermott, *Theology of Jonathan Edwards*, 551. For more on this theme, see Stuart Piggin, "The Expanding Knowledge of God: Jonathan Edwards's Influence on Missionary Thinking and Promotion," in *Jonathan Edwards at Home and Abroad: Historical Memories, Cultural Movements, Global Horizons*, ed. David W. Kling and Douglas A. Sweeney (Columbia: University of South Carolina Press, 2003), 266–296.

29 Douglas A. Sweeney, "Evangelical Tradition in America," in *The Cambridge Companion to Jonathan Edwards*, 223.

30 David L. Weddle, "The Melancholy Saint: Jonathan Edwards's Interpretation of David Brainerd as a Model of Evangelical Spirituality," *Harvard Theological Review* 81.3 (July 1988): 299. Weddle argues that Brainerd is not the best example of Edwardsean

In 1768, John Wesley published a revised version of Brainerd's diary which downplayed the latter's Calvinism but held him up as a model of missions-minded spirituality for the Methodist movement in the Church of England.[31] Evangelicals across the theological spectrum were drawn to Brainerd's story.

Edwards' spirituality also possessed an explicitly ethical bent to it. For Edwards, and contrary to the rationalists of his day such as Francis Hutcheson and the Earl of Shaftsbury, authentic spiritual affections flowed forth into a God-centred moral vision that shaped the rest of the Christian life. In 1738, Edwards preached a series of sermons on 1 Corinthians 13, which were later published in 1852 under the title *Charity and Its Fruits*. This work lays out much of Edwards' moral theology in a more theological (and pastoral) form. Edwards further advanced his ethical vision in a more philosophical form in *The Nature of True Virtue*, one of the two dissertations written during his final years at Stockbridge and published posthumously in 1765. The other dissertation, *The End for Which God Created the World*, provided the overarching worldview that sustained Edwardsean ethics.

According to Edwards, "True virtue most essentially consists in benevolence to Being in general. Or perhaps to speak more accurately, it is that consent, propensity and union of heart to Being in general, that is immediately exercised in a general good will."[32] He called his view "disinterested general benevolence" because our natural selfishness is redirected outward in love to God and other humans.[33] Edwards argues that the regenerate should so love God and delight in his beauty and perfection that we are led to look away from ourselves and toward others, for the glory of God. As George Marsden notes,

> God is love and the source of all love. True love, true benevolence, is love that resonates with God's love and is in harmony with it.... Intelligent beings are created with the very purpose of being

---

spirituality because of Brainerd's struggles with spiritual doubts, which in turn exercised an inordinate influence upon evangelical spirituality.

31 See John A. Grigg, *The Lives of David Brainerd: The Making of An American Evangelical Icon* (New York: Oxford University Press, 2009), 147–63.

32 Jonathan Edwards, *The Nature of True Virtue*, in *Ethical Writings*, WJE 8:540.

33 Edwards, *The Nature of True Virtue*, in WJE 8:617.

united in love with the Godhead. And to be united in love with the Godhead means to love all that God loves, or all being.[34]

For Edwards, ethics arise from spirituality. His moral theology was grounded in the character of God and emphasized the believer's communion with the Triune God.[35] True knowledge of God includes participation in God's knowledge of himself, partaking of divine love and allowing that love to transform our selfishness into disinterested benevolence toward others.[36]

Edwards passed on his vision of spirituality to his New Divinity successors. As William Breitenbach has argued, Edwards inherited and adapted the earlier Puritan commitment to both conversionist piety and grace-based morality. Each of these emphases were under attack in Edwards' day by antinomian evangelists who encouraged outlandish spiritual exercises and "Arminian" rationalists who discounted the centrality of conversion and personal piety. Edwards articulated a balanced approach between the extremes that he then bequeathed to New Divinity men such as Samuel Hopkins, Joseph Bellamy and Jonathan Edwards Jr.[37] As inheritors of this spiritual vision, the New Divinity men, in turn, continued to offer a fundamentally Edwardsean defense of the importance of spiritual awakenings and foreign missions.[38] They also extended his ethical vision of disin-

---

34 George M. Marsden, "Challenging the Presumptions of the Age: The Two Dissertations," in *The Legacy of Jonathan Edwards*, 109.

35 McClymond and McDermott, *The Theology of Jonathan Edwards*, 528.

36 John E. Smith, "Christian Virtue and Common Morality," in *The Princeton Companion to Jonathan Edwards*, ed. Sang Hyan Lee (Princeton: Princeton University Press, 2005), 150. See also see Kyle Strobel's introduction to Jonathan Edwards, *Charity and Its Fruits: Living in the Light of God's Love*, ed. Kyle Strobel (Wheaton: Crossway, 2012), 28–30.

37 William Breitenbach, "Piety and Moralism: Edwards and the New Divinity," in *Jonathan Edwards and the American Experience*, 177–204.

38 Despite obvious theological continuities and discontinuities between Edwards and the New Divinity men, most contemporary scholars emphasize the fundamentally Edwardsean shape of the New Divinity, particularly in the areas mentioned above. For example, see the introduction to Douglas A. Sweeney and Allen C. Guelzo, ed., *The New England Theology: From Jonathan Edwards to Edwards Amasa Park* (Grand Rapids: Baker Academic, 2006), 13–24, and many of the essays in Crisp and Sweeney, ed., *After Edwards*.

terested benevolence into evangelical activism, most notably opposition to race-based slavery.[39] Edwardsean spirituality continued to influence American evangelicalism into the nineteenth century. It also influenced British evangelicals such as Andrew Fuller.

Fuller's Edwardsean spirituality

In 2006, Michael Haykin published an essay examining the spirituality of seventeenth- and eighteenth-century Particular Baptists. He noted that because of the roots of these Baptists in the Reformation and Puritanism, they were characterized by a "spirituality of the Word." For this reason, the three key means of grace the Particular Baptists emphasized were preaching, the ordinances and prayer. They believed that the Spirit worked through the preached (and read) Word to draw the lost to saving belief and to strengthen the faith of God's people. Baptism marks out believers as spiritually separated from the world and promotes piety in the newly baptized and those who witness the ordinance. Many Particular Baptists embraced the Reformed emphasis upon feeding by faith on the spiritually present Christ in communion. Those who focused more on the memorial aspect of the Lord's Supper also believed the ordinance is central to cultivating authentic spirituality. Prayer occupied an important place in Particular Baptist piety, undergirding the others means of grace. Particular Baptist prayer was not a devotional practice unto itself, but was a means of communing with Christ.[40]

While Fuller was representative of the basic piety of Particular Baptists, he and many of his friends also embraced a distinctively

---

39 See Charles E. Hambrick-Stowe, "All Things Were New and Astonishing: Edwardsian Piety, the New Divinity, and Race," in *Jonathan Edwards at Home and Abroad*, 121–136. This was an extension of the Edwardsean ethical vision since Edwards himself owned slaves, though he did condemn the transatlantic slave trade. See Thabiti Anyabwile, "Jonathan Edwards, Slavery, and the Theology of African Americans," address delivered at the Jonathan Edwards Center, Trinity Evangelical Divinity School (February 1, 2012); available online at http://thegospelcoalition.org/blogs/justintaylor/files/2012/02/Thabiti-Jonathan-Edwards-slavery-and-theological-appropriation.pdf; accessed February 22, 2013.

40 Michael A.G. Haykin, "'Draw Nigh unto My Soul': English Baptist Piety and the Means of Grace in the Seventeenth and Eighteenth Centuries," *The Southern Baptist Journal of Theology* 10, no. 4 (Winter 2006): 54–73.

Edwardsean spirituality.[41] Like Jonathan Edwards, Fuller's spirituality emphasized the importance of authentic religious affections. He periodically mentions *Religious Affections* in his diary, extracts of which were incorporated into the biography of Fuller that John Ryland Jr. published after his friend's death. For example, in August 1780, Fuller wrote "Some savour to-day [*sic*], in reading *Edwards on the Affections*."[42] A couple of months later, Fuller claimed he was "Much affected this morning in reading Edwards' thoughts on evangelical humility in his *Treatise on the Affections*. Surely there are many that will be found wanting in the great day. 'Lord, is it I?'"[43] In February 1781, Fuller spoke to the influence of *Religious Affections* on his personal spirituality and his ministry:

> I think I have never yet entered into the true idea of the work of the ministry. If I had, surely I should be like Aaron, running between the dead and the living. I think I am by the ministry, as I was by my life as a Christian, before I read *Edwards on the Affections*. I had never entered into the spirit of a great many important things. O for some such penetrating, edifying writer on this subject!... O rather that the Holy Spirit would open my eyes, and let me see into the things that I have never yet seen.[44]

Chris Chun has demonstrated that Fuller used *Religious Affections* extensively in his critique of the Sandemanian belief that repentance

---

41 For the influence of Edwards on John Sutcliff, see Fuller's comments in his funeral sermon for Sutcliff in Andrew Fuller, "Principles and Prospects of a Servant of Christ," in *The Complete Works of Andrew Fuller*, ed. Joseph Belcher (Philadelphia: American Baptist Publication Society, 1845), 1:350–351. Hereafter *WAF*. For the influence of Edwards on John Ryland Jr., see L.G. Champion, "The Theology of John Ryland: Its Sources and Influences," *Baptist Quarterly* 28.1 (January 1979): 18–19. For Edwards influence upon Carey, especially through Brainerd's diary, see Grigg, *The Lives of David Brainerd*, 165–168.

42 John Ryland Jr., *The Work of Faith, the Labour of Love, and the Patience of Hope, Illustrated; In the Life and Death of the Rev. Andrew Fuller, Late Pastor of the Baptist Church at Kettering, and Secretary to the Baptist Missionary Society, From its Commencement, in 1792*, 2nd ed. (London: W. Button & Son, 1818), 78.

43 Ryland, *The Work of Faith*, 79.

44 Ryland, *The Work of Faith*, 74.

Andrew Fuller
1754–1815

is not intrinsic to saving faith.[45] Fuller's polemic, though theological in nature, was born out of a concern for authentic spirituality. Fuller believed that Sandemanianism was too rationalistic and downplayed experiential piety. In 1799, Fuller made his first visit to Scotland on behalf of the Baptist Missionary Society (BMS). In October 1799, Fuller and John Sutcliff visited with a Dr. Watts, a Baptist pastor in Glasgow. Sandemanian views were popular among the "Scotch Baptists" such as Alexander McLean, a convert to Sandemanianism. Sutcliff asked Watts if the Sandemanian view "allowed a proper and spiritual place for the exercise of the *affections?*" Fuller noted that, "To us it seemed that where these principles prevail, they operate to quench the religion of the heart."[46]

Chun further argues that "*Religious Affections* so saturated Fuller's thinking" that it pervaded his writings "even when he did not explicitly cite Edwards."[47] He cites as one example Fuller's 1784 sermon, "The Nature and Importance of Walking by Faith," which was preached against antinomianism. The sermon makes a very similar argument to Part 2, section 11 of *Religious Affections*, contending that walking in faith helps one achieve spiritual insight. Faith is the mind's eye through which the believer perceives invisible and spiritual realities.[48] Tom Nettles contends that Fuller also echoes *Religious Affections* in a sermon titled, "The Inward Witness of the Spirit."[49] In another sermon titled, "The Reception of Christ the Turning Point of Salvation," Fuller speaks of receiving Christ as involving all the faculties or powers of the soul, which includes both the will and the affections. Edwards used this same language in *Religious Affections*.[50] Each of these sermons deal

---

45 Chun, *Legacy of Jonathan Edwards in the Theology of Andrew Fuller*, 120–131.

46 Ryland, *The Work of Faith*, 159.

47 Chun, *Legacy of Jonathan Edwards in the Theology of Andrew Fuller*, 132.

48 Chun, *Legacy of Jonathan Edwards in the Theology of Andrew Fuller*, 132–133. See also Andrew Fuller, "The Nature and Importance of Walking By Faith," in *WAF* 1:117–134; Edwards, *Religious Affections*, in *WJE* 2:167–181.

49 Tom Nettles, "Edwards and His Impact on Baptists," *Founders Journal* (Summer 2003): 1–18, available online at http://www.founders.org/journal/fj53/article1.html; accessed February 22, 2013. See also Andrew Fuller, "Inward Witness of the Spirit," *WAF*, 1:624–626.

50 Andrew Fuller, "The Reception of Christ the Turning Point of Salvation," *WAF* 1:270; Jonathan Edwards, *Religious Affections*, in *WJE* 2:96–100.

with the nature of Christian spirituality; Fuller does not directly cite *Religious Affections* or any other of Edwards' writings in either sermon.

A common theme in *Religious Affections,* and one that is periodically mentioned by Fuller, is the danger of spiritual pride. Edwards argues, "Spiritual pride is man's chief temptation, and the true danger lies in the fact that a pride of this order is a real possibility only for the man with religious concern."[51] In a 1785 circular letter titled, "Causes of Declension in Religion, And Means of Revival," Fuller specifically mentions spiritual pride as one cause of religious declension.[52] Fuller also wrote a short essay on the topic of spiritual pride. Like Edwards, Fuller warned of the danger of spiritual pride in the context of revival, when individuals make their particular religious experiences the measure of authentic spirituality.[53] Edwards addressed this issue in both *Religious Affections* and *The Distinguishing Marks of a Work of God* (1741).[54]

Like Edwards, Fuller's spirituality was also a missions-minded piety. As many scholars have shown, Edwards' *Freedom of the Will* (1753) influenced Fuller to abandon his commitment to High Calvinism and embrace evangelical sentiments. Like most Particular Baptists, Fuller initially gave a negative answer to the so-called "modern question" of whether or not the non-elect were obligated to believe the gospel. But after reading *Freedom of the Will*, Fuller adopted Edwards' distinction between natural and moral ability, arguing that it is the latter that prevents the sinner from believing in Christ for his salvation. Fuller's Edwardsean Calvinism was publicly articulated in his personal confession of faith for the Kettering Church (1783) and put on full display in *The Gospel Worthy of All Acceptation, or the Duty of Sinners to Believe in Jesus Christ* (1785), which argued for indiscriminate gospel preaching to all people.[55] Fuller's views in turn influenced William Carey, and the

---

51 Edwards, *Religious Affections*, in *WJE* 2:36.

52 Andrew Fuller, "Causes of Declension in Religion, and Means of Revival," *WAF* 3:321.

53 Andrew Fuller, "Spiritual Pride: Or the Occasions, Causes, and Effects of High-Mindedness in Religion; With Considerations Exciting to Self-Abasement," *WAF* 3:564–578.

54 Edwards, *Distinguishing Marks*, in *WJE* 4:277.

55 The first edition of *Gospel Worthy* was replaced by the second edition in 1801. Fuller introduced significant changes inbetween the two editions. Robert Oliver is editing critical versions of both editions in one volume as part of the forthcoming

two of them were instrumental in forming the BMS and launching the modern missions movement in the English-speaking world.[56]

Edwards influenced Fuller's missions-minded spirituality in other ways. Fuller became acquainted with *The Life of David Brainerd* around the same time he read *Freedom of the Will*. The example of Brainerd played a key role in helping Fuller to see Edwardsean Calvinism as a more biblical alternative to High Calvinism. As Fuller noted in the preface to the second edition of *The Gospel Worthy of All Acceptation*,

> Reading the lives and labours of such men as Elliot [*sic*], Brainerd, and several others, who preached Christ with such success to the American Indians, had an effect upon him. Their work, like that of the apostles, seemed to be plain before them. They appeared to him, in their addresses to those poor benighted heathens, to have none of those difficulties with which he felt himself encumbered.[57]

Andrew Gunton Fuller, who edited a memoir of his famous father, quotes the elder Fuller making this point in a reflection on his change of sentiments. Fuller recounts that in 1776 he first met John Ryland Jr. and John Sutcliff. That same year, he began reading the writings of Edwards, Joseph Bellamy and David Brainerd. The combination of these new friendships and his reading had caused Fuller to begin "to doubt the system of false Calvinism" he had heretofore embraced.[58]

As helpful as *The Life of David Brainerd* was, it proved less influential than Edwards' *Humble Attempt*. In 1784, the Scottish Presbyterian John

---

Works of Andrew Fuller project. Fuller's confession is available in many places, most recently as Appendix I in Paul Brewster, *Andrew Fuller: Model Pastor-Theologian*, Studies in Baptist Life and Thought (Nashville: B & H Academic, 2010), 181–187.

56 See Chun, *Legacy of Jonathan Edwards in the Theology of Andrew Fuller*, 32–65; Peter J. Morden, *Offering Christ to the World: Andrew Fuller (1754–1815) and the Revival of Eighteenth Century Particular Baptist Life*, Studies in Baptist History and Thought 8 (Carlisle: Paternoster, 2003), 23–51; Gerald L. Priest, "Andrew Fuller, Hyper-Calvinism, and the 'Modern Question,'" in *'At the Pure Fountain of the Thy Word': Andrew Fuller as an Apologist*, Studies in Baptist History and Thought 6, ed. Michael A.G. Haykin (Carlisle: Paternoster, 2004), 43–73.

57 Andrew Fuller, *The Gospel Worthy of All Acceptation*, in WAF 2:329. Fuller refers to himself in the third person in the preface.

58 Andrew Gunton Fuller, *Memoir*, in WAF 1:16.

Erskine, an erstwhile correspondent of Edwards, sent a copy of *Humble Attempt* to John Ryland Jr., who in turn shared the pamphlet with Sutcliff and Fuller. The men were profoundly moved by Edwards' call for a concert of prayer for revival, Christian unity and global evangelization. When Fuller preached the aforementioned "The Nature and Importance of Walking by Faith" at the Northamptonshire Association's annual meeting, he echoed the themes of *Humble Attempt*. Sutcliff then persuaded those present to issue a "Prayer Call" on behalf of the association, commending a monthly concert of prayer in all the churches. In 1789, Sutcliff republished *Humble Attempt* with a new preface. Fuller and his friends embraced the revival-minded, missionary spirituality of Jonathan Edwards and were praying for global missions nearly a decade before the BMS was formed.[59]

Fuller mentions *Humble Attempt* periodically in his own journals.[60] Chun argues that *Humble Attempt* significantly shaped Fuller's missiology. Edwards held to a what Chun calls a "missiological optimism" that was driven by his particular eschatological views. Some of his convictions were simply tied to his postmillennialism, though he also advanced an idiosyncratic reading of the slaying of the witnesses in Revelation 11. Because Edwards believed that the allegedly antichrist religion of Roman Catholicism was rapidly declining in his lifetime, he was persuaded the slaying of the witnesses had to refer to Catholic persecution of medieval sectarians. Later evangelicals, including Sutcliff, rejected this view. But Fuller agreed with Edwards, adopting the latter's interpretation of Revelation 11 in his own *Expository Discourses on the Apocalypse* (1815). Though exegetically suspect, Edwards' views lent themselves to an optimistic missiology that foresaw worldwide revival and the imminent advance of the gospel to all peoples. Fuller embraced the same optimistic missiology, which comprised a key component of his own missionary spirituality.[61]

Fuller's missions-minded spirituality manifested itself in his preaching and writing. In 1793, he preached a sermon commissioning Carey

---

59 The story of the Prayer Call of 1784 is recounted in many places, including Michael A.G. Haykin, *One Heart and One Soul: John Sutcliff of Olney, His Friends, and His Times* (Darlington: Evangelical Press, 1994), 153–171.

60 Ryland, *The Work of Faith*, 85–86.

61 Chun, *Legacy of Jonathan Edwards in the Theology of Andrew Fuller*, 66–84.

and John Thomas as the BMS's first missionaries, shortly before they left for India. He noted that Christ was the One ultimately sending them on their mission, and their errand would be successful if they followed Christ's example and used his appointed means of gospel advance.[62] In 1810, he wrote a circular letter titled, "The Promise of the Spirit the Grand Encouragement in Promoting the Gospel." Nearly twenty years after founding the BMS, Fuller remained optimistic about worldwide evangelization. Missionary success is grounded, not in the efforts of the missionaries themselves, but on the sure prophecies of God that foretell the salvation of the nations. Missionaries should trust that the same Spirit who inspired the prophets will bring his promises to pass through the proclamation of the gospel.[63] In a sermon titled, "Conformity to the Death of Christ," Fuller argued, "It is not for ministers only to take an interest in the salvation of men; the army of the Lamb is composed of the whole body of Christians. Every disciple of Jesus should consider himself a missionary."[64]

Of course, Fuller also evidenced his missionary spirituality by serving as secretary of the Baptist Missionary Society from 1792 to 1815, a position he held in addition to his pastoral responsibilities. Fuller not only spoke on behalf of the BMS and raised funds for its support, but he also kept up an active correspondence with the missionaries and engaged in village preaching to spread the gospel among the unevangelized in England.[65] Morden argues that Fuller's evangelical (Edwardsean!) spirituality deepened over time through his involvement in promoting foreign missions.[66] In fact, through his travels on behalf of the BMS and his extensive correspondence, Fuller even

---

62 Andrew Fuller, "The Nature and Encouragements of the Missionary Work," in *WAF* 1:510–512.

63 Andrew Fuller, "The Promise of the Spirit the Grand Encouragement in Promoting the Gospel," in *WAF* 3:359–363.

64 Andrew Fuller, "Conformity to the Death of Christ," in *WAF* 1:315.

65 See Peter J. Morden, "Andrew Fuller and the Baptist Missionary Society," *Baptist Quarterly* 41.3 (July 2005): 134–57; Paul Brewster, "Out in the Journeys: Village Preaching and Revival among Eighteenth-Century Particular Baptists, Part I," *The Andrew Fuller Review* 1 (September 2011): 5–11; Paul Brewster, "Out in the Journeys: Village Preaching and Revival among Eighteenth-Century Particular Baptists, Part II," *The Andrew Fuller Review* 2 (Spring 2012): 5–14.

66 Morden, *Offering Christ to the World*, 167.

served as an unofficial "spiritual director" to Particular Baptist missionaries and pastors.[67] Fuller also published an influential book titled, *Memoirs of the Late Rev. Samuel Pearce* (1800). Pearce was a close friend and pastor of the Cannon Street Baptist Church in Birmingham. He was also an indefatigable supporter of missions who had wanted to serve as a missionary himself, though the BMS rejected his application. In the *Memoirs*, Fuller held up Pearce as a Baptist version of Brainerd, a model of spirituality to be emulated by others.[68]

As with Edwards, Fuller was committed to a spirituality that worked itself out morally in an ethic of disinterested benevolence. According to Chris Chun, Fuller was very familiar with *The Nature of True Virtue*, from which he adopted Edwards' approach to concepts such as self-love and self-denial. In doing so, Fuller embraced the Edwardsean notion that holy affections prefer holy actions.[69] In arguing against rationalists that a doctrine of Christian rewards does not constitute a "mercenary spirit," Fuller laid out his own Edwardsean approach to ethics. "The only method by which the rewards of the gospel are attainable, faith in Christ, secures the exercise of disinterested and enlarged virtue." True Christian morality includes "devotedness to God and benevolence to men; and this, if anything deserves that name, is true, disinterested, and enlarged virtue."[70] Fuller is echoing Edwards, albeit without citing him directly.

In 1799, Fuller wrote *The Gospel Its Own Witness* as a polemic against Deism, particularly the version advanced in Thomas Paine's *Age of Reason* (1794–1795). Fuller opened his broadside with a moral critique of Deism. Fuller argued that disinterested benevolence is central to Christian morality. He also argued that one of the key indicators that Deism is a false system is its inherent selfishness, which stands in opposition to disinterested benevolence.[71] Though it is rarely men-

---

67 Morden, *Offering Christ to the World*, 171–172.

68 See Adam Covington, "Swallowed Up in God: The Impact of Samuel Pearce on Modern Missions," White Paper 27, The Center for Theological Research, Southwestern Baptist Theological Seminary (January 2009); available online at http://www.baptist-theology.org/documents/SwallowedUpinGod-SamuelPearce.pdf; accessed February 23, 2013); and Michael A.G. Haykin, ed., *Joy Unspeakable and Full of Glory: The Piety of Samuel and Sarah Pearce*, Classics of Reformed Spirituality (Kitchener: Joshua Press, 2012).

69 Chun, *Legacy of Jonathan Edwards in the Theology of Andrew Fuller*, 134–138.

70 Andrew Fuller, *The Gospel Its Own Witness*, in WAF 2:25.

71 Fuller, *The Gospel Its Own Witness*, in WAF 2:16–17, 21.

tioned in modern studies of Paine or Deism, Haykin notes that *The Gospel Its Own Witness* was one of Fuller's most popular books during his lifetime, earning praise from the likes of William Wilberforce.[72]

Fuller offered a very similar critique of Socinianism in *The Calvinistic and Socinian Systems Examined and Compared as to Their Moral Tendency* (1794). Socinianism was an early form of Unitarianism that denied the full deity of Christ and his substitutionary atonement for sin. According to Fuller, Socinians such as Joseph Priestley identify benevolence with an irenic spirit toward others, including a latitudinarian position toward contentious doctrinal matters. Calvinists, by virtue of their tight doctrinal system, are not benevolent toward Socinians and others who question Reformed theology. Fuller counters that true benevolence is concerned with goodwill toward men, which has nothing to do with esteeming those who promulgate false doctrine. Authentic benevolence cares more for men's souls than their opinions. Fuller explicitly holds up Edwards as an example of authentic benevolence versus the false benevolence advanced by the Socinians.[73]

As with the examples of affections and missions, the ethical component to Fuller's Edwardsean spirituality was manifested beyond his polemical writings. In "The Prayer of Faith, Exemplified in the Woman of Canaan," a sermon on Matthew 15:21–28, Fuller criticized the disciples for seeking to send away a demonized Gentile woman. Jesus, of course, healed her. In contrast to Christ, Fuller claimed the disciples' treatment of the woman was "mean and pitiful; it does not appear to have a spice of benevolence in it, but to have been merely the effect of self-love." Fuller criticized the disciples' spirituality because, in that moment at least, they were not Edwardsean enough in their moral vision.[74]

In "The Increase of Knowledge," a sermon preached before the British and Foreign School Society, Fuller combined the ethical and

---

72 Michael A.G. Haykin, "'The Oracles of God': Andrew Fuller's Response to Deism," in *At the Pure Fountain of Thy Word*, 128–129. See also Alan P.F. Sell, *Enlightenment, Ecumenism, Evangel: Theological Themes and Thinkers, 1550–2000*, Studies in Christian History and Thought (Bletchley, Milton Keynes: Paternoster, 2005), 111–143.

73 Jonathan Edwards, *The Calvinistic and Socinian Systems Examined and Compared as to Their Moral Tendency*, in *WAF* 2:161–170.

74 Andrew Fuller, "The Prayer of Faith, Exemplified in the Woman of Canaan," in *WAF* 1:240.

missionary elements of his spirituality. He argued that God's knowledge will spread to all peoples, in fulfillment of biblical prophecy. Gospel advance will usher in the millennial kingdom, when the plight of the poor will be eased due to the spread of "genuine benevolence" as an outflow of the gospel. Edwardsean spirituality will become commonplace in the coming kingdom.[75] Much like with the New Divinity men, a commitment to disinterested benevolence led Fuller to embrace evangelical activism. For Fuller, the most important form of activism—a theme also picked up from Edwards—was foreign missions.

Because of Edwards' emphasis on disinterested benevolence, he believed that self-love is the cardinal vice. In his sermon "Love Your Enemies" from Matthew 5:43–48, Fuller argued, "If the love of God be not in us, self-love, in one shape or other, will have possession of our souls." He goes on to argue that self-love is the governing principle of unbelievers, and they often assume it is the same with Christians. But Christians are characterized by a God-centred benevolence that results in them *actually* loving their enemies and desiring for them to become friends of God.[76] In his sermon on "The Nature and Importance of Love to God," Fuller brings together his Edwardsean emphasis on true religious affections and disinterested benevolence. In an important passage, Fuller argues,

> A complacency in the Divine character still enters into the essence of love. There may be affections where this is not; but there can be no true love to God. We may be greatly affected by an apprehension that our sins are forgiven us; and this merely from self-love; but such affections will not abide.... The love of God will lead us to prize the way of salvation which, in making provision for our necessities, secures the Divine glory.[77]

This is the sort of God-centred, disinterested love for God that Edwards constantly advocated in his own writings. Like authentic affections and missionary zeal, it was in the background of Fuller's own spirituality, even when he did not explicitly mention the New England pastor.

---

75 Andrew Fuller, "The Increase of Knowledge," in WAF 1:417–419.

76 Andrew Fuller, "Love Your Enemies," in WAF 1:574.

77 Andrew Fuller, "The Nature and Importance of Love to God," in WAF 1:305.

Conclusion

Andrew Fuller was influenced by Jonathan Edwards' spirituality just as much as he was shaped by the famed pastor's theology. In fact, as this essay has demonstrated, it would be artificial to make a distinction between theology and spirituality in either man's thought. Through his reading of Edwards' treatises and sermons, Fuller came to embrace an Edwardsean spirituality that emphasized authentic spiritual affections, a revival characterized by world missions and disinterested benevolence. Like Edwards, Fuller wed these themes together into a robust evangelical spirituality that gave rise to a wider tradition—"Fullerism," a uniquely Baptist version of Edwardsean theology. Much like his New Divinity contemporaries in New England, Fuller represents a legitimate and influential extension of Edwardsean spirituality, his differences with the New Divinity men notwithstanding.[78]

In a well-known letter to John Ryland Jr., written shortly after John Sutcliff's death, Fuller summarized the appreciation he and his circle of friends had for Edwards' theological vision. As this essay has demonstrated, he was also speaking of the shaping influence of Edwards' spirituality. Fuller's words seem like a fitting conclusion to this chapter.

> We have some, who have been giving out, of late, that "if Sutcliff, and some others, had preached more of Christ, and less of Jonathan Edwards, they would have been more useful." If those who talk thus, preached Christ half as much as Jonathan Edwards did, and were half as useful as he was, their usefulness would be double what it is. It is very singular, that the Mission to the East should have originated with men of these principles; and pretending to be a prophet, I may say, if ever it falls into the hands of men who talk in this strain, it will soon come to nothing.[79]

---

78 Haykin discusses how Fuller and his friends represented a Baptist Edwardseanism in "Great Admirers of the Transatlantic Divinity." For one important example of a difference between Fuller and the New Divinity men, see "A Significant Letter from John Ryland to Samuel Hopkins," transcribed and edited by Daniel T. Weaver and Michael A.G. Haykin, *The Andrew Fuller Review* 3 (Summer 2012): 29–33.

79 Letter from Andrew Fuller to John Ryland Jr., April 28, 1814, in Ryland, *The Work of Faith*, 332–333.

20

BAPTISTS

The piety of James Petigru Boyce

By Tom J. Nettles

EMBEDDED IN THE context of James P. Boyce's (1827–1888) love and respect for his childhood pastor, Basil Manly Sr., one may see clearly his vision of Christian piety. In the middle of his public ministry, twenty years before his death and twenty years after his first public words of Christian ministry, Boyce preached the funeral sermon for his beloved mentor, friend and spiritual guide, the coryphaeus of Southern Baptist beginnings. Within a luxuriant verbal meadow, one may contemplate and savour Boyce's picture of the godliness that is the high calling of a Christian.

> It is a life in which God is made the chief end of being. To Him are given the best affections of the heart. Obedience to His law is a true delight. Communion with Him is earnestly sought. His rule is acknowledged, and dependence upon Him is a heartfelt joy. It is a life in which is recognized the true nature of the human brotherhood. God is seen in man, as the common Creator, in whose image we have been made. His fellow Christians are linked to him by the common Savior, in whose blood we have been redeemed. The blessings that surround in life awaken gratitude toward the Divine Giver. The sufferings and ills that befall are known as chastisements from a Father's hand, Thus in the

surrounding of his life, as well as in its Author and Preserver, does God, and only God, enter into his soul.[1]

The importance of piety

Boyce believed that genuine piety harboured a truly supernatural power that was useful for the furtherance of the cause of God in the world. At the start of the American Civil War (1861–1865), Boyce emphasized the necessity, even the prior importance to everything else, of increasing the "Christian reliance upon God in the present state of public affairs."[2] Being sustained in wartime, or even achieving victory through this reliance, will not be the only effect of this spirit of reliance, for "the flame of piety is not easily limited. It will burst beyond the immediate object for which it was kindled." Because of the fervent piety of the Baptists during the Revolutionary War, revivals of religion sprang up. "Should not our hearts yearn, should they not burn, that in like manner," Boyce proposed, "even in the midst of war, the Spirit of God may speak to the hearts of the penitent the peace that Jesus gives, that peace which passeth all understanding?"[3]

In an 1852 article demonstrating the importance of church discipline, Boyce stressed, first, that consistent discipline was necessary for "the purification of the visible church." Second, he stated that "the exercise of discipline leads to the advancement of personal piety among the members of the church." The disciples of Christ need every inducement "for their increase in holiness." Boyce mentioned the "many motives to be found in God's word, and his providential dealings" as means of piety but pointed to church discipline standing prominent. The churches that have the strictest discipline also "are universally filled with the most vital piety." The members know their duty, a standard of excellence is placed before them, and, because of the high aim, "they are constantly advancing in piety."[4]

---

1   James P. Boyce, "Life and Death the Christian's Portion," in *James Petigru Boyce: Selected Writings*, ed. Timothy George (Nashville: Broadman Press, 1989), 127.

2   *Stray Recollections, Short Articles, and Public Orations of James P. Boyce*, ed. Tom J. Nettles (Cape Coral: Founders Press, 2009), 115. This collection contains editorials, letters, newspaper articles and other works of and about Boyce.

3   *Stray Recollections*, 116.

4   *Stray Recollections*, 57.

Foundation of Word and Spirit

One of the first evidences and the most fundamental means for the advancement of piety is the Word of God, or as Boyce put it, the "many motives to be found in God's word." Not only, however, are many motives to be found in God's Word, the Bible, but a humble submission to the verdicts of God's Word under the conviction that the Bible is God's Word is the first indication that the foundation of true piety has been established. The first London Confession of 1644 placed belief in the Scripture within this framework.

> That faith is the gift of God wrought in the hearts of the elect by the Spirit of God, whereby they come to see, know, and beleeve the truth of the Scriptures, & not only so, but the excellencies of them above all other writings and things in the world, as they hold forth the glory of God in his attributes, the excellency of Christ in his nature and offices, and the power of the fulnesse of the Spirit in its workings and operations; and thereupon are inabled to cast the weight of their soules upon this truth thus beleeved.[5]

Boyce accepted the immediate, unilateral and absolute authority of the Bible. In speaking of the necessity of authoritative preaching, Boyce reminded a candidate for ministry of the increased efficiency of preaching when one remembers the character of Scripture as God's Word and treats it as such.

> It is not man only that tells of sin and offers a Savior; not man only that presents promises of acceptance through Christ; not man only that calls his fellows to repentance and trust in Jesus; not man only that invites to a life of full consecration to God, and gives assurances to help in the attempt to lead that life.

Rather, one must know that it is the voice of God and the invitation of Christ and the Holy Ghost "whose sword is thus unsheathed to convict of sin, of righteousness and of a judgment to come." God no more truly spoke to Christ at his baptism, nor to the apostles at the transfigura-

---

5   William L. Lumpkin, *Baptist Confessions of Faith* (Valley Forge: Judson Press, 1969), 162. Original spelling is retained.

tion, nor to the Jews at Pentecost, nor to Paul on the road to Damascus than he presently speaks his message "through the men of like passions with ourselves, through whom even in our day his gospel is preached unto their fellows."[6] Man's sinful condition, God's patience because of purposes of mercy, the fact and means of pardon for sin, the suitableness of Christ's person and work for such pardon, the universal rejection of the offer of pardon "anterior to God's compelling grace" and God's future purposes—all these are the statements of fact contained in and known only from divine revelation. The way in which they are applied for restoration of the divine image in sinners, that is, true piety, is also a matter of divine revelation.[7]

This Word of revelation, the Bible, is in one sense, the only means of sanctification and, therefore, of true holiness, true piety. All other means are not only secondary, "but actually subordinate means to the word of God." They furnish occasions for the more forceful application of truths revealed in the Word of God. Such are providence, afflictions, chastisement, dangers, good works, prayer, the Lord's Day, fellowship with other believers, the ministry and the ordinances. To each of these Boyce concedes nothing of intrinsic sanctifying power apart from their appointed connection with divine truth. As he said of the ministry so he said of all, "even these, though officially appointed, cannot either of themselves, or by virtue of their office, confer or increase spiritual grace."[8] He concluded his entire discussion of sanctification by reiterating that which he insisted on at each step along the way, "It is thus seen that all the means of sanctification are connected with the truth, and are secondary to it. They only become such, as they convey truth, or as they suggest truth, or as they are employed in the recognition of some truth."[9] The relationship of this to preaching seemed plain to Boyce: "Let the word of God, then, be simply declared, made known, spoken forth and such, and men called upon to receive it as such, and the most effective preaching must be attained."[10]

---

6 *Selected Writings*, 70.

7 Lumpkin, *Baptist Confessions of Faith*, 71.

8 James P. Boyce, *Abstract of Systematic Theology* (Philadelphia: American Baptist Publication Society, 1887), 420.

9 Boyce, *Abstract of Systematic Theology*, 425.

10 *Selected Writings*, 71.

But, as set forth clearly in the First London Confession just quoted, as well as the Charleston Confession ["Nevertheless we acknowledge the inward illumination of the Spirit of God, to be necessary for the saving understanding of such things as are revealed in the Word"] upon which Boyce cut his theological teeth, truth landing on rocky soil produces no fruit to holiness. The soil of the heart must be prepared, and that is the office of the Spirit. Boyce treated sanctification in the context of its being virtually an extension of regeneration. "In sanctification," Boyce wrote, "the Spirit moves as mysteriously as we are taught that he does in regeneration." And though it is done in accordance with the laws of mind and spiritual life, "we know no reason why there is not a place for supernatural action in sanctification as well as in regeneration."[11]

A man "must be rescued," it seems, "even to understand and appreciate the truth of God." The Spirit operates immediately on the heart, therefore, preparing the way for truth by recreating the affections, since "a new nature must be attained which will love and seek after holiness, and struggle forward, dissatisfied until it shall be perfected."[12] When one affirms, therefore, that the Word of God is the sword of the Spirit, he must understand that it is peculiarly so "to the heart prepared for it by his illuminating influences, which reveal its beauties and its suitableness, and by the aid of the memory which recalls, and the conscience which applies, and the affections which lay hold upon it."[13]

The expansive scope of piety—time and action

To the heart so prepared and continually conformed, joyfully and willingly, to the whole truth as well as the particular truths of Scripture, all of life becomes a gift from God, the personal property of the Christian, and an opportunity to give glory to him. That life is the property of the Christian means that every moment and aspect of life enters into the knowledge of God that one attains before entering into the eternal state. Boyce's early grasp of this in his Christian experience induced a time-intensive piety that was evident in his words and actions until death. The family of James P. Boyce lived somewhat under the pressure of

---

11 Boyce, *Abstract of Systematic Theology*, 417–418.

12 Boyce, *Abstract of Systematic Theology*, 411.

13 Boyce, *Abstract of Systematic Theology*, 376.

Boyce's keen sense of the value of time and noted "his anxiety always to be on time." "He never failed," so they recalled, "to be at an appointment some minutes before the time, watch in hand ready to pounce upon the tardy comer for his failure to come up to time."[14] It was also so in his classes and the latecomer feared the look of dissatisfaction on Boyce's face. His arrival at train stations an hour early, his starting for appointments to allow at least a quarter of an hour for possible delay, and his bag of reading material alongside to occupy any vacant minutes, arose not from any neurotic compulsion but from piety.

Boyce's piety emanated partly from his perception of how he saw time and life in relation to death and eternity. In an editorial entitled, "I Blot out a Day" on December 20, 1848, three weeks before his twenty-second birthday, Boyce contemplated the meaning of a day in the life of a Christian.[15] He called it a "Friend, a most precious friend of my best welfare" on an "errand of kindness" to provide a "longer probation, an opportunity to do something more for my own eternal welfare, something more for the eternal good of others." A day is an opportunity for improvement and usefulness that involved the active, busy, responsible existence of his soul. Though Boyce may blot it out on his calendar with the black marker he kept handy on his desk, the day now has a history and none of its events can he take back into non-existence—no emotion, no action, no word, all its facts stand to influence the next day for good or ill.

A well-spent day, Boyce urged, "augments the moral power of spending another day as well or better." On the other hand, a "mis-spent day weakens the power of principle, and increases the probability of another one being mis-spent." The indelible nature of each day's activities and the moral energy that is thrust into all future days does not end when the person's life ends but shall "live and come to meet me at the judgment."[16]

Boyce maintained this principle of accumulation in principles of holiness. One's works done as an expression of "life through the Spirit" naturally becomes "the means of further sanctification." Always in connection with the truth of God,

---

14 *Stray Recollections*, 6.

15 From November 1848 to May 1849, Boyce edited *The Southern Baptist*, a Baptist newspaper published in Charleston, South Carolina.

16 *Stray Recollections*, 33.

the new development will always be in the direction of the particular truths, contemplated in their performance. These will furnish the motives to further action, the strength for additional duty, the earnest purpose of deeper consecration, or whatever else the Spirit may graciously use for a more complete sanctification of the believer.[17]

The theme of time still haunted Boyce in his editorial for December 27, 1848, as he contemplated the end, not only of a day, but of a year. "How much has it assisted you to prepare for heaven?" he asked his readers. Did we regard it as precious time given to us, not for the acquisition of wealth, the pursuit of pleasure or the gratification of ambition, but to "prepare us for heaven, to enable us to assimilate ourselves to Christ, and to enforce upon us the fulfillment of our obligations to our heavenly Father." "The ticking of the clock beats the rapid march" with which the last hour of the year approaches. Its final days should be spent in "atoning for the past" by preparing for a more consistent future, engagement in serious self-examination and preparation to enter on the duties of the coming year, perhaps the last of our lives, with renewed energy.[18]

Obviously, Boyce could not avoid the same theme in the first article of the new year, on January 3, 1849, including in the second sentence the clause, "Let us be warned by the past to be more careful for the future" to be joined in intent with a phrase in the next sentence enjoining a review of the "mass of delinquencies" so that one would be the more "carefully, considerately, and determinedly" devoted to the service of the Lord. The turn of the calendar calls the Christian to conquer a besetting sin, perform acts of benevolence, grow in love for God and to a variety of duties "to the strict performance of which we are indebted for much of the happiness and still more of the piety which during the year may bless ourselves or those with whom we are associated."[19]

Matured by two more decades of life, war, work and theological reflection, this idea, more richly adorned but substantially unchanged, appeared in the funeral sermon for Manly. Contemplating the blessed-

---

17 Boyce, *Abstract of Systematic Theology*, 419–420.

18 *Stray Recollections*, 35.

19 *Stray Recollections*, 36.

ness of life itself for the Christian and special advantage of a long life, Boyce observed, "But this life is also seen to be the portion of the Christian from the fact that he carries it with him in all its entireness into the eternal world. Not a particle of it is left behind." The new life upon which the Christian enters is not stripped of those things that have constituted life here, but "we carry our past life with us, to be made a constituent part of that we are about to enjoy."[20] All of it, though perhaps forgotten by us, was hid with Christ in God and anew becomes our possession. Boyce envisioned a heavenly scene in its perfect intersection with the temporalities of earthly existence.

His crown is now studded with the stars placed there by his earthly labors. The garments which clothe him have been whitened by the blood of Christ, but they also mark the tribulations through which he has passed. The palms in his hand speak of the victories he had achieved. With all others, he casts all that he is and has at the feet of the Lamb, acknowledging that he has been rescued and purified and glorified only by His blood and His power and His grace. Yet it is in that life of earth thus translated to the skies that he is able to comprehend with all saints what is the breadth and length and depth and height of the love of Christ. For in it he sees himself a monument of grace, erected as a pillar in the house of God, to His infinite praise and glory.[21]

Given the issue of the use of time as a component of piety, it would come as no surprise that Boyce's piety was not quietistic, but activist. Activism as an element of piety appears throughout Puritan literature, and Boyce was a product of a Puritan worldview. Benjamin Keach's representation of the confrontation between true godliness and poverty shows how damning were sloth and lack of industry, not only in this life but in the life to come, in Puritan thinking.[22]

Very soon after his conversion, Boyce began his life of activity in defense of divine revelation, personal holiness and the efforts to see

---

20 *Selected Writings*, 129–130.

21 *Selected Writings*, 130.

22 Benjamin Keach, *The Travels of True Godliness* (Vestavia Hills: Solid Ground Christian Books, 2005), 75–95.

conversions. He spoke to Unitarians, Universalists and the spiritually careless, personally prayed for revival and urged his correspondents to do the same, as well as labour for the conversion of friends. During the spring of his senior year at Brown University, in 1847, numbers of conversions were reported. Boyce wrote his friend, H.A. Tupper, with a narrative of the most remarkable aspects of this movement and closed with this note:

> Never have I felt until this revival what a blessed privilege it is to save a soul. May my prayer evermore be to God that he may make me instrumental in his hands in the salvation of many! It is indeed a glorious and blessed privilege to labor in the vineyard of my Master.[23]

Little more than a year after his graduation, Boyce became editor of *The Southern Baptist*. His salutatory editorial made good on his earlier commitment to faithful labour and presented an outline of his ideal of Christian discipleship. He stated his intent to make the paper succeed and be useful in the lives of South Carolina Baptists by means of the "zeal, the industry, and the untiring perseverance which we are determined to give to the paper."[24]

Frequently, Boyce would point to the opportunities for fruitful labour that divine providence afforded Christians. With the opening of France to evangelical witness, Boyce urged "it becomes our duty to labor and toil. Our heavenly Father has work for us to do and how should we be straitened until it is done." In addition, one must not "overlook the many other interests which demand our care." With so many opportunities before the Christian, and those increasing continually, we must pray for "new motives to holy action."[25]

Among the many advantages that affliction offers the Christian, one must not overlook the opportunity for more extensive exertions of labour. When God removes pillars of the church by death, he not only consoles by his secret operations but calls the Christian to "labor

---

23 John A. Broadus, *Memoir of James Petigru Boyce* (New York: A.C. Armstrong & Son, 1893), 51.

24 *Stray Recollections*, 29.

25 *Stray Recollections*, 36.

earnestly, faithfully, diligently, that the place of the departed may not be unsupplied." He saw it as the duty of "everyone to strive to supply the place of a departed worthy. Let him labor as if God had appointed him to that work, and as though he was looked to for its due performance." If in the death of one, twenty come to life in genuine labours, how would that brighten the prospects of a Christian in leaving this world? "Let us then work while it is day," Boyce called; "work not without interest nor without fear—but as those who have a work to do, and who are straitened until it is accomplished." With a call to action, Boyce closed, "Wake up Israel—Zion awake. Put on the full armour of God, and fight valiantly for his cause."[26]

The close of the second session of the The Southern Baptist Theological Seminary in June 1861,[27] coincided with the first months of the Civil War and offered an unusual opportunity for students to trade one kind of labour for another—a "recreation from study" as Boyce called it, "a period of rest in labor in which you seek recreation for the wanted energies of student life, to other forms of activity for God." The best rest, so Boyce taught, was not a cessation of activity, "absolute inaction," but rest obtained by a "change in the direction of activity." He commended to them, therefore, labours in ministry of various sorts. Again employing the phrase "rest in labor" Boyce said that the period of vacation afforded an opportunity to "unbend the energies already overstrung" and engage in that work that, according to "the wish of the founders of this institution," should constitute a part of the training of its students, that is, "active personal labor as colporteurs, missionaries, and in other ways."[28]

According to Boyce, the unparalleled labours of the young Kingman Nott should inspire each of the students. He employed his vacations from study in ceaseless labours in "places where others had long labored and gathered in no fruit." Nott, however, by God's grace found his labours fruitful. In 1857, he succeeded Spencer Cone as pastor of First Baptist Church in New York City but he died within two years. Nott's soul had been strengthened and his character

---

26 *Stray Recollections*, 39.

27 Boyce was instrumental in the founding of The Southern Baptist Theological Seminary in 1859 and was one of its four original faculty members.

28 *Stray Recollections*, 113.

moulded by such labours and, though "cut off prematurely, as man judges, in the very vigor of incipient manhood, left behind him a record which may awaken thousands of others to the same labors and to like eminent usefulness." Wistfully, Boyce concluded his reference to Nott, "Would that the spirit of such a laborer might be found in every one connected in every way with this Seminary, in the past, the present, or the future."[29]

Boyce believe that "the pious heart" could not rest short of a "consecration of constant service to God." The object of the glory of God and the salvation of man is enough to enforce such claims. A person of genuine piety "longs daily to do some work for" God, and, returning to a theme of thirteen years earlier, "reviewing every day thus unblessed," would exclaim, "I have lost a day."[30]

Such labours for the divine glory are the proper operations of the human will and human energy. Boyce, of course, never viewed these labours apart from divine sovereignty expressed through decree and the co-temporal divine empowerment in every movement of the human will, thought of the human mind and action of the human body. Our present sanctification and eventual perfection in holiness comes by the operation of the triune God; he secures the final result and "the eternal purpose of God with respect to it shall assuredly be attained."[31]

That divine immanence and operation, however, does not make the labour any less ours. In his funeral sermon for Basil Manly Sr., Boyce viewed the human and the divine as necessarily united. Speaking of the Christian, Boyce said,

His life is also to be his own creation. Upon what he does is his growth to depend. He is himself to work out his own salvation. And the position that he shall occupy hereafter is determined by his position here—by the spirituality he attains, the knowledge he acquires, the intimacy of his communion with God, and the spirit of activity and sacrifice he exhibits.[32]

---

29 *Stray Recollections*, 116.
30 *Stray Recollections*, 117.
31 *Selected Writings*, 128.
32 *Selected Writings*, 128.

The work of man determines his future reward from the standpoint of differentiations that will exist in eternity. "God works as though man had nothing to do, and requires man to work as though God had left him to himself." Though God overrules everything as to its final result, an elemental aspect of the operation of grace in many of its outcomes is the coincident operation of human effort and human freedom. "According to his toils and cares, his sufferings and trials, his temptations and struggles, his yearnings after and prayers to God, and in all of these according to the use he makes of such opportunities in life, is the reward which God gives."[33]

Boyce described the journey of the Christian pilgrim with an emotion and perception that must have arisen from an existential immediacy. The Christian's experience of being swallowed up in the difficulty and turmoil of each successive path often renders any awareness of progress, any sense of difference from former days and ways, murky and indistinct; yet on he goes, secretly sustained by grace though often shut up in darkness. Then comes the end, and Boyce described how death belongs to the Christian as the end of a life in which God's "magic power...invigorates our wearied limbs" and "makes firm our tottering steps."[34]

> The Christian arrives at his heavenly home, humbled because of his life, glorying only in Christ. He knows that he has no merit, He feels that, with his best efforts, he is but unprofitable. He is ready to ascribe all to God. The life he has lived he feels to have been too unworthy of the grace he has received. The language of his heart is, "I am not worthy to be called Thy son." But he finds the countenance of his Savior filled with joy, because of the life, which the soul crucified with Him and in whom He has lived, has been able to live in the flesh by the faith of the Son of God. He learns how God had made him his co-worker to this end; and as he looks back upon the life he has achieved, he perceives how truly that life has been to him a blessed portion bestowed by God.[35]

---

33 *Selected Writings*, 128.

34 *Selected Writings*, 129.

35 *Selected Writings*, 129.

James Petigru Boyce
1827–1888

So it was with Boyce as he took his final steps toward death. Lizzie Boyce, the eldest of three Boyce daughters recorded the brief interview that Boyce had with Charles Spurgeon just weeks before Boyce's labours ceased. After exchanges about their common malady, gout, and an invitation from Spurgeon to speak at the Pastors' College, Lizzie recalled, "Father was so much excited by this interview with the great preacher that he became pale and exhausted." Upon leaving to return to the hotel, Boyce, with eyes filled with tears said, "How little I have accomplished compared with that man. If I can only get well and live a few years longer, I'll make greater efforts."[36] To Boyce this was a resolution of unvarnished piety.

The life of the mind In the presence of means

Boyce's activism, however, by no means precluded the conviction that genuine holiness and piety was enhanced by a robust life of meditation. Boyce would have the Christian gain confidence through pondering the infinitely transcendent wisdom of divine providence, the majestic and mysterious reality of the Saviour's person and the completeness of his redemptive work; he would have us grow in humility by meditating on the utter freeness of grace; he would have us abandon ourselves to service by embracing Christ's infinite condescension in the incarnation; and he would have us embrace death as ours by viewing it as a door into the presence of God.

By the contemplation of death, God "draws the soul away from this world and ripens it for heaven." It seems that God forces this contemplation of death on us in virtually every aspect of the Christian life. Adam's sin brought death, regeneration finds us dead in trespasses and sins; the law as a covenant, brings death, and to escape its curse we must become dead to it by the death of Christ. To follow Christ we must be crucified to the world, and our public profession of faith is a symbol of our death in Christ and our resurrection from the dead. The supper is a memorial of the death of Christ, a memorial of his ultimate humiliation to be celebrated until he comes again.[37]

These divinely instituted points of meditation on death show that the "contemplation of death is one of the most potent means of

---

36 *Stray Recollections*, 21.
37 *Selected Writings*, 132–133.

advancing the Christian's life and securing his happiness." What is gained in such meditation?

> It is thus that we are led never to forget that we are pilgrims and strangers, who have no abiding city, and hence are induced to seek the citizenship that is in heaven. It is thus that eternity is kept ever before us, that in the remembrance of it we may be diligent in the earthly kingdom of our Lord. It is thus that amid our trials and sufferings we may be consoled by their short duration. It is thus that amid persecutions for righteousness' sake we should not forget the future Judge that will avenge, yea, even the Savior that endured. It is thus that sin is restrained by the beatific visions that are called to mind. It is thus that the ties that bind to earth are broken, and the affections are set on Christ above. It is thus that the soul is taught to yearn for that life into which shall come no sorrow, and which shall have no end in death. It is thus that God alone is felt to be the satisfying portion of the soul.[38]

The contemplation of death necessarily involves the contemplation of affliction in this life. As a young editor, Boyce could write about the "Blessedness of Affliction" to prompt his readers to consider "how truly blessed are those who suffer under the afflicting hand of God." If any situation provides an opportunity for Satan to prompt the Christian to stagger at the biblical affirmation of the goodness of God, it will be in times of great affliction when he can encourage an inclination "to feel a disposition to murmur against the dispensations of Providence." These afflictions, however, when they have finished their proper work, draw us near to God, remove from us worldly hearts "so much at variance with his service" and, by this divine chastening, in the absence of earthly comfort, we find ourselves drawn nearer to the heavenly Comforter and into more "intimate union with Christ."[39]

The submission to affliction in reverential fear for the sake of greater piety arises from an enlarged vision of the providence of God and his good intentions for his people. This vision is ineluctably Trinitarian, as no action of God can be so reduced as to exclude any person of the

---

38 *Selected Writings*, 133.
39 *Stray Recollections*, 37.

Trinity from some operation as cause and receiver of glory as the ultimate effect. God's purposes are inseparably connected with innumerable secondary causes in which each individual Christian stands as though "for himself alone had God created or ruled the universe or sent forth His Son to redeem." All things happen for each one. "All the purposes and acts of God, which respect either the future or the past, are concentrated on each one, as though there were no other."[40]

Afflictions and infirmities carry no punishment for the Christian but rather a cleansing and chastening effect from the hands of a loving Father. Such fatherly affection comes to us by the blood of Christ that has removed punishment from our afflictions, but are given so that by "godly exercises he may grow up unto the full stature of a man in Christ Jesus." Grace is bestowed, and "the Holy Spirit dwells within the hearts, sanctifying by its presence and leading on to the perfection, which it is God's purpose" that the Christian "shall finally attain."[41]

This emphasis on the sanctifying presence of the Spirit of God recalls again the consideration of Boyce's substantial emphasis on the work of the Spirit in the Christian life. Equally important with the love of the Father in giving his only begotten Son, and the love of the Son in laying down his life, so must we contemplate the greatness of the love "which the Holy Spirit bears toward our race." Boyce, writing at twenty-one years of age, believed that "the love of the Spirit has been a theme untouched." If God is love, why do we not recognize that the Spirit shares that attribute equally with the Father and the Son? We should praise the Spirit for his love no less that we praise the Father and the Son. "Why do we neglect," Boyce asked, "to praise that Spirit by whom Christ is made known and enforced upon our unwilling hearts until we are convicted, converted, and sanctified as His followers?" When the gifts of Christ are bestowed on us, it is right that we should praise and thank Christ, but is it right that we should neglect to praise and thank the Spirit "who has bestowed it so freely on us?"[42]

The greatest mystery, in fact, connected with the union of God with man, and the greatest act of condescension consummates, neither in the presence of the Shekinah glory in the tabernacle, nor in the divine

---

40 *Selected Writings*, 126.
41 *Selected Writings*, 127.
42 *Stray Recollections*, 51–52.

Son's assumption of human nature, but in the Holy Spirit's indwelling of sinful humanity. Certainly the way for this was prepared by the removal of guilt through Christ's atonement, through the imputation of his righteousness, and indeed by the whole work of the One who of God is made unto us wisdom righteousness, sanctification and redemption. And, in the sacrifice of the Saviour, more of love and grace may be evident, but "neither in the incarnation itself, nor in the former indwelling of God with man, do we see such depth of condescension as in the indwelling of the Holy Ghost." Christ took to himself a sinless human nature, but the Spirit condescends to dwell *within* sinful human individuals and be the agent that wars against the remnants of sin yet within them.[43]

The implications of this for holy living, in Boyce's estimation, are enormous. The indwelling of the Spirit suggests, according to the apostle, that "we should eschew all defilement of our bodies." The Christian must consistently make his body a more fit residence for its heavenly visitor. Moreover, we should learn to recognize that our fellow Christians are temples of the Holy Spirit.

And while we learn to love them for the fruits they display, we would be shirking from offending them, from doing them any injury, from exercising toward them any malice for injuries received. Because with all its deformity, we behold a temple of God, sanctified to us by its holy inhabitant.[44]

The Son of Man

Given all the elements of the human and the divine in the production of piety in God's chosen, Boyce pointed to one fact as the quintessential marker of God's paradigm of piety—the incarnation. The mystery of the union of the human and divine in the person of Jesus Christ offered to Boyce the most delightful hours of contemplation and theological and ethical rigour throughout his life. The first article he published after his initial salutatory as editor of *The Southern Baptist*, entitled "Purity of Heart," pointed to Christ as the ultimate exemplar of genuine purity of heart. Boyce began,

---

43 *Selected Writings*, 119–120.
44 *Selected Writings*, 120.

> If there were no other proof of the divinity of Christ's mission, we would find it in the unearthly doctrines which he taught. Himself a pattern of purity, without an unchaste thought or an unholy motive, he taught his disciples to look upon purity of heart as one of the most desirable of attainments.[45]

The world does not know this nor relish this. Neither purity nor the sight of God has any attraction to the one whose pleasures and fears are derived from this present order. But to others, "there is a sacred pleasure, as well as a holy fear, in beholding God. God is to him, the image after which he would be formed, and he delights in the opportunity to behold the noble majesty of the perfect model," that is, Jesus Christ. "He knows that to see Him is to be made like unto Him, and there is nothing greater that he can desire." But who is the man that so loves purity of heart and has attained it? To be pure in the sight of God, "is to be pure as He is pure, in whom was found no guile. It is to be pure as He was pure who knew no sin. It is to be pure as He was into whose heart never entered the least sinful thought, or the least unholy desire." You are pure in this way only if Christ's own purity and righteousness are imputed to you. Union with Christ comes to those that are "actuated in all things by the propelling influences of God's grace." Those that have such grace will humble themselves at the throne of grace, and ask for a more abundant manifestation of his glory, that they "may be made the more earnest in His cause and the more devoted in His service."[46]

A sermon on the prayers of Jesus investigated this phenomenon of Christ's humanity as a model for ours in encouraging us to rely on prayer as Christ did. Boyce preached that Christ really did rely on the aid afforded him in his human nature by prayer. "As a man he calls upon God for aid and receives it according to human conditions." From this, Boyce deduced that no life can ever be lived successfully apart from prayer because of our weakness and dependence. Whatever our

> spiritual endowments, though the Spirit were given to us also without measure, still we are not above the necessity of prayer.

---

45 *Stray Recollections*, 31.
46 *Stray Recollections*, 31–32.

It is only thus that we can meet the power of the tempter. Thus only that we can live a worthy life in the performance of that work which God has given us to do.[47]

Thirteen years later, as Boyce bid farewell to the seminary students after the second session at the newly-minted seminary, he speculated whether some might soon be ministering in the war camps. Any to whom this opportunity comes "must maintain a life of unexampled piety, of super-human devotion to God, accompanied by habits of genial intercourse, by which, as it was in the life of the Great Teacher, the religion of Christ will be commended." Boyce then described the perfect integration of spiritual attributes that such delicate yet masculine ministry demanded.

Grave yet not austere; pleasant and genial, yet free from levity; instant in season and out of season, and yet not unseasonable; in his labors ever watchful for opportunities of doing good, yet seeming never, unwelcomed, to thrust in religion; subject to the neglect, the scorn, perhaps the hatred of those whom he came to bless; peculiarly liable to temptation, yet living among those who would be ever alive to the slightest faults, word or action, of omitted duty or committed sin—frequently misconceived after all and blamed for acts which deserve the highest praise and gratitude of his accusers—as the mind dwells upon the requirements of such a position, it is impressed with the fact, that never, save in one man, and he the sinless, perfect one, were combined the needed qualification. The more readily his example can be imitated; his temper caught and displayed; his love even for those who despised and injured him, cherished; and above all, that spirit of prayer exercised which kept him ever in communion with God, the more possible will it be to perform its arduous duties.[48]

Nineteen years later in an address to Southwestern Baptist University in Jackson, Tennessee, Boyce delivered a lecture entitled, "The Christian Ethical System; Its Nature, its basis, its exemplar, and The

---

47 *Selected Writings*, 104–105.
48 *Stray Recollections*, 114–115.

motives to its obedience." He spoke first of the nature of the ethical system showing that it went beyond simple justice or natural law and, in viewing the gospel as its driving force, surrenders rights to others and views oneself as a debtor to the world in spiritual matters. A comparison of Christianity with the ethics of the most venerated and venerable religions on earth have "only ended in proving the immeasurable superiority of its precepts."[49]

The basis on which this rests is what Boyce called the "voluntary nature of God." He does not deny that God's moral attributes are necessary, immutable and eternal. The gospel, however, though perfectly consistent with those eternal attributes of justice and holiness arises from something in the nature of God beyond that. "And as that which is voluntarily done can be known only by the declarations and the actions of the one willing," Boyce reasoned, "it was essential that God should reveal Himself in the character He would assume."[50]

From Old Testament to New Testament, the revelation gains clarity. Within the Old, mysterious assertions of the New appear, until within the teaching and the person and the actions of the Son of God, both the necessary and voluntary character of God have their full expression. "It is Jesus that has thus revealed God unto us." Boyce's narrative cannot disguise the sheer delight that he felt in such revelation.

> He who is in the bosom of the Father hath taught us what He is. It is the peculiarity of Christianity that its founder has thus made God known.... The duties he enjoins find their counterpart in the acts and revealed character of God and give force to the injunction, "Be ye therefore perfect, even as your father which is in heaven is perfect" [Matthew 5:48].[51]

But can the finite resemble the infinite, and the creature the Creator? Both the moral law and the voluntary standard of ethics "have been embodied in a perfect human example," that is, in the life of Jesus. Drawing upon his full commitment to historic Christological orthodoxy, Boyce sketched the picture, "Possessed of full divinity—so

---

49 *Stray Recollections*, 172.
50 *Stray Recollections*, 172–175.
51 *Stray Recollections*, 175–176.

that as the one in the bosom of the Father he has revealed him, he has also perfect humanity so that in his human nature he can set forth a perfect human example to us."[52]

Boyce continually insisted that the Christian not diminish the importance of Christ's humanity. Neither redemption nor righteousness is available without it, and apart from it, the injunction to be perfect as the heavenly Father is perfect becomes a pure chimera.[53] "He no more truly reveals the perfect God than He does the perfect man," Boyce repeated. Then after an extended recitation of the depths of compassion demonstrated by the human Jesus in his human relations under literally excruciating events, he inquired, "Where can you find such a character? Where could such a life be depicted with any appearance of reality save in Him? Where has there been such indication of that higher nature of God upon which Christian ethics are based?" This perfection brought salvation to sinners—none but Christ could do it—and at the same time established a picture of godliness, that, though not innately within the grasp of any of the sons of Adam produced by ordinary generation, is nevertheless the legitimate goal of any person made in the image of God. "No such character was ever innate and natural save in Jesus," Boyce declared. Nevertheless, "the perfect pattern of Christian ethics may be imitated and approached with increasing perfection by those who can do all things through Christ which strengtheneth them [Philippians 4:13]."[54]

When Edwin Arnold sought to argue that the ethical system presented in the life of Gautama, founder of Buddhism, matched that of Christ, Boyce could barely restrain himself to civility in investigating the claim and comparing the two men. At one point in the description of the life of Gautama, Boyce retorted, "How unworthy is one capable of such ignorance to be compared with him who saw Nathanael under the fig tree."[55]

After a noble attempt at close analysis, one pursued under the conviction that "the inferiority of Gautama and his ethical system, to Christ and his can be easily shown," Boyce minted a striking description of Christ:

---

52 *Stray Recollections*, 176.

53 Or illusion.

54 *Stray Recollections*, 176–181.

55 *Stray Recollections*, 180.

[Jesus] was no monk, no ascetic; so far from this his enemies actually reproached him because he ate the ordinary food and lived the customary life of men. He sought to prepare men to preach the glad tidings he had come to proclaim. He held familiar intercourse with them. He made known to them his human side, even in its weaknesses. He taught them constantly truth which he knew, not what he was seeking, and thus prepared them to go forth and teach others the lessons given them by their Great Teacher. His was a work of ministration not of meditation.

Then, within a substantial series of epitomized summaries of the actions and attitudes of Jesus, Boyce triumphed,

I contend therefore, none can see the resemblance of Gautama to Jesus save those whose ideas of Christian sanctity and holy life have been affected by the glamour of monkery and of mendicant hermit life.

Finishing his condensed recitation of Jesus' excellencies in his earthly life, Boyce noted that Jesus

was no selfwrapt, inward looking, world forgetting, pain despising, or piteously whining, dried up, sanctimonious, secluded separatist from his fellow men. He lived in them and with them, as he lived for them, that they also might not only live for him, but in him and with him.[56]

Then, in consideration of this highest possible life that was a demonstration of the most immaculate, far-reaching ethic and finally given in the blood drenched cross for the salvation of his fellow men and at the same time his sinful creatures, Boyce urged the implications.

Here, more than all elsewhere, we see the spirituality of the law, here the duty to pardon offenses, the refusal to avenge, the love for enemies, the blessing of those that despitefully use and persecute. Here is the motive to service to others, and of that service

---

56 *Stray Recollections*, 179–182.

not only to the good and gentle but even to the forward. From what standpoint too could sympathy go out so worldwide, and readiness to labour for every creature, so well as from that cross where the redeeming work for mankind was accomplished? When could we love more than when standing in the shadow of his love? When sacrifice more than when the very ground we tread is reddened with the mingled water and blood that came from his flowing side? [57]

Conclusion

In conclusion, I shall attempt a definition of piety based on the observations of James P. Boyce:

> *Piety consists of a life of worship characterized by increasing conformity in heart and actions to Christ as Son of Man, manifesting the mercies of God as experienced in redemption, under the holy and effectual influence of the Spirit of God, through the means of revealed truth, in anticipation of eternal life that overflows to the glory and praise of God.*

---

57 *Stray Recollections*, 184.

BAPTISTS

A gregarious spirituality: the personal piety of Charles H. Spurgeon

By Donald S. Whitney

ACCORDING TO THE late Carl F.H. Henry, American theologian and founding editor of *Christianity Today*, "Charles Haddon Spurgeon (1834–1892) is one of evangelical Christianity's immortals."[1] The purpose of this chapter is to examine the personal spirituality of this immeasurably influential preacher. Spurgeon is one of church history's most iconic preachers, but what about the piety behind the pulpit presence? Spurgeon was a breathtakingly busy man who, although he ministered in Victorian London, lived at a pace of life recognizable to contemporary readers. And yet, in the midst of the pressure of unending responsibilities and ever-looming deadlines, he maintained a consistent,[2] vibrant, gregarious spirituality.

Priority

Spurgeon manifested such an effervescent piety because his relationship with his God was at the pinnacle of his priorities. His piety was

---

1 Lewis A. Drummond, "Charles Haddon Spurgeon" in *Baptist Theologians*, ed. Timothy George and David Dockery (Nashville: Broadman, 2000), 11.

2 Consistent, that is, except for the noteworthy exceptions of the depressive aftermath of the Surrey Gardens Music Hall disaster and the episodic depression related to his health issues.

the means by which he cultivated and experienced the reality of the divine/human relationship, and so nothing was more important to him. "The chief element of Spurgeon's entire career," Arnold Dallimore declares, "was his walk with God."[3] When it came to the exercise of his pastoral influence, he must at times have felt the temptation to rely on his extraordinary gifts, his exceptional mental faculties and his abundant stock of tangible resources instead of those that were the fruit of his spiritual piety. Nevertheless, he recognized:

> It will be in vain for me to stock my library, or organize societies, or project schemes, if I neglect the culture of myself; for books, and agencies, and systems, are only remotely the instruments of my holy calling; my own spirit, soul, and body, are my nearest machinery for sacred service; my spiritual faculties, and my inner life, are my battle axe and weapons of war.[4]

Spurgeon believed this same priority of piety held true for every minister. At the very outset of his published lectures to his Pastors' College students, he mandated for them what he had found essential for himself: "True and genuine piety is necessary as the first indispensable requisite; whatever 'call' a man may pretend to have, if he has not been called to holiness, he certainly has not been called to the ministry."[5] Moments later in the same lecture, he reiterated the precedence of piety, both for their personal lives and their ministry effectiveness:

> Recollect, as ministers, that your whole life, your whole pastoral life especially, will be affected by the vigor of your piety. If your zeal grows dull, you will not pray well in the pulpit; you will pray worse in the family, and worst in the study alone. When your soul becomes lean, your hearers, without knowing how or why, will find that your prayers in public have little savor for them; they will feel your barrenness, perhaps, before you perceive it

---

3 Arnold Dallimore, *Spurgeon* (Chicago: Moody Press, 1987), 177.

4 Charles H. Spurgeon, *Lectures to My Students*, 4 vols. (1881; reprint, Pasadena: Pilgrim Publications, 1990), 1:2.

5 Spurgeon, *Lectures to My Students*, 1:3.

yourself. Your discourses will next betray your declension. You may utter as well-chosen words, and as fitly-ordered sentences, as aforetime; but there will be a perceptible loss of spiritual force. You will shake yourselves as at other times, even as Samson did, but you will find that your great strength has departed. In your daily communion with your people, they will not be slow to mark the all-pervading decline of your graces.[6]

Christocentric

Knowing Christ and being conformed to Christ were the passions that propelled Spurgeon's devotion. "Spurgeon saw in Jesus Christ spirituality exemplified," writes Lewis Drummond. "The Lord...became Spurgeon's model and the pattern for true spirituality.... His entire spiritual experience was predicated upon a personal experience of Christ as grasped in the Scriptures."[7]

Spurgeon's Christocentricity was a primary characteristic not only of his personal spirituality, but also of all his preaching and publishing, and of all his educational and social ministries. These were, to Spurgeon, expressions of his affection for Christ and of his desire that through these things others might know Christ. There is no evidence that Spurgeon, through these many activities, was attempting to build a personal empire, or that he thought he could earn God's favour or gain acceptance into heaven through his many contributions to society.[8] So even though the number and scope of Spurgeon's enterprises was remarkably expansive, they were uniformly focused on knowing Christ and making him known. Thus, in a sense, the breadth of Spurgeon's endeavours reflects the gregarious nature of his own personality, and their coherent focus on the edification of Christians and the evangelization of non-Christians echoes the motivations of his own Christ-centred piety.

---

6 Spurgeon, *Lectures to My Students*, 1:9–10.

7 Lewis A. Drummond, *Spurgeon: Prince of Preachers* (Grand Rapids: Kregel, 1992), 570.

8 His bestselling book, *All of Grace*, would serve as one of many pieces of evidence contrary to the notion that Spurgeon believed he would merit a place in heaven because of his manifold accomplishments.

God the source

Despite the intensity of his devotion, Spurgeon did not believe his spiritual inclination was the natural propensity of his own personality. Very soon after his conversion on a snowy day in January 1850, young Spurgeon attributed his Godward orientation to the grace of God, a grace mediated to him through the Scriptures:

> Well can I remember the manner in which I learned the doctrines of grace in a single instant.... When I was coming to Christ, I thought I was doing it all myself, and though I sought the Lord earnestly, I had no idea the Lord was seeking me. I do not think the young convert is at first aware of this. I can recall the very day and hour when first I received those truths in my own soul—when they were, as John Bunyan says, burnt into my heart as with a hot iron.... One week-night, when I was sitting in the house of God, ...the thought struck me, "How did you come to be a Christian?" I sought the Lord. "But how did you come to seek the Lord?" The truth flashed across my mind in a moment,—I should not have sought Him unless there had been some previous influence in my mind to make me seek Him. I prayed, thought I; but then I asked myself, "How came I to pray?" I was induced to pray by reading the Scriptures. "How came I to read the Scriptures?" I did read them; but what led me to do so? Then, in a moment, I saw that God was at the bottom of it all, and that He was the Author of my faith; and so the whole doctrine of grace opened up to me, and from that doctrine I have not departed to this day, and I desire to make this my constant confession, "I ascribe my change wholly to God."[9]

Spurgeon's view is sharply differentiated from the theology of spirituality that assumes that each human has, in his or her natural condition, an innate capacity to experience God by some means of self-effort. He rejected views of humanity wherein, as an advocate described it, "the presumption is that God is already within the soul...the eternal

---

9   C.H. Spurgeon, *C.H. Spurgeon's Autobiography: Volume 1: The Early Years, 1834–1859*, comp. Susannah Spurgeon and Joseph Harrald (1897–1900; rev. ed., Edinburgh: The Banner of Truth Trust, 1962), 164–165.

deity within each individual soul,"[10] awaiting discovery by the person's consciousness. Similarly, Spurgeon opposed the teaching popularized by those such as Quaker founder George Fox who believed that a divine "spark" or light is a constituent part of the composition of *Homo sapiens*, and that he "was commanded to turn people to that inward Light, Spirit, and Grace, by which all might know their salvation and their way to God; even that Divine Spirit which would lead them into all truth, and which I infallibly knew would never deceive any."[11] To the degree that the literature on Christian spirituality uses terms such as "ladder," "ascent," "climbing," etc., to optimistically refer to an intrinsic desire and ability of people to pursue a relationship with God, Spurgeon dismissed it as unscriptural and overly reliant upon human initiative. In summary, while he emphasized the responsibility of a individual to seek God, and the indispensability of a person's repenting of sin and believing in the gospel of Jesus Christ in order to know God, nevertheless Spurgeon maintained that the entire process of coming into a relationship with God—including these essential components—was *All of Grace*.[12]

The Bible

While he believed that God was both the source and goal of his piety, the unquestioned guide and authority for Spurgeon's piety, and indeed for all aspects of his life, was the Bible. Although he read widely and voluminously, no book rivalled the preeminence he gave to the Bible. He believed it to be the self-revelation of God, and that not only the ideas contained in the Bible, but the very words of Scripture were inspired by the Holy Spirit, and thus without error in all they intend to convey.[13] The Down Grade Controversy makes clear that Spurgeon

---

10 Michael Cox, *Handbook of Christian Spirituality* (New York: Harper and Row, 1983), 22.

11 George Fox, *The Journal of George Fox* (Richmond: Friends United Press, 1976), 101.

12 C.H. Spurgeon, *All of Grace: An Earnest Word with Those Who Are Seeking Salvation by the Lord Jesus Christ* (1892; reprint, New York: Fleming H. Revell Company, n.d.).

13 Spurgeon's beliefs about the inspiration of the Bible may be found in many places, but two of the most extensive treatments are in C.H. Spurgeon, "The Bible," in *The New Park Street Pulpit*, 6 vols. (1855–1860; reprint, Pasadena: Pilgrim Publications, 1981f), 1:109–116 and C.H. Spurgeon, "The Bible Tried and Proved," in *The Metropolitan*

was certainly not unaware of other views regarding the inspiration of Scripture;[14] he simply was not persuaded by them. He considered the Bible to be the terminus of divine revelation, and could not accept the belief promulgated by many Quakers in his day, that "the same Spirit that gave forth the Scriptures could lead the faithful into new truth,"[15] that is, that "revelation was not closed nor confined to Scripture."[16] To the end of his life he never wavered from the bibliology with which he had begun his ministry.[17] A very personal glimpse into how Spurgeon prized Scripture is provided by James J. Ellis:

> The following sentences are written in Mr. Spurgeon's study Bible: "C.H. Spurgeon. 1856. The lamp of my study."
> "The light is bright as ever! 1861."
> "Oh, that mine eyes were more opened! 1864."
> "Being worn to pieces, rebound 1870. The lantern mended, and the light as joyous to mine eyes as ever!"[18]

Perhaps these personal exclamations, hidden away in the Bible he kept in his study, may tell almost as much about his view of Scripture as

---

Tabernacle Pulpit, 57 vols. (vol. 7–63) (1861–1917; reprint, Pasadena: Pilgrim Publications, 1981f), 35:253–264.

14 Although Spurgeon was brilliant, widely-read, and exceptionally self-taught, he was not a trained academic. So he did not evaluate the textual nuances of the various views of inspiration as an expert in the biblical languages, but he was not unskilled in Hebrew and Greek. W.Y. Fullerton provides an interesting anecdote on this point, referring to "Dr. William Wright of the Bible Society, formerly of Damascus, himself a scholar," who observed Spurgeon preparing sermons with lexicons of the biblical languages adjacent to his Bible. W.Y. Fullerton, *C.H. Spurgeon: A Biography* (London: Williams and Norgate, 1920), 198.

15 Michael Birkel, "Quaker Spirituality," in Philip Sheldrake, ed., *The New Westminster Dictionary of Christian Spirituality* (Louisville: Westminster/John Knox Press, 2005), 522.

16 Carole Spencer, "Quaker Spirituality," in *Dictionary of Christian Spirituality*, ed. Glen Scorgie, Simon Chan, Gordon T. Smith and James D. Smith III (Grand Rapids: Zondervan, 2011), 705.

17 Note that regarding the two sermons about the Bible cited in the footnote above, the former is from Spurgeon's very first volume of sermons preached in London, and the latter was published just two years prior to his death.

18 James J. Ellis, *Charles Haddon Spurgeon* (London: James Nisbet & Co., 1892), 145.

any of the sermons he wrote to be examined by the thousands who regularly read his publications. It is also revealing that the initial entry was written by a zealous young man of twenty-two, and yet the final one, penned by a hard-working, ministry-seasoned pastor of thirty-six, reflects an equally high regard for the Book.

Spurgeon, like the biblical Timothy, had "from childhood...been acquainted with the sacred writings" (2 Timothy 3:15). There was no significant formative influence on Spurgeon as a child or youth who did not cherish the Bible, and as he grew he accepted without reservation the teachings of the Bible as true. So by the time Spurgeon was just sixteen, and preaching regularly but not yet pastoring at Waterbeach, the basic contours of his daily personal piety were already formed. For as biographer W.Y. Fullerton said of him in those days: "In the early morning he was up praying and reading the Bible" before school.[19]

Few knew Spurgeon as well as G. Holden Pike, who worked closely with him for three decades. It was Pike who maintained that recognizing the centrality of Scripture to Spurgeon's spirituality is essential for all who attempt to understand the preacher and his piety:

> The fact of his being mighty in the Scriptures...was a characteristic of which particular notice had to be taken by anyone who wished to understand Spurgeon.... The habit of diligently reading the Bible, which he no doubt acquired while living under the care of his aunt and grandfather at Stambourne, was continued throughout his busy life. Even among great preachers, a man has rarely been found who knew the Scriptures so thoroughly as Spurgeon.[20]

But an analysis of additional literature by and about Spurgeon indicates that Pike failed to mention one important aspect of Spurgeon's approach to Scripture: meditation. Spurgeon did not merely read the Bible, he also meditated on it. His keen grasp of Scripture and the impact it had upon him was not attained by reading alone,

---

19 Fullerton, *Spurgeon: A Biography*, 47.
20 G. Holden Pike, *The Life and Work of Charles Haddon Spurgeon*, 6 vols. (1894; reprint, Pasadena: Pilgrim Publications, 1991), 5:79.

nor could it be explained by much reading and the constant study of the Bible which his many preaching responsibilities necessitated. Instead one must also factor into these spiritual habits Spurgeon's practice of meditation on Scripture. He referred to such meditation as "holy thought," the "fresh fuel" with which "the flame of zeal in the renewed heart…must be continually fed."[21]

For Spurgeon, the "holy thought" which constituted his discipline of Scripture meditation assumed two primary forms: direct and indirect. The direct method was simply to meditate upon a particular biblical text or a scriptural principle. If there was a specific or consistent structure to Spurgeon's thought patterns as he meditated on a phrase or verse from the Bible, he did not disclose it. In other words, he left no record of any particular method or process that he followed when he would meditate on Scripture. His extraordinary facility for the use of imagery in his speaking and writing, however, argues for an unusually active imagination at work when he was engaged in meditation on Scripture. Regardless of his methodology, the principle of Christ-centredness in his piety remains constant in this aspect of Spurgeon's piety as well, as indicated by this exhortation to meditation:

> Long more and more to see Jesus. *Meditation*…[is] often like windows of agate, and gates of carbuncle, through which we behold the Redeemer. Meditation puts the telescope to the eye, and enables us to see Jesus after a better sort than we could have seen him if we had lived in the days of his flesh. Would that our conversation were more in heaven, and that we were more taken up with the person, the work, the beauty of our incarnate Lord. More meditation and the beauty of the King would flash upon us with more resplendence.[22]

Spurgeon's indirect method of meditation consisted of his habit of considering how something related to or conveyed biblical truth. He believed that almost everything could be used to illustrate something from Scripture, and hardly a paragraph passed from his pulpit or pen

---

21 Spurgeon, *Lectures to My Students*, 2:155.

22 C.H. Spurgeon, "November 16, Evening," in *Morning and Evening* (1868; reprint, Peabody: Hendrickson, 1995), 643.

without such a comparison. He did this occasionally by means of a brief anecdote, but most commonly by metaphor or simile. For instance, in a sermon where he mentioned John Bunyan, Spurgeon exclaimed, "Why, this man is a living Bible! Prick him anywhere; his blood is Bibline."[23] Before his sermon one Sunday morning in 1880 he prayed, "Shall we not find even in Thy rod [of discipline] a sweetness, as Jonathan did, when he dipped his rod in the honey?"[24] and "When Thine arrows stick fast in the conscience, may we know how to apply the balm of Jesus' wounds."[25] He delivered seven entire lectures to his students on the subject of illustrations, including one on where to find them,[26] concluding with, "Try with all your might to get the power to see a parable, a simile, an illustration, wherever it is to be seen."[27] When something caught his attention, Spurgeon seemed to have cultivated the habit of frequently asking himself, "To what does that compare in Scripture?"

Scripture was the soil in which all of Spurgeon's spiritual disciplines grew. "His spirituality…found its essential roots in the Bible."[28] The Bible—above all other influences—regulated Spurgeon's piety, for although his reading habits were wide-ranging, he was never known to experiment with devotional practices not found in the Bible, or to seek spiritual experiences not sanctioned by Scripture, because he was convinced that God had inspired Scripture and that Scripture contained all the spiritual disciplines necessary for knowing and enjoying God. "Spurgeon believed in the inexhaustibility of the Scriptures to impart life and to develop spirituality."[29] For Spurgeon, Scripture was sufficient to guide and to sustain his spirituality.

---

23 C.H. Spurgeon, "The Last Words of Christ on the Cross," in *The Metropolitan Tabernacle Pulpit*, 45:495.

24 Spurgeon was referring to the story of King Saul's son, Jonathan, in 1 Samuel 14:27.

25 C.H. Spurgeon, *The Pastor in Prayer* (1893; reprint, Edinburgh: The Banner of Truth Trust, 2004), 132–133.

26 Spurgeon, "Where Can We Find Anecdotes and Illustrations?," in *Lectures to My Students*, 3:54–70.

27 Spurgeon, *Lectures to My Students*, 3:70.

28 Drummond, *Spurgeon: Prince of Preachers*, 569.

29 Drummond, *Spurgeon: Prince of Preachers*, 571.

Prayer

Although the Bible occupied the preeminent and foundational position both in Spurgeon's piety and ministry, he regarded a sincere practice of Christian prayer as the *sine qua non* of the Christian life:

> If any one should ask me for an epitome of the Christian religion, I should say it is in that one word—"prayer." If I should be asked, "What will take in the whole of Christian experience?" I should answer, "prayer." A man must have been convinced of sin before he could pray, he must have had some hope that there was mercy for him before he could pray. In fact, all the Christian virtues are locked up in that word, prayer. Do but tell me you are a man of prayer and I will reply at once, "Sir, I have no doubt of the reality, as well as the sincerity, of your religion."
>
> ...Some say, "How can I discover whether I am God's elect? I am afraid I am not God's elect." Do you pray? If it can be said, "Behold, he prayeth," it can also be said, "Behold he is a chosen vessel."[30]

For Spurgeon to insist that "all the Christian virtues are locked up in that word, prayer," and that prayer is the "epitome of the Christian religion" seems to contradict Jesus' declaration in John 13:34–35 that Christlike love—not prayer or any other activity or quality—is the primary characteristic that distinguishes a Christ follower.[31] But it is likely either that Spurgeon was overstating his case as a sermonic device or was indicating what he believed to be the private experience most representative of the Christian rather than the foremost relational manifestation of true Christianity, for elsewhere he affirmed the primacy of love.[32] In any case, this statement reflects Spurgeon's view that prayer is at the core Christian piety, and implies that he would have considered a piety without prayer to be a piety undeserving of the name Christian.

---

30 C.H. Spurgeon, "Paul's First Prayer," in *The New Park Street Pulpit*, 1:122.

31 In John 13:34–35, Jesus says, "A new commandment I give to you, that you love one another: just as I have loved you, you also are to love one another. By this all people will know that you are my disciples, if you have love for one another."

32 As in C.H. Spurgeon, "Christ's New Commandment," in *The Metropolitan Tabernacle Pulpit*, 51:241–251.

Charles Haddon Spurgeon
1834–1892

Some uncertainty exists about Spurgeon's personal prayer habits. There is some reason to believe that he regularly engaged in what might be described as episodic prayer, that is, periods of sustained prayer. Spurgeon himself lends support to this, at least by implication when he writes, "The habit of regular morning and evening prayer is one which is indispensable to a believer's life, but the prescribing of the length of prayer, and the constrained remembrance of so many persons and subjects, may gender unto bondage, and strangle prayer rather than assist it."[33] Similarly, he gives the impression of encouraging periods of uninterrupted prayer when he exhorts his students, "You cannot pray too long in private. We do not limit you to ten minutes there, or ten hours, or ten weeks if you like. The more you are on your knees alone the better."[34] J.C. Carlile maintains that Spurgeon engaged in frequent episodic prayer, stating that "Spurgeon would sit at the end of [his study] with his back to the little private sanctum to which he often retired for prayer.... Spurgeon would dictate by the hour and then go to his little room and in a few moments return to begin again."[35] Although his description of Spurgeon's habits in regard to private prayer indicates knowledge of quite a few specifics, and though he was a student in the Pastors' College[36] and thus might have observed Spurgeon's activities in his study firsthand, Carlile does not cite a source for this information.[37]

A larger body of evidence indicates that Spurgeon's personal practice of prayer would better be characterized as more continual than episodic. It is reasonable to assume that virtually all Christians who consider themselves prayerful would affirm that they pray brief prayers at moments throughout the day, even in the midst of routine activities such as driving or working. But it seems that when Spurgeon and others refer to his praying throughout the day they mean something more than this. In one sermon he spoke of his experience of

---

33 Spurgeon, *Autobiography: Volume 1*, 103.

34 Spurgeon, *Lectures to My Students*, 1:62.

35 J.C. Carlile, *Spurgeon: An Interpretive Biography* (London: Religious Tract Society, 1933), 195–196.

36 Carlile, *Spurgeon: An Interpretive Biography*, 24.

37 Carlile also acknowledges the help he received from Spurgeon's sister for some of the information in the biography (Carlile, *Spurgeon: An Interpretive Biography*, 5).

praying short prayers all throughout the day, an experience he does seem to believe is normative for Christians:

> I always feel that there is something wrong if I go without prayer for even half an hour in the day. I cannot understand how a Christian man can go from morning to evening without prayer. I cannot comprehend how he lives, and how he fights the battle of life without asking the guardian care of God while the arrows of temptation are flying so thickly around him. I cannot imagine how he can decide what to do in times of perplexity, how he can see his own imperfections or the faults of others without feeling constrained to say, all day long, "O Lord, guide me, O Lord, forgive me; O Lord, bless my friend!" I cannot think how he can be continually receiving mercies from the Lord without saying, "God be thanked for this new token of his grace! Blessed be the name of the Lord for what he is doing for me in his abounding mercy! O Lord, still remember me with the favour that thou showest unto thy people!" Do not be content, deal brethren and sisters in Christ, unless you call pray everywhere and at all times, and so obey the apostolic injunction, "Pray without ceasing."[38]

Beyond this, however, Spurgeon had a reputation for praying brief prayers like those described above almost continually throughout the day. The resulting impression caused biographers like Dallimore to write, "Spurgeon was ever a man of prayer. Not that he spent any long periods of time in prayer but he lived in the spirit of communion with God."[39] Likewise, in his introduction to a collection of Spurgeon's pulpit prayers, Dinsdale Young says, "Prayer was the instinct of his soul, and the atmosphere of his life."[40] It would seem, however, that the knowledge of how inwardly prayerful Spurgeon actually was would be impossible to ascertain unless either he prayed aloud or else

---

38 C.H. Spurgeon, "Peter's Shortest Prayer," in *The Metropolitan Tabernacle Pulpit*, 56:98.

39 Dallimore, *Spurgeon*, vi.

40 Dinsdale T. Young in C.H. Spurgeon, *C.H. Spurgeon's Prayers*, ed. Dinsdale T. Young (1905; reprint, Grand Rapids: Baker, 1978), vi.

Spurgeon himself disclosed the information. In fact, he may have done both, for Fullerton suggests:

> If we may venture to observe the inner life of this man so greatly honoured of God in the world, we shall not find Spurgeon often on his knees; and that not because he did not pray, but because he prayed incessantly.... Between the closing of one book and the opening of another with Spurgeon there were the shut eyes and the moving lips. "I always feel it well just to put a few words of prayer between everything I do," he once said to an intimate friend.[41]

The "intimate friend" mentioned by the biographer may indeed have been Fullerton, who was a younger friend and protégé of Spurgeon.

Spurgeon himself encouraged such a prayerful lifestyle in a lecture to the students at his Pastors' College:

> I take it that as a minister *he is always praying.* Whenever his mind turns to his work, whether he is in it or out of it, he ejaculates a petition, sending up his holy desires as well-directed arrows to the skies. He is not always in the act of prayer, but he lives in the spirit of it. If his heart be in his work, he cannot eat or drink, or take recreation, or go to his bed, or rise in the morning, without evermore feeling a fervency of desire, a weight of anxiety, and a simplicity of dependence upon God; thus, in one form or other he continues in prayer. If there be any man under heaven, who is compelled to carry out the precept—"Pray without ceasing," surely it is the Christian minister.[42]

From what others have written about him, Spurgeon's description here of what it means to "pray without ceasing"[43] may have been more autobiographical than he expressed. In an excerpt from one of his sermons on prayer, he explicitly conveys his compulsion for continual prayer: "Minute by minute, moment by moment, somehow or other,

41 Fullerton, *Spurgeon: A Biography*, 178.
42 Spurgeon, *Lectures to My Students*, 1:40–141.
43 1 Thessalonians 5:17.

my heart must commune with my God. Prayer has become as essential to me as the heaving of my lungs, and the beating of my pulse."[44]

The most revealing piece of data about the matter comes from Spurgeon's own description of his private prayer practice:

> Prayer is bringing God's promise to mind, and pleading it with him. That is the essence of prayer. To use a very homely simile, the throne of grace is the bank, and prayer takes the promise, like a cheque, and lays it down upon the counter, and comes away with the cash. It gets what God has promised to give. Now, there are some prayers that do not succeed, because there is no promise quoted in them. Many prayers are very defective from the want of a promise. I may ask God what I will, but I am bound to tell him, "Thou hast promised this," or "Thou hast promised that." That is putting the cheque down on the table, and I can go away. I know I pray very differently from some people. I cannot pray by the half-hour together very well, my thoughts begin to wander; but when I get God's promise I go and put it down before him, and I know he will give it me, and I expect to get it. It seems to me for fellows to go loafing in a bank for the half-hour together, without presenting the cheque, would not show much confidence in the banker. You need not think, therefore, that prayer will be a thing of a few minutes, and soon over. No; because you will have another promise, and another, and another, and another, to come back again within a moment.[45]

So here Spurgeon makes plain that, due to wandering thoughts (caused in part, no doubt, by so many heavy responsibilities), he could not "pray by the half-hour together very well." However, it seems that at least occasionally he did so. Twice in his life he was known to pray through the night.[46] In one sermon on prayer, he urged upon Christians the imperative of making time for "your engagement with God,"

44 C.H. Spurgeon, "Unseasonable Prayer," in *The Metropolitan Tabernacle Pulpit*, 49:476.

45 C.H. Spurgeon, *Speeches Home and Abroad* (London: Passmore and Alabaster, 1878), 42.

46 Fullerton, *Spurgeon: A Biography*, 180.

especially when there seems to be no time for prayer,[47] saying, "You will, if you are a watchful Christian, have your times of daily devotion.... Never give up the morning prayer, nor the evening prayer, nor the prayer at midday if such has grown to be your habit."[48] And yet, in the same message he continued,

> between these times of devotion, labour to be much in ejaculatory prayer...in broken sentences and interjections.... Let short sentences go up to heaven, ay, and we may shoot upwards cries, and single words, such as an "Ah," an "Oh," and "O that;" or, without words we may pray in the upward glancing of the eye or the sigh of the heart.[49]

The reality was that Spurgeon's prayer life was both episodic and continual. It was not uncommon for Spurgeon to devote himself entirely to prayer—at least for a few minutes—yet he also prayed "in broken sentences and interjections," both silently and audibly all through his day. But it does seem that, from both Spurgeon's own words and the observations of others, his prayer life was characterized more by continual prayer than by daily episodes of prayer.

That Spurgeon was distinguished more by continual prayer than episodic, and perceived to be so by others, can be illustrated in a passage from Fullerton's biography, a section that also splendidly demonstrates the gregarious nature of Spurgeon's spirituality:

> Archibald G. Brown tells how in a railway journey with him they knelt down and spent a time in prayer. Dr. Wayland Hoyt says, "I was walking with him in the woods one day just outside London, and, as we strolled under the shadow of the summer foliage, we came upon a log lying athwart the path. 'Come,' said he, as naturally as one would say it if he were hungry, and bread were put before him, 'Come, let us pray.' And kneeling beside the log, he lifted his soul to God in the most loving outpouring and yet

---

47 C. H. Spurgeon, "Pray Without Ceasing," in *The Metropolitan Tabernacle Pulpit*, 18:140–141.

48 Spurgeon, "Pray Without Ceasing," 18:137–138.

49 Spurgeon, "Pray Without Ceasing," 18:138.

reverent prayer. Then, rising from his knees as naturally, he went strolling on, talking about this and that. The prayer was no parenthesis interjected. It was something that belonged as much to the habit of his mind as breathing did to the habit of his body." Dr. Cuyler bears a similar testimony. In one of the Surrey woods they were conversing in high spirits when suddenly Spurgeon stopped and said, "Come, Theodore, let us thank God for laughter." That was how he lived. "From a jest to a prayer meant with him the breadth of a straw."[50]

Whether in his study or in public, with only an assistant to silently observe or with friends in conversation, whether pausing in his activities or in the midst of them, Spurgeon was said to have lived in a spirit of prayer. He did not consider himself unusual in this regard; rather he believed that the heart of every Christian, regenerated by the Holy Spirit, always finds itself inexorably reverting heavenward. As Spurgeon put it, "Our heart, renewed by the Holy Ghost, must be like the magnetized needle, which always has an inclination toward the pole."[51]

Although many commented about Spurgeon's private prayer practices, others were more impressed by his public prayers.

Journaling

By far, the disciplines directly related to the Bible and to prayer were the most influential and most frequently practiced by Spurgeon. But besides these, he also engaged in several other personal spiritual disciplines. He kept a spiritual diary, but only once—in 1850 when he was sixteen. Following his conversion on January 6, Spurgeon began keeping a record of his spiritual experiences on April 6 and continued daily—with one exception—until June 20, a period of less than three months. Each entry was but a few lines. He wrote of his baptism, sermons he heard, things he prayed and people with whom he had spiritual conversations. He recorded his longings for God and for holiness, his desires to grow in grace, and his aspirations for more effectiveness as a Christian witness. In his diary he confessed his sins, made observations about church matters and expressed his joy in

---

50 Fullerton, *Spurgeon: A Biography*, 178–179.
51 Spurgeon, "Pray Without Ceasing," 18:138.

being a Christian. A representative entry illustrates not only the nature of the contents of the diary, but also provides a glimpse of Spurgeon's early views about the relationship of his piety with his ministry:

> April 20.—Went round with my tracts; could not feel the Spirit of the Lord upon me. I seemed to have a clog upon my feet and my tongue. I have richly deserved this, for I have not prayed, or studied my Bible as I ought. I confess mine iniquity, and my sin is ever before me. Mercy! It is all mercy! Wash me anew, O Saviour, in Thy sin-atoning blood![52]

Spurgeon never explained why he discontinued his journal, but the reason might have been nothing more than that his habits were interrupted by his relocation to Cambridge not long after his June 20 entry, and that the routines he developed in his new surroundings simply did not lend themselves to the resumption of journaling. It is possible that such an outgoing personality as Spurgeon's found the discipline too introspective or simply not worth the exchange of time required from the opportunities he was beginning to have for ministry to others. Whatever the reason, he never returned to this particular discipline. Nevertheless, he considered the activity valuable as this excerpt from a sermon six years later attests: "I have sometimes said, when I have become the prey of doubting thoughts, 'Well now, I dare not doubt whether there be a God, for I can look back in my Diary and say, on such a day in the depths of trouble I bent my knee to God, and or ever I had risen from my knees the answer was given me."[53] The entry to which he alludes is uncertain. But referring to the benefit provided by his diary in this case implies that he saw value in the practice for both himself and others.

Spurgeon's diary remained unpublished until after his death when Susannah included it in his autobiography.[54] She introduces it with a somewhat curious anecdote:

---

52 Spurgeon, *Autobiography: Volume 1*, 128.

53 C.H. Spurgeon, "Manasseh," in *The New Park Street Pulpit*, 2:415.

54 Spurgeon, *Autobiography: Volume 1*, 123–143.

Not very long after our marriage, my husband brought to me, one day, a small clasped book, and putting it into my hand with a grave and serious air, he aid, "That book contains a record of some of my past spiritual experiences, wifey; take care of it, but I never want to see it again." He never did, and to me also it was a sealed book, for I did not dare to open it; and it has lain, unrevealed, for certainly forty years since the day I first saw it.[55]

Why did Spurgeon not want to see his diary again? Was it an embarrassing reminder of his relative spiritual immaturity in those days? That seems doubtful, in light of the unusual rate of spiritual progress which he made. Furthermore, his pastoral experience would have taught him to understand and accept the perspective of a recent teenage convert such as he was in the days of his diary. There certainly is nothing recorded in the entries which would have injured his reputation had it been revealed or which should have pained him to remember it. Perhaps he was simply telling Susannah that she should keep it safe without bothering to keep it accessible to him. Ultimately, one can only speculate why he made the remark.

Regardless of this, and despite the possible spiritual benefits one may conjecture that Spurgeon might have enjoyed by attempting to keep a journal in the midst of his demanding schedule, Drummond crystallizes the significance of Spurgeon's short-lived journal as it relates to the purposes of this thesis: "The diary makes it abundantly clear that young Spurgeon had embarked upon an intimate walk with Jesus Christ. Prayer, Bible study, service, and the Christian disciplines had become central in his life."[56]

Solitude

It is no surprise that Spurgeon rarely engaged in extensive periods of solitude. While still in his teens he began to have a rapidly escalating number of responsibilities as a minister of a growing church, responsibilities he assumed with the utmost seriousness. Several times each week he had to prepare to stand before an ever-increasing congregation, and he believed that on each occasion souls were in the balance

---

55 Spurgeon, *Autobiography: Volume 1*, 123.
56 Drummond, *Spurgeon: Prince of Preachers*, 152.

between heaven and hell. People were often coming to him for counsel regarding their relationship with God, and when they were not he was seeking out those who had visited his church or who were in need. As the years went by, the burdens placed upon him and the numbers of those wanting to see him quickly proliferated to suffocating levels. As much as Spurgeon must have occasionally longed for a lengthy retreat to solitude, he may have thought it irresponsible to walk away very often from what he considered the stewardship of great, God-given tasks.

But it may also be that his extroverted personality contributed to the infrequency of his solitudes. Spurgeon was what is today referred to informally as a "people person." He loved people and people were attracted to and felt comfortable with him. He often seemed to find a kind of refreshment in people that others more often find in solitude. Carlile, for example, admired Spurgeon because, "It was amazing the amount of work he got through. He would dictate to three secretaries in succession and then turn to the study of a fresh subject as though he were just beginning his work for the day."[57] Many would have found such intense engagement with people draining, but, says Carlile, it was not so with Spurgeon. Nor does he appear to have been the kind of person who disliked being alone: he simply did not require solitude for spiritual replenishment as frequently as do many other Christians.

Despite this, Spurgeon knew that regardless of the individual differences each may possess, every Christian benefits from solitude, especially that which is for purposes of piety. Just as those who most enjoy solitude also need the benefits of the more relational spiritual disciplines, so it is that those who—like Spurgeon—thrive most from interaction with others also need solitude. Knowing this, Spurgeon wrote, "Believer, pray often in solitude,"[58] and:

> There are times when solitude is better than society, and silence is wiser than speech. We should be better Christians if we were more alone, waiting upon God, and gathering through meditation on His Word spiritual strength for labor in His service.... Why is it that some Christians, although they hear many sermons,

----

57 Carlile, *Spurgeon: An Interpretive Biography*, 212.
58 C.H. Spurgeon, "March 22, Morning," in *Morning and Evening*, 164.

make but slow advances in the divine life? Because they neglect their closets, and do not thoughtfully meditate on God's Word.[59]

In these selections, Spurgeon is clearly appealing to Christians to enjoy the benefits of drawing aside each day for times of prayer and meditation on Scripture, a practice we saw him advocating above (though here the stress is more on the context of solitude for prayer and meditation than on the activities themselves). We saw that Spurgeon himself sometimes withdrew from the company of others in order to engage in these disciplines. But he also advanced the idea that it is beneficial for withdrawal for much longer periods than that which would normally be associated with daily, devotional Bible meditation and prayer. Here we read of Spurgeon commending to his students this type of isolation:

> I would seriously recommend to you, when settled in the ministry, the celebration of extraordinary seasons of devotion. If your ordinary prayers do not keep up the freshness and vigour of your souls, and you feel that you are flagging, get alone for a week, or even a month if possible. We have occasional holidays, why not frequent holy days? ...Our silence might be better than our voices if our solitude were spent with God.... Sometimes [we should] say to our people when we felt moved to do so, "Dear friends, we really must be gone for a little while to refresh our souls in solitude."[60]

While it is not known that he ever got "alone for a week, or even a month," according to Susannah, her husband occasionally permitted himself to disengage from his strenuous routines for several slow-paced, relaxing hours in a countryside carriage ride. But it appears that he typically brought someone with him, and that the purpose was as much for physical rest and mental diversion as spiritual devotion:

> One of my dear husband's most congenial recreations consisted in spending a long day in the country;—driving over hill and

---

59 C. H. Spurgeon, "October 12, Morning," in *Morning and Evening*, 572.
60 Spurgeon, *Lectures to My Students*, 1:51.

dale, and through the lanes and pretty villages of our charming county of Surrey. Many sweet days of rest have thus been snatched from weeks of heavy toil, and a furlough of a few hours has helped to restore and refresh the overworked brain and heart. He would go out in good time, taking with him some choice companion, or, perchance, another weary worker; and, driving slowly, they would jog along till noon, when, at a pleasant wayside inn, they would rest the horse, and have their luncheon, returning in the cool of the evening for high tea at home at six or seven o'clock.[61]

Here again, Spurgeon's gregarious spirituality manifests itself. Apparently he found these occasions more restorative for both body and soul if he had a companion than if were alone.

Did Spurgeon suffer spiritually—and perhaps eventually even physically—from a lack of solitude? Did his devotional life become a victim of the busyness that resulted from his ministerial success? For apart from forthcoming evidence to the contrary, one might argue that Spurgeon failed to "practice what he preached" when he said in passages like the excerpt above, "We should be better Christians if we were more alone, waiting upon God,"[62] especially if by that he meant something more than the brief moments of solitude he had throughout the day when in his study and the few seconds of silent prayer between books he was reading. If the gregarious Spurgeon, apparently seldom alone by the half-hour or more, is judged by the standards of Jonathan Edwards quoted in a previous chapter, then his piety was greatly out of balance. Edwards writes:

Some are greatly affected when in company; but have nothing that bears any manner of proportion to it in secret, in close meditation, prayer and conversing with God when alone, and separated from the world. A true Christian doubtless delights in religious fellowship and Christian conversation, and finds much

---

61 C.H. Spurgeon, *C.H. Spurgeon's Autobiography: Volume 2: The Full Harvest, 1860–1892*, comp. Susannah Spurgeon and Joseph Harrald (1897–1900; rev. ed., Edinburgh: The Banner of Truth Trust, 1973), 219.

62 C.H. Spurgeon, "October 12, Morning," in *Morning and Evening*, 572.

to affect his heart in it; but he also delights at times to retire from all mankind, to converse with God in solitude.... True religion disposes persons to be much alone in solitary places for holy meditation and prayer.... It is the nature of true grace, however it loves Christian society in its place, in a peculiar manner to delight in retirement, and secret converse with God.[63]

But the reality with Spurgeon, unlike Edwards and others, seems to be that his true self was revealed as much "in company" as when alone. And it was not that Spurgeon experienced no "delight in retirement, and secret converse with God," but rather his personality was such that he did not require as much solitude as Edwards and others to gain the same amount of spiritual benefit, as well as the fact that he was simply unable to devote as much time to it as they. Anthony Storr, in his book *Solitude*, puts his finger precisely on the point: "People vary widely in how much they value experiences involving human relationships and how much they value what happens when they are alone.... The *need* to be alone differs from the *capacity* to be alone."[64] Spurgeon had the *capacity* to be alone, but apparently not as much *need* to be alone as many other pious Christians. He seemed to be able to commune with God in the daily routines when others were present in ways that some can hardly experience except when alone.

In time, however, Spurgeon would reluctantly find solitude more frequently accessible to him. From the 1870s until his death, ill-health forced Spurgeon to withdraw from the Metropolitan Tabernacle for weeks or even months at a time. Typically he went to Menton on the southern coast of France for a more healthful climate. These were the episodes that afforded him occasions for solitude almost as often and for as long as he chose (though there were always several assistants of various types in his travelling party). Still, while these journeys were often refreshing to him spiritually, their primary purpose was always physical recovery.

---

63 Jonathan Edwards, *The Works of Jonathan Edwards, Volume 2: Religious Affections*, ed. John E. Smith (1746; reprint, New Haven: Yale University Press, 1959), 374.

64 Anthony Store, *Solitude* (New York: The Free Press, 1988), 93.

Singing

Unlike Jonathan Edwards a century earlier, Spurgeon left no indication of singing aloud in his personal devotional life. Nevertheless, it would not be a great revelation to discover that he did so, for clearly Spurgeon was a man of Christian song. Not only was he raised in churches where psalms and hymns were almost certainly sung, but his paternal grandmother took pains to instill these into her grandson at an early age. In his autobiography, Spurgeon—humorously, no doubt—reports:

> My dear grandfather was very fond of Dr. Watts's hymns, and my grandmother, wishing to get me to learn them, promised me a penny for each one that I should say to her perfectly. I found it an easy and pleasant method of earning money, and learned them so fast that grandmother said she must reduce the price to a halfpenny each, and afterwards to a farthing, if she did not mean to be quite ruined by her extravagance. There is no telling how low the amount per hymn might have sunk, but grandfather said that he was getting overrun with rats, and offered me a shilling a dozen for all I could kill. I found, at the time, that the occupation of rat-catching paid me better than learning hymns, but I know which employment has been the more permanently profitable to me. No matter on what topic I am preaching, I can even now, in the middle of any sermon, quote some verse of a hymn in harmony with the subject; the hymns have remained with me, while those old rats for years have passed away, and the shillings I earned by killing them have been spent long ago.[65]

According to Robert Shindler's chapter, "Mr. Spurgeon as a Hymn-Writer," at eighteen Spurgeon wrote a six-stanza hymn, "Immanuel."[66] In 1866, the pastor compiled *Our Own Hymn-Book: A Collection of Psalms and Hymns for Public, Social, and Private Worship*.[67] It consisted

---

65 Spurgeon, *Autobiography: Volume 1*, 26–27.

66 Robert Shindler, *From the Usher's Desk to the Tabernacle Pulpit* (London: Passmore and Alabaster, 1892), 257–258.

67 C.H. Spurgeon, comp., *Our Own Hymn-Book: A Collection of Psalms and Hymns for Public, Social, and Private Worship* (London: Passmore and Alabaster, 1866).

of more than 1,060 songs, including at least one version of all 150 Psalms. Most were taken from the two songbooks the congregation had been using for years, namely the one by Watts and the volume from the church's former pastor, John Rippon. But the collection also contained "about a dozen psalms, and as many hymns, from the compiler's own pen."[68] A decade after Spurgeon's death, Charles Ray indicated that the resource had "been adopted by a large number of congregations all over the country."[69] Although it was reprinted in 2002,[70] it is not known to be widely used, and likely is purchased more for its historical value, by students of hymnody and by those interested in Spurgeon, than for use in congregational singing.[71]

So while Spurgeon may or may not have sung to God in private worship, the evidence leads to the belief that he loved to declare his devotion to God in song, and especially—in accordance with his gregarious spirituality—in company with his fellow believers at the Metropolitan Tabernacle, and as we shall soon see, with his wife, sons and guests in family worship as well.[72]

Fasting

Drummond affirms that "Spurgeon believed in a disciplined spirituality.... He also believed in fasting.... Spurgeon saw discipline in all these areas [that is, in meditation on Scripture, prayer and fasting] as vital if one aspires to be spiritual."[73] However, since Spurgeon kept no journal (other than the brief one from 1850) in which he might have recorded and reflected upon the occasions when he fasted, nearly all that can be known about Spurgeon on this subject are the things he

---

68 Shindler, *From the Usher's Desk to the Tabernacle Pulpit*, 258.

69 Charles Ray, *The Life of Charles Haddon Spurgeon* (London: Passmore and Alabaster, 1903), 464.

70 Spurgeon, comp., *Our Own Hymn-Book: A Collection of Psalms and Hymns for Public, Social, and Private Worship* (1866; reprint, Pasadena: Pilgrim Publications, 2002).

71 Perhaps Spurgeon's best-known hymn today is one he wrote for singing at the observance of the Lord's Supper, "Amidst us our Beloved Stands" in *Grace Hymns* (London: Grace Publications Trust, 1975), 480. This hymnal is primarily used by Baptists in the United Kingdom and English-speaking Calvinistic Baptists worldwide.

72 C.H. Spurgeon, "Hallelujah! Hallelujah!," in *The Metropolitan Tabernacle Pulpit*, 41:332.

73 Drummond, *Spurgeon: Prince of Preachers*, 573.

said about it in his sermons and books. But it should be helpful to remember that he lived in England during a time when days of national humiliation and fasting were sometimes called by the British government and Spurgeon himself was asked to speak at a gathering observing such an event on October 7, 1857, when more than 23,000 heard him in London's Crystal Palace.

Spurgeon seemed to be keen on striking what he believed to be a biblical proportionality regarding fasting. Thus on the one he hand he preached, "Our Lord Jesus Christ never made much of fasting. He very seldom spoke about it." Yet in the next sentence he said, "But, still, Holy Scripture does speak of fasting, in certain cases it advises fasting, and there were godly men and godly women, such as Anna, the prophetess, who 'served God with fastings and prayer night and day.'"[74] Then he was quite direct about the matter, and even refers to a personal experience while fasting:

I do not mean to spiritualize this away. I believe, literally, that some of you would be a great deal the better if you did occasionally have a whole day of fasting and prayer. There is a lightness that comes over the frame, especially of bulky people like myself; we begin to feel ourselves quite light and ethereal. I remember one day of fasting and prayer, in which I realized to myself,... there is a lightness, an elevation of the spirit above the flesh, that will come over you after some hours of waiting upon God in fasting and prayer. I can advise brethren sometimes to try it; it will be good for their health, and it certainly will not harm them. If we only ate about half what is ordinarily eaten, we should probably all of us be in better health; and if, occasionally, we put ourselves on short commons, not because there is any virtue in that, but in order to get our brains more clear, and to help our hearts to rest more fully upon the Saviour, we should find that prayer and fasting have great power.[75]

---

74 C.H. Spurgeon, "The Secret of Failure," in *The Metropolitan Tabernacle Pulpit*, 42:104.

75 Spurgeon, "The Secret of Failure," 42:104–105.

What Spurgeon meant by descriptions such as "light and ethereal" and "a lightness, an elevation of the spirit above the flesh" is a matter of speculation. Was he referring primarily to a physical sense of feeling somewhat lighter simply due to the absence of food in the stomach for a matter of hours? The use of "ethereal" and "elevation of the spirit" seem to argue against a purely physiological explanation of the experience. If he was attempting to describe a somewhat enhanced state of spirituality, it is important to note that he clearly connected it with "hours of waiting upon God in fasting and prayer," not merely the absence of food.

Consistent with his tendency to think of spirituality not just in terms of private experience but also in conjunction with others, Spurgeon often referred to the significance of fasting as it related to the church. He does so in the following passage, and again he associates its practice with prayer, and speaks of the spiritual power that may result from practicing the disciplines in tandem:

> The church of God would be far stronger to wrestle with this ungodly age if she were more given to prayer and fasting. There is a mighty efficacy in these two gospel ordinances. The first links us to heaven, the second separates us from earth. Prayer takes us into the banqueting-house of God; fasting overturns the surfeiting tables of earth. Prayer gives us to feed on the bread of heaven, and fasting delivers the soul from being encumbered with the fullness of bread which perisheth. When Christians shall bring themselves up to the uttermost possibilities of spiritual vigour, then they will be able, by God's Spirit working in them, to cast out devils which to-day, without the prayer and fasting, laugh them to scorn.[76]

Based upon such statements in his sermons and books, and the fact that he lived in a place and time when fasting was even part of the national culture, it is reasonable to assume that Spurgeon fasted at least occasionally. But it must be acknowledged that, based upon many photographs of him, the heavier-than-average ("bulky," in the self-description above) girth to which Spurgeon attained later in

---

76 C.H. Spurgeon, *Flashes of Thought* (London: Passmore and Alabaster, 1874), 327.

life—a condition which may have been compounded by illness—lends support to the view that he did not fast with any unusual degree of frequency.

Family worship

Leading the daily worship of God in the Spurgeon home for all family members and guests present was an essential part of Charles Spurgeon's piety. Despite the absence of a clear proof-text, he believed such a devotional expression to be a thoroughly biblical practice, "in accord with the genius and spirit of the gospel [and] commended by the example of the saints.[77]

In the doctrinal statement of the Metropolitan Tabernacle, a document Spurgeon treasured so highly that he placed a copy—along with a Bible—in a box over which his pulpit was built, one passage explicitly prescribed family worship:

> God is to be worshipped everywhere in spirit and in truth, whether in private families daily, in secret by each individual, or solemnly in the public assemblies. These are not to be carelessly or willfully neglected or forsaken, when God by His Word and providence calls us to them.[78]

Anyone seeking to understand Spurgeon's piety must take into account not only Spurgeon's own ancestral habits in family worship, but also the seriousness with which he embraced his church's confession of faith. Many spiritual traditions—the monastic one being an obvious example—have not emphasized this aspect of piety. But for Spurgeon, there were three spheres of devotion: personal, familial and congregational.

At six o'clock each evening, all the household gathered in Spurgeon's study for worship.[79] The event would consist of three primary elements. Referring to the famous Bible commentator, Matthew Henry, Spurgeon affirmed these elements:

---

77 C.H. Spurgeon, "Restraining Prayer," in *The Metropolitan Tabernacle Pulpit*, 51:327.
78 The 1689 Second London Confession of Faith, section 22.6.
79 Dallimore, *Spurgeon*, 178.

> I agree with Matthew Henry when he says, "They that pray in the family do well; they that pray and read the Scriptures do better; but they that pray, and read, and sing do best of all." There is a completeness in that kind of family worship which is much to be desired.[80]

After the Bible reading, the host typically added a few spontaneous observations and/or applications related to the passage.[81]

In addition to the basic devotional purposes of family worship, Spurgeon also considered it an important part of influencing children in the things of God and an indispensible way for parents to present a consistent Christian example to their children. But he feared that some families in his church were neglecting this great privilege and opportunity:

> Brethren, I wish it were more common, I wish it were universal, with all professors of religion to have family prayer. We sometimes hear of the children of Christian parents who do not grow up in the fear of God, and we are asked how it is that they turn out so badly. In many, very many cases, I fear there is such a neglect of family worship that it is not probable that the children are at all impressed by any piety supposed to be possessed by their parents.... If we want to bring up a godly family, who shall be a seed to serve God when our heads are under the clods of the valley, let us seek to train them up in the fear of God by meeting together as a family for worship.[82]

Spurgeon was convinced that the disregard of the piety expressed in family worship resulted in serious consequences:

> The house in which there is no family altar can scarcely expect the divine blessing.... The mournful behaviour of many of the

---

80 C.H. Spurgeon, "The Happy Duty of Daily Praise," in *The Metropolitan Tabernacle Pulpit*, 32:289.

81 Dallimore, *Spurgeon*, 178.

82 C.H. Spurgeon, "A Pastoral Visit," in *The Metropolitan Tabernacle Pulpit*, 54:362–63.

children of professing parents is mainly due to the neglect or the coldness of family worship; and many a judgment has, I doubt not, fallen upon households because the Lord is not duly honoured therein. Eli's sin still brings with it the visitations of a jealous God. That word of Jeremiah bears hard upon prayerless families, "Pour out thy fury upon the households that call not upon thy name." ...If neglect of family prayer should become general throughout our churches it will be a dark day for England. Children who observe that their parents are practically prayerless in the household will grow up indifferent to religion, and in many cases will be utter worldlings, if not altogether atheists.[83]

Children with "mournful behaviour," and who become indifferent to religion, worldly, and even atheistic could be the price parents pay for the neglect of family worship. Spurgeon believed family worship so vital to Christian piety that without it "many a judgment" from God could fall. So important was it that—even as a pastor of a large church with many ministry positions to keep filled—he announced, "Public usefulness must not injure private piety; church work must not push family worship into a corner. It is ill to offer God one duty stained with the blood of another."[84]

Perhaps the greatest testimony to the place family worship held in Spurgeon's spirituality is simply the fact that he made it a *priority* despite all his other responsibilities. Though he pastored such an enormous church, presided over dozens of ministries, preached several times each week, felt the pressure of publishing deadlines constantly before him and had an unending stream of people wanting to see him, Spurgeon made sure that none of them crowded out his commitment to family worship. According to Susannah, even when they were travelling:

We had family prayer, whether we lodged in some rough inn on the mountains, or in the luxurious rooms of a palatial hotel in a city; and the blessed "abiding in Christ," of which many of us say, "It is high, I cannot attain unto it," was to him the natural

---

83 C.H. Spurgeon, "Hindrances to Prayer," in *The Metropolitan Tabernacle Pulpit*, 20:506–507.

84 C.H. Spurgeon, "July 18, Evening," in *Morning and Evening*, 401.

atmosphere of his soul;—he lived and breathed in the presence of God.[85]

Understandably, it is possible that Susannah, writing as an elderly widow, was reflecting wistfully upon happy days long-departed. Even so, she was an eyewitness to far more occasions of family worship led by Spurgeon than anyone else. Despite her subjectivity, she can describe the nightly scene from a unique perspective:

> After the meal was over, an adjournment was made to the study for family worship, and it was at these seasons that my beloved's prayers were remarkable for their tender childlikeness, their spiritual pathos, and their intense devotion. He seemed to come as near to God as a little child to a loving father, and we were often moved to tears as he talked thus face to face with his Lord.[86]

Dallimore quotes a visitor to the Spurgeon home who corroborates much of what Susannah reported, but adds some additional observations, both about Spurgeon's method and his spirit:

> One of the most helpful hours of my visits to Westwood was the hour of family prayer. At six o'clock all the household gathered into the study for worship. Usually Mr. Spurgeon would himself lead the devotions. The portion read was invariably accompanied with exposition. How amazingly helpful those homely and gracious comments were. I remember, especially, his reading of the twenty-fourth of Luke: "Jesus Himself drew near and went with them." How sweetly he talked upon having Jesus with us wherever we go. Not only to have Him draw near at special seasons, but to go with us whatever labor we undertake.... Then, how full of tender pleading, of serene confidence in God, of world-embracing sympathy were his prayers.... His public prayers were an inspiration and benediction, but his prayers with the family

---

85 C.H. Spurgeon, *C.H. Spurgeon's Autobiography*, comp. Susannah Spurgeon and Joseph Harrald, 2 books in 4 vols. (1897–1900; reprint, Pasadena: Pilgrim Publications, 1992), 3:103.

86 Spurgeon, *C.H. Spurgeon's Autobiography*, 4:64.

were to me more wonderful still.... Mr. Spurgeon, when bowed before God in family prayer, appeared a grander man even than when holding thousands spellbound by his oratory.[87]

While these accounts may contain the embellishments of beloved memories, when considered in conjunction with what Spurgeon said above on this subject, it is not surprising that he declared of family worship, "I esteem it so highly that no language of mine can adequately express my sense of its value."[88] That would be a remarkable statement by Spurgeon on any subject, as he was renowned for his facility with the English language. In this instance it is an especially noteworthy commentary on Spurgeon's view of the significance of this particular aspect of piety.

Conclusion

By any measure, Charles Haddon Spurgeon lived one of the most extraordinary lives of any preacher in Christian history. At points, the accolades about Spurgeon from his family, church members, friends, admirers and biographers strain credulity, and yet the facts about him seem to sustain that strain with remarkable success, even with the increasing objectivity given to the evaluation of his life and influence added by the distance of so many years since his death in 1892. Spurgeon was human, thus he was flawed, even if the conventions of Victorian England and the biases of his many hagiographers concealed his weaknesses and character defects.

At the outset of his London ministry, his most vocal critics were the newspapers, and their criticism of him ran along the lines of lampooning him as a young upstart from the country with stylistic differences with the established church, or disparaging the self-references in his sermons, an unconventional practice in Spurgeon's day.[89] From today's perspective, the charges sound petty or motivated by jealousy. Eventually, his detractors were mostly theological critics, that is, those who did not accuse him of personal faults so much as they differed with

---

87 Dallimore, *Spurgeon*, 178–179.

88 Spurgeon, "Hindrances to Prayer," 20:506.

89 Spurgeon devoted a chapter to the subject of "Early Criticisms and Slanders" in his autobiography. Spurgeon, *Autobiography: Volume 1*, 303–327.

him doctrinally.[90] By the time of Spurgeon's death, the fruit of his ministry had quelled so much of the criticism that all the papers carried important articles about him, praising him for his labours. But when as a young man he was becoming so quickly a household name in London, both the barbs and the praises in the press were trying to him spiritually. One of his letters from that time—to Susannah in 1855—reveals that his chief concern was not with the public's impression of him or with the media's possible impact on church attendance, but rather with the influence it could have on the intimacies of his relationship to God:

> I shall feel deeply indebted to you, if you will pray very earnestly for me. I fear I am not so full of love to God as I used to be. I lament my sad decline in spiritual things. You and others may not have observed it, but I am now conscious of it, and a sense thereof has put bitterness in my cup of joy. Oh! what is it to be popular, to be successful, to have abundance, even to have love so sweet as yours,—if I should be left of God to fall, and to depart from His ways?[91]

Spurgeon had countless devoted supporters and he had detractors. But whatever his opponents in any sphere or at any time in his life said

---

90 The plainest instance of this is the Down Grade Controversy. Theological differences are still the basis for nearly all the relatively few published detractors of Spurgeon today. Such is the case with Kruppa, for example. Though she lauded him in many ways, in the last paragraph of her 1982 work, she concluded that Spurgeon was ultimately a tragic failure because his views did not prevail in the Down Grade Controversy: "It was Spurgeon's tragedy that he lived long enough to witness the comfortable intellectual assumptions of evangelicalism disrupted by the twin challenges of science and higher criticism." Patricia S. Kruppa, *Charles Haddon Spurgeon: A Preacher's Progress* (New York and London: Garland, 1982), 478. To the end, Spurgeon was confident that he was on the side of truth: "For my part, I am quite willing to be eaten of dogs for the next fifty years; but the more distant future shall vindicate me. I have dealt honestly before the living God." C.H. Spurgeon, *An All Round Ministry: Addresses to Ministers and Students* (1900; reprint, Edinburgh: The Banner of Truth Trust, 1978), 360. One's theological presuppositions, and whether they incline more toward Kruppa's or Spurgeon's, along with one's reading of Christian history since Spurgeon's time will likely determine whether one believes that Spurgeon has been vindicated.

91 Spurgeon, *Autobiography: Volume 1*, 298.

of him, no one ever cast suspicions on Spurgeon's piety. Though he was many things to many people, in all roles and relationships Charles Haddon Spurgeon was a man of intense and practical spirituality. "He was," writes Drummond, "a spiritual man in every sense of the word. His spirituality profoundly touched lives."[92]

Spurgeon's piety is easily traceable in his pastoral relationships, in his preaching (including the public prayers he offered immediately prior to preaching) and throughout his pastoral publications. The heart of his piety was Jesus Christ—experiencing, loving, following, and proclaiming him. The Bible regulated Spurgeon's spirituality and was its ultimate authority for, as Drummond explains, "It was Spurgeon's deep conviction that the Bible imparts life, and that constitutes the essential secret of his spirituality."[93]

Perhaps what is most remarkable, given his incessant schedule and the innumerable demands made upon him, is simply that he would become and remain a consistently pious and prayerful person. The pressures of time did not produce in him, as they sometimes do in the hectic lives of busy leaders, a shallow or hypocritical spirituality, rather they resulted—in tandem with his outgoing personality—in what we have characterized as a "gregarious spirituality." This may conflict with the picture that many associate with a life of prayerful piety, a life they envision as one in which long, lingering hours are often invested in solitude and prayer. This is not the picture history provides of Spurgeon. Both the man himself and his associates speak of Spurgeon as one who lived in a spirit of prayer, meaning that whether alone or with others, whether aloud or silently, whether at length or only with a sentence, Spurgeon prayed in moments all throughout the day. And all this impressed others, not as an act or contrived, but as thoroughly sincere. In Ernest Bacon's view:

> Earnestness in spiritual things, and urgency in the service of the Lord, were outstanding characteristics with him. He lived for God, in the pulpit, in the study, in the home, in the street, in the college, in the orphanage.... [Others] talk of God, but do not seem to walk closely with Him. Spurgeon did. There was a trans-

---

92 Drummond, *Spurgeon: Prince of Preachers*, 569.
93 Drummond, *Spurgeon: Prince of Preachers*, 570.

parent sincerity about him, and an attractive simplicity, that proclaimed him to be a true man of God.[94]

When the name of Spurgeon is referenced from Christian history, too often a single identity—typically something such as "great preacher"—is associated with his memory. This chapter sets forth the proposal that the identity of "deeply pious pastor" is another that should be conjoined with that name. Spurgeon's sermons will long be remembered; equally so should be the reputation of his piety.

---

94 Ernest W. Bacon, *Spurgeon: Heir of the Puritans* (London: George Allen & Unwin, 1968), 172.

BAPTISTS

Thomas Todhunter Shields: the spirituality of separation

By Douglas Adams

THE STUDY OF the life and ministry of Thomas Todhunter Shields (1873–1955) is a fascinating subject providing the student of church history with a panorama of paradoxical extremes. In early twentieth-century Ontario, Shields was one of the most loved and most hated figures ever to grace the ecclesiastical landscape. Loved by his supporters, he was likened to Spurgeon, Jeremiah, the apostle Paul and Luther.[1] His opponents were not so kind. The media treated him to such designations as "'dictator,' 'hypocrite,' 'vain,' 'egotistical,' 'destructive' and... 'a man without a Christian heart.'"[2] Shields' career saw him elevated to positions of political and international distinction as a "distinguished Canadian,"[3] but also earned him the contempt of Canada's prime minister on the floor of Parliament.[4] In the Fundamentalist

1   Leslie K. Tarr, *Shields of Canada* (Grand Rapids: Baker Book House, 1967), 3. According to the fly-leaf, one of the first to call him this was Sir W.R Nicoll, editor of *The British Weekly*. It is a comparison often made in both Canadian and British newspapers. See *Toronto Telegram*, May 9, 1921; H.C. Slade "Forward" in Tarr, *Shields of Canada*, 3.

2   Tarr, *Shields of Canada*.

3   T.T. Shields, Circular letter, August 3, 1915. (MS) Jarvis Street Baptist Church Archives [henceforth JSBCA], Toronto.

4   T.T. Shields, "The Gospel Witness is Discussed in Parliament," *Gospel Witness*

controversies of the 1920s, Shields went from a celebrated leader of the Baptist Convention of Ontario and Quebec to a marginalized outcast. In Shields' early career he was an otherworldly evangelist but by the 1930s he had become a social and political activist. At one point in Shields' career, he was used as a denominational conciliator. However, the same denomination that once used him to heal schisms found itself torn apart by Shields in one of the most contentious divisions in its history. The highs and lows of Shields' career are equally noteworthy and provide significant lessons in the study of Christian spirituality.

To understand the character of Shields' spirituality, a brief overview of his Christian career is in order. The first reference to spiritual interest on Shields' part was recorded in his father's sermon diary.[5] In November 1889, his father noted "Heard of a young man who asked for prayer. Young man was Tod."[6] In February of the following year, Shields' father recorded the beginning of an evangelistic campaign in his sermon diary. This was a common practice among Baptist churches of this period, and often these would run for two or three weeks, with guest evangelists brought in to preach at special evening services. On this occasion, Shields Sr. had invited Pastor McDonald to preach for the week of February 12th and Pastor Sheldon for the following week. The results were positive and Shields noted in his diary: "Revival began." Even more rewarding for the father was the conversion of his two oldest sons: "Irwie and Todda professed a change of heart Feb. 18th. To God be all Praise."[7] Thomas Jr., or Tod as his father called him, was sixteen years old.

It should be noted that this event clearly occurred in Plattsville in the third year of the elder Shields' pastorate there. His Plattsville pastorate lasted from December 1888 to February 1892. From Plattsville, the Shields family moved to Tiverton, where the younger Shields was first introduced to the ministry. In January 1894, Shields Sr. suffered with a sickness that kept him from the pulpit for a month. Looking for pulpit suppliers, the elder Shields turned to his son. This event proved

---

5   T.T. Shields Sr., *Sermon Diary*, JSBCA, Toronto.

6   Shields Sr., *Sermon Diary*.

7   Shields Sr., *Sermon Diary*.

to be a turning point in his career and in his son's life. Shields Sr. wrote in his diary: "This sickness opened the way for Tod going into the ministry and also cleared the way for me going to Vittoria."[8]

Thomas Todhunter Shields Jr.'s ministerial career began with a series of pastorates in rural southwestern Ontario, including Florence, Dutton and Delhi. Shields was a few days shy of his twenty-first birthday when he entered the pastorate and was twenty-three years old at the time of his ordination in Dutton in 1897.

In 1900, at the age of twenty-seven, Shields took up his first urban pastorate at Hamilton's Wentworth Street Baptist Church. He served there for nearly three years but, by June 1903, felt so burdened with the call to evangelism that he withdrew from the pastorate and served as a full-time evangelist with the Baptist Convention of Ontario and Quebec.

In September 1904, he accepted the call to London's Adelaide Street Baptist Church. He pastored there for five-and-a-half years until he received the momentous call to Jarvis Street Baptist Church in Toronto. Shields served as Jarvis Street's pastor for forty-five years until his death in 1955.

During his years in Toronto, Shields quickly rose to prominence in a number of spheres. As pastor of Jarvis Street Baptist Church, the premier church in the convention, Shields was soon drawn into the denominational hierarchy where he sat on a number of boards and committees. Significantly, he was also named to the Board of Governors of McMaster University. In 1913, 1915, 1917, 1918 and 1919, Shields ministered in London, England, in Spurgeon's Metropolitan Tabernacle.

A pivotal experience in the shaping of Shields' subsequent life and ministry was his invitation to be a guest of the British Ministry of Information in 1918. During a four month period, he was given a tour of Ireland, was invited to inspect all the major armament factories, was taken on an inspection of the Grand Fleet and was shown the many scenes of devastation on the war front in France and Belgium.

When Shields returned to Canada early in 1919, he was a different man, and the differences soon evidenced themselves in a series of controversies that shook his own church and the denomination. Shields led the charge against every manifestation of liberalism in

---

8   Shields Sr., *Sermon Diary*.

what some have called "the Battle for the Book." In the 1919 convention, Shields took issue with the publishing of a liberal editorial in the *Canadian Baptist* magazine. He challenged the growth of liberalism and the use of liberal professors at McMaster University, and was so militant in his stance that he was driven from the Baptist Convention in 1926. He led the excluded churches in forming the Union of Regular Baptist churches, and became its president. In 1919 and 1920, Shields helped organize and lead the Baptist Forward Movement in Ontario. He founded the *Gospel Witness* magazine in 1922 as his weapon of choice in the developing fight. He became formally involved with the international Fundamentalist cause and became president of the Baptist Bible Union in 1923. Under the auspices of this organization, he led the abortive attempt to purchase and run Des Moines University as a Fundamentalist Christian liberal arts university. With the failure of Des Moines, he established his own institution of higher learning—Toronto Baptist Seminary.

Shields continued as leader of the Baptist Bible Union through the 1930s and most of the 1940s until a tragic split occurred in Toronto Baptist Seminary in 1948. When leaders of the Union expressed criticism of his handling of that split, Shields withdrew from the Union and formed a small splinter group known as the Association of Regular Baptist Churches. He again became involved with a fundamentalist group in 1948, working together with American Carl McIntyre (1906–2002) to form the International Council of Christian Churches.

During the last two-and-a-half decades of his life, Shields became fixated on the threats he saw forming against the western ideological model—unionism, socialism, communism and especially Catholicism. In 1941, he helped form the Protestant League and renamed his magazine *The Gospel Witness and Protestant Advocate*. Shields died in 1955 at the age of eighty-two.

Consideration of the successes and failures of Shields' ministry relates in a large way to the matter of his spirituality. His greatest achievements clearly lay in the spiritual sphere. Where he fought spiritual battles with spiritual weapons, he knew extraordinary blessing. Where he became entangled with carnal battles and engaged his opponents with carnal weapons, his ministry diminished. This paper seeks to trace the evolution of Shields' spirituality.

1889–1910

Most of the significant elements of Shields' mature spiritual character found their roots in his early Christian development. One historian has tried to make a case for a cold formalism in Shields' approach to his Christian walk. Mark Parent, in his doctoral thesis "The Christology of T.T. Shields: The Irony of Fundamentalism," argued that in his Fundamentalist crusade Shields deviated from evangelical orthodoxy in his Christology. Parent argued that for Shields, the authority of the Bible itself displaced an "experientially based faith" in Christ. Parent, therefore, worked hard to find in Shields' earliest religious experiences a cold formalistic or rationalistic approach to Christianity. He concluded: "Lacking an ecstatic conversion experience, Shields could not appeal to an experientially based faith for authority. A more external authority was required. This he found in the Holy Scriptures."[9] On the surface, Shields' accounts of his conversion seem to validate Parent's position. When Shields spoke of the event in subsequent years, he deliberately played down the emotional aspect of the event, noting that for him the significant matter was belief in and acceptance of God's Word of promise:

> It was a simple, matter-of-fact business transaction. I rested in the Word of the Lord and I said, "If that is the Word of the Lord, either I am now a Christian or God is a liar—one or the other." And seeing he cannot lie, I believed all my sins were forgiven for His Name's sake. I dared to believe and to rest upon His Word. But I could not have shouted, "Hallelujah!" at that moment. I did not feel particularly like it. I just accepted the promise, and then I went forward and applied for baptism.[10]

Over thirty years after the event, Shields spoke in much the same fashion of the experience as he lectured on homiletics and pastoral theology to his young theology students. Arnold Dallimore remembered Shields' testimony of his conversion as a response to the text of Scripture used that evening by the evangelist Rev. McDonald, "If we

---

9 Mark Parent, "The Christology of T.T. Shields: The Irony of Fundamentalism" (Ph.D. dissertation, McGill University, 1991), 42.

10 Tarr, *Shields of Canada*, 28.

confess our sins, he is faithful and just to forgive us our sins and to cleanse us from all unrighteousness" (1 John 1:9). Shields commented:

> I remember when I received the word that Jesus was my Saviour, and when I believed that all my sins were laid upon Him, I believed just what that verse said. I did not feel that any miracle had been performed; I did not feel any kind of electric shock; I did not feel any great accession of joy and gladness. It was a simple matter-of-fact business transaction.[11]

Parent's contention that Shields' early development was a trajectory toward cold formalism and rationalism is deeply flawed. Parent wrenched one descriptive comment by Shields of his conversion, a comment for which he only has secondary authority, out of the whole context of Shields' first fifteen years of ministry. Upon this solitary evidence, Parent built an incredible fabrication that ignored countless evidence to the contrary. Shields' roots were anything but cold formalism and every fibre of his youthful being resonated with pietistic fervency!

The first evidence of the development of an acute spiritual awareness in the young Shields was the almost ecstatic experience of his baptism. Shields' biographer, Leslie Tarr, correctly observed that though "his conversion was not accompanied by any unusual emotional upheaval, he acknowledged that it was otherwise with regard to his baptism."[12] This experience for Shields was intensely emotional:

> I remember stepping down into the waters of baptism, and I should like to have had a congregation of at least a million just then to witness my confession. I remember emerging from those waters, and the joy that came to me! I did not hear a voice from heaven, saying, "This is my beloved son"—although I was His beloved son—but I had this testimony that God by His infinite grace had put one simple duty plainly before me, about which

---

11 Arnold Dallimore, "Thomas Todhunter Shields: Baptist Fundamentalist" (Unpublished manuscript, in author's possession), 8.

12 Tarr, *Shields of Canada*, 28.

there could be no doubt. I had done just as He commanded me and He said, "Well done, I am pleased with you tonight."[13]

Shields, by his own devotional practices, clearly believed that any consciousness of divine presence was contingent on a commitment to prayer and Bible study. His attention to this in his own life and in the life of all his churches was paramount. Any success he achieved, he attributed to God's answers to prayer. Speaking of Shields' first pastorate, Arnold Dallimore testified of Shields' practice: "T.T. immediately commenced the pattern of life that characterized the whole of his ministry. First thing every morning, after a time with his hymn-book and his Bible he sought God's presence in prayer."[14]

In addition to his private devotional exercises, Shields understood and emphasized the importance of corporate prayer. For Shields, the church was "a spiritual post-office or telegraph office...a place to receive and send messages from and to heaven."[15] All of his ministry, in one sense, moved to this end; that is, to achieve and to lead his people to achieve right relationship with God and intimate communion with him. Indeed, in more than one of the churches he pastored, *The Baptist Year Book* recorded two or more prayer meetings a week. Shields' success in promoting the prayer meeting had to do in part with the deep enjoyment and fulfillment he himself drew from such Christian fellowship.

One of his students, Arnold Dallimore, recalled Shields' expressions of delight with recollected experiences of spiritual *camaraderie*. One example related to his fellowship with a ministerial friend. Speaking of some of Shields' early ministerial relationships he recollected: "Another was with Rev. Walker of Wortley Road Baptist Church and when teaching his class in Toronto Baptist Seminary, T.T. mentioned how he and Mr. Walker often walked in the fields on a Saturday afternoon and spent their time in fellowship and prayer. He spoke with animated delight of the remembrance of these sessions."[16]

---

13 Dallimore, "Thomas Todhunter Shields," 9.

14 Dallimore, "Thomas Todhunter Shields," 11.

15 T.T. Shields, "Oh Earth, Earth, Earth, Hear the Word of the Lord," *Gospel Witness*, 18, no. 47 (March 28, 1940): 1.

16 Dallimore, "Thomas Todhunter Shields," 17.

Prayer then, for Shields, was the *sine qua non* of the Christian experience. Not only was it the source of Christian fellowship but also the vehicle of understanding God's will. Shields' sermon preparation was one illustration of his deep commitment to divine guidance. He later told a story from his early ministry of how he had been experiencing a very fruitful time of sermon preparation in which he was very conscious of the leading and blessing of God's Spirit but then went out to get his mail. Shields testified that he suddenly felt an inner urge to go and visit an unlikeable old fellow who never seemed to listen. However, he convinced himself it was a waste of time. But, when he returned to his sermon preparation, he discovered that the "fire of inspiration" had gone out. He commented:

> At length it flashed upon me as a revelation, that the fruitlessness of my labour was due, not to sudden intellectual disability, but to moral delinquency: I had refused to do what I knew I ought to do. Then I ran away and made that call! When I came back I found as Ezekiel found in his temple vision, "The glory of the Lord came into the house by the way of the gate whose prospect is toward the east"—through the door by which it had departed![17]

Shields would always hesitate to lay claim to direct divine communication in terms of visions or revelations, but he would often speak of a deep sense and assurance of God's will communicated into his heart. This was quite important to him in his early pastorates and particularly in the important decisions he had to make. The most obvious illustration of this was the decision to resign from his Delhi charge and to take up a pastorate in Hamilton. He related the inner compulsion he had to suddenly write out his resignation and present it to the church—without even having thought about it beforehand— to the inner promptings of the Holy Spirit. This sense of an inner prompting was seemingly confirmed to him later when he discovered that this had occurred at precisely the same hour the deacons in Hamilton were praying about his call. When he made the decision

---

17 T.T. Shields, "Faith and a Good Conscience," in *Other Little Ships* (Toronto: The Hunter-Rose Co., 1935), 203.

to resign his pastorate in London, he made the same kind of claim to his Adelaide Street congregation:

> I feel…that our relations as pastor and people…have been so exceedingly happy, and our united labour has been fraught with such large spiritual blessing, that I owe it to you and to myself to assure you that nothing but the clearest indication that such is the divine will could lead me to bring about a severance of our present relationship.[18]

Due, perhaps in part, to this professed dependence upon intimacy with the Divine, Shields soon developed a prophetic demeanor in his ministry as he regularly delivered the Word that God had laid upon his heart. This prophetic aspect was a characteristic that would become far more pronounced in his later period. While he would always attempt to find biblical warrant for his pronouncements, believing God never contradicted himself, nevertheless, there were times that his claims demonstrated a certainty that bordered on assertions of infallibility. Certainly, the time would soon come when he would lay claims to the honours that were due a prophet of the Lord.

Another significant aspect of Shield's early spirituality was his self-lessness as he sought to redeem the time in a sacrificial ministry to others. There can be no question that, from the outset, Shields manifested a very high work ethic. His dogged work habits continued throughout his life and were perhaps the single biggest factor in the success and influence he achieved. Shields' first pastorate in Florence, Ontario, saw an energetic young man who far surpassed the minimum requirements of the job.

Shields began a routine that carried on until the early 1920s. Following his father's practice, he carefully handwrote every sermon he preached and bound the finished product with string. He spoke later of the "laborious preparation to which I habituated myself for so long."[19] In another place, he noted that "most of them represented hours of

---

18 "Among the Churches," *Canadian Baptist* 56 (April 21, 1910): 9.

19 T.T. Shields to Rev. Theodore Anderson, August 13, 1940, box 1, "Shields' Correspondence," JSBCA, Toronto.

midnight and early morning toil."[20] Over 1,500 of these sermons still exist in the archives of Jarvis Street Baptist Church.

Every Sunday, Shields looked for other opportunities to preach the gospel and every Sunday afternoon through this busy year Shields travelled to neighbouring villages to hold a preaching service. Even though he usually travelled the ten plus kilometres by bicycle, he was always back in time for his own evening service. This would be his regular practice throughout his rural pastorates. However, his formal ministry was not limited to Sundays and every week had at least one prayer meeting in which he again emphasized biblical teaching. As noted above, his own devotional life and intimate dependence on prayer translated into a heavy emphasis on the prayer meeting. By the time of his Hamilton pastorate, he had so pressed the issue that the church was able to report for the *Baptist Year Book* three regular weekly prayer meetings, the most of any church reporting in the denomination.[21] In addition to Sunday services and prayer meetings, Shields also engaged in extended campaigns in which he would preach throughout the week as well.

With all of the tasks that Shields performed in these early pastorates, tasks that multiplied as he matured in the pastorate, and that multiplied again as his obvious homiletic and administrative talents led to increased demand for his services, it raised the question as to how he ever found the time to do all that was demanded of him. An intimate letter to his sister many years later gives some rather interesting insights into the question. In 1951, at the age of seventy-seven, Shields lamented the fact that he had not as of yet been able to publish his father's sermons. His life was so busy that he complained "duties follow each other in procession like cars in a traffic jam, crawling bumper to bumper, so that there is no chance to get between them to cross the street." Yet, the problem for Shields was not a lack of time, but rather a lack of energy. "I don't mean to say that I have no time to do it, or that I am so crowded that I cannot do it, but I find that *Anno Domini* has not passed me by, and when I get through with one duty, I am not

---

20 T.T. Shields, "A Sermon Thirty-Three Years Old," *Gospel Witness* 18, no. 47 (March 28, 1940): 4.

21 "Churches, Pastors, Clerks, etc.," *Baptist Year Book* (Baptist Convention of Ontario and Quebec, 1901), 241.

so ready for the next as I used to be, and sometimes have to rest between." While most men might look forward to rest as a well earned break from their labours, Shields always seemed to see rest as a hindrance to the work he wanted to accomplish. With a note of resignation, Shields struggled to give in to the inevitable. "I suppose that is natural. Most men retire many years before they reach my time of life. But I still have all my administration duties to attend to, two sermons on Sunday, and two lectures a week." His last comment, however, gave a sense of the life he led as a young man. "If I could do as once I did, work all night, and begin again early next morning unwearied, I could get through with things; but I find now that that is beyond me."[22] His early ambivalence toward necessary rest was reflected in his holiday times as well. Shields did take holidays during these first fifteen years of ministry, however, his idea of a holiday was to exchange pulpits with another minister and to assume his responsibilities for the period of absence from his own church.

Above all, Shields was dedicated to the task of ministry. There was really but one duty and that was the work of preaching the gospel and winning souls. Everything else he did moved to that end. He did not waste time on anything else, including necessary rest. Even his marriage seemed to be very low profile and, throughout his ministry, his wife stayed in the background, offering support but avoiding any sort of distraction to his "holy" calling.[23] In his mind, the man who accepted a calling of this sort had to be willing to make the necessary sacrifices and to exercise "a vigorous and aggressive service." He was more than critical of the man who wanted to sustain himself by the ministry but who was unwilling or incapable of exercising that kind of intense service.[24]

A vigorous work ethic and an aggressive commitment to ministry were, in these early years, accompanied by a deep commitment to self sacrifice for the sake of gospel service. Shields gave little attention in these early years to his own comfort. When he first moved to the Adelaide Street ministry, the only accommodations he could initially

---

22 T.T. Shields to Miss Ethel Shields, March 1, 1951, Shields Correspondence, JSBCA, Toronto.

23 George Greenway, "Triumphant," *Gospel Witness* 11, no. 14 (August 18, 1932): 1.

24 T.T. Shields, *The Plot That Failed* (Toronto: Gospel Witness, 1937), 302.

find were in a boarding house on Princess Street.[25] Shields, though pastor of one of the larger churches in the city, was content with his lot and went about his ministry without complaint. In the previous pastorate, his example of self sacrifice was the instrument whereby Wentworth Street was able to free itself of dependence on Home Missions funds and become a self-sustaining entity. Shields' leadership in this matter was held out to the denominational churches by C.J. Cameron, the Home Missions secretary as exemplary:

> Among the many lessons of value that may be received from a study of the work undertaken so successfully by the Wentworth St. church is one we wish in closing to emphasize. That is, the willingness on the part of both pastor and people to sacrifice largely in order that their fellow-citizens in other parts of the home-land destitute of the Gospel might receive the means of grace they so richly enjoy.
>
> Is not the first obligation of a Home Mission church, before contributing largely to other missions outside of itself, to become self-supporting, and thus enable the Board to use the money thus saved in entering open doors in other districts? Are there not many other mission churches willing to follow the worthy example of Wentworth St., and by reducing or cancelling completely their application for aid to share in sending the Gospel to many a destitute district whose people anxiously wait for the coming of the missionary with the living and life-giving message of peace?[26]

Another dimension of Shields' early spiritual development consisted in the tools of his trade. In one of the most notable contrasts to the post-war period, Shields in his early pastorates relied almost exclusively on what he considered "spiritual" weapons. Of course, weapons presupposed a war and, very early on, Shields regarded himself as being engaged in a desperate struggle for men's souls, the classic struggle between good and evil.

---

25 Tarr, *Shields of Canada*, 43.

26 C.J. Cameron, "Wentworth St. Baptist Church, Hamilton," *Canadian Baptist* 49 (June 26, 1902): 5.

War is a terrible expedient, and on Christian lips it represents an absolute necessity. It is indicative of *the divine attitude toward evil*. God has declared war. The sword has been unsheathed. Evil is to be searched out, and driven to its last hiding place—out of the sight of God. That too is to be *the Christian attitude*.[27]

Shields' commitment to this warfare was, in large part, a response to the challenge of Jude v.3, "Beloved, when I gave all diligence to write unto you of the common salvation, it was needful for me to write unto you, and exhort you that ye should earnestly contend for the faith which was once delivered unto the saints." The challenge of this text to "earnestly contend" was an admonition that Shields, in future years, would use to justify his militant approach to nearly every issue he confronted.

On September 2, 1911, a year-and-a-half after beginning his pastorate at Jarvis Street Baptist Church, Shields preached a sermon entitled, "The Weapons of our Warfare," a sermon that reflected the attitudes he exhibited throughout his early pastorates. This was likely a development upon an earlier sermon preached in Delhi, November 4, 1899, entitled, "Warfare, Weapons, Victory." The handwritten manuscript of this sermon contained only an outline of Shields' message on that occasion, suggesting a familiarity with the subject that made him comfortable going to the pulpit without a polished sermon in hand. Both sermons dealt with the biblical text from 2 Corinthians 10:4, "For the weapons of our warfare are not carnal, but mighty through God to the pulling down of strongholds." Though we do not have the full text of Shields' sermon, his outline was very significant. There was little doubt that, for Shields, every Christian was by virtue of his faith involved in a war. He noted that "Enemies were abroad," that "Watchfulness was needed," and that "Fighting was imperative." As to the weapons that were to be used, he made several significant observations. "Our weapons," he wrote are "Not Carnal—Therefore Spiritual." Subsidiary points in his message expanded on this principle. "All fleshly weapons [are] condemned.... Apostolic weapons are not obsolete. Spiritually modern warfare differs in no respect from conflicts of

---

27 T.T. Shields, "The Weapons of Our Warfare," September 2, 1911, sermon #913, "Shields' Sermon Manuscripts," JSBCA, Toronto.

ancient times." As to the promised victory, he concluded that it was "Certain," "Complete," and "Wrought by God's power." The weapons then that Shields believed were to be employed in this battle were prayer, evangelism and biblical preaching and teaching. Significantly, he also noted that victory was in one sense "conditional," not being "promised to carnal engagements."[28]

It is not surprising then to discover that the most distinctive characteristic of Shields' early pastorates was his aggressive evangelism. His first pastorate witnessed the beginning of a practice that characterized all of his first five pastorates. Shields would announce the beginning of an evangelistic campaign and, after extended preparations in prayer and visitation, he would begin meetings that would extend from one to five weeks. In most of these, he would do the bulk of the preaching himself. He preached every night of the week except Saturday, and then usually three times on Sunday. His first such campaign in Florence lasted three weeks. Once in his Adelaide Street pastorate in London, he led a five month campaign, though on that occasion he did rely fairly heavily on other pastors to supplement his own preaching. It has already been noted that after his Hamilton pastorate, Shields dedicated over a year to nothing but evangelism.

1910–1920

The first decade of Shields ministry in Jarvis Street Baptist Church proved to be a pivotal period for Shields' spiritual development. In some ways, his understanding of spirituality grew and matured; in other ways, distractions to that same spirituality began to appear in his life. Two factors in particular contributed to this maturation and decline in his spiritual development: the demographic context and the impact of the First World War.

The demographic factor came to expression in the culture of respectability that Shields first encountered in Jarvis Street Baptist Church. Shields, the otherworldly evangelist, was suddenly confronted with the materialistic constraints prevalent among those of a higher social class than his previous ministerial charges. When Shields came to Jarvis Street, he was suddenly confronted with a very different

---

28 T.T. Shields, "Warfare, Weapons, Victory," November 4, 1899, sermon #389, "Shields' Sermon Manuscripts," JSBCA, Toronto.

demographic construct. Now, for the first time, Shields faced the challenge of ministering to the social elite of both the ecclesiastical realm and the secular. Jarvis Street's membership list was like a "Who's Who" of Toronto's social elite as well as the denominational hierarchy of the Baptist Convention. The first casualty of Shields' earlier spiritual deportment came in this period with the loss of the evangelistic campaign. Revival services were characteristic of sect-type Christianity, and received little acceptance in the more respectable church-type Christianity found among the socially respectable members of Jarvis Street.[29] Shields himself identified the restraints of "worldliness" and "respectability" and concluded, "I had to wait eleven years for my full liberty as a preacher of the gospel."[30]

However, not only was the evangelistic campaign displaced, Shields' view of spiritual success was also reshaped. It is interesting to reflect upon Shields' own assessment of his church and ministry during this period. By his own account in *The Plot that Failed*, Shields claimed to have enjoyed, for a few years at least, a harmonious and generally successful ministry. Shields was anxious to attribute the troubles that he finally encountered in Jarvis Street to outside interference from McMaster interests rather than from any ministerial failings on his part. Shields tried hard to paint a rosy picture of the period but it is clear that all was not well, either with his congregation or with his own ministry. While Shields spoke highly of his congregation from this early period, he also acknowledged a deep-seated ambivalence toward them. On the one hand, he lauded them as "delightful people

---

29 Concerning the distinction between church and sect, see S.D. Clark, *Church and Sect in Canada* (Toronto: University of Toronto Press, 1948.) Clark sought to examine the struggle between church and sect; the struggle between the organized religious structure which sought order and accommodation with the community versus the otherworldly separatists who had little or no concern with the ungodly society around them. This struggle revolved around the issue of social stability which when present favoured the church and when absent encouraged the sect form of religious organization. Thus the church grew out of the conditions of mature society while the sect was a product of frontier conditions of social life. For more on the religious shift toward respectability among the Methodists of this period, see Marguerite Van Die, *An Evangelical Mind: Nathaniel Burwash and the Methodist Tradition in Canada, 1839–1918* (Kingston: McGill-Queen's University Press, 1989).

30 Shields, *The Plot That Failed*, 196.

on the whole" who "walked circumspectly before the world." On the other hand, he castigated them in the same breath as being worldly and lacking in spirituality. They "had not learned the principle of entire separation 'unto the gospel of Christ.'"[31] The ambivalence Shields felt toward his people had to reflect upon his own record during this period, a record that essentially caused him to redefine his definition of success. Clearly, upon ascending to the pulpit of Jarvis Street Baptist Church, Shields had achieved the first of two lifelong dreams. In this he had been eminently successful, and Shields was not the least bit reticent about gloating over his triumph in wresting this choicest "plum" from the sphere of McMaster patronage. Having achieved this honour, it is clear that he was not going to let it slip from his grip for anything except a call to Spurgeon's Metropolitan Tabernacle, despite the character of the congregation he had inherited. Nevertheless, hints of the inner struggle he faced surfaced time and again as he reflected upon this early period of ministry. His idealistic assumptions about this premier Baptist church did not at all line up with the reality he encountered. He quickly found himself mired in the culture of "respectability." In his previous pastorates, Shields calculated his success in terms of the measure to which he had brought glory to Christ and extended the kingdom of heaven. The results of his evangelistic efforts were his only barometer of success. By surrendering the evangelistic campaign, Shields had to measure himself by different standards, standards that focused far more on his own abilities and accomplishments.

The second factor that helped reshape Shields' spirituality during these years was his experience of the First World War. When Shields returned home from England in 1918 from his experiences on the warfront, he was both more committed and more militant. On the one hand, his spirituality came to a maturity of expression that was directly instrumental in the years of revival that characterized his ministry of the 1920s, but, on the other hand, seeds of spiritual distraction were sown that would haunt his latter decades of ministry and rob it of the spiritual vibrancy of earlier periods.

There can be little doubt that upon his return from England in 1918, things quickly changed in Shields' ministerial demeanor and outlook.

---

31 Shields, *The Plot That Failed*, 24.

Thomas Todhunter Shields
1873–1955

Over the next few years, the same man who had never suffered through a church split and had been used by the denomination for his conciliatory skills, now witnessed a serious division within his own church—and dragged the whole denomination into the most bitter rupture in its history.

At home in Jarvis Street, a faction was becoming increasingly restless under a ministry they found to be progressively more controversial. They complained: "Dr. Shields' ways do not appeal to a quiet peace-loving people, such as we are. He is a fighter all the time."[32] In the pivotal 1926 convention at First Avenue Baptist Church, one delegate was led to the observation:

> Three years ago in the Emmanuel Baptist Church there was not a man who would not have voted for Dr. Shields and followed his leadership; to-day I challenge anybody to find a single man who has any confidence in any statement that Dr. Shields makes.

Moments later the same delegate remarked,

> These things are crippling the Lord's work. If slandering the brethren is Satan's work, if robbing men of God of their good name is dishonourable, if disrupting churches and sowing disunion is wicked, if undermining the health of noble and Christian men is cruel, then I beseech Dr. Shields to come to repentance, for he has committed every one of these offences.[33]

It should be noted that both of these examples are expressions of those who were willingly blind to the issues Shields was trying to confront. However, both inside his church and outside, a new and more caustic Dr. Shields was emerging. Shields would have explained the changes in his demeanor as a necessary response to the enormity of the threat

---

32 "Retired Deacons Tell of Jarvis Church Case," *The Toronto Daily Star* (October 12, 1921), sec. 1, 2.

33 T.T. Shields, "Ichabod, McMaster's New Name" *Gospel Witness* 5, no. 26 (November 4, 1926): 155–156. This was an expanded issue of the *Gospel Witness*. In its earliest form, the magazine commonly ran to 8 pages. As controversy unfolded, editions began to run over 20 pages. This particular edition was 176 pages in length and was printed as a separate booklet.

facing evangelical Christianity. Shields now viewed himself as a heroic warrior, set for the defense of the faith. While the import of the issues being fought over certainly contributed to the magnitude and speed of his metamorphosis, it is equally arguable that Shields' immersion in the affairs of war over the previous four years led to significant shifts in his outlook and behaviour.

War now increasingly became the defining metaphor in Shields' view of the Christian faith. Early in his career and before his involvement in the First World War, Shields had a much more *otherworldly* view of the warfare in which he was to be engaged. The connection between "great conflicts" of the physical and spiritual realms lay in the sphere of principles. In his early sermons, Shields was quick to find illustrations in contemporary battles of spiritual realities. Nevertheless, the connection between the two realms was tenuous and served primarily to provide illustrative material. "In every great conflict," he argued, "the warring peoples are representative of warring principles, and from the issue of such battles useful lessons may always be learned." For instance, at the conclusion of the war between Russia and Japan, he impressed upon his congregation the importance of making peace with God. At that time, though, he was quick to note: "I am aware that the now historic conflict between Russia & Japan can only partially illustrate the battle between the soul and God."[34] However, with the advent of the Great War, the connections between physical and spiritual dimensions quickly deepened.

Arguably, one of the most dramatic consequences of this growing conflation of spiritual and physical was the loss of the otherworldly aspect so characteristic of Shields' early ministry. While this element never entirely disappeared, it became less and less prominent in subsequent years. There was a subtle elevation in Shields' mind of the significance of contemporary events and a growing tendency to spiritualize such events. The war marked the genesis of this trend and set the trajectory toward his later absorption in political matters in the 1930s and thereafter. His fascination with the unfolding scenes of war increasingly diverted his attention from the eternal to the temporal. Shields' justification for his obsession with the temporal

---

34 T.T. Shields "The End of the War" (London: 1905), JSBCA, Sermons and Lectures, Box 2, File 656–660, Sermon 659.

affairs of war was to find spiritual meanings in events, often elevating the importance of temporal circumstances so as to speak of them in a spiritual fashion.

It is not surprising then that, with Shields' changing outlook, the war would evoke practical and significant changes in the manner of his ministry. These could be summarized as a new military leadership model, a new military service model and a new military operational model.[35] It was in Shields' military service model and his evolving expectations of his congregation that some of the most idealistic and the most mature expressions of Shields' spirituality were found.

By the end of Dr. Shields' first decade in Jarvis Street, his relationship with his congregation was becoming increasingly strained. Though the changing character of Shields' leadership style played a part in this tension, the heightened expectations that Shields was developing for those under his pastoral care certainly contributed to the friction. The beginnings of this trend began mid-decade as Shields began to challenge the social elite and their culture of respectability. The call to holiness in the matter of fiscal responsibility was his first battle.[36] When, however, Shields began to attack the badges of social respectability that had for so long defined their "dear old Jarvis Street," the war was on.[37] The struggle over the choir was but the first round of a vicious fight that came very close to ousting Shields from the church and issued in a significant fracture of the congregation in 1921. The reasons for Shields' magnified expectations arose from several factors that all converged for him in 1919. In that year, Shields emerged victorious from the Ottawa convention, the first of many skirmishes over theological liberalism within the convention. As Shields reflected on the ramifications of the liberal assault, he began to realize that

---

35 For a fuller discussion of the impact of the First World War on Dr. Shields' ministry, see Doug Adams, "The Call to Arms: Reverend Thomas Todhunter Shields, World War One and the Shaping of a Militant Fundamentalist," paper presented to The Canadian Baptist Historical Society, March 3, 2012.

36 See Shields, *The Plot That Failed*, 32–33. Cf. Paul Wilson, "Baptists and Business: Central Canadian Baptists and The Secularization of the Businessman at Toronto's Jarvis Street Baptist Church, 1848–1921" (Ph.D. dissertation, University of Western Ontario, 1996), 220–224.

37 In the climactic battle to evict Shields from Jarvis Street, the rallying cry was "save dear old Jarvis Street." Cf. Shields, *The Plot That Failed*, 240, 244.

there was a significant alliance of cultural liberalism with the theological liberalism manifesting itself within the denomination at large.

Though his members objected violently to being painted with the "liberal" brush and even protested in the press about false accusations of "worldliness" and "modernism,"[38] Shields believed that business interests and social obligations had made them intolerant to the demands of biblical holiness. Shields later reflected that when he brought the matter of theological liberalism within the denomination before his church, to his surprise, his concern was resisted:

> I can see that Sunday morning congregation as I write. Had I measured the personal conviction of each one by his or her profession, I should have estimated there were few opposed to the position I had taken.... I have since learned that men who are seemingly true to evangelical positions are as houses built upon the sand.... But their evangelicalism is based upon the sands of heredity, education, and expediency. They are as those hearers who have not root in themselves, and when "tribulation or persecution ariseth because of the word, by and by (they are) offended."[39]

Realizing that many within his congregation were indifferent to the denominational controversy or openly resistant to his position, Shields began a campaign to call his congregation to self-denial. Shields acknowledged he had not fully understood the concept until that Sunday morning sermon:

> I had not then learned the profound philosophy our Lord's saying: "Think not that I am come to send peace on earth: I came not to send peace, but a sword. For I am come to set a man at variance against his father, and the daughter against her mother.... He that loveth father or mother more than me is not worthy of me: and he that loveth son or daughter more than me is not worthy of me. And he that taketh not his cross, and followeth after me

---

38 "Retired Deacons Tell of Jarvis Church Case," 2.
39 Shields, *The Plot That Failed*, 125.

is not worthy of me. He that findeth his life shall lose it: and he that loseth his life for my sake shall find it."[40]

Nearly a decade after Shields had initiated the battle with modernism in his own church, he would reflect back upon the hostility that he provoked by his call to self-denial. In a sermon entitled, "Crucified with Christ," he noted the character of true spirituality and its consequences:

It was Christ's insistence upon the spirituality of the law which called forth the hostility which uttered itself in the Cross; it was the violation of the law's spiritual requirements which made the divine judgment of the Cross necessary. It was an unspiritual religion, fashioned in its externals after a divine pattern, which brought Jesus to the Cross. And if you and I take Christ's spiritual law of life as a standard for the regulation of our inner life, our thinking, and desiring, and willing; if we take it with us into our homes and apply it to all our social relations, if we erect it as a standard of conduct in our places of business, if we bring it to bear upon our distinctively religious activities, if we make Christ's spiritual law of life the touchstone to which the whole of life is brought for spiritual appraisement, we shall be crucified with Christ. Try it to-morrow in the office. Try it to-day in the home; try it this moment in the pew, let us judge ourselves by Christ's interpretation of the deep spirituality of God's law, and in everyone of us the principle of evil, which spoke in the ancient Pharisee, and the principle of holiness which wrought in Christ will come again into conflict, and with this dual significance a Cross will be erected for us."[41]

The second factor that heightened Shields' expectations for his congregation came from his involvement with the Baptist Forward Movement. Shields became heavily involved with that denominational effort, organizing it and travelling extensively to promote its goals.[42]

---

40 Shields, *The Plot That Failed*, 125. cf. Matthew 10:34–39.

41 T.T. Shields "Crucified with Christ," *Gospel Witness* 6, no. 21, (September 29, 1927), 5.

42 Shields, *The Plot That Failed*, 161–184. Cf. T.T. Shields, *The Inside of the Cup* (Toronto: Jarvis Street Baptist Church, 1921), 16.

In the course of his travels he met with the deacon of a church who informed him that the biggest obstacle to spiritual revival in his own church was a divided attitude about worldliness:

> This man told me he was a Deacon of the Baptist church in the city where he lived, and that his fellow Deacons were all fine men, but they were about equally divided on spiritual matters. He said half of the Deacons desired to see the church spiritually aggressive, and athrob with the power of the Holy Ghost, but that the others were content with a respectable worldliness. Many of their members he said, were fond of card-playing, and had their little dancing parties, and saw no inconsistency in being found frequently at the theatre.[43]

Later when visiting that church in the course of his preaching tour with one of his own deacons, Shields determined to make an appeal: "I then appealed to Ministers and Deacons, and all present, if they felt God's call to a deeper consecration, to leave their seats and come forward and say so."[44] Shields was profoundly moved by the following scene:

> In the congregation I saw the friend whose guest I had been, and who had been described to me as one of the worldly Deacons. He whispered to his wife, and they immediately left their seats and walked up to the front, and without invitation, knelt before the platform, the Deacon putting his arm about his wife's shoulders as they knelt to pray. My Deacon-friend [Shields' co-presenter], deeply moved, and with tears upon his cheeks, stepped down from the platform—it was only about eighteen inches high—and knelt beside the Deacon, putting his arm upon his shoulder. Then the procession started—Ministers and Deacons came forward until there was a great company—I would not dare to say how many—on their knees before God. I can only add that we continued with confessions, and petitions, and praises, until long past the midnight hour. We sang the Doxology together, and

---

43 Shields, *The Plot That Failed*, 203.
44 Shields, *The Plot That Failed*, 207.

bowed as a closing prayer was offered, leaving the place feeling that God had visited His people.[45]

The question of worldly amusements, "notably, dancing, card-playing, and theatre-going," soon became one of the hot issues for the Forward Movement.[46] Shields became convinced that these things were the major obstacles to revival blessings falling upon the denomination and his church. He began to preach about the necessity of "entire separation." It would be this factor more than any other that drove the wedge between him and the social elites within his congregation. Reflecting back upon the congregation that he served in that first decade at Jarvis Street he noted: "In those days, few members of Jarvis Street had learned to give the Lord all their time apart from that which was necessary for their business and their home life…some had not learned the principle of entire separation 'unto the gospel of Christ.'"[47] In the years following the eventual split of 1921, Shields preached and insisted upon this principle of entire separation, and, not incidentally, the church experienced the richest years of revival in its history.

The third factor in Shields' inflated expectations was the contextualization of the whole struggle in terms of the world war that had just been concluded. Shields was determined to bring his new military perspective to bear on the question:

It were folly for anyone to join the army in wartime on condition that he be not required to leave his wife and family, business associates, and the country he loves! Hence our Lord insisted that no one could truly be His disciple who would not put allegiance to Him before all other considerations of life.[48]

Having witnessed firsthand the deprivations of war and the stupendous cost at which victory was achieved, he now firmly believed that the wars of the Spirit could be won with no lesser sacrifice:

---

45 Shields, *The Plot That Failed*, 207.
46 Shields, *The Plot That Failed*, 211.
47 Shields, *The Plot That Failed*, 23.
48 Shields, *The Plot That Failed*, 125.

I have a vivid recollection of seeing the military trains leave
Charing Cross and Waterloo stations in Old London during the
War. I saw officers and men standing on the platform with their
wives and children and other loved ones about them. And as the
warning signal was given these splendid men each took his wife
and his children into his arms, and often as tears streamed down
their manly faces bade their loved ones good-bye. And after the
doors of the carriages were closed, and the train began slowly
to move out, I have seen them stretch out their arms that the
wife and mother might once more put the baby into the father's
arms for a parting kiss. In those great days, yes, GREAT, though
terrible, no one was ashamed to shed tears. But why did these
men go? Was it because they did not love their wives and children? Certainly not! It was because they loved duty more. And
for the sake of the world's freedom they separated themselves
even from those they loved the best that, unhindered, they
might, amid scenes of blood, do their utmost to preserve the
liberties of the world. And if we are to make progress in the work
of the Lord the same principle must be applied, and the same
spirit must be exemplified.[49]

1920–1955

While the war brought about a maturation of Shields' attitudes toward
self denial and entire separation, it also introduced a new militancy
that at the same time eroded the spiritual gains made in the sphere of
consecration. Shields' earlier dependence upon spiritual tools rapidly
morphed during the early 1920s into an appeal to weapons of a more
carnal nature. As Shields entered the 1919 Ottawa Convention and
became the chief protagonist in the inspiration controversy, his reliance upon spiritual resources was still paramount. His description of
his preparations for that battle spoke of his reliance upon prayer and
the Word of God:

Having prayed, as I continued to meditate, it appeared to my
mind that I should be most likely to find a word of special guid-

---

49 T.T. Shields, "A Holy War" *Gospel Witness* 2, no. 6 (June 21, 1923): 3. Emphasis
mine.

ance in the pastoral epistles, since they were written by a veteran to a younger preacher. I therefore turned to Timothy. Opening the Book, I came upon the concluding verses of the last chapter of Second Timothy, and my eyes fell upon these words: "At my first answer no man stood with me, but all me forsook me: I pray God that it may not be laid to their charge. Notwithstanding the Lord stood with me, and strengthened me; that by me the preaching might be full known, and that all the Gentiles might hear: and I was delivered out of the mouth of the lion. And the Lord shall deliver me from every evil work, and will preserve me unto his heavenly kingdom; to whom be glory for ever and ever. Amen."

I despair of conveying to my readers an accurate understanding of that moment. I was to speak the next day in defense of the Bible as the Word of God. At that moment I knew, as perhaps I had never known before, how truly it is the Word of God. If the words had been uttered out of the open heaven, or communicated by some special visible and audible heavenly messenger, it would have been impossible that I should have been more thrilled than I was at that moment. I went into my wife's room, and wakened her, and asked her to rise and join with me in thanksgiving for the victory God was to give on the morrow.[50]

Such was the case in late 1919.

However, as Shields encountered more and more resistance to his stand against modernism in his own church, the militancy of his response stiffened and his weaponry become increasingly carnal in its nature. Over the months and years that were to follow, Shields became more and more inclined to a denunciatory ministry, jingoistic diatribes, political machinations and out-and-out character assassinations. The pulpit and the press became the primary vehicles of his militant fulminations. In his own pulpit at Jarvis Street Baptist Church, Shields' growing militancy came to expression in what many of his members identified as knocking, or "hitting."[51] The temptation toward a denunciatory ministry seems to have become a common one during this period. One correspondent to *The Canadian Baptist* noted: "During

---

50 Shields, *The Plot That Failed*, 141.
51 Ryrie to T.T. Shields, March 14, 1918, in *The Inside of the Cup*, 49.

the war we developed a spirit of battle, and perhaps one of the results of that has been a tendency to fall into the way of opposing everyone with whom there may be any ground for a difference."[52] The "pew-sitters" in Jarvis Street were particularly sensitive to Shields' growing addiction to the trend.

As the struggle for control of Jarvis Street heated up in 1920 to 1921, a huge political campaign was waged by his opponents in an attempt to drive Shields from the pulpit. Initially, Shields refused to respond in kind, but eventually gave in to the temptation to engage in his own political maneuvering:

> I reached the conclusion that, notwithstanding we had been on our knees for nearly six months before God, praying for victory, we must use ordinary prudence in preparation for the great conflict; and inasmuch as every member of the church had been canvassed again and again throughout the six months by the opposition, and we had done nothing in that direction, it would be well to select a band of people who would visit the membership to urge the members to come out and vote.[53]

Shields then conducted his own visitation campaign by hand picking 110 loyal members, secretly meeting with them off site, asking them to visit all the undecided members and then having them mail in a card identifying the position held by each of those so visited.[54] Much the same thing happened later in his fight with McMaster University. By 1925, Dr. Shields was through with "playing nice" and commented:

> We intend to fight on. As a matter of fact the war has just begun... We promise those who would lead the denomination to destruction, that if they have feared *The Gospel Witness* before, they shall fear it a hundred-fold more in the future. We have long endeavoured to maintain diplomatic relations but that effort is at an end. We propose to bring the enemy out of his dugout.... We

---

52 J.L. Gilmour, "Conference Impressions," *Canadian Baptist* 65 (March 13, 1919): 8.
53 Shields, *The Plot That Failed*, 315.
54 Shields, *The Plot That Failed*, 315.

have avoided anything like organization. Now we intend to work for it.... We shall also endeavour to enlist churches as such to present a solid front to the enemy."[55]

One historian has noted that Shields now engaged his enemies on six fronts: (i) *The Gospel Witness*; (ii) the pulpit; (iii) protest rallies; (iv) withdrawal of support; (v) rival educational institutions; and (vi) secession meetings.[56] Having learned something of the power of the pen in his rapid publication of *The Inside of the Cup*, a feat he accomplished in less than twenty-four hours, Shields noted:

> Since that time, on scores of occasions, I have spent all night in the printer's office, in editorial work, on some jobs that were far bigger than "The inside of the Cup." Our success, however, in that venture demonstrated the possibilities of quick reply, which I have very frequently made use of since then.[57]

When the violence of his language both from the pulpit and in the pages of his magazine provoked a backlash of condemnation, Shields was quick to defend himself:

> The question we propose now to discuss is whether "violent language" can be justified.... There can be but one answer: when the things of the spiritual world become as real as submarines and bombing aeroplanes, and their victims, when the murder of a soul is as vividly realized as the crimes of Hickman or Loeb or Leopold—when, indeed, men actually believe the Bible to be God's Word, and therefore to be true, they will find no language too strong with which to describe the sin of rebellion against God.[58]

As the fight heated up within his church, as he wrestled with denominational leaders and finally as he waged war on the interna-

---

55 T.T. Shields, "Creeping in Unawares," *Gospel Witness* 4, no. 25 (October 22, 1925): 4.

56 John D.E. Dozois, "Dr. Thomas Todhunter Shields (1873–1955) in the Stream of Fundamentalism" (B.D. dissertation, McMaster University Divinity School, 1963), 78.

57 Shields, *The Plot That Failed*, 346.

58 T.T. Shields, "Violent Language," *Gospel Witness* 8, no. 2 (May 30, 1929): 1, 6.

tional scene as president of the Baptist Bible Union, Shields gradually perfected his skills of denunciation and condemnation. By the end of the 1920s, Shields' dependence upon carnal weaponry had insinuated its way into nearly every area of his spiritual life. His fellowship with many who could have stood with him was destroyed and from 1930 to the end of his life Shields was increasingly marginalized in his larger spiritual impact.

The First World War most certainly helped shaped Shields' militant responses to the issues of his age, and contributed to the rapid dependence on carnal weaponry. However, it also undermined his otherworldly perspective by creating an increasing fascination with the temporal concerns surrounding him. In so doing, it not only affected his choice of weapon but also the *character* of the warfare in which he was engaged. Prior to the war, Shields' whole focus had been evangelistic and kingdom oriented. With the death of the Baptist Bible Union and the popularity of the Fundamentalist cause in the late 1920s, Shields' attentions turned more and more to the threats facing the Western ideological model. From this point, Shields meddled more and more in socio-political matters. The media was fascinated with his exploits. In his 1949 article in *Maclean's* magazine entitled, "The Battling Baptist," Gerald Angelin catalogued a list of his skirmishes:

> T.T. has gone scalping after gamblers, card players, burlesque comedians, the United States of America and women. He has attacked beverage rooms ("trapdoors to hell"), bobbed hair ("The Lord never intended women to go to the barber") and athletics ("The Lord hath no pleasure in the legs of a man").
>
> Laying about at his fellow believers, he has denounced Methodists, Anglicans, the United Church and the Oxford Group. More than any of these he has attacked the Roman Catholic Church, but he has lashed out at brother Baptists more relentlessly and more vehemently than at all other objects of his wrath combined.[59]

By 1935, Shields was increasingly consumed with his running battles with leading politicians. Kenneth Johnston of *The Standard* noted something of Shields' record in the social and political arena:

---

59 Shields, "Violent Language": 1, 6.

The year 1935 was the year of Dr. Shields' big campaign on Mitch Hepburn, and for once Mitch had met his match in the gentle art of invective. First he announced that Hepburn was a vulgarian demagogue. Then he noticed that Hepburn strongly resembled Hitler. He asked the pertinent question: Did Rome assist Hepburn? Finally he lit upon the golden phrase of 'Hepburn's Alliance with Rum and Rome.'

Noting that the past few years had posed some few problems for Shields he concluded,

However, his great crusade goes on with unabated and uninhibited fervour. He still calls for the ousting of Mackenzie King, Premier Drew, the Catholic church, the Baptist Modernists, the Baptist Fundamentalists who oppose him, Labour Unions and cartels.... But these are merely a few of the things that Dr. Shields opposes and combats with pen and voice. Just you name something else and he will be against it, providing, of course, that it isn't Pastor Shields himself.[60]

Conclusion

To his credit, throughout the years, Shields continued to preach the same gospel of grace that he had preached when he began his career. Many within his church were largely insolated from the socio-political commentary that won him such public notoriety. He was a capable administrator and he built up a large Sunday School, a significant training institution for Baptist ministers and continued to pastor effectively one of the largest Baptist churches in Ontario. Within the walls of his church he was deeply loved and respected to the end.

His defense of the fundamentals of the faith was important, but his reliance upon carnal weapons contributed to Fundamentalism's ultimate fracture. His resistance to the rising tide of secularism and pursuit of a more righteous society was commendable but the distractions of those interests served only to undermine the otherworldly perspective that made him such an effective evangelist in his youth. In the end, his efforts in the socio-political sphere were largely counter-

---

60 Kenneth Johnstone, "Toronto's Dr. Shields," *The Standard* (1946): 10–11.

productive, as his militancy left him marginalized. As one modern commentator has noted: "Too much sanctimony in the marketplace of ideas, renders a person and/or institution less than relevant."[61]

Shields' greatest contribution to spirituality came in his insistence upon entire separation. So long as Shields insisted upon that in his own life and ministry, he saw years of unparalleled spiritual success. Shields was right to bring the question of social pastimes under scrutiny and to insist upon separation from worldly amusements. Separation from the world to the ministry of prayer and evangelism was a distinguishing characteristic of the revivals of the 1920s. Shields was amazingly successful in instilling such ideals into his congregation. However, the otherworldly focus that he achieved there was undermined in his own life by his militant response to the world in which he lived. The social distractions Shields condemned in the social elite of his congregation paled into insignificance beside the social and political morass into which Shields ultimately found himself entangled. His intentions were honourable but, in the end, Shields' spirituality suffered from the violation of the very principle that had generated such spiritual power and vitality. Entire separation, by its very definition, demands application in every sphere of life.

---

61 Charles Adler, "Jesus had a Human Face Too," *Toronto Sun* (May 24, 2006), 21.

IN HONOUR

23

IN HONOUR

Michael A.G. Haykin: historian of the Spirit

By Clint Humfrey

He who has an ear, let him hear what the Spirit
says to the churches (Revelation 2:7).

Deep roots are not reached by the frost.
—J.R.R. Tolkien[1]

LUKE TELLS US that when the apostle Paul met the Ephesians he asked
if they had been baptized by the Holy Spirit. They replied that they
had not even heard of a Holy Spirit (Acts 19:2). Since then that
response has been the foil for the church's confession. It is a response
that reminds the church of the life of the Spirit at work in the body of
Christ. From the days of Pentecost until now, Christians have engaged
in the task of collecting, recording and announcing the Spirit's work.
As broad as this Christian consciousness may be, there have always
been a few in the church who have taken up Luke's example and
become archivists of ecclesiastical life. They are historians of the Spirit.
Michael Haykin is one of their company.

---

1   Dr. Haykin used this line on the cover page of many of his syllabi. The source
is the poem *All That's Gold Does Not Glitter*, also called *The Riddle of Strider* in J.R.R.
Tolkien, *The Fellowship of the Ring* (London: George Allen & Unwin, 1954).

First impressions

I first came across Michael Haykin's name in a handwritten subscription renewal notice for the magazine *Reformation Today*, edited by Erroll Hulse, of which Haykin was the Canadian agent at the time.[2] Haykin's characteristic blue ink script from a fountain pen would be familiar to me in later years when I became a student of his and then later a colleague. The number of imitators of his Moleskine journals and fountain pens is now lost in the faddish wake of urban hipster culture.

As a student of Haykin's essential course, "Puritan and Evangelical Spirituality," I met the historian of the Spirit for the first time.[3] Never before had I been exposed to the sublime reflections of the Christian tradition on the person of the Holy Spirit. Like a man's limb gone numb with temporary paralysis, churches in my experience had recoiled sharply from the charismatic movement and the subjectivism of Keswick hybrids. They were nearly incapable of acknowledging pneumatology except as an abstract necessity. So it was a functional awakening for me to learn about the history of the Spirit from Haykin. Compared to the happenings of Azusa Street, this history recalled more depth but less novelty.[4] The Spirit's orchestration of Christian piety which Haykin opened to me was like "an untravelled world."

Interest in the Spirit's work in the church
1. THE CHURCH FATHERS

By that point in his career Haykin had already developed his triad of interests in the Spirit's work in the church. The first of these was the church fathers in general, and the Cappadocians in particular. Haykin had first taken an interest in Basil of Caesarea's work on the Spirit as a new convert in the charismatic movement prevailing among

---

2 Reformation Today Trust published an early and important book by Haykin, which Robert Oliver described in the "Foreword" as one that "needed to be written." Michael A.G. Haykin, *Kiffin, Knollys and Keach: Rediscovering Our English Baptist Heritage* (Leeds: Reformation Today Trust, 1996).

3 For the book form of these lectures see Michael A.G. Haykin, *The God Who Draws Near: An Introduction to Biblical Spirituality* (Darlington: Evangelical Press, 2007).

4 The "Azusa Street Revival" was a Pentecostal revival meeting that took place in Los Angeles, California, in 1906, and is considered the origin of the worldwide Pentecostal movement.

Michael A.G. Haykin
1953–

Christian university students in the 1970s.[5] This interest led to his doctoral thesis on the Pneumatomachian controversy with focus on the use of Paul's Corinthian letters by defenders of the deity of the Holy Spirit.[6] The Cappadocians were impressed to summarize what the Scripture said concerning the Holy Spirit. They were part of that Spirit-led process of developing and refining doctrine. Throughout the church's history, this development has been occasioned by errors and confusion which required pastoral attention and the application of Scriptural truths with spiritual sensitivity.[7] The Arian controversy was a watershed for clarifying and confessing the deity of Christ, but it also lead necessarily to the clarification of the Spirit's divinity.[8]

A Baptist writing on Patristics was rare in the twentieth century. Most patristic work was done by Roman Catholic or Eastern Orthodox scholars.[9] With this concern for doctrinal development in matters at the core of the Christian faith, the Cappadocians would have stood tall for an historian of the Spirit. For modern evangelicals, practitioners like Billy Graham or D.L. Moody may appear mountain-like in their significance.[10] But for an historian of the Spirit like Haykin, the church fathers were more significant. He was like the man who entered the wide plain in order to see the whole range of mountains, many of which dwarfed the ones in his nearer proximity. In this way, distance

---

5   For a brief account of Haykin's conversion and early Christian experience see "An Introductory Word" in his book, *The Empire of the Holy Spirit* (Memphis: Borderstone Press, 2010), i. See also G. Stephen Weaver Jr. and Ian Hugh Clary, "Michael A.G. Haykin: a biographical sketch," in this book, *The pure flame of devotion*, 3–14.

6   The thesis was published as Michael A.G. Haykin, *The Spirit of God: The Exegesis of 1 and 2 Corinthians in the Pneumatomachian Controversy of the Fourth Century* (Leiden: E.J. Brill, 1994).

7   See Michael A.G. Haykin, *Defence of the Truth: Contending for the Faith, yesterday and today* (Darlington: Evangelical Press, 2004).

8   See "Defending the Holy Spirit's Deity: Basil of Caesarea, Gregory of Nyssa, and the Pneumatomachian Controversy of the 4th Century" *The Southern Baptist Journal of Theology* 7, no. 3 (Fall 2003): 74–79.

9   See Haykin's reflections on his mentor John Egan, a Roman Catholic Jesuit scholar, in Michael A.G. Haykin, *Rediscovering the Church Fathers: Who They Were and How They Shaped the Church* (Wheaton: Crossway 2011), 150–151.

10   Haykin's reflections on the continuities and discontinuities of evangelicalism with the past, especially concerning the influence of the Enlightenment are taken up in Michael A.G. Haykin, Kenneth J. Stewart, ed., *The Advent of Evangelicalism: Exploring Historical Continuities* (Nashville: B & H Academic, 2008).

permitted scope of judgement and scope of judgement permitted a deeper appreciation.[11]

2. THE EIGHTEENTH-CENTURY BAPTISTS

The second part of this triad of interests was Haykin's research into the English Calvinistic Baptists of the eighteenth century. Haykin taught at Central Baptist Seminary in Toronto after graduating from the University of Toronto in 1982. At this time, the churches in the seminary's constituency were not enthusiastic about special lectures on church fathers. Partly in response, Haykin developed his research interest into the history of English Calvinistic Baptists. During the eighteenth century they experienced profound renewal and saw the dawn of modern Protestant missions. Although William Carey, the pioneer missionary to India, was well known, the pastors and churches that banded together to send him across the globe were not.[12] Haykin mined much of this forgotten history, bringing to light the engines which propelled a remarkable enterprise. It is no surprise that the components working behind the Serampore Mission were frequent Haykin themes: prayer, the Word of God preached, the sovereignty of God, the use of means and the activity of the Spirit.[13] Haykin's massive work on John Sutcliff of Olney compiled these findings in a way that featured the virtually unknown efforts of Baptist pastors alongside William Carey's famous efforts.[14] As an historian of the Spirit, Haykin traced the source of that profound transcontinental missionary enterprise to the pious, theologically-driven devotion of ordinary pastors animated by Word and Spirit.[15]

---

11 The influence of the church fathers on Haykin is illustrated by his recollection of a study of Irenaeus' view of the future after the death of Haykin's mother, Theresa Haykin, in *Rediscovering the Church Fathers*, 152.

12 For example Samuel Pearce, who was described as "another Brainerd" and was much admired in his day yet who is relatively unknown today. See Michael A.G. Haykin, ed., *Joy Unspeakable and Full of Glory: The Piety of Samuel and Sarah Pearce*, Classics of Reformed Spirituality (Kitchener: Joshua Press, 2012).

13 See Michael A.G. Haykin, ed., *The Armies of the Lamb: The Spirituality of Andrew Fuller*, Classics of Reformed Spirituality (Dundas: Joshua Press, 2001).

14 Michael A.G. Haykin, *One Heart and One Soul: John Sutcliff of Olney, His Friends and His Times* (Darlington: Evangelical Press, 1994).

15 Haykin introduced the reprint of Andrew Fuller's memoir of Samuel Pearce. The new edition's title reflected the pivotal role Pearce played in Carey's Indian mission,

3. EVANGELICAL SPIRITUALITY

The third peg of his triad of interests is Haykin's concern for a truly Protestant and evangelical spirituality. During the latter half of the twentieth century, the charismatic movement brought a focus to the so-called "forgotten person of the Trinity," the Spirit. At the same time, the New Age movement revived interest in pagan, Buddhist and Hindu spiritualities. During this time, many evangelicals sought to find resources for Christian spirituality which led them into the tradition of the Roman Catholic mystics. Haykin argued for a distinctly Protestant and evangelical spirituality that was superior in depth and biblical fidelity. For example, he saw the Protestant emphasis on Word and Spirit in Puritanism and described it as a "spirituality of the Word."[16] Looking to theologians such as John Calvin, John Owen and Jonathan Edwards, he drew out their emphases on the Spirit, and in consequence, their spirituality.[17] With these resources, there was no need to look to the popularized versions of spirituality advanced by Roman Catholic mysticism.

Erasing caricatures

Haykin made important contributions toward erasing caricatures about the evangelical church. For example, he challenged the caricature that Calvinistic doctrine leads to atrophy in missions.[18] His documentation of the theological basis for William Carey's mission showed that the doctrines of election and particular redemption did not hinder, but actually promoted the use of extraordinary means for the conversion of sinners globally.

Haykin's work gave a response to another caricature, namely that Baptists are a-theological or anti-intellectual. He showed that among

---

though he never visited the field. See "Introduction," in Andrew Fuller, *A Heart For Missions: The Classic Memoir of Samuel Pearce* (Birmingham: Solid Ground Christian Books, 2005).

16 "An introductory word" in Michael A.G. Haykin, *The Reformers and Puritans as Spiritual Mentors: "Hope is kindled"* (Kitchener: Joshua Press, 2012), 4.

17 Haykin, *The Reformers and Puritans as Spiritual Mentors*; Michael A.G. Haykin, ed., *A Sweet Flame: Piety in the Letters of Jonathan Edwards* (Grand Rapids: Reformation Heritage Books, 2007).

18 See Michael A.G. Haykin, "'A Sacrifice Well Pleasing to God': John Calvin and the Missionary Endeavor of the Church," *The Southern Baptist Journal of Theology* 13, no. 4 (Winter 2009): 36–43.

the many self-taught Baptist pastor-theologians like Andrew Fuller, there was a keen interest in sound doctrine, theological precision and confessional orthodoxy.[19] For example, Haykin brought attention to Baptist theologian John Gill who was comfortable drawing from Rabbinic and Patristic sources to defend the doctrine of the Trinity at a time when other denominations were letting error destroy their theology.[20]

Another common caricature charged that evangelicals had no concept of a tradition of spiritual practice. Haykin's numerous articles show not only that Protestants were concerned about spiritual practice, but they had profound insights on spirituality in the most basic elements of Christian life. Whether insight from Robert Hall on how to hear a sermon or from John Bunyan on to how to pray, Protestant piety was extremely practical, but no less profound in reflection.[21]

Toronto Baptist Seminary

When I graduated from seminary and moved to a single-wide mobile home with my new bride, those wind worn prairies felt a long way from Haykin's historical world of catacombs and closed communions. But the following summer, on a blue sky day I was fixing the tin roof on the trailer lean-to when he called from Ontario. He had recently accepted the role of principal at Toronto Baptist Seminary and Bible College (TBS) and he was wondering if I would be interested in returning there to teach New Testament Greek.[22] I easily accepted his offer and we moved to inner-city Toronto later that summer.

For the next three years, as a faculty member, I had the honour of working alongside Michael Haykin. He brought a warm catholicity to

19 For example see the treatment of Andrew Fuller and the Sandemanian controversy in Michael A.G. Haykin, "At the Pure Fountain of Thy Word": Andrew Fuller as an Apologist (Milton Keynes: Paternoster 2004), 223–236.

20 Haykin edited a volume on John Gill: The Life and Thought of John Gill (1697–1771): A Tercentennial Appreciation (Leiden: Brill 1997).

21 See Michael A.G. Haykin, "Hearing The Word: Robert Hall's Reflections On How Best To Profit Spiritually From Preaching," Reformation and Revival Journal 9.1 (Winter 2000): 137–146; Michael A.G. Haykin, "John Bunyan on Praying with the Holy Spirit" in Joel R. Beeke and Brian G. Najapfour, ed., Taking Hold of God: Reformed and Puritan Perspectives on Prayer (Grand Rapids: Reformation Heritage Books, 2011), 109–119.

22 Haykin's own facility in Greek was noted by a classmate who bought him a paperback edition of the Greek text of Athanasius' On the Incarnation of the Word. See Haykin, The Empire of the Spirit, 137.

the confessionally Baptist school. Portraits of various Reformed worthies were added to the walls of the seminary building as a pictorial reminder of the emphasis. He even insisted that a portrait of John Wesley be hung up in the midst of the Calvinists.

Toronto Baptist Seminary had a new atmosphere of freshness and optimism with Haykin as principal. However, he would be the first to agree that he was not an administrator. Haykin could recollect an entry from the minute book of an eighteenth-century village church but forget a double-booked engagement. Yet his enthusiasm for live orthodoxy rubbed off on everyone and overcame any limits he may have had as an administrator. Soon TBS was swirling with activity as new students, fresh lecturers and widely-known chapel speakers came to the corner where Jarvis Street crossed Gerrard.

Southern Baptist Theological Seminary

He returned to his primary calling when he left the principal position at TBS to assume classroom and research duties at The Southern Baptist Theological Seminary (SBTS) in Louisville, Kentucky.[23] The switch to an institution that served as one of the hubs of a renewed interest in Calvinistic theology gave Haykin a much wider span of influence for his writing and teaching. An example of this influence was his book, *Rediscovering the Church Fathers* that introduced Haykin to a wider American evangelical readership. By 2011, when the book was published, the study of the early church had become a faddish novelty for many evangelicals, and Haykin offered a steadying introduction.[24]

Southern also offered greater opportunity for Haykin's nascent Andrew Fuller Center for Baptist Studies. Through the work of the Center at Southern, he was able to establish conferences, a journal, and most importantly, the beginnings of a multi-volume critical edition of Andrew Fuller's *Works*. This endeavour provided Haykin with

---

23 Haykin continued to live in Ontario but commuted each week during the school year to Kentucky.

24 Michael A.G. Haykin, *Rediscovering the Church Fathers: Who They Were and How They Shaped the Church* (Wheaton: Crossway, 2011). Seeing an imbalanced novelty in the church fathers, Haykin had earlier written a response to one of these books: "Recovering Ancient Church Practices: A Review of Brian McLaren, *Finding Our Way Again: The Return of the Ancient Practices*," *The Southern Baptist Journal of Theology* 12, no. 2 (Summer 2008): 62–67.

a fitting *magnum opus* to labour toward. It was a surprisingly neglected work considering that Andrew Fuller may be arguably the greatest Baptist theologian in church history.

Churchmanship

Haykin is not a mere academic however; he has always been a churchman. He has served as an elder at Trinity Baptist Church in Burlington, Ontario, through the bulk of his seminary career.[25] Many Sunday School lessons have been recorded where he shared vivid biographical studies of figures from every age of church history.[26] Added to that have been the recurring lectures at pastors' fraternals providing historical perspective on issues related to the practicalities of ministry.[27] Certainly in Canada there is no other single disseminator of eighteenth-century English Calvinistic Baptist piety and mission more ubiquitous than Michael Haykin.

Haykin loves the church, but even that love could be put to the test. Haykin was challenged by Toronto pastor Paul Martin of Grace Fellowship Church to teach the history of Christianity in *one day*—a near impossible task! Haykin accepted the challenge and gave a sense of the church's historic scope to Martin's congregation in a way that they had likely never known before or since. As an historian of the Spirit, he has been constant in his interest in applying the fruits of the Spirit's operation in history to believers today who are eager to keep in step with the Spirit.

Naturally, Haykin's interest in the Spirit and the mission of the church as heralds of the gospel of Jesus Christ have led him to be concerned for other cultures and nations with their need for Christ. Whether it has been in French Canada teaching at Séminaire Baptiste Évangélique du Québec (SEMBEQ) or in Northern Ireland teaching at Irish Baptist College, he has been intentional about supporting gospel work beyond his local church.

---

25 Haykin wrote a history of the church on the occasion of its fortieth anniversary: *"Declaring the Whole Counsel of God": Celebrating the History of Trinity Baptist Church, Burlington, Ontario, 1972–2012* (Burlington: Trinity Baptist Church, 2012).

26 Many of these biographical studies are hosted online at www.sermonaudio.com.

27 During this time, Haykin spoke frequently to pastors from associations such as The Sovereign Grace Fellowship of Canada, The Fellowship of Evangelical Baptist Churches of Canada and other evangelical ministerials.

Spiritual friendship

Throughout Haykin's labours he has known many people and developed many friendships. His friendships are not the haphazard type of modern social media. Rather they are born out of extended reflection on friendship as a key component of Christian fellowship.[28] Christian friendship is a Spirit produced reality, and it is not surprising that it would be a point of reflection by an historian of the Spirit.

In one TBS chapel address, Haykin spoke on the theme of Christian friendship and cited the example of John Ryland Jr. and Andrew Fuller.[29] They had disagreed strongly on the obligations of open or closed communion, but they still preserved their friendship. I was despondent after the message because I was estranged from a close friend. Haykin urged me strongly to work at reconciliation, even offering to help mediate it. On Haykin's part, this kind of interest in the practical applications of lessons from history showed that the Spirit of history was still working in our personal history.

Prayer

Few things can epitomize Haykin as an historian of the Spirit quite like his attentiveness to prayer. Frequently Haykin taught on the theme of prayer during his many courses on Christian spirituality. One of the elements in these courses was the Concert of Prayer. Taking his cue from the Prayer Call of 1784, Haykin adopted the pattern used by John Sutcliff and the eighteenth-century English Baptists and employed it in a day long Concert of Prayer.[30] It was usually on a Saturday near the end of the scheduled classes; a decidedly Christian supplement to an academic course. Anyone who has prayed with Haykin will know that his deep interest in the activity of the Holy Spirit has not been merely a scholarly abstraction. Haykin at prayer is the consequence of the historian of the Spirit. For it is in prayer where the Spirit, active in history meets the Spirit, active in the heart.[31]

---

28 See "The Holy Spirit and Love of The Brethren" in *The Empire of the Holy Spirit* (Memphis: Borderstone Press, 2010), 129–141.

29 On this friendship, see Haykin, ed., *The Armies of the Lamb*, 42–46.

30 On the Concert of Prayer, see Michael A.G. Haykin, "John Sutcliff and the Concert of Prayer," *Reformation & Revival* 1.3 (Summer 1992): 65–88.

31 I am grateful for the privilege of adding my reflections to this volume in celebration of the Christian service which Michael Haykin, my dear friend, has rendered to

Historian of the Spirit

Time and distance have limited the occasions when I can see Haykin. Neither Louisville, Kentucky, nor Hamilton, Ontario, has moved any closer to the Rocky Mountains. So, at our local conference, I brought Haykin to the mountains. His time was spent seeing the natural beauty of Lake Louise with his wife Alison, and then speaking to pastors and laypeople on his evergreen theme, the Spirit's work in the church.

Seeing Haykin in action again was a treat for me. He spoke five times in two days without diminishing. The attendees, most of whom had not heard him before, were enthralled with Haykin's encyclopedic knowledge of English Calvinistic Baptist history. But it was Haykin's deep earnest in the Spirit that made the details of the Spirit's work in the past become sharply focused for the attendees that day. The same Spirit was operative, even as Haykin spoke with that mysterious enabling unction.

Haykin's Spirit-chrismed ministry at our church was merely the most recent in a long line of works which he has offered to Christ's church. He continues to be an historian of the Spirit. This aim in his life parallels Basil of Caesarea who had what Haykin described as, "a lifelong passion to be a holy man." Haykin said further:

> He rightly understood that the Christian life is not simply an embrace of certain orthodox notions, just as the church catholic is far more than a coherent system of orthodox beliefs. For both the individual Christian and the church, it is the life of holiness lived in humility for the glory of God. True Christianity is both orthodoxy and "orthopraxy," and both of these, for Basil, are rooted in the life-giving work of the Holy Spirit.[32]

Haykin's description of Basil applies to himself. To be an historian of the Spirit, one must be "rooted" in the Spirit. Such roots lay deeper below the frostline than even Tolkien imagined.

---

the church and to our Lord Jesus Christ.

32 Haykin, *Rediscovering the Church Fathers*, 117

Afterword

THE YEAR WAS 1988 and the day was Tuesday, September 6. On that fateful morning, a somewhat younger and smaller version of me walked into the registrar's office of what was then known as Central Baptist Seminary in Toronto, Ontario. I was to finalize all necessary paperwork and embark on a three-year journey studying the various facets of biblical theology, with the hope of one day entering full time Christian service.

The policy of the school's administration was to assign each student a faculty advisor to facilitate class selection and artfully maneuver him or her through the labyrinth of academic bureaucracy. My advisor that year was none other than the man we are honouring with this small token of esteem and affection. Then, I called him Dr. Haykin. Now, I call him Michael and, in private moments, a number of other choice but privileged covenantal epithets.

Our first encounter was less than auspicious. He confessed he thought me to be a hard-driving, aggressive businessperson; an odd sort of individual seeking to acquire a Christian education. I was! I thought him to be a reclusive—withdrawn, erudite and unpersonable. I am delighted to say that our relationship has lasted well beyond graduation day and, twenty-five years later, I consider Michael to be one of my closest friends. So much for first impressions!

In the intervening years, there has not been a single season of ministry in which our lives did not intertwine. Many were the nights spent at Starbucks where we dreamed and schemed, mapping our chicanery upon soggy, coffee-stained napkins. We started journals together, wrote books together, started a publishing enterprise together, taught together, laughed together and sometimes cried together. Together we have rejoiced at those moments of earthly delight and together we have strengthened each other in those moments of darkest despair.

To me, and countless other students, Michael has not merely been an educator extraordinaire. His love of all things past, and the manner in which he brings bygone days to life, has influenced my personal ministry. In fact, it would not be an overstatement to say that Michael's passion and example finds its way into most things upon which I write or speak today. That would be legacy enough for most people.

But, it is as a godly mentor that Michael's real strength shines. He is a living laboratory of how a Christ-follower ought to conduct himself in grace, gentleness, compassion and humility. He does so quietly, without affectation. Michael lives and breathes the truths that he teaches.

This book has been produced by former students, friends and peers who wish to express their admiration, respect and love for Michael's dedicated service to the church of Jesus Christ. He has impacted and inspired us in ways that may never be fully known. Each of the varied contributors have expressed the joy and privilege of knowing him.

For my part, I would like to make the following addition to the manuscript:

Thank you and God bless you, Michael. May the God of all glory grant you strength, endurance and wisdom for another thirty years of service and friendship.

HEINZ G. DSCHANKILIC
Executive Director
Sola Scriptura Ministries International

Select bibliography of Michael A.G. Haykin

MICHAEL HAYKIN HAS written and edited over thirty books, and countless academic and popular articles. As we go to print, he has a number of other volumes set to be published. Below is only a sample of his work, chosen to reflect the wide range of his interests (arranged chronologically).

Books

The Spirit of God: The Exegesis of 1 and 2 Corinthians in the Pneumatomachian Controversy of the Fourth Century. Leiden: E.J. Brill, 1994.

One heart and one soul: John Sutcliff of Olney, his friends, and his times. Darlington: Evangelical Press, 1994.

Kiffin, Knollys and Keach: Rediscovering Our English Baptist Heritage. Leeds: Reformation Today Trust, 1996.

Edited. *The Life and Thought of John Gill (1697–1771): A Tercentennial Appreciation*. Leiden: E.J. Brill, 1997.

Edited. British Particular Baptists, 1638-1910. 3 Volumes. Springfield: Particular Baptist Press, 1998–2003.

Edited and introduced. *"To honour God": The Spirituality of Oliver Cromwell*. Dundas: Joshua Press, 1999.

Edited and introduced. *The revived Puritan: The Spirituality of George Whitefield*. Dundas: Joshua Press, 2000.

Edited and introduced. *The Armies of the Lamb: The Spirituality of Andrew Fuller*. Dundas: Joshua Press, 2001.

Edited. *'At the Pure Fountain of Thy Word': Andrew Fuller as an Apologist*. Carlisle: Paternoster Press, 2004.

Jonathan Edwards: The Holy Spirit in Revival. Darlington: Evangelical Press, 2005.

The God Who Draws Near: An Introduction to Biblical Spirituality. Darlington: Evangelical Press, 2007.

Edited and introduced. *"A Sweet Flame": Piety in the Letters of Jonathan Edwards*. Grand Rapids: Reformation Heritage Books, 2007.

Edited and introduced, with Steve Weaver. *"Devoted to the Service of the Temple": Piety, Persecution, and Ministry in the Writings of Hercules Collins*. Grand Rapids: Reformation Heritage Books, 2007.

Edited with Kenneth J. Stewart. *The Emergence of Evangelicalism: Exploring Historical Continuities*. Nottingham: Apollos/Inter-Varsity Press, 2008.

With Victoria J. Haykin. *The Christian Lover: The Sweetness of Love and Marriage in the Letters of Believers*. Orlando: Reformation Trust, 2009.

With Roger D. Duke and A. James Fuller. *Soldiers of Christ: Selections from the Writings of Basil Manly, Sr., & Basil Manly, Jr.* Cape Coral: Founders Press, 2009.

The Empire of the Holy Spirit: Reflecting on Biblical and Historical Patterns of Life in the Spirit. Memphis: BorderStone Press, 2010.

Rediscovering the Church Fathers: Who They Were and How They Shaped the Church. Wheaton: Crossway, 2011.

Edited with Mark Jones. *"Drawn into Controversie": Reformed Theological Diversity and Debates Within Seventeenth-Century British Puritanism*.

Reformed Historical Theology, vol. 17. Göttingen: Vandenhoeck & Ruprecht, 2011.

The Reformers and Puritans as Spiritual Mentors: Hope is Kindled. Kitchener: Joshua Press, 2012.

Edited and introduced. *Joy Unspeakable and Full of Glory: the Piety of Samuel and Sarah Pearce.* Kitchener: Joshua Press, 2012.

Articles

"'The Spirit of God': The Exegesis of I Cor. 2:10–12 by Origen and Athanasius," *Scottish Journal of Theology* 35 (1982): 513–528.

"Makarios Silouanos: Silvanus of Tarsus and His View of the Spirit," *Vigiliae Christianae* 36 (1982): 261–274.

"The Fading Vision? The Spirit and Freedom in the Pastoral Epistles," *The Evangelical Quarterly* 57 (1985): 291–305.

" 'In the Cloud and in the Sea': Basil of Caesarea and the Exegesis of 1 Cor 10:2," *Vigiliae Christianae* 40 (1986): 135–144.

"And Who Is the Spirit? Basil of Caesarea's Letters to the Church at Tarsus," *Vigiliae Christianae* 41 (1987): 377–385.

"'A Sense of Awe in the Presence of the Ineffable': 1 Cor. 2:11–12 in the Pneumatomachian Controversy of the Fourth Century," *Scottish Journal of Theology* 41 (1988): 341–357.

"'The Oracles of God': Andrew Fuller and the Scriptures," *Churchman* 103 (1989): 60–76.

"'The Sum of All Good': John Ryland, Jr. and the Doctrine of the Holy Spirit," *Churchman* 103 (1989): 332–353.

"John Ryland, Jr. (1753–1825) and Theological Education," *Nederlands Archief voor Kerkgeschiedenis/Dutch Review of Church History* 70 (1990), 173–191.

"Hanserd Knollys (ca.1599–1691) on the Gifts of the Spirit," *Westminster Theological Journal* 54 (1992): 99–113.

"'A Habitation of God, Though the Spirit': John Sutcliff (1752–1814) and the revitalization of the Calvinistic Baptists in the late eighteenth century," *The Baptist Quarterly* 34 (1991–1992): 304–319.

"'Where the Spirit of God Is, There Is Power': An Introduction to Spurgeon's Teaching on the Holy Spirit," *Churchman* 106 (1992): 197–208.

"'Hazarding all for God at a Clap': The Spirituality of Baptism among British Calvinistic Baptists," *The Baptist Quarterly* 38 (1999–2000): 185–195.

"Particular Redemption in the Writings of Andrew Fuller (1754–1815)" in David Bebbington, ed., *The Gospel in the World: International Baptist Studies* (Studies in Baptist History and Thought, vol. 1; Carlisle: Paternoster Press, 2002), 107–128.

"'His soul-refreshing presence': The Lord's Supper in Calvinistic Baptist Thought and Experience in the 'Long' Eighteenth Century" in Anthony R. Cross and Philip E. Thompson, ed., *Baptist Sacramentalism*, Studies in Baptist History and Thought, vol. 5 (Carlisle: Paternoster Press, 2003), 177–193.

"Defending the Holy Spirit's Deity: Basil of Caesarea, Gregory of Nyssa, and the Penumatomachian Controversy of the 4th Century," *The Southern Baptist Journal of Theology* 7, no. 3 (Fall 2003): 74–79.

"'The Oracles of God': Andrew Fuller's Response to Deism" in Michael A.G. Haykin, ed., *'At the Pure Fountain of Thy Word': Andrew Fuller as an Apologist* (Carlisle: Paternoster Press, 2004), 122–138.

"Andrew Fuller and the Sandemanian Controversy" in Michael A.G. Haykin, ed., *'At the Pure Fountain of Thy Word': Andrew Fuller as an Apologist* (Carlisle: Paternoster Press, 2004), 223–236.

"Eighteenth-Century Calvinistic Baptists and the Political Realm, with Particular Reference to the Thought of Andrew Fuller" in Philip E. Thompson and Anthony R. Cross, ed., *Recycling the Past or Researching History? Studies in Baptist Historiography and Myths,* Studies in Baptist History and Thought, vol. 11 (Milton Keynes, U. K. /Waynesboro, Georgia: Paternoster Press, 2005), 264–278.

"'Glory to the Three Eternal': Benjamin Beddome and the Teaching of Trinitarian Theology in the Eighteenth Century," *The Southern Baptist Journal of Theology* 10, no. 1 (Spring 2006): 72–85.

"'Draw Nigh unto my Soul': English Baptist Piety and the Means of Grace in the Seventeenth and Eighteenth Centuries," *The Southern Baptist Journal of Theology* 10, no. 4 (Winter 2006): 54–73.

"'Come to the Father': Ignatius of Antioch and his calling to be a martyr," *Themelios* 32, no. 3 (May 2007): 26–39.

"Andrew Fuller on Mission: Text and Passion" in Ian M. Randall and Anthony R. Cross, ed., *Baptists and Mission: Papers from the Fourth International Conference on Baptist Studies*, Studies in Baptist History and Thought, vol. 29 (Milton Keynes: Paternoster, 2007), 25–41.

"'For Those who Spurn the Sprinkled Blood!' Praying with Charles Wesley for Muslims," *Southwestern Journal of Theology* 49, no. 2 (Spring 2007): 186–198.

"'Soldiers of Christ, in Truth Arrayed': The Ministry and Piety of Basil Manly Jr. (1825–1892)," *The Southern Baptist Journal of Theology* 13, no. 1 (Spring 2009): 30–44.

"Benjamin Beddome (1717–1795): His Life and His Hymns" in John H.Y. Briggs, ed., *Pulpit and People: Studies in Eighteenth Century Baptist Life and Thought*, Studies in Baptist History and Thought, vol. 28 (Milton Keynes: Paternoster, 2009), 93–111.

"'A Sacrifice Well Pleasing to God': John Calvin and the Missionary Endeavor of the Church," *The Southern Baptist Journal of Theology* 13, no. 4 (Winter 2009): 36–43.

"'A Glorious Inebriation': Eucharistic Thought and Piety in the Patristic Era" in Thomas R. Schreiner and Matthew R. Crawford, ed., *The Lord's Supper: Remembering and Proclaiming Christ Until He Comes*, NAC Studies in Bible & Theology, vol. 10 (Nashville: B & H Publishing Group, 2010), 103–126.

"'We Trust in the Saving Blood': Definite Atonement in the Ancient Church" in David Gibson and Jonathan Gibson, ed., *"From Heaven He Came and Sought Her": Definite Atonement in Historical, Biblical, Theological, and Pastoral Perspective* (Wheaton: Crossway, 2013), 55–72.

Other titles available from Joshua Press...

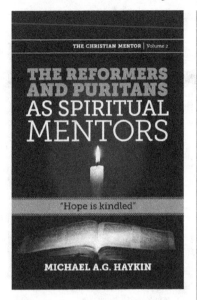

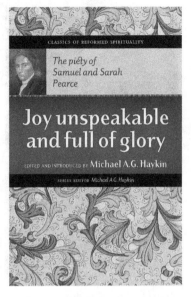

The Christian Mentor | Volume 2

Classics of Reformed spirituality

The reformers and Puritans as spiritual mentors
"Hope is kindled"

By *Michael A.G. Haykin*

REFORMERS SUCH as Tyndale, Cranmer and Calvin, and Puritans Richard Greenham, John Owen, etc. are examined to see how their display of the light of the gospel provides us with models of Christian conviction and living.

ISBN 978–1-894400-39-8

Joy unspeakable and full of glory
The piety of Samuel and Sarah Pearce

By *Michael A.G. Haykin*

SAMUEL PEARCE played a key role in the formation and early days of the Baptist Missionary Society in eighteenth-century England. Through Samuel and Sarah's letters we are given a window into their rich spiritual life and living piety.

ISBN 978–1-894400-48-0

Other titles available from Joshua Press...

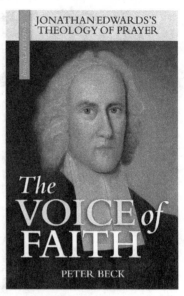

Great themes in Puritan preaching
Compiled and edited
By Mariano Di Gangi

DRAWING FROM a gold mine of Puritan writings, this book provides a taste of the riches of Puritan theology and its application to life. This title will whet your appetite and stir your faith to greater views of Christ, his Person and his work.

ISBN 978–1-894400-26–8 (HC)
ISBN 978–1-894400-24–4 (PB)

The voice of faith
Jonathan Edwards's theology of prayer

By Peter Beck

EXPLORING THE sermons and writings of Jonathan Edwards, Dr. Beck draws a comprehensive picture of his theology of prayer and why Edwards believed God would hear the prayers of his people. Interspersed are three external biographies that set the historical and theological scene.

ISBN 978–1-894400-33–6 (HC)
ISBN 978–1-894400-32–9 (PB)

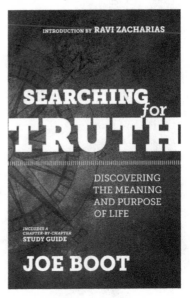
The grace of godliness

An introduction to doctrine and piety in the Canons of Dort

By Matthew Barrett

BARRETT opens a window on the synod's deliberations with the Remonstrants and examines the main emphases of the canons, with special attention on their relationship to biblical piety and spirituality.

ISBN 978-1-894400-52-7 (PB)

Searching for truth

Discovering the meaning and purpose of life

By Joe Boot

BEGINNING WITH a basic understanding of the world, Joe Boot explains the biblical worldview, giving special attention to the life and claims of Jesus Christ. He wrestles with questions about suffering, truth, morality and guilt.

ISBN 978-1-894400-40-4

Deo Optimo et Maximo Gloria
To God, best and greatest, be glory

www.joshuapress.com

CPSIA information can be obtained
at www.ICGtesting.com
Printed in the USA
LVHW091650081220
673648LV00018B/372/J